Dictionary of Literary Biography

Documentary Series

13 *The House of Scribner, 1846-1904,* edited by John Delaney (1996)

14 *Four Women Writers for Children, 1868-1918,* edited by Caroline C. Hunt (1996)

15 *American Expatriate Writers: Paris in the Twenties,* edited by Matthew J. Bruccoli and Robert W. Trogdon (1997)

16 *The House of Scribner, 1905-1930,* edited by John Delaney (1997)

17 *The House of Scribner, 1931-1984,* edited by John Delaney (1998)

18 *British Poets of The Great War: Sassoon, Graves, Owen,* edited by Patrick Quinn (1999)

19 *James Dickey,* edited by Judith S. Baughman (1999)

Yearbooks

1980 edited by Karen L. Rood, Jean W. Ross, and Richard Ziegfeld (1981)

1981 edited by Karen L. Rood, Jean W. Ross, and Richard Ziegfeld (1982)

1982 edited by Richard Ziegfeld; associate editors: Jean W. Ross and Lynne C. Zeigler (1983)

1983 edited by Mary Bruccoli and Jean W. Ross; associate editor: Richard Ziegfeld (1984)

1985 edited by Jean W. Ross (1986)

1986 edited by J. M. Brook (1987)

1987 edited by J. M. Brook (1988)

1988 edited by J. M. Brook (1989)

1989 edited by J. M. Brook (1990)

1990 edited by James W. Hipp (1991)

1991 edited by James W. Hipp (1992)

1992 edited by James W. Hipp (1993)

1993 edited by James W. Hipp, contributing editor George Garrett (1994)

1994 edited by James W. Hipp, contributing editor George Garrett (1995)

1995 edited by James W. Hipp, contributing editor George Garrett (1996)

1996 edited by Samuel W. Bruce and L. Kay Webster, contributing editor George Garrett (1997)

1997 edited by Matthew J. Bruccoli and George Garrett, with the assistance of L. Kay Webster (1998)

Concise Series

Concise Dictionary of American Literary Biography, 6 volumes (1988-1989): *The New Consciousness, 1941-1968; Colonization to the American Renaissance, 1640-1865; Realism, Naturalism, and Local Color, 1865-1917; The Twenties, 1917-1929; The Age of Maturity, 1929-1941; Broadening Views, 1968-1988.*

Concise Dictionary of British Literary Biography, 8 volumes (1991-1992): *Writers of the Middle Ages and Renaissance Before 1660; Writers of the Restoration and Eighteenth Century, 1660-1789; Writers of the Romantic Period, 1789-1832; Victorian Writers, 1832-1890; Late-Victorian and Edwardian Writers, 1890-1914; Modern Writers, 1914-1945; Writers After World War II, 1945-1960; Contemporary Writers, 1960 to Present.*

Dictionary of Literary Biography® • Volume Two Hundred Two

Nineteenth-Century American Fiction Writers

Dictionary of Literary Biography® • Volume Two Hundred Two

Nineteenth-Century American Fiction Writers

Edited by
Kent P. Ljungquist
Worcester Polytechnic Institute

A Bruccoli Clark Layman Book
Gale Research
Detroit, Washington, D.C., London

Library of Congress Cataloging-in-Publication Data

Nineteenth-century American fiction writers / edited by Kent P. Ljungquist.
    p. cm.–(Dictionary of literary biography; v. 202)
"A Bruccoli Clark Layman book."
Includes bibliographical references and index.
ISBN 0-7876-3096-9 (alk. paper)
1. American fiction–19th century–Dictionaries. 2. American fiction–19th century–
Bio-bibliography–Dictionaries. 3. Novelists, American–19th century–Biography–
Dictionaries. I. Ljungquist, Kent, 1948-   . II. Series.
PS377.N56 1999
813'.309'03–dc21   98-49304
[b]   CIP

10 9 8 7 6 5 4 3 2 1

For my friends and colleagues at the American Antiquarian Society,
with thanks for assistance on this project and others

Contents

Plan of the Series

The advisory board, the editors, and the publisher of the *Dictionary of Literary Biography* are joined in endorsing Mark Twain's declaration. The literature of a nation provides an inexhaustible resource of permanent worth. We intend to make literature and its creators better understood and more accessible to students and the reading public, while satisfying the standards of teachers and scholars.

To meet these requirements, *literary biography* has been construed in terms of the author's achievement. The most important thing about a writer is his writing. Accordingly, the entries in *DLB* are career biographies, tracing the development of the author's canon and the evolution of his reputation.

The purpose of *DLB* is not only to provide reliable information in a convenient format but also to place the figures in the larger perspective of literary history and to offer appraisals of their accomplishments by qualified scholars.

The publication plan for *DLB* resulted from two years of preparation. The project was proposed to Bruccoli Clark by Frederick C. Ruffner, president of the Gale Research Company, in November 1975. After specimen entries were prepared and typeset, an advisory board was formed to refine the entry format and develop the series rationale. In meetings held during 1976, the publisher, series editors, and advisory board approved the scheme for a comprehensive biographical dictionary of persons who contributed to North American literature. Editorial work on the first volume began in January 1977, and it was published in 1978. In order to make *DLB* more than a reference tool and to compile volumes that individually have claim to status as literary history, it was decided to organize volumes by

**From an unpublished section of Mark Twain's autobiography, copyright by the Mark Twain Company*

topic, period, or genre. Each of these freestanding volumes provides a biographical-bibliographical guide and overview for a particular area of literature. We are convinced that this organization—as opposed to a single alphabet method—constitutes a valuable innovation in the presentation of reference material. The volume plan necessarily requires many decisions for the placement and treatment of authors who might properly be included in two or three volumes. In some instances a major figure will be included in separate volumes, but with different entries emphasizing the aspect of his career appropriate to each volume. Ernest Hemingway, for example, is represented in *American Writers in Paris, 1920–1939* by an entry focusing on his expatriate apprenticeship; he is also in *American Novelists, 1910–1945* with an entry surveying his entire career, as well as in *American Short-Story Writers, 1910–1945, Second Series* with an entry concentrating on his short stories. Each volume includes a cumulative index of the subject authors and articles. Comprehensive indexes to the entire series are planned.

Since 1981 the series has been further augmented by the *DLB Yearbooks,* which update published entries and add new entries to keep the *DLB* current with contemporary activity. There have also been *DLB Documentary Series* volumes which provide biographical and critical source materials for figures whose work is judged to have particular interest for students. One of these companion volumes is entirely devoted to Tennessee Williams.

We define literature as the *intellectual commerce of a nation:* not merely as belles lettres but as that ample and complex process by which ideas are generated, shaped, and transmitted. *DLB* entries are not limited to "creative writers" but extend to other figures who in their time and in their way influenced the mind of a people. Thus the series encompasses historians, journalists, publishers, book collectors, and screenwriters. By this means readers of *DLB* may be aided to perceive literature not as cult scripture in the keeping of intellectual high priests but firmly positioned at the center of a nation's life.

DLB includes the major writers appropriate to each volume and those standing in the ranks behind them. Scholarly and critical counsel has been sought in deciding which minor figures to include and how full their entries should be. Wherever possible, useful references are made to figures who do not warrant separate entries.

Each *DLB* volume has an expert volume editor responsible for planning the volume, selecting the figures for inclusion, and assigning the entries. Volume editors are also responsible for preparing, where appropriate, appendices surveying the major periodicals and literary and intellectual movements for their volumes, as well as lists of further readings. Work on the series as a whole is coordinated at the Bruccoli Clark Layman editorial center in Columbia, South Carolina, where the editorial staff is responsible for accuracy and utility of the published volumes.

One feature that distinguishes *DLB* is the illustration policy–its concern with the iconography of literature. Just as an author is influenced by his surroundings, so is the reader's understanding of the author enhanced by a knowledge of his environment. Therefore *DLB* volumes include not only drawings, paintings, and photographs of authors, often depicting them at various stages in their careers, but also illustrations of their families and places where they lived. Title pages are regularly reproduced in facsimile along with dust jackets for modern authors. The dust jackets are a special feature of *DLB* because they often document better than anything else the way in which an author's work was perceived in its own time. Specimens of the writers' manuscripts and letters are included when feasible.

Samuel Johnson rightly decreed that "The chief glory of every people arises from its authors." The purpose of the *Dictionary of Literary Biography* is to compile literary history in the surest way available to us–by accurate and comprehensive treatment of the lives and work of those who contributed to it.

The *DLB* Advisory Board

Introduction

The essays in *Dictionary of Literary Biography 202: Nineteenth-Century American Fiction Writers* suggest the richness, depth, and diversity of American fiction in a century marked by both national expansion and regional division. Although some authors discussed in the volume have been attracting the attention of scholars and critics in the past two decades, most of these writers received no more than passing mention in standard histories of American fiction such as Arthur Hobson Quinn's *American Fiction: An Historical and Critical Survey* (1936) and Alexander Cowie's *Rise of the American Novel* (1948) and remain neglected. The inclusion of many of these writers in *DLB 202*, then, marks the first meaningful assessment of their lives and roles, significant or marginal, in the literary and cultural history of the United States.

The works of several authors in *DLB 202* represent the roots of American fiction in the early national period, a time when objections to the novel as merely a meretricious or frivolous form of entertainment were still common. These cultural strictures against fiction may seem quaint to the modern reader, but they were not easily refuted or quickly overcome. James McHenry (1785–1845), Robert Montgomery Bird (1806–1854), William Joseph Snelling (1804–1848), and Frederick William Thomas (1806–1866) attempted to write fiction at a time when there was no accepted tradition of professional authorship in America. Like almost all fiction writers of the nineteenth century, these authors pieced together their literary careers, writing for periodicals as well as struggling to find publishers for their books.

The early careers of such figures illustrate that literature was more of a calling than a profession, for each of these men could have followed more-acceptable social pathways than that offered by the publication of stories and novels. The professional options available to McHenry, who was born in Ireland, were law, medicine, or religion. Upon his arrival in America, he became a physician, opened a medical office, and published two medical papers. Like McHenry, Bird also studied medicine, practiced it for a little over one year, and briefly taught at a medical college. Through family connections Snelling seemed destined for a career in

military service, but his assignment to an army outpost in the upper Midwest exposed him to experiences that he eventually incorporated into tales for newspapers and magazines. Thomas was admitted to the bar and practiced law for more than a decade while also pursuing journalistic activities. Although these men ultimately turned more and more to literature, it is certain that many other aspiring authors chose more practical careers.

Budding fiction writers in the United States, especially in the 1820s and 1830s, felt the need to shed the inherited tradition of British letters. In his oft-quoted preface to *Edgar Huntly* (1799), novelist Charles Brockden Brown exhorted American authors to turn away from Gothic castles and chimeras, which he associated with an inherited British tradition, in favor of indigenous settings. Citizens of a young nation with no independent literary or cultural traditions, American authors were faced with what James Fenimore Cooper in his *Notions of the Americans* (1828) called "a poverty of materials" and sought to uncover distinctively American subjects. Few writers were as bold as George Lippard (1822–1854), who exploited the vogue of French writer Eugéne Sue to write a novel about crime and hypocrisy in Philadelphia. Lippard's *The Quaker City; or, The Monks of Monk-Hall*, distinctive for its urban Gothic setting, appeared in 1844.

For Bird, McHenry, Snelling, and Thomas, the frontier seemed a promising subject. (In the 1830s and 1840s the West comprised the area west of the Ohio River as well as the Kentucky and Missouri frontiers.) McHenry, eager to overcome objections of readers to "works of fancy," explored the fictional potential beyond civilization in *The Wilderness* (1823) and also became the first American author to examine the Irish immigrant in fiction. Thomas made varied contributions to the "emigrant literature" of westward expansion in such works as *The Emigrant* (1823) and *East and West* (1836). Snelling's *Tales of the Northwest* (1830) was one of the earliest story collections by a native author. He drew upon firsthand, rather than imagined, experience of the frontier, particularly in his richly authentic portrayal of the lives and lore of Native Americans. Initially inspired by Washington Irving's tales of imperial conquest, Bird fixed on exotic locales in his early works, but for his most significant novel he used a setting closer to home, combining frontier and Gothic elements in *Nick of the Woods; or, the Jibbenainosay* (1837). Other authors covered in *DLB 202* sought variously to exploit the literary potential of the West: Emerson Bennett (1822–1905) transformed Cooperesque elements into popular formulae; John Beauchamp Jones (1810–1866) vigorously portrayed "wild Western scenes"; and Charles Wilkins Webber (1819–1856?) recounted his adventures on the Texas frontier.

Despite their eagerness to advance the cause of a national fiction, early American authors were hampered by the absence of an international copyright law. American publishers were able to reprint, without permission and without providing remuneration to the author, the works of British novelists. The so-called mammoth newspapers, huge folio-sized papers that anticipated the story papers later in the century, were notorious for offering the works of Charles Dickens and, particularly, Edward Bulwer-Lytton as fictional supplements. In a column in the 16 November 1844 issue of *New-York Saturday Emporium,* one of the mammoth newspapers, an editorialist articulated the gratitude of American publishers to Bulwer-Lytton: "I and my brethren have lived and grown fat upon your brain. . . . But you had a copyright in England; and that's enough for an author. Yet Sir Lytton, we feel indebted to you for most of our substance; and wish to repay you for all we have taken." With money to be made so easily from proven British authors, American publishers had little incentive to promote the work of their countrymen. Indifference or inaction on the copyright issue by Congress intensified the concerns of American authors.

The critical climate was also difficult for American authors. The charge of imitation or derivativeness was often leveled against writers who were judged to fall short of the models provided by British authors such as Sir Walter Scott and Bulwer-Lytton and American successes such as Irving and Cooper, who were popular both in the United States and in Europe. Edgar Allan Poe, for example, characterized Bird's *The Hawks of Hawk-Hollow* (1835) as a "bad imitation of Sir Walter Scott." McHenry, though he attacked Scott as well as Irving and Cooper in stinging critical essays, was also labeled an imitator of Scott.

Even as the nineteenth century progressed, American authors had to contend with a reading public that was conflicted over the value of fiction. Although Nina Baym in *Novels, Readers, and Reviewers: Responses to Fiction in Antebellum America* (1984) is not alone in claiming that the novel had become a respectable form by the middle of the century, other historians of reading argue that rising literacy rates did not necessarily lead to a predilection for

stories and novels. In *A Fictive People: Antebellum Economic Development and the American Reading Public* (1993) Ronald J. Zboray finds much evidence that the long-held antipathy to fiction was slow to die. The interest in factual information, embodied in newspaper reading, often crowded out any appetite for fiction. Even some supporters of education discouraged novel reading, a private form of entertainment that might dissipate the mind, in favor of instructive or informational reading.

One of the important factors that favored the emergence of a literary culture was a flourishing periodical market. Beginning in 1833 *The Knickerbocker Magazine,* which took its name as a tribute to Irving's *Knickerbocker History of New York* (1809), served as the organ for a group of writers, led by Irving, William Cullen Bryant, and James Kirke Paulding, who were recognized as the Knickerbocker school. Writing with Irving's amiable humor, the Knickerbocker writers were more interested in tone and atmosphere than the intricacies of plot. Prose works in the magazine were highly descriptive, deeply influenced by the tradition of the Irvingesque sketch and his use of framing devices and the tale-within-a-tale technique. In its miscellaneous nature, *The Knickerbocker* reflected many of the varied fictional practices of the nineteenth century.

Two of the lesser known authors of the Knickerbocker school were Frederic S. Cozzens (1818–1869), a wine merchant in New York State, and Richard Burleigh Kimball (1816–1892), a lawyer. Cozzens's sketches of suburban life on the banks of the Hudson River appeared in both *The Knickerbocker* and *Putnam's Magazine,* and Kimball wrote lively novels about businessmen and their predicaments. The appeal of both writers was to the urban and cosmopolitan values of magazine readers. Such works as Cozzens's *Prismatics* (1853) and *The Sparrowgrass Papers* (1856) and Kimball's *Romance of Student Life Abroad* (1853) are representative examples of the writing that first appeared in *The Knickerbocker.*

Though Irving was a model for the Knickerbocker school, the guiding spirit of *The Knickerbocker* was Lewis Gaylord Clark, whose temperamental conservatism colored its editorial columns and its general contents. Wholesome subject matter was standard fare in *The Knickerbocker,* and nothing was permitted that was potentially offensive to literary taste or to Clark's genteel sensibility. Clark became the spokesman for the continuity of an established American literary tradition that enshrined Irving and Cooper as demigods. Those who emulated Irving, such as sketch and story writer Theodore S. Fay (1807–1898), were welcomed to *The Knickerbocker* fold; those who attacked Cooper, such as McHenry, were despised.

The example of *The Knickerbocker* shows how sectional rivalries, cultural politics, and even personal antagonisms governed the publication and reception of American fiction. Like other literary periodicals, *The Knickerbocker* was not averse to literary warfare, as a series of contretemps between Clark and the combative Poe indicate. In his editorial columns Poe attacked two of Clark's pets. He wrote a slashing attack on Fay's novel *Norman Leslie* (1835) in the December 1835 *Southern Literary Messenger;* lampooning the obvious deficiencies in Fay's narrative, Poe displayed his scorn for literary cliques in general and for the excessive praise that New York editors lavished on their local favorites. Poe also gleefully critiqued *Ups and Downs in the Life of a Distressed Gentleman* (1836) by William Leek Stone (1792–1844) for its superficiality. Clark turned on the attacker by dubbing him "Mr. POH," and he dished out as many personal insults as compliments from his "Editor's Table." After Poe attacked Henry Wadsworth Longfellow, another contributor and favorite of *The Knickerbocker,* verbal insult nearly erupted into physical assault when Clark met a drunken Poe on the New York streets in 1845.

Poe, of course, did not limit himself to attacking the Knickerbocker writers. He included the poet and novelist Thomas Dunn English (1819–1902) along with Clark in his satiric essay "The Literati of New York City," published in *Godey's Lady's Book* in 1846. In *Poe's Literary Battles* (1963) Sidney P. Moss documents Poe's literary warfare with the antebellum literati, but the entries in *DLB 202* on Fay, English, Webber, Jones, and Stone offer new information from the perspective of Poe's contemporaries on these conflicts as well as on the contexts that engendered them. These entries take note of the struggles endured by Poe and his contemporaries for financial security and artistic autonomy in an unstable, contentious, and antagonistic literary marketplace.

The Knickerbocker survived until the end of the Civil War, but even by the 1850s much of its writing took on a predictable and sentimental cast, an Irving "alpenglow," as Fred Lewis Pattee characterized its devolution. The first decade of the latter half of the nineteenth century has been derided by Pattee as the "feminine fifties," for it ushered in a period in which women's fiction came to dominate the literary marketplace. Magazines such as *Godey's Lady's Book* rose to prominence, providing a forum for women's fiction and offering useful patterns for social behavior. *The Knickerbocker* published the work of one of the more unconventional of these woman authors, Caroline Chesebro' (1825–1873), who also contributed to *Graham's Magazine* and *Holden's Dollar Magazine.* The readership for many 1850s periodicals was female, and editors worked to attract women readers with familial subjects and domestic themes.

Scholarly interest in nineteenth-century women's fiction—much of which was the most popular literature of its time—has evolved since the 1970s. No longer dismissed as trivial or simply sentimental, this body of fiction is studied to clarify the role of authorship as a profession for women, to understand the place of reading in women's lives, and to examine the social conventions that female writers reflected and often challenged. Although familial and domestic subject matter predominated, women's fiction was not monolithic in its reliance on sentimental conventions. Chesebro', for example, presented unconventional heroines. Frances Whitcher (1812–1852) lightened or even subverted the cult of female domesticity through humor. Elizabeth Stoddard (1823–1902) even mocked the formulaic conventions of women's fiction. Others used fiction to explore overtly political issues. Lillie Devereux Blake (1833–1913), for example, was a fiction writer and a suffragette. While Chesebro', Stoddard, and Blake never reached a wide readership, women authors such as Mary Jane Holmes (1825–1907) most surely did. The majority of her work was serialized in the *New York Weekly* before being published in book form.

Several women can be grouped under the general heading of regional fiction, which bridged a gap between romanticism and the realism of the late nineteenth century. Although literary regionalism was anticipated in works such as *Clovernook* (1852) by Alice Cary (1820–1871), stories of rugged farming life in the Ohio River valley, it became one of the most vigorous movements in American fiction primarily after the Civil War. Other regional writers in *DLB 202* include Ruth McEnery Stuart (1849?–1917), who wrote of Louisiana; Sherwood Bonner (1849–1883), who wrote of Mississippi; and Mary Hallock Foote (1847–1938), who wrote of the West. Literary regionalism fostered a strong sense of place and encouraged attention to natural scenery. Regional writers emphasized local customs, mores, dialects, and often used stereotypical characters.

While some regional, or local-color, writers might be accused of uncritically celebrating regional characteristics, a harder edge of realism often surfaced. By exploring the tensions between past and present, stasis versus change, regionalists introduced thematic complexity. In the more mature works of Stuart, Bonner, and Foote, simplistic characterization, especially as regards to their central female characters, is supplanted by complexity of motive and perspective. Bonner's *Like Unto Like* (1878) presents an unconventional heroine independently sorting out her life choices. Stuart's *The Cocoon* (1915)—like Charlotte Perkins Gilman's "The Yellow Wallpaper," a response to the rest cure developed by S. Weir Mitchell (1829–1914)—is a pointed exploration of feminist themes. The main character of Foote's *Edith Bonham* (1917) must choose among the values of personal fulfillment, self-sacrifice, and the ties of female friendship. By portraying female protagonists of insight and independence, these novels reflect cultural trends at the end of the nineteenth and dawn of the twentieth centuries.

The local-color movement, weakened by many writers' excessive reliance on dialects, did not survive far into the twentieth century; however, vestiges of regional writing can be detected in two novels that became best-sellers at the turn of the century. The rustic setting and language of *David Harum* (1899) by Edward Noyes Westcott (1846–1898) suggest its affinities with the local-color movement, but its author seems to be more intent on harkening back to the lost values of the preindustrial world. Apparently fed by nostalgia for the rural values of Westcott's Homeville, New York, turn-of-the-century readers devoured his novel. Early printings were exhausted in a few months, and the novel sold more than 400,000 copies in its first two years. In *Eben Holden* (1900) Irving Bacheller (1859–1950) drew upon his own knowledge of the setting, dialect, and folklore of upper New York State. Sounding many of the same notes as *David Harum*, Bacheller's novel also became a popular sensation, selling more than 250,000 copies within one year. Both *David Harum* and *Eben Holden* were dramatized for the stage.

Authors such as Westcott and Bacheller apparently sensed the promise in the combination of the growing commercial appeal of the novel and an appeal to the values of a simpler past. Many other American writers after the Civil War returned to the past by writing historical novels or romances. Whatever the historical acumen and authority of Jane Goodwin Austin (1831–1894), Amelia Barr (1831–1919), Robert W. Chambers (1865–1933), Winston Churchill (1871–1947), Foote, Charles Major (1856–1913), Mitchell, Daniel Pierce Thompson (1795–1868), and Lew Wallace (1827–1905)—and there is considerable evidence that each of these writers took the study of history seriously—one suspects that at least in part they were delving into the past, as Jay Martin suggests in *Harvests of Change: American Literature 1865–1914* (1967), to escape a confusing present. The leap into the past, in several cases, was accompanied by an impulse to retreat from American soil, as exemplified by Wallace's *Ben Hur* (1880) or Chambers's novels of the Franco-Prussian War or Major's *When Knighthood Was in Flower* (1898). Historical fiction satisfied readers' appetites for color, pageantry, and excitement while transporting them to presumably more fixed and stable periods in the past. While writers at the beginning of the century felt that Americans had no history, no sense of the past comparable to Great Britain, romancers at the end of the century manufactured their own versions of the past.

The historical romance, the adventure story, and the mystery story—these emerging popular genres are well represented by the authors covered in *DLB 202*. The concerns of the American author had shifted from the issues of morality and literary nationalism at the beginning of the century to marketability at its end. For authors such as Cozzens, English, Fay, Foote, and Kimball, the popular periodical served as a medium that helped to shape the form and content of fictional products. Writers who were sensitive to the literary market tailored their stories to particular periodicals. In an entry from his personal diary Cozzens claimed, "Authorship has become a business." Such a statement suggests the distance traveled from the tradition of writing fiction as a gentlemanly avocation to its status as a practical profession.

In the case of Bacheller, in particular, periodicals and books became part of a system of syndication that both reflected and shaped readers' changing tastes in fiction. Through his syndicate, which operated from 1887 to 1898, he was instrumental in establishing a system by which fiction writers could increase their rate of payment and expand their audiences. The entertainment value of fiction was becoming ever more important as readers were becoming consumers, enjoying more leisure time, and looking for escapist fare.

DLB 202 contains discussions of two genres, pioneered in the nineteenth century by Poe, that became more firmly established in the twentieth century: the detective story and the supernatural tale. Anna Katharine Green (1846–1935), whose most famous work was *The Leavenworth Case* (1878), and Frederick Irving Anderson (1877–1947), whose contributions to the field of crime fiction came after 1900, were important early practitioners of the detective story. Chambers's *The King in Yellow* (1895) represents the Poe-esque influence that was ultimately filtered through him to a more famous inheritor of the supernatural tradition, H. P. Lovecraft.

The primary objective of *DLB 202: Nineteenth-Century Fiction Writers* is straightforward: to provide profiles of fiction writers of the nineteenth century who have not been treated previously in the Dictionary of Literary Biography series. (Only two of the forty-seven subjects, Whitcher and Foote, have appeared in previous volumes). The application of the term *fiction* is broad and is not determined by any arbitrary criterion of length. Short-story and sketch writers are included, and as evidenced by the number of popular writers, the volume is not limited to the domain of belles lettres. Writers who melded fictional and nonfictional techniques, such as J. Ross Browne (1821–1875), Samuel Post Davis (1850–1918), and Anne Warner (1869–1913), are also included. The editor hopes that the list of "Books for

Further Reading" at the end of this volume will encourage the reader to further exploration of the history of American fiction.

– Kent P. Ljungquist

Acknowledgments

This book was produced by Bruccoli Clark Layman, Inc. Karen L. Rood is senior editor for the Dictionary of Literary Biography series. George Anderson was the in-house editor. He was assisted by Charles Brower, Jan Peter F. van Rosevelt, Karen L. Rood, Phil Dematteis, Penelope M. Hope, and Tracy Simmons Bitonti.

Administrative support was provided by Ann M. Cheschi, Tenesha S. Lee, and Shawna M. Tillman.

Bookkeeper is Neil Senol.

Copyediting supervisor is Phyllis A. Avant. The copyediting staff includes Brenda Carol Blanton, Jannette L. Giles, Thom Harman, Melissa D. Hinton, Beth Peters, Raegan E. Quinn, and Audra Rouse. Freelance copyeditors are Brenda Cabra, Rebecca Mayo, Nicole M. Nichols, and Jennie Williamson.

Editorial associate is Jeff Miller.

Layout and graphics staff includes Janet E. Hill, Mark J. McEwan, and Alison Smith.

Office manager is Kathy Lawler Merlette.

Photography editors are Margo Dowling, Charles Mims, and Paul Talbot. Photographic copy work was performed by Joseph M. Bruccoli.

Production manager is Marie L. Parker.

SGML supervisor is Cory McNair. The SGML staff includes Linda Drake, Frank Graham, Jennifer Harwell, and Alex Snead.

Systems manager is Marie L. Parker.

Database manager is Javed Nurani. Kimberly Kelly performed data entry.

Typesetting supervisor is Kathleen M. Flanagan. The typesetting staff includes Karla Corley Brown, Pamela D. Norton, and Patricia Flanagan Salisbury. Freelance typesetters include Deidre Murphy and Delores Plastow.

Walter W. Ross and Steven Gross did library research. They were assisted by the following librarians at the Thomas Cooper Library of the University of South Carolina: Linda Holderfield and the interlibrary-loan staff; reference-department head Virginia Weathers; reference librarians Marilee Birchfield, Stefanie Buck, Stefanie DuBose, Rebecca Feind, Karen Joseph, Donna Lehman, Charlene Loope, Anthony McKissick, Jean Rhyne, and Kwamine Simpson; circulation-department head Caroline Taylor; and acquisitions-searching supervisor David Haggard.

The editor would like to thank Dennis Berthold, Lawrence Berkove, Robert Burkholder, Benjamin F. Fisher, Thomas Knoles, Wesley T. Mott, and Daniel Wells for recommending potential contributors. He also thanks John F. Carney, vice president and provost at Worcester Polytechnic Institute, who granted a sabbatic leave to complete the research and editing of the volume. Much of the research and editing was done during a two-month period as a research associate at the American Antiquarian Society (AAS). The editor is grateful for the assistance and cooperation of the staff at the AAS, particularly research librarian Joanne Chaison. The list of authors to be included in this volume was developed by the editor after consulting a preliminary list prepared by William Cagle, Lilly Library, Indiana University.

Penny Rock and Margaret Brodmerkle provided invaluable clerical assistance at WPI.

Nineteenth-Century American Fiction Writers

Dictionary of Literary Biography

Frederick Irving Anderson
(14 November 1877 – 24 December 1947)

Benjamin F. Fisher
University of Mississippi

BOOKS: *The Farmer of Tomorrow* (New York: Macmillan, 1913);

Adventures of the Infallible Godahl (New York: Crowell, 1914);

Electricity for the Farm: Light, Heat and Power by Inexpensive Methods from the Water Wheel or Farm Engine (New York & London: Macmillan, 1915);

The Notorious Sophie Lang (London: Heinemann, 1925);

The Book of Murder (New York: Dutton, 1930).

MOTION PICTURES: *The Notorious Sophie Lang,* screenplay by Anderson, Paramount, 1934;

The Return of Sophie Lang, screenplay by Anderson, Paramount, 1936;

Sophie Lang Goes West, screenplay by Anderson, Paramount, 1937.

SELECTED PERIODICAL PUBLICATIONS–
UNCOLLECTED:

FICTION:

"The Unknown Man," *Adventure,* 2 (August 1911): 645–650;

"Come Ahead Slow," *Adventure,* 4 (June 1912): 319–325;

"Beyond a Reasonable Doubt," *Adventure,* 4 (October 1912): 67–74;

"The Purple Flame," *Adventure,* 5 (November 1912): 11–17;

"The Man Who Couldn't Go Home," *Saturday Evening Post* (29 March 1914): 17–19, 77–78;

"An Hour of Leisure," *Saturday Evening Post* (25 July 1914): 3–5, 38–40; (1 August): 16–18, 44–47; (8 August): 19–21, 36–37; (15 August): 19–21, 41–42; (22 August): 19–21, 41; (29 August): 18–19, 36;

Frederick Irving Anderson

"The Makeshift," *Saturday Evening Post* (5 September 1914): 3–5, 46–47;

"Vanities," *Saturday Evening Post* (14 November 1914): 12–13, 65–66;

"The Alchemists," *Saturday Evening Post* (2 January 1915): 9–10, 33;

"The Flame in the Socket," *Saturday Evening Post* (26 February 1916): 26–30;

"The Worldling," *Pictorial Review,* 17 (October 1916): 13–14, 56–58;

"The Touch on His Shoulder," *McClure's Magazine,* 50 (March 1918): 20–21, 36–38;

"The Golden Fleece," *Saturday Evening Post* (4 May 1918): 20–21, 98, 101–102, 104;

"The Mad Hour," *McClure's Magazine,* 50 (June 1918): 13–14, 36, 39;

"Dumbkopf!" *McClure's Magazine,* 50 (October 1918): 22–24, 33–34;

"The Siamese Twin," *Saturday Evening Post* (8 February 1919): 34, 37–38, 40, 43;

"Hokum!" *Saturday Evening Post* (12 April 1919): 8–9, 99, 102, 104;

"The Phantom Alibi," *McClure's Magazine,* 52 (November 1920): 27–28, 45–46;

"The Half-Way House," *American Magazine,* 93 (May 1922): 48–51, 73–74;

"Dolores Cay," *Chicago Tribune,* fiction supplement, 23 January 1921, pp. 2–3, 12;

"The Assassins," *Pictorial Review,* 22 (February 1921): 12–13, 80, 102–103;

"Wild Honey," *Saturday Evening Post* (26 November 1921): 6–7, 33–34, 36, 39, 41;

"The Man Killer," *Chicago Tribune,* fiction supplement, 12 March 1922, pp. 2, 11;

"The Half-Way House," *American Magazine,* 93 (May 1922): 48–51, 73–74;

"The Follansbee Imbroglio," *Saturday Evening Post* (29 July 1922): 17–19, 52, 54, 59–60, 62; (5 August): 20–21, 24, 26, 28, 30;

"Fifty-Fifty," *Saturday Evening Post* (6 December 1924): 5, 102–104, 109–110;

"The White Horse," *Saturday Evening Post* (20 June 1925): 16–17, 38, 41, 42;

"The Man on Post," *Saturday Evening Post* (12 November 1932): 6–7, 37, 40–41.

NONFICTION

"The Man Who Heard Voices," *Harper's Weekly,* 52 (15 February 1908): 10–12;

"The French Think Wilbur Wright Is a Bird," *Harper's Weekly,* 52 (24 October 1908): 30;

"The Full Dinner Pail," *Everybody's Magazine,* 27 (July 1912): 33–34;

"From Hand to Mouth," *Everybody's Magazine,* 28 (May 1913): 656–657;

"The Automobilist's Dream," *Scientific American,* 116 (13 January 1917): 61.

Beginning his career in the nineteenth century as a writer for newspapers in his native Illinois, Frederick Irving Anderson became widely known for his creation of two of the most compelling criminal rogues in early twentieth-century American detective fiction: the Infallible Godahl and the alluring but elusive Sophie Lang. These lawbreakers were featured in two volumes of crime stories, *Adventures of the Infallible Godahl* (1914) and *The Notorious Sophie Lang* (1925). Readers were also gripped by the antagonists of these criminals: Deputy Parr of the New York City detective police force; his subordinates, the handsome lady-killer Morel and the shabby, beggar-like Pelts; and his great cohort Oliver Armiston, a former author of crime fiction.

Anderson's literary creations spring from mainstream nineteenth-century fiction. His Godahl and Sophie descend from the confidence men and women of Edgar Allan Poe, Nathaniel Hawthorne, Herman Melville, and Mark Twain although they revel in their abilities to hoodwink to a greater degree than do many of their literary ancestors. Anderson is also notable for his skillful handling of dialect and slang of the flashy New York urban set and the duller-seeming but nonetheless quick-witted New-England rural folk. Revealing an ear as sensitive to language nuances as that of Twain or George Washington Harris, Anderson contributed to American regional fiction.

Frederick Irving Anderson, son of Andrew and Elizabeth Adling Anderson, was born 14 November 1877 in East Aurora, Illinois. He began his career as a journalist with stints on the *Aurora News* in 1895 and 1896 and worked on the *New York World* from 1898 through 1908. In the late 1890s he attended the University of Pennsylvania, taking classes in the Wharton School of Business and in the College of Liberal Arts, but he never pursued a business career. He married Emma Helen de Zouche on 23 March 1908. A pioneer feminist, she also worked many years for the *New York World.* Anderson's first book was *The Farmer of Tomorrow* (1913), which was originally serialized in part from August to October 1912 in *Everybody's Magazine.* He also wrote a second scientific book, *Electricity for the Farm: Light, Heat and Power by Inexpensive Methods from the Water Wheel or Farm Engine,* which was serialized in *Country Gentleman* and published independently in 1915.

Like his pair of great rogues, Anderson is an elusive figure. Although he moved in journalistic circles of New York from 1907 to 1937, little is known about his personal life. His literary production virtually ceased in 1932, though he did publish an occasional story thereafter in *Ellery Queen's Mystery Magazine,* for which he unfailingly received editorial accolades. After his wife died on 26 July 1937, he spent much of his time with his sister, Mabel L. Anderson, on a farm in southern Vermont, near East Jamaica. There are few reminiscences of Anderson; he left few significant personal papers and apparently no literary manuscripts or typescripts. In his accounts of visits to Anderson at the farm, Charles Honce mentions a folder of correspondence from fans of Anderson in which the author's techniques and methods were discussed, but apparently that folder was lost. The seventy-year-old Anderson died suddenly on 24 December 1947 in Pittsfield, Massachusetts, where he was visiting friends.

Apart from his newspaper columns, Anderson's first signed article, "The Man Who Heard Voices," appeared in *Harper's Weekly* for 15 February 1908. Even in this early sketch, which treats Frank W. Sandford's founding of the "Holy Ghost and Us" sect, Anderson's narrative bent is evident. He creates an omniscient storyteller to introduce the subject but then quickly switches to a more sober journalistic account.

Blends of the factual with the fantastic typify Anderson's fiction: one moment readers are nearly overwhelmed by the mundane detailing of subjects such as gold plating or automotive mechanics, and the next instant they are whirled through less tangible subjects, such as those dealing with the supernatural or quasi-supernatural, abstract art, or drama criticism. Such methodology comes naturally for Anderson by way of old masters. Throughout his writings he alludes to Charles Dickens, William Shakespeare, the Pre-Raphaelites, Sir Thomas Browne, and Edgar Allan Poe—all of whom mingled sensationalism and verisimilitude.

Anderson's first detective story, "The Unknown Man," appeared in the August 1911 issue of *Adventure*. Like Poe's C. Auguste Dupin, Anderson's sleuth, Mr. White, cuts through sensationalism to reveal the simplicity inherent in the seemingly insoluble mystery. The story thus introduces a pattern and a technique, the surprise ending, that Anderson followed in all his succeeding crime stories, though Mr. White was soon replaced by the duo of Deputy Parr and Oliver Armiston. Parr's mystification is commonly cleared away by imaginative Armiston, the one-time creator of ingenious criminals and plots for magazine stories. Oliver's quick wits and urbanity prevent many situations from becoming dull or else facilely melodramatic.

Anderson's first Godahl story, "The Infallible Godahl," was published in the 15 February 1913 issue of *The Saturday Evening Post*. Five more stories appeared in the magazine before they were all collected in *Adventures of the Infallible Godahl* the next year. The name Godahl carries suggestive, symbolic implications, as God and all connote the character's apparently limitless abilities. Originating as a character created by Armiston for a magazine story, Godahl continually dons and doffs guises after the manner of an actor playing multiple roles. He is convincing in the highest and the humblest roles, from a fashionable dilettante or a gourmand to a mechanic or a plumber. His most unlikely role occurs in the concluding story, "An All-Star Cast," where Godahl masquerades as a good guy. Anderson's readers enjoy Godahl's delightful gulling of his pursuers. Melville Davisson Post's Uncle Abner and E. W. Hornung's Raffles have been mentioned as prototypes for Anderson's rogue, but clearly he drew upon other models as well. Wilkie Collins's influence upon "The

Illustration for Anderson's "The Man on Post," his last detective story to appear in The Saturday Evening Post *(12 November 1932)*

Infallible Godahl" is unmistakable, and Anderson also reveals a knowledge of situation and psychological characterization in Henry James's fiction.

"The Infallible Godahl," in which the rogue dupes Annission into revealing the means of stealing a rare white ruby, is the showpiece of the collection because of its subtlety in characterization and language. Anderson's relish for involved wordplay is evident in the games he plays concerning the value or worth of the gem. For example, the owner of the ruby is Mrs. Billy Wentworth, whose name suggests the ultimate decline of the value of the ruby, which loses its financial worth when Godahl returns it to the sacred setting from which it was originally stolen.

Anderson's padded novelette featuring Godahl, "An Hour of Leisure," which ran serially in *The Saturday Evening Post* during July and August 1914, was less successful than his stories and may have led him to turn away from the character. Most of his fiction until the beginning of the 1920s employs either situations connected with the New York stage and music halls or—in a series for *McClure's Magazine* beginning in early 1918— spy-story activities. One of his best stories from this period is "The Phantom Alibi," which appeared in the November 1920 issue of *McClure's*. In this short tale featuring Parr and Armiston, handwriting analysis reveals the criminal's identity during an emotional courtroom scene.

Anderson introduced his second great rogue, Sophie Lang, in "The Signed Masterpiece," which ran in *McClure's* in the June–July 1921 issue. The subsequent stories in the series appeared in *The Saturday Evening Post* between September 1922 and March 1924. The stories were published as *The Notorious Sophie Lang* by Heinemann of London but were not published in book form by an American publisher. A feminine counterpart to Godahl, Sophie is alluring, audacious, and adaptive. With the facility of a chameleon she takes on such varied roles as lady, lady's maid, model, and disfigured soldier. Like Godahl, she is a genuine cosmopolitan who has a ready knowledge of languages, elegant dining, modish dress, the subtleties of gems, and the finer points of legal documents. She can also be ruthless if the situation warrants. Her poisoning of an unwanted "husband" and vicious attack on Parr's cohort Pelts occasion her no great distress.

The Sophie Lang stories are tensely dramatic. She is above all a splendid actress, and her varied disguises entertain readers just as much as they baffle Deputy Parr, who tirelessly trails her. She is likened to a "noon-day shadow" and always manages to elude Parr and company. Even Morel, the "handsome man of the type called 'fatal'," gives way before her charms. Sophie's world is that of New York City's high society, and her overriding love is a desire for valuable jewels. She walks coolly out of an apparently impregnable fortress of a gem merchant with an opulent string of pearls—after so hypnotically charming the old owner that he forgets his suggestion that she try them on. The concluding story, "The Peacock," is especially dramatic as readers wonder whether Sophie, garbed as a model, will escape the determined Parr one last time.

Like Godahl, who functions as a fictional character within a fiction, Sophie at times seems to be a phantom. Several times her actual existence is questioned, and such ambiguities only drive Parr farther into frustration and rage. Thus Sophie intermittently functions like contemporaneous "ghostly" personages in Edith Wharton's tales of the uncanny or those in most stories from Ellen Glasgow's *The Shadowy Third* (1923). She is also literary kin to the better known femmes fatales in the plays of Eugene O'Neill or in the fiction by Ernest Hemingway, F. Scott Fitzgerald, and William Faulkner who threaten male egos, sexuality, and professions. Engaging but frightening, Sophie will not scruple to eliminate some man who proves an obstacle to her goals. She remains "the uncaught," too fine a creation to yield to Parr's "gorilla" hands and a facial expression "ape-like in its ferocity." Sophie's popularity was such that the character inspired three movies for which Anderson wrote the screenplays: *The Notorious Sophie Lang* (1934), *The Return of Sophie Lang* (1936), and *Sophie Lang Goes West* (1937).

Beginning with "Wild Honey," a story in *The Saturday Evening Post* of 26 November 1921, Anderson turned more and more to producing fiction that emphasized detection and featured Parr, Armiston, Morel, and Pelts. The last of these stories, "The Man on Post," appeared in the *Post* on 12 November 1932. These works divide along regional lines, with some set in New York City and others in rural New England. In the rural stories Armiston and Parr are assisted by constable Orlando Sage, another sleuth, though one less aggressive about his position than Parr. Sage's name is another Andersonian pun, as the constable exemplifies an unobtrusive, though pungent, sagacity. In his rural stories Anderson also features Jason Selfridge, a college-educated farmer, and Aunt Ivy Cotton, a farm widow.

Many of the Armiston-Parr stories set in rural New England also offer glimpses into country life that compare with those in the best regional fiction of Mary Wilkins Freeman, Sara Orne Jewett, and Edith Wharton. In "The Dead End," a story collected in *The Book of Murder* (1930), an everyday chore takes on the dimensions of art when Jason Selfridge and old Noah Seymour's trip to the latter's old home in search of a tombstone leads to their assisting in laying a crime to rest. Aunt Ivy Cotton's firing up her kitchen stove makes a homely counter to the conniving of a would-be swindler who begs her hospitality. In "The Golden Fleece," a story that was published in the 4 May 1918 issue of *The Saturday Evening Post*, Jason's daydreaming about his rural home, its warmth and its cyclical activities centered in securing a living from the land cheer him while he is far away and lonely in wintery New York City.

In 1930 Anderson gathered ten stories for *The Book of Murder*, a title subsequently included in the Haycraft-Queen "Cornerstone" library of detective fiction. Three pieces have a New England setting, and seven are set in New York. Anderson chose to lead the collection with "Beyond All Conjecture," an enticing account of suspense aroused by an ingenious murder. Reminiscent of Poe in "The Murders in the Rue Morgue," Anderson satisfactorily explains the seemingly outré circumstances of the story. Other stories in the volume also involve the reader in mind-teasing detection.

The Book of Murder is a more carefully selected and arranged volume than Anderson's previous collections. In the earlier books he had simply included all of the stories about his protagonists that he had then published, generally in the order they appeared (he did rearrange the sequence of the Sophie stories to conclude with "The Peacock"). He had about forty stories from which to choose for his last collection, though. He generally chose his best work, though one may wonder at the exclusion of "Wild Honey" and "The Half-Way House," which he evidently decided against because they included quasi-supernatural occurrences. In closing *The Book of Murder* with "The Door Key," Anderson deftly intertwined all the strands of his New York and New England fiction. The urban detectives enter the country and wind up pursuing a murder investigation nearly as impossible as that in the opening story, and a case of concealed identity connects both regions.

The major weakness of the book is the repetition from story to story of epithets and of character features, especially in the characterizations of Parr, Armiston, Morel, and Pelts. Had Anderson revised such passages in these magazine stories before book publication, he could have eliminated some tediousness for the reader reading straight through the collection. Anderson may have been discouraged by the initial small sales of *The Book of Murder* or the rapid remaindering of the stock; in any case, he composed little fiction thereafter.

Anderson deserves greater critical attention than he has received. His detective fiction builds on the genre developed in the nineteenth century, and his stories featuring roguish characters, with their violence and brutality as well as their reliance on colloquial language, may be seen to adumbrate the hard-boiled school of detective fiction that blossomed in the late 1920s. Beyond its relevance to detective fiction, though, Anderson's work in its local color and realism is tied to the mainstream trends of the nineteenth as well as the twentieth centuries. Many of his stories are masterpieces in richly textured expression and psychological character portrayal.

Bibliography:
Benjamin F. Fisher, *Frederick Irving Anderson (1877–1947): A Biobibliography* (Madison, Ind.: Brownstone Books, 1987).

References:
Benjamin F. Fisher, "Frederick Irving Anderson and the Infallible Godahl," *Clues,* 9 (Fall/Winter 1988): 9–19;

Fisher, "Frederick Irving Anderson's Godahl: Con Man Extraordinaire," *WHIMSY,* 3 (April 1985): 26–28;

Howard Haycraft, *Murder for Pleasure: The Life and Times of the Detective Story* (New York & London: Appleton-Century, 1941): 160–163; 304;

Charles Honce, *Mark Twain's Associated Press Speech and other News Stories on Murder, Modes, Mysteries, and Makers of Books* (New York: Privately printed, 1940): 50–57;

Ellery Queen, ed., *The Female of the Species: The Great Women Detectives and Criminals* (Boston: Little, Brown, 1943): 375–394;

Queen, ed., *101 Years of Entertainment: The Great Detective Stories, 1841–1941* (Boston: Little, Brown, 1941).

Papers:
Frederick Irving Anderson's papers are held by the Harry Ransom Center for the Humanities, University of Texas at Austin.

Jane Goodwin Austin

(25 February 1831 – 30 March 1894)

Jane Atteridge Rose
Georgia College and State University

BOOKS: *Fairy Dreams; or, Wanderings in Elf-Land* (Boston: Tilton, 1859);

Kinah's Curse! or, The Downfall of Carnaby Cedars (Boston: Elliott, Thomes & Talbot, 1864);

Dora Darling: The Daughter of the Regiment (Boston: Tilton, 1865);

The Novice; or, Mother Church Thwarted (Boston: Elliott, Thomes & Talbot, 1865);

The Outcast; or, The Master of Falcon's Eyrie (Boston: Elliott, Thomes & Talbot, 1865);

The Tailor Boy: Wreck of the Nautilus (Boston: Tilton, 1865);

Outpost (Boston: Tilton, 1867);

Cipher: A Romance (New York: Sheldon, 1869);

The Shadow of Moloch Mountain (New York: Sheldon, 1870);

Moonfolk: A True Account of the Home of the Fairy Tales (New York: Putnam, 1874; London, 1882);

Mrs. Beauchamp Brown (Boston: Roberts, 1880);

A Nameless Nobleman (Boston: Osgood, 1881);

The Desmond Hundred (Boston: Osgood, 1882);

Nantucket Scraps: Being the Experiences of an Off-Islander, in Season and Out of Season, Among a Passing People (Boston: Osgood, 1883);

The Story of a Storm (New York: Lupton, 1886);

Standish of Standish: A Story of the Pilgrims (Boston: Houghton, Mifflin, 1889; London: Ward, Lock, 1892);

Dolóres (New York: Lupton, 1890);

Dr. LeBaron and His Daughters (Boston: Houghton, Mifflin, 1890);

Betty Alden: The First-Born Daughter of the Pilgrims (Boston: Houghton, Mifflin, 1891);

David Alden's Daughter and Other Stories of Colonial Times (Boston: Houghton, Mifflin, 1892);

It Never Did Run Smooth (New York: Lupton, 1892);

Queen Tempest (New York: Ivers, 1892);

The Twelve Great Diamonds (New York: Lupton, 1892);

The Cedar Swamp Mystery (New York: Lupton, Lovell, 1901).

Jane Goodwin Austin

Jane Goodwin Austin deserves much of the credit for mythologizing America's Pilgrim forebears. She wrote twenty-four books, including children's books and adult sensation novels, but her reputation rests on her five novels that treat colonial life in Plymouth. The history of Plymouth Colony was a natural subject for Austin. She was a descendent of at least eight *Mayflower* Pilgrims–including Myles Standish and William Bradford–through both her mother and her father. She also claimed other ancestors who were notable in Plymouth history, such as Francis and Lazarus LeBaron. She used this family lore in her best fiction.

The author known as Jane Goodwin Austin was born as Mary Jane Goodwin on 25 February 1831 (some sources incorrectly state January) in Worcester, Massachusetts, to Isaac Goodwin and Elizabeth Hammatt Goodwin. Her writing shows the influence of both her parents. A lawyer and a scholar, her father was also a respected antiquarian and genealogist. Though her father died when she was young, Jane Goodwin grew up in a home filled with his books and papers, which visitors often came to consult. She was reared primarily by her mother, who cherished the oral, anecdotal history of the region. Elizabeth Hammatt Goodwin also enjoyed local fame as a poet and songwriter. The strength of these parental influences is also evident in Jane Goodwin's brother, John A. Goodwin, who was also drawn to the study of his roots. He authored *The Pilgrim Republic* (1888), considered at the time the best history of Plymouth.

Jane Goodwin received a good education, attending private academies in Boston. In school she demonstrated both a fascination with family history and a desire to write, circulating stories among friends. However, her marriage at nineteen to Loring H. Austin of Boston and the birth of her four children (three survived) in the years immediately following, delayed her pursuit of a professional writing career. When Austin did begin publishing in 1859, her first volume reflected her maternal focus. It was a collection of children's fairy tales, *Fairy Dreams; or, Wanderings in Elf-Land*. As she developed as a writer and turned for material to colonial history Austin used the approaches of both her parents. She never lost her fascination with hearing the old stories of the community and browsing through crumbling gravestones. She also became a committed student of old records, particularly after the historic license she took in her first efforts was criticized. As a result Austin's mature use of the colonial material is good historical fiction–imaginatively enriched with human insight and sensitivity but not in violation of the facts.

During the 1860s and 1870s Austin became a frequent contributor to the popular literary journals of the period: *Harper's, Atlantic, Lippincott's, Putnam's,* and *Galaxy*. Many of her stories and serials received subsequent book publication. In addition to juvenile pieces, Austin's early writing reflects the conventional taste of her reading audience–sentimental romances and sensational thrillers–with titles such as *The Novice; or, Mother Church Thwarted* (1865) and *The Outcast; or, The Master of Falcon's Eyrie* (1865).

An interesting piece from this period is *Dora Darling: The Daughter of the Regiment* (1865), which Susan Sutton Smith describes as "in many ways Austin's most charming novel." The story occurs during the Civil War. Twelve-year-old Dora Darling and her mother are

Union sympathizers in the South. After her mother's death, young Dora flees an unloving family, and following a series of adventures, eventually finds refuge in the Union army. There she is befriended by soldiers who protect and educate her. With them, she continues to experience the tribulations of the war. Brave and noble, she is a fine example of the sentimental heroine so popular in nineteenth-century fiction. *Outpost* (1867) continues the saga of Dora Darling out West.

In the late 1860s the Austin family lived for some time in Concord, Massachusetts. Their house was located on Main Street, near the home of Henry David Thoreau's mother. She became friends with Louisa May Alcott. Though only Austin is listed on the title page of *Cipher: A Romance* (1869), Madeleine Stern in her *Louisa May Alcott* (1950) asserts that Alcott assisted Austin in writing this wild, Gothic thriller, which was serialized in *Galaxy* and then published as a book. While Alcott, unlike Austin, had already found fame as well as her career focus, she never abandoned her fondness for sensational fiction and found ways to publish it anonymously. When Austin, on the other hand, found popularity and respect in the genre of historic fiction, she continued to publish occasional sensational thrillers under her own name.

In 1881, after more than two decades as a professional writer of juvenile, sentimental, and sensational fiction and with eleven books to her credit, Austin experienced her first big literary success with *A Nameless Nobleman*. This historical novel was reprinted at least thirty times and led to her eventual relationship with Houghton, Mifflin, the most prestigious publisher of her day.

Though fictionalized, Austin's source for this story is her family's oral history. In an aside to the reader at one point, she alludes to the repositories of such narrative gold, noting that "the gray old Sphinx of a town knows the answer to that riddle, and others, and tells them, too, to him who has ears and heart to listen, and eyes wherewith to see the sights she will show in the dim twilight on Burying Hill." The "nameless nobleman" of this tale is her great, great grandfather, Dr. Francis LeBaron. In the story Dr. LeBaron is an expatriate French nobleman originally named Francois, the younger son of Count de Montarnaud in the court of King Louis XIV.

The story opens with a family dispute that causes Francois to defy his father and wound his brother. The complicated plot that follows is driven not only by love and intrigue but also a conflict of values. In obedience to the king's whim, the count has arranged a marriage between his older son, Gaston, and his ward, Valerie. Though Valerie and Francois are in love, Francois discovers, after he fights his brother, that Valerie has agreed to the marriage. At this news Francois, with the

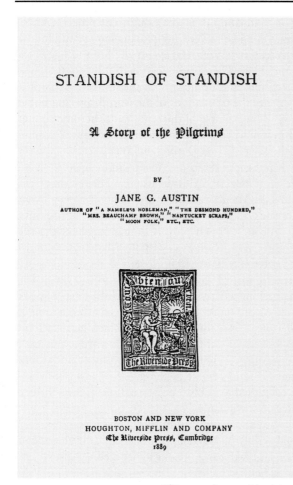

STANDISH OF STANDISH

A Story of the Pilgrims

BY
JANE G. AUSTIN
AUTHOR OF "A NAMELESS NOBLEMAN," "THE DESMOND HUNDRED,"
"MRS. BEAUCHAMP BROWN," "NANTUCKET SCRAPS,"
"MOON FOLK," ETC., ETC.

BOSTON AND NEW YORK
HOUGHTON, MIFFLIN AND COMPANY
The Riverside Press, Cambridge
1889

BETTY ALDEN

THE FIRST-BORN DAUGHTER OF
THE PILGRIMS

BY
JANE G. AUSTIN
AUTHOR OF "STANDISH OF STANDISH," "A NAMELESS NOBLEMAN," "DR.
LE BARON AND HIS DAUGHTERS," "THE DESMOND HUNDRED,"
"NANTUCKET SCRAPS," ETC.

BOSTON AND NEW YORK
HOUGHTON, MIFFLIN AND COMPANY
The Riverside Press, Cambridge

Title pages for two of Austin's novels that focus on the history of Plymouth Colony

help of Pere Despard, his tutor, sells his lands, rejects France and family entirely, and leaves to pursue a medical education. Clearly, the motivating factor for everyone but Francois is the wealth and privilege that come with court favor. A polarity of values–European decadence versus American integrity–is established early. The virtuous Francois is destined to be a new American.

Austin then shifts the scene to the coast of Cape Cod. It is the end of the seventeenth century, during the first outbreak of the French and Indian Wars. The reader is introduced to the heroine of the novel, Mary Wilder–daughter of Humphry Wilder, a proudly independent farmer, and his Quaker wife, Deborah–who lives near Falmouth. Austin's delineation of Mary is significant, for the character exemplifies how the new world seemed to develop "new women." Mary is one of the many Austin heroines marked by defiant independence, who make statements to male authorities such as "I deny your right to command, and I shall not obey."

Examples of American self-reliance, Francois and Mary make their own way. When a French warship, on

which Francois serves as a military physician, is wrecked on the coast, most the survivors are captured, but a few like Francois make it to shore safely. Home alone, Mary takes Francois in, nurses him, hides him from authorities, and renames him Francis LeBaron–mistaking in her democratic innocence his title for a last name. The two fall in love of course and are secretly married before he leaves to rejoin the army of Quebec. The preparations for the marriage–with disguises, danger, and intrigue–consumes about half the novel. When peace is declared between France and England, Francis returns for Mary. On his way there, however, he stops in Plymouth, where he is befriended by the community because as a doctor he is able to save a life. Plymouth, in need of a physician, offers him the job, so the LeBarons make their first and lasting home there.

While they value community, the integrity of Francis and Mary LeBaron keeps them always a little distanced from their neighbors. For instance, as Francis works out his contract with William Bradford and the selectman of Plymouth Colony, his religion becomes an issue. He is a non-practicing Catholic who nevertheless refuses to renounce his faith. They strike a deal that neither he nor the Puritans will ever bring up their religions to each other. Religious dissent and tolerance are important issues for Austin. Here and elsewhere, she has recurring instances of sympathetic, admirable characters refusing to participate in the religion of their communities and being accepted regardless.

Although this novel contains conventional improbabilities, it is a compelling narrative about sympathetic characters. Particularly in her delineation of New England rustics, Austin's characterizations have a truthful power. In dialogue she manages to depict archaic, formal speech with seeming accuracy, but at the same time to breathe humanity into it. For instance, when LeBaron dies, the reader feels the grief as his oldest friend laments to Mary: "I loved him more than ever I loved mortal before or since, and news of his fearful death has changed the face of all the world to me."

A Nameless Nobleman was the first of what were called Austin's Pilgrim books, though they would more accurately be described as her Plymouth books. The five novels that comprise the series cover the entire Colonial period. The sequel to *A Nameless Nobleman, Dr. LeBaron and His Daughters* (1890), is set during the American Revolution and focuses on the children of Dr. Lazarus LeBaron, the son of Francis and Mary, who continued his father's practice. Their various stories interweave with the lives of many other citizens of Plymouth and its environs as they struggle for or against the transition from colonial outpost to new nation.

The success of *A Nameless Nobleman* evidently increased Austin's appreciation for familiar material, but it does not seem to have immediately affected her writing style. The following year she published *The Desmond Hundred* (1882), an adventure-romance about Colonial Puritans. Her next volume, a collection of local-color stories called *Nantucket Scraps: Being the Experiences of an Off-Islander, in Season and Out of Season, Among a Passing People* (1883), suggests a continued fascination with her own New England locale. More telling of her development as a writer, however, is the decline in output after *Nantucket Scraps*. With the exception of a few stories, Austin published nothing until Houghton, Mifflin brought out *Standish of Standish: A Story of the Pilgrims,* arguably the most significant of her novels, in 1889. Certainly, this novel reflects her increased respect for history and a commitment to research.

Standish of Standish tells of the founding *Mayflower* Pilgrims. Two thirds of the novel covers the trials of their first year: landing at Plymouth, building their primitive settlement, struggling for food, losing half their number to disease, interacting with Indians (Samoset, Squanto, Chief Massasoit), and celebrating a feast of thanksgiving. The final third shows the colony evolving: adjusting to more relaxed citizens with the arrival of the second group of Plymouth colonists on the *Fortune,* handling Indian problems caused by Weymouth Colony, and coping with drought and famine. Throughout the story, but particularly after the plague decimates their settlement, they court, seeking personal and communal stability in marriage.

Much more than her previous historic subjects, Austin's approach to this material of national significance required extensive research into formal records, including William Bradford's *Complete History Of Plymouth Plantation,* which had been rediscovered in England in 1856. The result of her several years of research was a novel that had the significance of history and the power of fiction. It offers perhaps the best illustration of Austin's ability as a storyteller to infuse history with life. From the bare facts of record she creates poignant human moments. The reader must remember that it is fiction, however, for Austin freely develops parts of the story that are not clear in record. For instance, from the fact that Bradford's wife drowns at sea, Austin weaves a poignant human drama. She portrays Dorothy Bradford, obediently but miserably following her husband in his quest, and depicts her depression and suicide as well as Bradford's lifelong stoic guilt. For the sake of drama she invests these historical characters with personalities of her own creation that are not wholly admirable.

The title *Standish of Standish* is somewhat misleading, for Austin really tells the story of the fifty Pilgrims who survived the first winter. In addition to Captain Myles Standish, the primary players in the story are William Bradford, who became governor after the death of John Carver; John Alden, Standish's lieutenant; and Priscilla Molines, a young woman orphaned by plague. The focus on Standish allows Austin to negotiate two plots: the adventure of surviving in a wilderness and the romance of courtships. As the military leader of the colony, he was central in all their frontier exploits, both with the land and with the Indians. He was also a widower, whom history had already attached to romance.

Focus on Standish further allowed Austin to view the Pilgrim experience as both an insider and an outsider. While committed to the Pilgrims' enterprise, he was not one of them; though he continued to live in Plymouth throughout his life, he never abandoned the Anglican Church of England. This situation works well narratively, but it also seems to carry thematic issues for Austin. Like her great-great grandfather, Francis LeBaron, Standish–also an ancestor–is an outsider. He too is a displaced aristocrat, adopting democracy.

Austin also develops Myles Standish as an American emblem. A soldier whose role was to protect a community of faith as it colonized a strange land for the glory of God, he well encapsulates an important tension of the Pilgrim venture, one that haunts America to this day. In a variety of situations, this new "kingdom on a hill" is ironically a place of sin. Particularly in their dealing with natives, these people who sought to purify Christianity found it necessary to become killers. Austin was certainly sensitive to this paradox. She closes her novel by quoting from a letter written a few years after the colony was established. It explains that the lower part of the military fort was used "for their church, where they preach on Sundays and the usual holidays. They assemble by beat of drum, each with his musket or firelock."

Another instance in which Austin's perspective on history influences the story is in the depiction of Priscilla Molines (though usually Anglicized, Austin uses the French spelling) whose family were Huguenots who joined the separatists from Scooby, England, in Leydon, Netherlands. In many ways Priscilla, like Mary Wilder LeBaron, seems to belong more to the woman-question debate of the nineteenth century than the religious-freedom debate of the seventeenth. For instance, when Governor Bradford requests that all the men be called for the "first town-meeting," Priscilla angrily whispers to a friend, "But none of the women, mark you!"

While eight years had passed between *A Nameless Nobleman* and *Standish of Standish,* Austin published their sequels in quick succession. *Dr. LeBaron and His Daughters* appeared the next year, and her continuation of the Pilgrims' saga, *Betty Alden: The First-Born Daughter of the Pilgrims* (1891), followed in another year. Her Plymouth fiction was then so popular that Houghton, Mifflin brought out a collection of her earlier magazine stories treating the material: *David Alden's Daughter and Other Stories of Colonial Times* (1892). Regrettably, this last of the series is the least noteworthy. Many of the stories were written early in her career, before she developed an ethic of accuracy. In one of the stories, "The Love Life of William Bradford," she falsely authenticates her story with fabricated records. Other stories carry extreme examples of qualities that somewhat weaken her better work: sentimentalized lovers, sensationalized heroes, and villains.

The traits modern readers may count as faults, however, were typical of the age in which Austin wrote. In her own time and in modern times her historical fiction can be appreciated for its realistic texture of details. Her depiction of the New England milieu reveals the uniqueness of the Puritan character. Furthermore, she demonstrates the power of a good storyteller, with fiction that appeals to the sympathetic imagination. As one critic asserted at her death in the 1894–1895 volume of *The Book Buyer,* "No other writer has done as much to perpetuate the life and customs of the Pilgrim Fathers."

References:

Stanley Kunitz and Howard Haycroft, *American Authors 1600–1900* (New York: Wilson, 1938), p. 42;

Arthur Hobson Quinn, *American Fiction* (New York: Appleton-Century, 1936), p. 488;

"Rambler," *The Book Buyer,* third series, 2 (1894–1895): 194;

Susan Sutton Smith, "Jane Goodwin Austin," in *American Women Writers,* volume 1, edited by Lina Mainiero (New York: Unger, 1979), pp. 72–74;

Frances E. Willard and Mary A. Livermore, *A Woman of the Century* (Buffalo: Moulton, 1893); republished (Detroit: Gale, 1967), p. 36.

Papers:

Some of Jane Goodwin Austin's letters, manuscripts, and photos are held by University of Virginia, Stanford University, and University of Arizona.

Irving Bacheller

(26 September 1859 – 24 February 1950)

Charles Johanningsmeier
University of Nebraska-Omaha

BOOKS: *The Master of Silence* (New York: Webster, 1892);

The Still House of O'Darrow (London: Cassell, 1894; London: Cassell, 1894);

The Story of a Passion (East Aurora, N.Y.: Roycroft, 1899);

Eben Holden: A Tale of the North Country (Boston: Lothrop, 1900; London: Richards, 1901);

D'Ri and I: A Tale of the North Country; Memoirs of Colonel Ramon Bell, U.S.A. (Boston: Lothrop, 1901); republished as *D'ri and I: A Tale of Daring Deeds in the Second War with the British. Being the Memoirs of Colonel Ramon Bell, U.S.A.* (London: Richards, 1901);

Darrel of the Blessed Isles (Boston: Lothrop, 1903; London: Watt, 1903);

Vergilius: A Tale of the Coming of Christ (New York & London: Harper, 1904);

Silas Strong, Emperor of the Woods (New York & London: Harper, 1906);

Eben Holden's Last Day A-Fishing (New York & London: Harper, 1907);

The Hand-Made Gentleman: A Tale of the Battles of Peace (New York & London: Harper, 1909); republished as *Cricket Heron* (London: Unwin, 1909);

The Master (New York & London: Doubleday, Page, 1909);

In Various Moods; Poems and Verses (New York & London: Harper, 1910);

Keeping Up with Lizzie (New York & London: Harper, 1911);

"Charge It!" or Keeping Up with Harry (New York & London: Harper, 1912);

The Turning of Griggsby (New York & London: Harper, 1913);

The Marryers (New York & London: Harper, 1914);

The Light in the Clearing: A Tale of the North Country in the Time of Silas Wright (Indianapolis: Bobbs-Merrill, 1917; London: Collins, 1918);

Keeping Up With William (Indianapolis: Bobbs-Merrill, 1918);

Irving Bacheller, circa 1899

A Man for the Ages: A Story of the Builders of Democracy (Indianapolis: Bobbs-Merrill, 1919; London: Constable, 1920);

The Prodigal Village: A Christmas Tale (Indianapolis: Bobbs-Merrill, 1920);

In the Days of Poor Richard (Indianapolis: Bobbs-Merrill, 1922; London: Hutchinson, 1923);

The Scudders: A Story of Today (New York: Macmillan, 1923; London: Mills & Boon, 1924);

Father Abraham (Indianapolis: Bobbs-Merrill, 1925; London: Hutchinson, 1925);

Opinions of a Cheerful Yankee (Indianapolis: Bobbs-Merrill, 1926);

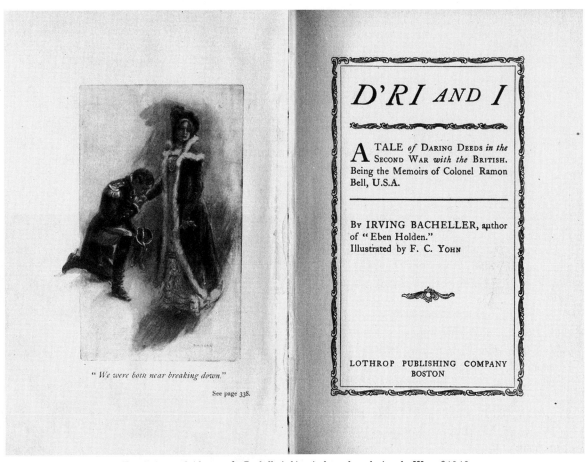

"We were both near breaking down."

See page 338.

D'RI AND I

A TALE of DARING DEEDS in the SECOND WAR with the BRITISH. Being the Memoirs of Colonel Ramon Bell, U.S.A.

By IRVING BACHELLER, author of "Eben Holden." Illustrated by F. C. YOHN

LOTHROP PUBLISHING COMPANY BOSTON

Frontispiece and title page for Bacheller's historical novel set during the War of 1812

Dawn: A Lost Romance at the Time of Christ (New York: Macmillan, 1927); republished as *The Trumpets of God: A Lost Romance of the Time of Christ* (London: Melrose, 1927);

Coming Up the Road: Memories of a North Country Boyhood (Indianapolis: Bobbs-Merrill, 1928);

The House of Three Ganders (Indianapolis: Bobbs-Merrill, 1928; London: Hutchinson, 1929);

A Candle in the Wilderness: A Tale of the Beginning of New England (Indianapolis: Bobbs-Merrill, 1930);

The Master of Chaos (Indianapolis: Bobbs-Merrill, 1932);

Great Moments in the Life of Washington, by Bacheller and Herbert S. Kates (New York: Grosset & Dunlap, 1932);

Uncle Peel (New York: Stokes, 1933);

The Harvesting (New York: Stokes, 1934);

The Oxen of the Sun (New York: Stokes, 1935);

A Boy for the Ages (New York & Toronto: Farrar & Rinehart, 1937);

From Stores of Memory (New York & Toronto: Farrar & Rinehart, 1938);

The Winds of God: A Tale of the North Country (New York & Toronto: Farrar & Rinehart, 1941).

OTHER: "The Syndicate Matter," *Journalist,* 17 April 1886, p. 3.

Copies of Irving Bacheller's novels, especially his popular *Eben Holden: A Tale of the North Country* (1900), can be found on the shelves of almost any antiquarian or used bookshop, but few people recognize his name or are familiar with his work. These books are a testament to Bacheller's widespread popularity between approximately 1900 and 1920 but also to the rapid decline of his reputation. Like so many of his contemporaries who rejected literary modernism, he and his works were long ago relegated to the shadows of American literary history. This does not mean, though, that they deserve to remain there. While Bacheller's writing is often marred by deficiencies in authorial technique, several of his novels are good specimens of twentieth-century regionalist writing. Further, the novels in which he is critical of the moral and social decay of America are representative of the type of middle-brow culture described in Joan Shelley Rubin's *The Making of Middle-brow Culture* (1992).

Constructing an accurate account of Bacheller's life has been hindered in large part by Bacheller's two desultory autobiographies, *Coming Up the Road: Memories of a North Country Boyhood* (1928) and *From Stores of Memory* (1938), which include few specific dates. The one available biography on Bacheller, a 1952 doctoral dissertation, relies heavily on these autobiographies, as do most of the hagiographic accounts of his life written by those who knew him. Only in the 1990s has scholarly work been carried out on Bacheller's early life that has employed sources other than the autobiographies in order to confirm or correct Bacheller's accounts.

Born on 26 September 1859, Addison Irving Bacheller—named by his mother, who revered writers Joseph Addison and Washington Irving—came from old New England stock. The family of his father, Sanford Paul Bacheller, emigrated from Vermont in the 1830s to the St. Lawrence River valley area of Upstate New York, and his mother, Achsah Ann Buckland Bacheller, was from Massachusetts and a descendant of *Mayflower* settlers John Alden and Priscilla Mullins. Irving was the sixth of seven children, with two older sisters, Elvira and Sarah, and four brothers, Loren, Burton, Arthur, and Wilbur; all his siblings, except Elvira and Wilbur, died at relatively young ages. Bacheller grew up on a farm in Pierrepont, New York, a few miles south of Canton.

When he was thirteen, Bacheller moved with his family to Canton and attended Canton Academy. He spent much of his time in the pool hall, though, and after graduation drifted in and out of a series of odd jobs. At the age of nineteen Bacheller convinced A. C. Gaines, president of St. Lawrence University in Canton, to admit him as a "select" student on probation. Never a model scholar, Bacheller as an undergraduate was best known for having founded the first chapter in the North of the southern fraternity Alpha Tau Omega. Bacheller graduated from St. Lawrence University in 1882 and later received an M.S. degree in 1891. Eventually he became one of the university's leading alumni, and in recognition of his work on its behalf he received honorary M.A. and L.H.D. degrees in 1901 and 1911, respectively.

Like so many young men from rural areas at the time, Bacheller soon after graduation made his way to New York City, eager to make his place in the world. During his first two years there he occupied a variety of journalistic positions, including a stint as drama editor of the *Brooklyn Daily Times*. Serving in this capacity in 1883, he met the English novelist Joseph Hatton, who was accompanying dramatist Henry Irving on tour. Inspired by the syndication of fiction in Britain by Tillotson's *Newspaper Fiction Bureau*, Hatton suggested that Bacheller act as his agent and sell the serial rights to his latest novel, *The Mystery of Margaret Willoughby*, to American newspapers. Bacheller was only able to sell the novel to the *New York Ledger*, but that sale brought $3,500 and earned him $500 as a commission. Encouraged by this experience and by his syndication of a series of London letters that Hatton sent to him in 1884, Bacheller in early 1885 quit his post at the *Brooklyn Daily Times* and began working full-time at syndicating fiction to multiple American newspapers for simultaneous serial publication.

Bacheller may have wished to be remembered for his work as a novelist, but his greatest contribution to literature in America was probably his work as a syndicator. His name appears in the footnotes of many famous authors' biographies and bibliographies because of the role he played in their careers, and what little scholarly work has been carried out on Bacheller has focused on syndication. From the beginning of his syndicate until he sold it in early 1898, Bacheller ran a relatively successful enterprise that bought and sold the first serial rights to hundreds of works, including many by Sarah Orne Jewett, Mary E. Wilkins, Hamlin Garland, Bret Harte, Sir Arthur Conan Doyle, Rudyard Kipling, Thomas Hardy, and Joel Chandler Harris. Bacheller and other syndicators deserve some of the credit for raising the rates of pay for American authors and expanding their audience. In 1886 Bacheller succinctly stated his mission to readers of *The Journalist*: "If the great public can get hold of the wholesome productions of literary genius, it will thank God for deliverance from the reign of rot."

As a syndicate manager Bacheller is best known for the significant role he played in the career of a struggling young author named Stephen Crane. After his manuscript for *The Red Badge of Courage* had been rejected by *McClure's Magazine* in 1894, Crane submitted it to Bacheller's syndicate. Bacheller, who later recalled that he was "thrilled by its power and vividness," immediately accepted the work and published it in at least ten American newspapers in December 1894, long before Appleton brought out the book version in the fall of 1895. Unfortunately for readers, however, the constraints of Bacheller's contracts with his newspaper-editor clients dictated that the work be shortened from the fifty thousand words in Crane's manuscript to fifteen thousand words, and in almost every newspaper these were doled out in six installments.

For his part in the publication of shortened versions of Crane's masterpiece, Bacheller has earned an undeserved reputation as a commercially minded editor with little literary taste. Yet it should be remembered that he was bound by his contracts with editors who wanted no more than six short installments of any work. Furthermore, Crane was quite pleased at the time to receive the reported $90 Bacheller paid him, and the success of *The Red Badge of Courage* subsequently led to

An illustration by F. C. Yohn for D'Ri and I

more work with the Bacheller syndicate. In 1895 Crane traveled throughout the West for Bacheller, gathering material for sketches and stories published via the syndicate, and in January 1897 he was engaged by Bacheller to go to Cuba as a news correspondent. When Crane's ship went down off the coast of Florida, though, he reported that he had to jettison the $700 in gold that Bacheller had advanced him for expenses. While Crane used the experience as the basis of one of his best short stories, "The Open Boat," the loss of the gold dealt a severe blow to the finances of the syndicate.

Bacheller always stated that the syndicate remained a profitable enterprise, but close examination of the historical record reveals otherwise. Even before the loss incurred by Crane, Bacheller had sought to make up syndicate losses by founding the *Pocket Magazine* in November 1895. With a circulation of approximately twelve thousand, this small magazine contained stories by famous authors reprinted from the syndicate service, and it continued in publication until December 1901. While still serving as editor and publisher of this magazine, Bacheller sold the syndicate business in early 1898 to John Brisbane Walker of *Cosmopolitan* magazine.

Bacheller remained as the salaried manager of the syndicate for three months and then quit to pursue his literary aspirations.

Bacheller had long entertained the dream of establishing himself as an author and had sought out the advice of prominent poet Edmund Clarence Stedman as early as 1889. He also received helpful criticism from members of the literary Lanthorne Club–including Stephen Crane–which Bacheller and others had founded in 1895. In the interstices of his busy syndicate work, Bacheller had managed to publish the war ballad "Whisperin' Bill" in 1890 and the novels *The Master of Silence* (1892) and *The Still House of O'Darrow* (1894). A measure of his growing recognition is the republication of his 1897 story "A Passion Study" in 1899 as *The Story of a Passion* in a deluxe, illuminated edition by Elbert Hubbard of the Roycroft Shop, East Aurora, New York.

In the spring of 1898 Bacheller devoted himself to writing a new novel. He managed to produce about thirty thousand words before his savings started running out and he accepted Joseph Pulitzer's invitation to become editor of the Sunday edition of the *New York World*. While working at the *World*, Bacheller submitted his novelette to *Harper's Round Table, St. Nicholas, Youth's Companion,* and *Century,* but all turned it down. Fortuitously, in 1899 an old friend of Bacheller's with the Lothrop publishing company of Boston contacted him, and the firm gave him an advance to finish his novel. Bacheller then asked Pulitzer for and received a leave of absence from his duties at the *World*. During the winter of 1899–1900 Bacheller finished writing *Eben Holden*.

Published in July 1900, *Eben Holden* is set in Bacheller's north country and draws heavily on his family's experiences there and on his own career in New York City journalism. It begins with the story of William, a young Vermont boy whose parents have drowned in a boating accident. Seeing that William is to be sent to live with a malicious uncle, a hired man named Eben Holden spirits William away and takes him west, traveling through the forest until they reach Paradise Valley in Upstate New York. Once there, William is adopted by the Brower family and grows up in a wonderfully nurturing environment. This part of the plot follows the outline of the life of Bacheller's father, who had been orphaned at a young age in Vermont and taken west to Paradise Valley. Like Bacheller himself, William Brower eventually leaves the north country for New York City. Brower finds journalistic work on Horace Greeley's *New York Tribune* and serves in the Civil War.

The plot and characters of this novel are unexceptional, with its chief interest coming in the depiction of north country life, folklore, and dialect, and it came as a great surprise to Bacheller and many others when his book became a runaway best-seller. Possibly because

Eben Holden sounded many of the same notes as E. N. Westcott's *David Harum* (1899)–which was published after Bacheller had already finished the first part of his novel–sales rose rapidly. The novel first appeared on the best-seller list of *Bookman* in October 1900 and remained near the top until July 1901. By April 1901 it had sold 250,000 copies, and it eventually sold more than one million copies. Its popularity led to its dramatization and presentation on the New York City stage in 1901 and by various traveling companies.

For the rest of his writing career, Bacheller tried but failed to recapture the dizzying success he enjoyed with *Eben Holden*. In life and in his obituaries he was known chiefly as the "author of *Eben Holden*." Yet for Bacheller *Eben Holden* marked just the beginning of his four-decade career as a full-time author of short stories and novels. He explored a variety of genres in his writing but was best known for novels of historical romance, regionalism, and social criticism.

Bacheller's first attempt at historical romance after *Eben Holden* was *D'Ri and I: A Tale of the North Country; Memoirs of Colonel Ramon Bell, U.S.A.,* which he published in March 1901. Because of *Eben Holden*'s phenomenal success, Bacheller was able to place *D'Ri and I* in the *Century* magazine for serial publication, and there were advance book sales of sixty-five thousand copies. In its first year it sold more than two hundred thousand copies, but the reviews were quite mixed. Most agreed that the novel was conventional in its improbable events and wooden love story. Col. Ramon Bell is the son of Vermonters transplanted to the St. Lawrence River valley, and his boon companion is the family's hired man, Darius (D'Ri) Olin. They go through a series of adventures during the War of 1812, being captured several times yet always managing to make daring escapes. Bacheller whitewashes the American historical figures, relieving them of any complex or self-serving motives. It is no surprise for the reader when Bell wins the hand of the beautiful French girl Louise.

During the course of his career Bacheller often wrote historical romances, some of which he set in the far past: *Vergilius: A Tale of the Coming of Christ* (1904), *Dawn: A Lost Romance of the Time of Christ* (1927), and *A Candle in the Wilderness: A Tale of the Beginning of New England* (1930). All of these novels were panned by reviewers and were commercial failures.

Bacheller, who firmly believed that Americans needed great men to lead them, also wrote novels with American historical figures at their center. *The Light in the Clearing: A Tale of the North Country in the Time of Silas Wright* (1917) deals with the legacy of the famous north country politician Silas Wright. Bacheller's hagiographic impulses were given further outlet in *In the Days of Poor Richard* (1922), about Benjamin Franklin, and *The Mas-*

ter of Chaos (1932), about George Washington. In his novel *The Oxen of the Sun* (1935) he chronicles the significant contributions of John D. Rockefeller, Thomas Edison, Philip Armour, Andrew Carnegie, and Alexander Graham Bell. Bacheller considered Abraham Lincoln to be the greatest man America had produced and wrote a trilogy on his life: *A Man for the Ages: A Story of the Builders of Democracy* (1919), which took Lincoln up to his election to Congress; *Father Abraham* (1925), about Lincoln's last years; and *A Boy for the Ages* (1937), about Lincoln's boyhood. In 1926 Bacheller's patriotism was rewarded when Bobbs-Merrill included six of his works in the Independence Bell Editions of historical romances.

Another genre Bacheller practiced with moderate success was regionalist fiction. To some extent he was personally responsible for defining Upstate New York as a "regional" literary area. Having lived in this area for his first twenty three years, Bacheller knew it well. The best scenes of *Eben Holden* take place in the early chapters, when William and Eben are living on the Brower farm in Paradise Valley. He also represents the local dialect well and incorporates north country folklore in novels such as *Darrel of the Blessed Isles* (1903), *Silas Strong, Emperor of the Woods* (1906), *The Hand-Made Gentleman: A Tale of the Battles of Peace* (1909), and *The House of Three Ganders* (1928).

Silas Strong is perhaps the best and most interesting of his regional novels. The title character is an Adirondack guide named Silas Strong–based on Bacheller's companion and guide Philo Scott–who actively resists the lumber companies that seek to destroy the wilderness. A love story is awkwardly included, but along the way Bacheller sympathetically portrays the people who live in the harsh environment of the Adirondacks. *Silas Strong* is notable, too, because it is the only novel Bacheller wrote that has an unhappy ending.

While the wise investment of profits from his first books made him a wealthy man and he did not need his novels to succeed financially, Bacheller did wish to make a difference in the lives of his readers. Around 1909 Bacheller discovered a subject that he believed would do so. On the lecture and after-dinner speaking circuit Bacheller began developing a theme that elicited a strong, positive reaction from his audiences: conservative social criticism. In these speeches and many of his subsequent novels Bacheller gave voice to many of the concerns conservative, older Americans had about the new, "liberated" and "Europeanized" ways of young Americans and the effects these were having on old-fashioned American values. In his speaking engagements Bacheller created the persona of "Socrates ("Sock") Potter, a sage elderly lawyer from Pointview,

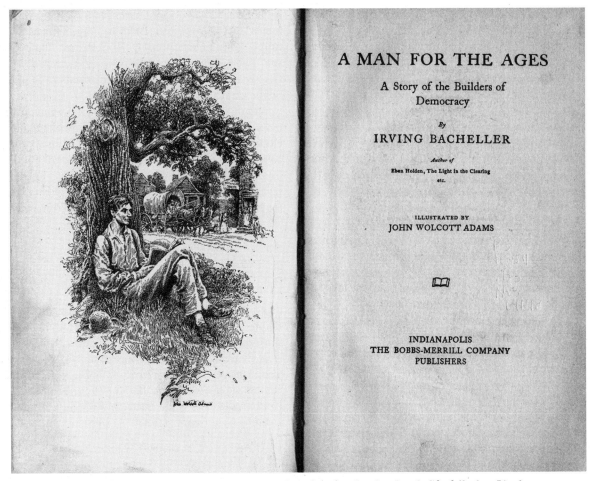

Frontispiece and title page for Bacheller's 1919 novel, the first of a trilogy based on the life of Abraham Lincoln

Connecticut, who wryly criticizes the many changes he observed in America during the previous decade.

Recognizing the great popularity of this character, Bacheller made him the narrator of his novel *Keeping Up with Lizzie* (1911). In this work the local grocer in Pointview has to raise his prices in order to keep his daughter Lizzie in the finest fashions, and all the other businessmen in town, whose daughters wish to emulate Lizzie, also raise their prices and go into debt until every family is living far beyond its means. All of this folly leads to great unhappiness, for everyone has lost touch with the important family values that Bacheller viewed as the foundation of America. Eventually, though, Socrates Potter helps Lizzie regain her senses and return to the virtues of diligence, thrift, and simple living, and the others follow suit. Such a theme struck a chord with many Americans: the novel sold 160,000 copies by 1917.

Bacheller brought Potter back as his surrogate preacher in four subsequent novels. For instance, in *"Charge It!" or Keeping Up with Harry* (1912) Potter criticizes the extravagance of credit, the changes brought about by the advent of the automobile, and modern novelists who appealed to readers with sex. Potter reappears in *The Marryers* (1914) to save the daughter of an American millionaire from marrying an avaricious European count. In *Keeping Up with William* (1918) Potter becomes concerned about Kaiser "William" and the German "leprosy" afflicting America, especially in the theaters and movie houses controlled by Germans. Socrates Potter's final appearance was as the narrator of *The Oxen of the Sun,* a rambling account of the great age of expansion in America after the Civil War. Socrates spends most of his time applauding the initiative of the great inventors and businessmen of the day, occasionally criticizing labor unions for their antiprogressive stance.

Bacheller was also capable of writing social criticism without using Socrates Potter. In *The Turning of Griggsby* (1913) and *The Prodigal Village: A Christmas Tale* (1920) Bacheller lectures on how Americans can save themselves from rampant moral deterioration simply by returning to good old-fashioned American values and by rejecting European influences. In *The Scudders: A Story of Today* (1923) Bacheller attacks families in which the men are so busy making money and the women so busy socializing that they neglect their children. His final work of social criticism, *Uncle Peel* (1933), is about the collapse of the Florida land boom that greatly depleted Bacheller's personal fortune.

Bacheller is representative of the many writers whose hearts and minds remained firmly rooted in the nineteenth century even though they lived well into the twentieth. Not only in his novels but also in short stories, speeches, and essays Bacheller returned time and time again to the idea that the modern world was a greatly diminished one. He believed that middle-class family life had fallen apart because parents were too concerned with making money and socializing and neglected to attend church, the fount of American morality.

The tendencies of modern life, Bacheller argued, were creating indulged, spoiled children who had no sense of self-restraint and believed that the best things in life could be had without working for them. Bacheller viewed the infiltration of European ideas into American life as especially dangerous to young Americans. Some of this antipathy stemmed from what he saw as a magazine war correspondent in France in 1917, but much of it resulted from his superficial reading and observation of American life. The three men he blamed most for having ruined Americans were Frederic Nietzsche, George Bernard Shaw, and Sigmund Freud. Bacheller's works of social criticism are of interest to literary historians because they serve as a counterbalancing reminder that not all Americans eagerly embraced the messages found in the works of such authors as Ernest Hemingway, F. Scott Fitzgerald, T. S. Eliot, Ezra Pound, Theodore Dreiser, Sherwood Anderson, Sinclair Lewis, Susan Glaspell, Eugene O'Neill, and Lillian Hellman.

Another interesting aspect of Bacheller's social criticism is its hypocritical nature. Hamlin Garland, who was Bacheller's best friend from approximately 1895 until Garland's death in 1940, railed against modern literature and morals, too, but he did so from the vantage point of a person who lived relatively simply. On the other hand, Bacheller, who was made wealthy by the success of his early novels and shrewd investments in land, lived a luxurious life. Bacheller's advice to Americans was to live a simple, frugal existence and be content with the enjoyment of one's family and immediate surroundings, but he did just the opposite. He owned substantial homes in Riverside, Connecticut, and Winter Park, Florida, and spent a great deal of time at his Adirondack "camp" set on four thousand acres of land. He entertained lavishly, had many servants, traveled widely (while insisting Americans need not), and used credit to full advantage.

Furthermore, this apostle of family life and morals spent much of his time away from home on business, and his adopted son spent much of his childhood in summer camps and boarding schools. Bacheller's hypocrisy is also evident in his contention that for America to be a great country again it must turn away from its Europeanized cities to the values and people of its small villages and rural areas to lead it out of its morass. Yet Bacheller himself had found farm work tiresome and smalltown life and people unfulfilling; this is why as soon as he could he fled to New York City. Garland was candid enough to admit that he could never return to the farms of his youth; Bacheller's response was to romanticize that part of his life and encourage others to see it as the ideal. In doing so he was not unlike millions of Americans of his era who, dismayed at what they believed were the liberated ways of the 1910s and 1920s and viewing the Depression as a natural result of societal licentiousness, escaped in nostalgia to an idealized golden age.

Bacheller's influence as an author declined appreciably in the 1920s, but he continued to write and remain active in other ways. He spent the final decades of his life not in New York's north country but rather in Winter Park, a town founded by transplanted New Englanders. From the time Bacheller first visited in 1918, the town regarded him as its leading citizen, and he was actively involved in civic affairs. He developed a close relationship with Rollins College, serving as a member of its board of trustees and bringing distinguished speakers to campus. Accompanying him as his partners in these endeavors were his first wife, Anna Detmar Schultz, who died in 1924, and then Mary Elizabeth Solace, whom he married in 1925 and who died in 1949. When the Florida land boom fizzled in 1929, Bacheller lost a great deal of money, but he soldiered on, writing novels that sold only a few thousand copies each, keeping in touch with old friends such as Garland, and writing diatribes against the corruption of modern life. His last published novel was *The Winds of God: A Tale of the North Country* (1941); at his death on 24 February 1950 he had completed two novels for which he could not find a publisher.

In the more than one hundred years since Bacheller published his first novel, not a single serious work of literary criticism dealing with his fiction has appeared. This is not surprising, since Bacheller's style of optimistic, didactic, and patriotic boosterism has never been popular within an academy that embraced modernism. As literary historians seek to present a more complete and accurate picture of American literature, however, more attention needs to be paid to the type of middlebrow fiction represented by Bacheller's works. At the same time, one must acknowledge Bacheller's relative lack of artistic skill. His novels are episodic and full of clichés, and his depictions of romances between men and women are predictable and unrealistic. Further, there is little psychological complexity to his characters; just as he painted social issues in black and white terms, he did not present gray characters. Finally, he appeared constitutionally unable to write an unhappy ending, with the single exception of *Silas Strong*. To his credit, he recognized his shortcomings as an author and always described himself as a "copyist" of life. This assessment is borne out by his work, the best of which describes the north country life that he knew so well.

Bibliography:

Alfred J. Hanna, "A Bibliography of the Writings of Irving Bacheller," *Rollins College Bulletin*, 35 (September 1939): 1–48.

Biography:

"Life Sketch of Irving Bacheller, Noted North Country Author," *Watertown* (N.Y.) *Times*, 25 February 1950, pp. 14–15.

References:

D. Lynn Case, "Eben Holden: Irving Bacheller's Folk Society," *St. Lawrence Historical Association Quarterly*, 23 (October 1978): 25–31;

Clarence Hurd Gaines, "Irving Bacheller: An Attempt at Interpretation," *Rollins College Bulletin*, 35 (September 1935): 11–14;

Hamlin Garland, *Companions on the Trail. A Literary Chronicle* (New York: Macmillan, 1931);

Garland, "Irving Bacheller: Interpreter of the Old America to the New," *Red Cross Magazine* (March 1920): 11–14, 79;

Garland, *Roadside Memories* (New York: Macmillan, 1930);

Charles Johanningsmeier, "Expanding the Scope of 'Periodical History' for Literary Studies: Irving Bacheller and His Newspaper Fiction Syndicate," *American Periodicals*, 5 (1995): 14–39;

Johanningsmeier, *Fiction and the American Literary Marketplace: The Role of Newspaper Syndicates, 1860–1900* (Cambridge: Cambridge University Press, 1997);

Joseph Katz, "Bibliography and the Rise of American Realism," *Studies in American Fiction*, 2 (1974): 75–88;

O. W. R., "The Newspaper Syndicate King," *Journalist*, 31 July 1886, p. 3;

Charles E. Samuels, "Irving Bacheller: A Critical Biography," dissertation, Syracuse University, 1952;

Samuels, "Irving Bacheller's Pioneer Syndicate," *Journalism Quarterly*, 34 (1957): 90–92.

Papers:

Irving Bacheller's papers are held by the Owen D. Young Library at St. Lawrence University, the Clifton Waller Barrett Collection of the Alderman Library, University of Virginia, and the Rollins College Library at Winter Park, Florida.

Amelia Edith Huddleston Barr

(29 March 1831 – 10 March 1919)

Bruce Guy Chabot
Texas A&M University

BOOKS: *Romances and Realities: Tales of Truth and Fancy* (New York: J. B. Ford, 1876);

The Young People of Shakespeare's Dramas For Youthful Readers (New York: Appleton, 1882);

Cluny MacPherson: A Tale of Brotherly Love (New York: Dodd, Mead, 1883);

Scottish Sketches (New York: American Tract Society, 1883);

The Hallam Succession (New York: Dodd, Mead, 1884);

Jan Vedder's Wife (New York: Dodd, Mead, 1885);

The Lost Silver of Briffault (New York: Philips & Hunt; Cincinnati: Cranston & Stowe, 1885);

Between Two Loves: A Tale of the West Riding (New York: Harper, 1886; London: Warne, 1894);

The Bow of Orange Ribbon: A Romance of New York (New York: Dodd, Mead, 1886);

A Daughter of Fife (New York: Dodd, Mead, 1886);

The Last of the MacAllisters (New York: Harper, 1886);

The Squire of Sandal-Side (New York: Dodd, Mead, 1886);

A Border Shepherdess: A Romance of Eskdale (New York: Dodd, Mead, 1887; London: Clarke, 190?);

Paul and Christina (New York: Dodd, Mead, 1887);

Christopher, and other Stories (New York: Philips & Hunt; Cincinnati: Cranston & Stowe, 1888);

In Spite of Himself: A Tale of the West Riding (London: Clarke, 1888);

Master of His Fate (New York: Dodd, Mead, 1888);

The Novels of Besant and Rice (New York: Dodd, Mead, 1888);

Remember the Alamo (New York: Dodd, Mead, 1888); republished as *Woven of Love and Glory* (London: Clarke, 1890);

Feet of Clay (New York: Dodd, Mead, 1889);

Friend Olivia (New York: Dodd, Mead, 1889);

The Beads of Tasmer (New York: Dodd, Mead, 1890; London: Clarke, 1893);

The Household of MacNeil (New York: Dodd, Mead, 1890);

She Loved A Sailor (New York: Dodd, Mead, 1890);

Amelia Edith Huddleston Barr, 1880

Love For An Hour Is Love Forever (New York: Dodd, Mead, 1891);

Mrs. Barr's Short Stories (New York: Bonner, 1891);

A Rose of A Hundred Leaves: A Love Story (New York: Dodd, Mead, 1891);

A Sister To Esau (New York: Dodd, Mead, 1891);

Michael and Theodora: A Russian Story (Boston: Bradley & Woodruff, 1892);

The Preacher's Daughter: A Domestic Romance (New York: Ward & Drummond, 1892);

Girls of a Feather: A Novel With Illustrations by J. O. Nugent (New York: Bonner, 1893);

The Lone House (New York: Dodd, Mead, 1893);

The Mate of the "Easter Belle" and Other Stories (New York: Bonner, 1893);

A Singer From the Sea (New York: Dodd, Mead, 1893);

Bernicia (New York: Dodd, Mead, 1895);

The Flower of Gala Water: A Novel With Illustrations by C. Kendrick (New York: Bonner, 1895);

A Knight of the Nets (New York: Dodd, Mead, 1896);

Winter Evening Tales (New York: Christian Herald, 1896);

The King's Highway (New York: Dodd, Mead, 1897);

Prisoners of Conscience (New York: Century, 1897);

Stories of Life and Love (New York: Christian Herald, 1897);

Maids, Wives, and Bachelors (New York: Dodd, Mead, 1898);

Trinity Bells: A Tale of Old New York (New York: Taylor, 1898);

I, Thou, and the Other One: A Love Story (New York: Dodd, Mead, 1899);

Was It Right To Forgive? A Domestic Romance (Chicago & New York: Stone, 1899);

The Maid of Maiden Lane: A Sequel to "The Bow of Orange Ribbon" A Love Story (New York: Dodd, Mead, 1900);

The Lion's Whelp: A Story of Cromwell's Time (New York: Dodd, Mead, 1901);

Souls of Passage (New York: Dodd, Mead, 1901);

A Song of a Single Note: A Love Story (New York: Dodd, Mead, 1902);

The Black Shilling: A Tale of Boston Towns (New York: Dodd, Mead, 1903);

Thyra Verrick: A Love Story (New York: Taylor, 1903; London: Unwin, 1904);

The Belle of Bowling Green (New York: Dodd, Mead, 1904);

Cecilia's Lovers (New York: Dodd, Mead, 1905);

The Man Between: An International Romance (New York & London: Authors and Newspapers Association, 1906); republished as *Love Will Venture In* (London: Chatto & Windus, 1907);

The Heart of Jessy Laurie (New York: Dodd, Mead, 1907);

The Strawberry Handkerchief: A Romance of the Stamp Act (New York: Dodd, Mead, 1908);

The Hands of Compulsion (New York: Dodd, Mead, 1909);

The House on Cherry Street (New York: Dodd, Mead, 1909);

A Reconstructed Marriage (New York: Dodd, Mead, 1910);

A Maid of Old New York: A Romance of Peter Stuyvesant's Time (New York: Dodd, Mead, 1911);

Sheila Vedder (New York: Dodd, Mead, 1911);

All the Days of My Life: An Autobiography, the Red Leaves of a Human Heart (New York: Appleton, 1913);

Three Score and Ten: A Book For the Aged (New York & London: Appleton, 1913);

Playing With Fire (New York & London: Appleton, 1914);

The Measure of a Man (New York & London: Appleton, 1915);

The Winning of Lucia: A Love Story (New York & London: Appleton, 1915);

Profit and Loss (New York & London: Appleton, 1916);

Christine, A Fife Fisher Girl (New York & London: Appleton, 1917);

Joan; A Romance of an English Mining Village (New York & London: Appleton, 1917);

An Orkney Maid (New York & London: Appleton, 1918);

The Paper Cap: A Story of Love and Labor (New York & London: Appleton, 1918);

Songs in the Common Chord: Songs for Everyone to Sing, Tuned to the C Major Chord of This Life (New York & London: Appleton, 1919).

Amelia Edith Huddleston Barr was a prolific writer of romance and historical novels, and she enjoyed tremendous popular success during the 1890s. Her historical novels, particularly *Remember the Alamo* (1888), are valuable as artistic representations of actual events and people. In her works of pure fiction, she usually invents plots in which a virtuous Christian character triumphs. Her main talent lies in creating enjoyable narratives and clear descriptions of real places.

Amelia Edith Huddleston was born on 29 March 1831 in Ulverston, a village in Lancashire, England, to William Henry Huddleston and Mary Singleton Huddleston. She spent her childhood in northern England and Scotland, attending several small private schools as her father, a Methodist minister, moved among pastoral assignments. In *All the Days of My Life: An Autobiography, the Red Leaves of a Human Heart* (1913), she writes of her happy childhood: "My physical being was well cared for by loving parents in a sweet orderly home, and my mental life well fed by books stimulating the imagination." As a child she enjoyed reading penny chapbooks, including adventure stories and travel narratives, as well as literature dealing with the supernatural, planting early seeds of her lifelong fascination with all things mystical and exotic. The birth of her younger brother and the reactions of the other family members made her feel less important and unhappy, and she was always resentful toward male-dominated societal mores.

While living on the Isle of Man during her teenage years, she made her first attempt at writing, a tragedy about the Roman senator and philosopher Seneca. Of it she said, "I had become very ambitious. I longed to write books and to travel and to see the great cities and the strange peoples I had read about."

When she was sixteen Huddleston started teaching to help alleviate the family's troubled financial situa-

It was only a trodden path used by fishermen, but coming swiftly up to it – as if to detain him Neil Semple saw Captain Hyde. The two men looked at each other defiantly & Neil Said with a cold meaning emphasis – "At your service, Sir."

"Mr Semple at your service." touching his sword –" to the very hilt, Sir."

"Sir, yours to the same extremity."

"As for the cause Mr Semple, here it is –" and he pushed aside his embroidered coat to exhibit to Neil the Bow of Orange Ribbon beneath it.

"I will dye it crimson in your blood," said Neil passionately.

"In the meantime I have the felicity of wearing it," and with an offensively deep salute he terminated the interview. Bow of Orange Ribbon

Amelia. E. Barr.

Page from the manuscript for The Bow of Orange Ribbon *(facsimile in Barr's* The Man Between, *1906)*

tion. One year later she went to Glasgow to continue her education. During her years there, she went on a steamboat excursion to St. Andrews in Fife, Scotland, an experience that would later serve as raw material for several of her novels, including *Jan Vedder's Wife* (1885), *A Daughter of Fife* (1886), and *Prisoners of Conscience* (1897).

In Glasgow she met Robert Barr, a wool merchant, after having first dreamed about meeting him. Throughout her life she reported having frequent dreams in which the future was revealed to her. On 11 July 1850 she married Robert Barr, who was, like her, the child of a minister. His family, who were Scots, opposed the marriage because Huddleston's family was English and poor. Amelia Barr eventually opposed the marriages of her own two eldest daughters, and the theme of parents opposing their daughters' marriages is found in many of her novels.

The married life of Amelia and Robert Barr was frequently plagued by financial troubles. Within a year of the wedding, Robert Barr's business failed and he declared bankruptcy. While still living in Glasgow the couple met Harriet Beecher Stowe and her brother Henry Ward Beecher, who persuaded them to move to America. They made plans to start over in the United States and arrived in New York on 5 September 1853 with their two daughters, Mary and Lilly. The family then traveled to Chicago, where Robert went to work as an accountant and Amelia attempted to open a school for girls. However, their fortunes did not turn around. Their third daughter died in infancy, and Robert made damaging blunders while trying to involve himself in local politics.

Deciding to move on, the Barrs sold their belongings and after stopping briefly in Memphis, Tennessee, arrived in Texas by ship. Upon learning of a yellow-fever epidemic in Galveston, their intended destination, they decided instead to settle in Austin. On the way there Barr saw the San Jacinto battlefield and heard stories about Sam Houston and the War for Texas Independence. She was fascinated by tales of the already legendary Houston and his eight hundred soldiers, who were reported to have wiped out the Spanish army under Santa Anna, thus securing religious and civil liberties for the American settlers in Texas. Barr would later turn the story into her most successful novel, *Remember the Alamo*.

The Barrs lived in Austin for nine years and had five more children there, two of whom died of diphtheria in infancy. Their life, however, was otherwise generally happy. While her husband worked for the state government as an accountant, Barr worked as a teacher in her own school and became active socially, attending parties and playing the organ for the Episcopal church choir. She immersed herself in Texas culture, and she came to know and admire Sam Houston. Relating local societal doings in a 15 February 1861 letter to a friend, Barr complained about the many "Yankee sympathizers" in Austin.

In 1867 the family moved to Galveston, where Robert Barr went to work for a cotton merchant. Amelia Barr had premonitions of misfortune and believed that their house was haunted by the ghost of the French pirate Jean Laffite, who had once lived there. Her misgivings proved prophetic because yellow fever soon killed her husband and three sons, the last of whom had been born in Galveston and lived only a few days. Two years later Barr and her three surviving daughters—Mary, Lilly, and Alice—moved to Ridgewood, New Jersey, where Barr started a private school and set out to write.

In 1869 Barr sold an article on the Texas Confederacy for $30 to *The Christian Union* magazine. She was helped and encouraged in her early writing career by several magazine editors, including George Merriam of *The Christian Herald* and Henry Ward Beecher of *The Christian Union*. At the age of thirty-nine, she moved to New York, where she began to write full-time, composing essays, stories, and poems for magazines such as *The Christian Herald, The Christian Union, Harper's Weekly, Harper's Bazaar, Frank Leslie's Magazine,* and *The Advance*. These works deal with historical matters as well as her reflections on love and life. Barr's first novel, *Eunice Leslie,* was serialized in *The Working Church* in 1872 but was not published in book form.

Though her income from writing was at first meager, Barr records in her autobiography that she was surprised and pleased at being able to publish her writing; she felt she had found her true vocation: "Inside there is a click, a kind of bell that strikes, when the hands of our destiny meet at the meridian hour. I only hope that every new writer may enter the gates of the literary life, as happily and hopefully as I did." Barr's abiding concern with spiritual matters is reflected in her phrasing here as it is in every phase of her life.

Serialized in 1876, *The Last of the MacAllisters* (1886), a novel of Scottish life, marked a turning point in Barr's career because its initial rejection by publisher Henry Holt, who sought works dealing with American subjects, led the writer to begin using American history as source material for many of her novels, starting with *The Bow of Orange Ribbon: A Romance of New York* (1886). Barr's practice was to research historical periods in preparation for writing about them. She spent long days studying in the fine arts alcove of the south hall of the Astor Library, which she believed she had seen years earlier in a vision as a "city of books." She also combed other libraries, searching through books of history, folklore, literature, and religion, gathering source material

"CORNELIA LINGERED IN THE GARDEN."

THE MAID
OF
MAIDEN LANE
A Sequel to
"The Bow of Orange Ribbon"

A LOVE STORY

BY
AMELIA E. BARR
Author of "Friend Olivia," "Jan Vedder's
Wife," "I, Thou and the Other One," *etc.*

NEW YORK
Dodd, Mead and Company
1900

Frontispiece and title page for Barr's 1900 book, one of her series of American historical novels

for her writing and making indices of information she found interesting.

Barr began to enjoy popular success with *Cluny MacPherson: A Tale of Brotherly Love* (1883) and *Jan Vedder's Wife* and quickly became one of the most popular of American novelists. Such was her success that some of her works were pirated by unauthorized publishers. In 1887 Barr purchased a typewriter, shortly after the machines were introduced to the public. She felt that the typewriter made her work much easier and faster, but with or without a typewriter, she wrote prolifically, averaging two books a year in the thirty-five year period from 1883 to 1918. Her habit was to write for at least eight hours almost every day.

Jan Vedder's Wife, for which she was paid the considerable sum of $800 by her publisher, shows the results of Barr's painstaking research into the backgrounds and lifestyles of her characters, in this case Dutch speech patterns, literary history, domestic life, and clothing styles. The novel, which tells the story of a woman who is suspected of ending her unhappy marriage by murdering her husband, received favorable

reviews, and Barr's dramatic style was likened to that of Jane Austen. Harriet Beecher Stowe praised the work in the June 1885 issue of *Bookbuyer:* "There is such an intense human nature that I could not help being sorrowful along in the first part where that unhappy woman was throwing her happiness away, and rejoicing in the last part, when she comes to her better and higher self. . . . When there are so many trashy, sentimental novels, with false moral teachings, put upon the public, I rejoice in a book whose moral is so noble and so nobly and strongly expressed." The high moral tone of Barr's novels always struck a responsive chord with her readers.

The Bow of Orange Ribbon, for which she was paid $600, was a commercial success. Set in New York during the British occupation of the city in 1765, the novel is rich with an atmosphere of anticipation of the Revolution as the Americans prepare to make their stand against British tyranny. As she details the intricacies of urban life, Barr unfolds the tale of Capt. George Hyde, a gold-digging opportunist who marries a wealthy young Dutch girl for money but redeems himself in the end by putting his military skills to use in helping the American colonists. Hyde is representative of many of Barr's protagonists, who often start out as villains but improve themselves and become heroes by the end of the story.

In *A Daughter of Fife* Barr tells the story of Maggie, a Scottish fishergirl who feels inferior to her more sophisticated and worldly lover and goes to Glasgow to work and gain an education. In evaluating this novel, the reviewer for the August 1886 *Bookbuyer* states that Barr's "characters are frequently, as in the case of this story, men and women of strong natural traits, largely modified by contact with society, and discovering, in an unaffected and ingenious way, those common traits and experiences which are the universal possession of the race. The transformation of the simple maiden of the fishing village into the trained and poised woman, able to hold her own in a world of society, may not seem at first glance entirely natural; but when one takes into account the native force of character with which Mrs. Barr endows her heroine, the change is by no means improbable."

One of Barr's strengths as a writer is her effective, lifelike depictions of her characters' worlds. Like the great writers of the Romantic period, Barr in many works deftly uses descriptions of the sea, the mountains, and the countryside to convey an understanding of the way environment reflects and shapes the lives of people. In *A Daughter of Fife* Barr's picture of life in the fishing village and the tribulations of people living in such coastal communities is especially convincing. Some years after the publication of the book, Barr received a letter from a woman who had grown up on the isle of Fife, saying that she had been touched by the verisimilitude of Barr's depiction of the people and their lives there.

Drawing upon her love for Texas lore and history, Barr in 1888 wrote *Remember the Alamo,* an historical romance based on events surrounding the 1836 battle at the mission. She begins the novel with vivid descriptions of the lush Texas countryside, suggesting its appropriateness as a setting for a fight for liberty and democracy. The coming of freedom-loving American settlers sets the stage for their inevitable conflict with the repressive Mexican government that has dominion over the land. Barr simplifies the complex issues surrounding the conflict and gives only the Anglo side, which she glorifies and to which she assigns moral superiority.

The protagonist is Robert Wolf, a physician from New York. Although Wolf had come to San Antonio to set up a medical practice, he eventually chooses to serve with General Houston's army. His foils include his Mexican wife, Maria, who is indolent and profligate, spending her days in her boudoir smoking cigarettes and consuming dainties. Santa Anna is depicted as a ruthless despot who orders the execution of the "Texian" settlers at Goliad. Another noteworthy character, a priest known as Fray Ignatius, is shown to be a devious plotter and despicable moral fraud. Such characters contribute to the clear bias in the novel against the Mexican side of the conflict, making Barr's unapologetic glorification of her American heroes all the more apparent.

Despite its propagandistic nature, the novel shows Barr's talent for crafting intricately detailed portraits of characters such as Houston and Davy Crockett, revealing their personalities through their attire, mannerisms, and actions. Houston's son wrote to thank Barr for her excellent representation of the social situation surrounding the historical incident and for her flattering tribute to his father. Barr once commented that she felt that the spirit of Sam Houston had helped her relate the story truthfully.

Modern readers may well fault *Remember the Alamo* for lacking accurate historical detail, for being too rich in purple prose, facile characters, and fanciful romantic dalliances, and for its underlying assumptions of racial and cultural superiority. Like any historical novelist Barr uses actual historical events as a starting point, inventing what is necessary to flesh out known facts into fiction. Her heroes are larger than life and more legendary than historical, but the work stands as an important reflection of lasting attitudes about the lore surrounding the Alamo and the emotionally charged roles of the major characters. Although the plot is often melodramatic, it is a stirring representation of a significant historical event.

While some contemporary critics noted defects in the construction of Barr's plots and faulted her wooden dialogue, most found much to applaud in her works. One of her most exuberant admirers was Oscar Fay Adams, who, writing in the March 1889 issue of *Andover Review,* favorably compared Barr to Austen for her contribution to realism and praised the way her plots excite the reader's attention from the first. Adams commented that *The Squire of Sandal-Side* (1886) is not plagued by the raw, crude qualities he perceives in much American fiction; he attributed Barr's superior "evenness of tone" to her English ancestry and noted that her use of English and Scottish settings and characters also contributes to the stable "atmosphere" he discerns in her prose. Adams admired Barr's depiction of the differences between members of different social classes, but most of all he praised the pacing of her narratives: "No matter how quiet the life portrayed may be, it is done with vigor and spirit, and the action never halts." Adams concluded that Barr's having embarked

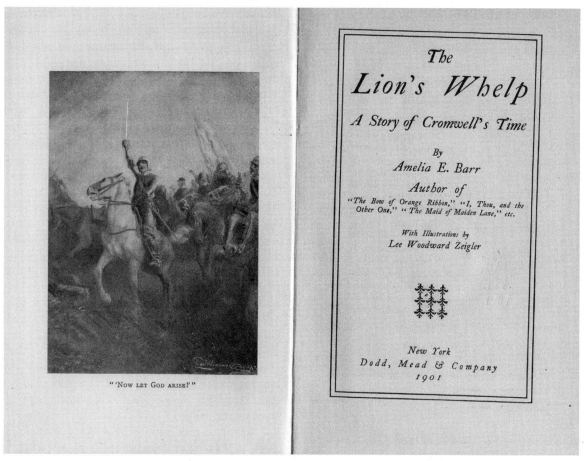

" 'Now let God arise!' "

The
Lion's Whelp
A Story of Cromwell's Time

By
Amelia E. Barr
Author of
"*The Bow of Orange Ribbon,*" "*I, Thou, and the Other One,*" "*The Maid of Maiden Lane,*" *etc.*

With Illustrations by
Lee Woodward Zeigler

New York
Dodd, Mead & Company
1901

Frontispiece and title page for the 1901 novel that expresses Barr's admiration for Puritan leader Oliver Cromwell

upon her writing career late in life enabled her to imbue her works with her own maturity and that her years of contributing to journals and other publications before beginning to write novels helped her gain experience and a smooth style.

During the last decade of the nineteenth century Barr's career was at its height; she enjoyed popular and financial success and appeared frequently on the lecture circuit at colleges and social functions. Her books were bought by the middle-class reading public and were especially favored by young people and college women. Dodd, Mead, and Company advertised her novels heavily in *Bookbuyer.* The September 1891 issue of that magazine carried an article on her by Hamilton Mabie, who wrote of her "hearty zest for sound and simple people; people who do not sophisticate, who have passions and are not ashamed of them; who love frankly and unreservedly; who believe in themselves and their fellows and God. It is good society which Mrs. Barr gives us for the most part; brave, honest men and pure, true-hearted women." Letters that she wrote to friends back in Austin in the 1890s, though, indicate that Barr

was lonely in New York, missed Texas, and still mourned the loss of her husband and sons. Late in the decade she began to suffer from poor health, diminishing eyesight, and bouts of depression, but she resolved to continue writing and to rely on her religious faith for strength.

Barr's notable books in the 1890s include *She Loved a Sailor* (1890), a story of the life of aristocrats in New York's Bowling Green in 1834. A well-written and historically valuable novel, it also contains much information about politics in President Andrew Jackson's time, as well as prevailing attitudes regarding slavery in the South. Barr was personally opposed to slavery but felt that slaves often fared better under their masters than on their own. In *A Rose of A Hundred Leaves: A Love Story* (1891) Barr creates heroine Aspatria Anneys, who feels socially inept compared to her upper-class husband and resolves to improve herself in order to be worthy of him. She becomes graceful, stylish, and witty. Her husband, Sir Ulfar Fenwick, after abandoning her, later suffers remorse and reforms, showing that it is actually he who must become worthy of her love.

Barr at eighty

In 1895 Barr wrote Bernicia, which was described in the December 1895 issue of *Bookbuyer* as "One of those semi-religious studies to which Mrs. Barr has been so successful in giving dramatic interest and quality. It is her good fortune to be something of an idealist, to write with her heart, and impart to her work the impress of her own vigorous personality."

Barr was supportive of the fledgling woman suffrage movement and lamented the inferior place of women in society and under the law. Such attitudes are reflected in her works, where female characters both are more clearly drawn and have stronger personalities than males. Her women are realistic, appealing individuals with simple, noble motives; she saw them as virtuous paragons and role models for readers. Often unyielding in their moral rectitude and expectations of life and of other people, they are rewarded for their virtue by the end of the story. Some of the ancillary male characters have flaws, are profligate, and have to develop to come closer to the spiritual worth of the women. Barr's plots routinely involve romantic love, religious faith, and devotion to duty. All of her novels have a high moral tone, and the major characters share

the same staunch religious faith and inner resilience Barr had observed in her own family.

The advent of a new century did not diminish Barr's productivity. Her notable works of the first decade include *The Lion's Whelp: A Story of Cromwell's Time* (1901). Barr admired the strength of Puritan leader Oliver Cromwell's spiritual convictions in opposing Parliament and the King; she portrays him as a military and political visionary who is, like many of her heroes, larger than life. Set in the Orkney Islands, *Thyra Varrick: A Love Story* (1903) is about the brilliant but blundering Prince Charles Stuart. She based her novel *The Black Shilling: A Tale of Boston Towns* (1903) on Cotton Mather and the New England witch hunts. Barr sets *The Strawberry Handkerchief: A Romance of the Stamp Act* (1908) in New York in 1765 and depicts the social consequences of the infamous tax act from the perspective of women. The novel was well received except for some objections to stilted dialogue. Faithful readers admired Barr for shedding light on history and for making her characters intriguing by revealing their motivations and feelings. A reviewer for the 24 April 1909 issue of *The New York Times* remarked: "There is about Mrs. Barr's work a sincerity, a direct simplicity, and a knowledge of the singular experiences of human life which gives to her books a real value."

At the age of eighty Barr wrote *A Maid of Old New York; A Romance of Peter Stuyvesant's Time* (1911). The focus of this historical novel is Stuyvesant, the last Dutch governor of New Netherland, which became New York when he handed it over to the English in 1664. The book skillfully conveys the manners and ideals of the period. Typically, Barr had carefully researched her subject. To the critics who argued that she showed disdain for the upper-class British Loyalists through her presentation of them as stilted, Barr responded that she had studied the correspondence of prominent figures such as Horace Walpole and Lord Chesterfield in order to glean from their most personal writings and thoughts a reliable understanding of the people and the society making up the court circles and their sympathizers.

In 1913 Barr published her autobiography, *All the Days of My Life,* an intensely candid account of a singularly eventful life that is as entertaining as her fiction. Critic P. F. Bicknell wrote in the 1 August 1913 issue of *The Dial* that Barr's book "is more variously interesting, richer in romance and strange adventure than is usual with the lives of literary folks. It holds the reader under its spell from beginning to end." Barr tells of her lifelong interest in spirituality, mysticism, and theosophy. The reader comes to know a woman who enjoyed reading, studying, and contemplating the Bible, who believed that she had prescient psychic powers and that she was comforted by a guardian angel during sad times. Barr explains that she felt sadness when concluding a novel because she was reluctant to say farewell to characters of whom she had become so fond and whom she believed she had known in some other incarnation. The autobiography shows Barr's spirit of optimism and her feeling that her life was blessed by God.

Barr's prose did not diminish in quality in her last years. On 10 May 1914 a reviewer for *The New York Times* wrote of Barr's *Playing With Fire* (1914): "There is no 'fine writing' anywhere in the book, but the simplicity and directness of Mrs. Barr's method is a real refreshment." In the novel Barr charms the reader through her story with the same gentle ease that marked her work throughout the years of her popularity. *The Paper Cap: A Story of Love and Labor,* Barr's last novel, was published in 1918. In 1919 she released a collection of poems composed through many years, titled *Songs in the Common Chord*. This book of folk wisdom contains hymns to trees, autumn, harvest, and other aspects of nature. Barr celebrates and expresses thanks for simple domestic joys.

Barr died on 10 March 1919 in Richmond Hill, New York, and is buried at Sleepy Hollow Cemetery. While a woman making a living as a writer was not unheard of in the late nineteenth and early twentieth centuries, she was remarkable for her popularity and for the astonishing amount of work she produced in her forty-year career. Though her narratives are often melodramatic and moralistic, containing little real suspense or humor, and her dialogue is not realistic, her characters are interesting and her pacing of events keeps the readers' interest. Although critics contend that the haste with which she produced her novels led to weakly constructed plots, Barr satisfied her readers and was perhaps the most popular woman novelist in America during her lifetime.

Biographies:

Hildegarde Hawthorne, "Amelia Barr: Some Reminiscences," *Bookman* (May 1920): 283–286;

Raymund A. Paredes, introduction to *Remember the Alamo* (Boston: Gregg Press, 1979).

References:

Oscar Fay Adams, "The Novels of Mrs. Barr," *Andover Review,* 11 (March 1889): 248–268;

Mary Eby Howard, "The Novels of Amelia Barr," M.A. thesis, University of Texas at Austin, 1943.

Papers:

Amelia Edith Huddleston Barr materials can be found in the archives at the state capitol in Austin and in the Eugene C. Barker Texas History Center at the University of Texas at Austin.

Emerson Bennett

(16 March 1822 – 11 May 1905)

Joseph L. Coulombe
University of Tennessee at Martin

BOOKS: *The Brigand: A Poem . . . in Two Cantos* (New York: Xylographic, 1842);

The Bandits of the Osage: A Western Romance (Cincinnati: Robinson & Jones, 1847);

The Renegade: A Historical Romance of Border Life (Cincinnati: Robinson & Jones, 1848); revised as *Ella Barnwell: A Historical Romance of Border Life* (Cincinnati: James, 1854);

Mike Fink: A Legend of the Ohio (Cincinnati: Robinson & Jones, 1848; revised edition, Cincinnati: James, 1852);

Kate Clarendon; or, Necromancy in the Wilderness. A Tale of the Little Miami (Cincinnati & St. Louis: Stratton & Barnard, 1848);

The Trapper's Bride; or, Spirit of Adventure (Cincinnati: Stratton & Barnard, 1848);

The Prairie Flower; or, Adventures in the Far West (Cincinnati & St. Louis: Stratton & Barnard, 1849; revised edition, Cincinnati: James, 1850);

Leni-Leoti; or, Adventures in the Far West (Cincinnati & St. Louis: Stratton & Barnard, 1849; revised edition, Cincinnati: James, 1850);

Miranda: A Tale of the French Revolution (New York: Stringer & Townsend, 1850);

Oliver Goldfinch; or, The Hypocrite (Cincinnati: Stratton & Barnard, 1850); republished as *The Forged Will; or, Crime and Retribution* (Philadelphia: Peterson, 1853);

The Forest Rose: A Tale of the Frontier (Cincinnati: James, 1850; revised edition, 1852);

The League of the Miami (Louisville & Nashville: Hagan, 1850);

The Traitor; or, The Fate of Ambition, Part 1 (Cincinnati & St. Louis: Stratton & Barnard, 1850); *Part 2* (Cincinnati: Stratton, 1850);

The Unknown Countess (Cincinnati: Stratton, 1851);

The Female Spy; or, Treason in the Camp. A Story of the Revolution (Cincinnati: Stratton, 1851; revised edition, Cincinnati: Edward & Goshorn, 1853);

The Pioneer's Daughter: A Tale of Indian Captivity (Philadelphia: Peterson, 1851);

Rosalie Du Pont; or, Treason in the Camp: A Sequel to the Female Spy (Cincinnati: Stratton, 1851);

Viola; or, Adventures in the Far South-West (Philadelphia: Peterson, 1852);

Walde-Warren: A Tale of Circumstantial Evidence (Philadelphia: Peterson, 1852);

Clara Moreland; or, Adventures in the Far South-West (Philadelphia: Peterson, 1853);

The Fair Rebel: A Tale of Colonial Times (Cincinnati: Rulison, 1853);

The Bride of the Wilderness (Philadelphia: Peterson, 1854; London: Piper, Stephenson, & Spence, 1854);

The Heiress of Bellefont (Philadelphia: Peterson, 1855);

Ellen Norbury; or, The Adventures of an Orphan (Philadelphia: Peterson, 1855);

Alfred Moreland; or, The Legacy (Cincinnati: Rulison, 1855);

The Artist's Bride; or, The Pawnbroker's Heir (New York: Garrett, Dick & Fitzgerald, 1856); republished as *Villeta Linden; or, The Artist's Bride* (Philadelphia: Claxton, Remsen & Haffelfinger, 1874);

The Border Rover (Philadelphia: Peterson, 1857);

Intriguing for a Princess: An Adventure with Mexican Banditti (Philadelphia: Bradley, 1859);

Wild Scenes on the Frontiers; or, Heroes of the West (Philadelphia: Hamelin, 1859); republished as *Forest and Prairie; or, Life on the Frontier* (Philadelphia: Bradley, 1860);

The Phantom of the Forest: A Tale of the Dark and Bloody Ground (Philadelphia: Claxton, Remsen & Haffelfinger, 1867; revised edition, Philadelphia: Potter, 1868); republished as *The Phantom of the Forest. A Romance of the Early Settlers of Kentucky* (Glasgow: Cameron & Ferguson, 187-?);

The Outlaw's Daughter; or, Adventures in the South (Philadelphia: Claxton, Remsen & Haffelfinger, 1874);

The Orphan's Trials; or, Alone in a Great City (Philadelphia: Peterson, 1874).

OTHER: *Casket*, edited by Bennett, 1 (15 April–7 October 1846);

Emerson Bennett's Dollar Monthly, edited by Bennett, 1 (January–December 1860);

Emerson Bennett's Weekly; The Great Literary Paper of the Age, edited by Bennett, 1, nos. 1–20 (6 December 1879–17 April 1880).

Emerson Bennett enjoyed great popularity among nineteenth-century readers of romances and westerns. Between 1847 and 1880 he published more than thirty books in addition to hundreds of short stories and serialized tales. His prolific output is largely formulaic: kidnappings, outlaw gangs, virtuous maidens, and surprise revelations abound. Bennett first gained fame with stories of the American West, and he relied heavily upon common Eastern conceptions of frontier adventure, degeneracy, and opportunity. His fiction also draws upon sentimental romance, in which stock characters, contrived plots, and idealistic endings often exaggerate the successes of Samuel Richardson and James Fenimore Cooper. Bennett's imitation of the latter, in particular, prompted the ridicule of that exponent of literary realism Mark Twain; in *Roughing It* (1872) Twain mocks the diction of Cooper's Indians, comparing their talk to the remarks "a Broadway clerk might make after eating an edition of Emerson Bennett's works."

Bennett benefited from the emerging mass-print culture of the United States. His romances first appeared in regional newspapers, and the ones that were well received were then distributed nationally in cheap editions and sometimes republished under a second title. The primary goal was to make money, not create art. While some of his later works exhibit a strong social purpose, most of his books reveal—and, in fact, rely upon—contemporary prejudices regarding class, race, religion, and gender. Students can learn much about nineteenth-century literature and culture from perusing his work, for Bennett gave his large audience of readers what they wanted: a temporary disruption of the status quo with an inevitable return to a safe, harmonious world. His life and career do not reflect such a secure world though, for he died alone and forgotten in Philadelphia.

Little is known of Bennett's early life. Born on 16 March 1822 on a farm near Monson, Massachusetts, he attended Monson Academy. After his father died in 1835 and his mother remarried, he left home at the age of sixteen and wandered for several years in the East, visiting Boston, Providence, New York, Philadelphia, and Baltimore. Bennett's first foray into the literary world was not propitious. A reviewer in the December 1842 issue of *The Knickerbocker Magazine* disparaged his first publication—*The Brigand: A Poem* (1842)—asking, "Why couldn't they [his friends] permit him to remain guiltless of ink-shed?" Moving to Philadelphia in 1843,

Bennett wrote his first short story, "The Unknown Countess," which he submitted to a contest held by the Philadelphia *Dollar Magazine.* Not only were his hopes for the prize money disappointed, but the *Dollar* also refused to return the only copy of his story or to set a date for its publication.

Bennett drifted west and arrived in Cincinnati, Ohio, in the spring of 1844. His various occupations during the next year included managing a hotel, peddling patent stamps for marking linen, and selling subscriptions for the *Western Literary Journal and Monthly Review.* Bennett never lost his literary ambition, however, and in December 1844 the editors of the *Western Literary Journal,* Edward C. Z. Judson (also known as dime novelist Ned Buntline) and Lucius A. Hine, published his poem "Sonnet." Although Bennett continued to write poems throughout his life, they never gained the popularity of his prose writings.

A strange coincidence brought Bennett fame. In 1845 to his surprise "The Unknown Countess" appeared in the *Cincinnati Dollar Weekly Commercial,* reprinted from the Philadelphia *Dollar Magazine.* The story gained instant acclaim in Cincinnati, and that issue of the magazine immediately sold out. When Bennett asked the editor of the *Dollar Weekly Commercial* for a copy, he was berated for not subscribing to the magazine. Not until after this initial meeting did Bennett identify himself as the author of the story to editor L. G. Curtis, who quickly contracted him to write more.

Cincinnati journals eagerly published his essays, stories, and poems. In March 1846 Curtis serialized *The League of the Miami,* which was published as a book in 1850. The plot revolves around Cicely Vandemore, a virtuous girl of mysterious background who is kidnapped by Aaron Burrand, a traitorous bandit based loosely on former Vice President Aaron Burr (a character Bennett returns to in *The Traitor; or, The Fate of Ambition*). When her suitor Edward Langley saves her, several surprise revelations—including that of her aristocratic background—allow the two lovers to retire to a life of marital bliss and comfort. In the tale Bennett uses a basic pattern that he would employ with more complex variations in his subsequent career.

Capitalizing on his new popularity Bennett moved to Lawrenceburg, Indiana, in 1846 to edit *The Casket,* in which he promoted education, reading, and regional pride among the middle classes. In his first issue of *The Casket,* which appeared on 15 April 1846, he announced: "We believe there is talent in the West, as well as in the East; we not only believe, but we know it; and we believe the people are, also, awakening to the importance of learning, and literary acquirements." To further this awakening Bennett published his own poetry, prose, and fiction in every issue of *The Casket,* along with works by Alice and Phoebe Cary, Edward Melancthon, Sophia H. Oliver, C. B. Gillespie, B. St. James Fry, and his former publisher, Lucius Hine. Bennett's contributions included the serialized romance "Helena Ashton" (never republished) and poetic rhapsodies on nature and death. *The Casket* ceased publication after its last issue appeared on 7 October 1846.

Bennett ultimately secured his reputation (and a $500 prize) with the serialization of *The Bandits of the Osage: A Western Romance* in the *Dollar Weekly Commercial* between 6 May and 17 June 1847. The *Commercial* sold out all three thousand copies immediately, and the book—published only one week after the final installment—sold an amazing twenty thousand copies by the end of 1848. *The Bandits of the Osage* utilizes many common western themes and situations. The West is portrayed as a bountiful, beautiful land "infested with bands of lawless desperadoes," and the tale is replete with adventure, violence, love intrigues, and supernatural occurrences. Emily, a woman of mysterious birthright but noble demeanor, is kidnapped on two separate occasions. Reminiscent of Richardson's heroines Pamela and Clarissa, Emily is not only pious, patient, and selfless but also strong and forthright when her virtue is threatened. Ultimately she is saved by her upper-class lover, Edward, with the help of a Natty Bumppo-type frontiersman.

In this as in his other romances Bennett links social class and moral integrity to physical beauty. Inevitably the good succeed, and the bad fail. In *The Bandits of the Osage* the principal bandit, Ronald Bonardi, is of noble origin and ultimately helps Emily escape from the clutches of the two evil kidnappers: her stepbrother and the "Jew." In terms of negative stereotypes, the Jew is unsurpassable and ultimately receives a bullet through the forehead execution-style, with the approbation of a large crowd (as well as the author). His executioner, Bonardi, on the other hand, dies in grand style, using several barrels of gunpowder to blow himself and his hideout into the sky. Bonardi's legions of followers, his sacred oaths, and his vow to protect women recall the objects of satire in Mark Twain's *Adventures of Tom Sawyer* (1876) and *Adventures of Huckleberry Finn* (1885). Moreover Bonardi's promise to war "only on the rich and avaricious" and to help the poor draws upon the legend of Robin Hood.

In June 1847 Bennett traveled home to Massachusetts flushed with success and in September married Eliza G. Daly in Philadelphia. They returned to Cincinnati before the year ended, and in 1850 Emerson Bennett Jr. was born. With a family to support and hoping to benefit from his popularity, Bennett wrote prolifically and sales were extremely high. *Kate Clarendon; or, Necromancy in the Wilderness. A Tale of the Little Miami* (1848)

THE

BANDITS OF THE OSAGE.

A WESTERN ROMANCE.

BY EMERSON BENNETT,
AUTHOR OF THE "LEAGUE OF THE MIAMI," "UNKNOWN COUNTESS," "SILVER BIRD,"
AND OTHER TALES.

CINCINNATI:
ROBINSON & JONES.
1847.

Title page for Bennett's first novel, in which the West is depicted as a bountiful land "infested with bands of lawless desperadoes"

appeared first in the Cincinnati *Dollar Weekly Commercial*, and its editors credited their circulation of nearly one hundred thousand to Bennett's story. Three other novels, *Mike Fink: A Legend of the Ohio* (1848), *The Prairie Flower; or, Adventures in the Far West* (1849), and its sequel *Leni-Leoti; or, Adventures in the Far West* (1849) were serialized between May 1848 and March 1849 in *The Great West*. All three were quickly published as books, along with *The Renegade: A Historical Romance of Border Life* (1848), which was later republished as *Ella Barnwell: A Historical Romance of Border Life* (1854).

The popular Bennett acquired some notoriety by being charged with plagiarism. After the publication of a revised edition of *The Prairie Flower* in 1850, Sidney Moss, who had traveled to California in 1842 and given his story to Overton Johnson for publication in the East, charged Bennett with stealing his adventures for publication. Bennett claims in the preface of his novel to have received the story from a western adventurer, and he ponders whether his role is "the author,

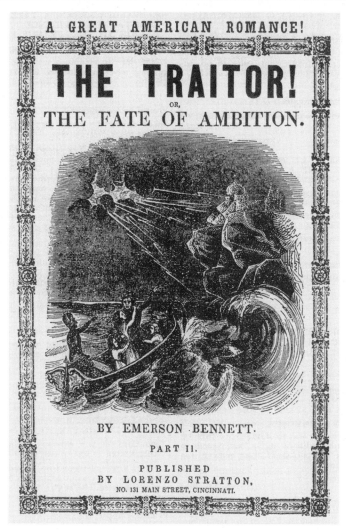

Cover for the second part of one of five books Bennett published in 1850

compiler, or editor." In his introduction to the 1973 republication of *The Forest Rose: A Tale of the Frontier* (1850) Thomas H. Smith argues that Moss's claim is false because *The Prairie Flower* and its sequel *Leni-Leoti* were submitted for publication together, and they show a consistency of design and style that indicates Bennett was their sole author.

Controversy also surrounds Bennett and the authorship of *The Trapper's Bride; or, Spirit of Adventure* (1848). Although the title page states "By the Author of the *Prairie Bird*," Charles L. Camp argues that the style of Charles Augustus Murray's *The Prairie-Bird* is too unlike *The Trapper's Bride,* and he points to Bennett as the author, suggesting that Bennett tried to augment sales by borrowing Murray's name and popularity. On the other hand, Smith contends that Bennett's own popularity had reached a high point—*The Renegade* and *Mike Fink* had each sold forty-five thousand copies in 1848 alone—and so he needed no help from Murray. Nevertheless, the novel is usually credited to Bennett.

Mike Fink, a novel untouched by these difficulties, contains many popular motifs of frontier literature. Bennett begins by celebrating the transformation of wilderness land into civilized territory. Then Fink introduces himself as a combination of "the Kaintuck warhorse, the snapping turtle, and Massassip alligator," a description that recalls the style of Southwestern humorists such as George Washington Harris and Thomas Bangs Thorpe. Readers encounter fortune-tellers, "murderous and implacable savages," and a beautiful heroine of mysterious background, Aurelia Fontaine. The story teems with fabulous revelations and contrived twists. The most interesting character is the kidnapper, Camilla, whose mixture of good and evil recalls Lovelace in Richardson's *Clarissa* (1748–1749).

To modern readers Bennett's romances may seem overwrought and predictable. Bennett intended, though, to evoke a mood and to entertain his contemporaries. In the preface to *Mike Fink* he explains his authorial freedoms in "the legitimate field of romance."

Not claiming to write a "verifiable history," he instead seeks to use Fink as a character to illustrate "a certain portion of events which took place during the period that he was known as a boatman on the Ohio." Similarly in the preface to *The Forest Rose* Bennett outlines his goals: "The chief beauty of fiction, in our humble opinion, consists in its representation of scenes and incidents so like to nature and facts, that the reader can *feel*, as it were, that they are *realities*." The sentimental "realities" he achieves through stylized plots and one-dimensional characters undermine the verisimilitude of his tales.

The Forest Rose exposes another problem with Bennett's claim to realism. Rather than creating his own characters and situations, Bennett borrows heavily from Cooper. Like Cooper's Natty Bumppo, Bennett's scout, Lewis Wetzel, wears buckskins, shuns society, speaks in dialect, has a "peculiar" laugh, and carries a long rifle. Wetzel reflects the motifs of popular fiction more than "nature and facts." The details that pass for Bennett's facts, though, often can be offensive to a modern sensibility. For example, the scout calls his long rifle "Killnigger" and refers to American Indians as "red niggers"; American Indians appear either as shrieking "savages" or as noble "sons of the forest." Cultural and racial inconsistencies appear as at least one set of "realities" in the fiction of both Cooper and Bennett.

Bennett's romance is not wholly derivative, however. The freshest element in the novel is the heroine, Forest Rose. Captured and adopted by Indians, she learns to defend herself and to think for herself. When Wetzel and her lover, Albert, arrive to save her, they become hopelessly trapped. Rose ignores their advice, grabs a gun, defends the men expertly, and leads them all to safety. While she transcends stereotypes of helpless damsels in distress, Bennett reverts to his formula and marries her contentedly to Albert.

In *Oliver Goldfinch; or, The Hypocrite* (1850) Bennett shifts the setting of his novels from the West to New York City, but the story nevertheless shares much with his previous works. Beginning with the cliché, "It was a dark and stormy night," Bennett spins a complex tale of deceit and death, though as a critic for the 19 January 1850 issue of *The Great West* wrote, "some of the characters are a little overwrought, and conversation at times becomes too dramatic." In this and other works Bennett uses highly stylized language to depict character. While heroes and heroines typically speak in a formal, melodramatic manner, lower-class characters and villains reveal their status through colloquial dialect and uncouth sentiment.

Although Bennett was primarily interested in making money through his writing, some of his productions also seem aimed at promoting social and political change. For example, in his two-volume romance about the American Revolution, *The Female Spy; or, Treason in the Camp. A Story of the Revolution* (1851) and *Rosalie Du Pont; or, Treason in the Camp: A Sequel to the Female Spy* (1851), the plot centers around the efforts of Captain Edgar Milford and Rosalie Du Pont to capture Benedict Arnold. The novels radiate with patriotic pride and national harmony. In the preface Bennett writes that he was motivated by "one single desire to see that Union preserved that cost our fathers so much to establish." Bennett was responding to the growing divisiveness between the North and the South over slavery, and he uses his romance to champion solidarity. He promotes unity again in *Viola; or, Adventures in the Far South-West* (1852) and *Clara Moreland; or, Adventures in the Far South-West* (1853), which are patterned after William Shakespeare's *Romeo and Juliet*. In both works Bennett shows how the feuding of two families destroys the lives of their children.

Bennett deals with social issues more overtly in *Ellen Norbury; or, The Adventures of an Orphan* (1855), a novel intended to raise awareness of injustice in the legal system. Influenced by the ideas of William James Mullen, a Pennsylvania prison reformer to whom Bennett dedicated the book, Bennett visited a Philadelphia prison to gather information for his book. In the preface he laments how "our statute laws, as construed and abused by here and there an unfeeling, unscrupulous magistrate, are made most terribly oppressive to the poor wretch who has neither money nor friends." Similarly, in *The Artist's Bride; or, The Pawnbroker's Heir* (1856), the hero, Julian St. Cloud, observes, "The world sets a value upon a man's purse, rather than his brain."

Bennett's laudable political and social goals in *The Artist's Bride*, however, did not lead him to break the romance formula or to soften his recurring anti-Semitism. Plotting villains, false names, and bank robberies are balanced with virtuous women, sensitive heroes, and happy revelations. The story begins in medias res: the heroine, Villeta, is cheated by a Jewish pawnbroker, Isaac Jacobs, described as "the personification of Avarice." Unlike Forest Rose, though, Villeta never rises above a stock heroine, and she resumes her privileged position only with the help of lawyer Amos Vincent and artist Julian St. Cloud, whom she marries.

Throughout the 1850s Bennett continued to write prolifically for serial publication. As early as 1852 he had contributed regularly to *The Saturday Evening Post*, and in 1853 Bennett was the only male author included among its advertised "Brilliant Array of Genius." His foremost literary outlet, *The Columbian and Great West*, folded in 1856, but in September of that year the *New York Ledger*—with the largest circulation in the United States—announced its exclusive rights to Bennett's literary productions. Bennett wrote three romances for the

Ledger: The Refugees; An Indian Tale of 1812 (1857), *Blanche Bertrand; or, Perils of the Border* (1858), and *Hubert, the Foundling, A Mystery in Paris* (1859), none of which was republished in book form. Although his popularity had begun to wane, Bennett still commanded a sizable audience. Most of the 262 short stories he wrote before 1865 appeared in the back pages of the *Ledger.*

To gain other outlets for his work, Bennett started two more magazines of his own. In 1860 he joined John L. Hamelin to edit *Emerson Bennett's Dollar Monthly* in Philadelphia. Here he serialized *The Mountain Lily; or, Adventures in the Wilderness,* advertised as "a companion to 'Prairie Flower'" probably to capitalize on his earlier fame. The magazine lasted less than one year. After a long period of sporadic writing and ebbing popularity, Bennett in late 1879 began another journal, *Emerson Bennett's Weekly; The Great Literary Paper of the Age,* which lasted only twenty weeks.

Bennett largely dropped from the public eye for the last two decades of his life. He died at the Masonic Home in Philadelphia, where he had lived for three years before he died at the age of eighty-three. A four-line obituary in *The New York Times* called him a "com-poser" whose best "song productions were 'Prairie Flower' and 'Leni Leoto'" [sic].

Bennett's importance as a literary figure stems from the rise of the immensely popular dime novels in the latter half of the nineteenth century. The rise of mass culture in the United States both helped and hurt his career. He gained immediate popularity with the reading public but, just as quickly, lost its approbation to other writers, other methods, and other matters. Bennett failed to learn the prevailing law of popular culture: art must change with the times to influence the times.

References:

R. V. Mills, "Emerson Bennett's Two Oregon Novels," *Oregon Historical Quarterly,* 41 (1940): 367–381;

Herbert B. Nelson, *The Literary Impulse in Pioneer Oregon* (Corvallis: Oregon State University Press, 1948), pp. 44–51;

Richard C. Poulsen, "Black George, Black Harris, and the Mountain Man Vernacular," *Rendez-Vous,* 8 (Summer 1973): 15–23;

Thomas H. Smith, introduction, *The Forest Rose: A Tale of the Frontier* (Athens: Ohio University Press, 1973).

Robert Montgomery Bird

(5 February 1806 – 23 January 1854)

Justin R. Wert
University of Mississippi

BOOKS: *Calavar; or, the Knight of the Conquest; a Romance of Mexico,* anonymous, 2 volumes (Philadelphia: Lea & Blanchard, 1834; revised edition, 1847); republished as *Abdalla the Moor, and the Spanish Knight: A Romance of Mexico,* as Bird, 4 volumes (London: Newman, 1835);

The Infidel; or, The Fall of Mexico; a Romance, as by the author of *Calavar,* 2 volumes (Philadelphia: Carey, Lea and Blanchard, 1835); republished as *Cortes, or, The Fall of Mexico,* as Bird, 3 volumes (London: Bentley, 1835); republished as *The Infidel's Doom; or, Cortes and The Conquest of Mexico,* as Bird (London: Cunningham, 1840);

The Hawks of Hawk-Hollow; A Tradition of Pennsylvania, as by the author of *Calavar,* 2 volumes (Philadelphia: Carey, Lea & Blanchard, 1835); as Bird, 3 volumes (London: Newman, 1837);

Blackbeard: A Page from the Colonial History of Philadelphia, anonymous, 2 volumes (New York: Harper, 1835);

Sheppard Lee: Written by Himself, anonymous, 2 volumes (New York: Harper, 1836);

Nick of the Woods; or, The Jibbenainosay; a Tale of Kentucky, as by the author of *Calavar . . . ,* 2 volumes (Philadelphia: Carey, Lea & Blanchard, 1837); republished as *Nick of the Woods: A Story of Kentucky,* as by the author of *Spartacus,* etc., 3 volumes (London: Bentley, 1837); republished as *Nick of the Woods; or, Adventures of Prairie Life,* 1 volume (London & New York: Routledge, 1851?); revised as *Nick of the Woods; or, The Jibbenainosay: A Tale of Kentucky,* as Bird, 1 volume (New York: Redfield, 1853);

Peter Pilgrim; or, a Rambler's Recollections, as by the author of *Calavar, Nick of the Woods,* etc. (2 volumes, Philadelphia: Lea & Blanchard, 1838; 1 volume, London: Cunningham, 1838);

The Adventures of Robin Day, as by the author of *Calavar . . . ,* 2 volumes (Philadelphia: Lea & Blanchard, 1839); republished as *Robin Day; or, The Rover's Life,* as Bird, 1 volume (London: Cunningham, 1840);

Sketch of the Life, Public Services, and Character of Major Thomas Stockton, of New-Castle: The Candidate of the Whig Party for the Office of Governor of Delaware (Wilmington, Del.: Porter & Naff, 1844);

A Brief Review of the Career, Character & Campaign of Zachary Taylor (Washington, D.C.: Gideon, 1848);

A Belated Revenge: From the Papers of Ipsico Poe, by Bird and Frederic Mayer Bird (Philadelphia: Lippincott, 1889);

The Life and Dramatic Works of Robert Montgomery Bird, edited by Clement E. Foust (New York: Knickerbocker, 1919);

The City Looking Glass: A Philadelphia Comedy, edited, with an introduction, by Arthur Hobson Quinn (New York: Colophon, 1933);

The Cowled Lover & Other Plays by Robert Montgomery Bird, edited by Edward H. O'Neill (Princeton, N.J.: Princeton University Press, 1941).

PLAY PRODUCTIONS: *The Gladiator,* New York City, Park Theater, 26 September 1831;

Oralloossa; Son of the Incas, Philadelphia, Arch Street Theater, 10 October 1832;

The Broker of Bogota, New York, Bowery Theater, 12 February 1834.

OTHER: *The Broker of Bogota,* in *Representative American Plays,* edited by Arthur Hobson Quinn (New York: Century, 1917), pp. 209–251;

"From the Papers of Robert Montgomery Bird: The Lost Scene from *News of Night,*" *University of Pennsylvania Library Chronicle,* 24 (Winter 1958): 1–12;

Richard Harris, ed., "A Young Dramatist's Diary: The Secret Records of Robert Montgomery Bird," *University of Pennsylvania Library Chronicle,* 25 (Winter 1959): 8–24.

SELECTED PERIODICAL PUBLICATION–UNCOLLECTED: "Community of Copy-Right Between the United States and Great Britain," *Knickerbocker Magazine,* 6 (October 1835): 285–289.

A prizewinning dramatist in the early 1830s, Robert Montgomery Bird turned to fiction in the middle of the decade and produced historical romances about the American frontier and satirical romances in which he examines American culture. A writer with wit, tragic sensibilities, dramatic instincts, and extensive knowledge of American history, Bird won both popular and critical acclaim during his lifetime. His work, however, has since received little scholarly attention.

A descendant of a prominent Delaware family, Bird was born on 5 February 1806 and raised with the social and intellectual advantages of wealth in New Castle, Delaware. However, the death of his father, John Dearborn Bird, when Bird was only four precipitated a difficult passage into adulthood. As is shown by an autobiographical section of Bird's last novel, *The Adventures of Robin Day* (1839), the harsh corporal punishments that the young man endured at the New Castle Academy were not forgotten and provided material for some of his most poignant satire.

In 1818 Bird was put under the guardianship of his uncle the Honorable Nicholas Van Dyke while his mother was forced by economic hardship to live with his older brother, James Madison Bird, in Philadelphia.

The strict Van Dyke did not take kindly to young Bird's habit of sleeping in–his "morning indulgence" as he phrased it in a letter to Bird's mother. While the boy's studies suffered under the no-nonsense rule of his guardian, they improved when in 1820 he rejoined his family in Philadelphia. He did especially well in the art of sketching. A year later Bird returned to his hometown to attend New Castle Academy and to prepare for college. In 1823 he enrolled in Germantown Academy, which had an even better reputation than New Castle Academy, in order to ensure his entrance into a professional program in college. The following year Bird achieved "distinguished literary rank" among his fellow students and received his diploma. His school sketches reveal that he had begun to develop his writing skills, and he had already placed some of his poetry in local periodicals.

In the fall of 1824 Bird enrolled in the medical program at the University of Pennsylvania. While studying medicine he read widely and wrote verse, prose, and dramatic pieces. By the end of 1827 he had placed seven of his prose and verse works in *The Philadelphia Monthly Magazine,* initiating a writing career that would bring him considerable literary attention and moderate financial success. Two of Bird's medical school acquaintances, Dr. Black and John Grimes, were influential early in Bird's literary career. His two visits to the Delaware Water Gap with Black and Grimes proved essential to the conception and setting of his novel *The Hawks of Hawk-Hollow; A Tradition of Pennsylvania* (1835). In addition Black's accounts of frontier life in Kentucky stimulated Bird's desire to see the West and in some measure inspired the novel *Nick of the Woods; or, The Jibbenainosay; a Tale of Kentucky* (1837).

In the spring of 1827 Bird graduated from the University of Pennsylvania Medical School. Soon after graduation he set up practice in Philadelphia, but he was unhappy in the profession and closed his office within a year. He continued writing during his brief medical career, finishing his fourth apprentice play, which was published in 1933 as *The City Looking Glass: A Philadelphia Comedy,* and published poems and sketches in *The Philadelphia Monthly Magazine.* Despite his publications, Bird's financial situation was insecure until 1830 when his play *Pelopidas* won an award from Edwin Forrest, a well-known dramatic actor and producer who was searching for tragedies that he could produce successfully in the Northeast. Even though *Pelopidas* was never produced, it earned Bird a prize of $1,000. The play was published in *The Life and Dramatic Works of Robert Montgomery Bird* (1919), edited by Clement E. Foust.

Bird earned three more of Forrest's prizes–from a committee that included William Cullen Bryant–and considerable popular recognition and critical acclaim

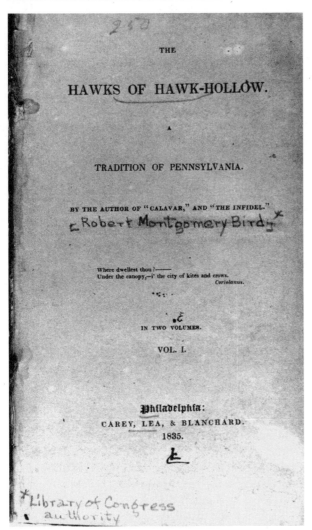

THE

HAWKS OF HAWK-HOLLOW.

A

TRADITION OF PENNSYLVANIA.

BY THE AUTHOR OF "CALAVAR," AND "THE INFIDEL."

Robert Montgomery Birds

Where dwellest thou?——
Under the canopy,—i' the city of kites and crows.
Coriolanus.

IN TWO VOLUMES.

VOL. I.

Philadelphia:
CAREY, LEA, & BLANCHARD.
1835.

Library of Congress authority

Title page for Bird's third novel, which was inspired by his visit to the
Delaware Water Gap with two fellow medical-school students
(courtesy of Special Collections, Thomas Cooper Library,
University of South Carolina)

Robert Montgomery Bird). On the eve of the production of each play, the theaters in New York, Boston, and Philadelphia were sold out. Critics were particularly impressed with *The Broker of Bogota* and were full of praise for its staging and Forrest's acting. The principal role of Baptista Febro, the broker in the play, became a staple of Forrest's stage career.

During the years that Bird and Forrest collaborated so successfully, they traveled extensively throughout the southern and western states as well as through Mexico and Peru. In addition to learning much about stage production and acting from Forrest, Bird extended his knowledge of these regions far beyond what he had read in books and travel sketches, enabling him to write convincingly of these places in his plays and in novels such as *Nick of the Woods* and *Sheppard Lee: Written by Himself* (1836). Even as he continued to work in theater, though, Bird was beginning his career as a novelist, for his first three novels were written before he ceased writing plays.

Bird's first two novels, *Calavar; or, the Knight of the Conquest; a Romance of Mexico* (1834) and *The Infidel; or The Fall of Mexico; a Romance* (1835), deal respectively with Cortez's conquest of the Aztecs and the aftermath of that conquest. In writing these historical romances about South America, Bird was following the lead of Washington Irving, whose sketches and histories of Columbus and the conquistadores were then popular. Having originally planned to write a detailed and accurate history of the Indians of Mexico and of Cortez's conquests in Mexico, Bird brings formidable historical knowledge to his romances, but at times his quirky dramatic effects, especially in *Calavar*, render the books a bit farcical. Overall, though, the excitement of the adventure stories does not detract from the historical significance of his work. Writing in the *Southern Literary Messenger* (June 1835), Edgar Allan Poe praised *The Infidel* and attributes to Bird "a fertility of imagination rarely possessed by his compeers."

Bird turned away from drama because of financial disagreements with Forrest, which came to a head in 1837. Forrest had paid Bird for only three of his prizewinning plays, and despite Bird's claim that the two had agreed orally to share the profits of the productions of the plays, Forrest refused to offer any. Prompted by his fiancée, Mary Mayer, whom he married on 13 July 1837 in Philadelphia, Bird sought to receive $6,000 dollars in back pay; but Forrest, like many dramatic producers of the era, maintained that the manuscripts and the productions from them were his property, not Bird's. Even though an attempt was made in 1851 to bring Forrest to court over the matter, damages could not be recovered as the witnesses to Bird and Forrest's oral agreement were by then all dead.

for *The Gladiator*, his second prizewinner, which was also collected in *The Life and Dramatic Works of Robert Montgomery Bird*. First produced at the Park Theater in New York on 26 September 1831, *The Gladiator* brought Bird and Forrest to the forefront of popular American drama, where they would remain until 1837, when for financial reasons Bird stopped writing plays. *The Gladiator* enjoyed an especially strong reception because of the talents of Forrest, who was exceptional in the starring role of Spartacus, and because of Bird's blank verse, which was praised by contemporary critics.

Before his withdrawal from the American stage Bird wrote two more successful tragedies, his third and fourth prizewinning plays: *Oralloossa: Son of the Incas,* which premiered in Philadelphia in 1832, and *The Broker of Bogota,* which opened in New York in 1834 (both plays were published in *The Life and Dramatic Works of*

Bird's plays have seldom received scholarly attention. Although Arthur Hobson Quinn in the 3 August 1916 issue of *The Nation* championed *The City Looking Glass* and had high praise for *The Broker of Bogota,* later critics have found the plots of the plays overly complex and unrealistic and the action melodramatic. Moreover, Bird's four prizewinning plays are less interesting to American critics because they are South American romances or Greek/Roman restorations set outside of the United States.

Though Bird's third novel, *The Hawks of Hawk-Hollow,* is full of fine descriptions of the Delaware Water Gap, the complexity of its plot renders the novel rather tedious. He was more successful in his subsequent novels, *Sheppard Lee: Written by Himself* and *Nick of the Woods,* which are less complicated and more dramatic and compelling. Bird's characters give these narratives a vibrancy and authenticity lacking in his earlier romances. During part of this period of intense writing—Bird wrote five novels between 1834 and 1837 in addition to his theater work—he was also editing *The American Monthly,* and his health was sometimes adversely affected by the late, strenuous hours he was keeping.

Sheppard Lee: Written by Himself is full of sharp cultural commentary and satire. In his September 1836 review for the *Southern Literary Messenger* Poe praised it as "exceedingly unaffected and . . . well adapted to the varying subjects." Bird's ability to represent such different subjects as farming, politics, and northern and southern aristocratic life makes his novel a fascinating study of American culture in the 1830s. Bird's use of the popular psychological and physiological notion of metempsychosis renders the narration, and hence the satirical point of view, intriguing and hilarious. Particularly poignant is Bird's political satire aimed at the aristocracies of the North and the South into which the stealthy Sheppard Lee transplants himself by means of metempsychosis with comical unease.

Poe's interest in Bird's romance lay primarily in the theme of metempsychosis, which provides the theoretical basis for Sheppard Lee's life essence passing from his dead body into the dead bodies of other people: a Squire Higgins; a gentleman, Mr. I. Dulmer Dawkins, Esq.; a barber, Abram Skinner; a philanthropist, Mr. Zachariah Longstraw; an abolitionist, Nigger Tom, who is lynched; and finally Mr. Arthur Megrim, who then transforms into a chicken, a coffee pot, a clock, and the Emperor of France before reverting back to Sheppard Lee at the end. Clearly Bird satirizes metempsychosis and its popularity. Absurd as it may seem to modern readers, metempsychosis was a popular scientific topic at the time. Some of Poe's own tales, such as "A Tale of the Ragged Mountains," "Ligeia," and "Metzenger-

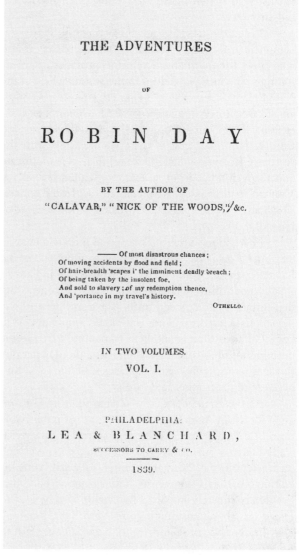

THE ADVENTURES

OF

ROBIN DAY

BY THE AUTHOR OF
"CALAVAR," "NICK OF THE WOODS," &c.

———— Of most disastrous chances ;
Of moving accidents by flood and field ;
Of hair-breadth 'scapes i' the imminent deadly breach ;
Of being taken by the insolent foe,
And sold to slavery ; of my redemption thence,
And 'portance in my travel's history.
OTHELLO.

IN TWO VOLUMES.
VOL. I.

PHILADELPHIA:
LEA & BLANCHARD,
SUCCESSORS TO CAREY & CO.
1839.

Title page for Bird's last novel, in which he depicts his experiences at New Castle Academy in Delaware

stein," employ metempsychosis and thus also exploit the popular appeal of the subject.

Nick of the Woods; or, The Jibbenainosay; a Tale of Kentucky, Bird's most financially successful novel, centers upon the struggles between Kentucky pioneers and Native Americans. Traveling in 1782 through the Salt River wilderness of northern central Kentucky, the protagonist, Roland Forrester, and his cousin Edith arrive at a fort where Colonel Bruce tells them of Nick of the Woods, a mysterious, Gothic figure known to the Indian tribes as the Jibbenainosay. Leaving the fort, the two encounter Ralph Stackpole, a sharp-witted horse thief who speaks a thick Kentucky dialect, and "Bloody" Nathan Slaughter, a roving hunter and self-proclaimed pacifist who is ridiculed by the pioneers for not killing Indians at will.

When the travelers are threatened by Shawnees, Slaughter leads them to an old cabin where they might rest safely for the night. The cabin provides a Gothic setting–a gloomy place deep in the woods where some Native Americans once slaughtered a pioneer family–and foreshadows an attack by the Shawnees. The travelers try to flee but are captured, and Edith is separated from Roland. The rest of the romance deals with the rescue of Roland by Slaughter and their plans to locate and recover Edith from an evil chief called "the Black Vulture" and Braxley, Roland's old foe. In the conclusion Slaughter, the pacifist, is revealed to be the dreaded Nick of the Woods.

In addition to the brisk plot and the vivid characters, *Nick of the Woods* is an interesting examination of the Kentucky pioneers and their conflict with the Indians of that region. Bird deliberately provides a contrasting depiction of Native Americans to the more sympathetic depictions offered by James Fenimore Cooper and William Gilmore Simms in their romances. His Gothic descriptions of the untamed wilderness, though, parallel those of Simms, who also emphasizes the darkness and mystery of the frontier and forests.

As the romances of Sir Walter Scott in England and Cooper in America had set the tone for publishable prose, Bird's hard work was compensated not only critically but also financially. Although he did not get rich on book royalties, he made enough to supplement his editing work. His regimen of little sleep and poor diet eventually severely impaired his health, and he had to resign his editing position in order to recover. Not long after this episode of failing health, his wife gave birth to a baby, Frederick, in June 1838.

For two years Bird recovered, resting and looking forward to moving onto a farm he purchased not far from Elkton, Maryland, near Chesapeake Bay. Bird arrived there on 13 March 1840. The three-hundred-acre farm, called "Cabin Cove," was located on the Elk River, a beautiful location as Bird described it in a letter to his wife: "Never was there a more beautiful river. . . . I wish you could have seen it yesterday in the glorious misty calm,–the piney headlands, blue hills and gleaming waters." Under a less strenuous daily schedule Bird's health and spirits recovered. He did little literary work while at Cabin Cove, however, as he was engaged both with the daily workings of the farm and with the pursuit of his own interests in agriculture.

Most of his writings, seven volumes of journals, dealt with farming methods and crop production. He did edit *Pelopidas* in an attempt to have it produced in Philadelphia by William Burton, but he withdrew it

from production even though Burton had agreed to reasonable terms. Perhaps, as the play was to appear on the same night in the same city as a play produced by Forrest, Bird decided not to engage in any sort of rivalry. He never gave Burton an explanation for not pursuing the production of the play, however, and simply never sent the manuscript.

In September 1840 Bird moved back to New Castle to be with his family. Not long thereafter, he began a career in teaching at a new medical college in Philadelphia, which suited him well until the college closed in 1844. Bird returned to teaching in the fall of 1844 at a Philadelphia high school before accepting the directorship of a bank in New Castle in 1846. His friend John Clayton, a Delaware statesman who suggested the bank directorship to Bird, then offered to help him buy a one-third share in *The North American Magazine and United States Gazette,* whose editor, Robert Conrad, was a well-known Philadelphia dramatist and poet. Despite his hard work and good intentions, the financial situation of *The North American* declined, along with Bird's health, as a result of the ill-advised speculations of one of the other owners, George Graham. Bird's tenure as an editor of *The North American* lasted from 1847 until his death in 1854.

In 1853 Bird was approached by George H. Boker about a "Dramatic Author's Bill" that he hoped would pass through Congress that year. Bird supported the bill and commented on how it would have affected his life in his 31 January 1853 letter to Boker: "if there had been such a law in existence twenty years ago, I should not have abandoned dramatic writing, as I did, in what was the moment of Success and the period of youthful vigor and enthusiasm." The rest of that year brought on worsening health for Bird. He left Philadelphia for Cape May, New Jersey, and then returned once again to the Delaware Water Gap, where he wrote what would prove to be his last pieces for *The North American.* He died on 23 January 1854.

Robert Montgomery Bird's contributions to American drama and fiction in the 1830s were significant. As a professional writer in an era unsupportive of authors with literary ambitions, Bird deserves respect for his perseverance. Though his aesthetic appeal has diminished, he occupied a vital place in early American culture and letters.

Letters:

C. Seymour Thompson, ed., "Travelling With Robert Montgomery Bird," *University of Pennsylvania Library Chronicle,* 7 (March 1939): 11–22; 7 (June 1939): 34–50; 7 (October–December 1939): 75–90; 8 (April 1940): 4–21.

Biographies:

Mary Meyer Bird, *Life of Robert Montgomery Bird,* edited by C. Seymour Thompson (Philadelphia: University of Pennsylvania Library, 1945);

Clement E. Foust, *Robert Montgomery Bird* (New York: Knickerbocker Press, 1919).

References:

Curtis Dahl, *Robert Montgomery Bird* (New York: Twayne, 1963);

Clara Louise Dentler, ed., "Robert Montgomery Bird and Hirman Powers," *University of Pennsylvania Library Chronicle,* 27 (Winter 1961): 63–79;

Joan Joffe Hall, "*Nick of the Woods:* An Interpretation of the American Wilderness," *American Literature,* 35 (May 1963): 173–182;

Edgar Allan Poe, review of *The Infidel,* in *The Complete Works of Edgar Allan Poe,* volume 8, edited by James A. Harrison (New York: AMS Press, 1965), pp. 32–37;

Poe, review of *Sheppard Lee,* in *The Complete Works of Edgar Allan Poe,* volume 9, edited by Harrison (New York: AMS Press, 1965), pp. 126–139;

Arthur Hobson Quinn, "Dramatic Works of Robert Montgomery Bird," *Nation,* 103 (3 August 1916), pp. 108–109.

Papers:

Many of Robert Montgomery Bird's private papers, including his medical thesis and lectures, speeches, manuscripts of plays and fiction, and financial records, can be found at the University of Pennsylvania Library.

Lillie Devereux Blake

(12 August 1833 – 30 December 1913)

Grace Farrell
Butler University

BOOKS: *Southwold: A Novel,* as Lillie Devereux Umsted (New York: Rudd & Carleton, 1859);

Rockford; or, Sunshine and Storm, as Umsted (New York: Carleton, 1863);

Zoe (Oswego, N.Y.: American News Company, 1866);

Forced Vows; or, A Revengeful Woman's Fate (New York: Beadle & Adams, 1870);

Fettered for Life; or, Lord and Master. A Story of To-day (New York: Sheldon, 1874);

The Fables (New York: Blaber, 1879);

Woman's Place To-day. Four Lectures, in Reply to the Lenten Lectures on "Woman" by the Rev. Morgan Dix (New York: Lovell, 1883);

A Daring Experiment and Other Stories (New York: Lovell, Coryell, 1892).

Edition: *Fettered For Life,* afterword by Grace Farrell (New York: Feminist Press, 1996).

SELECTED PERIODICAL PUBLICATIONS–
UNCOLLECTED: "My Last Conquest," anonymous, *Harper's Weekly,* 1 (14 November 1857): 734;

"A Tragedy of the Mammoth Cave," anonymous, *Knickerbocker Magazine,* 51 (February 1858): 112–121;

"Despair," anonymous, *Knickerbocker Magazine,* 51 (May 1858): 449;

"John Owen's Appeal," as Lillie D. Umsted, *Harper's New Monthly Magazine,* 22 (December 1860): 72–81;

"A Lonely House," anonymous, *Atlantic Monthly,* 7 (January 1861): 40–51;

"A Ball and a Duel," as Essex, *Forney's War Press,* 1 (1 February 1862): 1, 8;

"The Lieutenant's Courtship," as Essex, *Forney's War Press,* 1 (8 February 1862): 1;

"A Wild Night Ride," as Essex, *Forney's War Press,* 1 (1 March 1862): 1;

"The Rescued Fugitives," as Essex, *Forney's War Press,* 1 (22 March 1862): 4;

"The Beautiful Rebel," as Essex, *Forney's War Press,* 1 (12 April 1862): 1; (19 April 1862): 1;

"Carrying False Colors," as Essex, *Forney's War Press,* 1 (3 May 1862): 1, 8;

"The Casket of Letters," as Essex, *Forney's War Press,* 1 (31 May 1862): 1;

"A Duel For a Flirt," as Essex, *Forney's War Press,* 1 (14 June 1862): 1;

"Contraband of War," as Essex, *Forney's War Press,* 1 (5 July 1862): 1;

"A Romance of the Battle of Fair Oaks," as Essex, *Forney's War Press,* 1 (26 July 1862): 1, 8;

"Leona Somers," as Essex, *Forney's War Press,* 1 (16 August 1862): 1;

"A Midsummer Sail," as Essex, *Forney's War Press,* 1 (20 September 1862): 1, 8;

"Stories of Two Refugees," as Essex, *Forney's War Press,* 1 (4 October 1862): 1;

"Life on the Mountains," as Essex, *Forney's War Press,* 1 (24 October 1862): 1; (1 November 1862): 1; (8 November 1862): 1, 8;

"The Slave's Revenge," as Essex, *Forney's War Press,* 2 (15 November 1862): 1;

"My Cruise in the Dream," as Mrs. L. Devereux Umsted, *Home Journal,* no. 48 (29 November 1862): 1; (6 December 1862): 1;

"A Soldier's Letter," as Essex, *Forney's War Press,* 2 (6 December 1862): 1, 8;

"Brothers by Birth–Foes in the Field," as L. Devereux Umsted (Essex), *Forney's War Press,* 2 (21 March 1863): 1; (28 March 1863): 1; (4 April 1863): 1; (11 April 1863): 1;

"Shot through the Heart," anonymous, *Knickerbocker Magazine,* 61 (May 1863): 413–421;

"The Social Condition of Woman," anonymous, *Knickerbocker Magazine,* 61 (May 1863): 381–388;

"The Tenant of the Stone House," as Mrs. Lillie Devereux Umsted, *Frank Leslie's Illustrated Newspaper,* 16 (1 August 1863): 297–298; (8 August 1863): 313–314;

"The Gloved Lady," as L. Devereux Umsted, *Frank Leslie's Illustrated Newspaper,* 16 (22 August 1863): 345–346; (29 August 1863): 361–362;

Lillie Devereux Blake

"A Visit to a Fortuneteller," as Lillie Devereux Umsted, *Frank Leslie's Illustrated Newspaper,* 18 (2 July 1864): 229–230;

"In Prison," as Essex, *New York Weekly Mercury,* 28 (27 May 1865): 6–7; (3 June 1865): 5–6;

"A Stormy Courtship," as Essex, *New York Weekly Mercury,* 28 (30 September 1865): 3;

"The Dead Letter," as Essex, *New York Weekly Mercury,* 28 (11 November 1865): 3;

"A Clap of Thunder," as Di Fairfax, *New York Ledger,* 21 (27 January 1866): 3;

"Found Drowned," *New York Weekly Mercury,* 30 (5 October 1867): 4;

"Reparation," *Galaxy,* 11 (April 1871): 592–593;

"Who Won the Prize," *Saturday Evening Post* (21 October 1871): 2;

"Love and Death," *Galaxy,* 16 (November 1873): 661;

"Ten Years' Devotion," *New York Sunday Times,* 22 August 1875, pp. 1;

"The Sea People," *Galaxy,* 20 (December 1875): 789;

"Roses and Death," *Short Stories,* 29 (January 1898): 98–101.

Lillie Devereux Blake, novelist, short-story writer, journalist, essayist, and lecturer, was a cultural critic who commented on a wide range of social conventions,

especially those regarding women, in a career that stretched for more than half a century. Blake served in Washington, D.C., as a Civil War correspondent for major New York and Philadelphia papers. Later she became a successful political organizer for the suffrage movement. During her career in New York she pushed legislative action that proved instrumental in modifying discriminatory laws against women. Largely because of her leadership, Civil War nurses became eligible for pension benefits; women were enabled to hold civil service positions; mothers were made joint guardians of their children; and for the first time women were allowed to serve on school boards and work wherever women were incarcerated. She also initiated actions that led to the founding of Barnard College of Columbia University. Blake attained such prominence as a feminist that in 1900 Elizabeth Cady Stanton supported her to succeed Susan B. Anthony as president of the National American Woman Suffrage Association.

Blake's fiction, which spans the whole of her career and evolves during the rise of American realism, moves from sentimental to realistic forms. She published in well-regarded literary magazines such as *Atlantic Monthly* and *Harper's,* but her life circumstances also forced her to write for the mass market of popular magazines. She covertly challenged, even as she gave voice to, the views of her popular audience. Her work shows the ongoing evolution of cultural codes and values during and after the Civil War, a period in which the life of women and the culturally coded notions of femininity were profoundly changed.

Blake was born Elizabeth Johnson Devereux in Raleigh, North Carolina, on 12 August 1833 to Sarah Elizabeth Johnson and George Pollok Devereux. She was a descendant of Jonathan Edwards on both her maternal and paternal sides. Her maternal great-great-grandfather, Samuel Johnson, had been the first president of Kings College, and his son, her great-grandfather William Samuel Johnson, had been the first president after the Revolution, when its name was changed to Columbia College. In 1873, under portraits of both ancestors, Blake would present President F. A. O. Barnard with a petition to admit women to Columbia, an action that later led to the founding of Barnard College.

Lillie Devereux's father died in 1837 at the age of forty-two, and her mother, pregnant with their second daughter, Georgina, returned to her maternal home in Stratford, Connecticut. Her mother soon moved to New Haven, where Lillie was educated at the Anthorpe school until the age of fifteen. She was then tutored by a Yale theological student following the Yale undergraduate curriculum. In June 1855 Lillie Devereux married Frank Umsted, a lawyer from Philadelphia, with whom she had two daughters: Elizabeth, born in February 1857, and Katherine, born in July 1858.

After the birth of her first daughter Lillie Devereux Umsted began writing. Her first story, "My Last Conquest," appeared in November 1857 in *Harper's Weekly;* a second story, "A Tragedy of the Mammoth Cave," and a poem, "Despair," appeared respectively in February and May 1858 in *The Knickerbocker Magazine.* The early stories swerve from the conventions of courtship narratives in their sympathetic depictions of women as courageous, independent, and capable of murderous rage. The *Knickerbocker* pieces are confessions of women nearing death, haunted by acts of aggression.

After her second daughter's birth, Umsted began writing her first book, *Southwold* (1859), which sold so quickly that second and third printings were required within two weeks. The novel was a critical as well as a popular success. The reviewer for the *Philadelphia Home Journal* wrote on 23 February 1858 that the author was "a tragedienne out of place on the tame sidewalk of common life." The novel continues Umsted's combination of a conventional romance with an unconventionally strong female protagonist. The sensuous, intelligent Medora Fielding is confined within a social system that limits feminine endeavors to the acquisition of a husband. Her restless energy eventually turns into a rage

that results in murder and suicide. Undermining the Romantic stereotypes of feminine frailty and purity, Umsted in this early work shows that women share in the human capacity for desire and violence.

Three months after *Southwold* appeared, Frank Umsted, twenty-six, killed himself with a pistol shot to the head. The mystery surrounding his death was never resolved, although his wife's fortune, which had become his upon their marriage, was believed to be completely gone, as was some of her mother's property. His death was commonly presumed to be a suicide, but the coroner's verdict was indecisive, and Lillie Devereux Umsted never resolved for herself whether his death was an accident or a suicide. In either case the tragedy left her in poverty, abandoned to support two small children. She was traumatized by memories of the incident, unable to comprehend his financial betrayal and/or incompetence, apprehensive about the future, and overwhelmed with grief over his loss.

Umsted's journals reveal that she resisted remarriage as a solution to her widowhood and the precarious financial situation she faced. Instead she fought off grief by immersing herself in writing. Written a few months after Frank Umsted's death, "A Lonely House" draws on the archetype of the Cain and Abel story and concerns two brothers who kill one another after their widowed mother dies. Her *Atlantic Monthly* editor, poet James Russell Lowell, wrote of the story on 3 April 1860: "It is rather savage, perhaps, but I liked it for leaving the ordinary highway." Although Umsted never gave direct public voice to the private grief that is evident in her journals, her situation is clearly suggested in the figure of the widow who sequesters herself in the house after her husband's death. Through fiction she was able to convert her private grief into a meditation on concealment and self-slaughter, displacing the violent suicide of her own husband and the suppressed rage of the widow in the story into a reciprocal fratricide. The brothers subtly become one another's double; thus, each kills himself by killing the other.

Less artistically realized and a commercial failure, Umsted's second novel, *Rockford; or, Sunshine and Storm,* written in 1860 and published in 1863, also dealt with the theme of grief, but it is complicated by adultery and the suggestion of incest. The death of George Sandys is the occasion for innuendos regarding his sexual relationship with Claudia Rockford and the paternity of her son, who falls in love with Sandys's daughter. The sexual relationship between George and Claudia is never directly admitted, remaining always as the unspoken deed of the novel. Through the text's careful silence, the lost relationship comes to double for the unspeakable loss and absence of death. Although flawed by Umsted's heavy-handedness in developing the innuendos, the novel is a significant attempt to deal with erotic passion within a cultural code of sexual reticence.

To earn her living Umsted contracted as a Washington-based Civil War correspondent with the *New York Evening Post, New York World, Philadelphia Press,* and *Forney's War Press.* She also published fiction, frequently in *Forney's War Press* under the pseudonym Essex. Her stories form a bridge between the home and the battleground. Domestic concerns push tentatively against the boundaries of war; marriage plots collide with war plots; via disguises, women cross over from the female haven of the home into the male arena of the battleground. Umsted's chosen pseudonym is itself a disguise, a male-sounding name that allows her safe passage between a woman's world of popular fiction and the mixed audience of the *War Press.*

Appealing to a readership used to sentimentality in their newspaper fiction, Umsted in the earliest of these stories transfers sentimental elements into a martial context: conflict over possession of a woman often mirrors the conflict over possession of land, and the war plot parallels the romance plot in depicting skirmishes, advances, retreats, and final triumphs and surrenders. The realities of the Civil War pushed against the conventions of sentimentality, however. In ways that parallel the public's evolving perception of the war–a perception that shifted from an optimistic, if not frivolous, view of the war as a kind of chivalric parade that would soon be over to a deepening realization of its deadly consequences–her stories move from sentimental to realistic styles as she cautiously introduces violence into her fiction. At each step Umsted attempts to maintain distance, to keep death from intruding upon the domestic circle, but the progression of the war soon made the unthinkable a matter of everyday reality. The realities of war reports, printed side by side with her *War Press* fiction, soon intruded upon the content of her stories. She wove in realistic settings and actual events, dealt with a range of social classes, and overrode sentimental evasions to deal with death and loss.

In 1866 Umsted married Grinfill Blake, a New York businessman several years her junior, but continued to support herself through her writing. Under her real name, Lillie Devereux Blake, and a variety of pseudonyms–Essex, Charity Floyd, Violet, Aesop, Tiger Lily, Di Fairfax, Lulu Dashaway–she routinely sold stories to a wide variety of periodicals, including Frank Leslie's publications as well as *Harper's Weekly, The Saturday Evening Post, The New York Leader,* and *The New York Sunday Times.* Typical of her novels was *Forced Vows; or, A Revengeful Woman's Fate* (1870), a romance of abductions and betrayals that also gives voice to female desire, revealing the pain of thwarted ambition and imprisonment within the domestic sphere.

By the 1870s Blake had found her work as an activist against social injustice and her voice as a lecturer for the suffrage movement. Within the context of the women's movement, Blake published her best-known novel, *Fettered for Life; or, Lord and Master. A Story of To-day* (1874). Declared a "thrilling story . . . a powerful book" by the reviewer for the 6 May 1874 *Home Journal* and "among the most readable and notable books of the year" by the critic for the 13 April 1874 *New York World, Fettered for Life* has since been praised as "a feminist classic" by *The Feminist Companion to Literature in English* (1990) and "the most comprehensive women's rights novel of the nineteenth century" by David S. Reynolds in *Beneath the American Renaissance* (1989). The novel was reprinted in 1885, shortly after a collection of Blake's essays appeared.

Fettered for Life interweaves women's rights issues, abolitionist allusions, and temperance concerns with the plight of urban seamstresses. It addresses the post-Civil War status of women and documents broad social concerns resulting from industrialization, immigration, and an increasing urban population. Blake sets sentimentality against realism to alert her readers to the entrapments that the culture of sentiment held for women. Twenty-five years before Kate Chopin's *The Awakening* (1899) appeared, Blake dealt with the stultifying life of a society wife whose every attempt at meaningful work is trivialized or condemned and who as a result attempts suicide by drowning. Her novel was a precursor of works by such writers as Chopin and Charlotte Perkins Gilman, who sympathetically depicted women who awakened to their own selves and desires in the face of a patriarchal culture that did not acknowledge that they had any needs beyond fulfilling those of others.

In 1883 Blake's public lectures in response to Dr. Morgan Dix–*Woman's Place To-day. Four Lectures, in Reply to the Lenten Lectures on "Woman" by the Rev. Morgan Dix* (1883)–earned public recognition for her and drew ignominy down on him. Published by popular demand, the collection, writes Elinore Hughes Partridge in *American Prose and Criticism, 1820–1900* (1983), "created a sensation in the contemporary press and did much to awaken women into active workers for suffrage." Calling Dix a "theological Rip Van Winkle," Blake systematically refutes each of his biblically based arguments for the subjugation of women. She maintains her lifelong position, radical in the nineteenth century, that people share a common nature but are trained in gender roles. In other words she held that gender is socially constructed and historically contingent.

Blake's last book, a collection of short stories, went to press in 1892 but because of the financial problems of her original publisher did not appear until

1894. *A Daring Experiment and Other Stories* reprints three previously published pieces along with fifteen additional stories. Blake's aesthetic strength lies in her descriptions, as for example her evocation of the arctic circle in "Lost in the Ice." Several of the stories deal with the social and marital implications of democracy and the inequities of class and wealth. These issues were central to realism as well as to the development of the American literary canon, and Blake's engagement with them seems more subtle than her treatment of feminist issues in *Fettered For Life*. For example, in an allegory on gender issues, "A Divided Republic," Blake treats William Dean Howells and Henry James as political writers. She implies that their work prompts aesthetic rather than political comment only because their sexual politics reflect the status quo.

Blake's radical politics kept her at the margins of the literary mainstream. She fought for sexual equality at a time when even the suffrage movement worked from the premise that men and women were radically different. Instead she created female characters who participate in a full range of desires, needs, and ambitions. Her last published story, "Roses and Death" (1894), shows just such a fully realized human being—an eighty-five-year-old woman—dying, "alone . . . the sole occupant of a wide emptiness of space," remembering a soul-surrendering "wild embrace" of love. As she dies, she is linked momentarily to the world by the sensuousness of life, its scent of roses.

Biography:

Katherine Devereux Blake and Margaret Louise Wallace, *Champion of Women* (New York: Revell, 1943).

References:

Grace Farrell, afterword to *Fettered for Life* (New York: Feminist Press, 1996), pp. 381–430;

Farrell, "Legacy Profile: Lillie Devereux Blake," *Legacy*, 14 (Fall 1997): 68–75;

David S. Reynolds, *Beneath the American Renaissance: The Subversive Imagination in the Age of Emerson and Melville* (New York: Knopf, 1988).

Papers:

The major collection of Lillie Devereux Blake's documents, including her diaries, autobiography, correspondence, and clippings, is in the Missouri Historical Society Library in St. Louis. A smaller collection is in the Sophia Smith Collection of the Smith College Library.

Sherwood Bonner
(Katharine Sherwood Bonner McDowell)
(26 February 1849 – 22 July 1883)

Anne Razey Gowdy
Tennessee Wesleyan College

BOOKS: *Like Unto Like* (New York: Harper, 1878); republished as *Blythe Herndon* (London: Ward, Locke, 1882);

Dialect Tales (New York: Harper, 1883);

Suwanee River Tales (Boston: Roberts, 1884);

Dialect Tales and Other Stories, edited, with an introduction, by William L. Frank (Albany, N.Y.: NCUP, 1990);

"The Uncollected Works of Sherwood Bonner (Katharine Sherwood Bonner McDowell, 1849–1883): An Annotated Edition," edited by Anne Razey Gowdy, dissertation, University of Mississippi, 1996.

Editions: *Dialect Tales,* facsimile edition (Freeport, N. Y.: Books for Libraries Press, 1972);

Suwanee River Tales, facsimile edition (Freeport, N.Y.: Books for Libraries Press, 1972);

Like Unto Like, introduction by Jane Turner Censer (Columbia: University of South Carolina Press, 1997).

When the nineteenth-century, Mississippi-born author Katharine Sherwood Bonner McDowell earns mention in American literary history, it is usually on the basis of the short fiction she published in national—that is, northern—magazines between 1875 and 1884. Most often praised as a humorist and as one of the first and foremost creators of local-color dialect fiction, she and her work faded from memory as literary tastes shifted. Scholars interested in her career have lamented how little work she left when her life was cut short by cancer at age thirty-four. However, the breadth of Bonner's achievement is being reappraised as previously buried works have been rediscovered and delivered into the hands of interested readers. A comprehensive estimation of her literary career must include primary texts long slighted because they have been largely inaccessible: a range of short fiction, a novella, a novel, two series of journalistic travel letters, celebrity profiles, his-

Sherwood Bonner

torical/autobiographical sketches, and poems. A broader perspective on her work makes clear that she was a talented writer as well as an observant practitioner of literary trends of her time.

During most of the twentieth century the literary reputation of the writer known as Sherwood Bonner rested largely upon two slender volumes of short fiction selected when she was literally on her deathbed. With the help of her friend Sophia Kirk, she gathered twenty-nine stories for the volumes *Dialect Tales* (1883) and *Suwanee River Tales* (1884) in an urgent attempt to provide a financial legacy for her young daughter, Lilian. In search of saleable material that would appeal to contemporary popular tastes, she chose from her publications of the previous decade a group of light romances, stories for young readers, and stories heavy in the dialects of the South. Until recently more than half of Bonner's published work, often difficult to locate, remained uncollected.

Since much of her work was buried in periodical archives, Bonner was overlooked even by many scholars seeking to reclaim the writing of nineteenth-century American women. However, the more than fifty recovered Bonner publications gathered in "The Uncollected Works of Sherwood Bonner (Katharine Sherwood Bonner McDowell, 1849–1883): An Annotated Edition" (1996) testify eloquently to the diversity or her career. Her later, decidedly less romantic, tales set in Tennessee and Illinois anticipate the turn to realism and even naturalism in the American fiction of the later nineteenth century. Recurring subtexts on the plight of the talented woman who did not feel the need to be or to remain married permeate Bonner's essays and her fiction, notably her favorably reviewed novel, *Like Unto Like* (1878). Helen Taylor in *Gender, Race, and Region in the Writings of Grace King, Ruth McEnery Stuart, and Kate Chopin* (1989) labels *Like Unto Like* "one of the first strongly feminist American novels," but the novel did not become easily available until a modern edition was published by the University of South Carolina Press in 1997.

Catherine Sherwood Bonner was born in the north Mississippi town of Holly Springs on 26 February 1849, the first surviving child of an Irish immigrant physician, Dr. Charles Bonner, and his wife, Mary Wilson Bonner, daughter of a local planter family. Kate, as she was called, experienced the Civil War firsthand, including the occupation of Holly Springs by Federal forces under Gen. Ulysses S. Grant. She received most of her education in a local academy, except for a term she spent during the war at Hamner Hall, an Episcopal boarding school in Montgomery, Alabama. From her early years she read widely in her father's well-stocked library of British literature and experimented with writing and high-spirited dramatics.

Bonner's diary entries for 1869, the year she sold her first fiction for publication, reveal a romantic young woman enjoying the attentions of a serious beau while also imagining possible alternatives to marriage. On St. Valentine's Day 1871 she married Edward McDowell in Holly Springs; their daughter Lilian was born there on 10 December of the same year. Like many other southerners, the young family moved west for a new postwar beginning, joining relatives of Edward McDowell in Texas. Kate Bonner McDowell, however, returned with their daughter to Holly Springs in the fall of 1873 when it became clear that none of her husband's impracticable schemes would support them.

Within a few weeks the young mother left her baby with disapproving relatives in Mississippi and went alone by train to Boston in search of further education and opportunities to earn her own way. She had corresponded with editor Nahum Capen; he and his family helped her to find lodging, schooling, and work. Initially she supported herself with secretarial jobs for Capen, for charismatic health and temperance reformer Dr. Dio Lewis, and then for the revered poet Henry Wadsworth Longfellow, who became her literary patron and lifelong friend. Through these notable men and her friend James Redpath, director of Boston's first Lyceum Bureau, she promptly gained entrée to prominent social and literary circles.

Kate Bonner McDowell spent most of the next ten years building a successful freelance writing career, which peaked with the publication of *Like Unto Like* by Harper Brothers. Although she was eventually able to bring Lilian and her aunt Martha Bonner to her household in Boston, her ambiguous marital circumstances and Bohemian lifestyle scandalized patrons who had initially supported and sponsored her. Her personal life thereafter suffered successive blows. In 1878 her father and brother died in the yellow-fever epidemic that swept the South. After several attempts to reconcile with her husband, she obtained a divorce in Illinois in 1881 on the grounds of abandonment and nonsupport.

Soon after the divorce, Bonner's recurring episodes of ill health were diagnosed as breast cancer. She returned to Holly Springs and died in the summer of 1883 in the home where she had spent much of her childhood. In that small southern town the author is most often recalled in her role as secretary to Longfellow, the twice-widowed poet who may have been "sweet on her." In his critical biography *The Prodigal Daughter: A Biography of Sherwood Bonner* (1981) Hubert Horton McAlexander provides a fascinating, well-documented account of Bonner's extraordinary life.

Three romances, thought to be Bonner's earliest publications and authenticated as hers although they do not bear her name, appeared in the *Massachusetts Ploughman and New England Journal of Agriculture* in 1869: an Italian gothic thriller, "Laura Capello: A Leaf from A Traveller's Note Book"; a melodramatic two-part quest for a British inheritance, "The Heir of Delmont"; and a bridal dream fantasy, "Saved." The last story, written two years before her marriage to Edward McDowell, examines some consequences of choosing the wrong husband. Through the device of a dream, Bonner saves her heroine Marion Moore from the "mistake" of an imprudent choice. (Five years after becoming McDowell's wife, she complained in a letter to her sister of a real-life nightmare: "my life blighted by marriage with a man utterly unworthy.") While Bonner's first published stories—with their exotic foreign settings, complicated family relationships, mysterious plots, crucial documents, ill-fated romances, melodramatic dialogue, and questions of illegitimacy or secret marriage—may strike the modern reader as improbable, they represent credible examples of literary genres immensely popular at the time. Some early stories of Louisa May Alcott or Henry James are just as unlikely.

During her first years in Boston, Bonner struggled to find an identity as a writer. Her earliest publications there are signed Katherine McDowell, and then Kate McDowell or Kate Bonner, but by early 1875 she settled on the gender-ambiguous nom de plume Sherwood Bonner. Locating information about the writer or her publications requires searching all of these names, as well as the frequent misspelling MacDowell. George Polhemus's article in the July 1960 *Notes and Queries,* based on her family's own records, establishes the correct spellings as Katharine Sherwood Bonner McDowell. Biographer McAlexander clarifies that she changed her given first name from Catherine, after her Irish grandmother Bonner, to Katharine. Bonner and her daughter—later Lilian Kirk Hammond—both used the McDowell name as little as possible.

While working at other jobs, Bonner began to see her work in print. Her introduction to Boston readers occurred with a satiric poem attributed to "D. Scribe," which was published in the *Boston Times* on 8 May 1875. In "The Radical Club: A Poem, Respectfully Dedicated to 'The Infinite' by an Atom" Bonner borrows the prosody of Edgar Allan Poe's "The Raven" and draws humorous, unflattering caricatures of revered figures, including Bronson Alcott, "an ancient Concord bookworm"; Elizabeth Peabody, "the Kindergarten mother"; John T. Sargent, "Mr. Pompous"; and Ednah Dow Cheney, "another *magnum corpus* with a figure like a porpus." The lasting notoriety that surrounded the poem and its author, when she was revealed, brought Bonner instant celebrity but eventually led to her ostracism from circles where she had previously been welcomed. From 1875 on, she regularly sold her work to leading magazines, including *Harper's Monthly, Harper's Weekly, Lippincott's Magazine, Youth's Companion, Cottage Hearth, Harper's Young People, St. Nicholas,* and *Our Continent.* Her other published poetry comprises a few verses for children and several touching personal lyrics written near the end of her life.

Like many other aspiring writers, Bonner sharpened her skills as a newspaper special correspondent. In 1874–1875 she sold to the *Memphis Avalanche* seven long letters from Boston that focused on a southern woman's first impressions of the New England city that styled itself as the "Hub of the Universe." When she went abroad in 1876, she earned expense money with signed front-page European travel letters sold to both Memphis and Boston newspapers. Although she designated these "a woman's letters," she developed a humorous, irreverent, and self-deprecatory personal voice much in the style of Mark Twain's best-selling travel book *The Innocents Abroad* (1869). The genre of the loosely constructed travel letter allowed Bonner to create a strong narrative persona and to practice devices that would serve her well as a writer of fiction: dialogue, dialects, observation and description, characterization, literary allusion, and embedded stories.

Shortly after her arrival in Boston, Bonner forwarded some of her stories to a family friend, Dr. Theodore Dwight at Columbia University, and related that she was considering a move to New York. Responding at length on 21 February 1874, he observed that Boston was a place more congenial to a woman's success and praised her "real power for story telling." Dwight also offered some on-target criticism in his self-described "sermon": "The only considerable fault I found was, that the influence of your reading was noticeable through every composition. . . . Your modes of expression often, but oftener the plan of your story was unconsciously based on the conventional plan."

Dwight's judgment is borne out by the 1875 story "Who Won the Crown?," the earliest known fiction Bonner published in Boston. Although it is strong in the localized detail of the town "Hollywell," a re-creation of Holly Springs, this sketch about a group of young people enjoying a chivalric tournament in the South owes heavy debts, in the telling as much as in the customs it describes, to Sir Walter Scott's *Ivanhoe* (1819). In search of new models, Bonner later that year shaped a true Civil War event into the romantic tale of "Miss Willard's Two Rings," which is clearly built on a formula that had lately brought success to Bret Harte: an outcast in rough circumstances turns out to have a heart of gold. She apparently took Dwight's criticism seriously, though, for four months after her Scott-like story appeared in *The Youth's Companion,* she published there "Gran'mamy's Last Gift," a story that was expanded and collected in *Suwanee River Tales* as "Gran'mammy's Last Gifts." It was the first of a series of tales that won praise for their freshness and realism.

Bonner's Gran'mammy tales published between 1875 and 1880 were, according to Dorothy Gilligan in her "Life and Works of Sherwood Bonner" (1930), among the earliest and best of the immensely popular black dialect stories published in national magazines

Bonner's husband, Edward McDowell, and her daughter, Lillian McDowell

after the Civil War. Wade Hall in *The Smiling Phoenix: Southern Humor from 1865–1914* (1965) asserts they were "probably the first Negro dialect stories widely read in the North." Hall claims that Bonner was "the first Southern woman to deal with the Negro, and the first writer to treat him separately from the white man."

The literary character of Gran'mammy was modeled on Molly Wilson, the African American matriarch who had nurtured Bonner's family for three generations before the war. Often both narrator and central character, Gran'mammy relates real events from her life with Kate's mother and maternal grandmother. Following the death of Bonner's mother in 1865, Gran'mammy, by then a free woman, had continued to care for the three surviving Bonner children—Kate, Ruth, and Sam—even after Dr. Bonner's sister Martha came to live with them.

Bonner's experiences within her family doubtless account for the sentimental overtones in some of the Gran'mammy reminiscences. In her 1881 novella "The Valcours," when the motherless Eva loses her grandmother, only her Maum Lucy can comfort her: "Eva clung to her with that simple affection a Southern girl never loses for her 'black mammy': afterward it seemed to her she could never have lived through those first dreary days but for the comfort of that faithful pres-

ence." Lovingly drawn mammy figures appear throughout Bonner's fiction.

Gran'mammy's first appearance antedates both Joel Chandler Harris's Uncle Remus, who first appeared in the *Atlanta Constitution* in 1876, and Irwin Russell's popular dialect poem "Christmas Night in the Quarters" (1878), landmarks of the genre. Martha Cook in *American Women Writers* (1981) claims that Bonner "creates one of the finest literary portraits of the black mammy" when she moves Gran'mammy to center stage as an individualized narrator. The six Gran'mammy sketches that open the *Suwanee River Tales* expand Gran'mammy's literary role and became Bonner's most anthologized short fiction. Long identified simply as black dialect fiction, the Gran'mammy tales may be seen alternatively as family lore, carefully shaped memoir in the guise of fiction.

In 1878 Bonner's Boston literary career reached its pinnacle when Harper Brothers published *Like Unto Like,* a regional romance set in the Deep South during Reconstruction. Bonner's version is not typical of the so-called reconciliation novels of the period, where national reunion was often symbolized by the marriage of a southern beauty to a northern hero. Like George Eliot's *Middlemarch* (1871–1872)—one of many literary works alluded to in the novel—*Like Unto Like* parallels the courtships of three young provincial women. Patient Mary Barton, with her womanly "gentle reserve," wins the heart of her childhood love Van Tolliver, but only after he recognizes the shallowness of his first love, Betty Page. Betty, a shameless flirt, meanwhile pursues the Yankee Captain Silsby to a marriage of convenience and an extended European honeymoon.

The strength of the somewhat autobiographical novel lies in the lively delineation of Blythe Herndon, an unconventional southern heroine who quotes Margaret Fuller: "To give her hand with dignity, woman must be able to stand alone." At the conclusion Blythe does stand alone, having broken her engagement to Roger Ellis, a most unlikely hero for a literary romance. In his 1987 article in *Southern Studies,* "Some Thoughts Concerning the Love Life of Sherwood Bonner," Daniel E. Sutherland explores evidence that Ellis is modeled on Bonner's friend, Boston lyceum director James Redpath—also a middle-aged radical Republican Yankee—and suggests that the North-South romance of the novel was not altogether fictional.

Beyond its romantic plotlines, *Like Unto Like* is remarkable for its frank exploration of Reconstruction-era politics. While Blythe's steely-eyed grandmother clings unforgivingly to the Lost Cause, Blythe strives in the critical election year of 1876 to formulate her own positions on race, party politics, and national reunion. Because "she had not that charming docility which in many women leads them to accept the *dictum* of the nearest man . . . with no questions asked . . . Miss Herndon made up her mind to decide on a political creed." She solicits—and Bonner presents—an evenhanded range of southern Democrat and northern Republican views, extremes as well as moderates in each camp. Yet when Blythe and Roger clash initially, her anger is more about gender issues than regional loyalties: when she becomes outraged at his defense of General Butler's insulting tactics in managing the subversive women of occupied New Orleans, Ellis calls her "a desperate little rebel." She quickly corrects him: "it is not as a Southerner I resent what you have said, but as a *woman.*" McAlexander observes, "Twenty years before Kate Chopin wrote so powerfully of a woman's search for her self, in *Like Unto Like* Sherwood Bonner had explored another southern woman's awakening."

The novel is strong in local color. A variety of realistic dialects portray characters struggling with the class and race displacements in the Alabama town of Yariba (a fictional blend of Huntsville, Alabama, and Holly Springs, Mississippi) as a result of the recent war. The black child Willy, humorously nicknamed by the townspeople "Civil Rights Bill," emerges as a sympathetic and developing character, though he dies in the course of the novel. Jane Turner Censer in her 1997

introduction praises *Like Unto Like* because "Sherwood Bonner broke new ground both in acknowledging the importance of race in southern attitudes and in creating a range of African American characters, some of whom transcend stereotype." Later episodes of the novel set in New Orleans describe in authentic detail the French Market, the Garden District, the wharfs, and a carnival parade and ball, scenes familiar to the author and similar to those popularized nationally in the 1870s by George Washington Cable.

Bonner's subsequent work evolved in new directions as she perceived shifts in American literary fashion. Her romance "The Revolution of Mr. Balingall" (1879), included in *Dialect Tales and Other Stories* (1990), was set in the aftermath of the 1878 yellow-fever epidemic. Mr. Balingall's future seems settled when he becomes engaged to Fanny Vancourt, the spoiled daughter of a renowned physician who will set him up in practice after they marry. Balingall, though, cannot forget a mysterious woman he saw only once, as she was hurrying to the aid of her fiancé in Kilbuck, a southern town devastated by the plague. Balingall's obsession with Idalia destroys his assured future with the Vancourts and sends him on a lonely journey after he hears that Idalia is dead, a victim of the epidemic. Although he unexpectedly finds her alive in Kilbuck, prostrate upon the grave of Fane Evans, her fiancé, there is no quick resolution or certain happy ending for Balingall. As he builds a new life for himself in Kilbuck, "Idalia has not recognized him, and he has not yet spoken to her. But in his heart he has vowed to win her back to forgetfulness and a new love." Balingall's once predictable life has undergone a revolution, but as the tale closes and Idalia wastes away in grief, "the future holds her secrets securely." Ambiguous endings are not standard fare in the sentimental romances of the period. This fanciful story, published just a year after Bonner lost her father and brother to the fever, seems far more controlled than "The Yellow Plague of '78: A Record of Horror and Heroism," her account of actual experiences written a few months earlier for *The Youth's Companion.*

In even some of her most realistic short stories Bonner uses sentimental endings, presumably because 1880s readers—and therefore editors—demanded them. "A Volcanic Interlude" (1880), a story Claude Simpson includes in *The Local Colorists: American Short Stories, 1857–1900* (1960) and calls one of her strongest stories, is an explosive Louisiana mixture of illegitimacy and miscegenation. When it appeared in *Lippincott's,* its sensational themes caused some readers to cancel their subscriptions in protest. The three daughters of wealthy plantation owner Dufresne return from Madame Crozat's boarding school in New Orleans and press their father to give them information about their mothers, whom they have never known. Dufresne is forced by the family priest, Father Marquette, to reveal to them first that he has never been married. Irene, the oldest at nineteen, learns that her mother was "the daughter of a neighbor's overseer . . . pretty, passionate and ignorant." Cora, just seventeen, is horrified to discover that her mother was "a ballet-dancer at the Varieties Theatre" who had many lovers. Zoe, the youngest, has the rudest shock; she is the daughter of "your grandmother's waiting-maid, a slave." An epilogue explains that Dufresne's social position allows him to arrange comfortable marriages for the older two daughters, but mixed-race Zoe is abandoned even by her sisters and is consigned to a convent. In what Simpson judges to be an "anticlimactic final paragraph," the reader learns that Zoe dies at eighteen. Likewise, in 1893, more than a decade after Bonner's story appeared, the same "acceptable" literary fate is the only available resolution for tragic mulatta characters in Kate Chopin's often-anthologized "Desiree's Baby" and in Grace King's "The Little Convent Girl."

Dialect stories proliferated in part because writers after the end of the Civil War sought to capture America's diverse regional speeches before, as many expected, they would blend and disappear in the reunited country. Some of Bonner's black characters follow nineteenth-century conventions, functioning largely to provide humor by emphasizing dialects and attitudes that shaped a wave of popular comic writing in the 1870s and later. Stories such as Bonner's "Hieronymous Pop and the Baby," first published in 1880, and "Aunt Anniky's Teeth" (1882) led early critics to cite Bonner's humor as her greatest gift.

"Hieronymous Pop and the Baby," a comic narrative republished in Edward Mason's multivolume *Humorous Masterpieces of American Literature* (1886), is about a lad designated by his family to watch the baby, Tiddlekins, while the adults go to view a hanging. Hieronymous gets into trouble for his inventive solution for keeping the baby cool while he goes off to watch a dogfight: "'If I wuz ter hang Tiddekins down de well,' he reflected, 'twouldn't be no mo' dan three jumps of a flea befo' he's as cool as Christmas.'" The second story, "Aunt Anniky's Teeth," was included in Kate Sanborn's *The Wit of Women* (1885), an anthology designed to show that women could write in modes other than the sentimental or the melancholy. In the story Aunt Anniky's prized false teeth are ruined when Uncle Ned, in a fit of fever, mistakes them for ice in a glass of water. When she and Ned cannot agree how he will repay her, they take the case to the plantation owner, who offers new teeth as a wedding gift if Anniky and Ned will marry. Uncle Ned at first agrees, on the grounds that she will then have to obey him. When Uncle Ned reconsiders and leaves to go fishing, Aunt Anniky delights in the

teeth, given to her anyway, because, she explains, "it wuz de teef I wanted, not de man!" Changing sensibilities have led to the removal of such once-popular jokes based on class and race from mainstream literature, but feminist readers can find another way to appreciate Aunt Anniky's pronouncement.

In his 1965 analysis of southern humor Hall acknowledges that some Bonner stories represent the old mode of finding humor implicit in the upward strivings of newly freed blacks, but he cites her raucous tale "The Gentlemen of Sarsar" (1882) as a prime example of a hoax tale. This story involves an elaborate plot of rural blacks and whites who cooperate to bilk an outsider from the city, with all sharing in the profit. While northern critics celebrated this story as an authentic picture of life in the distant South, southern readers recognized it as a caricature. Later critics point out that a good deal of Bonner's popular dialect humor, full of exaggeration and impolite jokes, clearly belongs to the rowdy masculine tall-tale tradition rather than to the more subtle subversive domesticity of Frances Whitcher and Marietta Holley, early female humorists.

In "Writing in A Different Direction: Women Authors and the Tradition of Southwestern Humor, 1875–1910" (1996) Kathryn B. McKee examines the work of Bonner and three other women whose writing was often misunderstood because it was such an unfamiliar variation on conventionally gendered literary patterns. McKee shows that Bonner finds humor in the displacement of many southern classes during Reconstruction, the white male establishment as well as the newly freed slaves. For example, "Dr. Jex's Predicament" (1880) depicts the prim village doctor, a white man "speckless, spotless, gloved, scented, curled," trying to minister to corpulent Uncle Brimmer, a black man stuck in a small window at the top of the barn where he has taken up residence. When an angry bull knocks away the doctor's ladder, Uncle Brimmer is persuaded to hang on to the "pompous and self-important" Dr. Jex while the other black servants below lingeringly debate the price they might ask for sending an emissary to summon help. The bedraggled, terrified doctor is finally rescued, suffering most from his loss of dignity. Uncle Brimmer visits the doctor soon after to claim the rewards he has negotiated: a cravat, a cane, and other fine attire that readers then would have seen as hilariously inappropriate for a black servant.

The four broadly comic stories involving Hieronymous Pop, Aunt Anniky, the Gentlemen of Sarsar, and Dr. Jex—all included in *Dialect Tales*—owe their distinctly unladylike tone to the literary tradition of Thomas Bangs Thorpe, George Washington Harris, Augustus Baldwin Longstreet, and other "sporting" writers of American Southwestern humor dating from the 1830s.

Bonner's strength in re-creating vernacular speech patterns, recognized and praised as part of the realism of the rising local-color movement, has been extended and refined by twentieth-century southern writers indebted to the same traditions, notably William Faulkner, Eudora Welty, and Flannery O'Connor.

Besides using the multiple dialects that she knew from her life in Mississippi, Bonner also experimented successfully with recording the speech and scenic descriptions of other locales. Capitalizing on the reading tastes of her time, she made fictional forays into Cable's New Orleans and Mary Murfree's Tennessee mountains, places she visited. In two Louisiana stories, "C.G.; or, Lily's Earrings" (1878), which was later chosen for *Suwanee River Tales,* and "Two Storms" (1881), as well as in several European travel letters and stories, Bonner falls back on artificial conventions common at the time to suggest Creole or French accents, but elsewhere her characters speak with believable, if not precisely accurate, dialects.

In "Two Storms" Bonner builds a convoluted, melodramatic tale around the disastrous 1856 Gulf hurricane years before Lafcadio Hearn used it for his better-known romance *Chita* (1888) and before Chopin's Gulf island setting for parts of *The Awakening* (1899). Though the plot of "Two Storms" has been heavily criticized, the author convincingly re-creates the exotic setting, which she knew from the months the McDowells had spent in Galveston, Texas. In this story Dina, the motherless young heroine, comes dangerously close to suffering the fate so scandalous that it kept Louisa May Alcott's *A Long Fatal Love Chase* unpublished until 1995: eloping with an already married older man. In this story Bonner further refines the practice of dialect impressions by creating distinct black voices that successfully delineate two characters: the mammy figure, Maum Dulcie, and the old hoodoo witch, Sinai.

After Harper Brothers sponsored Bonner's trip to the Cumberland mountains of Tennessee in 1879, she produced four stories for *Dialect Tales* designed to build on interest in that region stirred by the stories of Mary Murfree, then writing as Charles Egbert Craddock. "The Barn Dance at Apple Settlement" (1881) offers more a picturesque scene than a plotted story. "Jack and the Mountain Pink" (1881) features the mountain girl, or pink, Sincerity Hicks, who is strong and clever enough to help the moonshiner (a requisite character of the genre) escape from the government agent sent to apprehend him. The Tennessee stories, though, go beyond superficial generic conventions of the mountain story to deeper concerns with the plights of heroines who face distinctly unromantic fates. "The Case of Eliza Bleylock" (1881) and "Lame Jerry" (1881) portray Eliza Bleylock and Cordy, the daughter of Lame Jerry,

Bonner at thirty

as women who are betrayed or abandoned by men and for whom there is no redeeming happy ending or even survival. Bonner's empathetic depictions of the mountain women engage reader sympathies in ways Murfree's outsider perspective cannot. Of Bonner's four Tennessee stories, biographer McAlexander contends that "no group of stories by a contemporary writer reflects so well the pattern of development in American literature from the Civil War to the end of the nineteenth century."

Bonner's novella "The Valcours," which was serialized in *Lippincott's* in 1881 and republished in *Dialect*

Tales and Other Stories, is set in Arnville, Louisiana, and Hot Springs, Arkansas. The characters and unfolding plot make gentle fun of romance conventions: the sympathetic heroine is a large, red-haired, freckle-faced, whistling girl from Kentucky, named by her grandfather for his favorite battle: Buena Vista Church. Her brother David edits the Arnville *Avalanche,* for which B. V. draws cartoons. The dashing hero Garoche' (Garry) Valcour represents reason and the future in a new South, though his father, General Valcour, "grieved sorely that his bones had not been left to whiten on a Southern battle-field rather than he should live to swallow the bitter results of defeat." Garry provides the romantic interest for B. V. and also for her friend Eva Charenton, the frail girl of mysterious parentage who comes to Arnville with her grandmother to escape a New Orleans epidemic. The identity of Eva's father forms a major subplot, as does B. V.'s scheme to send Garry and Eva off in different directions.

When Garry marries Eva, Buena Vista, "a gifted little creature," goes to Europe for three years to study art; the narrator concludes that she "allies herself to no selfish, exclusive lover.... So let no one pity B. V., who has lost earth and gained only–heaven." As in *Like Unto Like,* Bonner may have been rewriting her own life to explore options she had not been aware of when she married Edward McDowell. For its lighthearted, imaginative treatment of romance themes, McAlexander calls "The Valcours" "Sherwood Bonner's best piece of work."

Having followed Murfree's lead to Tennessee, Bonner later broke new regional ground when she wrote four stories, two of them collected in *Dialect Tales,* set in the farm country of the southern Illinois prairie. "Sister Weeden's Prayer" (1881) takes to task the narrow religious views of pious churchwomen quick to judge a neighbor, Sister Biscoe, who apparently has violated the Sabbath with her sewing. They are humbled when they learn that she was making a suit for a local man who needs it in time for the circuit preacher to baptize him at the river. An anonymous reviewer in the 24 March 1881 issue of *The Nation* praised the dialect and character portrayals in this "unusual story" and concluded that the talent of the author–assumed to be male–"is plainly considerable."

The grim "On the Nine-Mile" (1882) tells the tale of Janey Burridge, a farm girl who boasts, "I can do a'most anything that a man can." When she is crippled by a piece of heavy machinery, her fiancé, Charley Winn, breaks their engagement because, he reasons, "a man hes to marry a woman ter do her shear o' the work. And you can't do anything." Janey subsequently marries Alexander Farley, a reformed drinking man whose weakly wife "up an' died." Satisfying the popular demand for a sentimental ending, the epilogue shows Janey a few years later, walking and carrying their new baby. Yet this final obligatory celebration of domesticity and motherhood is undercut by the words of another neighbor in the story, Nancy Jones, who describes as her burdens "Twins the first year o' my marriage, an' a baby ten months after! I am fairly dragged out with nursin', an' I suppose I shell have a baby in my arms es long es I am able to move." Ambivalent subtexts in this Bonner story and others reflect dilemmas about marriage and motherhood central to the woman question of the nineteenth century.

Two posthumously published Bonner stories from the Illinois prairie, "At the Wool-Picking" (1883) and "The Tender Conscience of Mr. Bobberts" (1884), show her increasing confidence in the strength of women to resolve difficulties. Deb Hornish, the young heroine of "Wool-Picking," kills a dangerous snake to save the life of a crippled girl and later marries the girl's brother. Leila Raney, the bride in "Mr. Bobberts," deftly outsmarts a mean-spirited neighbor who threatens her husband with character defamation; she relies on Providence, the sisterhood of other women, and her own wits to pursue evidence that will rescue her husband. Along the way she triumphs over an uncompromising legal system and exposes the hypocrisy of Mr. "So-so" Bobberts and the community church. The underlying message, though, is strongly Christian in spirit: true justice is based on the higher law of God that dictates charity and compassion rather than adherence to the letter of a rigid law. Bonner's four Illinois stories, written during the year she lived near relatives while her divorce was pending, demonstrate clearly her turn toward more realistic fiction, her growing facility in re-creating dialogue, and strong undertones of social criticism.

Like many other professional writers of her time, Bonner sold lighthearted entertainments for young readers. Eight juvenile stories, written during the years Lilian lived with her in Boston and in Illinois, were subsequently collected in *Suwanee River Tales* under the heading "A Ring of Tales for Younger Folks," and two more are preserved in "The Uncollected Works." "The Angel in the Lilly Family" (1880) features characters named for Lilian and other Bonner family members. When Katharine Kirk Lilly, one of the many children in the story, is seriously injured in a fall, her nurse receives gifts accompanied by a note from "a glorious poet": "MY DEAR MRS. LILLY.–I send you a little book for your sick child, and some medicine for her broken back. The peculiarity of this medicine is that in order to produce any good effect it must be taken by the nurse. This is rather hard upon the nurse; but if she is a good nurse she will not mind it much." An identical message sent with candy to Lilian from her godfather, Longfellow, can be found in his collected correspondence. A charming illustration at the end of Bonner's story reveals what readers will have guessed: the fourteen children are Lilian's dolls. Another rollicking juvenile tale, "The Terrible Adventures of Ourselves and the Marshal," features a prodigious spider clan with names such as "Rumtickle, Ramtickle, and little Rumdumburrow."

Assessing Bonner's development as a writer is complicated by the brevity of her career, the diversity of her literary efforts, and the fact that some of her posthumously published stories were completed hastily during her illness or afterward by her executor. Among those late publications but not at all in the mode of the novels or the Tennessee and Illinois stories, "Christmas Eve at Tuckeyhoe" (1884) features a southern belle heroine courted by a handsome hero in a traditional plantation romance, an emerging literary mode at the time. "Tuckeyhoe" is among the earliest examples of sentimental local-color Christmas fiction, a subgenre subsequently made famous by Thomas Nelson Page, Grace King, Ruth McEnery Stuart, Mary Murfree, Octave Thanet, Bret Harte, and Virginia Frazer Boyle. It is unclear how much editorial revision "Tuckeyhoe" incorporates; however, it exhibits Bonner's penchant for comedy, especially in several ostensibly romantic scenes. Notably, the female characters, black and white, are compassionate, caring, and forgiving, in contrast to a central male character, old Mr. Erskine, who is for most of the story bitter, vindictive, and unforgiving of his own daughter and of her faithful mammy as well.

Bonner's early literary models had been magazine romances derivative of British trends, but after her move to Boston she incorporated techniques borrowed from popular contemporary American male writers: Edgar Allan Poe, Mark Twain, Bret Harte, and the Southwest humorists. Bonner's later stories are often woman-centered but darker, although sometimes with obligatory endings that acknowledge lingering popular preferences for sentiment. Driven always by economic necessity, Bonner experimented widely rather than developing her talent in a single literary direction. Her one professional decade did not allow her the luxury of time. Her better-known contemporaries such as Sarah Orne Jewett, Stuart, Frances Hodgson Burnett, Murfree, Chopin, King, and Mary Wilkins Freeman all enjoyed long careers.

One other novel deserves mention in connection with Bonner. The *Story of Margaret Kent* (1886) appeared initially under the pseudonym Henry Hayes but was later credited as the work of novelist Ellen Olney Kirk, stepmother of Bonner's friend and literary executor, Sophia Kirk. Recognizable at once as a thinly veiled account of Bonner's Boston years, this successful novel reached its thirty-fourth printing in 1890. The title page in 1886 advertises that the authors behind the mask of Hayes "are confidently reported as the late Katherine McDowell ('Sherwood Bonner') and Sophia Kirk, the former the originator and writer of the story, the latter the reviser and finisher."

McAlexander notes that the veiled revelations contained in the novel were the last straw for Boston conservatives, who thereafter abjured all mention of the lady from Mississippi. Citing content and differences in writing styles in early and late portions of the novel, he argues convincingly that *Margaret Kent* is in part an autobiographical roman à clef. The finished version contains information that would have been known only to Bonner, including some details of her fall from grace in Boston circles. It presents some of the best-known descriptions of Lilian and depicts the aging poet Herbert Bell as a suitor pressing for the hand of the lovely Margaret Kent. The circumstances of authorship will probably always remain clouded, but the narrative, blurring fact and fiction, adds to the fuller understanding of Bonner's life and career.

Nineteenth- and twentieth-century critics have compared Bonner's heroines to those of George Eliot, Jane Austen, and William Thackeray. Her work has been included in anthologies of humor, of women's writing, of American literature, of Southern writing, and of local-color stories. In "The Woman Question in the Life and Work of Sherwood Bonner" (1989) Darlene Pajo concludes that Bonner's portrayals of women set her ahead of her time. Her peculiar marital situation took her outside of traditional domesticity, and she wrote about and sympathized with other women who carved out new roles. She used journalistic articles about prominent women–Mary Clemmer Ames, Julia Ward Howe, Louise Chandler Moulton, Elizabeth Avery Meriwether, and Helena Modjeska–to present her positions on marriage, divorce, careers, and public roles for women. Lisa Pater Faranda in her 1988 essay "A Social Necessity: The Friendship of Sherwood Bonner and Henry Wadsworth Longfellow" concludes that "Bonner was no feminist, but she came close to being one."

Researchers continue to find additional Bonner publications, and tantalizing hints suggest that others remain to be discovered. Two of the *Suwanee River Tales* have not been located in their periodical versions, although Kirk asserts in her preface that the stories collected had all been previously published. Before she married, Bonner may have published "A Flower of the South" in a music journal, not yet identified, and her notes say she submitted as-yet-unfound pieces that may have been published by a Frank Leslie journal and a

Mobile newspaper at about the same time that she sold her first three stories to the *Massachusetts Ploughman.*

Sherwood Bonner was an astute, talented, witty observer of the American scene whose work reveals much about cultural and literary trends during crucial decades of the nineteenth century. Faced with the necessity of writing to support herself, she was quick to notice and to try what she thought would sell; not all of her experiments were successful, but as McAlexander observes, "Of all her contemporaries, she is the most varied." Her irrepressible sense of humor, lighthearted but not always tempered by discretion, got her into difficulty on more than one occasion. Her candid southern views, broadened but unintimidated by brushes with the elite of New England, provide an alternative perspective for understanding postwar regional differences; her southern correspondence to the Memphis newspaper paints an outsider's superior local-color view of Reconstruction-era Boston. Her skepticism about organized religion shapes characters and plots. Most important, her articulation of emerging feminist concerns weaves recurring threads throughout her literary fabric. New readers of her work will discover that Sherwood Bonner has been too lightly estimated and too narrowly classified.

Letters:

Jean Nosser Biglane, "An Annotated and Indexed Edition of the Letters of Sherwood Bonner," M.A. thesis, Mississippi State University, 1972.

Bibliographies:

Thomas McAdory Owen, "A Bibliography of Mississippi," *Annual Report of the American Historical Association,* 1 (1900): 654;

Jean Nosser Biglane, "Sherwood Bonner: A Bibliography of Primary and Secondary Materials," *American Literary Realism,* 5 (1972): 38–60.

Biographies:

Alexander Bondurant, "Sherwood Bonner–Her Life and Place in the Literature of the South," *Publications of the Mississippi Historical Society,* 1 (1899): 43–68;

Hubert Horton McAlexander, *The Prodigal Daughter: A Biography of Sherwood Bonner* (Baton Rouge: Louisi-

ana State University, 1981); republished, with a new introduction, by McAlexander (Knoxville: University of Tennessee Press, 1999).

References:

Nash Kerr Burger Jr., "Katherine Sherwood Bonner: A Study in the Development of a Southern Literature," M.A. thesis, University of Virginia, 1935;

Lisa Pater Faranda, "A Social Necessity: The Friendship of Sherwood Bonner and Henry Wadsworth Longfellow," in *Patrons and Protegees: Gender, Friendship, and Writing in Nineteenth-Century America,* edited by Shirley Marchalonis (New Brunswick, N.J.: Rutgers University Press, 1988), pp. 184–211;

Dorothy Gilligan, "Life and Works of Sherwood Bonner," M.A. thesis, George Washington University, 1930;

Wade Hall, *The Smiling Phoenix: Southern Humor from 1865 to 1914* (Gainesville: University of Florida Press, 1965);

Ellen Olney Kirk, *The Story of Margaret Kent* (Boston: Ticknor, 1886);

Sophia Kirk, preface to *Suwanee River Tales,* by Sherwood Bonner (Boston: Roberts, 1884);

Kathryn B. McKee, "Writing in a Different Direction: Women Authors and the Tradition of Southwestern Humor, 1875–1910," dissertation, University of North Carolina–Chapel Hill, 1996;

Darlene Pajo, "The Woman Question in the Life and Fiction of Sherwood Bonner," M.A. thesis, University of Louisville, 1989;

Daniel E. Sutherland, "Some Thoughts Concerning the Love Life of Sherwood Bonner," *Southern Studies,* 26 (1987): 115–127.

Papers:

Some personal correspondence, an unpublished manuscript poem, a fragment of a Revolutionary War story, and other miscellaneous papers of Sherwood Bonner are held by the Mississippi Department of Archives and History in Jackson. Some Bonner materials exist in the special collections of the libraries of the University of Mississippi in Oxford and Mississippi State University in Starkville, as well as in the Marshall County Public Library in Holly Springs.

J. Ross Browne

(? January 1821 – 9 December 1875)

Joseph Csicsila
Eastern Michigan University

BOOKS: *Confessions of a Quack; Or the Autobiography of a Modern Aesculapian* (Louisville, Ky.: James Marshall, 1841);

Etchings of a Whaling Cruise, with Notes of a Sojourn on the Island of Zanzibar; with a History of the Whale Fishery (New York: Harper, 1846; London: John Murray, 1846);

Report of the Debates in the Convention of California on the Formation of the State Constitution in September and October 1849 (Washington, D.C.: J. T. Powers, 1850);

Yusef; Or the Journey of the Frangi, a Crusade in the East (New York: Harper, 1853; London: Low, 1853);

Crusoe's Island: A Ramble in the Footsteps of Alexander Selkirk, with Sketches of Adventure in California and Washoe (New York: Harper, 1864; London: Sampson Low & Marston 1864);

An American Family in Germany (New York: Harper, 1866);

Report upon the Mineral Resources of the United States (Washington, D.C.: Government Printing Office, 1867);

The Land of Thor (New York: Harper, 1867);

Report of J. Ross Browne on the Mineral Resources of the States and Territories West of the Rocky Mountains (Washington, D.C.: Government Printing Office, 1868);

Adventures in the Apache Country: A Tour through Arizona and Sonora, with Notes on the Silver Region of Nevada (New York: Harper, 1869; London: Marston, 1869).

SELECTED PERIODICAL PUBLICATIONS–
UNCOLLECTED: "Melhatchee, the Enchanted Warrior," *Southern Literary Messenger,* 6 (June 1840): 466–450;

"Yoo-Ti-Hu," *Graham's Magazine,* 18 (January 1841): 10–12;

"The Confessions of a Miser," *Graham's Magazine,* 18 (January–March 1841): 83–87; 102–104; 189–191;

"Misfortunes of a Timid Gentleman," *Graham's Magazine,* 19 (September, December 1841): 120–123; 289–292;

"A Peep at Washoe," *Harper's Monthly,* 22 (December 1860 – February 1861): 1–17; 145–162, 289–305;

"A Dangerous Journey," *Harper's Monthly,* 24–25 (May, June 1862): 741–756; 6–19;

"Washoe Revisited," *Harper's Monthly,* 30–31 (May–July 1865): 681–696; 1–19; 151–161.

J. Ross Browne (for his first name, John) is routinely cited as a minor literary influence on Herman Melville and Mark Twain. His *Etchings of a Whaling Cruise, with Notes of a Sojourn on the Island of Zanzibar; with a*

History of the Whale Fishery (1846), for instance, has long been considered by critics to have inspired key aspects of *Moby-Dick* (1851). Readers since the mid nineteenth century have also recognized more than a few striking similarities between several of Browne's travel narratives written in the 1850s and 1860s and Twain's *Innocents Abroad* (1869), *Roughing It* (1872), and *A Tramp Abroad* (1880).

While such distinctions have proved helpful in sustaining limited interest in Browne's writings in the last century and a half, he clearly deserves recognition in his own right. A nascent realist, Browne crusaded against romantic literature a generation before American writers collectively took up the cause of literary realism. Although Browne utilized the travel book format throughout his career, he regularly approached his craft as a writer of prose fiction, introducing the styles, techniques, and characters of American frontier humor to one of the most conventional–and financially lucrative–genres of his times.

The second son of Elana Elizabeth Buck Browne and Thomas Egerton Browne–a celebrated literary and political figure in his native Ireland and a friend of William Makepeace Thackery–John Ross Browne was born the third of seven children in Beggarsbush, Ireland, a small village situated just north of Dublin, in January 1821. Family tradition and Browne's earliest biographer, Francis J. Rock, give 11 February 1821 as Browne's date of birth; however, in the late 1960s, Lina Fergusson Browne, wife of Browne's grandson, uncovered church documents in the parish of Donnybrook, Ireland, that record the christening of John Ross Browne almost three weeks earlier on 23 January 1821. Unfortunately, these recently discovered papers provide no date of birth.

In addition to literary aspirations J. Ross Browne (he typically used only the initial for his first name) inherited from his father an activist's hatred for social injustice. As the editor of three Dublin news publications in the early 1830s, the elder Browne waged a successful war against the notorious tithe system imposed on the impoverished Irish peasantry by the Church of England. By 1833 the British government had apparently considered Browne's campaign effective enough to charge him with "seditious libel and inciting to revolt," and on 28 January he was found guilty, fined two thousand pounds, and sentenced to a year in the Dublin Newgate prison. Browne served only a few months before his wife and several friends convinced the courts to remit the fine and commute the sentence to banishment from Ireland for seven years. Shortly thereafter, sympathetic Dubliners raised a considerable sum of money for his benefit. Upon Browne's release from jail, the family immigrated to the United States.

When the Brownes arrived in America in late 1833, they settled near Cincinnati, where Thomas Egerton Browne established a sawmill and ferry business on the Ohio River. Less than a year later when the venture proved unprofitable, the family moved downriver to the still primitive village of Louisville, Kentucky. Here the Brownes opened the Young Ladies Seminary, which provided J. Ross Browne, now thirteen, with the only formal education he would ever receive. During his short-lived career as a student, Browne's parents demanded that he master the classics, but the headstrong teenager resisted. He rejected the Greek and Roman writers not because he found them inaccessible or difficult but because he judged their epics absurdly fantastic. Browne instead devoured more modern books that he would later describe as literature of "the real life," tales of travel and adventure including *Don Quixote* (1605), *Gil Blas* (1715–1735), and his beloved *Robinson Crusoe* (1719).

By the age of seventeen Browne resolved that wandering the globe vicariously through his reading could no longer satisfy his yearnings for travel and adventure. In 1838 he hired out as a deckhand on a flatboat trading between Louisville and New Orleans. For the next year he rambled up and down the Ohio and Mississippi Rivers, working and soaking up the folk culture of the Mississippi River valley. Like Samuel Clemens after him, Browne encountered the Jim Doggetts of the Old Southwest spinning yarns and met the backwoods roughs, sage frontiersmen, and credulous greenhorns who inspired them. By the time Browne turned eighteen he had already covered an astounding 2,200 miles of the United States and ventured as far west as Texas. Sometime in early 1839 he left the flatboat and returned home, but the experience of those few months on the river provided him a rich store of materials from which he would later draw–and only whetted his appetite for more extensive travels.

Once back in Louisville Browne took a job as the police reporter for the *Advertiser* and worked as an occasional correspondent for Cincinnati and Columbus newspapers. He attended medical school for a short while but quickly recognized that he was better suited to be a writer and began writing short fictional sketches for local journals. In 1840 Browne realized his first major success as an author by placing his tale "Melhatchee, the Enchanted Warrior" in the *Southern Literary Messenger*. The story is the work of a novice, unquestionably inspired by James Fenimore Cooper's Leather-stocking series, yet significant nonetheless in that it features two traits that would become hallmarks of Browne's mature writings: a humorous approach to his subject and a satirical treatment of romantic literature.

Illustrations from Browne's second book, Etchings of a Whaling Cruise *(1846)*

In 1841 Browne published three more stories in Edgar Allan Poe's *Graham's Magazine.* While family legend holds that Browne received "encouragement" from Poe, it is more probable that Poe's endorsement of the twenty-year-old writer from Louisville was limited to the magazine's acceptance of his manuscripts. Two of the tales, like "Melhatchee, the Enchanted Warrior," are essentially imitative. "Yoo-Ti-Hu" is a fantasy piece written in the vein of the "Arabian Nights," and "The Confessions of a Miser" is a story set in medieval Italy reminiscent of Cervantes's shorter fiction. With the third piece, however, Browne for the first time capitalized on the quasi-autobiographical materials he would exploit for the rest of his career. A much more original piece than his earlier stories, "Misfortunes of a Timid Gentleman," recounts the escapades of a young man as he negotiates the codes and mores of Louisville society.

In April 1841 Browne published his first book, *Confessions of a Quack; Or The Autobiography of a Modern Aesculapian.* The slim volume consists of a series of sketches (some of which had appeared elsewhere in a slightly different form) revolving around the peculiar deeds of a medical fraud. Most critics agree that *Confessions of a Quack* represents something of a false start for Browne. An essentially humorless story, the prose is stiff, affected, and verbose. Biographer Rock argues, however, that the style of *Confessions of a Quack* may owe much to the "exaggerated mode of Ben Jonson's *The Alchemist.*" Browne's earliest book also contains evidence of more contemporary influences, most notably a

distinctive naming of characters, such as "Graball" and "Killcure," a practice common to many novels by authors from Laurence Sterne to Charles Dickens.

Although Browne may be seen as too indebted to earlier writers for certain features of his first book, other qualities of *Confessions of a Quack* show his progress in the development of his own style. As in the case of "Misfortunes of a Timid Gentleman," Browne transformed the raw materials of autobiography into a fictionalized narrative that includes wholly created scenes and characters. Additionally, *Confessions of a Quack* illustrates Browne's intense hatred of shams and fraud that underlies practically everything he ever published. Writing that the book was conceived as a satire on "quackery in general and quack doctors in particular," Browne in publishing *Confessions of a Quack* likely had been driven as much by a desire to expose the deceit within the medical profession as by literary ambition.

After the publication of *Confessions of a Quack,* probably in late spring or early summer 1841, Browne's father accepted a job in Washington, D.C., as a reporter for the *Congressional Globe,* the precursor to the *Congressional Record.* Browne remained in Louisville after his father moved the family east, but by November he decided to relocate to Washington. Apparently "Misfortunes of a Timid Gentleman" created something of a scandal in Louisville that autumn as many in Browne's hometown judged it a too thinly veiled portrait of the author and his acquaintances. Distressed by the commotion he had created, Browne later expressed regret for ever publishing "Misfortunes of a Gentleman," conceding in a letter dated November 1841: "I made a very particular ass of myself writing that fulsome thing." Coupled with his recent rejection by a Louisville belle, the reaction of his community surely made the decision to follow his family all the more pragmatic.

Browne took a job with his father at the *Globe* after his arrival in Washington. With the ultimate hope of saving up enough money for an extensive trip abroad, a "grand tour" as he put it in *Etchings of a Whaling Cruise,* Browne spent the winter of 1841–1842 transcribing Senate speeches and reporting congressional proceedings. He worked eagerly and diligently those first few months, but the longer he spent on Capitol Hill the more he became sickened by the varieties of corruption and demagoguery he witnessed, as he later recalled in his whaling book: "The profession I had chosen enabled me to see behind the scenes and study well the great machinery of government, and I can not say that I saw a great deal to admire. Such life had no attractions for me. I looked forward with anxiety to the close of the session." By late spring, though he had not yet acquired sufficient funds for his trip abroad, he left his position at the *Globe.* He decided that he would rather work his way to Europe than endure another session of Congress.

Browne had initially planned to travel with two young men whom he had met in Washington. By early July one of the acquaintances backed out, so Browne and the remaining friend, Henry Wilson, an employee of the Treasury Department originally from Ohio, left the capital by train for New York. With just forty dollars between them (well short of the six to eight hundred dollars they figured they would need to sail to Europe in style), Browne and Wilson signed on a New Bedford whaler as sailors before the mast. On the morning of 17 July 1842 the *Bruce,* a ship designed to carry one thousand barrels of oil and provisions for twenty-seven months at sea, embarked for a planned sixteen- to twenty-month expedition.

In September 1842 the *Bruce* had reached the Azores where several of the crew, including Browne's friend from Ohio, were let off because of failing health. Browne continued on without his companion and spent another nine months aboard the whaler. According to the journal he kept throughout the voyage, the rest of the expedition was a typical whaling experience. The drudgery of hard, disgustingly dirty labor, substandard fare, and many monotonous months spent unaccompanied at sea all combined to make Browne lament his decision to sign on to the *Bruce.* In late spring 1843 the ship reached the island of Zanzibar, where Browne was able to purchase his release from the whaler for ten dollars, his entire sea chest of clothes, and by providing a

man to serve in his place. Several weeks later Browne secured passage back to America on another vessel, the *Rolla,* which afforded him considerably better conditions. Arriving in New England in early November, Browne by the end of the month was back in Washington, D.C., and working as a reporter in the Senate. In November 1844 he married Lucy Anna Mitchell, daughter of a Washington physician, after a courtship that lasted a year.

Browne began work on what he called his "whaling book" almost as soon as he settled in Washington. He spent the next two years transforming his two-volume journal into a semifictional account of life aboard a whaling ship. In *Etchings of a Whaling Cruise* he achieved a skillful blend of autobiography, romance, and propaganda. The broad outline of the book follows Browne's experience at sea with a chapter or two near the end tracing briefly the lives of Henry Wilson and several of the crew in the months after their voyages aboard the *Bruce.* Browne supplies many technical details of the whaling profession–including diagrams of tools and weapons that he drew himself–as well as comprehensive descriptions of many of the places he visited along the way.

Although it follows the basic conventions of the travel book, *Etchings of a Whaling Cruise* is a considerably more complex book than at first it might appear and qualifies as a bona fide fictional narrative. Browne transforms Captain Alden of the *Bruce,* by most accounts a stern but not uniquely harsh officer, into Captain A–, a tyrannically cruel seaman who governs his ship, the *Styx,* with malice toward all. Conversely, Browne portrays himself and his companion as innocents whose constant romantic expectations are invariably disappointed when confronted by reality. Not only does Browne thus provide himself the opportunity to satirize literary romanticism through such naive characters, but he also sets up as the central conflict a struggle between good and evil, virtue and vice. In addition to his exaggerated characterizations Browne combined and deleted scenes from his journals and wholly created some incidents to present a compelling narrative designed as much to entertain as to expose the deplorable conditions in the whaling industry.

Etchings of a Whaling Cruise was reviewed favorably in both the United States and England when it appeared. Lewis Gaylord Clark in the November 1846 issue of the prestigious *Knickerbocker Magazine* praised its "naturalness of style" as well as Browne's "detestation of inhumanity in the petty tyrants of the deck." Herman Melville commended *Etchings of a Whaling Cruise* in the 6 March 1847 issue of *The Literary World* by pointing out its similarities with Richard Dana's *Two Years Before the Mast* (1840): "What Mr. Dana has so admirably done in describing the vicissitudes of the merchant-sailor's life, Mr. Browne has credibly achieved with respect to that of the hardy whaleman's." The *London Athenaeum* of 23 January 1856 was slightly less charitable than American reviewers, characterizing Browne a lesser Dana and questioning outright whether the author of *Etchings of a Whaling Cruise* could have actually served as a seaman. But in the end the English reviewer conceded that the "work as regards its main design has a powerful claim on our sympathy."

Etchings of a Whaling Cruise brought Browne recognition as a writer, especially in the United States, but it did not make him wealthy. In early 1845 he had taken a position as a clerk in the Treasury Department. Not long after he became Treasury Secretary Robert J. Walker's personal assistant. For the next three and a half years Browne spent most of his time in Washington but also traveled throughout the Northeast with Walker performing an ever increasing amount of secretarial work. By late 1848 Browne's health was beginning to fail under the stress of the job, so Walker arranged a special assignment for him as a revenue inspector in California. Leaving his wife and their two infant children in Washington, Browne left New York in January 1849 on the long voyage around the Horn to California, a trip that furnished him with more material for his writing. During the voyage the captain was removed by trial in Rio de Janeiro for unacceptable treatment of his passengers. Browne was able to to explore Juan Fernandez, the small island off the coast of Chile immortalized by Daniel Defoe in *Robinson Crusoe*. He arrived in San Francisco on 5 August 1849.

Although Browne discovered within a month that he had lost out on the treasury assignment, he took advantage of his newly acquired freedom to attend the California Constitutional Convention as its recording secretary. He secured the rights to the minutes later that year and published them as *Report of the Debates in the Convention of California on the Formation of the State Constitution in September and October 1849* (1850). The publication was a runaway bestseller as the recent discovery of gold at Sutter's Mill had created a tremendous demand across the United States for anything in print about California. In its first year alone Browne made more than ten thousand dollars, a small fortune for the time.

Browne was able to return to Washington in time to spend Christmas 1849 with his family, and in 1851 he took part of the money he made from *Report of the Debates* and spent a year with his family in Europe. He eventually settled them in Florence, Italy, while he traveled through central Europe, Italy, Greece, the Middle East, and Egypt as a wandering correspondent for the *National Intelligencer,* a Washington journal. In the fall of 1852 Browne brought his family back to Washington.

The next January *Harper's Monthly* began running a series of his irreverent sketches based on his adventures in Europe and the Middle East. Browne combined these articles with his letters that had appeared in *National Intelligencer* to form *Yusef; Or the Journey of the Frangi, a Crusade in the East* (1853), the book that made his name as a writer.

Though on the surface a conventional travel book, *Yusef* is a milestone in American humorous literature. Playing off the sort of blind adoration of things exotic that had become a fundamental component of the travel book, Browne as narrator subverts the genre by ridiculing practically everything he encounters—landmarks, customs, local inhabitants. Browne's satire clearly undermines idealized European culture, and he even occasionally explicitly asserts the superiority of American political and social values. Of course, American humorists had always felt comfortable mocking the manners of Europeans visiting the United States, but rarely before Browne had an American writer dared to deride Europeans in Europe. *Yusef,* then, can be seen as a model for *Innocents Abroad,* the book that effectively launched the career of Mark Twain.

With *Yusef,* Browne hit his stride not only as an original American humorist but also as a literary craftsman. The portrayal of the narrative's central character Yusef, the wily dragoman who supplies the story with much of its vitality, is masterful. A braggart of Old Southwestern proportions, Yusef professes to be known throughout the East as "the destroyer of robbers." The narrator and his fellow travelers gullibly accept the dragoman's tall tales of having single-handedly fought, maimed, and killed innumerable bedouin marauders. Yet, any time the narrator actually witnesses Yusef confronted by real danger, the ridiculous and cowardly guide conveniently manages to disappear or somehow otherwise escape jeopardizing his own safety.

Browne also uses other techniques characteristic of the school of Old Southwest humor in *Yusef.* Throughout the narrative, for example, Browne and the unsuspecting "greenhorn" travelers are swindled by the seemingly charitable local guides, traders, and merchants. Equine humor, another staple of the frontier tradition, accounts for much of the amusement in *Yusef.* At one point Browne is thrown from a mule that he claims holds a prejudice against him. Other comic scenes develop around encounters with horses that are maimed. "The animal upon which I rode," Browne wryly notes at the beginning of his journey, "was intended for a horse, I believe, but it bore very little resemblance to that noble animal." Later the depictions and the humor become considerably more grim. Among the most macabre is the "genuine Syrian" horse that Yusef furnishes Browne, a horribly disfigured animal reminiscent

Browne's portrait of himself meeting San Francisco financiers (from Crusoe's Island*)*

of the images in Augustus Baldwin Longstreet's *Georgia Scenes* (1835).

Yusef was the best known of Browne's books during his lifetime, and it generated a demand for his writing in the 1850s and 1860s by distinguished periodicals such as *Harper's Monthly*. But as with *Etchings of a Whaling Cruise, Yusef* did not make Browne financially secure. In 1853 he again fell back on government service to support his family, taking a job as a special agent for the Treasury Department. For the next seven years he traveled throughout the country inspecting customhouses, surveying conditions on Indian reservations, and sending reports of his observations back to Washington. In 1860, following a brief two-month stint prospecting for silver in the newly discovered Comstock Lode of Nevada, Browne moved his family to Germany, where they would reside until 1863.

During Browne's second European sojourn, he spent much of his time touring Germany, Russia, and Scandinavia and writing travel sketches for *Harper's Monthly,* where his contributions almost always ran as the lead articles. Encouraged no doubt by his growing popularity as a writer, Browne returned to New York in the winter of 1862–1863 to try his hand at lecturing, a potentially lucrative avocation open to authors in the nineteenth century. However, Browne's first experience on the lecture circuit was a failure. By April he was back with his wife and children in Europe.

In 1863 Browne moved his family to California. He made a short trip through Arizona during the winter of 1863–1864. In August he returned to Virginia City, one of the boom towns sprung up with the discovery of the Comstock Lode, as a celebrated writer. Browne had made a reputation for himself on the West

Coast in the early 1860s with a series of sketches in *Harper's* about Nevada mining titled "A Peep at Washoe." In 1864 Browne collected these and other writings, including his 1849 visit to Juan Fernandez and subsequent travels in California and the Pacific Northwest, as *Crusoe's Island: A Ramble in the Footsteps of Alexander Selkirk, with Sketches of Adventure in California and Washoe.*

Crusoe's Island consists of four sections, each devoted to disparate episodes in Browne's life. The first one-third of the book, titled "Crusoe's Island," is autobiographical only in the broadest sense. As in *Etchings of a Whaling Cruise* and *Yusef,* Browne supplies the sketch with many fictional scenes and characters to embellish his narrative and develop its principal themes, especially the humorous debunking of the romantic sensibility.

Browne continuously deflates romantic sentiment throughout *Crusoe's Island* by repeatedly subjecting quixotic characters to the hard, mostly disappointing facts of experience and reality. Early in the section the romantic narrator discovers an earthen pot he presumes to be a relic of Alexander Selkirk, the sailor who was an inspiration for Defoe's Crusoe. The vessel is undamaged except for one side that bears the partial inscription "A S . . . 170," which he deciphers as Selkirk's name and the date of the sailor's arrival on the island. Near the end of the section the narrator, who has become disillusioned, learns that the piece of pottery did not belong to Selkirk but to an American hermit. The glorious inscription he took for Selkirk's signature actually reads, "A Saucepan made by W. Pearce, 17 Oct." This technique of satirizing romantic tendencies in literature is the same Browne employed nearly two decades earlier in *Etchings of a Whaling Cruise.* It is, moreover, the narrative strategy that Mark Twain—who conceivably could have been directly influenced by Browne's work—and other post–Civil War realists frequently exploited.

The second section of *Crusoe's Island,* "A Dangerous Journey," is based on Browne's first few months in California during his initial visit to the West Coast in 1849. At the center of the account is the comical relationship between Browne and his willful mule. Like the Southwest humorists, Browne also uses humor to countervail the graphic violence underlying most of the episodes in the story, particularly the narrator's overnight visit with a family of cannibals, the fight he witnesses between a bear and a bull, and his extended encounter with three banditos. Offering an authentic portrait of the mid-nineteenth-century California wilderness, "A Dangerous Journey" is a minor classic of American regionalist literature as well as a tour de force in frontier humor.

The last two sections of the collection, "Observations in Office" and "A Peep at Washoe," consist mostly of straightforward description and commentary. As such, they read much more like traditional travel sketches than the first two pieces. "Observations in Office" recounts Browne's mid-1850s excursion through the Pacific Northwest, during which he reported on the wretched treatment of the Native American peoples of California and Oregon. "A Peep at Washoe" deals with Browne's mining trip to the Comstock Lode in 1860. It is a fairly reliable—and oftentimes critical—history of Carson City, Virginia City, and the early days of the Nevada Silver Boom.

The final decade of Browne's life was marked by his declining prominence as a writer. At the time of the publication of *Crusoe's Island* Browne was at the height of his literary fame. *Harper's* continued to publish his sketches and he became a successful lecturer, but his popularity fell precipitously in the next few years. Most modern critics attribute Browne's waning reputation to the rise of a generation of new writers, among them Bret Harte and Mark Twain. The year 1866 is at least symbolically significant, for Browne met and advised the young Mark Twain as he embarked on his first lecture tour, and *Harper's* effectively dropped Browne as one of its major contributors.

Browne published three more books with Harper and Brothers in the 1860s. All three were moderately successful, but none of them generated the acclaim of *Yusef* or *Crusoe's Island.* The first two volumes, *An American Family in Germany* (1866) and *The Land of Thor* (1867) are humorous but relatively conventional travel narratives that recount Browne's tours of Europe in 1860 and 1861. Although Browne again satirizes European institutions, these books lack the dynamic central character and spirit that made *Yusef* so memorable. Chronicling his 1864 travels through Arizona and the Southwest desert, Browne's last book, *Adventures in the Apache Country: A Tour through Arizona and Sonora, with Notes on the Silver Region of Nevada* (1869), relies more on straightforward description and documentation than on the more literary qualities of action and characterization. It is highly regarded as an accurate record of nineteenth-century pioneer Arizona.

In addition to writing travel books, Browne spent time in the late 1860s assembling respected reports for the government on the mineral resources of the western states: *Report upon the Mineral Resources of the United States* (1867) and *Report of J. Ross Browne on the Mineral Resources of the States and Territories West of the Rocky Mountains* (1868). Except for an appointment to China in 1868 as Envoy Extraordinary and Minister Plenipotentiary of the United States and a few miscellaneous trips to England, Browne lived the rest of his life in California at Pagoda Hill, the home he built for his family in the hills near Tamescal. He died suddenly on 9 December 1875 at the age of fifty-four from acute appendicitis.

During his last years Browne was disappointed by the lack of interest in his writing, yet he never grew embittered. He lived long enough to see a younger generation of authors realize immense success by utilizing virtually the same narrative methods and material he had pioneered decades earlier. He exerted a minor though indisputable influence on not just the individual careers of Herman Melville and Mark Twain but the development of American letters as a whole.

Letters:

J. Ross Browne: His Letters, Journals, and Writings, edited by Lina Fergusson Browne (Albuquerque: University of New Mexico Press, 1969).

Biographies:

Francis J. Rock, *J. Ross Browne* (Washington, D.C.: Catholic University of America, 1929);

Richard H. Dillon, *J. Ross Browne, Confidential Agent in Old California* (Norman: University of Oklahoma Press, 1965);

David Michael Goodman, *A Western Panorama, 1849–1875, the Travels, Writings and Influence of J. Ross Browne* (Glendale, Cal.: Arthur H. Clark, 1966).

References:

Lina Fergusson Browne, "J. Ross Browne in the Apache Country," *New Mexico Quarterly,* 35 (1965): 5–28;

R. D. Madison, "Melville's Review of Browne's Etchings," *Melville Society Extracts,* 53 (February 1983): 11–13;

Franklin Walker, *Irreverent Pilgrims: Melville, Browne, and Mark Twain in the Holy Land* (Seattle: University of Washington Press, 1974).

Papers:

J. Ross Browne's correspondence is held by the Harvard University Library, the Massachusetts Historical Society, and the New York Historical Society.

Alice Cary

(26 April 1820 – 12 February 1871)

Heidi M. Schultz
University of North Carolina at Chapel Hill

BOOKS: *Poems by Alice and Phoebe Cary* (Philadelphia: Moss & Brother, 1850);

Clovernook; or, Recollections of Our Neighborhood in the West (New York: Redfield, 1852);

Hagar: A Story of To-Day (New York: Redfield, 1852);

Lyra and Other Poems (New York: Redfield, 1852);

Clovernook; or, Recollections of Our Neighborhood in the West, Second Series (New York: Redfield, 1853);

Clovernook Children (Boston: Ticknor & Fields, 1854);

Poems by Alice Cary (Boston: Ticknor & Fields, 1855);

Married, Not Mated; or, How They Lived at Woodside and Throckmorton Hall (New York: Derby & Jackson / Cincinnati: Derby, 1856);

The Adopted Daughter (Philadelphia: Smith, 1859);

The Josephine Gallery (New York: Derby & Jackson, 1859);

Pictures of Country Life (New York: Derby & Jackson, 1859);

Ballads, Lyrics, and Hymns (New York: Hurd & Houghton, 1866);

The Bishop's Son: A Novel (New York: Carleton / London: Low, 1867);

Snow-Berries: A Book for Young Folks (Boston: Ticknor & Fields, 1867);

A Lover's Diary (Boston: Ticknor & Fields, 1868).

Edition & Collections: *Ballads for Little Folk,* by Alice and Phoebe Cary, edited by Mary Clemmer Ames (New York: Hurd & Houghton, 1874);

Early and Late Poems of Alice and Phoebe Cary (Boston & New York: Houghton, Mifflin, 1887);

Clovernook Sketches and Other Stories, edited by Judith Fetterley (New Brunswick, N.J.: Rutgers University Press, 1987).

SELECTED PERIODICAL PUBLICATIONS–
UNCOLLECTED: "Annie Heaton," *Ladies' Repository,* 11 (May 1851): 169–177;

"Prayer for a Poet," *Graham's Illustrated Magazine,* 39 (September 1851): 158;

"Lost," *Ladies' Repository,* 12 (April 1852): 137;

Eng.ᵈ by A H Ritchie.

"Duties and Beauties of Life," *Ladies' Repository,* 12 (July 1852): 262–264;

"A Vision," *Ladies' Repository,* 14 (January 1854): 17–18;

"Our Fast Age," *Graham's Illustrated Magazine,* 49 (August 1856): 148–151.

Alice Cary, as Mary Clemmer Ames records in *A Memorial of Alice and Phoebe Cary* (1872), wrote to a friend during the last decade of her life: "I am ashamed of my work. The great bulk of what I have written is poor stuff. Some of it, maybe, indicates ability to do better–that is about all." Despite Cary's deprecating self-evaluation, nineteenth-century readers and critics valued her work. Her first collection of short stories, *Clovernook; or, Recollections of Our Neighborhood in the West* (1852) was popular for more than thirty years, until at least 1884 when a new edition of the collection was published. Critic Edward Eggleston recognized Alice Cary as "the first native of the Ohio Valley who attempted to interpret the region in fiction" and dubbed her "the founder of the tradition of honest interpretation of the West." Indeed, Cary's "honest interpretation" required her readers to face in print the challenges she experienced growing up in rural Ohio. As Cary remarked in the second series of her *Clovernook* recollections (1853), poverty, a situation with which "none of us voluntarily mate ourselves" but which "gives birth to the sweetest humanities," shaped her literary focus.

Several nineteenth-century commentators on female poets in the United States recognized the importance of Cary's writing. In *The American Female Poets* (1848) Caroline May praised Alice Cary's creative output, which exhibits "a nobility and independence of thought" wherein "we see the genuine poet." Thomas Buchanan Read in *The Female Poets of America* (1852) included an entry on Cary and her sister, Phoebe. Acknowledging the sisters' lack of formal education, Buchanan wrote, "But surely in the wild hills and vales of their native West they have found 'Tongues in trees, books in the running brooks, / Sermons in stones, and good in everything.'"

Referring to Cary in his *The Female Poets of America* (1848) Rufus Griswold asserted that America has "perhaps no other author, so young, in whom the poetical faculty is so largely developed." Through Griswold's promotion of her poetry Cary reached a national audience. The reviewer of Griswold's anthology in the February 1849 issue of the *Southern Literary Messenger* described Cary's "Pictures of Memory" as "decidedly the noblest poem in the collection" and characterized her as "the most imaginative" poet.

Born in Mt. Healthy, Ohio, on 26 April 1820, Cary was the fourth of eleven children (seven daughters and two sons) born to Elizabeth Jessup Cary and Robert Cary. She was raised in a house her father built on a small farm in Hamilton County, Ohio, eight miles north of Cincinnati near the village of Mt. Healthy. As Ames records in *Memorial of Alice and Phoebe Cary,* Cary's younger sister Phoebe reminisced that the one-and-a-half-story frame house was "small, unpainted, without the slightest pretensions to architectural beauty." Around their home were planted some fruit trees "and a luxuriant sweet-brier, the only thing near that seemed designed solely for ornament." Alice Cary based the Clovernook of her fiction on her family's homestead, the nearby village, and the surrounding farms.

In 1832 the Cary family moved into a new house on the property. While the new home represented the family's financial success, the move also foreshadowed personal sorrow. When she was in her late forties Cary recounted a strange event to Ames that occurred prior to the family's move to their new home. Looking from the doorway of the old house to the new, the family saw Cary's older sister Rhoda holding her young sister Lucy. However, when the family called out to the two girls across the yard, Rhoda came downstairs in the old house where she had left Lucy sleeping. Then, Cary said, the entire family saw "the woman with the child in her arms slowly sink, sink, sink into the ground, until she disappeared from sight. . . . Since the apparition in the door, never for one year has our family been free from the shadow of death." Sisters Rhoda and Lucy died within the year after the family settled into their new home.

Cary's mother died in 1835, and two years later her father married his second wife. Although the seventeen-year-old Cary had developed an interest in writing and reading, her stepmother insisted that she spend her time on household chores. Cary scrubbed floors and milked cows during the day, and at night she read, according to W. H. Venable in his biographical sketch in *Beginnings of Literary Culture in the Ohio Valley* (1949), by the light of a "saucer of lard with rag wick." When she had time Cary and Phoebe read such works as *History of the Jews,* Lewis and Clarke's *Journal, Charlotte Temple,* Pope's "Essay on Man," and a Universalist newspaper published in Boston titled *The Trumpet.* When she was almost fifty years old Cary remembered with emotion that fewer than "a dozen books" rested on the "family shelf. . . . There was little time to study, and . . . no chance to learn but in the district school-house, down the road" which she attended but sporadically. Despite their insufficiency, the books Cary was able to read served as her literary models. She had also been inspired by her sister Rhoda, who she remembered as "the most gifted of all our family." Rhoda told stories on their walks home from school together that "had in them the germ of the most wonderful novels."

When she turned eighteen Cary's first published poem, "The Child of Sorrow," appeared in *The Sentinel,* Cincinnati's Universalist paper that was later renamed *The Star in the West.* Cary began regularly placing poems in about a dozen periodicals, including *The Casket,* a literary magazine published in Cincinnati, but it was not until 1847 that she was paid for her work. Writing under the pen name "Patty Lee," she received her first payment, $10, from *The National Era,* the paper that four years later published Harriet Beecher Stowe's *Uncle Tom's Cabin.* Cary's poetry then began to appear in magazines such as the Boston-based *Ladies' Repository* and *Graham's Magazine.* In a 3 July 1848 letter to Griswold she asserted that she often wrote "two or three poems in a day." Cary's success prompted Horace Greeley's visit to Mt. Healthy in 1850. That year Cary and her sister published their first volume, *Poems by Alice and Phoebe Cary,* for which their Philadelphia publisher paid them $100.

During the summer of 1850 Alice and Phoebe Cary visited New York and Boston. They also spent some time in Amesbury, Massachusetts, where they met John Greenleaf Whittier, their favorite poet, who memorialized the visit in a poem titled "The Singer," published after Alice Cary's death. That trip prompted the then thirty-year-old Cary to move permanently to New York City in November. Twenty years later in 1870, the year before her death, Cary reminisced, "Ignorance stood me in the stead of courage. Had I known the great world as I have learned it since, I should not have dared; but I didn't. Thus I came."

Cary evidently had several reasons for her move to the East. Ames suggests that she left Ohio for New York upon reading in the newspaper about the marriage of a man whom she desperately loved. Cary may also have moved in part because she wanted to be closer to Griswold, to whom she had formed a romantic attraction. She of course may also have been thinking of attaining social success in New York, which was then emerging as a literary center. Soon after her move Cary began writing for the New York-published *Ladies' Repository.* From 1858 until her death Cary's works appeared in the *Atlantic Monthly.*

In April 1851 Cary's younger sisters Phoebe and Elmina joined her in New York, where they lived at the American Hotel during their first year in the big city. Reminiscing about the sisters' move to New York in the 11 March 1871 obituary he wrote for the *New York Ledger* not long after Cary died, Greeley indicates that he did not encourage the move because the literary culture of the city—its journals, financial resources for writers, and methods of distribution—was just beginning to develop. Greeley writes that the Cary sisters were undeterred; they "hired two or three modest rooms, in an unfashionable neighborhood, and set to work resolutely to earn a living by the pen." Cary continued her correspondence with Griswold and confessed her attraction to him. She suffered another disappointment when he married another woman late in 1852.

In New York, Cary began to write of memories of Ohio country life and the deaths of her sisters and mother almost two decades earlier. According to Judith Fetterley in her introduction to a 1987 edition of *Clovernook Sketches and Other Stories,* "Alice Cary was a writer with a subject." Cary's memories provided the material for her first story collection, *Clovernook; or, Recollections of Our Neighborhood in the West,* which she dedicated to Griswold "who sent to me while we were strangers the first praise that cheered me in the pursuits of literature."

Cary's sister Phoebe (from Mary Clemmer Ames's A Memorial of Alice and Phoebe Cary, *1874)*

In the stories of *Clovernook,* Cary depicts nineteenth-century Ohio Valley farm life with what she in her preface describes as "the simplest fidelity." She maintains that "there is surely as much in the simple manners, and the little histories every day revealed, to interest us in humanity, as there can be in those old empires." The collection reveals an overriding melancholy, with deathbed scenes included in many of the stories, that led some critics to characterize it as too dark. Even though Cary certainly experienced her share of loss her younger brother Asa told Venable that she was "'melancholy by nature,' not by circumstances."

Despite its melancholy tone *Clovernook* sold well. The publisher, Redfield, promoted the book by reprinting several reviews on the first edition's end sheet in praise of the collection. These reviewers compared Cary to "Poe or Hawthorne," suggested she possessed "perhaps the strongest imagination among women of this country," and described her stories as "almost unequaled." According to Annette Kolodny in *The Land Before Her: Fantasy and Experience of the American Frontiers, 1630–1860* (1984), Cary's focus on a fertile landscape, in which "the unremitting labors of her characters are . . . granted material reward," saves the collection. Cary indeed does show that the fertile land yields an abundance of "Beans, radishes, raspberries, and currants" to the industrious inhabitants.

In *Clovernook; or Recollections of Our Neighborhood in the West, Second Series* Cary defended her prose against the standards found in the fiction of other contemporaneous female writers "who have essayed to amuse or instruct society" based upon their connections to "wealth and splendor." For readers accustomed to opulent descriptions, Kolodny comments, Cary's depictions of "debt-encumbered farms, the daily penalties of pinched circumstances and pinched lives, and the frustrations of a lifetime" could seem somber indeed. Still, Cary's second Clovernook series proved even more successful than the first, even though she replaces her celebration of rural Ohio's progress in the first series with ambivalence.

Although progress created for second and third generations an easier life than that experienced by the first generations in the area, it also brought the problems associated with city life. Cary simply felt she could no longer focus on an agrarian utopia isolated from progress. Kolodny argues that "The outcome is a book that yearns toward an arrested agrarian past, even as it identifies the irrevocable seeds of change sown in that past." According to Fetterley, Cary's Clovernook series as well as *Pictures of Country Life* (1859) warrant inclusion in America's literary history because of their accurate regional descriptions based on her attention to minute details.

In 1855 Ticknor and Fields published the complete collection of Alice Cary's poems to date as *Poems by Alice Cary,* which she again dedicated to Griswold. Although the volume established Cary's reputation as a poet and placed her fully in the public eye, some reviewers criticized it harshly. One review for *Putnam's Monthly* indicated her collection was "a sob in three hundred and ninety-nine parts. Such terrific mortality never raged in a volume of the same size before. It is a parish register of funerals rendered into doleful rhyme."

Six years after they arrived in New York, the Cary sisters bought a house on 20th Street. Herein, the sisters hosted their popular Sunday evening receptions, described by Ames as "the centre of one of the choicest and most cosmopolitan circles" in the city. Alice Cary always organized these receptions, which were well attended by such figures as Greeley, Elizabeth Cady Stanton, Richard Henry Stoddard, Bayard Taylor, John Greenleaf Whittier, William Lloyd Garrison, Sarah Helen Whitman, and Phineas T. Barnum. The receptions provided a forum for intellectual exchange for more than fifteen years.

Cary died at age fifty on 12 February 1871 at her home in New York, probably the victim of cancer and paralysis. She was buried two days later in Brooklyn's Greenwood Cemetery. Eleven years later on 24 June 1881 friends and family dedicated the Carys' childhood home as a memorial to Alice and Phoebe. Their brother Asa brought Alice Cary's career full circle when he traced his sister's inspiration to the meadows, the barn, the well, and the walks of the homestead.

References:

Mary Clemmer Ames, *A Memorial of Alice and Phoebe Cary, with Some of Their Later Poems* (Boston: Houghton, Mifflin, 1874);

Joy Bayless, *Rufus Wilmot Griswold* (Nashville: Vanderbilt University Press, 1943);

Rufus W. Griswold, "Alice and Phoebe Cary," *The Female Poets of America with Additions by R. H. Stoddard* (New York: James Miller, 1877), pp. 372–379;

Annette Kolodny, "Alice Cary and Caroline Soule," *The Land Before Her: Fantasy and Experience of the American Frontiers, 1630–1860* (Chapel Hill: University of North Carolina Press, 1984), pp. 178–199;

Caroline May, *The American Female Poets: with Biographical and Critical Notices* (Philadelphia: Lindsay & Blakiston, 1848);

Frank Luther Mott, *A History of American Magazines, 1741–1850* (Cambridge: Harvard University Press, 1939);

Thomas Buchanan Read, *The Female Poets of America: With Portraits, Biographical Notices, and Specimens of Their Writings* (Philadelphia: Butler, 1852);

Henry Nash Smith, *The Virgin Land: The American West as Symbol and Myth* (New York: Random House, 1961);

W. H. Venable, "Alice Cary," *Beginnings of Literary Culture in the Ohio Valley: Historical and Biographical Sketches* (New York: Peter Smith, 1949), pp. 482–503.

Papers:

Alice Cary's papers are held by the Boston Public Library, Huntington, University of Virginia, and the Historical Society of Pennsylvania.

Robert W. Chambers

(26 May 1865 – 16 December 1933)

Bennett Lovett-Graff

BOOKS: *In the Quarter,* anonymous (Chicago & New York: Neely, 1894; London: Chatto & Windus, 1895);

The Red Republic: A Romance of the Commune (New York & London: Putnam, 1895);

The King in Yellow (Chicago: Neely, 1895; London: Chatto & Windus, 1895);

With the Band (New York: Stone & Kimball, 1896);

A King and a Few Dukes: A Romance (New York & London: Putnam, 1896);

The Maker of Moons (New York: Putnam, 1896);

The Mystery of Choice (New York: Appleton, 1897);

Lorraine: A Romance (New York & London: Harper, 1898);

The Haunts of Men (New York: Stokes, 1898; London: Bowden, 1899);

Ashes of Empire: A Romance (New York: Stokes, 1898; London: Macmillan, 1898);

Outsiders: An Outline (New York: Stokes, 1899; London: Richards, 1900);

The Cambric Mask: A Romance (New York: Stokes, 1899; London: Macmillan, 1900);

The Conspirators: A Romance (New York & London: Harper, 1900); republished as *A Gay Conspiracy* (London & New York: Harper, 1900);

Cardigan: A Novel (New York & London: Harper, 1901);

The Maid-at-Arms (New York & London: Harper, 1902);

Outdoorland: A Story for Children (New York & London: Harper, 1902);

The Maids of Paradise (New York & London: Harper, 1903);

Orchard-Land: A Story for Children (New York & London: Harper, 1903);

River-Land: A Story for Children (New York & London: Harper, 1904);

In Search of the Unknown (New York & London: Harper, 1904);

A Young Man in a Hurry and Other Short Stories (New York & London: Harper, 1904);

Forest-Land (New York: Appleton, 1905);

Iole (New York: Appleton, 1905; London: Constable, 1906);

Robert W. Chambers

The Reckoning (New York: Appleton, 1905; London: Constable, 1905);

The Fighting Chance (New York: Appleton, 1906; London: Constable, 190.');

The Tracer of Lost Persons (New York: Appleton, 1906; London: Murray, 1907);

Mountain-Land (New York: Appleton, 1906);

The Tree of Heaven (New York: Appleton, 1907; London: Constable, 1908);

Garden-Land (New York: Appleton, 1907);

The Younger Set (New York: Appleton, 1907; London: Constable, 1907);

The Firing Line (New York: Appleton, 1908; London: Amalgamated Press, 1911);

Some Ladies in Haste (New York: Appleton, 1908; London: Constable, 1908);

The Danger Mark (New York & London: Appleton, 1909);

Hide and Seek in Forest-Land (New York & Chicago: Appleton, 1909);

Special Messenger (New York: Appleton, 1909; London: Laurie, 1909);

Ailsa Paige: A Novel (New York & London: Appleton, 1910);

The Green Mouse (New York & London: Appleton, 1910);

The Common Law (New York & London: Appleton, 1911);

The Adventures of a Modest Man (New York & London: Appleton, 1911);

Blue-Bird Weather (New York & London: Appleton, 1912);

The Streets of Ascalon: Episodes in the Unfinished Career of Richard Quarren, Esqre. (New York & London: Appleton, 1912);

Japonette (New York & London: Appleton, 1912);

The Business of Life (New York & London: Appleton, 1913);

The Gay Rebellion (New York & London: Appleton, 1913);

The Hidden Children (New York & London: Appleton, 1914);

Between Friends (New York & London: Appleton, 1914);

Anne's Bridge (New York & London: Appleton, 1914);

Quick Action (New York & London: Appleton, 1914);

Athalie (New York & London: Appleton, 1915);

Police!!! (New York & London: Appleton, 1915);

Who Goes There! (New York & London: Appleton, 1915);

The Girl Philippa (New York & London: Appleton, 1916);

The Better Man (New York & London: Appleton, 1916);

Barbarians (New York & London: Appleton, 1917);

The Dark Star (New York: Appleton, 1917);

The Laughing Girl (New York & London: Appleton, 1918);

The Restless Sex (New York & London: Appleton, 1918);

The Crimson Tide: A Novel (New York & London: Appleton, 1919);

In Secret (New York: Doran, 1919; London: Hodder & Stoughton, 1919);

The Moonlit Way: A Novel (New York & London: Appleton, 1919);

The Slayer of Souls (New York: Doran, 1920; London: Hodder & Stoughton, 1920);

The Little Red Foot (New York: Doran, 1921; London: Hodder & Stoughton, 1921);

The Flaming Jewel (New York: Doran, 1922; London: Hodder & Stoughton, 1922);

Eris (New York: Doran, 1922; London: Hodder & Stoughton, 1923);

The Hi-Jackers (New York: Doran, 1923);

The Talkers (New York: Doran, 1923; London: Unwin, 1925);

America; or, The Sacrifice, a Romance of the American Revolution (New York: Grosset & Dunlap, 1924);

The Girl in Golden Rags (London: Cassell, 1925; New York & London: Appleton-Century, 1936);

Marie Halkett: A True Story (London: Unwin, 1925; New York & London: Appleton-Century, 1937);

The Man They Hanged (New York & London: Appleton, 1926);

The Drums of Aulone (New York & London: Appleton, 1927);

The Gold Chase (London: Cassell, 1927; New York & London: Appleton-Century, 1935);

The Rogue's Moon (New York: Appleton, 1928; London: Cassell, 1929);

Beating Wings (London: Cassell, 1928; New York & London: Appleton-Century, 1936);

The Sun Hawk (New York: Appleton, 1928; London: Cassell, 1928);

The Happy Parrot (New York: Appleton, 1929; London: Cassell, 1929);

The Mask and Other Stories (Racine, Wis.: Whitman, 1929);

The Painted Minx (New York & London: Appleton, 1930);

The Rake and the Hussy (New York & London: Appleton, 1930);

Gitana (New York & London: Appleton, 1931);

War Paint and Rouge (New York & London: Appleton, 1931);

Whistling Cat (New York & London: Appleton, 1932);

Whatever Love Is (New York & London: Appleton-Century, 1933);

Secret Service Operator 13 (New York & London: Appleton-Century, 1934); republished as *Spy No. 13* (London: Allan, 1935);

The Young Man's Girl (New York & London: Appleton-Century, 1934);

Love and the Lieutenant (New York & London: Appleton-Century, 1935);

The Girl in Golden Rags (New York & London: Appleton-Century, 1936);

The Fifth Horseman (New York & London: Appleton-Century, 1937);

"Cardigan and Silver Heels," *frontispiece for Chambers's* Cardigan *(1901), one of several romances he set during the American Revolution*

Smoke of Battle (New York & London: Appleton-Century, 1938).

Robert W. Chambers was one of the most prolific and most popular American authors in the first half of the twentieth century. However, Chambers's influence on American letters, unlike that of his best-selling contemporary Jack London, diminished rapidly after the publication of his last work. Instead of altering American literary sensibilities, Chambers was commonly criticized by writers and reviewers for pandering to popular tastes. His significance as a writer, then, derives less from his role as a shaper than as a mirror of American tastes. In his heyday Chambers was the king of the historical romance, but his only works that remain in print are his supernatural tales. As for the rest of his fiction, it is unlikely that the nearly ninety novels and short-story collections, long out of print, will see publication again.

Chambers's reputation as a writer of tales of terror is due in large part to the success of his short-story collection *The King in Yellow* (1895), regarded by his contemporaries and later critics as an important achievement in the development of the Gothic short story. *The King in Yellow* was particularly praised by Howard Philips Lovecraft, after whose death in 1939 scholars of supernatural fiction began to explore Chambers's influence on Lovecraft.

Chambers was a remarkably consistent author throughout his career. In the years from 1894 to 1933,

the year of his death, and even five years beyond to 1938, not a year passed without the publication of at least one book—sometimes as many as four—by Chambers. Although he wrote a variety of works, including society novels, parodies, children's books, and even poetry, he produced not one work of nonfiction prose and left no direct account of his life. The important sources on his biography were written by others: Joyce Kilmer's interview with him in *Literature in the Making by Some of Its Makers* (1917) and Frederic Taber Cooper's sketch in *Some American Story Tellers* (1911).

Born in Brooklyn on 26 May 1865, Robert William Chambers became an active member of the Art Students' League in New York. In 1886 he left for Paris, where he studied with fellow American Charles Dana Gibson at the Ecole des Beaux Arts and the Académie Juliene for seven years. Several of his paintings were accepted to the Salon in 1889. Chambers returned in 1893 to New York, where he became an illustrator for *Life, Truth,* and *Vogue* magazines. A year later he decided to try his hand at writing. Cooper notes that "the tangible realities of his student's life in Paris formed the raw material for a first novel, *In the Quarter* (1894), while the yet undisciplined extravagances of his imagination found outlet in the short stories of uncanny and haunting power that make up the volume titled *The King in Yellow*. It was the cordial recognition accorded this second volume that decided Mr. Chambers' subsequent career." *In the Quarter* follows from Chambers's conviction that a writer's material derives less from mystical inspiration than from hard-won experience. In his interview with Kilmer, Chambers asserted that "If we are to devote ourselves to the production of pictures of humanity according to our own temperaments, we must have this vivid interest in life; we must have intense curiosity." He maintained that writers "must have their basis in real life."

A melodramatic, class-conscious, semi-sentimental tale, *In the Quarter* is focused on the artist Reginald Gethryn, one of several American and British painters studying art in France. Like Chambers, Gethryn studies at the Académie Juliene and has one of his paintings exhibited in the Salon. The colorful setting, though, is secondary to the romantic plot involving Gethryn and Yvonne, a lovely French singer. After he rescues Yvonne from a riot, Gethryn soon learns that, though he has not seen her before, she just happens to live in the flat below his. When he later observes her giving money to the yellowish, villainous Emmanuel Pick, the disgusted Gethryn confronts her, shouting, "And that,–Jew was in your rooms? That Jew!" Unaware that the connection was thrust upon Yvonne by her dissolute sister, Nina, Gethryn is led to question the wisdom of their relationship.

Yvonne's leaving Paris to tend her sick mother throws into doubt whether she and Gethryn will ever see each other again, and meanwhile Gethryn on an excursion in the country nearly falls in love with another woman, Ruth. When the characters return to Paris, though, Gethryn and Yvonne reconfirm their love while Ruth marries a friend of Gethryn whose heart had been broken by the infamous Nina's running off with the despicable Pick. Gethryn is murdered by Pick when he decides to marry Yvonne because Nina wants her to wed Blumenthal, a compatriot of Pick. In the end Nina and Pick are captured by the police, but this offers little solace to Gethryn's friends.

Despite the tragic ending–a rare gesture for Chambers–*In the Quarter* is typical of his romances. The loose plot is made unnecessarily complex because of his reliance on awkward coincidences. There is no reason Gethryn should first meet Yvonne during a riot rather than on the stairwell, and only Chambers's pleasure in coincidence can explain why Yvonne's sister should be the same woman who jilted Gethryn's friend. Chambers also makes full use of stereotypes to accommodate the prejudices of his perceived audience, from the benign suggestions of the blue-bloodedness of his heroes and heroines to the anti-Semitic shorthand employed in the characterization of Pick and Blumenthal. A capable recycler of material, Chambers wrote again of artists and their amours in several of his early short stories as well as in such works as *The Common Law* (1911) and *Between Friends* (1914).

The success of *The King in Yellow* convinced many reviewers that Chambers's true strength lay not in the novel but in the short story. His first attempts at short fiction were effective in large part because he focused on visual imagery and avoided sentiment. Modern critics especially cite the first four tales, all of which are linked to one another by allusions to an invented dramatic work called *The King in Yellow,* the perusal of which literally drives its reader insane. In "The Mask" Chambers creates a powerful supernatural love story in which, reversing the legend of Pygmalion, the female love interest is turned to stone by her lover, a mad scientist. In the three subsequent stories–"The Repairer of Reputations," "The Yellow Sign," and "The Court of the Dragon"–Chambers jettisons stock conventions to write tales of dreamlike horror that strongly suggest Edgar Allan Poe's influence. As the reviewer for *The Bookman* pointed out, "Mr. Chambers succeeds where so many try and fail. . . . He belongs to the school of his compatriot Poe, though his workmanship is of another stamp, and though he is perhaps a trifle more sensational."

The success of *The King in Yellow* led Chambers to write more books in the fantastic vein, including *The Mystery of Choice* (1897) and *The Haunts of Men* (1898), both of which include some of his best supernatural fiction. Because of his interest in other types of fiction, though, he often incorporated the conventions of other genres into his fantastic tales. In the interlocking short stories of *The Maker of Moons* (1896), a collection that shows his early interest in spy thrillers, Chambers mixes romance, anti-Asian chauvinism, black magic, and the secret service. The title and lead tale, "The Maker of Moons," later served as the basis for his novel *The Slayer of Souls* (1920), which added the threat to American society of Bolsheviks, unionists, and all manner of leftists recast as the descendants of devil-worshiping Yezidee Kurds.

Chambers also mixes romance and the supernatural in *The Tree of Heaven* (1907), an interconnected story cycle of supernatural romances, as well as in *In Search of the Unknown* (1904) and *Police!!!* (1915), two romantic parodies featuring the humorous adventures of Archie Goodwin, hunter of preternatural oddities. In the Goodwin stories, which show the influence of Sir Arthur Conan Doyle and H. G. Wells, the hero encounters such creatures as a half-man, half-amphibian ("The Harbor-Master"), the last living dinosaur ("A Matter of Interest"), and a giant worm ("Un Peu d'Amour"). Each tale includes a love interest who Goodwin inevitably fails to win through some comic deus ex machina.

Chambers's strength as a writer of historical romances was rooted in his attention to detail, a strength refined by his habit of returning in novel after novel to favorite historical epochs. *The Red Republic: A Romance of the Commune* (1895), *Lorraine* (1898), *Ashes of Empire*

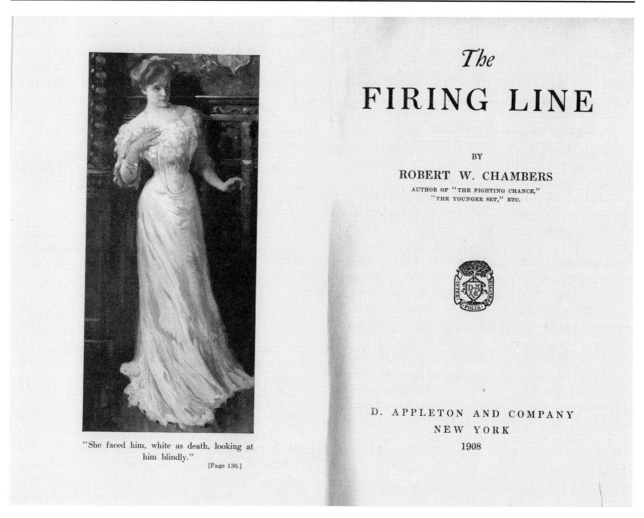

"She faced him, white as death, looking at him blindly."
[Page 136.]

The

FIRING LINE

BY

ROBERT W. CHAMBERS

AUTHOR OF "THE FIGHTING CHANCE,"
"THE YOUNGER SET," ETC.

D. APPLETON AND COMPANY
NEW YORK
1908

Frontispiece and title page for Chambers's 1908 novel treating high society

(1898), and *The Maids of Paradise* (1903) record the heroic and romantic deeds of dashing young American men in France during the Franco-Prussian war. *Cardigan: A Novel* (1901), *The Maid-at-Arms* (1902), *The Reckoning* (1905), *The Hidden Children* (1914), *America; or, The Sacrifice, a Romance of the American Revolution* (1924), and *Love and the Lieutenant* (1935) take as their background the American Revolution, particularly the local troubles in New York State. His Civil War romances deal with espionage: *Special Messenger* (1909), which is notable for its depiction of a female protagonist as a Union spy, *Whistling Cat* (1932), and *Secret Service Operator 13* (1934). Chambers also turned to a more contemporary setting, churning out a series of World War I romance-espionage thrillers that included *Who Goes There!* (1915), *The Girl Philippa* (1916), *Barbarians* (1917), *The Dark Star* (1917), *In Secret* (1919), and *The Moonlit Way* (1919).

Chambers explored other historical settings in single works: the War of 1812 in *The Rake and the Hussy*

(1930), the beginning of the Mexican War of 1846–1848 in *Gitana* (1931), and the French and Indian Wars in *War Paint and Rouge* (1931). *The Sun Hawk* (1928) treats the reign of the seventeenth-century French Canadian governor Comte Louis de Buade de Frontenac; *The Man They Hanged* (1926) is a dramatic memorialization of Captain Kidd. Chambers was so prolific in the genre that a reviewer for *The New York Times* wrote in frustration on 14 December 1919 of *The Crimson Tide:* "One pictures Mr. Chambers awakened by the alarm clock of destiny to the realization that the hour is striking in which he must begin to write a new novel and saying to himself with infinite boredom: 'What in thunder is there left in the world that I haven't written about? Bolshevism? Is Bolshevism among my titles?'"

The Conspirators: A Romance (1900), which records the foiling of a German plan to invade Belgium, is typical of the novels Chambers wrote that are set against a contemporary backdrop. A summary of the plot in the first quarter of the book suggests the author's love of convolution. The hero is Gilbert Hardy, who has been sent as military attaché to the American legation in Belgium. En route he is forced at gunpoint to exchange passports with German prince Stanerl von Elbe, who finds in Hardy—who closely resembles Elbe—his opportunity to enter Belgium under another name. Having no choice but to use Elbe's passport, Hardy is mistaken for the prince by the Belgian authorities, who arrest and jail him. In jail Hardy meets the Countess of Wilverwiltz, disguised as the Duchess of Luxembourg. Mistaking Hardy for the German prince, the countess in her role as the duchess pretends to be in love with him. Assuming that the prince reciprocates the duchess's love, she attempts to extract from him a promise never to return to Belgium. Why Elbe seeks to enter Belgium under false pretenses, why the Belgians are seeking to jail the true prince, and why the Countess of Wilverwiltz, pretending to be the Duchess of Luxembourg, seeks promises from Elbe to stay away are traps laid for the reader by Chambers. The situation suggests how Chambers relies on strained coincidences, masquerades, lovers' misunderstandings, and duplicitous acts to grab and keep the reader's interest.

Another type of novel Chambers wrote was the high-society romance. *The Fighting Chance* (1906), *The Younger Set* (1907), *The Firing Line* (1908), and *The Danger Mark* (1909) were naturalistic experiments in dark romance that featured eugenic theories of conjugal compatibility. In romantic satires such as *Iole* (1905) and *The Gay Rebellion* (1913) Chambers freely ridicules hypocritical suffragettes, overenthusiastic eugenicists, foppish bohemians, and back-to-nature idealists. Chambers's love of fantasy also revealed itself in the romantic fictions *Some Ladies in Haste* (1908) and *The Green Mouse* (1910), both of which depend on premises grounded in science fiction.

Some of Chambers's most interesting romances are those that feature his version of the "New Woman," for his attempts to write traditional romances with atypical heroines led him to challenge stock conventions and raise narrative tensions above the level of cat-and-mouse games. In the short novel *Blue-Bird Weather* (1912), for example, Chambers presents a straightforward romance across class lines. When John Marche, the last surviving member of the Foam Island Duck Club, inherits the Virginia marshes the club owned, he decides to go hunting to see the property. He meets there the ground warden's beautiful, quiet daughter, Molly Herold, who acts as his "bayman," handling the decoys. After hunting together for a few weeks, Marche falls in love with Molly. When he proposes marriage to

her, though, he discovers that her father is a former employee of his who stole securities from him. Meeting face to face, Marche learns from Molly's father that before the latter could make restitution he was compelled by Marche's former business partner to flee New York. After Marche hears the full confession, he offers to reinstate Molly's father and asks him for his daughter's hand in marriage.

Although Chambers uses several standard romantic plot gimmicks in this tale, he marshals them in a far more satisfying manner than in his other romances. Instead of just throwing his lovers together, he provides a rationale for their meeting. The attraction across class lines, a rare gesture for Chambers, is made all the more interesting by Chambers's disturbance of sexual roles. Casting Molly as the competent bayman aiding the novice duckhunter Marche lets Chambers stretch the limits of traditional romance without bursting them. In the woods the captain of industry is shown to be a bumbling boy while the slight girl is depicted as a competent hunter. By playing with traditional gender roles Chambers generates just enough dramatic tension and comic relief to make his lovers' coming together pleasurable.

The heroine created along the lines of Molly, strong enough to take care of herself yet always in need of the assuring masculinity of a male protagonist, would be used by Chambers again in such novels as *Anne's Bridge* (1914) and *The Business of Life* (1913), in which the female lead not only runs her own antique shop but also is an expert appraiser of arms and armor. In such works as "The Tree of Dreams," a story from his 1907 collection *The Tree of Heaven,* and *Japonette* (1912), Chambers's heroines are the impoverished scions of once wealthy families who must work to survive but eventually recover their financial place.

Chambers's novels represent an uneven mixture of romance and adventure. He appears to have made no effort to formalize his ideas about writing, a point that is clear from his interview with Kilmer: "A writer should not be convinced all the while that he is a realist or a romanticist; he should not subject himself deliberately to some special school of writing, and certainly he should not be conscious of his own style. The less a writer thinks of his technique the sooner he arrives at self-expression." This idea of how one should write was bolstered by Chambers's heartfelt belief that writing is "just like ordinary conversation" and that a "writer should be known by his untrammeled and unembarrassed expression." This conviction, although it served Chambers well in the financial short term, did not contribute to his posthumous reputation. Had he brought discipline to his writing, he might have become a far more original and interesting, albeit less prolific, author.

Interview:

Joyce Kilmer, "What Is Genius? Robert W. Chambers," *Literature in the Making by Some of Its Makers* (New York & London: Harper, 1917), pp. 75–85.

Bibliography:

Theodore Hornberger, "American First Editions at Texas University: V. RWC (1865–1933)," *Library Chronicle of the University of Texas,* 2 (Spring 1947): 193–195.

References:

Charles C. Baldwin, "Robert William Chambers," in his *The Men Who Make Our Novels* (New York: Moffat, Yard, 1919), pp. 119–123;

Martha Banta, "Artists, Models, Real Things, and Recognizable Types," *Studies in the Literary Imagination,* 16 (Fall 1983): 7–34;

Everett F. Bleiler, introduction, *The King in Yellow, and Other Horror Stories* (New York: Dover, 1970);

Marion Zimmer Bradley, "The (Bastard) Children of Hastur," *Nyctalops,* 6 (1972): 3–6;

Frederic Taber Cooper, "Robert W. Chambers," in his *Some American Story Tellers* (New York: Holt, 1911), pp. 68–90;

Will Murray, "Lovecraft, Blackwood, and Chambers: A Colloquium of Ghosts," *Studies in Weird Fiction,* 13 (Summer 1993): 2–8;

Grant Overton, "Robert William Chambers and the Whole Truth," in his *Authors of the Day* (New York: Doran, 1924), pp. 366–379;

William J. Scheick, "Chambered Intimations: *The King in Yellow* and *The Descendant,*" *Ellen Glasgow Newsletter,* 34 (Spring 1995): 1, 4, 8–9;

John Curtis Underwood, "Robert William Chambers and Commercialism," in his *Literature and Insurgency: Studies in Racial Evolution* (New York: Kennerley, 1914), pp. 447–480;

Lee Weinstein, "Robert William Chambers and *The King in Yellow,*" *Romantist,* 3 (1979): 51–57;

Blanche Colton Williams, "Robert W. Chambers," in her *Our Short Story Writers* (New York: Moffat, Yard, 1920), pp. 55–72.

Papers:

The major collections of Robert W. Chambers's works are housed at the University of Virginia Library; Colgate University Library; the Houghton Library, Harvard University; and the Beinecke Library, Yale University.

Caroline Chesebro'

(30 March 1825 – 16 February 1873)

S. J. Wolfe
American Antiquarian Society

BOOKS: *Dream-Land by Daylight: A Panorama of Romance* (New York: Redfield, 1851);

Isa: A Pilgrimage (New York: Redfield, 1852);

The Children of Light: A Theme For the Time (New York: Redfield, 1853);

The Little Cross-Bearers (Auburn, N.Y.: Derby & Miller / Buffalo, N.Y.: Derby, Orton & Mulligan, 1854);

The Beautiful Gate and Other Tales (New York & Auburn, N.Y.: Miller, Orton & Mulligan, 1855);

Getting Along: A Book of Illustrations, anonymous, 2 volumes (New York: J. C. Derby / Boston: Phillips, Sampson / Cincinnati: H. W. Derby, 1855); republished as *Susan, the Fisherman's Daughter; or, Getting along: A Book of Illustrations*, 2 volumes (New York: Derby / Boston: Phillips, Sampson / Cincinnati: H. W. Derby, 1855);

Philly and Kit; or, Life and Raiment (New York: Redfield, 1856);

Victoria; or, The World Overcome (New York: Derby & Jackson / Cincinnati: H. W. Derby, 1856);

Blessings in Disguise; or, Pictures of Some of Miss Haydon's Girls (New York: Carlton & Porter, 1863);

Peter Carradine; or, The Martindale Pastoral (New York: Sheldon / Boston: Gould & Lincoln, 1863);

The Sparrow's Fall; or, Under the Willow and Other Stories (New York: Carlton & Porter, 1863);

Amy Carr; or, The Fortune-Teller (New York: Dodd, 1864);

The Fishermen of Gamp's Island; or, Ye Are Not Your Own (New York: Carlton & Porter, 1865);

The Glen Cabin; or, Away to the Hills (New York: American Tract Society, 1865);

The Foe in the Household (Boston: Osgood, 1871).

OTHER: "The Prince at Land's End," in *Gifts of Genius: A Miscellany of Prose and Poetry* (New York: Davenport, 1859), pp. 62–88;

"Victor and Jacqueline," in *Atlantic Tales: A Collection of Stories From the Atlantic Monthly* (Boston: Ticknor & Fields, 1866), pp. 180–247;

"Probationer Leonhard; or, Three Nights in the Happy Valley," *Lippincott's*, 12 (January–March 1873).

Caroline Chesebro'

Caroline Chesebro' was one of the most unappreciated women writers of the nineteenth century. Contemporary critics derided her plots as emotional and slow and found her dialogue conventional. While her stories are full of old-fashioned sentiments and moralizing, she occasionally wrote vivid, realistic descriptive passages that provide flashes of brilliance in some of her works. For the most part grave in tone, her writing focuses on the emotions of characters rather than on their appearance or actions—a tendency that is typical of much of the writing by nineteenth-century women.

Chesebro's primary subject was women. Employing the formula that characterizes most nineteenth-century women's fiction, she created domestic, sentimental plots that lead to moral lessons. Her strong-minded, strong-willed heroines are righteous, long-suffering, and compassionate martyrs who persevere to virtuously remedy the ills of their worlds–caused chiefly by merciless, rigid men. The women's uncomplaining self-sacrifices and unadorned goodness lead eventually to just rewards. The children's tales Chesebro' wrote are full of noble, suffering children who overcome abuse, loss of family, destitution, or other maladies by sincere introspection and the desire to live godly, exemplary lives. As with her adult heroines, the children in her stories are rewarded for their virtues once they have recognized and learned to live by them. When Chesebro' attempted to avoid stereotypes and portray the complexity that would enable her to better tell her stories, her characters show hints of originality and unpredictability.

While the changing political and social roles of women are referenced in her works, Chesebro' focuses more on the spirituality of her heroines. Although the religious didacticism that permeates her writing may at first be mistaken for conventional Protestantism, she neither champions nor attacks any one specific religion. Her primary concern seems to be pointing out the difficulties faced by women trying to live under religious rules made and administered by men. She believes that women are God's chosen emissaries and that God speaks through women in their dreams, making them His agents of moral regeneration. The spiritual knowledge thus obtained is used by her characters to temper justice with mercy and add compassion to the interpretation of doctrine. Her aggrandizement of the characters' morality, however, often wreaks havoc with plot and style as her religious zeal overwhelms her desire to portray real people.

Born 30 March 1825, Caroline Cheseborough was the fifth child of Betsey Kimball Cheseborough and Nicholas Goddard Cheseborough of Canandaigua, New York. She was a direct descendant of William Cheseborough, who left England in 1630 to settle in Salem, Massachusetts, and later became one of the founders of Stonington, Connecticut. Her father, Nicholas, born in Stonington, was a hatter, wool dealer, and postmaster in Canandaigua. He was also a Freemason, master of the lodge at Canandaigua, and was one of the conspirators in the William Morgan kidnapping of 1826, for which involvement he was convicted and served a year in the common jail. Caroline grew up in the town of her birth and attended Canandaigua Seminary.

She was twenty-three when she changed the spelling of her name to "Chesebro'" and produced her first literary works, a series of fanciful tales and sketches that appeared in *Graham's Magazine* and *Holden's Dollar Magazine* in 1848. She won newspaper prizes in Philadelphia and New York for two of her short stories, and soon she was writing for *Knickerbocker Magazine, Putnam's Magazine,* and *Harper's.* In her career she wrote short stories for both adults and children, novellas, novels, and poetry.

Chesebro's first book, *Dream-land by Daylight: A Panorama of Romance* (1851), was a collection of fanciful, introspective, and sometimes somber short stories and sketches, reminiscent of her magazine work. In her foreword Mrs. E. F. Ellet, a writer well known for her own magazine contributions and a member of Edgar Allan Poe's circle, praised Chesebro' as one who "possessed powers of imagination unsurpassed by any female writer of the country." Her inventiveness was also cited by the reviewer for the January 1852 issue of *Harper's New Monthly Magazine,* who asserted that the work had "unmistakable evidences of originality of mind, an almost superfluous depth of reflection for the department of composition to which it is devoted." The reviewer went on to lament Chesebro's lack of mastery in expressing her lively fancy and intensity of thought and remarked her "almost masculine energy . . . destitute of the sweet and graceful fluency which would finely temper her bold and striking composition."

Chesebro's masculine style, which was alluded to in reviews of her later works as well, was apparently one of the prevailing reasons for her lack of popular appeal. Her writing was also criticized for repetitiveness. She wanted to get her points across with no misunderstanding and so hammered things home again and again. Chesbro' was either unaware or did not care that her writing was perceived as clashing with conventions and so failed to fulfill the expectations of her readers. On the other hand, her work was also faulted for being too feminine. A reviewer for the *Literary World* of 18 December 1852 contended that "diffusiveness is the main fault of Miss Chesebro', as of many other lady writers."

Chesebro's first novel, *Isa: a Pilgrimage* (1852), tells the story of an orphan who is rescued from the poorhouse and ultimately rewarded for her goodness. Although such a plot summary makes the book seem similar to many novels of the time by women, the heroine Isa is far from conventional. She manages to grow beyond the usual opportunities for woman's success and eventually winds up in Europe with a radical, freethinking lover, and together they pursue careers in teaching and writing. Isa dies an infidel but otherwise is not punished for her unconventionality.

Isa is clearly a role model for women of genius, but Chesebro' makes clear that Isa's way is not the way for all women. Isa's sex is subordinated in the novel to her freethinking, and she is endowed with outlooks and capabilities that do not mirror other heroines of the period or their real-life prototypes. The subplot, which

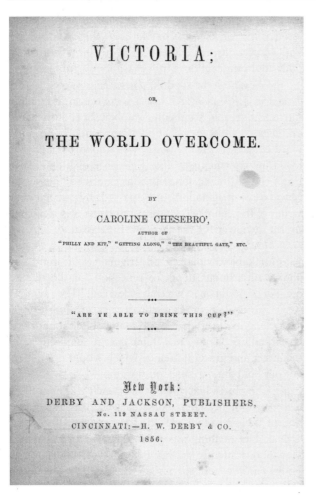

VICTORIA;

OR,

THE WORLD OVERCOME.

BY

CAROLINE CHESEBRO',

AUTHOR OF

"PHILLY AND KIT," "GETTING ALONG," "THE BEAUTIFUL GATE," ETC.

"ARE YE ABLE TO DRINK THIS CUP?"

New York:

DERBY AND JACKSON, PUBLISHERS,
No. 119 NASSAU STREET.
CINCINNATI:—H. W. DERBY & CO.
1856.

Title page for Chesebro's 1856 novel about the plight of women in Puritan society

centers around Mary, a more conventional heroine, validates the prevailing conventions regarding feminine behavior. When Mary tries to follow the example of Isa and lead an unconventional life, she compromises herself, finds solace in religion, and in the end dies rather than submit to a former lover's seduction.

Chesebro' is one of the few authors of the time to imply that social questions concerning a woman's place in society could be raised by new interpretations of traditional male-oriented Calvinistic religious views rather than being the cause of those new interpretations. Her novel presents the reader with the question of whether or not unorthodox social behavior is directly linked to religious infidelity. The reviewer in the May 1852 issue of *Harper's New Monthly Magazine* praised its insight and originality of characterization, complimented its "power of reflection . . . intensity of passion . . . and subtlety of discrimination" but decried the tale as "too somber." John Seely Hart in his 1852 anthology, *The Female Prose Writers of America,* called it a "novel of highly original

character, and one which gave rise to the greatest contrariety of opinions." In later novels Chesebro' largely ignores political and social issues in her focus on a didactic religious message.

Chesebro' asserted in its preface that her second novel, *The Children of Light: A Theme For the Time* (1853), was "wrought in no careless, thoughtless manner." As in *Isa,* Chesebro' again juxtaposes a traditional heroine, Vesta, who dedicates her life to the redemption of a fallen clergyman only to be spurned for a more simple-minded woman, and an unconventional heroine, Asia, who becomes an actress, aspires to an upper-class marriage, and is also rejected for a less individualistic woman. Vesta channels her need to serve others into reclaiming Asia's life, and the two women refuse to let humiliation rule their lives. Chesebro' thus shows that exceptional women cannot hope for conventional destinies. Instead of marriage the two women end their days in a community of women, Maderon House, where their talents are appreciated and nurtured. Chesebro' drives home the point that gifted women, no matter how traditional a lifestyle they embrace, cannot succeed in that life because their superiorities will not be appreciated by men. Instead of becoming "flower-crowned victims offered up to the human lords of creation," gifted women should pursue their talents and vocations with the support of the "sisterhood."

In 1854 Chesebro' published *The Little Cross-Bearers,* a collection of tales. The following year she completed a collection of short stories for children titled *The Beautiful Gate and Other Tales.* Her children's stories, perhaps more than any others, display her didactic side most clearly. The stories are highly moralistic and emphasize that life's rewards come to those who seek to do good with their lives.

Chesebro's third novel, *Getting Along: A Book of Illustrations* (1855), is her most ambitious work—two volumes, well over six hundred pages, with a cast of some twenty major interconnected characters. Both men and women are featured, though the roles of women are more seriously considered. The plots concern choices and commitments to vocations, with each character weighing his or her dreams against the realities of familial obligations and social expectations. Chesebro' treats those who eschew money, luxury, and status more generously than those who dedicate their lives to self-gratification and exploitation. The female characters' gender is most often the determining factor in their choices. Seeming neither to favor nor to deprecate marriage as an institution, Chesebro' shows that in each case a marriage must be judged upon its own merits. Her stories indicate that women should strive for fulfilling lives and certainly not settle for the subjugation of spirit or self beneath the demands of domineering husbands. Her message is that the ideal life satisfies the need of self-expression as well as one's obligations to others without compromising either.

Reviews of the novel were mixed. While the reviewer of the June 1855 issue of the *Knickerbocker Magazine* argued that "the canvas, though full, is not crowded," the critic for the *Tribune* of 30 March 1855 disagreed, indicating that the novel was "diminished by the attempt to introduce too many conspicuous personages crowding the foreground of the picture, and impairing the projections essential to the harmony of the whole." The reviewer for the *Harper's New Monthly Magazine* of May 1855 complained that "the materials employed in the construction of the plots are sufficient for half a dozen novels. Such a profuse outlay on the part of the writer indicates a consciousness of power, of a rich store of resource—but not a talent for organization which is essential to the success of a great imaginative work." The reviewer praised the writing as "sinewy and masculine, often highly picturesque. . . . we much prefer the robust and well compacted phraseology of this work, animated as it is by the workings of an original and active mind, to the safe and polished sweetness of many of our fashionable sentence makers."

Victoria; or, The World Overcome (1856), perhaps Chesebro's best realized work despite its misleading introduction, is a novel of witchcraft that explores the position of women in hierarchical, male-dominated Puritan society. Like many other anti-Puritan novels of the late nineteenth century, the work points out that a culture based on Puritanism destroys women who do not fit into strictly defined, traditional roles. Chesebro' effectively shows how both accusers and accused are victimized by a system created and administered by men. In the same year *Philly and Kit; or, Life and Raiment* was published, a work as disparate from *Victoria* as could possibly be imagined. The book consists of two novellas that were typical social-reform stories, wherein Chesebro' attempted to inculcate in her audience an appreciation of the hardworking poor. The heroines are poor women who embrace the middle-class values of industry, thrift, and decency and find self-fulfillment in doing their jobs to the best of their abilities.

In 1865 Chesebro' began teaching English composition at the Packer Collegiate Institute in Brooklyn, New York. She lived with her brothers and sister at Piermont on the Hudson until her death. Revered by her students, she taught at the school until her death. According to the *Dictionary of American Biography,* one student described her as "of slight build, with blue eyes that could flash, full brows framed by wavy hair, features that indicated sensitiveness and ideality."

During the Civil War, Chesebro' wrote mainly for gift books and literary magazines, including *Harper's*

New Monthly Magazine, Aldine, Lippincott's, and *Knickerbocker Magazine.* She also wrote for literary newspapers such as the *New York Independent,* whose other authors included Harriet Beecher Stowe, Elizabeth Barrett Browning, Horace Greeley, and Ralph Waldo Emerson. Although she does not mention the war or its consequences in any other of her writings of the time, she shows a patriotic fervor for the Northern cause in the *New York Independent.* One of her early poems in the paper, "The Traitor's Wife," dated 2 May 1861, is a severe castigation of Varina Davis, the wife of the president of the Confederacy, Jefferson Davis, to whom she refers as the "lost daughter of a hero." In a later poem she attacks Leonidas Pope, the "Fighting Bishop" of the Confederacy, berating him in a scathing poem titled "Church and State." Her anti-Southern feelings are evident in her many articles, short stories, and verses that were published in the paper during the war.

Seven years passed before Chesebro' wrote another novel. Often considered her best novel, *Peter Carradine; or, The Martindale Pastoral* (1863) is, of all her works, the one that conforms most closely to the accepted patterns of women's fiction of the time. It revolves around a triad of heroines, and the contrast between traditional and untraditional lives that appeared in her early novels is replaced in *Peter Carradine* by the presentation of more conventional choices between lives of service or lives of dissipation. The paths to rewards are clearly shown, instead of developing slowly as the result of struggle and soul-searching. This change to a more recognizable and familiar story line brings Chesebro' firmly into the ranks of her contemporaries.

In 1863 she also wrote two collections of stories for children, *The Sparrow's Fall; or, Under the Willow and Other Stories* and *Blessings in Disguise; or, Pictures of Some of Miss Haydon's Girls.* The heroines of these stories are all ostensibly pupils of a beloved teacher who is retiring. She gives each of her pupils a small token of affection, which contains a Bible passage. Most of the girls put their gifts away until events in their lives sow discontent and unhappiness. The rediscovery of the gifts and the effects of living according to the Bible passages change each pupil's life significantly, as each young woman discovers inner peace through a greater understanding of God and a commitment to doing His will. In the next two years she wrote three more novels: *Amy Carr; or, The Fortune-Teller* (1864), *The Fishermen of Gamp's Island; or, Ye Are Not Your Own* (1865), and *The Glen Cabin; or, Away to the Hills* (1865).

Chesebro's last published novel, *The Foe in the Household* (1871), was originally serialized in the *Atlantic Monthly.* It tells the story of a woman's disastrous secret marriage to a man outside of her Mennonite sect and the consequences of that action upon her children and family. Again Chesebro' depicts the harshness of a religion ruled by men and the hardships of exceptional women who must live within the rigid rules. The reviewer in the September 1871 issue of *Harper's New Monthly Magazine* said it "Ranks with the best of American fictions and is surpassed only by Hawthorne's romances and Mrs. Stowe's greatest work . . . no book of our time has contributed such high qualities of art and morals with greater success." Chesebro' was working on yet another book when she died in 1873.

In his assessment of Chesebro's career in the *New York Tribune,* George Ripley praised her realism:

> As a general rule, she has no sympathy with the darker passions of our nature; no delight in the delineation of scenes of repulsive wickedness; but she selects her materials from the common heart of every-day humanity. . . . Hence the singular reality of all her characters, none of whom is without a distinct purpose, or fails in the exhibition of consistency and unity, which, in her writings, produce a more powerful impression than any desire of artificial dramatic skill. The record of their experience, which is less startling than natural, reads more like personal biography than a creation of art, and we become interested in their fortunes as in the adventures of people whom we have known.

Modern readers are especially drawn to her portrayals of women of strong purpose. Although her heroines are quite unconventional for their time, they find happiness rather than censure.

References:

Nina Baym, *Novels, Readers and Reviewers; Responses to Fiction in Antebellum America* (Ithaca, N.Y.: Cornell University Press, 1984);

Baym, *Woman's Fiction: A Guide to Novels By and About Women in America, 1820–1870* (Urbana: University of Illinois Press, 1993), pp. 208–230;

Herbert Ross Brown, *The Sentimental Novel in America, 1789–1860* (Durham, N.C.: Duke University Press, 1940);

Ann Douglas, *The Feminization of American Culture* (New York: Knopf, 1977);

Evert A. Duyckinck and George L. Duyckinck, *Cyclopaedia of American Literature* (Detroit: Gale, 1965);

Marjorie Jane Hunt, "Short Stories of Caroline Chesebro'," thesis, George Washington University, 1970.

Winston Churchill

(10 November 1871 – 12 March 1947)

Wade Hall
Bellarmine College

BOOKS: *The Celebrity: An Episode* (New York & London: Macmillan, 1898);

Richard Carvel (New York & London: Macmillan, 1899);

The Crisis (New York & London: Macmillan, 1901);

Mr. Keegan's Elopement (New York & London: Macmillan, 1903);

The Crossing (New York & London: Macmillan, 1904);

The Title-Mart: A Comedy in Three Acts (New York & London: Macmillan, 1905);

Coniston (New York & London: Macmillan, 1906);

Mr. Crewe's Career (New York: Macmillan, 1908; London: Macmillan, 1908);

A Modern Chronicle (New York: Macmillan, 1910; London: Macmillan, 1910);

The Inside of the Cup (New York: Macmillan, 1913; London: Macmillan, 1913);

A Far Country (New York: Macmillan, 1915; London: Macmillan, 1915);

The Dwelling-Place of Light (New York: Macmillan, 1917; London: Macmillan, 1917);

The Faith of Frances Craniford (New York, 1917);

A Traveller in Wartime; With an Essay on the American Contribution and the Democratic Idea (New York: Macmillan, 1918);

Dr. Jonathan: A Play in Three Acts (New York: Macmillan, 1919);

The Crisis: A Play in Four Acts (New York & London: S. French, 1927);

The Uncharted Way: The Psychology of the Gospel Doctrine (Philadelphia: Dorrance, 1940).

SELECTED PERIODICAL PUBLICATIONS–
UNCOLLECTED: "Modern Government and Christianity," *Atlantic,* 109 (January 1912): 12–22;

"The Modern Quest for Religion," *Century,* 87 (December 1913): 169–174;

"A Plea for the American Tradition," *Harper's,* 132 (January 1916): 249–256;

"The Knowledge of Good and Evil," *North American Review,* 215 (April 1922): 483–500;

Winston Churchill

"An Uncharted Way," *Yale Review,* 11 (April 1922): 526–545.

During the first two decades of the twentieth century, the American novelist Winston Churchill was better known than his British namesake. In little more than twenty years he had published twelve highly popular books to considerable critical acclaim. He had also played an important role in New Hampshire politics, serving in the state legislature, campaigning for political reform, and twice running as a progressive candidate for governor. In 1919, however, he retired from an activist life, putting aside his pen and going into seclusion.

A 14 March 1947 editorial in *The New York Times* upon his death did not overstate his earlier fame and promise. "At the turn of the present century there were two Winston Churchills who were somewhat in the news. One was a young Englishman, who had had a dashing career as a correspondent and soldier but who still had to be identified as a son of Lord Randolph Churchill. The other was the author of *Richard Carvel,* an American historical novel which beat all selling records. In 1900, even after the British Churchill had been taken prisoner by the Boers and dramatically escaped, there was no question in this country as to which Churchill was *the* Winston Churchill." Indeed, as both men were becoming celebrities and their names were often confused, the Briton wrote the American suggesting that one of them should modify his name. The American agreed but suggested that since the Briton was three years younger he should make the change. The future Sir Winston Churchill agreed and thereafter signed himself Winston S. Churchill.

While the future British prime minister's fame increased, the American writer's reputation waned, and at his death few people knew who he was. No one knows for sure why he abandoned his literary career. He said he was simply tired of writing. Perhaps this man of considerable talent had become a wealthy dilettante, who despite his initial professionalism saw authorship as an obstacle to the life he wanted to live. Except for a final book in 1940, he wrote only as a diversion for his own amusement and that of his friends. His abbreviated career was not, however, without its significance. *The New York Times* credited his big achievement: "He set a pattern in the writing of historical fiction, giving it a solid basis of research." In fact, he did this and more. He thoroughly prepared himself for writing by visiting the places he would cover in his books and by reading biographies, histories, memoirs, letters, and period newspapers and taking notes like a graduate student. Moreover, he was a hardworking, meticulous craftsman who rewrote *Richard Carvel* five times. Most important, he knew how to fashion a good story. More than one contemporary called him "a born storyteller."

Churchill was born on 10 November 1871 in St. Louis, Missouri, into a prominent and wealthy family. The son of Edward Spalding Chuchill, an import merchant, and Emma Bell Blaine Churchill, he was descended on both sides from colonial ancestors. Through his father he was related to John Churchill, who landed at Plymouth in 1641. Through his mother

he was descended from the eminent New England minister and author Jonathan Edwards. He was educated at Smith Academy in St. Louis and at seventeen was appointed to the U.S. Naval Academy in Annapolis, where he was an outstanding scholar and all-round athlete, especially skilled in fencing and such outdoor sports as rowing.

After graduating from Annapolis twelfth in his class in 1894, Churchill briefly took editorial positions with *The Army and Navy Journal* in New York City and *Cosmopolitan Magazine* in Irvington, New York, of which he was managing editor for nine months. On 22 October 1895 he married Mabel Harlakenden of St. Louis and settled on a large estate near Cornish, New Hampshire, on the Connecticut River, where he raised his children—Mabel, John, and Creighton—wrote his books, and lived the rest of his life. He died of a heart attack at age seventy-five on 12 March 1947 at Winter Park, Florida, where he had spent several winters. He left a considerable literary legacy that earns him at least a modest place in American letters.

Churchill began his literary career with *The Celebrity: An Episode* (1898), an amusing social satire. After spending the winter of 1895–1896 preparing a draft of the book, he left the unfinished manuscript with Macmillan in April of 1896 and sailed for Europe. Readers at the publishing house were so impressed with the work they encouraged him to complete it. After several failed efforts at completion and revision, the twenty-six-year-old author had his book accepted and published to immediate acclaim and popularity.

Churchill soon began work on *Richard Carvel* (1899), which was one of the most widely discussed and praised books of the year and eventually sold more than a million copies. Exhaustively researched and documented, the book was hailed by *The New York Times* as "the most extensive piece of semi-historical fiction which has yet come from an American hand." The critic for *The Saturday Review* of London said, "When we say that Mr. Churchill has achieved a success where Thackeray achieved masterpieces, that is a form of praise no writer need resent in these degenerate days."

With this novel Churchill began a series that would investigate historic forces and ideals in American history. *Richard Carvel* is a chronicle from the American colonial period through the Revolution of the Carvel family of Maryland, whose adventures include Atlantic sea battles and European sojourns. The title character and narrator serves during the Revolution under John Paul Jones and is wounded in the battle between the *Bonhomme Richard* and the *Serapis*. There is also a love story of young passion, long separation, and eventual reunion. It is a roomy, epic Victorian novel with a large cast of historical and invented characters, violent

Frontispiece for Churchill's Richard Carvel *(1899), which traces a Maryland family from the colonial period through the Revolution*

encounters, romantic interludes, intriguing entanglements, daring rescues, adventures over land and sea, and comfortable conclusions. The historical personages intermingle convincingly with the fictional characters.

Along with its Victorian virtues of thoroughness and earnestness, the novel also has faults typical of the popular fiction of the day. Like many Victorian authors, Churchill seems obsessed with death and treats its occurrence sentimentally. The soon-to-be-orphaned narrator offers a clichéd depiction of his young mother's death: "She drooped like the flower she was, and one spring day my grandfather led me to receive her blessing and to be folded for the last time in those dear arms. With a smile on her lips she rose to heaven to meet my father." Churchill, of course, knew his audience. As he writes in his afterword, "No one may read the annals of these men, who were at once brave and courtly, and of these women, who were ladies by nature as well as by birth, and not love them." Despite a sometimes stilted dialogue, stiff narrative style, and sticky sentimentality, however, this historical romance is as readable as any by Washington Irving or Sir Walter Scott.

After the publication in 1901 of *The Crisis,* an historical novel of the Civil War, Churchill was recognized as one of America's foremost novelists. The story is centered in St. Louis before and during the war and features several descendants of Richard Carvel. The hero is Stephen Brice, a Union man from Boston who settles in St. Louis to practice law and falls in love with the daughter of Colonel Carvel, a Confederate sympathizer. Virginia Carvel spurns the Yankee, however, and becomes engaged to Clarence Colfax, who is captured

during the war as a Confederate spy. Meanwhile, Brice is wounded in the Union army and later becomes an aide to President Lincoln. Eventually, the North and South are reunited symbolically as Virginia breaks with Colfax and marries Stephen. The war was still fresh in the memories of many Americans, and the novel quickly became a popular and critical success.

Another historical romance, *The Crossing* (1904), is considered by most readers and critics to be Churchill's finest novel. This story of the settling of Kentucky and the role of the frontier in the American Revolution is a patriotic celebration of manifest destiny and the heroism of the American pioneer. Again, Churchill smoothly blends historical figures such as John Sevier, Daniel Boone, and Simon Kenton with purely fictional characters.

The hero and narrator of the novel is David Ritchie, who as a boy is sent by his father from their North Carolina home on the frontier to live with the Temple family in Charleston, South Carolina. He and Nick Temple, a boy of his own age, become fast friends. After receiving news of his father's death in the Revolutionary army, David returns to the frontier, is befriended by a newly married couple, and accompanies them to a settlement in Kentucky. When his foster father becomes a soldier under George Rogers Clark, the eleven-year-old David goes with the army into the Illinois country as a drummer and aide to Clark. After David grows up back home in Kentucky, he attends law school in Virginia and at twenty-one returns to Kentucky to practice. He is joined by his boyhood friend Nick, who reveals that they are cousins and both grandsons of a Scottish earl. The two young men go to New Orleans, where David meets and marries a beautiful French exile and brings her back to the Kentucky frontier. Despite its contrived plot, *The Crossing* is a fast-paced, gripping story told in authentic language.

Churchill showed his interest in politics, fostered by his meeting Theodore Roosevelt, by winning a seat in the New Hampshire legislature, where he served from 1903 to 1905; he then ran unsuccessfully for governor in 1906. His first literary treatment of contemporary politics was *Coniston* (1906), in which Churchill used the approaches and techniques he had developed in his popular romances. The novel concerns political ethics—or lack of them—in a mid-nineteenth-century New England town and state. The central character is Jethro Bass, a warmhearted but unscrupulous and power-hungry politician who uses his base in the town of Coniston to become the political boss of the state. Because of his lack of principles, he is rejected by Cynthia Ware, who marries another man, has a daughter, and dies. When her widower moves to the town with his daughter, Bass befriends them and to please them even ends a lengthy struggle with corporation defender Isaac Worthington, whose son is in love with the girl. The novel ends happily when Worthington agrees to let his son marry her. Bass, who sacrifices his political power in order to ensure the happiness of the daughter of the only woman he ever loved, is one of Churchill's most complex and striking characters.

Reviews for the novel were again laudatory. The reviewer for the 7 September 1906 issue of *The North American Review* praised Churchill's ability to make the New England village setting come alive: "Reading *Coniston* is very like spending a week in a remote New England village, stopping one's newspaper and keeping away from the post-office." The critic for *The Review of Reviews* for August 1906 called the novel not merely "a sermon on civic righteousness" but a great love story. With this novel, said the reviewer in *The Athenaeum* of London (28 July 1906), Churchill placed himself "at the head of contemporary American novelists."

The reviewer for the 9 May 1908 *New York Times* called Churchill's next book, *Mr. Crewe's Career* (1908), a reform novel designed "to purify politics." Despite its title, the novel is the story of Austin Vane, the son of the legal counsel and chief power in the railroad that controls a New England state, presumably New Hampshire. The younger Vane campaigns to free the state from the railroad monopoly but refuses to be nominated for governor for fear of hurting his father and the railroad president, who is the father of his fiancée, Victoria Flint. The reform nomination is then given to the unprincipled Humphrey Crewe, who loses the election to the candidate backed by the railroad interests. The

campaign, however, reveals the reduced power of the railroad. Although some critics held that the novel was more a pamphlet than a work of art, it was generally praised for its vitality and idealism and for its analysis of American politics.

In *A Modern Chronicle* (1910) Churchill turned his attention to another social problem, divorce. The heroine, Honora, is a social-climbing woman of beauty and ambition who grows up in a St. Louis foster home, spends a year in a New York finishing school, and marries a man who seems to offer her the opportunity for social advancement. After he fails her, she divorces him and marries another man, who also disappoints her. Finally, as a more mature and wiser woman chastened by experience, she finds happiness in the arms of a successful St. Louis lawyer who has always loved her. Although the book was not universally acclaimed, most critics praised the Churchill's style and found it an entertaining "modern novel" with natural humor. The reviewer for the 23 April 1910 issue of *The Outlook* concluded that the novel would enhance Churchill's "reputation for careful writing and delicate treatment of a difficult subject."

Perhaps the most popular of Churchill's reform or muckraking novels was *The Inside of the Cup* (1913), in which he calls upon the church to face the social problems of modern life. The message is told through the story of the Reverend John Hodder, an Episcopal clergyman who leaves a secluded New England parish to pastor St. John's, a church in a large midwestern city. St. John's is still a fashionable church controlled by rich men, but its once fashionable location has become a home to poverty and vice. Hodder's experience of the stark realities of urban life awakens in him a stronger faith and a commitment to social service. Many of his readers, however, disliked his sermonizing in fiction and longed for a return to his premuckraking days of *Richard Carvel* and *The Crisis*. As the reviewer for *The Catholic World* (October 1913) lamented, "We took up Mr. Churchill's book to be entertained, but we must confess we were bored instead." The critic for the 9 August 1913 *Outlook,* however, asserted that "this novel has the lift and invigorating air of a mountain."

The title of Churchill's 1915 novel, *A Far Country,* comes from the story of the prodigal son in the New Testament. The protagonist, Hugh Paret, is a highly successful lawyer who has wandered into a far country of lost honor and wasted ideals. Set in the early 1880s during the height of the Robber Baron era, the novel traces Paret's life from boyhood to maturity and his joining a large firm of corporation lawyers in his hometown. The novel preaches the reform of industry and big business and the development of a social conscience. For many readers, however, Paret was a character in an

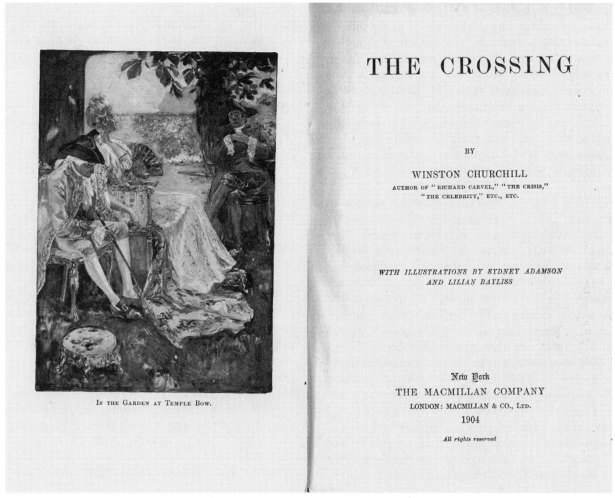

THE CROSSING

BY

WINSTON CHURCHILL

AUTHOR OF "RICHARD CARVEL," "THE CRISIS,"
"THE CELEBRITY," ETC., ETC.

WITH ILLUSTRATIONS BY SYDNEY ADAMSON
AND LILIAN BAYLISS

New York
THE MACMILLAN COMPANY
LONDON: MACMILLAN & CO., LTD.
1904
All rights reserved

IN THE GARDEN AT TEMPLE BOW.

Frontispiece and title page for Churchill's 1904 novel, in which he explores the effect of the settling of Kentucky upon the American Revolution

allegory, not a man of blood and flesh. The reviewer for the 24 June 1915 issue of *The Nation* found "not a gleam of humor to relieve the dronings of that long-winded and rather dull person."

In *The Dwelling-Place of Light* (1917) Churchill attempted to address such problems of industrialization as the insensitive treatment of workers by mill owners and the sometimes violent clashes between labor and capital. The story is set in the Massachusetts mill city of Hampton, where the status quo of exploited workers and profiteering is disrupted when the chapter of the International Workers of the World (I.W.W.) begins to demand reforms and goes on strike. The central figure is Janet Bumpus, confidential secretary to Claude Ditmar, the mill manager. She is personally involved with several men on both sides of the dispute but eventually supports the I.W.W.

The novel is notable for its gritty realism in depicting the sordid conditions among the poor as well as the details of the strike. The reviewer for *Publishers' Weekly* (20 October 1917) complimented Churchill for his knowledge

and insight of the broad ranges of "the feminine temperament" in his portrayal of Janet and unrequited love and her contrasting sister Lise, who displays the morals of a courtesan. While some criticized Churchill for poorly imitating the realism of Theodore Dreiser and dealing with people and conditions he did not understand, the reviewer for the 11 October 1917 issue of *The Nation* was impressed with his command of the new material: "Mr. Churchill has rendered with extraordinary breadth and sympathy the New England manufacturing city, with its enterprise and squalor, its huge industrial plants driving always remorselessly for increased dividends, its polyglot hordes kept within bounds."

Churchill's *A Traveller in Wartime; With an Essay on the American Contribution and the Democratic Idea* (1918) is a nonfiction account of his impressions of war-torn Europe, his assessment of the American involvement, his optimism for a lasting peace, and the need for a League of Nations to referee international disputes. He followed this with *Dr. Jonathan: A Play in Three Acts* (1919), which is based on the premise that the real aim of the just-concluded war was industrial democracy. It is set in a New England mill village, where three generations of Pindars have controlled the mill and its people. The present owner, Asher Pindar, is as autocratic as his predecessors. Representing the new democratic movement are his sons, Dr. Jonathan Pindar, a scientist, and George Pindar, a returning war veteran. The conflict is resolved when the father is won over to the new views of democratic management. Churchill's drama was almost universally dismissed for its cardboard characters and technical weaknesses. It was apparently never produced.

From 1920 until 1940 Churchill withdrew from the literary world, with the exception of a 1927 stage version of *The Crisis.* He lived quietly with his family on his New Hampshire estate, painting, carpentering, and reading. Occasionally he wrote short pieces that he shared with friends. His last published book, *The Uncharted Way: The Psychology of the Gospel Doctrine* (1940), is a profession of faith in which he examines the Old Testament prophets and the parables of Jesus for the roots of religion, science, human conduct, and human hope. He concludes that the Biblical prophets were all pointing to a form of energy that would free the individual from desire, fear, and death. The Gospels, he maintained, describe this force with the Greek word *agape,* a non-possessive, selfless love–a force as real as electricity. While many readers welcomed the book as the final testament of acceptance from a man who had once been a literary force, most critics called it a muddled and muddy piece of work from a man who had lost his literary powers.

Winston Churchill deserves to be remembered for his literary accomplishments. His obituary in *The New York Times* sums up his achievement well: "Perhaps the outdoor pageantry of *The Crossing,* with its epic picture of the movement over the Wilderness Trail into Kentucky, lingers longest. He was American to the heart, deeply feeling and warmly expressing a great tradition. All who now read historical fiction and all who write it owe much to him."

Bibliography:

Eric Steinbaugh, *Winston Churchill: A Reference Guide* (Boston: Hall, 1985).

Biography:

Robert W. Schneider, *Novelist to a Generation: The Life and Thought of Winston Churchill* (Bowling Green, Ohio: Bowling Green University Popular Press, 1976).

References:

Geoffrey Blodgett, "Winston Churchill: The Novelist as Reformer," *New England Quarterly,* 47 (December 1974): 495–517;

Joseph Blotner, "Winston Churchill and David Graham Phillips: Bosses and Lobbies," in his *The Political Novel* (Garden City, N.Y.: Doubleday, 1955), pp. 36–37;

Phyllis Franklin, "Winston Churchill," *American Literary Realism, 1870–1910,* 8 (Summer 1975): 225–256;

Richard and Beatrice Hofstadter, "Winston Churchill: A Study in the Popular Novel," *American Quarterly,* 2 (Spring 1950): 12–28;

Helen V. Parsons, "*The Tory Lover, Oliver Wiswell,* and *Richard Carvel,*" *Colby Library Quarterly,* 9 (December 1970): 220–231;

Robert W. Schneider, "Novelist to a Generation: The American Winston Churchill," *Midwest Quarterly,* 3 (January 1962): 163–179;

Morris Edmund Speare, "Mr Winston Churchill and the Novel of Political Reform," in his *The Political Novel: Its Development in England and America* (New York: Oxford University Press, 1924), pp. 306–321;

Warren I. Titus, *Winston Churchill* (New York: Twayne, 1963);

Titus, "Winston Churchill (1871–1947)," *American Literary Realism,* 1 (Fall 1967): 26–31;

Charles Child Walcutt, "The Romantic Compromise of Winston Churchill," in his *American Literary Naturalism: A Divided Stream* (Minneapolis: University of Minnesota Press, 1956), pp. 157–179.

Papers:

Manuscripts, scrapbooks, and personal papers of Winston Churchill are deposited in the Baker Memorial Library at Dartmouth College, Hanover, New Hampshire.

Frederic S. Cozzens
(Richard Haywarde)
(11 March 1818 – 23 December 1869)

Kent P. Ljungquist
Worcester Polytechnic Institute

BOOKS: *Prismatics,* as Richard Haywarde (New York & London: Appleton, 1853);

The Sparrowgrass Papers; or, Living in the Country (New York: Derby & Jackson / Cincinnati: Derby, 1856);

Acadia; or, A Month with the Blue Noses (New York: Derby & Jackson, 1859);

Colonel Peter A. Porter: A Memorial Delivered Before the Century in December, 1864 (New York: Van Nostrand, 1865);

The Sayings of Dr. Bushwhacker, and Other Learned Men, by Cozzens and others (New York: Simpson, 1867; revised and enlarged, New York: Hurd & Houghton, 1871);

Fitz-Greene Halleck: A Memorial . . . Read Before the New York Historical Society, January 6, 1868 (New York: Trow & Smith, 1868).

OTHER: *Cozzens' Wine Press: A Vinous, Vivacious Monthly,* edited by Cozzens (1854–1861);

"Captain Belgrave," in *The Knickerbocker Gallery,* edited by Richard B. Kimball, Frederick W. Shelton, and others (New York: Hueston, 1855), pp. 163–184;

Samuel Ferguson, Father Tom and the Pope, or A Night in the Vatican, preface by Cozzens (New York: Moorehead, Simpson, & Bond, 1868).

SELECTED PERIODICAL PUBLICATIONS–
UNCOLLECTED: "Sir Clod his Undoinge," anonymous, *Yankee Doodle,* 1 (13 March 1847): 242;

"The Mythological History of the Heavens," anonymous, *Yankee Doodle,* 1 (20 March 1847): 256;

"Lender's Books–No. II," as Richard Haywarde, review of *Mardi,* by Herman Melville, *Graham's Magazine,* 35 (August 1849): 130;

"A True History of the Colony of New Plymouth," as I. B., A Descendant of Anne Bradstreet, *New York Ledger,* 14 (1 January 1859 – 28 January 1860);

"Leaves from the Journal of Frederic S. Cozzens," edited by Arthur D. F. Randolph, *Lippincott's Monthly Magazine,* 45 (May 1890): 739–748;

"The Sound of a Voice; or, The Song of the Debardeur," *Lippincott's Monthly Magazine,* 47 (March 1891): 283–344.

A businessman and editor, Frederic S. Cozzens pursued literature as an avocation. Often adopting the pseudonym Richard Haywarde, he wrote stories, sketches, and poems for many periodicals, most notably *The Knickerbocker Magazine,* in the 1840s and 1850s. His most popular work was *The Sparrowgrass Papers; or,*

Living in the Country (1856), humorous stories of a city couple who take up a country residence in Yonkers, New York. The collection initiated the tradition of the suburban domestic sketch. His imitations of famous authors—notably Charles Lamb, Washington Irving, and Donald Grant Mitchell—displayed cleverness and skill, as did his literary burlesques in the Knickerbocker tradition of the early nineteenth century.

Born in New York City on 11 March 1818, Frederic Swartwout Cozzens professed an early dislike for history, though he eventually immersed himself in ancestral and antiquarian lore. His Quaker grandfather, who distinguished himself in the American Revolution, married a descendant of Richard Hayward, who was known as "Old Father Hayward," the founder of the Moravian Church in Newport, Rhode Island. Though Richard Hayward was not known as a jocular man, Cozzens added an *e* to his surname to create the pseudonym he used in publishing humorous sketches and stories.

Cozzens's father, Frederick Smith Cozzens, a member of several scientific societies, was a physician whose interests extended to chemistry, natural history, and geology. Young Cozzens developed a fascination for these subjects as well, and he became a collector of minerals, shells, coins, and Native American curiosities. Scientific references and allusions spice his literary works, and his fondness for the natural world is particularly evident in his elaborate landscape descriptions. Although little is known of his mother, it is clear that his maternal grandmother, a Cumberland woman from northern England, played a primary role in Cozzens's imaginative life. She introduced him to the songs, legends, and supernatural tales of her native region, and he drew from their interactions an abiding love of poetry and humor. Perhaps because of the influence of his grandmother, indulgent aunts, and grandmothers, mysterious female figures frequently appear in his sketches.

As a teenager Cozzens studied anatomy, chemistry, and mechanics. Hardly a stranger to manual labor, he worked for three years at the forge, anvil, and lathe. He learned as well the practices of engraving and typesetting, practical skills that would prove useful when he entered the realm of periodical literature. He later passed down his interest in engraving to his eldest son. At the age of twenty-one Cozzens entered the grocery and wine business of Clark and Bininger on Vesey Street in New York City. From all accounts he became successful in this enterprise. He is credited with introducing domestic wines, specifically the native Longworth wines of Ohio, into New York State.

In 1845 or 1846 Cozzens married Susan Meyers of Philadelphia, with whom he had three sons and two daughters. Still in his twenties, he began to submit his writings to the New York periodicals, and he was apparently able to balance working as a wine merchant during the day and writing in the evenings and on weekends. In 1847 Cozzens published a humorous imitation of Spenser in the satirical periodical *Yankee Doodle,* most famous for Herman Melville's spoof of General Zachary Taylor, "Authentic Anecdotes of 'Old Zack.'" In the same year Cozzens published a poem in *The Knickerbocker,* commencing a cordial relationship with the periodical that lasted more than eight years. He also became a founding member of the Century Association, a New York literary club that included William Cullen Bryant, Irving, George Bancroft, H. T. Tuckerman, and Gulian Verplanck.

During his association with *The Knickerbocker* Cozzens produced works in a range of genres; however, few readers of the magazine knew his actual identity since the pieces appeared either anonymously or under the name Richard Haywarde. Among his notable submissions to the magazine was the essay "On Wit and Humor," published in December 1850, which set forth some of his principles for humorous writing. He also discussed this topic on the lecture platform. According to Cozzens, humor offers a more "genial" tone than wit, for the former combines the laughable with love, tenderness, and sympathy. The objective of humor is mirth while wit might carry a more caustic tone in pursuing its target. Wit can be antagonistic and rapier-like; humor is higher, finer, more agreeable. Cozzens further notes, "We still make a reservation in favor of a more genial quality; not that we love wit less, but we love humor more: for humor is of nature, and wit is of artifice." Reviewers of Cozzens's own works, when they were collected into volumes later in the 1850s, commented on his mixture of humor and pathos, aligning him with a tradition of "genial humor" that had precedence in the works of Irving. Other writers Cozzens admired included Lamb, Oliver Goldsmith, Henry Fielding, Charles Dickens, and fellow *Knickerbocker* contributor F. W. Shelton.

In 1851 Cozzens moved his family to Yonkers, New York, on the banks of the Hudson River, and began to contemplate the collection of his fugitive pieces. Appearing as by Richard Haywarde, *Prismatics* (1853) was illustrated by John Kensett, F. O. C. Darley, and others. In content the volume is a miscellany reminiscent of Irving, and the plight of the poor is a recurrent theme. In his essays Cozzens demonstrates the value of seeing life through the "prism of humor." A reviewer in the July 1853 issue of *The Knickerbocker* praised its "keen observation of men and manners," the "clear limnings of the beautiful in nature," and the "truthful delineations and contrasts of character."

The varied collection includes burlesques such as "A Chronicle of the Village of Babylon," a history in the vogue of Diedrich Knickerbocker's *History of New York* (1809), and "The First Oyster-Eater," a mocking scientific description in the manner of Lamb. In "Old Books" Cozzens explicitly acknowledges his affection for Lamb and manifests his interest in the typography that characterizes prized antiquarian specimens. "Orange Blossoms" is a fictionalized travelogue with Niagara and Trenton Falls serving as scenic backdrops. An evocation of the Revolutionary spirit, "Bunker Hill: An Old Time Ballad" was undoubtedly inspired by the exploits of Cozzens's grandfather Issachar, who supported the retreating patriot troops during the famous battle. The narrators of the stories in the volume, which are highly melodramatic, attach themselves to women who serve as surrogate mother figures, as for example the grandmother in "The Last Picture" or the title character of "Aunt Miranda."

In 1854 Cozzens began editing his own periodical, *Cozzens' Wine Press: A Vinous, Vivacious Monthly.* He knew the world of publishing from a hands-on perspective and chose his title to play on the business of printing as well as on the enterprise from which he derived most of his income, the sale of domestic wines. While the focus of the monthly was on articles about wine, liquors, and alcohol-related topics and much of its humor derived from playfulness about drinking and sexuality, the *Wine Press* also included poems, stories, essays, and biographical sketches on topics reflecting the editor's wide-ranging interests. Cozzens kept the periodical going for seven years, until 1861.

Yonkers was the setting of the sketches and stories that made up *The Sparrowgrass Papers; or, Living in the Country.* The stories ran under the heading "Living in the Country" in *Putnam's Magazine* from December 1854 to March 1855, but the series had actually begun in *The Knickerbocker* in June 1854. Editor Lewis Gaylord Clark introduced his "'prismatic' friend and correspondent, Richard Haywarde, who loves the country with a mother's affection." What eventually became the first chapter of the volume thus appeared as part of Clark's "Editor's Table," giving the impression of a letter from the country to urban readers. A model for Cozzens was "Letters from Up the River" by Frederick W. Shelton, to whom *The Sparrowgrass Papers* was dedicated. Shelton's epistolary sketches had also appeared in *The Knickerbocker* and were eventually published in *Up the River* (1853) with a chapter dedicated to Richard Haywarde.

Cozzens derives humor from the "annoyances" endured by a "Cit," an urban dweller named Samson Sparrowgrass who moves to Chestnut Cottage on the banks of the Hudson with his wife and five children. Mr. Sparrowgrass, the narrator, endures a series of pas-

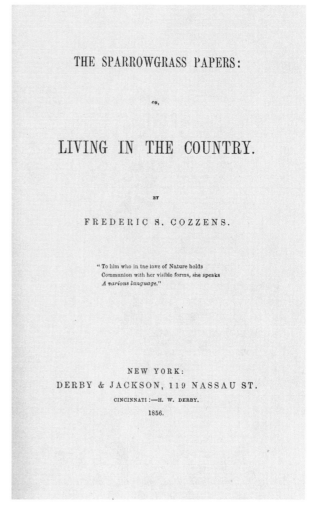

THE SPARROWGRASS PAPERS:

OR,

LIVING IN THE COUNTRY.

BY

FREDERIC S. COZZENS.

" To him who in the love of Nature holds
Communion with her visible forms, she speaks
A *various language.*"

NEW YORK:
DERBY & JACKSON, 119 NASSAU ST.
CINCINNATI :—H. W. DERBY.
1856.

Title page for Cozzens's 1856 collection of humorous sketches about city people in the country

toral predicaments to please his fussy wife, a Philadelphian who devises complicated stratagems to acclimate her family to country living. The domestic comedy and rural setting recall Irving's tale of Rip van Winkle, and Mrs. Sparrowgrass in particular suggests Irving's female characters, who are portrayed as intruders into the realm of male tranquility. Cozzens includes suggestions of rustic talk and pays close attention to rural customs. Although the family encounters many difficulties, the volume celebrates domestic life. Cozzens's appeal to urban values is evident in the Sparrowgrasses' eventual decision to end their sojourn in the country and return to the city.

Apparently hitting upon a formula with appeal to magazine subscribers and the book-reading public, Cozzens begins many chapters with an effusive paean to life in the country, only to have the narrator's expectations deflated. The tone of hopeful expectation is struck in the opening chapter:

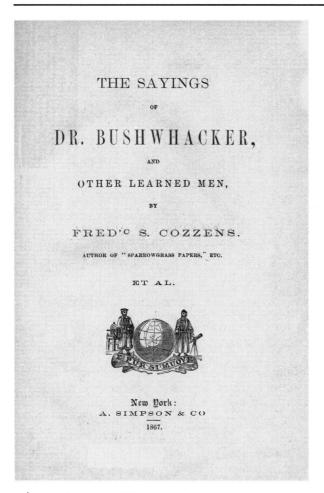

Title page for Cozzens's fifth book, whose title character is a loquacious knickerbocker

It is a good thing to live in the country. To escape from the prison-walls of the metropolis—the great brickery we call "the city"—and to live among blossoms and leaves, in shadow and sunshine, in moonlight and starlight, in rain, mist, dew, hoar-frost, and drouth, out in the open campaign, and under the blue dome that is bounded by the horizon only. It is a good thing to have a well dripping with buckets, a porch with honey-buds, and sweet-bells, a hive embroidered with nimble bees, a sun-dial mossed over, ivy up to the eaves, curtains of dimity, a tumbler of fresh flowers in your bedroom, a rooster on the roof, and a dog under the piazza.

Cozzens's catalogues sometimes take on an exclamatory tone reminiscent of Donald Grant Mitchell's *Reveries of a Bachelor* (1850). While some sketches lapse into slapstick or just rollicking fun, a result of the Sparrowgrasses' recognition that their "preconceived no tions had to be abandoned, and some departures made from the plans laid down" in their city apartment, other sketches are touching or sentimental. Cozzens aims to unite laughter with pathos, fulfilling the objectives of his so-called genial humorist. The comedy and picturesque

"word-painting" of *The Sparrowgrass Papers* struck a chord with readers, and the volume sold more than five thousand copies within a week of its initial publication. As Mary Moss recalls in "An Impression of the Fifties," her 1908 article for *Putnam's Magazine,* the collection helped originate a new American comic theme—"the beginning of the suburban joke!" Cozzens also included "Captain Davis: A Californian Ballad," a verse epic about three miners attacked by bandits, in his volume of suburban sketches.

In the late 1850s Cozzens traveled widely, first touring Nova Scotia and then attending the International Copyright Convention in Brussels as a delegate of the Century Club. His sojourn in Canada resulted in *Acadia; or, A Month with the Blue Noses* (1859), a collection of travel sketches in which he treats the towns of Halifax, Louisburg, and Sydney as well as several villages. Cozzens plays off his readers' knowledge of Nova Scotia by developing a series of counterpoints to Henry Wadsworth Longfellow's *Evangeline, A Tale of Arcadie* (1847). He also invokes the humorous writings of Thomas Chandler Haliburton, the Canadian creator of Sam Slick, whose shrewd observations on human nature had a Yankee pungency.

Primarily descriptive, Cozzens's *Acadia* lacks the penetrating satire and dialect humor characteristic of Haliburton, and only in Cozzens's sharp comments on the "wretched" and "penurious" Scots population of Nova Scotia does he deviate from his usual genial tone. Few contemporary issues are addressed, though the narrator briefly touches on sectional divisions in the United States with a fellow traveler named Picton. By the end of this fast-paced travelogue, with its few digressions about Canadian history, the narrator has overcome his prejudices about Nova Scotia, and claims every confidence in the province's future.

Ever the creature of the periodical world, Cozzens produced a fifty-two chapter burlesque of Pilgrim history for Robert Bonner's *New York Ledger,* which was serialized as *A True History of the Colony of New Plymouth* from 1 January 1859 to 28 January 1860. Published under the pseudonym I. B., "A Descendant from Anne Bradstreet," this burlesque is broader in outline than its title might suggest and includes several chapters on the Dutch colony in New York.

Cozzens did a significant amount of writing for *Hearth and Home,* and many of his pieces were copied into other newspapers. In looking back on his forays into a range of periodical outlets and miscellaneous writings, Cozzens acknowledged that roughly three-quarters of his output was never directly attributed to him. A case in point was "La Creche," an account of a pediatric hospital in Paris. This piece and other articles were collected in *The Sayings of Dr. Bushwhacker, and Other*

Learned Men (1867), which achieved wide sales. Cozzens's title character is a bushy-headed old knickerbocker who serves as his spokesman on miscellaneous topics, notably wines and potables. "Notables and Potables" serves to demonstrate that all men of intelligence are wine drinkers. "A Talk About Tea" is another imitation of Lamb. In "Wives and Weathercocks" Cozzens returns to the domestic and suburban setting of *The Sparrowgrass Papers*.

The interests of Dr. Bushwhacker and his "learned" colleagues range far and wide. In "A Literary Curiosity" Cozzens's character addresses figures in American history, especially George Washington, about whom Cozzens planned to write a full-length biography. Cozzens's interest in science is again evident in "What Is the Cause of Thunder?" "My First Drama," on the other hand, is a fanciful sketch that reflects his long-standing fascination with the theater. Throughout the collection the bibulous and talkative Dr. Bushwhacker fuels his discourse with drink and peppers it with maxims.

By the late 1860s Cozzens was in ill health, though he continued to write about foreign travel, the modern prison system, and sites in New York City for *Hearth and Home* until nearly the time of his death. One of the last pieces he wrote was "The Sound of a Voice; or, The Song of the Debardeur," a story of an American in Paris who has a flirtation with a peasant girl, which was published posthumously in the March 1891 issue of *Lippincott's Monthly Magazine*. By March 1869 he had sold the Yonkers estate and moved to Rahway, New Jersey. Long suffering from asthma, he died of congestive heart failure while visiting a friend in Brooklyn at the end of the year.

Proud of the Knickerbocker tradition from which he sprang, Cozzens developed friendships with the authors he admired and who influenced him. Through Bryant he got to know Irving well, and he relished personal visits with him. He wrote a memorial for the poet Fitz-Greene Halleck, who, like Cozzens, divided his time between business and literary pursuits. The first edition of *The Sayings of Dr. Bushwhacker* was dedicated to fellow Century Club member Verplanck. Indeed much of Cozzens's literary output is a celebration of a Knickerbocker tradition that had been vital in the 1820s and 1830s.

By the 1850s and 1860s the Knickerbocker tradition had become a staple of American culture, and much of the periodical literature of this period was colored, in the words of Fred Lewis Pattee in *The Feminine Fifties* (1940), by a "Washington Irving alpenglow." Although literary historians have found little originality in Cozzens's derivative burlesques, he is a representative popular author of his period. While the jesting, the seriocomic tone of Knickerbocker writing–buoyed by the economic and social forces that shaped New York's emerging literary culture in the early nineteenth century–was not destined to long outlast the conditions that engendered it, mid-century writers such as Cozzens won ready acceptance and praise from magazine editors, publishers, and critics well after the most important Knickerbocker writers had passed from the literary scene.

References:

John Bryant, *Melville and Repose: The Rhetoric of Humor in the American Renaissance* (New York: Oxford University Press, 1993), pp. 28, 265;

Lewis Gaylord Clark, "Editorial Historical Narrative of the Knickerbocker Magazine," *Knickerbocker,* 55 (May 1860): 541–548;

J. C. Derby, *Fifty Years among Authors, Books and Publishers* (New York: Carleton, 1884), pp. 538–544;

"Literary Notices," review of *Prismatics, Knickerbocker,* 42 (July 1853): 73–76;

"Literary Notices," review of *The Sparrowgrass Papers, Knickerbocker,* 47 (June 1856): 621–623;

Mary Moss, "An Impression of the Fifties," *Putnam's Magazine,* 3 (January 1908): 389–401;

Fred Lewis Pattee, *The Feminine Fifties* (New York: Appleton-Century, 1940), pp. 203–205, 260–261;

Richard Alan Schwartz, "Cozzens' Wine Press," *American Humor Magazines and Comic Newspapers,* edited by David E. E. Sloane (New York: Greenwood Press, 1987), pp. 61–62;

Frederick W. Shelton, *Up the River* (New York: Scribner, 1853);

James Grant Wilson, *Bryant, and His Friends: Some Reminiscences of the Knickerbocker Writers* (New York: Fords, Howard, & Hulbert, 1886), pp. 421–424.

Papers:

Many of Frederic S. Cozzens's letters are at the New York Historical Society.

Samuel Post Davis

(4 April 1850 – 17 March 1918)

Lawrence I. Berkove
University of Michigan–Dearborn

BOOKS: *Short Stories* (San Francisco: Golden Era, 1886);
The History of Nevada, 2 volumes (Reno, Nevada, & Los Angeles: Elms, 1913).

OTHER: "Sam Davis," in Comstock Bonanza, edited by Duncan Emrich (New York: Vanguard, 1950): 279–316.

Samuel Post Davis, like other authors of the short-lived Comstock era of Nevada such as Dan De Quille, Joseph Thompson Goodman, and Rollin Mallory Daggett, has been seriously neglected and undervalued. An influential figure in Nevada politics and one of the state's most respected journalists, Davis left a legacy of probity, courage, and effectiveness. He was best known in his own time for his journalism and humor, but his fiction, poetry, and drama as well as his writing as a historian and memoirist are likely to provide the enduring foundation for his evolving reputation.

Assessing Davis's career is complicated by the lack of a full bibliography of all of his writing. He wrote far more than the two books he published during his life, but because he wrote mainly for periodicals, it is difficult to determine how much he published or when and where his works first appeared. Although an examination of the Sylvia Crowell Stoddard collection of Davis's papers suggests that he apparently attempted to keep copies of his publications, he did so in a haphazard and inconsistent fashion. He often clipped articles without identifying information and pasted them into notebooks. Other writings he stored in boxes along with manuscripts of both published and unpublished works.

Identifying and cataloguing Davis's literary works is an ongoing project made more difficult by his idiosyncrasies. His handwriting is nearly indecipherable and his spelling notoriously bad. Ambrose Bierce relates an anecdote of Davis not being able to read his own writing in a letter he had sent to Bierce. Letters exist in which Davis misspelled someone's name three different ways, and even handwritten corrections in his

Samuel Post Davis (courtesy of Lawrence I. Berkove and Sylvia Crowell Stoddard)

manuscripts are sometimes misspelled. Additionally, Davis often recycled his material, either retelling the same stories after a lapse of years or telling them in different forms. This practice complicates dating, muddles categorization, and also makes difficult the job of separating fact from fiction, especially when different details of the same story appear in versions purporting to be memoirs, humor, and fiction. Despite these difficulties, there can be no doubt that Davis was richly endowed with the literary gifts of phrasing and verbal precision as well as narrative, and excelled in all fields of writing. Although a large portion of his writings remain uncertain as to provenance, it is possible to at least glimpse the range of his literary activity.

Born in Branford, Connecticut, on 4 April 1850 Davis was one of four children of Sylvia Nichols Davis and the Reverend George R. Davis, an Episcopal priest. Following the Reverend Davis's career as he accepted new pulpits, the family moved to Ansonia, Connecticut, and as the years passed, westward to Newark, New Jersey; Brownsville, Nebraska; and Vallejo and Nevada City, California. When he was fifteen and his family was living in Nebraska, Davis was sent to attend Racine College, a theological school in Wisconsin. He studied Latin and Greek with little success but excelled in cricket, a sport the college promoted, and developed a taste for journalism by editing the college newspaper. Deemed unsuitable for the clergy because of his lack of distinction as a scholar and his fondness for pranks, Davis was expelled before he could graduate. He then decided to seek his livelihood as a journalist.

Davis's first newspaper job was in Nebraska with the *Brownsville Democrat* at $3 a week. He also worked for the *Brownsville Advertiser* and the *Nebraska City News* before advancing to the *Omaha Herald*, where he wrote a series of harsh exposés of legislators. He succeeded in arousing the electorate, but offended legislators threatened his life and hired thugs to kill him at his boardinghouse. After Davis escaped out a window and made it to another town, he hired a friendly journalist to continue the exposés under his name. He thus baffled his enemies and made a name for himself locally. Davis next joined the *Lincoln Statesman*, where he boldly continued to attack incompetence and venality. At the *St. Louis Republican* he attempted to liven up his column by passing fiction off as fact and was fired in the first week. Davis also worked at the *Chicago Times* and the *Chicago News*. He may have first met Mark Twain, a fast friend in later years, when the lecturing author stopped in Chicago.

In 1872 Davis followed his family to California. He worked on the *Vallejo Independent* and subsequently on the *Colusa Independent*, the *Marysville Appeal*, and a variety of San Francisco papers—the *Chronicle, Evening Post, Morning Ledger*, and *Stock Report*. With two friends he launched the *The Open Letter*, a short-lived weekly that combined news and literary efforts. He also began his lifelong practice of writing poetry and contributed verse to a San Francisco newspaper, the *News-Letter*. While in San Francisco Davis became a friend of Ambrose Bierce and of Joseph Goodman, Mark Twain's friend, adviser, and former employer.

Davis's fondness for practical jokes earned him some notoriety in 1874 when he covered a San Fran-cisco horse race for a *Vallejo Chronicle* reporter. As reported in the *Argonaut* (22 March 1879), Davis concocted a story in which the heats were intermingled with two earthquake shocks, the first of which destroyed the grandstand at the cost of hundreds of lives—but did not stop the race and its exciting result—and the second of which "swallowed up several thousand people." The *Vallejo Chronicle* editor did not doubt Davis's dispatches because they came under his colleague's name. Extra issues of the newspaper were published, and Vallejo residents chartered a boat to San Francisco to view the tragedy. The hoax was fully revealed the next day when Davis sent the editor a $12.50 bill for the story: $10 "For earthquake item—two shocks at $5 per shock," and $2.50 for "a small boy to cut the wires" so that no San Francisco papers could telegraph their own dispatches. He then offered to fill orders for future "exclusive items" on the shortest notice.

To prove he could write as well as Bret Harte, Davis on another occasion published a poem in *The Open Letter* about a heroic railroad engineer, "Binley and '46,'" under Harte's name. The poem was widely republished across the country as Harte's work. *Frank Leslie's Illustrated Magazine* gave it a full page with an accompanying illustration on 2 May 1874. Davis eventually admitted that the poem was a hoax in a note in *Short Stories* (1886) and described it as a "successful literary forgery."

In 1875 Davis took a position at the *Evening Chronicle* in Virginia City, Nevada, a boom town that had sprung to life with the discovery of the Comstock Lode, a four-mile-long enormously rich deposit of silver and gold in the western part of the state. The move was fateful for Davis as the Comstock and its population of daring, hoax-loving, unconventional free spirits appealed to his nature. Davis devoted the rest of his life and all of his talents to studying Nevada, writing its history, and serving and defending the state from incompetent or dishonest officials and detractors. The process of becoming a Nevada author began immediately, for in addition to his newspaper work he sent poetry and humorous sketches to such mainstream West Coast periodicals as the *Argonaut* and the *Alta California*.

Almost as much as poetry, theater was a passion for Davis. He attended plays, reviewed and acted in them, and interviewed and befriended actors and actresses, and his memoirs contain many delightful anecdotes about his connection with the theater. Those memoirs are, in fact, important sources of information about Comstock theater. Of his early plays there is only scanty knowledge. An undated clipping from the *Virginia City Chronicle* reports that one of his plays, about to be produced locally, involves two reporters and a corpse. In the play a *Chronicle* reporter finds a corpse and in order to keep an *Enterprise* reporter from learning about it, brings it to his room. Troubles multiply, and the *Chronicle* reporter is charged with murder and is "put to direst extremities to evade arrest, etc." Another unidentified clipping mentions another play, *The Bohemian's Blunder,* which lampooned recognizable Comstock personalities. Yet another play, *The Sculptor's Daughter,* is dated 1879, but no other details about it are known. The unfinished and undated text of *The Triple Plated Honeymoon; A Chinese Comedy* that has been saved in the Stoddard Collection is undistinguished and appears to be no better and no less stereotypical than were the host of dramatic works about exotic subjects that played briefly each season on West Coast stages and then disappeared forever.

In 1879 Davis moved to nearby Carson City to work on the *Morning Appeal,* managed by Nellie Verrill Mighels, widow of its recently deceased editor. Davis married her in 1880, accepted her four children as his own, and subsequently had two daughters with her. Davis enhanced the standing of the *Appeal,* already an influential newspaper, with his fearless reporting and wit. One of his humorous sallies that became a Comstock legend was the *Wabuska Mangler.* It began as a private joke between Davis and E. P. Lovejoy, a relative of the famous journalist Elijah Lovejoy who lived in nearby Wabuska. Davis pretended that the *Mangler* existed and that Lovejoy was its editor. He ascribed ridiculous stories to it and criticized Lovejoy and his editorial policies. Other Nevada newspapers joined in the fun and took sides in the disputes.

Davis's *Appeal* promoted Nevada interests and good government. A supporter of free silver, the movement advocating the unlimited coinage of silver, the paper was the first in the state to call for a silver party, which was soon organized. The *Appeal* favored economic diversification and promoted agriculture, leading the campaign to encourage tree planting that resulted in the state's adoption of Arbor Day. It attacked the railroads for their unfair rates and criticized the incompetence and crookedness of elected officials. In a state where most newspapers depended upon the patronage of the railroads, mining companies, and political entities, the *Appeal* was financially independent. In 1892 Davis went to jail rather than reveal a source, and in 1895 he again defiantly used a secret source to comment on a Carson City Mint investigation. By way of putting Nevada in the national limelight, Davis was influential in bringing the lucrative Corbett-Fitzsimmons prize fight to Carson City in 1897, which his wife covered for a Chicago newspaper. He also helped create and supported the exhibits for Nevada and the '49 Mining Camp at the California Midwinter Fair of 1894

and the Nevada exhibit for the Panama-Pacific International Exposition of 1915, both held in San Francisco.

Davis became increasingly involved in political affairs. He was appointed deputy secretary of state in 1895 and was elected in 1898 on the Silver Party ticket and reelected in 1902 on the Silver-Democratic slate to the position of state controller, and he also served as ex-officio state insurance commissioner. Davis revoked the license of a New York insurance company in 1905 for misusing funds for political purposes and for attempting to bribe him. The president of the company was forced to resign, and the misused funds were restored. In 1906, when a powerful earthquake devastated much of San Francisco and insurance companies attempted to default on their fiscal responsibilities, Davis on his own announced that only companies that paid one hunderd cents on the dollar on California claims would be allowed to do business in Nevada. When other states showed signs of following Nevada, the insurance companies yielded. His last political appointment, from 1907 to 1911, was as chairman of the Publicity and Industrial Commission of Nevada. He worked especially to protect mining investors from chicanery, running regular newspaper ads warning against purchasing shares on the deceptive installment plan.

While state controller, Davis conceived of the idea of erecting a statue to John Mackay, the most famous and beloved of the Comstock silver magnates. Largely at his own expense, he went to New York to persuade Clarence Mackay to authorize the sculptor Gutzon Borglum to create a statue of his father. This led Clarence Mackay to further endow the University of Nevada School of Mines Building in Reno, before which the statue stands. Also typical of Davis's public spiritedness was his decision, when nominated to run for governor in 1906, to instead persuade the incumbent, Gov. John Sparks, to run again with his support.

Although Davis put down deep roots in Nevada, he was by no means a mere regionalist. He was a sophisticated man whose education did not stop when he left Racine College. His reading of both current and classical literature is exemplified by a Davis commentary in the *Appeal* (3 March 1889) on changing literary tastes in which he alludes to *Tristram Shandy* (1759–1767), *Tom Jones* (1749), and Giovanni Boccaccio as well as several contemporary novelists. Davis visited the East often enough to be familiar with the region and traveled to Europe more than once, sending back humorous travel letters that were published in the *San Francisco Examiner* and other western papers.

Davis enjoyed friendly relationships with many outstanding figures in a variety of fields. In addition to his friendships with writers and political leaders in

Nevada and California and with such men as Bierce, Twain, and Mackay, he also was respected by such internationally known actors as Edwin Booth, Madame Modjeska, and Sarah Bernhardt. It is related that Bernhardt so enjoyed an interview with him in 1907 that she kissed him afterwards, saying "The right cheek for the *Appeal,* the left for the *Examiner,* and the lips for yourself." Davis wittily replied without a moment's hesitation: "I also represent the Associated Press, which serves 380 papers west of the Mississippi alone!" Davis's correspondence also includes personal letters from the writer Irvin Cobb, P. T. Barnum, and Theodore Roosevelt. In short, Davis was among Nevada's most well-connected and influential citizens.

Davis's achievements as a newspaperman and a public figure overshadowed his solid and serious literary work during his lifetime. Like most authors, Davis wrote for a variety of reasons—to express himself, to make money, to gain fame. His once describing himself as having written for "Eastern publications" suggests that he took some pride in being known beyond the West. Family tradition has it that Ambrose Bierce persuaded Davis to select some of his pieces to be published in a collection. The resulting book, misleadingly titled *Short Stories* (1886), contains nineteen stories, six humorous essays, and nine poems, including "Binley and '46.'" Containing some of his best stories, *Short Stories* received many strongly favorable reviews in which Davis was compared to Twain, Harte, and De Quille.

The most justly famous story in the collection is "A Christmas Carol," later republished under the better-known title "The First Piano in Camp." Like other Comstock authors, Davis was fascinated by hoaxes and attracted to both sentiment and irony. In this well-wrought story about a disguised gambler who robs a mining camp on Christmas Eve after his piano playing makes the miners feel sentimental, Davis shrewdly assesses the delicate balance between faith and gullibility.

Another oft-reprinted story, "The Typographical Howitzer," recounts how Twain and De Quille, with a wagon full of columns of set type for a newspaper, are surrounded by hostile Indians in the mountains. They have an antique army cannon with them and some powder but no shells. In a flash of inspiration they decide to charge the cannon with type. The devastation that is caused is directly related to the particular authors and writings represented in each salvo. Inasmuch as Davis uses the names of contemporary authors, including Twain, the story is a rollicking but good-natured send-up of the writers mentioned.

As originally published in the *San Franciscan* (16 February 1884), "The Reporter's Revenge" ironically portrays a professional but shallow Christian who

Davis and his wife, Nellie, at Niagara Falls

undergoes rapid transformations from despair to hypocrisy and then to self-delusion. Apart from its intrinsic interest, the story, which Bierce almost certainly read, makes some observations about the mind's "blaze" occurring in the interval between the beginning and end of a hanged man's fall to his death that qualify it as a possible precursor of Bierce's classic 1890 tale, "An Occurrence at Owl Creek Bridge." The later book version of the story appends some imaginary letters that turn the story's composition into a joke and thus dilute its original impact.

Other fine pieces are also included. "A Day with Bill Nye" is an admiring spoof of the Wyoming humorist and judge who lies to get at the truth and acts illegally in order to effect justice. "A Carson Poker Incident," originally published in the *Argonaut* (23 March 1878) under the title of "Hold the Fort," is the account of an epic contest between Virginia City and Carson City poker players who risk large sums of their own money for the honor of their respective towns. "The Pocket-Miner" is really two stories in one: a sentimental narrative of a good-hearted prospector whose wealth benefits others but not him and a macabre parody of the Comstock malady of speculation. Davis shows that mining profits benefit stockbrokers far more than they do miners. In "A Sage-brush Chief" Davis records how De Quille, the master hoaxer of the Comstock, used the Piute Indian chief Captain Bob to out-hoax some fellow journalists.

It is very likely that none of these stories are entirely fictitious. Davis early demonstrated a disposition to work with complex subject matter on the borderline between opposite values and to evoke feelings of ambivalence in his readers. Davis typically retains the main features of some dramatic real-life incident from Nevada or California while heightening its fictional possibilities with a few imaginative touches of his own. Davis's genuine love of Comstock character sometimes leads him to discover the best qualities of the unsaintly personalities he depicts in his stories.

Humor was a large part of Davis's personality. He had a naturally prankish disposition that, early and late, led him to play good-natured practical jokes on his friends and associates and to engage in ongoing rivalry with his western colleagues in person and in print that continuously honed the edge of his wit. It manifested itself also in his quick and unlabored expression of humor in oral or written form. He was in great demand as an entertaining speaker; his yarns and witticisms were frequently reprinted in Western periodicals; and his escapades were a favorite topic of editorial note. Much of his written work, both published and unpublished, has a humorous cast.

For many years Davis was a popular contributor to the *San Francisco Examiner,* especially in 1888–1889. This was probably because the newspaper, acquired in 1887 by William Randolph Hearst as his first venture into publishing, sought out the best authors to establish its reputation and paid well for their contributions to its Sunday supplement. It is possible that Bierce, then a staff member of the paper, recommended Davis to the Sunday editor. In his own Sunday columns Bierce occasionally mentioned Davis in a bantering way.

Many of Davis's Sunday items are dryly humorous—written versions of poker-faced oral delivery. Writing in the guise of letters to the editor, Davis pretends to be factual and is seemingly unaware that his remarks are funny. Amusing illustrations often accompany these items, but intermixed with them are the same sort of stories Davis published elsewhere, fictionalized versions of real-life incidents. The pieces vary widely in quality from potboilers to choice work.

Davis did not publish any more books of fiction after *Short Stories,* but he continued for the rest of his life to probe the complexities of human nature in fiction. "My Friend, the Editor," published in the *San Francisco Examiner* (21 July 1889), is loosely based on James

"Lying Jim" Townsend, one of the Comstock's most accomplished liars. Townsend once revived an abandoned press in a deserted mining town and for months single-handedly published a newspaper that represented the lonely place as a lively town whose mines were active and profitable. He then sent copies of the newspaper to associates in England who used them to hoax potential investors. Davis takes many liberties with the facts in presenting his readers with the paradox of a protagonist who, compartmentalizing his life, is both good and bad.

"When Booth Was Not Booth," published in the *San Francisco Examiner* (20 October 1895), is again apparently based on an actual incident, as Davis's memoirs indicate. Davis relates how an admirer of Edwin Booth's Shakespearean roles was given an opportunity to achieve a dream of taking the actor's place. Mutual friends detained Booth while the amateur took up the role of Hamlet at a production of the play in San Francisco. For four acts the amateur turned in a stunning performance. Just before the last act Booth showed up and took over, but he built his interpretation on the amateur's lead and played the role as he had never done before. The psychologically insightful story thus suggests the creative possibilities of reversing a model/pupil relationship.

"The Loco Weed," dated 1899, is a powerful, almost brutal story in the realistic tradition in which Davis hauntingly describes the effect that the hallucinogenic loco weed has on horses and men. The story reveals that men, rather than being a higher class of beings, are ultimately only animals. Davis shows, too, that nature is no more benevolent toward men than horses.

"The Mystery of the Savage Sump," perhaps originally published in 1901, may be Davis's most powerful, subtle, and skillful work of social criticism. Based on De Quille's famous 1876 hoax "Eyeless Fish That Live in Hot Water," Davis in his story also imagines a hole in the bottom of Lake Tahoe that drains water into the Comstock mines. Davis's story quickly goes its own way, however, by depicting an unscrupulous character whose discovery of the hole allows him to manipulate the stock market by controlling whether or not water floods the mines. This character bears some striking resemblances to the Silver King and former U.S. senator James Fair, whom Davis in the *Appeal* openly charged with murder. Knowledge of the background of the story may add to the reader's appreciation of this chilling exposé of the power that greed can have over a ruthless individual.

The stories that can be dated following the publication of *Short Stories* suggest that Davis as a fiction writer progressed in ability, strength, and complexity; however, the question of his growth as an artist cannot be fully gauged because several stories in manuscript in the Stoddard collection have no indication of their date of composition and may or may not have been published. Few of these stories are finished products worthy of publication, but they do have value in that they cast light upon Davis's processes of conception, composition, and revision. Some of them are formulaic potboilers. "The House of Mystery," for example, is a melo- dramatic romance in which the loyalty of true love is rewarded. Only slightly better is "The Battle of the Jewels," another melodrama of a young woman from a nouveau riche Nevada family who has to learn how to overcome her wealth. Davis joins De Quille as the only Comstock writers who go so far as to entertain the notion that the pursuit of wealth for its own sake may be an evil.

Davis's ambivalence about his religious upbringing and education is reflected in at least two stories. "The Western Way" is a marginally credible tale of deep hypocrisy being overcome by even deeper goodness. In it, a con man swindles money from a church congregation but returns the loot after he has a change of heart. A much more substantial story is "The Conversion of Champagne Liz." Three versions of it show Davis wrestling with the theological issues of individual salvation by faith or by deeds. He depicts Champagne Liz, a woman of ill repute and a scoffer, whose death on a mission of mercy has unintended consequences that complicate the issue of moral judgment.

Religious and moral considerations also play a part in one of the longest and the most intriguing of Davis's incomplete manuscripts, "The Divorcon." The story defines a *divorcon* as one whose divorce is pending, as opposed to a divorcée, a woman whose divorce has been legally accomplished. The forty-nine-page typed manuscript is a sensitive and thoughtful probing of the emotional and moral complications that can result when a bachelor lawyer comes to know his attractive client intimately. Davis makes his reader consider the validity of laws, legal or religious, that bind two people together who have ceased to love and keep apart those who are in love with each other. Despite some stilted language and clichés, the draft shows considerable promise in the ways Davis avoids loading the story to an obvious conclusion, shifts back and forth between the perspectives of believable protagonists, and subtly undermines with a phrase an otherwise persuasive argument.

Living in Nevada, where divorce laws were the most liberal in the United States, naturally forced Davis to come to grips with both the phenomenon and industry of divorce. Earlier editorial comments in the *Appeal* indicate that although Davis had many reservations about the divorce industry, he considered divorce a national problem rather than a local one. He defended Nevada from the charge that it was guilty of any special iniquity for washing the dirty laundry that other states were relieved to be able to send it. However, the draft of "The Divorcon," which is set just before the outbreak of World War I and includes a final scene on the ill-fated *Lusitania,* reaches far beyond these obvious topical concerns to complex ironies and suggests a strong but not quite coalesced moral vision.

Another interesting find among the manuscripts in the Stoddard Collection is the complete text of a charming comic opera titled *The Prince of Timbuctoo,* dated 1905. Davis's talents for humor, poetry, drama, and social commentary happily blend together to form an impressive artistic achievement in this three-act opera that has a delightfully improbable plot of lovers triumphing over evil political machinations. The cast consists of the king of Timbuctoo, his unjustly banished son, the son's Zulu sweetheart, a mercenary adventuress from San Francisco, a New York agent for Carnegie Steel and his Irish valet from Chicago, a native shyster lawyer, "Priscilla Primrose, of Boston, and her six Puritan maidens," attendants, dancing girls, and members of the royal household. The libretto makes topical allusions to the British losing battles to the Boers in South Africa, Roosevelt's "big stick" policy, the growth of trusts, American economic imperialism, the practice of ballot-box stuffing, and the notorious court case over the will of Charles Fair, the son of silver magnate James Fair. These allusions date the opera's composition no earlier than 1902. Without the music, which appears to have been lost, there is no way of telling how well everything worked together, but judging only from the sprightly and sparkling vernacular of the libretto it appears that *The Prince of Timbuctoo* might have been a noteworthy American contribution to the tradition of Gilbert and Sullivan.

Although much of Davis's poetry probably has not been located, none of his extant pieces suggest that he was more than a minor poet. Some of his light verse is imitative of popular ballads. In "Bill Magee of Pine Nut; An Epic of a Nevada Mining Camp," for example, he uses the same meter and stanza form that Robert Service popularized with "The Cremation of Sam Magee" (1907). Davis even ends his first stanza with "The day the boys laid out the corpse of poor old Bill Magee." After the first several stanzas, however, Davis becomes fully original and ironic with the story line of how the discovery of a gold nugget in the grave dug for Bill Magee turns a solemn funeral into a free-for-all that strips the superficial piety from the "mourners" and makes everybody but the coroner losers. Another popular work, Carolyn E. S. Norton's "Bingen on the Rhine," which begins "A soldier of the Legion lay

Davis and his family at their ranch near Carson City, Nevada

dying in Algiers," was the inspiration for Davis's ballad "Just from Dawson," which has the first line, "A Dawson City mining man lay dying on the ice."

Davis wrote much of his poetry in the dated style of elevated diction that was popular in the nineteenth century. The few poems he wrote that rise above this artificial loftiness and become memorable are marked either by their homespun wisdom, their wit, or their sincerity. Davis's most famous poem—and it remains famous at least in Nevada—is "The Lure of the Sagebrush." It is typical of Davis that his love of his state led him to find beauty in the sagebrush, a plant whose only previous distinction had been that it would grow where nothing else could.

So remarkable and unique was the Comstock era that almost all writers who lived through it recollected it with genuine nostalgia. Davis was no exception and began as early as the 1880s to write anecdotes and memoirs of its colorful personalities and their extraordinary deeds. It was inevitable that he repeat himself and, given his penchant for touching up historical and biographical events, it is sometimes difficult to ascertain where truth ends and fiction begins in a given document. In the last decade of his life, however, Davis became involved with two retrospective projects that alone ensure his lasting reputation but also make it a little easier to infer accuracy in his memoirs. One was his participation in an ongoing series of mainly pseudonymous Comstock memoirs whose publication began in 1908 and continued at least until 1914. The other was

his preparation of the two-volume *The History of Nevada* (1913).

In 1908 the *Nevada Mining News,* a weekly trade newspaper out of Reno, began to publish a regular feature column of reminiscences titled "By-the-Bye" contributed by the best surviving writers from the Comstock era. Since the heyday of the Comstock was some thirty years before and most of those involved in its history had died or moved away, the writers were free to set the record straight as they saw it and say the things that they might have suppressed out of concern for the living or fear of retaliation. As a result "By-the-Bye" is richly loaded with fascinating and sometimes startling details of Comstock history seldom or never before revealed. Because the different writers occasionally contradicted or corrected each other, the series has an accuracy check that is missing from the usual single-author memoirs, and it is likely that contributors tended to be more scrupulous about sticking to the facts. Davis was one of the major contributors to this series. He was at the peak of his ability, and his columns were some of the highlights of the series.

Perhaps inspired by the "By-the-Bye" series, Davis undertook the editing of *The History of Nevada.* The previous standard histories of Nevada and the Comstock area were De Quille's *The Big Bonanza* (1876), Myron Angel's *History of Nevada* (1881), and Eliot Lord's *Comstock Mining and Miners* (1883). Davis assigned some chapters to local specialists and wrote others himself. Although he appropriated text by

Joseph Goodman into one of his own chapters without acknowledging his source (but apparently without an objection from Goodman) and sometimes followed Angel closely, the *History* is nevertheless an impressive achievement.

It is a credit to Davis that, staunchly standing up for his principles and ethics, he made many enemies as well as friends. Perhaps in his last years experiences of ingratitude from individuals and the state he had done so much for contributed to the feeling of disillusionment that somberly characterizes "The Gleaners," a poem that according to family tradition was the last thing that Davis wrote. It is moving and eloquent in its plain and sincere statement of a hard truth, a sad reflection on how few true friendships there are among the chaff of one's acquaintanceships. When Davis died, however, many friends responded with laudatory assessments of his life and work. The writer and editor Sam Dunham observed that Davis "was the last of that august company of magicians of the pen who told from first-hand knowledge the wonderful story of the Builders of the West." At his best Davis transcends a regional identification, but he will always be associated with the incomparable Comstock outlook and spirit.

Biographies:

Lucy Davis Crowell, "One Hundred Years at Nevada's Capital," oral history transcription, University of Nevada, Reno, 1965;

Daniel Edward Small, *Sam Davis of The Morning Appeal,* M.A. thesis, University of Nevada, Reno, 1978;

Sylvia Crowell Stoddard, *Sam Knew Them When* (Reno: Great Basin, 1996).

References:

Sherilyn Cox Bennion, "Nellie Verrill Mighels Davis: The 'Spirit of Things Achieved,'" *Nevada Historical Society Quarterly,* 34 (Fall 1991): 400–414;

Lawrence I. Berkove, "A New Comstock Letter of Mark Twain," *Nevada Historical Society Quarterly,* 41 (1999);

Berkove, "Samuel Post Davis," *American National Biography* (New York: Oxford University Press, 1999);

Sally Springmeyer Zanjani, "The United States Government Meets the Nevada Mule: The Humor of Sam Davis," *Nevada Historical Society Quarterly,* 23 (Spring 1980): 36–42.

Papers:

The largest and most important collection of Samuel Post Davis's papers is privately owned in Carson City by Sylvia Crowell Stoddard, a granddaughter of Davis. Other collections include the Bancroft Library at the University of California, Berkeley, and the University of Nevada, Reno Library. The Oral History Program at the University of Nevada, Reno, has an unpublished autobiographical dictation by Davis's daughter, Lucy Davis Crowell, that contains much information about Davis.

Thomas Dunn English

(29 June 1819 – 1 April 1902)

William Crisman
Pennsylvania State University, Altoona

BOOKS: *Zephania Doolittle: A Poem, From the Manuscripts of Montmorency Sneerlip Snags, Esq.* (Philadelphia: Alexander, 1838);

1844; or, The Power of the "S. F.": A Tale: Developing the Secret Action of Parties during the Presidential Campaign of 1844 (New York: Burgess, Stringer/Graham/ Long/Tuttle/Dexter, 1847);

Walter Woolfe; or, The Doom of the Drinker (New York: Smith, 1847);

The French Revolution of 1848: Its Causes, Actors, Events and Influences, by English and G. G. Foster (Philadelphia: Zieber, 1848);

The Mormons; or, Life at Salt Lake City, A Drama in Three Acts (New York: S. French, 1858);

Ambrose Fecit; or, The Peer and the Printer: A Novel (New York: Hilton, 1867);

Zara; or, the Girl of the Period: A Novel (New York: Hilton & Syme, 1869);

Gasology: A Satire, as John Donkey (Philadelphia: John Donkey, 1878);

American Ballads (New York: Harper, 1879); enlarged as *The Boy's Book of Battle-Lyrics: A Collection of Verses Illustrating Some Notable Events in the History of the United States of America, from the Colonial Period to the Outbreak of the Sectional War* (New York: Harper, 1885);

Jacob Schuyler's Millions: A Novel, anonymous (New York: Appleton, 1886);

The Rules of Order Governing Public Meetings, together with the Methods of Organizing and Conducting Societies, Associations . . . etc., as F. M. Payne (New York: Excelsior, 1887);

Model Speeches for All School Occasions, Containing Original Addresses and Orations on Everything Appertaining to School Life, as Christol Ogden (New York: Dick & Fitzgerald, 1888);

Skeleton Essays; or, Authorship in Outline, Consisting of Condensed Treatises on Popular Subjects, With Copious References to Sources of Information and Directions How to Enlarge Them into Essays or Expand Them into Lectures, Fully

Thomas Dunn English

Elucidated by Example as Well as Precept, as Ogden (New York: Dick & Fitzgerald, 1890);

The Select Poems of Dr. Thomas Dunn English (Exclusive of the "Battle-Lyrics"), edited by Alice English (Newark: Published by private subscription, 1894);

Fairy Stories and Wonder Tales, edited by Florence English Noll (New York: Stokes, 1897);

The Little Giant, The Big Dwarf, and Two Other Wonder-Tales for Boys and Girls From Eight to Eighty Years Old (Chicago: McClurg, 1904).

OTHER: *Aurora,* edited by English (1844);

Aristidean, A Magazine of Reviews, Politics and Light Literature, edited by English (1845);

John Donkey, edited by English (January–July 1848);

The Book of Rubies: A Collection of the Most Notable Love-Poems in the English Language, edited by English

(New York: Scribner, 1866); revised as *Half Hours With the Poets: A Collection of Choice Poems from Chaucer to Tennyson* (New York: Miller, 1874);

The Old Guard, edited by English (1870).

SELECTED PERIODICAL PUBLICATIONS–
UNCOLLECTED: "Two Open Letters From Dr. English to Mr. Ingram," *Independent,* 38 (15 April 1886): 455; 38 (22 April 1886): 488–489;

"Reminiscences of Poe," *Independent,* 48 (15 October 1896): 1381–1382; 48 (22 October 1896): 1415–1416; 48 (29 October 1896): 1448; 48 (5 November 1896): 1480–1481.

The assessment of Thomas Dunn English's career has changed significantly from the period of his greatest productivity, to the time of his death, to the present day. Modern students remember English, if at all, as an editor of failed journals and the unsuccessful defendant in a libel suit initiated by Edgar Allan Poe. Toward the end of his life, however, he was appreciated as an indefatigable poet, novelist, and dramatist. English's son-in-law, Arthur Howard Noll, in an essay that won a prize from *The Midland Monthly* for Best Original Descriptive Paper in 1897, extolled the "vast amount of literary work accomplished by [English] in an extraordinarily long and busy career." His obituary in *The New York Times* of 2 April 1902 echoes the same sentiment.

Born near Philadelphia on 29 June 1819 English was of Norman-Irish Quaker ancestry, with the Norman surname "Angelos" anglicized at some point to "English." His family immigrated to North America in 1682 or 1683 and received a William Penn land grant at Mt. Pleasant, New Jersey. This land was still known as "the English Farm" at the end of the nineteenth century. There is some doubt about who English's father was and how long he lived. The account in *American Authors 1600–1900: A Biographical Dictionary of American Literature* (1938) suggests that his father was "probably Robert English" without explaining the apparent uncertainty. Noll claims that Robert English died in Thomas's early childhood, but on the basis of unpublished papers William H. Gravely Jr. is convinced that Robert was still very much alive in his son's maturity.

English was educated at Wilson's Academy in Philadelphia and the Friends' Boarding School in Burlington, New Jersey. At the age of sixteen he was working for newspapers, publishing in *Paulson's Advertiser,* and earning enough money to study medicine under Dr. Paul D. Goddard at the University of Pennsylvania. Before matriculating, however, he served briefly as an employee of the Pennsylvania Geological Survey, and his knowledge of mineralogy appears in his later literary descriptions of nature. In *Walter Woolfe; or, The Doom of the Drinker* (1847), for instance, a quarry presents "a perpendicular wall of gneiss rock . . . and its micaceous particles glittered." His interest in ores, coals, and geological education figure prominently in *Ambrose Fecit; or, The Peer and the Printer: A Novel* (1867) and *Jacob Schuyler's Millions: A Novel* (1886). He maintained geological interests throughout his life. He lamented the loss of his mineral collection in a house fire in the 1860s at Fort Lee, New Jersey, and in 1890 gave William and Mary College a collection of minerals he had subsequently acquired.

After his geological interlude English received his medical degree with an 1839 thesis on phrenology. Apparently obeying his father's desire that he learn something useful, Thomas also took up carpentering and became a lawyer in 1842. Throat problems kept him from courtroom advocacy, however, and he returned to medicine.

Beginning in 1839 English contributed regularly to *Burton's Gentleman's Magazine,* one of whose editors was Poe. The two started their acquaintance on friendly terms, but the relationship became acrimonious by 1846, devolving into a physical, literary, and legal squabble. In 1843 Nathaniel P. Willis and George P. Morris revived the *New York Mirror* and asked English for a sea chantey. The result was his most famous work, "Ben Bolt." English registered misgivings about the poem, but it became quite popular and was often quoted or alluded to in nineteenth-century novels, drama, and song. It appears as a song in George Washington Cable's *Dr. Sevier* (1885) and in George du Maurier's *Trilby* (1894). Noll explains that its popularity was due in part to "the exquisite melody to which it is now wedded." English's first attempt to set the poem to music failed, but its musical adaptation in *The Battle of Buena Vista* (1846), a jingoistic melodrama by actor Nelson Kneass, made the lyrics nationally popular.

Addressed to a real person, a sailor lost or absent at sea, "Ben Bolt" has few characteristics of a sea chantey. Indeed, the sea has no presence until the last line, when Bolt's friend, the speaker of the poem, remarks "the salt-sea gale." Most of the poem is a sad catalogue of childhood and countryside vistas that are gone. The poem becomes a poignant list of transient experiences, reminiscent of Thomas Gray and an eighteenth-century penchant for sensibility. Nonetheless, its popularity continued until the turn of the twentieth century, and English had to contend with false boasts from others that they had actually written it.

In the 1840s English became involved in Whig politics. In addition to giving speeches in favor of President William Henry Harrison and his successor John Tyler, he edited *Aurora,* which Noll calls "the organ of President Tyler's administration," phrasing ironically close to that of

Poe who in his 1846 satiric essay characterized English as a stooge for Tyler. English's politics probably started the rift with Poe. During this period English attended a party in the capital at which Poe embarrassed himself through drunken behavior and apparently ridiculed English's huge, walruslike mustache. The scene deeply offended English, who lacked ironic detachment and as an avowed "Washingtonian" temperance member had remonstrated with Poe before about his drinking. Although it is not certain that English took action, Poe may well have suspected that English's influence with the Tyler administration denied him an appointment to the Philadelphia Customs House, where a Robert English was installed instead. If, as Gravely argues, this is Thomas English's still-living father, the slight to Poe would be considerable.

In the aftermath of the party, English started writing "The Doom of the Drinker, or, Revel and Retribution," which was first serialized in *Coldwater Magazine* in 1843 and published in book form with its originally conceived title, *Walter Woolfe; or, The Doom of the Drinker,* four years later. The novel is partly a temperance and antigambling novel and partly a roman à clef. At its heart, though, it is a conspiracy novel in which Walter's drunkenness and gambling are induced and orchestrated by his half brother, whose mother Walter's father had "ruined." The novel is marked by lyric passages, such as the description of a river that "wound through the near valley, and seemed, beneath the red rays of the dying sun, like some golden serpent writhing amid the trees and rocks." It also is interesting for the homoerotic edge of English's portrayal of his protagonist, who in college is attracted to a man of "girlish beauty." He later drunkenly drives his wife into the snow to her death so that he can remain with his bachelor friends.

Walter Woolfe increased English's estrangement from Poe, in part because the description of one character was widely recognized as an unflattering caricature of Poe–a "pale, gentlemanly looking personage" who "made no ceremony . . . in appropriating the ideas of others when it suited his turn; and as a man, was the very incarnation of treachery and falsehood." The vignette also makes fun of Poe's "peculiarly shaped forehead," a piece of physical ridicule that perhaps inspired Poe's later physical caricature of English. Beyond the satiric caricaturing of the "pale personage," however, Walter's own career bears spot resemblances to Poe's life. Married to a "little wife" and fascinated by the "childlike innocence" of girls, Walter goes on drunken trips while his wife is dying of tuberculosis. If Poe perceived Walter's characterization, with its implication that homosexuality underlay the attraction to little girls and the drunken abuse of women, also as a personal attack, his later antipathy for English is all the more understandable.

In 1845 English edited the Aristidean, a short-lived journal to which Poe contributed, but between the serial and book publication of Walter Woolfe an event occurred that certainly broke their already strained friendship. In a dispute over indiscreet letters that Poe claimed were sent to him by the writer Elizabeth Ellet, the two men had a brief fistfight in 1845 that both claimed to have won. English asserted that he struck Poe so hard as to confine him to bed, a claim that most biographers take as more likely than Poe's boastful accounts of victory.

The course toward English's legal dispute with Poe began in full with Poe's publication of the satiric sketch "Thomas Dunn English" in *Godey's Lady's Book* of 20 June 1846, in which he ridicules English primarily for bad grammar but also pokes fun at him for his failed journals and physical appearance. Three days later two New York newspapers, the *Morning Telegraph* and the *Evening Mirror,* printed English's scathing counterattack, which includes the imputation that Poe's mother came from a kennel. More critical from a legal standpoint, however, was English's assertion that Poe had committed forgery and borrowed money without repaying it. Poe won the ensuing libel suit on 17 February 1847, receiving from English a punitive damage compensation of $225.06.

Serialized in 1846, English's long novel *1844; or, The Power of the "S. F.": A Tale: Developing the Secret Action of Parties during the Presidential Campaign of 1844* (the *S. F.* stands for Startled Falcon) was published as a book in 1847 before *Walter Woolfe* came out in hardcover. Set in the infamous Five-Points area of Manhattan and exploiting all its lurid environment, *1844; or, The Power of the "S. F."* is about a secret society of underhanded Democrats trying to defeat the Whigs in the election of that year. Interwoven with the political intrigue is a sordid family plot about personal revenge and confused identities. English again attacks Poe, who appears in unflattering vignettes as the character Marmaduke Hammerhead, the unlettered author of the poem titled "Black Crow."

In 1848 English edited the satiric journal *John Donkey* and collaborated with G. G. Foster on a book about the 1848 revolution in France. A long spell of ill health led English to retreat from politics. He then turned to drama and wrote about twenty plays. One of these, *The Mormons; or, Life at Salt Lake City, A Drama in Three Acts,* was produced by Junius Brutus Booth, premiering at Burton's Theatre in March 1858, and published in 1858. Along with "Ben Bolt," *The Mormons* is responsible for the literary fame English enjoyed during his lifetime.

The play is a thorough melodrama–complete with a ruined sister driven out into the snow–that presents the Mormons as anti-American conspirators whose every waking hour is spent plotting to entrap new, naive converts into the bonds of polygamy. The presentation of Mormon polygamy alternates between Gothic scenes in which hooded figures with torches threaten torture if the converts do not take second wives and comic scenes in which polygamous buffoons appear in domestic contretemps. The conspiracy against monogamy is thwarted by the arrival of the cavalry.

English married Annie Maxwell Meade in 1849, and they had four children in their forty-year marriage that ended with her death in 1889. Between 1852 and 1857 he worked both as lawyer and doctor in Lawnsville, Virginia, where he was also town mayor. For two years he edited the official journal of President Buchanan's administration. In 1858 he moved to Fort Lee, New Jersey, a state that was to be his home for the rest of his life. A sympathizer with the South, he served as a member of the state legislature in 1863 and 1864.

In *Ambrose Fecit; or, The Peer and the Printer: A Novel* English writes without the Whiggish political agenda or the personal rancor of his earlier novels. Although the novel is certainly a mystery—with such devices as orphans of unknown identity, mysterious Spanish monks, crossed lineages, and misconceptions about who is and is not dead—it is difficult to say what it is really about. English drops hints but does not develop themes. The reader searches in vain for a coherent pattern in seemingly significant points. One wonders why Ambrose is an ardent language student and becomes a printing apprentice to a distant relative of Johannes Gutenberg or what it means that the orphan Ambrose's name comes from the lettering "Ambrose Fecit" ("Ambrose Made It") on the town clock, which he calls "Godfather." The subtitle implies an investigation of class, but though he turns class identities topsy-turvy, English evidently has no deeper purpose. He certainly plays with Gothicism—mentioning Ann Radcliffe by name and surely invoking Ambrosio in Matthew Lewis's *The Monk* (1796) through the name "Ambrose"—yet the novel is far from a consistent satire or parody. At best it seems a collection of momentarily entertained themes.

In 1870 English took over and edited the soon-to-perish journal *Old Guard*—even after the war an anti-Lincoln, pro-Confederacy periodical—in which he mocked Poe eleven years after his death. The same year he was awarded an honorary L.L.D. from William and Mary College. In 1878 he was working as a newspaper staff member for the *Sunday Call* of Newark. He also served as private secretary to the mayor of Newark.

English, according to Noll, had begun doing his literary work "with the aid of an amanuensis." He was probably preparing his first poetry collection, *American Ballads* (1879). Harper reissued the collection in considerably augmented form in 1885 as *The Boy's Book of Bat-*

tle-Lyrics: A Collection of Verses Illustrating Some Notable Events in the History of the United States of America, from the Colonial Period to the Outbreak of the Sectional War. Noll reports that the title of the enlarged collection is half the result of the publisher not wanting to repeat a title already used by its press and half a desire to alliterate *B*. The book is not children's literature and indeed has a form unusual for adults as well.

Starting with the Spanish colonizers of America, English writes a prose account of a battle, often quite long, that he then celebrates with a poem. The combination shows the same impulse to get the facts straight that informed the treatment of politics in *1844; or, The power of the "S. F."* The *Battle-Lyrics* is in the main a textbook and the poems serve as illustrations. Interestingly, the last detailed prose accounts concern the Mexican War. As English moves briefly into the Civil War era the prose accounts become clipped. He admits that their foundation is "rather slender." Of the poem "The Charge by the Ford" English acknowledges, "The story may be correct, or not." One has to suspect that the "slenderness" of these accounts connects to English's Civil War politics as a Southern sympathizer in the North. He apparently was reluctant to describe in detail the Union victory.

Jacob Schuyler's Millions: A Novel, English's last, was published in 1886. As in *Ambrose Fecit* English constructs an elaborate mystery involving conspiratorial double-dealing. His particular concern here is a lost will and the question of inheritance within a complicated family. It is an historical novel dealing with the events surrounding the 1848 revolution, and the sometimes elaborate landscape descriptions constantly evoke this historical distance. Intersecting the mystery plot is a courtship drama of who will marry whom, and it is in this subplot that English approaches a psychological study. In addition to narrating dreams, he also creates two characters, Barculo and Barent, whose alliterative names, contrastive types (hardy and frail), and contradictory actions as savers and betrayers of one another, suggest that they are split parts of the same personality. Exactly what English wants to accomplish by staging this psychological split, however, remains unclear. Nevertheless, the novel is more cohesive than *Ambrose Fecit*, if only because English has a stronger focus on class. Barculo saves Barent at the barricades in Europe during the 1848 revolution, and a traveling European shows up to present a set speech on class struggle. Presiding over the action, the sage and eccentric old Colburn, both a doctor and a lawyer, clearly presents a flattering and affectionately self-mocking version of English himself.

Jacob Schuyler's Millions was English's last piece of fiction for adults. Between 1887 and 1890 he published three books of models for public speaking: *The Rules of Order Governing Public Meetings, together with the Methods of*

Organizing and Conducting Societies, Associations . . . etc. (1887), *Model Speeches for All School Occasions, Containing Original Addresses and Orations on Everything Appertaining to School Life* (1888), and *Skeleton Essays; or, Authorship in Outline, Consisting of Condensed Treatises on Popular Subjects, With Copious References to Sources of Information and Directions How to Enlarge Them into Essays or Expand Them into Lectures, Fully Elucidated by Example as Well as Precept* (1890). *Fairy Stories and Wonder Tales* (1897), edited by his daughter Florence Noll, was published in 1897, and *The Little Giant, The Big Dwarf, and Two Other Wonder-Tales for Boys and Girls from Eight to Eighty Years Old* appeared posthumously in 1904.

During much of the 1890s English was occupied with Democratic politics. During his successful 1890 race for Congress, his old poem "Ben Bolt" became a nightly Democratic chant. He defended his seat in the 1892 election but lost it in 1894, the year his daughter Alice published *The Select Poems of Dr. Thomas Dunn English (Exclusive of the "Battle Lyrics")*. Claiming in her introduction that "a number of gentlemen" had called for the volume, Alice English divides the more than seven hundred pages into five sections: "Legends and Lays," "Rural Sketches," "Dialect Studies," "Bizarre Rhymes," and "Miscellaneous." The book is prefaced by "Kallimais," a ballad about changelings that won some fame in English's time because of the speed with which he wrote it. While the title heroine turns into a tiger at night because she was once uncharitable to a beggar, the ballad finally shows that her action has little moral consequence, for the spell is broken by a local hermit who once dabbled in magic.

English considered balladeering his main talent as a poet, and the first two sections constitute about two-thirds of the collection, with "Ben Bolt" included in "Rural Sketches." "Dialect Studies" and "Bizarre Rhymes," in which he makes use of local dialects, are slight sections. Of greatest interest are the poems Alice collected under "Miscellaneous," which, like "Ben Bolt," are generally elegiac in tone. In poems such as "The River," "Oblivion," and "The Island of the Soul" English depicts sometimes gorgeous, sometimes drab landscapes with strong agnostic or even atheistic implications. In "The Island of the Soul" he describes a seeming paradise: "There rise the lilac mountains; / There palms their leaves unfold; / There bubble life-renewing fountains, / Pellucid, crystalline, and cold, / Through sands of gold." Nevertheless, in this "life-renewing" island "Nothing that breathes is found." In "Oblivion" English imagines another disturbing landscape: "It is the realm of Nowhere, where / The listless dwellers have no care, . . . / Hence from their eyes that vacant stare."

Apart from their poignancy, English in some of his miscellaneous poems explores in more concentrated form the themes and interests that are diffuse in his novels. In "The Telegraph Wires," for instance, he focuses on the mysteries of language and communication that occupied him increasingly from *Ambrose Fecit* to *Jacob Schuyler's Millions*. In "Song of Fire" he returns to his early interest in geology, which he kept at the periphery of his novels.

When English died on 1 April 1902 he was nearly blind. A crabbed and vindictive personality, English was often more concerned with historical accuracy than artistic merit. His lack of originality is also an important reason for his lack of enduring fame. Though a nineteenth-century author, English was an anachronism, generally working in the mode of the late eighteenth century, the pre-Romantic elegy and the Gothic conspiracy novel.

Biography:

William H. Gravely Jr., "The Early Political and Literary Career of Thomas Dunn English," dissertation, University of Virginia, 1954.

References:

William H. Gravely Jr., "Poe and Thomas Dunn English: More Light on a Probable Reason for Poe's Failure to Receive a Custom-House Appointment," in *Papers on Poe: Essays in Honor of John Ward Ostrom*, edited by Richard P. Veler (Springfield, Ohio: Chantry Music, 1972), pp. 165–193;

Perry Miller, *The Raven and the Whale: The War of Words and Wits in the Era of Poe and Melville* (New York: Harcourt, Brace, 1956), pp. 160–161, 169, 173, 177;

Sidney P. Moss, *Poe's Literary Battles: The Critic in the Context of His Literary Milieu* (Durham: Duke University Press, 1963);

Moss, *Poe's Major Crisis: His Libel Suit and New York's Literary World* (Durham: Duke University Press, 1970);

Frank Luther Mott, *A History of American Magazines, 1850–1865* (Cambridge, Mass.: Harvard University Press, 1938), pp. 181, 544–546;

Arthur Howard Noll, "The Truth about 'Ben Bolt' and Its Author," *Midland Monthly*, 7 (January 1897): 3–10;

Kenneth Silverman, *Edgar A. Poe: Mournful and Never-Ending Remembrance* (New York: HarperCollins, 1991), pp. 261, 266, 284, 290–291, 335, 410;

Dwight Thomas, "Poe, English, and *The Doom of the Drinker*: A Mystery Resolved," *Princeton University Library Chronicle*, 40 (Spring 1979): 257–268.

Edgar Fawcett

(26 May 1847 – 2 May 1904)

John D. Cloy

University of Mississippi

BOOKS: *Short Poems for Short People* (New York: Felt, 1872);

Purple and Fine Linen: A Novel (New York: Carleton / London: Low, 1873);

Ellen Story: A Novel (New York: Hale, 1876);

Fantasy and Passion (Boston: Roberts, 1878);

A Hopeless Case (Boston: Houghton, Mifflin, 1880);

A Gentleman of Leisure: A Novel (Boston: Houghton, Mifflin, 1881);

An Ambitious Woman (Boston: Houghton, Mifflin, 1884);

Tinkling Cymbals: A Novel (Boston: Osgood, 1884);

Song and Story: Later Poems (Boston: Osgood, 1884);

The Buntling Ball: A Graeco-American Play, Being a Poetical Satire on New York Society (New York: Funk & Wagnalls, 1884; London: Funk & Wagnalls, 1885);

Rutherford (New York & London: Funk & Wagnalls, 1884);

The Adventures of a Widow: A Novel (Boston: Osgood, 1884);

The New King Arthur: An Opera Without Music . . . , anonymous (New York & London: Funk & Wagnalls, 1885);

Social Silhouettes (Being the Impressions of Mr. Mark Manhattan) . . . (Boston: Ticknor, 1885);

Romance and Revery: Poems (Boston: Ticknor, 1886);

The Confessions of Claud: A Romance (Boston: Ticknor, 1887);

The House at High Bridge: A Novel (Boston: Ticknor, 1887);

A Man's Will: A Novel (New York & London: Funk & Wagnalls, 1888);

Miriam Balestier: A Novel (Chicago: Belford, Clarke, 1888);

Olivia Delaplaine: A Novel (Boston: Ticknor, 1888);

Divided Lives (Chicago: Belford, Clarke, 1888);

Agnosticism and Other Essays (New York: Belford, Clarke / London: Drane, 1889);

Blooms and Brambles (London: Stock, 1889);

A Demoralizing Marriage (Philadelphia: Lippincott, 1889);

Solarion: A Romance (Philadelphia: Lippincott, 1889);

The Evil That Men Do (New York: Belford, 1889);

Edgar Fawcett

A Daughter of Silence (New York: Belford, 1890);

Fabian Dimitry: A Novel (Chicago: Rand, McNally, 1890);

How a Husband Forgave: A Novel (New York: Belford, 1890);

A New York Family: A Novel (New York: Caswell, 1891);

A Romance of Two Brothers (New York: Minerva, 1891);

Women Must Weep: A Novel (Chicago: Laird & Lee, 1891); republished as *A Story of Three Girls (Women Must Weep)* (Chicago: Laird & Lee, 1895);

Loaded Dice (New York: Tait, 1891);

Songs of Doubt and Dream (Poems) (New York: Funk & Wagnalls, 1891);

The Adopted Daughter (Chicago & New York: Neely, 1892);

An Heir to Millions (Chicago: Schulte, 1892);

American Push (Chicago: Schulte, 1892);

The New Nero: A Realistic Romance (New York: Collier, 1893);

Her Fair Fame: A Novel (New York: Merrill & Baker, 1894; London: Ward, Lock & Bowden, 1894);

A Martyr of Destiny (New York: Collier, 1894);

A Mild Barbarian: A Novel (New York: Appleton, 1894);

Outrageous Fortune (New York: Dillingham, 1894);

The Ghost of Guy Thyrle (New York: Collier, 1895);

Life's Fitful Fever, Being the Memoirs of Clarence Disoway Torington . . . , 2 volumes (New York: Collier, 1896);

A Romance of Old New York (Philadelphia & London: Lippincott, 1897);

New York: A Novel (New York & London: Neely, 1898);

Voices and Visions: Later Verses (London: Nash, 1903);

The Vulgarians (New York & London: Smart Set, 1903);

Some Reminiscences of Old Victoria (Toronto: W. Briggs, 1912);

"The Pride of Intellect," edited by Stanley Harrison, dissertation, Michigan State University, 1964.

PLAY PRODUCTIONS: *A False Friend,* New York, Union Square Theater, 21 June 1880;

Our First Families, New York, Daly's Theater, 23 September 1880;

Sixes and Sevens, New York, Bijou Opera House, March 1881;

Americans Abroad, New York, Daly's Theater, 5 October 1881;

The Earl, New York, Hollis Street Theater, 11 April 1887.

SELECTED PERIODICAL PUBLICATIONS– UNCOLLECTED: "Mr. Aldrich's Poetry," *Atlantic Monthly,* 34 (December 1874): 671–674;

"Douglas Duane," *Lippincott's Monthly Magazine,* 39 (April 1887): 529–631;

"A Few More Words About Miss Rives," *Lippincott's Monthly Magazine,* 42 (September 1888): 390–394;

"Solarion," *Lippincott's Monthly Magazine,* 44 (September 1889): 294–369.

Though little read today, Edgar Fawcett during his lifetime was well known as novelist, poet, dramatist, and essayist. Decidedly a minor figure in American letters, Fawcett was nonetheless one of the earliest purveyors of realism and naturalism in American literature. His fiction, which almost exclusively treats the New York of his day, generally condemns the wealthy Dutch aristocracy, nouveau riche plutocrats, and corrupt politicians that abounded in his native city. He also wrote several slum novels and some supernatural fiction. The prolific Fawcett produced such a quantity of material

that contemporary critic Richard Henry Stoddard lamented, "Won't somebody please turn this Fawcett off?" While much of his work is barely above the level of hack writing, Fawcett in the 1870s and 1880s began to blaze a trail that more talented authors such as William Dean Howells, Frank Norris, and Stephen Crane pursued in the development of realism.

Fawcett knew many of the literary luminaries of his day, and his comments about their abilities in his voluminous correspondence provide an interesting perspective on the American writing scene of the latter nineteenth century. He counted as close friends Paul Hamilton Hayne, Frank Saltus, James Maurice Thompson, Julian Hawthorne, and Thomas Bailey Aldrich. He greatly admired Howells, Henry James, John Greenleaf Whittier, Henry Wadsworth Longfellow, Oliver Wendell Holmes, and Hamlin Garland, all of whom he had met. Among contemporary British authors, Fawcett applauded the work of Robert Browning, Algernon Charles Swinburne, Alfred Tennyson, and Oscar Wilde. A man of violent likes and dislikes, Fawcett seldom minced words in his letters and did not value the writing of Elizabeth Barrett Browning, Sidney Lanier, James Russell Lowell, or Walt Whitman. Serving as a sounding board for his critical pronouncements on the literary efforts, particularly the poetry, of fellow writers, most of his extant letters were sent to Hayne. Fawcett's favorite American poet was Aldrich, whom he considered a master craftsman, and he considered Tennyson, Swinburne, and Wilde the premier British poets of their generation.

Little is known of Fawcett's early life or family connections. He was born in New York City on 26 May 1847, the only son (he had several sisters) of Frederick Fawcett and his wife, Sarah Lawrence Fawcett. His father, an Englishman, became a wealthy leather merchant in the city, and his mother was a member of a patrician New York family. A voracious reader and composer of juvenile verse and prose, Fawcett attended New York public schools. At the age of sixteen he entered Columbia College and was involved in undergraduate literary culture. He graduated in 1867 and stayed on to receive an M.A. from Columbia in 1870. Because of his family's financial position, Fawcett was relieved of the uncomfortable necessity of earning a living and was thereby enabled to devote himself entirely to literature, although his father had intended that he study law.

In a letter to his friend William Rideing, Fawcett recalled that his first publication occurred around 1865, when he sent a wretched poem to *The Banner of Light,* a spiritualist periodical to which his father subscribed. Bowled over that his submission was printed, Fawcett became addicted to authorship. Rideing maintained that Fawcett could have entered society had he chosen, but the lure of literature and an innate distaste for frippery and sham dissuaded him. He characterized Fawcett as loving toward his friends but somewhat irascible, hypersensitive to criticism, and staunchly unforgiving when wronged. Despite his many acquaintances in the literary world, he had few close associates. He never married and spent much of his time at various clubs when not writing.

One of Fawcett's earliest novels, *Purple and Fine Linen* (1873), indicts the practice of arranged marriages between wealthy families. Nouveau-riche Helen Jeffries is shepherded into wedlock with the scion of a decayed aristocratic clan, Fuller Dobell, by her social-climbing mother, whose relentless machinations are worthy of Machiavelli. Mrs. Jeffries promotes the liaison despite her prior knowledge of Dobell's illicit relationship with the courtesan Edith Everdell. Helen is devastated to learn of Dobell's infidelity after their marriage. Much to the horror of her mother, who counsels her daughter to make the best of a bad situation, she threatens to leave Dobell if he does not drop Everdell but finds that the adulterer sneeringly refuses to alter his behavior. After Helen's former suitor Melville Delano wounds Dobell severely in a duel and her husband is convalescing in the home of his paramour, Helen contrives to enter the woman's home disguised as a nurse and arranges to demonstrate to the weakened Dobell that his lover has been unfaithful to him with an old friend, Driscoll. The repentant husband then returns to Helen and vows to love her as she deserves.

Helen is a strong character who triumphs in the teeth of overwhelming odds. She defies the conventions of New York society by exposing her aristocratic mate's dalliances and overcoming her mother's powerful influence. She rises above the set roles for nineteenth-century women by taking an active part in her own affairs but sacrifices none of her femininity and wins through female wiles. Fawcett uses the attractive, moral Helen to reveal the decadent shallowness of New York society filled with transparent illusion. Through her, he promotes the democratic ideal of the worth of individuals over the presumed superiority of blood and wealth.

Although chiefly remembered as a novelist, Fawcett was praised for his poetry by contemporaries such as Lowell, Hawthorne, and Stoddard. Perhaps his highest encomium came from Howells, who wrote in the *Atlantic Monthly* (May 1878) that Fawcett "seems first among American poets; we do not know why we should stop short of saying among all the English-writing poets of our time. Possibly Leigh Hunt surpasses him in our literature; we shall not try to establish his place too definitely, for criticism must not leave time

with nothing to do." Fawcett's poetry often shows his dark, introspective side. "Darkness," a poem in his 1878 collection, *Fantasy and Passion,* is an anguished dirge reminiscent of the work of Edgar Allan Poe:

> I had a dream of a wild-lit place
> Where three dark spirits met face to face.
>
> One said: "I am darkest; I had birth
> In the central blackness of mid-earth."
>
> With a sneer one said, below his breath:
> "I am still more dark, for I am Death."
>
> But the third, with voice that bleaker pealed
> Than freezing wind on a houseless field,
>
> Cried, where he stood from the rest apart,
> "I am that darkness which fills man's heart
>
> "When it aches and yearns and burns for one
> It has loved as the meadow loves the sun!"
>
> Now I gazed on him from earth's mid-reach,
> And now on the spirit of death; and each,
>
> Though dark with a darkness to affright,
> Beside that third was a shape of light.

Fawcett, whose conception of darkness is closely akin to Poe's idea of beauty, was apparently drawn to the extreme poetic tenets of the American writer and Charles Baudelaire. Although he remarked in a 22 September 1875 letter to Hayne that he found the Frenchman "an excessively immoral poet" who seemed "to denounce and renounce all idea of virtue," he nevertheless composed a sonnet titled "Baudelaire" in *Fantasy and Passion.* Fawcett's later, more naturalistic writings are not inconsistent with the romantic tendencies of both Poe and Baudelaire to depict horrifying images.

In *An Ambitious Woman* (1884), probably his best-known novel, Fawcett skillfully depicts a wide cross-section of character types as he shrewdly combines an unusual rags-to-riches tale with adroit criticism of the American upper crust. The book concerns Claire Twining, the polished, scholarly daughter of a younger son of a gentlemanly English family. Her father is an amiable failure who squanders much of the legacy of his wife and daughter on unsound speculations. After his death Claire leaves her mother, a shrew of the sort belonging to stage farce, when she refuses to part with some of the remaining money for a decent burial of her spouse, who ends up in Potter's Field.

Claire seeks out Sophia Bergemann, a coarse, good-natured brewer's daughter whom she had met at a finishing school she briefly attended in better days. The

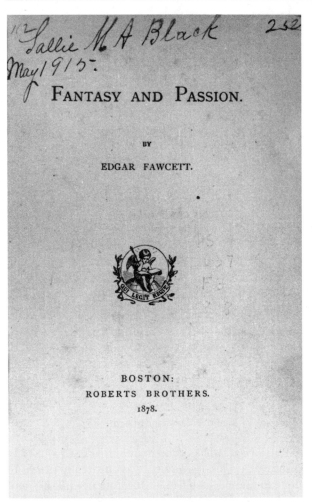

Title page for Fawcett's 1878 poetry collection, which shows the influence of Edgar Allan Poe and Charles Baudelaire (courtesy of Special Collections, Thomas Cooper Library, University of South Carolina)

friendly Sophia invites Claire to live with her as a companion, and soon Claire is launched into the Bergemann family's nouveau-riche society. Driven by the desire to dominate the champagne-and-caviar set of old New York, Claire calculatingly sets about gaining introductions to Knickerbocker family balls. She meets and bewitches an older aristocratic lawyer, Beverley Thurston, who proposes to her. Although she rejects him, the would-be suitor continues to aid her. She eventually marries a promising young stockbroker, Herbert Hollister, who seems sufficiently well connected to further her ambition. Claire quickly rises to social prominence with the help of a friend, Mrs. Diggs, a social climber who has managed over a considerable period to insinuate herself into the graces of the best families.

When at the pinnacle of her social success her husband is bankrupted by a stock market collapse, Claire begins to reconsider her motives. Taking Thurston's fatherly advice, she resolves to support her hus-

band in his noble attempt to right himself financially and pay off his creditors. She then discovers Hollister's fine qualities and comes to love him unreservedly, eschewing ambition for the more satisfying life of study and reflection that she had earlier pursued.

Despite her beauty, poise, and intelligence, Claire is not an admirable character. She typifies for Fawcett the pushy Americans who create their own aristocratic status through money. Usually immensely wealthy, these parvenus exhibit a lack of culture that shocks the truly refined, who were nevertheless often willing to endure their company in order to exploit their bounty. Even Claire's later decision to live in bookish seclusion is selfish as she cares little for the destitution of many of her fellow New Yorkers.

In *Tinkling Cymbals* (1884) Fawcett again attacks New York aristocracy. The story concerns Leah Romilly, a beautiful middle-class girl who becomes enamored of Tracy Tremaine, a shallow aristocrat, during a visit to fashionable Newport. Despite the objections of Tracy's family that Leah is common, the two marry. Leah's mother, a former platform speaker for radical causes, and Leah's former suitor, Lawrence Rainsford, a painter, both disapprove of the union on the grounds that Tremaine and his friends are too superficial for her.

Fawcett characterizes Tremaine's mother as a typical period snob when she visits Leah's mother to solicit her aid in preventing the marriage:

> Oh, I was prepared to find you very clever. I had heard of that. It is your profession to be clever. I won't attempt to cross wits with you. Tracy has been fascinated by your daughter. Very well—let him marry out of his set if he pleases. But you will gain nothing, madam, by such a union. I think we will none of us acknowledge it. I wished to talk peacefully with you, but you make that impossible. When I say 'we' I mean our whole large family. The Tremaines and Tracys have been noted for their sensible marriages. We have scarcely had a single mesalliance [*sic*] for four or five generations.

Leah soon has cause to repent of her nuptials as Tremaine drinks to excess and proves unfaithful. Humiliated by her spouse's open infidelity, she gives him an ultimatum of reformation or divorce. Tremaine accedes to her demands, and the two live a sham marriage until Leah catches him again in adultery. During a quarrel over her leaving, Tremaine strikes her. He immediately goes on a bender from which he never recovers, dying within a month. The heroine then pledges her troth to Rainsford, who has become a success in the art world. Although the book contains some worthy passages regarding the inappropriateness of an American version of European nobility, it would prove to be the first of a series of formulaic tirades on the subject.

Like many of his British and American contemporaries, Fawcett sometimes indulged in supernatural fiction. "Douglas Duane," which appeared in *Lippincott's Monthly Magazine* in April 1887, was a departure from the writer's society novels. The book concerns madness and has otherwordly undertones. Duane, a cold rationalistic scientist, possesses as his only friends a reclusive young couple, Floyd and Millicent Demotte. Unknown to both, Duane falls desperately in love with Millicent and plots to trade bodies with Demotte by employing an electrical device that he has successfully used on plants.

The book opens after Floyd apparently has killed Millicent and then turned the gun on himself. Demotte does not die immediately and is transferred to an asylum, where he pens the story of the incident, which is taken as the raving of a lunatic by the two young detectives who investigate the crime, Ford Fairleigh and Hiram Payne. The man claims that he is actually Duane and that he murdered Demotte with his invention, appropriated his body, and, after disposing of his own body, impersonated Demotte in order to possess Millicent. She, however, recognized him as Duane, even in her husband's form. Insane with remorse, Duane devised the murder and suicide, imagining that he and Millicent might be united in the afterlife.

With "Douglas Duane" Fawcett tapped into the philosophical themes that were prevalent in late nineteenth-century American literature. Duane is Nietzschean in his desire to overcome fleshly limitations; his worship of science and rational thought make him a man who will stop at nothing to gain his ends. The validity of the Frankenstein-style experiment that transforms Duane into Demotte is left open to the reader's conjecture because there is no concrete evidence that Demotte was actually Duane, whom the papers had reported as missing several weeks before the shooting. The official version—that he killed his wife because of insanity—may be true.

In 1888 Fawcett published the novel *A Man's Will*, a surprisingly insightful study of alcoholism from a hereditary perspective. The protagonist, Edmund Saltonstall, inherits the predisposition to drink excessively from his father, Johnston, a successful businessman who is a periodic binge drinker. Though carefully monitored by his doting wife, Johnston dies disgracefully in a dive while on a spree. Johnston's wife and daughter, Judith, who together managed to conceal his illness until his scandalous death, then convince the twelve-year-old Edmund to take a lifelong temperance oath by frightening him with the example of his father's excesses.

All goes well until Edmund, influenced by peers, breaks his pledge at a college party and becomes disgustingly intoxicated. Although he vows to be more careful in the future, he finds that drinking becomes more and more important to him. After years of trying to drink "normally," Edmund becomes an inveterate alcoholic, obsessed by liquor and constantly remorseful at his failure to control his craving. He is eventually saved by an enlightened physician, Allsop, who warns him that even one drop is too much for a person with his mental and physical makeup and that he must remain forever on his guard against the first drink.

In a scene where a nervous Edmund is called upon to make a public address Fawcett shows the insidious charms that liquor presents to those afflicted with the disease of alcoholism:

> A glass of champagne shone golden and infinitely tempting at his side. He reached out his hand, lifted it, and drained it at one draught. Just then an obsequious servant was passing. The glass was no sooner emptied than replenished. As the yellow, creamy fluid slipped forth, its effervescence had for Saltonstall the delicate hiss of a snake. But already a new courage, a careless and exquisitely comforting self-possession, had begun to diffuse its influence through his spirit. More slowly, and with the growing surety that in a little while he would acquit himself at least with the requisite composure and fluency which his future auditors were justified in expecting from him, he drained the contents of this second glass.

Fawcett exhibits remarkable understanding of the tragedy of alcoholism at a time when the problem was viewed primarily as a moral question. He saw that the injunction to "drink like a gentleman" killed many alcoholics. Allsop, speaking for Fawcett, tells Edmund that he will never be completely safe from intoxicants, that the compulsion could rear its head at any moment.

Fawcett's distrust of Christianity is a key factor in understanding his philosophy and fiction. An avowed rationalist, he viewed Christ's tenets as impractical in modern society and little short of ludicrous. He found the idea that Christians could rest assured in the knowledge that God was in control of their destinies and would provide for them especially distasteful. In the title essay of *Agnosticism and Other Essays* (1889) Fawcett maintains that "about the real agnostic spirit there is much more sincerity than diplomacy. It means, in its finest sense, a courageous envisaging of the awful problems of life and death, and an admission of their total insolubility." In the same essay he goes on to ridicule the accuracy of the Bible: "The very existence of that particular Christ whose life and death are recorded in the New Testament is by no means a proven fact. The ridiculous story that he was born of a virgin is scarcely less to be respected by unbiased judges than the story that he was ever born at all." The acceptance of Victorian Christian doctrine by most of his countrymen symbolized for Fawcett an exclusivity that separated the American upper-class haves from foreign and lower-class have-nots. This adherence to an outmoded religion that had been conveniently streamlined for the wealthy of the nineteenth century was more fuel for Fawcett's slow-burning fire of resentment toward the American aristocracy.

The Evil That Men Do (1889), one of Fawcett's more substantial efforts, is a naturalistic novel about Cora Strang, an exceptionally beautiful girl from a poor family who is orphaned in her late teens. She migrates to New York City from a small upstate town and ekes out a living as a seamstress. Attracting the unwelcome attentions of men of her class, she virtuously rejects them all. At a political fund-raising ball that she attends with her admiring neighbor, Owen Slattery, she meets Casper Drummond, son of a city alderman. Although Casper is far from cultured, to Cora he seems an aristocrat. Against her better judgment, she agrees to see him and incurs the wrath of Slattery, whom she drops immediately. Casper introduces the girl to alcohol and persuades her to move into a small house he owns until he can convince his father to allow their marriage. Drummond Sr., however, has other plans for his son. He forces Casper to wed a prosperous brewer's daughter for political reasons. Casper deserts the pregnant Cora, who ends in a charity ward and loses her baby.

After this betrayal Cora sinks rapidly into drunkenness and debauchery. When she hears of Casper's wedding, she appears at the ceremony intoxicated and makes a scene. When the police release her, the still inebriated woman encounters Slattery, now a skid-row denizen. The unkempt Irishman prevails upon her to drink with him in a low dive, after which the sodden Slattery murders Cora and kills himself in an effort to keep her with him always.

An environment that Cora seems unable to escape seems a key factor in her fate. Fawcett uses a set tone of fatalism that envelops many of the characters throughout the novel. Despite their good qualities, they are overwhelmed by circumstances and eventually bow to an inevitable doom. Cora remains chaste until Caspar Drummond enters the picture, but she then gives in as if to a power greater than herself. When Slattery and Cora have their fatal rendezvous, Fawcett comments on the forces at work against them:

There was something measurelessly pitiable in the meeting of these two destitute and accursed human souls. Each had made its own earthly hell, and amid the horrors of such a doom they sat and gazed at one another. . . . For them destiny pointed to one sure path. They could blame its misusage and cry out against its hardships as bitterly as they chose. It had left them nothing more dignified to do than to pass from a world which neither needed them nor could console them. It had left them nothing better to do than to die!

In 1889 Fawcett also brought out *A Demoralizing Marriage,* another salvo at the old Dutch aristocracy in New York. The story involves the union of Rosalind Maturin, daughter of a self-made millionaire, and society fop Carroll Remington. Caroline Casilear, Rosalind's sister, is frantic to enter New York's gilded circle and uses her wealth to give balls and other entertainments to attract the rich and influential. She encourages her sister to marry the shallow, handsome Remington in furtherance of her own ambitions. When Rosalind and Remington go abroad, she discovers his unfaithfulness and worthless character. Remington dies in Europe after she divorces him, leaving her free to marry the newly widowed Professor Trelawney, an early friend who is worthy of her intellect and personality.

This novel closely examines "social pushing" by those who do not belong to the old moneyed elite. The old Knickerbocker families looked askance at the nouveau riche, who could nonetheless break into society through wealth. Fawcett contrasts the sisters' ambitions with the down-to-earth attitude of their bachelor uncle, Seth Haviland, a confirmed cynic. Haviland has nothing but contempt for the aristocracy, bluntly giving his opinion of them when informed of Rosalind's intention to wed Remington:

They're most of 'em fools, you can see that with half an eye. A girl like Ros'lind could never stand 'em long, unless this head-over-heels attachment of hers lasted right on,—as I hope in the name of all that's merciful it may! They've got no place at all in our country. There isn't one of 'em that wouldn't have a king or an emperor here if he or she could be a grand duke or a princess.

The prejudice and hypocrisy exhibited by the upper crust and those who aspired to enter its ranks were a lifelong gall to Fawcett. He never passed up an opportunity to attack New York and American social pretensions, which he viewed as diametrically opposed to the democratic principles upon which the United States was founded.

Fawcett's most unusual work is the short novel *Solarion: A Romance* (1889), which illustrates the diversity of Fawcett's interests and his ability to present different types of material. The central figure of the tale is Kenneth Stafford, a wealthy, disfigured American who lives in seclusion at a Swiss chalet. He tells his story to his countryman Hugh Brookstayne, who is completing a scientific treatise at a local inn.

Before his disfigurement Stafford had been an eminent young scientist who specialized in electrical studies and experiments. While completing his education in Europe he had heard of a dying old scholar, Conrad Klotz, who possessed extraordinary knowledge on his chosen subject. Klotz reluctantly shared his insights with the persistent younger man, only withholding the contents of his last volume of electrical findings, still in manuscript. Intimating that the information was potentially harmful, Klotz on his death-bed extracted an oath from Stafford to burn the book without reading it.

The deceitful Stafford not only read the notes but also returned to New England to outfit a laboratory in which to conduct the required tests. Klotz had hypothesized that evolution could be pushed forward and sped up in lower animals by means of electrical stimulation of brain tissue. Stafford tries the process on several generations of dogs until he produces a magnificent leonine specimen, Solarion. The canine's intelligence is phenomenal, and he is soon able to speak and read, though the young scientist forbids him to do so out of his presence. Eventually, in the course of the many strange discussions Stafford and the animal have about love, immortality, and fame, they discover they are both in love with the same woman, Stafford's cousin Celia Effingham, who is attached to Solarion but does not love Stafford. When the horrified man forbids the dog to see Celia again, Solarion attacks and mutilates his face before being shot and killed by the scientist. A repentant Stafford then seeks exile in Switzerland.

In *The Adopted Daughter* (1892) Fawcett tries his hand at a more conventional romance. He conceives an idealized heroine and sets her against the backdrops of both promising America and decadent Europe, thus creating a fit conveyance for the triumph of virtue over entrenched corruption and avarice. Marie Rouncevalle, who lives in Europe with her American mother, is actually the daughter of a dishonest New York politico, Hugh Costello. When Costello decides he wants his child near him, she returns to the United States to visit. Contact with his pristine daughter gradually reshapes Costello into an honest man, after which Marie decides to remain in healthy robust America rather than risk the contaminations of the miasmic Old World.

Stanley Harrison points out that *The Adopted Daughter* reflects Fawcett's concept of an idealized society combining the attributes of both the New and Old Worlds: "a tempering of American crudeness with

LIPPINCOTT'S
MONTHLY MAGAZINE.

APRIL, 1887.

DOUGLAS DUANE.

THE PROLOGUE.

I.

LAMPS had begun to flicker in the wintry dusk. They gleamed with a flaring and very earthy mimicry of the first earlier stars which already had orbed clean little disks of silver above the city's numberless roofs. It was December, and though as yet slight snow had fallen with the dying year, an icy breath made the quick gusts cut like blades. The broad boulevard of lower Second Avenue gleamed quiet enough, for the hour that brings weary swarms of laboring-folk home from shops and factories across to the big East districts where so many of their dingy dwellings are huddled together, had not yet arrived. But the six-o'clock whistle soon sent its loud shriek, with eerie effect, to pierce the stillness of even this drowsy quarter. And then, in what seemed a strangely brief interval, the shabby throngs began pushing their way from a few of the near side-streets.

Varied indeed were the countless forms and faces for any eye that might care to look on them with more than indifferent heed. But none the less a universal sombreness and rustiness enfolded them in one visible fellowship of toil. Some of the men, women, girls or lads wore merry and smiling visages; others told of worriment and fatigue as plainly by their pallor and spareness as by the halting drag of their gait. The spacious avenue was suddenly alive with their dim swarms. Not a few, perhaps, were going hungry to boards where bread would greet them in no plenty and meat was yet more scarce. Along these same pavements, morning after morning and evening after evening, has passed for years this dreary procession, forever decimated by death yet forever swollen by fresh living recruits. It is a far more piteous parade than if mendicancy and not toil were the meaning of it; for here we

531

First page of Fawcett's serialized 1887 novel, in which he combines science fiction with a murder story

European manner and an enlivening of European stodginess with American vitality." American strength and resourcefulness are emphasized in the novel as father and daughter complement each other's qualities, with Marie through the strength of her purity aiding Costello to overcome his greed and crass ambition. Fawcett's love of his country is evident in this story, as the positive image of a wholesome American girl is portrayed as superior to that of both crooked upper-crust New York society and the doddering decadence of Europe. Fawcett felt a lifelong ambivalence toward the American republic. He was a great proponent of democratic principles while he was nonetheless more than a little abashed by the lack of polish and the cheerful ignorance displayed by many of his wealthy countrymen.

Fawcett shared many characteristics with Henry James and Edith Wharton. Like them, he was familiar with and disgusted by the upper-class American desire for recognition by old-world European nobility. All three writers were members of the upper class and explored misguided American social aspirations. Both James and Fawcett eventually settled in Britain, unable to stomach what they perceived as the shallow state of intellectual life in the United States.

In *American Push* (1892) Fawcett again writes of American expatriates in Europe and examines the yearning of the American nouveau riche for nobility. Alonzo Lispenard, a cultured artist, is second-generation wealthy and without many of the crass trappings of the more newly arrived. He is engaged to Kathleen Kennaird, the beautiful daughter of an ambitious mother who desires for her offspring a title as well as money. When Lispenard loses his money in a bank failure, the engagement is broken because of Mrs. Kinnaird's machinations. The artist's friend Eric Thaxton secures him a position as art administrator in the tiny country of Saltravia, ruled by the enlightened King Clarimond. Fawcett makes biting comments on the attitudes of Old World Europeans toward American upstarts. When Kathleen and her dreadful mother appear in Saltravia on a husband-hunting mission, two noblewomen discuss her case after they learn that she was once engaged to Lispenard:

> "Perhaps they had been married and then divorced," said the lady. "I have it on the best of authority that people in America marry there in one province (let us say Venezuela) this year, and are divorced with perfect ease the next year in some other province—let us say California."

Clarimond falls in love with Kathleen, much to her mother's delight, but gives her up to Lispenard when he discovers they are still attached. Fawcett shows that the "American push" is vulgar and suggests that sophisticated Europeans tolerate wealthy Americans in order to exploit them financially in return for useless titles and nebulous status.

Fawcett dedicated *New York* (1898), probably the best of his realistic slum novels, to James: "With the touch of a Velasquez you have painted many portraits. No living Briton or American ranks above you in your art. And so with reverence for the depth and reach of it, I venture to make you my modest offering, as one to whom your gifts have been for years a delight, and by whom your fame, now strengthening with time, was long ago foretold." Reminiscent of the grim urban fictions of his English contemporaries Arthur Morrison and George Gissing, the book accurately shows the bleak environment of many dwellers in turn-of-the-century industrial cities. Fawcett does not shy away from revealing the seedy side of America's largest metropolis,

the inevitable depravity that results when human beings live in close quarters and grinding poverty.

The novel chronicles the life of George Oliver, a promising young man of good family and a graduate of New York College who is drawn into an embezzlement scheme at the bank where he works. Manipulated by older men and a dishonest woman, the unfortunate youth draws a three-year prison sentence when the fraud is discovered. During his jail term his widowed mother loses her mind from grief and is cared for by his adopted sister Lydia, a mulatto. Almost immediately upon George's release, his mother dies and he gives the bulk of his inheritance to Lydia to reward her for her constancy.

Unable to find respectable employment, the repentant George goes to work in a bad part of the city, where he meets a Jewish slumlord, Lynsko, who discovers his past and attempts to blackmail him into participating in an arson scam. George exposes Lynsko with the help of a lawyer, Courtelyou, and the scoundrel is convicted of arson. The attorney, an emotionless egotist, refuses to aid George even after the youth is wounded in the apprehension of Lynsko.

An embittered George returns to obscurity and a fruitless search for work. At a mission service he meets philanthropist Frank Crevelling and his distant cousin, Doris Josselyn. After falling in love with Doris, George persuades her businessman father to employ him as secretary under an assumed name. He then wins Doris's love through upright conduct, despite the efforts of both Courtelyou and Crevelling to gain her affections for themselves. Doris serves as the catalyst that turns the former convict's introspective life outward; he is helped through his love for Doris to participate in life.

The book belongs to the realist tradition since it depicts lower-class life in New York without whitewash. A naturalistic theme is apparent in George's understanding of the forces shaping the lives of the slum denizens. While he is able to triumph over his environment because of his superior upbringing and education, others are not so fortunate. Police Captain Commisky, who commits suicide after a conviction for misappropriation of funds, is unable to comprehend the unraveling of his life brought about by powers beyond his control:

> He reviewed his past, from the time that he sold papers in lower Broadway, with a drunken father to beat him every night that he brought home less than a certain expected number of cents, to the time when he walked proudly in his gold buttons, conscious of how they became his manly beauty. Everything he had done of an immoral sort had seemed to him as natural as breathing. Nobody had ever blamed him; it had all literally been with him, as Doris had said to Courtelyou, like the teaching of the Spartan boy to steal.

Though never an Anglophile, Fawcett moved to England permanently in 1897; he died in the Chelsea district of London on 2 May 1904 after a short illness. He felt that the English publication conditions and literary environment were superior to those in America; his admiration for James, who had expatriated earlier, was another factor in his move. Fawcett also could not forgive his native land for its shallow society and lack of acceptance of his talent. His work had not received the critical attention he felt it deserved, and his bitter personal feuds with some of the New York newspaper critics still rankled.

Fawcett, who wrote too fast and too much, was not a great stylist, though nearly all his books contain something of value. The sheer volume of Fawcett's writing, besides the range of literary genres that he attempted, is impressive. In addition to his published books, he copyrighted more than twenty novels that never saw print. This massive ouevre, though not a viable excuse for sloppy writing, helps to explain the repetitiveness, dragging plots, and preachiness of which Fawcett was often guilty. Nonetheless, he was in his day a popular, innovative author who influenced younger writers by paving the way for American realism and naturalism. He also deserves respect for presenting an accurate portrait of upper-class New York society in the second half of the nineteenth century.

References:

Stanley R. Harrison, *Edgar Fawcett* (New York: Twayne, 1972);

Harrison, "Through a Nineteenth-Century Looking Glass: The Letters of Edgar Fawcett," *Tulane Studies in English,* 15 (1967): 107–157;

William H. Rideing, "Edgar Fawcett," in *The Boyhood of Living Authors* (New York: Crowell, 1887).

Rideing, "Edgar Fawcett," in his *Many Celebrities and a Few Others: A Bundle of Reminiscences* (New York: Doubleday, 1912);

Richard Henry Stoddard, "Edgar Fawcett," in *Poet's Homes,* by Stoddard and others (Boston: Osgood, 1879).

Papers:

The largest collection of Edgar Fawcett's manuscripts is held at the University of Virginia Library. Other archival material is held by the Library of Congress, Buffalo Public Library, Harvard University Library, Henry E. Huntington Library and Art Gallery, New York Public Library, Trinity College Library, and Yale University Library. Stanley R. Harrison also has several Fawcett manuscripts in his private collection.

Theodore Sedgwick Fay

(10 February 1807 – 24 November 1898)

Daniel A. Wells
University of South Florida

BOOKS: *Views in New-York and Its Environs from Accurate, Characteristic, & Picturesque Drawings, Taken on the Spot, Expressly for this Work* (New York: Peabody; London: O. Rich, 1831);

Dreams and Reveries of a Quiet Man, Consisting of the Little Genius and Other Essays, as One of the Editors of the *New-York Mirror* (New York: Harper, 1832);

Sketch of the Life of John Howard Payne, as Published in the Boston Evening Gazette, Compressed, (with Additions Bringing it Forward to a Later Period). By One of the Editors of the New-York Mirror: Now First Printed in a Separate Form, with an Appendix, Containing Selections of Poetry and Further Illustrations (Boston: Clapp, 1833);

Norman Leslie. A Tale of the Present Times, anonymous, 2 volumes (New York: Harper, 1835; London: Macrone, 1835; revised edition, New York: Putnam, 1869);

The Countess, 3 volumes (London: Bentley, 1840); republished as *The Countess Ida. A Tale of Berlin,* 2 volumes (New York: Harper, 1840);

The Double Duel; or, Hoboken, 3 volumes (London: Bentley, 1843); republished as *Hoboken: A Romance of New-York,* 2 volumes (New York: Harper, 1843); republished as *The Brothers; or, the Double Duel. A Romance of New York* (London: Bruce & Wyld, 1844);

Robert Rueful; or, A Lesson to Valetudinarians (Philadelphia: Godey, 1844);

Statement [relative to some business transactions with the Messrs. Harper & Brothers of New York, with correspondence] (Berlin, 1845);

Ulric; or, The Voices (New York: Appleton, 1851);

A Notice of the Death of Mrs. Laura Fay with Observations on Christianity, 2 parts (Bern, Switzerland, 1855–1856);

Die Sklavenmacht. Blicke in die Geschichte der Vereinigten Staaten von Amerika. Zur Erklärung der Rebellion von 1860–65 (Berlin: Stilke & Van Muyden, 1865);

Great Outline of Geography for High Schools and Families. Text-Book to Accompany the Universal Atlas (New York: Putnam, 1867);

Atlas to Fay's Great Outline of Geography for High Schools and Families, with a Text-Book (New York: Putnam,

1867); republished as *Atlas of Universal Geography for Libraries and Families* (New York: Putnam, 1869; revised, New York: Putnam, 1871);

Die Alabama-Frage (Leipzig: Brockhaus, 1872);

First Steps in Geography. A New Text-Book for Beginners (New York: Putnam, 1873);

The Three Germanys: Glimpses into Their History, 2 volumes (New York: Walker, 1889; New York & Chicago: Barnes, 1889; London: Low, 1889).

OTHER: *The New-York Mirror: A Weekly Journal Devoted to Literature and the Fine Arts,* edited by Fay, N. P. Willis, and G. P. Morris, 1–20 (1828–1835);

William Cox, *Crayon Sketches. By an Amateur,* 2 volumes, edited by Fay (New York: Conner & Cooke, 1833);

"American Deer-Hunt," in *The Premium; a Present for All Seasons: Consisting of Elegant Selections from British and American Writers of the Nineteenth Century* (Philadelphia: Carey, Lea & Blanchard, 1833), pp. 148–151;

"Snorers," "The Little, Hard-Faced Old Gentleman," "An Outline Sketch," "Editor's Study," and "The Author," anonymous, in *The Atlantic Club-Book: Being Sketches in Prose and Verse,* by various authors, 2 volumes (New York: Harper, 1834);

Epilogue, *Waldimar. A Tragedy in Five Acts,* by John J. Bailey (New York, 1834);

"Marie Jeanne," in *The Magnolia for 1837,* edited by Henry William Herbert (New York: Bancroft & Holley, 1836), pp. 149–174;

"Katrina Schuyler. A Tale of the Times of Charles II," in *The Token and Atlantic Souvenir. A Christmas and New Year's Present,* edited by S. G. Goodrich (Boston: Bowen, 1837), pp. 11–33;

"Song," "My Native Land," "Lines for Music," and "On Ship-Board," anonymous, in *The New-York Book of Poetry* (New York: Dearborn, 1837);

"The Death of Ulric," in *The Knickerbocker Gallery: A Testimonial to the Editor of the Knickerbocker Magazine from Its Contributors* (New York: Hueston, 1855), pp. 269–275.

SELECTED PERIODICAL PUBLICATIONS–UNCOLLECTED: "Beilage zu . . . der Deutschen Allgemeinen Zeitung . . . die Alabama-Frage," *Deutschen Allgmeinen Zeitung* (Leipzig), 12–24 March 1872;

"The Revolution of 1848 in Berlin. Personal Recollections," *Galaxy,* 16 (August 1873): 244–251; 16 (September 1873): 363–374;

"The Bearer of Dispatches in London," *Lippincott's Magazine,* 14 (September 1874): 370–375.

Theodore Sedgwick Fay was one of the most talented of the Knickerbocker school of writers who pursued a career in literature in the wake of the international success of Washington Irving. His popularity in the late 1820s, due to a facile, pleasant writing style and gentle, wry humor, led *New-York Mirror* editors George Pope Morris and Nathaniel Parker Willis to offer the twenty-one-year-old Fay coeditor status. In the mid 1830s Fay turned his talents to the novel, producing a best-seller with his first effort, *Norman Leslie. A Tale of the Present Times* (1835), which was attacked by Edgar Allan Poe in a famous slashing review. The success of *Norman Leslie* helped Fay win the first of a series of diplomatic appointments in Europe, where he spent the last sixty years of his life.

While he lived on the Continent, Fay published two more novels, including his best one, *The Countess* (1840); a book-length poem, *Ulric; or, The Voices* (1851); and a two-volume history of Germany, *The Three Germanys: Glimpses into Their History* (1889). His literary reputation, however, waned after his early success and descended into the obscurity that engulfed the entire Knickerbocker school, save for Irving. Fay nevertheless deserves appreciation as one of the most gifted magazine writers during the first golden age of American magazines, from the 1820s through the 1840s.

Fay was born on 10 February 1807 in New York City, the first child of lawyer John Dewey Fay and Caroline Broome Fay. His father, who had clerked in the law office of Alexander Hamilton, enjoyed the company of literary figures and the friendship of John Howard Payne and Samuel Woodworth. In his occasional column in the *Mirror* titled "The Little Genius," he lightly satirized the unusual events and odd characters of the New York scene. Fay began contributing his own articles to the magazine at the age of sixteen, continuing his father's "Little Genius" column after his father's death in 1825. Three years later he was admitted both to the New York bar and to the editorial staff of the *Mirror.*

In his essays in the *Mirror,* Fay cast a witty, perceptive eye on all facets of life in New York, producing just the kind of entertaining writing that Irving had pioneered and that New York readers loved. He wrote on literature, recommending writers such as Irving, James Kirke Paulding, and Joseph Addison, and politics, engaging in mild satire on municipal governance, presidential campaigns, and the influence of the press on elections. He ranged widely, commenting on everything from social problems, such as dirty streets, malodorous cemeteries, and wretched lives of the homeless, to the theater. The essays he collected in the two-volume *Dreams and Reveries of a Quiet Man, Consisting of the Little Genius and Other Essays* (1832) exhibit much more substance than implied by the title description and many more words than one would expect from "a quiet man."

Of particular interest is "Solitary Confinement," which in its style of manic speech and hyperactive memory anticipates Poe: "I am the most crushed and wretched of all beings. I have the horror of death, without its peace. I am *buried alive* . . . I am growing to be something different from other human beings. Could these massive walls be suddenly rent apart, and I appear to some festive assembly, what a sight of horror I should present. . . . No-no-no-madness–darkness . . . Merciful God!" More typical are the sarcastic extracts in "From the Diary of an Editor." He writes that the editor is misperceived as "a sort of divinity." Although many think that "mortals lay gifts at his shrine" and

NORMAN LESLIE.

A TALE OF THE PRESENT TIMES.

"You shall see anon; 'tis a knavish piece of work."
Hamlet.

IN TWO VOLUMES.

VOL. I.

NEW-YORK:

PUBLISHED BY HARPER & BROTHERS,
NO. 82 CLIFF-STREET.

1835.

Title page for Fay's first novel, which Edgar Allan Poe attacked as "a monstrous piece of absurdity and incongruity"

native city (though like Irving he spent a great deal of his life away from it) and a deep awareness of the impermanence of earthly things. Both are present in an introduction and historical note he wrote for a book of engravings, *Views in New-York and Its Environs from Accurate, Characteristic, & Picturesque Drawings, Taken on the Spot, Expressly for this Work* (1831), a type of book popular in a day when publishers sought to profit from the civic pride of Americans in the great new architectural monuments resulting from commercial expansion. At first Fay in his introduction stresses the theme of the coming of age of the city. But despite his celebration of change, Fay, in true Janus-like Knickerbocker fashion, cannot help but dwell on the alienating effect of change on a typical member of the older generation who, Rip Van Winkle-like, was so "full of curious yet mournful recollections" that the new city "which has thus grown up under his eye, only makes him feel like a stranger."

In 1833 Fay published two works. The first, *Sketch of the Life of John Howard Payne,* a biography of his father's friend, was a detailed, factual account of Payne's career up to his triumphant return to New York in 1832. He also edited English-born William Cox's *Mirror* contributions under the title *Crayon Sketches. By an Amateur.* The anonymous publication of *Crayon Sketches* and the similarity of the essays in it to Fay's led many to believe Fay was the author, a misconception he publicly denied. Fay, though, was responsible for the selections, the dedication—to Irving for "the treasures which you have added to the English language"—and the preface, in which he paid tribute to Cox's genius in transforming minutiae into telling caricatures of the age. Cox's essays, like Fay's, are "bombastically about nothing . . . struck out in the heat of the moment, intended but for a careless, passing glance, and then to be thrown aside and forgotten." Like all magazine writing, they were destined for oblivion unless preserved in book form. Fay was trying to do for Cox what *Dreams and Reveries of a Quiet Man* had done for him a year before.

Also in 1833 Fay married Laura Gardenier, and shortly thereafter the newlyweds embarked on a European trip that unexpectedly lasted three years. The trip was undertaken at the urging of doctors alarmed at a loss of weight so precipitous that Fay was unable to perform his editorial duties at the *Mirror.* The magazine's readers were told that Fay had become "an invalid, with slender hope of recovery." He was strong enough, however, to provide sketches of his travel experiences for the *Mirror* under the title "The Minute Book" from April 1834 to June 1835, the first of which was praised in *The Knickerbocker Magazine* (June 1834) for combining "the ease and grace of Goldsmith, and the quiet and oblique humor of Irving." The *Knickerbocker* announced that the essays would be published in book form, but

that contributors "supply him with specimens of every graceful and splendid treasure that genius or industry put forth," the reality is somewhat different, as a list of a typical morning's activities indicates: "read and reviewed three novels, a quarto dictionary, and three octavo volumes of travels; wrote an account of the present state of the world, cut up the legislature and the corporation, and criticised the performances at the two theaters last evening; also the grand oratorio, and Mr. Wiseacre's lectures on ornithology; received and rejected nine communications, and went to a dinner." Such passages illustrate the versatility, wit, and sophistication for which New York was known. Few produced them as readily as Fay, forming the basis of his contemporary reputation.

The other chief Knickerbocker characteristics Fay had in abundance were chauvinistic devotion to his no evidence exists that they ever were. In addition, five short pieces by the convalescing author made their way into *The Atlantic Club-Book: Being Sketches in Prose and Verse,* an 1834 anthology of New York authors. To cap a busy year for one so indisposed, Fay wrote an epilogue to John J. Bailey's *Waldimar. A Tragedy in Five Acts,* which was privately distributed among the playwright's friends.

Sometime during his stay in Europe, Fay completed his first novel *Norman Leslie. A Tale of the Present Times,* which was published before Fay returned to America. The first printing sold out in two weeks, and a dramatization drew crowds at the Bowery Theater. As further proof of its popularity, a single benefit performance in February netted the needy author $750. In New York literary circles Fay was well liked and well connected, so despite its weaknesses *Norman Leslie* won a warm critical reception. In Richmond, though, Poe, the eternal outsider, fumed. Jealous of the ways that New York and Boston literary cliques "bepuffed" and "beplastered" each other's works with extravagant praise, Poe launched a vicious attack on *Norman Leslie,* its author, and the New York literati in the December *Southern Literary Messenger,* the first number Poe edited, thus initiating for the sake of making his own reputation what Sidney P. Moss in his 1963 book called "Poe's Literary Battles."

For the most part Poe's rollicking excoriation of Fay and his novel is a just analysis. Fay's plot, he wrote, "is a monstrous piece of absurdity and incongruity"; his characters "have no character"; his style "is unworthy of a school-boy"; and as for grammar, "There is not a single page of *Norman Leslie* in which even a school-boy would fail to detect at least two or three gross errors." Altogether *Norman Leslie* is "the most inestimable piece of balderdash with which the common sense of the good people of America was ever so openly or so villainously insulted." *Norman Leslie* surely has its faults, especially in not adequately displaying Fay's wit and sprightly style, but it fares well when compared to the absurdities and crudities of plot, character, and style to be found in the best works of Fay's contemporaries. The author apologized for the shortcomings of his novel in a preface to the second edition late in 1835, admitting that "It was written with the unsettled mind of a traveller in the stolen intervals of more imperative occupations" and that he had sent the manuscript to the publishers "before it had received the time and care which it was my intention to bestow."

In January 1836 Fay wrote an essay for the *Mirror,* "The Successful Novel," in which he satirized Poe as "Mr. Bulldog" of the "Southern Literary Passenger." He also criticized other captious critics whose jealous scorn is heaped on any young writer who meets with popular success. Poe bore Fay no lasting enmity. He did belittle Fay once again in his "Autography" series in *Graham's* (November 1841) but also published eight of Fay's essays on Shakespeare in that magazine. Poe was forgiven in turn when he joined the *Mirror* staff in 1844 and took Fay's former position alongside Morris and Willis.

In Fay's tale the villain is the profligate Count Clermont, who is in a romantic tug-of-war with Leslie over the charms of the stately but cold Flora Temple of New York. Leslie is the traditional noble, brooding romantic hero, paralyzed by doubts, natural reticence, and "fatal necessity." He is not particularly ingenious or resourceful, but he is, like all of Fay's heroes, virtuous and patient. Clermont conspires to smear Leslie with charges of cowardice, gambling, and finally murder, of which Leslie is acquitted at the end of the first volume. After much plot contrivance, ten years, and much shape-shifting by the ever-resourceful villain who finally pays for his sins, Flora and Leslie are restored to each other in a happy ending. Into the fabric of the story Fay incorporates attacks on his favorite targets: duelling— that "dark unchristian" vestige of a medieval past, Roman Catholicism, the fashionable world of the wealthy, and the irresponsibility of the rabble-rousing press.

In the spring of 1836 Fay again returned to Europe for the restoration of his health, which, reported the *Mirror* in June, "was materially benefited, but not altogether restored by his former tour." Actually Fay was in England as secretary to the U.S. Minister to the Court of St. James, Irving's old post. Fay deserved the position, according to an assertion in the September 1836 *Knickerbocker,* because "he possesses a pure heart, pleasing manners, modest pretensions, and decided talent." He managed to find time to finish a short satire, "The Adventures of Mr. Robert Rueful," which was serialized in the *Mirror* in early 1837. (Seven years later it was published independently as *Robert Rueful; or, A Lesson to Valetudinarians,* a seventy-page book that was given away free with new subscriptions to *Godey's Lady's Book.*) Also in 1837 Fay contributed short pieces to the popular gift books *The Magnolia* and *The Token* and poems to *The New-York Book of Poetry.* By the end of the year President Martin Van Buren appointed Fay secretary to the American legation at Berlin, where he served for the next sixteen years.

Although Fay has been listed as the author of the anonymously published *Sydney Clifton; or, Vicissitudes in Both Hemispheres* (1839) by *Cyclopaedia of American Literature* (1855), *The National Union Catalogue,* and other usually reliable sources, contemporary evidence suggests otherwise. Fay's *Mirror* announced *Sydney Clifton* as a work by "one of our citizens" in the same paragraph of

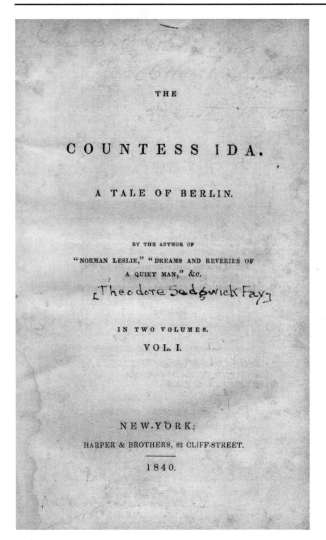

THE

COUNTESS IDA.

A TALE OF BERLIN.

BY THE AUTHOR OF
"NORMAN LESLIE," "DREAMS AND REVERIES OF
A QUIET MAN," &c.

Theodore Sedgwick Fay

IN TWO VOLUMES.

VOL. I.

NEW-YORK:
HARPER & BROTHERS, 82 CLIFF-STREET.

1840.

Title page for the American edition of Fay's second novel, in which he caricatures Poe

literary news that mentioned the imminent London publication of *The Countess,* making no connection between Fay and the novel. In addition, none of the title pages of Fay's subsequent books, which listed all of his published volumes, included *Sydney Clifton.* Internal evidence also discounts Fay's authorship. Although a few aspects of *Sydney Clifton* do suggest Fay–dueling, trips to Europe, the falsely accused hero, and a perfumed toad named Elton Arabesque who resembles Poe in drag and who tries to guess the authorship of Clifton's anonymously published stories–the prose style is stiff, awkward, and cliché-ridden, not at all like Fay's. The actual author of *Sydney Clifton* was George D. Strong, a New York bank president and a one-time West Indian merchant, unmasked as author by Lewis Gaylord Clarke in his August 1839 *Knickerbocker* review of the novel. Strong's identity as author was confirmed by Eugene Exman in his history of the house of Harper, *The Brothers Harper* (1965).

Contemporary critics viewed Fay's second novel, *The Countess,* which was published in London before being published in the United States as *The Countess Ida. A Tale of Berlin,* as his best work of fiction. In London the *Literary Gazette* called it "a sensation in the literary circles," and the *Court Journal* praised it as "*The* novel of the season." American reviewers remarked on the great advancement in Fay's powers as a novelist. The friendly *Mirror* (6 June 1840) referred to *The Countess Ida* as "the Best American novel of the day" and "much the best thing Mr. Fay has ever done." Even the staid *North American Review* (October 1840) opened its laudatory review by admitting that "the previous writings of Mr. Fay had not prepared us for the superior merit of the work before us." The reviewer praised the book for its polished writing style, vigorous characterizations, and weighty reflections on life. The dissenters were the reviewers for the *Casket* (July 1840) and the usually complimentary *Knickerbocker* (July 1840), which bemoaned the "piled-up agony" and likened it to a stage melodrama "in which the scene-shifters come in now and then to pick up the dead bodies, and sweep the stage for more distress in the next." *The Countess* was a natural for the theater, and a dramatization was prepared by the manager of the Bowery Theater.

The Countess is one of the earliest examples in American fiction of the international theme. Set in Berlin at the time of the French Revolution, the overwrought novel centers around Claude Wyndham's love for Ida Carolan, the daughter of proud aristocrats, and Wyndham's attempts to rescue her from a forced marriage to an English libertine, Lord Elkington, son of the Earl of Beverly, without resorting to chicanery or dueling, which he has foresworn. Wyndham's background is shrouded in mystery until the end of the novel, when he is revealed to be the eldest son of the Earl of Beverly, half-brother to Elkington. Interesting secondary characters appear in the form of the comical Digbys, English forerunners of Henry James's gauche, nouveau riche American travelers in Europe.

The most interesting minor character is an emaciated, brooding man "with a pale, melancholy face" and "uncommonly brilliant" eyes named Rossi, one of the earliest stand-ins for Poe in American fiction. Always "particularly anxious to appear well dressed" but now shabby in appearance with a countenance of profound grief, Rossi "ushered" Wyndham into his delapidated rooms, "desolate and almost unfurnished," that strike the hero "with peculiar mournfulness." Recently Rossi had been brought home "in a state of insensibility, which was succeeded by a raging delirium." Wyndham, who "never saw a more unhappy creature," offers Rossi financial support. But the ungrateful supplicant proves unworthy of sympathy as he succumbs to "intemperance" and dies, "a mind undisciplined–a heart not cultivated properly–passions without restraint or religion to govern them . . . [and a] want of education and moral principle." The scene, the description, Rossi's fascination with "intellectual beauty," and his manic speech make Rossi the second of Fay's public replies to the tormentor of Norman Leslie. The sequence with Rossi also reveals new social concerns in Fay's work, especially sympathy for the poor imprisoned for debt, which had been the chief social cause for Fay's lawyer-father.

In a novel of unusually complex plot twists, one of the oddest and most powerful is the final one, where the characters are thrown into the French Revolution at the height of the Reign of Terror. Fay vividly renders the violent anarchy of the age, the palpable fear of saying the wrong thing to the wrong person, the limp bodies hanging from lampposts, the bloodthirsty mobs, and the beheading of Wyndham's former servant. In this hell the hero proves his manhood by exposing the villainous Elkington, discovering his true identity, and rescuing and marrying Ida.

In his last novel, which was first published in London as *The Double Duel; or, Hoboken* (1843) and then in New York as *Hoboken: A Romance of New-York,* Fay again dwells on the evils of dueling, the pastoral "Elysian Fields" of Hoboken being the favored location for such contests. Through misperceptions and the conspiracies of others, rational and contemplative Harry Lennox and his impetuous brother, Frank, lose fortune and friends. In the climactic duel Frank Lennox even loses his life, plunging his brother into despair. Although the novel marks no advance in Fay's growth as a novelist, it accentuates a theme that did not appear as obtrusively before–his characters' thoughtful struggles with religious faith before finally and passionately embracing Christianity. Fay's denouement involves the conversion experience of Harry Lennox and his simultaneous rejection of godless materialism and the vestigial scientism of the Enlightenment.

In 1845 Fay's long-running discontent with his publisher became a matter of public record as he published his *Statement,* a seventy-eight-page document detailing his business dealings with the Harpers. As Exman reveals in *The Brothers Harper,* "no author was to give them [the Harpers] so much trouble as Theodore Sedgwick Fay." The Harpers' troubles with Fay began when they advanced him $1,000 for the second edition of *Norman Leslie* and for a promised second novel, as well as an additional loan of $1,500 for his subsequent trip to Europe. After waiting patiently for three years for the second novel, the Harpers threatened Fay with a lawsuit, upon which he sent them a completed manuscript of *The Countess Ida.* Sales almost immediately required a second printing of perhaps another thousand copies. The small printing of nine hundred copies of *Hoboken,* however, did not sell enough to pay the expenses of publication, leaving the beleaguered Fay still indebted to the Harpers for $1,200.

On 11 July 1844 Fay fired off a letter from Berlin to John Harper, now mayor of New York, demanding to know the basis of his continuing indebtedness and asking for justice. When he did not receive a satisfactory reply, Fay in March 1845 published a thirty-two-page pamphlet as an open letter laying out his side of the controversy, appealing to public opinion and hoping to wound the Harpers financially. He also appealed to Charles Sumner, whom he had befriended when the Bostonian visited Berlin in 1839 and to whom he had dedicated *Hoboken,* to intercede with the Harpers on his behalf. Sumner arranged for arbitration of the matter, but the arbitrators decided for the Harpers, and the copies of Fay's statement, which had arrived in New York via the steamship *Great Western,* were intercepted and suppressed. He then published his longer *Statement* (1845), a pamphlet that Exman with some exaggeration calls a "portrayal of a distraught and deeply disturbed mind searching to find evidence that will prove its own integrity." As it turns out, the Harpers' accounting was probably correct, and Fay must have overlooked his investment in a stock deal with his colleague Morris years before. The vengeful Fay was so angry, though, that he tried to convince William Hickling Prescott, a highly valued Harper author for whom Fay was acting as agent with German publishers, to seek a different publishing house for his next work.

The wordiness and didacticism that made *Hoboken* so tedious also mars Fay's one venture into extended narrative poetry, *Ulric; or, The Voices* (1851). Ulric is a German knight during the early years of the Protestant Reformation. The voices of the subtitle are his inner spirits, one of which, the Principle of Good, not surprisingly finally triumphs over the emissary of the devil. The poem reminded contemporary reviewers of the dueling voices of faith and skepticism in Alfred Tennyson's "The Two Voices" (1842).

Fay's conscientiousness as a diplomat in Berlin was rewarded in 1853 with his appointment as minister to Switzerland, a post he held until President Abraham Lincoln replaced him in 1861. During Fay's tenure in Bern his wife, Laura, died, eliciting from the stricken husband a thirty-two-page work, "An Account of the Death of his Wife, Mrs. Laura Fay, with Observations on Christianity" (1856). Upon retirement Fay settled in Germany, married a native German, and spent the rest of his life in Blasewitz, near Dresden, and in Berlin. There he abandoned fiction and poetry for geography and history, seeking to continue through his writings his ambassadorial role: he aimed to explain the United States to Germans in *Die Sklavenmacht. Blicke in die Geschichte der Vereinigten Staaten von Amerika* (1865) and *Die Alabama-Frage* (1872), and to enlighten Americans about the rest of the world in *Great Outline of Geography for High Schools and Families* (1867) and the accompanying *Atlas* (1867).

Perhaps as part of its agreement with Fay, Putnam, the publisher of his later nonfiction, brought out a revised version of *Norman Leslie* in 1869. In his preface Fay admitted that he did not "attempt to remove all its evidences of youthfulness and inexperience," a neglect that was only too evident to reviewers. The reviewer for *Harper's Monthly* (August 1869) said the book "would be twice as good if it were half as long" and called the brief preface the best part of the book. *The Overland Monthly* (December 1869) reviewer scorned Fay's romantic conventions as typical of the "marks of crudeness and immaturity" to be found in the fiction of forty years ago.

Fay's responsibilities during his quarter century of foreign service ranged from the usual looking after American travelers to courting influential Europeans, including Friedrich Wilhelm IV, the king of Prussia. In 1857, the year he obtained French and English visas for Herman Melville (who was visiting Bern), Fay was instrumental in avoiding an open conflict between Switzerland and Germany over control of the Swiss region around Neuchâtel. After intense personal diplomacy, including a special appeal to shared religious values directly with Friedrich Wilhelm, Fay succeeded in brokering an agreement that avoided bloodshed and ceded Neuchâtel to Switzerland, earning him praise and gratitude from all sides, especially from Otto von Bismarck. Fay was also a firsthand witness when revolution broke out in Berlin in 1848 and again in 1866 and 1870. In a two-part essay, "The Revolution of 1848 in Berlin. Personal Recollections," published in the August and September 1873 issues of *The Galaxy*, Fay wrote like an excited young reporter, recounting his experience of the kind of anarchistic violence he had only imagined in *The Countess*.

It is hardly surprising that Fay, like Irving so many years before, chose to focus on history in his final published work, a massive two-volume history of his adopted country, *The Three Germanys: Glimpses into Their History*. Having for sixty years beheld with his own eyes "as from a good seat in a theater" earth-shaking events, Fay traces through German history the victories of his own twin allegiances—democracy and Christianity—and attacks what he perceives to be the main threats to those allegiances—science, socialism, materialism, atheism, and Jesuitism. In some of his final printed words he warned that "Because the assertion that the masses are oppressed is true" and that "their misery is real," horrible revolution would sweep Europe and out of it would rise "a world dictator" who would inflict "a despotism such as has never yet been seen." Fay mercifully did not live to see his prediction come true. He died in Berlin on 24 November 1898 at the age of ninety-one.

References:

Anonymous, "Fay's *Countess Ida*," North American Review, 51 (October 1840): 434–457;

James T. Callow, *Kindred Spirits, Knickerbocker Writers and American Artists, 1807–1855* (Chapel Hill: University of North Carolina Press, 1967), pp. 111–130;

Eugene Exman, *The Brothers Harper* (New York: Harper, 1965), pp. 75–77, 98–99, 143–144, 211–229;

Edward Halsey Foster, foreward to *Norman Leslie* (New York: Garrett, 1969);

Sidney P. Moss, *Poe's Literary Battles: The Critic in the Context of His Literary Milieu* (Durham, N.C.: Duke University Press, 1963), pp. 39–46, 50–58, 60–68;

Frank Luther Mott, *A History of American Magazines, 1741–1850* (Cambridge, Mass.: Harvard University Press, 1938);

Edward C. Pierce, ed., *Memoirs and Letters of Charles Sumner, II* (Boston: Roberts, 1878);

Edgar Allan Poe, "*Norman Leslie*," Southern Literary Messenger, 2 (December 1835): 54–57;

Burton R. Pollin, "Poe's 'Mystification': Its Source in Fay's *Norman Leslie*," Mississippi Quarterly, 25 (Spring 1972): 111–130;

Thomas R. Price, "Samuel Woodworth and Theodore Sedgwick Fay: Two Nineteenth-Century Literati," dissertation, Pennsylvania State University, 1971;

Kendall B. Taft, "Theodore Sedgwick Fay," in his *Minor Knickerbockers* (New York: American Book, 1947), pp. 234–248.

Mary Hallock Foote

(19 November 1847 – 25 June 1938)

Kent P. Ljungquist
Worcester Polytechnic Institute

See also the Foote entries in *DLB 186: Nineteenth-Century American Western Writers* and *DLB 188: American Book and Magazine Illustrators to 1920.*

BOOKS: *The Led-Horse Claim: A Romance of the Mining Camps* (Boston: Osgood, 1883);

John Bodewin's Testimony (Boston: Ticknor, 1886);

The Last Assembly Ball, and The Fate of a Voice (Boston & New York: Houghton, Mifflin, 1889);

The Chosen Valley (Boston & New York: Houghton, Mifflin, 1892);

Coeur d'Alene (Boston & New York: Houghton, Mifflin, 1894);

In Exile and Other Stories (Boston & New York: Houghton, Mifflin, 1894);

The Cup of Trembling and Other Stories (Boston & New York: Houghton, Mifflin, 1895);

The Little-Fig Tree Stories (Boston & New York: Houghton, Mifflin, 1899);

The Prodigal (Boston & New York: Houghton, Mifflin, 1900);

The Desert and the Sown (Boston & New York: Houghton, Mifflin, 1902);

A Touch of Sun and Other Stories (Boston & New York: Houghton, Mifflin, 1903);

The Royal Americans (Boston & New York: Houghton Mifflin, 1910);

A Picked Company: A Novel (Boston & New York: Houghton Mifflin, 1912);

The Valley Road (Boston & New York: Houghton Mifflin, 1915);

Edith Bonham (Boston & New York: Houghton Mifflin, 1917);

The Ground-Swell (Boston & New York: Houghton Mifflin, 1919);

A Victorian Gentlewoman in the Far West: The Reminiscences of Mary Hallock Foote, edited, with an introduction, by Rodman W. Paul (San Marino, Cal.: Huntington Library, 1972);

Mary Hallock Foote

Idaho Stories and Far West Illustrations of Mary Hallock Foote, compiled by Barbara Taylor Cragg, Dennis M. Walsh, and Mary Ellen Williams Walsh (Pocatello: Idaho State University Press, 1988).

OTHER: "Gideon's Knock," in *The Spinners' Book of Fiction* (San Francisco: Elder, 1907), pp. 77–91.

SELECTED PERIODICAL PUBLICATIONS–
UNCOLLECTED: "A California Mining Camp," *Scribner's Monthly,* 15 (February 1878): 480–493;

"A Sea-Port on the Pacific," *Scribner's Monthly,* 16 (August 1878): 449–460;

"A Story of the Dry Season," *Scribner's Monthly,* 18 (September 1879): 766–781;

"Pictures of the Far West," *Century Illustrated Magazine,* 37–39 (November 1888 – November 1889);

"The Borrowed Shift," *Land of Sunshine,* 10 (December 1898): 13–24;

"How the Pump Stopped at the Morning Watch," *Century Illustrated Magazine,* 58 (July 1899): 469–472;

"The Eleventh Hour," *Century Illustrated Magazine,* 71 (January 1906): 485–493.

Mary Hallock Foote began her literary career by writing vivid stories, sketches, and novels about mining camps in the West. Unlike Bret Harte, who had little firsthand knowledge of the subject, Foote was able to study the locales, personalities, conflicts, activities, and business interests associated with Western mining in the nineteenth century. Married to an engineer whose career took his family to a variety of Western locales, she was often asked to provide stories and illustrations of these settings for Eastern readers. Tinged with romance and melodrama, her early stories reached a wide readership. As her fiction matured, romantic elements and stock situations diminished, and she explored the tensions between the dreams and professional aspirations of her male characters and the civilizing instincts and familial relationships cherished by her female characters. After the turn of the century she wrote several novels that surpassed her mining stories in refinement of theme and technique, but these later works failed to have a wide appeal.

Born Mary Anna Hallock on 19 November 1847 on a farm near Milton, a town not far from Poughkeepsie, New York, this writer who came to be associated with the West was educated in the East, and the values derived from her Quaker upbringing and Eastern background often surfaced in her fiction. Young Mary, who was called Molly, and her three older siblings, Philadelphia, Tom, and Bessie, were devoted to their mother, Ann Burling Hallock. Her father, Nathaniel Hallock, was an energetic farmer whose library was stocked with periodicals and volumes of poetry, the source of much of her early reading. Among the Victorian poets, she favored Alfred, Lord Tennyson. First attending Poughkeepsie Female Collegiate Seminary, she went on to study art at the women's school of design at the Cooper Institute. She had four of her drawings published in A. D. Richardson's *Beyond the Mississippi* in 1867 and soon established herself as an illustrator. Her drawings were featured in *The Century Illustrated Magazine* as well as in an 1874 edition of Henry Wadsworth Longfellow's *The Hanging of the Crane*

and an 1876 edition of Nathaniel Hawthorne's *The Scarlet Letter.*

One of Hallock's classmates at the Cooper Institute was Helena de Kay, with whom she developed the most intense and sustained friendship of her life. The daughter of a prominent New York family, Helena helped introduce Hallock to the social life of the city. After the two women married–Mary to Arthur De Wint Foote and Helena to Richard Watson Gilder, the founding editor of *The Century Illustrated Magazine*–and began living their disparate lives, they carried on an extensive correspondence, exchanging more than five hundred letters that bridged the social divide and the great distances that threatened to separate them. Some commentators on Foote feel that her correspondence with her friend is among her finest writing.

On 9 February 1876 Mary Hallock married Arthur DeWint Foote, an ambitious mining engineer who had studied at the Sheffield Scientific School of Yale University. The late nineteenth century was the era of the heroic engineer, whose drive, energy, imagination, and fortitude were instrumental in developing the frontier West. While Hallock must have been impressed by her future husband's professional commitment, she expressed mixed feelings about the marriage. Before proposing, Arthur Foote had completed an apprenticeship in civil engineering in Nevada and California. The mining of precious materials required a knowledge of marketing, machinery, and litigation and yet offered uncertain economic prospects. Following her husband's dream meant leaving the ties of friendship and family in the East and transplanting her life to inhospitable environments. Having worked hard to refine her technique in woodcut illustration, Hallock also had her own aspirations that she knew would be better served by remaining in the East. Despite her reservations, Mary Hallock Foote traveled west to join her husband in New Almaden, California, where Arthur was resident engineer in a quicksilver mine. As she acknowledged in her posthumously published autobiography edited by Rodman W. Paul, *A Victorian Gentlewoman in the Far West: The Reminiscences of Mary Hallock Foote* (1972), "No girl ever wanted less to 'go West' with any man, or paid a man a greater compliment by doing so."

The first literary fruit of Foote's California experience was her nonfiction description "A California Mining Camp," published in *Scribner's Monthly* in February 1878. She may have written the piece to please her friends the Gilders, who sensed the literary potential of the picturesque lives of the miners; however, critic Lee Ann Johnson suggests that this early sketch is a pastiche, the result of editorial intervention on the part of her Eastern friends, who patched together fragments from her letters. The New Almaden experience proved

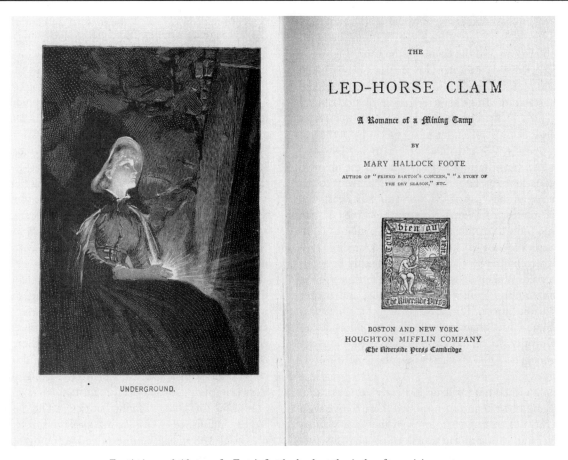

THE

LED-HORSE CLAIM

A Romance of a Mining Camp

BY

MARY HALLOCK FOOTE

AUTHOR OF "FRIEND BARTON'S CONCERN," "A STORY OF
THE DRY SEASON," ETC.

BOSTON AND NEW YORK
HOUGHTON MIFFLIN COMPANY
The Riverside Press Cambridge

UNDERGROUND.

Frontispiece and title page for Foote's first book, about the rivalry of two mining camps

short-lived as her husband took on freelance assignments outside the San Francisco area. With her first child, Arthur Burling Foote, who was born 29 April 1877, she took up temporary residence in Santa Cruz, southwest of New Almaden.

In a story from this period in her life, "In Exile," which was first published in *The Atlantic Monthly* in 1881 and later served as the title story of her first collection, *In Exile and Other Stories* (1894), Foote establishes several themes that surface in her later fiction. The story traces the fitful courtship of Frances Newell, a schoolteacher from the East, by Arnold, a young mining engineer. With its obvious parallels to the lives of the Footes, the story offers the theme of exile from the East and its values. Foote downplays romantic love in favor of submission to exigent circumstances. A series of incidents beyond the characters' control—Frances's illness, Arnold's rejection by an eastern amour—compel them to confront their loneliness and isolation. Seasonal imagery, as Johnson notes, accentuates Frances's predicament: her lassitude during the first dry season is followed by an illness during the second. The aridity of the West challenges and repels the female protagonist, replicating

Foote's responses. The matching of physical and emotional settings is skillfully handled, though the ending does not entirely avoid melodrama. As she writes in *A Victorian Gentlewoman in the Far West,* Foote felt that the first part of the story, "a dry-season episode, breaking off on a minor key," was faithful to the New Almaden setting. In response to William Dean Howells's comment that the somber opening was "too wantonly sad," Foote added "a second part ending in happiness and rains!"

In 1878, when her husband accepted a position in Deadwood, South Dakota, Foote returned home to Milton. South Dakota offered no permanent prospects, and when her husband turned to fresh opportunities in Colorado, Foote worked at home on illustrations and fiction. She did illustrations for works by the nature writer John Burroughs, and her story "Friend Barton's Concern" (1879), collected in *In Exile and Other Stories,* drew upon her Quaker background. During her adolescence she had read the poetry of John Greenleaf Whittier and tales such as Hawthorne's "The Gentle Boy," but she was impatient with fiction that failed to reflect accurately the lives of Quaker families. When the story was published, family members were bothered by what they thought was a challenge to the father's choice between family obligations and the claims of the Inner Light.

Acknowledging the tension that lay beneath the surface calm of the Quaker household, Foote is particularly interested in the characterization of her central female figure, Dorothy, whom she called, in *A Victorian Gentlewoman in the Far West,* "an early specimen of the girl of today with a will and mind of her own." Dorothy assumes significant family responsibility in the absence of her conscientious father, who is called away to air concerns about the War of 1812. She initially resists the romantic interest of Walter Evesham. Dorothy is like many of Foote's female protagonists—vigilant, composed, reserved but far too practical to qualify as a full-blown romantic heroine. The relationship between Dorothy and Walter does not develop until a violent rainstorm compels Walter to offer comfort and shelter to the Barton family. Their relationship blossoms less from romantic love than from the limited options available to Dorothy. Foote, moreover, skillfully develops the conflict between Quaker values and those of the Evesham family.

Foote visited her husband in Leadville, Colorado, in the spring of 1879 and then moved there to live with him in 1880. The carbonate ores in the area yielded both silver and lead and had transformed a small settlement into a community of nearly thirty thousand inhabitants. For most of her time in Leadville, she remained in a one-room cabin, distanced from the rambunctious life of the town. The Footes received some notable visitors during this period, including Clarence King of the U.S. Geological Survey and the novelist Helen Hunt Jackson.

After Arthur Foote assumed a managerial role in the Adelaide Consolidated Silver Mining Company, a bitter conflict erupted between miners and owners, leading to a strike, which was followed by a boundary dispute with a rival mine. In the standoff between the two mines Foote saw something akin to the Montague-Capulet feud, which she transformed into the plot of *The Led-Horse Claim: A Romance of the Mining Camps* (1883). In the relationship of George Hilgard, representing the Led-Horse mine, and Cecil Conrath, whose brother manages the Shoshone mine, Foote mixed romance with realism. She based characters on the personalities from her and her husband's circle of associates. Cecil's encounter with the dark, unsettling forces of nature, embodied in her descent into the Led-Horse mine, was based on Foote's own subterranean exploration. Looking back on her days in Leadville, she described herself in a 1922 letter as "one of the 'protected' women of that time," a perspective that may have prevented her from creating a fully developed

novel of realism. Though she preferred to end the story with the lovers never to see each other again, the publisher Gilder would not allow such a conclusion. She developed a subdued happy ending for the story, and the novel proved to be a modest popular success.

In 1882 Foote returned to Milton, where her daughter, Betty, was born on 9 September 1882. She and the children, along with her sister Bessie and Bessie's husband, John Sherman, joined her husband in Idaho at the site of his ambitious new project—the irrigation of arid land near the Snake River. Upon her arrival she turned to an unfinished Leadville fiction, which again was based on a boundary dispute between two mines. Though the title character of *John Bodewin's Testimony* (1886) is a rather muted frontier hero, Foote included sufficient local detail to fortify her reputation as a novelist of the West. She reported to Helena Gilder that she had begun to receive letters and clippings from miners, who saw her as an authentic reporter of their experiences. Unlike Harte, who relied on primitive character types and sentimental touches, Foote addressed the actual business of mining: land disputes, courtroom scenes, and the problematic financing of Western mining by multiple interests.

One of Foote's Idaho stories, "The Fate of a Voice," published in *The Last Assembly Ball, and The Fate of a Voice* (1889), can be interpreted autobiographically. Madeline Hendrie, during a visit to her sister in the Wallula River Canyon area, refuses the marriage proposal of a young mining engineer. In doing so, she rejects "the common destiny of woman" to follow her desire to become an accomplished singer. The climax of the story is the engineer's rescue of Madeline from a fall, resulting in a shock to her nervous system that deprives her of her voice. She moves back to the East to recover her lost voice. In a contrived episode the two are reunited, but the story ends on a note of regret at lost opportunity: "Somewhere in that vague and rapidly lessening region known as the frontier, there disappeared a few years ago, a woman's voice. . . . She threw away a charming career, just at its outset, and went West with a husband—not anybody in particular." Embodied in Madeline's predicament are Foote's ambivalent feelings about marriage and motherhood in the West. Foote felt cut off from the artistic refinements of culture, but a more important thrust of the story is the recognition that individual expression (musical or literary) may fail if supporting voices are lacking.

In *The Last Assembly Ball* Foote again draws on her experiences in Leadville and explores her theme of the Easterner exiled in the West. A mining engineer from New York, Frank Embury, lodges in the boardinghouse of Mrs. Dansken, who warns her young male boarders against marriage in the West. She is particularly apprehensive about an appealing servant named Milly who attracts Frank's attention. In this "Pseudo-Romance of the Far West," as the story was subtitled, Foote uses the makeshift boardinghouse as a social setting to probe the provisional, unstable lives of those who aspire naively for fortune and love. Despite Mrs. Dansken's warnings, Frank hopes that an announcement at the Assembly Ball of his marriage to Milly will allay all suspicions about their relationship. The ball, however, becomes the occasion of their public humiliation when it is revealed that Milly had concealed a previous marriage and a child. When her real background is exposed, Frank arranges a desperate defense of his wife's "honor," a duel that leads to his death. In contrast to her previous focus on the entrapment of female characters, Foote in *The Last Assembly Ball* presents a male protagonist victimized by emotional entanglements.

As in *John Bodewin's Testimony,* the protagonist of *Coeur d'Alene* (1894) is a figure whose motives are not apparent to those who initially observe him. Darcie Hamilton, using the assumed name of "Jack Darcie," covertly investigates the questionable finances of the Big Horn mine. As did John Bodewin, this dutiful figure faces a dilemma. He is caught between his obligation to report the suspect practices of the mine's alcoholic manager, Bingham, and his love for Bingham's daughter, Faith. In previous novels Foote had transformed personal experiences into fiction, but with this rendering of the violent strike that erupted in Idaho's Coeur d'Alene in 1892, she relied on newspaper reports and accounts from individuals who had participated in the dispute. The romantic plot is overshadowed by Foote's bitter portrayal of the ruthlessness of the union members, who massacre their opponents. Darcie and Faith manage to escape the carnage, but the tone of outrage that colors the final pages, as Johnson notes, "makes it unique among Foote's writings."

The failure of her husband's irrigation project may have contributed to the somber tone of several stories Foote published in *The Century Illustrated Magazine* in the following years. Collected in *The Cup of Trembling and Other Stories* (1895), these stories present characters cut off from social ties and in some cases in violation of social conventions. "Maverick" presents a character who has been disfigured while a captive of Native Americans, but the true outsider of the story is Rose Gilroy, with whom Maverick is infatuated. Repelled by her suitor, she tries to escape from her pitiful circumstances by eloping with a Swedish waiter, only to face death in Idaho's black lava fields. The setting of the title story of the collection, one of Foote's more polished tales, is equally bleak. In previous stories she had dealt with business corruption, alcoholism, violence, and social impropriety, but in "The Cup of Trembling" she deals

with "an ugly theme, adultery," that she felt needed to be confronted in Western fiction. Esmee flees her marriage from a "rough Western man," a mine owner in the Coeur d'Alene, running away with Jack Waring, a mining engineer. Snowbound during an Idaho winter, Esmee confronts the "ridiculous" and "squalid" situation into which she and her lover have fallen. The unanticipated visit of Jack's brother produces a chain of circumstances that causes Esmee to review her wrongs, and as with Rose Gilroy, her escape proves to be futile and fatal. The avalanche that destroys her may add a melodramatic touch to the story, but this dark tale of guilt and punishment appealed to Victorian readers and was particularly admired by Rudyard Kipling.

In 1895, assisted by his brother-in-law James Hague, Arthur Foote took a temporary position with the North Star Mining Company in Grass Valley, California. After their disappointments and wanderings, this appointment eventually offered the Footes the security that had eluded them in Colorado and Idaho. When her husband became superintendent of the North Star mines, the family settled into perhaps the most stable period of their lives, and Foote stopped taking commissions for book illustrations to devote her energies to her fiction, which took a more reflective turn. By 1903 she had collected her juvenile tales into *The Little Fig-Tree Stories* (1899); she had assembled her last collection of mature short fiction, *A Touch of Sun and Other Stories* (1903); and she had published two more novels, *The Prodigal* (1900) and *The Desert and the Sown* (1902).

Two stories in particular stand out from this period. In "How the Pump Stopped at the Morning Watch," published in *The Century Illustrated Magazine,* Foote describes the death of a man who worked as a pump-man at the North Star mines. When a pump stops, human and mechanical breakdown are symbolically joined. The man's absorption in the subterranean world of the pumps is so intense that he becomes a worn-out cog in the machinery. The relentless forces of nature overcome him, and his associates bear him home to his distressed wife. The story is told economically and without editorializing. The title story of Foote's last collection, "A Touch of Sun," establishes an atmosphere of "hasty fruition" or "blight in bloom," based on the overheated setting of North Star Cottage in Grass Valley. The roses blighted by a touch of sun match the mood of Mrs. Thorne, concerned about her son's premature engagement to a young woman known to have a questionable past. Foote carefully outlines the excessive concern of Mrs. Thorne and her husband only to reveal in the end that the son had learned long ago about his fiancée's past. Mrs. Thorne's lack of patience and faith is subtly upbraided, and the subdued conclu-

Foote with family members and a friend in Boise, circa 1894–1895: (back row) Foote, Bessie Hallock Sherman, and Nelly Linton; (front row) Foote's niece Mary Birney Sherman and Foote's three children, Agnes, Betty, and Arthur

sion avoids the melodrama of some of Foote's earlier stories.

The Desert and the Sown, which lacks the dramatic climaxes of her earlier fiction, is Foote's most ambitious novel, spanning two generations in the lives of its many characters and encompassing both Eastern and Western settings. The complicated plot is driven by the defiant Emily Van Elten, daughter of a wealthy New York family, who chooses to elope with Adam Bogardus, a hireling on her father's farm. The couple leads a desperate existence in the West, and in a major turning point Adam apparently deserts his pregnant wife and his son, Paul, when they are held captive and taunted by a sadistic stationkeeper. Communication between Adam and Emily is confused during this incident, and she is unaware that Adam had actually struck the stationkeeper dead. He flees in shame and dread to wander in the wilderness. With its sins-of-the-fathers theme, the novel focuses on the dilemma of young Paul, who undergoes his own ordeal in the Western wilderness. With its rich parallels to both the biblical story of Abraham and Hagar and that of the Prodigal Son, *The Desert and the Sown* suggests that Paul and representatives of his generation must confront the conflicted legacy of their heritage. While he achieves a degree of reconciliation with his father and his family's past, he is drawn away from his mother, who remains a figure of emotional hardness, a creature of the "stony hillsides" and "stony roads" of New York State.

In *The Royal Americans* (1910) Foote displays a talent for historical fiction. Ambitious in scope, the novel begins during the French and Indian War with the British surrender to Montcalm at the Battle of Fort Oswego. The historical setting may recall James Fenimore Cooper's *The Last of the Mohicans* (1826), but a more apt model is another entry in the Leatherstocking series, *The Deerslayer* (1841). Foote alludes to *The Deerslayer* early in her novel, and her setting recalls Cooper's in its evocation of an Edenic landscape marred by violence and warfare. Central figures in the novel are a British officer, Colonel Yelverton of the Royal Americans, and his daughter Catherine, who loses her mother during the war. Yelverton adopts a daughter whom he calls Charlotte, a part–Native American girl, whose tragic fate contrasts with that of Catherine. Foote devotes significant attention to the Quakers, and in the guise of Catherine's abortive romance with Francis Havergal, she offers critical commentary on the probity and inflexibility of her religious upbringing. Foote takes her characters up through the time of the American Revolution, and despite Catherine's complicated relationship with the Havergals and painful losses suffered by her family, she is united with the resolute and upright Bassy Dunbar. The novel ends on a note of reconciliation and hope for the future of the new nation.

Through the genre of historical fiction Foote skillfully shows how individual lives intersected with major national events. Between 1915 and 1919 Foote published her last three novels, *The Valley Road* (1915), *Edith Bonham* (1917), and *The Ground-Swell* (1919), each with a backdrop of national or international upheaval. Each of these novels is also a reminiscence of a departed loved one. Begun years before, *The Valley Road* looks back on the relationship between the Footes and the Hagues. At various points in Arthur's career, James D. Hague had been instrumental in assisting him in his professional exploits. Thomas Ludwell in *The Valley Road* is a fictional characterization of Hague, who had died in 1908, and the novel also shows how characters' lives are affected by the San Francisco earthquake of 1906.

In *Edith Bonham,* dedicated to her beloved friend Helena Gilder, Foote uses the device of Edith's diary to cleverly tell her story from a first-person perspective. She details Edith's close friendship with Nanny, who has married Douglas Maclay, a mining engineer. A subtly developed example of Foote's self-sacrificing women characters, Edith pledges to become a kind of governess to Nanny's daughter, Phoebe, when the girl is of proper age. When this plan is about to be implemented, Edith travels west to discover that Nanny has died. Since Edith's service has become a need rather than an expression of friendship, Edith stays to tend to Phoebe, who becomes seriously ill. Without assuming heroic scale, Edith becomes a figure of vigilance and renunciation of the world, evidenced by her resistance to premature romantic overtures by Nanny's widowed husband and his assistant, Dick Grant. The novel ends on a note of reconciliation, when Edith does eventually marry Douglas, Nanny's husband. The quietly resigned tone is accented by an epilogue told from Phoebe's perspective against the backdrop of World War I.

World War I also provides the backdrop for *The Ground-Swell.* Adopting once again a first-person perspective, Foote bases the novel on the correspondence between a concerned parent, Lucy Cope, and a friend. The setting of the book is Laguna Point in California, where Cope, married to a retired army general, hopes to settle after a lifetime of moving from place to place. The couple's three daughters have dispersed to various locations, but Cope hopes that her youngest daughter, Katy, will settle near them and perhaps marry Tony Kayding, a caretaker of the land on which they are staying. That relationship comes to fruition, a sharp contrast to the one between another daughter and her dissolute, philandering husband. In this novel Katy is the figure of self-sacrifice, renouncing personal happiness in favor of a life of service. She dies, somewhat mysteriously, in Europe while participating in the war effort, a victim of the cataclysm that engulfs all the characters in the book. The lively and appealing Katy is based on Foote's daughter Agnes, who died in 1904, and the novel constitutes a memorial to her.

It is hardly surprising that Foote, who often incorporated autobiographical situations and characters into her fiction, planned a full-length autobiography. She worked on "Backgrounds and Figures," as the work

was tentatively called, in the 1920s. It remained in family hands until an edited version of the manuscript was published in 1972 as *A Victorian Gentlewoman in the Far West.* In her narrative she devotes ample space to her Quaker background and her life in Colorado and California but tends to bury the painful memories of the Idaho years, though that period lasted much longer than her stays in Colorado and California. She touches briefly on the painful loss of Agnes. Perhaps because of the effect on Foote of this life cut short, her own autobiographical narrative, with little attention to her and her husband's years in Grass Valley, appears sharply truncated. Whatever principles of selectivity she observed in organizing her reminiscences, her autobiography compares favorably to other more celebrated examples of the genre. It merits consideration alongside other examples of Western life-experience writing such as Mary Austin's *Earth Horizon: An Autobiography* (1932).

Westerners for long periods of their lives, the Footes settled with the family of daughter Betty in Hingham, Massachusetts. Foote died on 25 June 1938, five years after her husband. Little attention was given to Foote's work in the early part of the twentieth century, even by students of regional writing. In 1958, in an anthology of realistic prose, Wallace Stegner included "How the Pump Stopped at the Morning Watch" with favorable comments. In 1971 Stegner published his Pulitzer Prize–winning novel *Angle of Repose,* in which his heroine, Susan Burling Ward, follows her husband, Oliver Ward, to a series of mining positions in New Almaden, Leadville, and Grass Valley. Readers familiar with Foote's writings will notice how intensely Stegner, a long-time student of Western literature, had immersed himself in the author-illustrator's correspondence and reminiscences. He took from Foote's autobiography many of the locales where she and her family lived, the title of his novel, and many of the personal traits of people she knew. Stegner, careful to distinguish his activities as a novelist from his obligations as a historian, imaginatively shaped Susan Ward's career from the raw materials of Foote's. In doing so he shed light on contemporary concerns.

Stegner found in the Footes' story a unique variant on the American dream of success, which is often defined in purely masculine terms. He played off the career aspirations of the mining engineer, signifying an American restlessness and rootlessness, against the nesting instincts of his wife. In the "protected woman's point of view" with its genteel values, Stegner sensed the strengths of patience, stoical courage, and endurance, attributes he clearly admired in Foote.

As Mary Hallock Foote's own career evolved, her fiction transcended the "protected" perspectives of her somewhat sappy heroines in romances such as *The*

Led-Horse Claim. In works such as *Edith Bonham* and *The Ground-Swell* Foote achieved a mature narrative perspective in which the West serves as a significant backdrop for fictional dramas of psychological subtlety and acuity.

Bibliographies:

Richard W. Etulain, "Mary Hallock Foote (1847–1938)," *American Literary Realism,* 5 (Spring 1972): 144–150;

Etulain, "Mary Hallock Foote: A Checklist," *Western American Literature,* 10 (Spring 1975): 59–65.

References:

Mary Lou Benn, "Mary Hallock Foote: Early Leadville Writer," *Colorado Magazine,* 33 (April 1956): 93–108;

Benn, "Mary Hallock Foote in Idaho," *University of Wyoming Publications,* 20 (July 1956): 157–178;

Helen de Kay Gilder, "Author Illustrators, II: Mary Hallock Foote," *Book Buyer,* 11 (August 1894): 338–342;

Melody Graulich, "Mary Hallock Foote (1847–1938)," *Legacy,* 3 (Fall 1986): 43–52;

Lee Ann Johnson, *Mary Hallock Foote* (Boston: Twayne, 1980);

James Maguire, *Mary Hallock Foote* (Boise, Idaho: Boise State College, 1972);

Carroll Smith Rosenberg, "The Female World of Love and Ritual: Relations Between Women in Nineteenth-Century America," *Signs,* 1 (Autumn 1975): 1–29;

Wallace Stegner, *Angle of Repose* (New York: Doubleday, 1971).

Papers:

Mary Hallock Foote's letters to Helena de Kay Gilder are at the Stanford University Library. Correspondence with James Hague and *The Century Illustrated Magazine* is at the Huntington Library in San Marino, California.

Anna Katharine Green

(11 November 1846 – 11 April 1935)

Barbara Ryan
Michigan Society of Fellows

BOOKS: *The Leavenworth Case: A Lawyer's Story* (New York: Putnam, 1878; London: Routledge, 1884);

A Strange Disappearance (New York: Putnam, 1879; London: Routledge, 1884);

The Sword of Damocles: A Story of New York Life (New York: Putnam, 1881; London: Ward, Lock, 1884);

The Defense of the Bride and Other Poems (New York: Putnam, 1882);

Hand and Ring (New York: Putnam, 1883; London: Ward, Lock, 1884);

XYZ; A Detective Story (New York: Putnam, 1883; London: Ward, Lock, 1883);

The Mill Mystery (New York & London: Putnam, 1886);

7 to 12 (New York & London: Putnam, 1887);

Risifi's Daughter, A Drama (New York & London: Putnam, 1887);

Behind Closed Doors (New York & London: Putnam, 1888);

The Forsaken Inn (New York: Bonner, 1890; London: Routledge, 1890);

A Matter of Millions (New York: Bonner, 1890; London: Routledge, 1890);

The Old Stone House and Other Stories (New York & London: Putnam, 1891);

Cynthia Wakeham's Money (New York & London: Putnam, 1892);

Marked "Personal" (New York & London: Putnam, 1893);

Miss Hurd: An Enigma (New York & London: Putnam, 1894);

The Doctor, His Wife, and the Clock (New York & London: Putnam, 1895);

Dr. Izard (New York & London: Putnam, 1895);

That Affair Next Door (New York & London: Putnam, 1897);

Lost Man's Lane, A Second Episode in the Life of Amelia Butterworth (New York & London: Putnam, 1898);

Agatha Webb (New York & London: Putnam, 1899);

The Circular Study (New York & London: McClure, Phillips, 1900);

A Difficult Problem, The Staircase at the Heart's Delight, and Other Stories (New York: Lupton, 1900; London: Ward, Lock, 1903);

Anna Katharine Green

One of My Sons (New York & London: Putnam, 1901);

Two Men and a Question (New York: Lupton Leisure Hour Library, 1901);

Three Women and a Mystery (New York: Lovell, 1902);

The Filigree Ball: Being a Full and True Account of the Solution of the Mystery concerning the Jeffrey-Moore Affair (Indianapolis: Bobbs-Merrill, 1903; London: Unwin, 1904);

The House in the Mist (Indianapolis: Bobbs-Merrill, 1905; London: Nash, 1910);

The Millionaire Baby (Indianapolis: Bobbs-Merrill, 1905; London: Chatto & Windus, 1905);

The Amethyst Box (Indianapolis: Bobbs-Merrill, 1905); republished as *The Amethyst Box and Other Stories* (London: Chatto & Windus, 1905);

The Woman in the Alcove (Indianapolis: Bobbs-Merrill, 1906; London: Chatto & Windus, 1906);

The Chief Legatee (New York & London: Authors and Newspapers Association, 1906); republished as *A Woman of Mystery* (London: Collier, 1909);

The Mayor's Wife (Indianapolis: Bobbs-Merrill, 1907);

The House of the Whispering Pines (New York & London: Putnam, 1910);

Three Thousand Dollars (Boston: Badger, 1910);

Initials Only (New York: Dodd, Mead, 1911; London: Nash, 1912);

Masterpieces of Mystery (New York: Dodd, Mead, 1913); republished as *Room Number 3 and Other Detective Stories* (New York: Burt, 1913);

Dark Hollow (New York: Dodd, Mead, 1914; London: Nash, 1914);

The Golden Slipper and Other Problems for Violet Strange (New York & London: Putnam, 1915);

To the Minute, Scarlet and Black: Two Tales of Life's Perplexities (New York & London: Putnam, 1916);

The Mystery of the Hasty Arrow (New York: Dodd, Mead, 1917);

The Step on the Stair (New York: Dodd, Mead, 1923; London: John Lane, 1923).

SELECTED PERIODICAL PUBLICATIONS–
UNCOLLECTED: Reprinted letter from Green, *Critic*, 19 (22 April 1893): 258–259;

"Personal Gossip About Authors," *Writer*, 26 (October 1914): 154–155;

"Anna Katharine Green Tells How She Manufactures Her Plots," *Literary Digest*, 58 (13 July 1918): 48;

"Why Human Beings Are Interested in Crime," *American Magazine*, 87 (February 1919): 38–39, 82–86.

As the "mother of detective fiction" and the most famous American mystery writer in her day, Anna Katharine Green helped to develop a popular genre. Arguably the next important writer to work in the genre after Edgar Allan Poe, the New York author's impressive corpus pleased mystery fans for almost half a century. Some of her books were translated into German, French, Italian, Spanish, Danish, Swedish, and Dutch. While Green's poetry and drama are justly forgotten, novels of detection such as *The Leavenworth Case: A Lawyer's Story* (1878) can still keep readers guessing. Also gripping are Green's ingenious tales of crimes that revolve around such devices as deadly mechanical hands and fatal daggers made of melting ice. Most sig-

nificant, Green is remembered for her early and perceptive explorations of the criminal mind and heart. "I do not put the emphasis on the *manner* of the act," she observed in "Why Human Beings Are Interested in Crime," an article published in the February 1919 issue of *American Magazine,* "but on the motives behind it and on the novel and strange situations which come in working out the mystery."

Born to New Englanders resident in Brooklyn on 11 November 1846, Green was a staunch Presbyterian all her life, and it is possible that religious faith helped inculcate the quality that Wilkie Collins praised as her "sincerity" in an 1883 letter to George Putnam, which Putnam published in the 28 January 1893 issue of *The Critic.* Yet it was interest in human nature that inspired her absorption in the reasons that people turn to crime. Her father, a lawyer, was an important influence. Her first and most famous book, *The Leavenworth Case,* was subtitled "A Lawyer's Story," and the character of Ebenezer Gryce, her shrewdest detective, was said to recall James Green. Her mother, Katherine Ann Whitney Green, was less influential because she died when Green was only three. Anna and her two brothers were raised by their sister, Sarah, in Connecticut and then Albany, New York. By the time of their third move, to Buffalo, New York, James Green was ready to remarry. His children learned to love their "Mother Grace," who encouraged her stepdaughter's literary dreams.

Green went to Ripley College in Vermont and became one of the nation's earliest female graduates in 1866. Pleased to be made president of the Washington Irving Association, she devoted herself to writing and prized an encouraging letter from Ralph Waldo Emerson. According to Mary R. P. Hatch's biographical sketch in the July 1888 issue of *The Writer,* after placing several poems in prominent literary magazines and learning that a long prose piece had been rejected, Green told her friend: "I eschew prose. Poetry is my forte; story telling is not possible to me." She changed her mind when her stepmother suggested she try prose again but kept her composition of *The Leavenworth Case* a closely guarded secret. When she finally presented the manuscript to her father, he agreed to help her approach an established literary critic and so find a publisher. Even then the aspiring poet told a literary friend: "I do not wish you to think I have any hopes for it in the way of giving me fame. I had to stop and throw out this story before I could get leave to settle down to my life work of writing poetry."

Perhaps in accepting Green's book Putnam recognized that he was publishing the first significant detective novel written by an American woman. Perhaps he also saw, as did Collins, that *The Leavenworth Case* was remarkable for "truth and subtlety." It is certain, how-

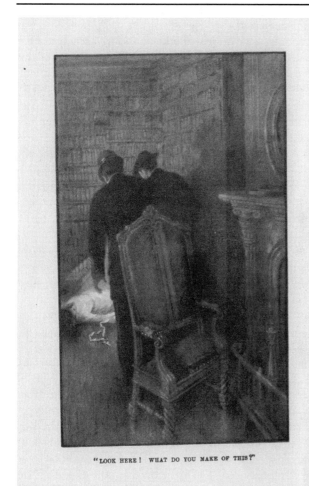

THE FILIGREE
BALL: BEING A FULL
AND TRUE ACCOUNT OF
THE SOLUTION OF THE
MYSTERY CONCERNING
THE JEFFREY-MOORE
AFFAIR

BY

ANNA KATHERINE GREEN

AUTHOR OF
THE LEAVENWORTH CASE

ILLUSTRATED BY C. M. RELYEA

THE BOBBS-MERRILL COMPANY
PUBLISHERS   INDIANAPOLIS

"LOOK HERE! WHAT DO YOU MAKE OF THIS?"

Frontispiece and title page for Green's 1903 novel, set in a mysterious mansion

ever, that neither Putnam nor Collins foresaw that Green's first book would become an immediate and lasting best-seller both at home and abroad. During Theodore Roosevelt's administration the plates used to print *The Leavenworth Case* wore out and had to be recast to keep up with demand. It sold more than a million copies by her death in 1935. Long before then, Green's importance to the genre was well understood. Not only was *The Leavenworth Case* used at Yale to demonstrate the unreliability of circumstantial evidence, but it was actually deemed by Supreme Court justice Morrison R. Waite to be "the greatest work ever written by a woman."

In *The Leavenworth Case,* Gryce and his associates investigate the murder of the wealthy Mr. Leavenworth, whose two beautiful wards are prime suspects. It is told in the first person, though not through Gryce's experienced and perceptive eyes. Instead, the narrator is a young attorney whose idealization of beautiful and privileged women leads him into confusion that the older

man sets straight with a smile. "I had a purpose in letting you follow your own lead for a while," the New York detective tells his "leg-man" with some complacency, for "while I did not hesitate myself as to the true explanation of the scene before me, I was pleased to find you accept a contrary one; as in this way both theories had a chance of being tested; as was right in a case of so much mystery." Gryce's openness to alternate theories contrasts sharply with other fictional detectives' smug toying with duller minds, and as it happens Gryce himself is surprised when Leavenworth's murderer confesses in a dramatic scene. Ever unassuming, Gryce admits that the criminal's revelations were unexpected, though he adds that he was never fooled by the wealthy lovelies who led his legal friend astray: "all the women in the world can't pull the wool over the eyes of Ebenezer Gryce when he is on a trail."

The seasoned Gryce is depicted as an ordinary man trained to do a job that requires patience, discipline, and acuity. Socially awkward, he provides the reader with glimpses into a monied and self-consciously exclusive world. "I can enter a house," Gryce tells his lawyer-friend,

> "bow to the mistress of it, let her be as elegant as she will, so long as I have a writ of arrest in my hand, or some such professional matter upon my mind; but when it comes to visiting in kid gloves, raising a glass of champagne in response to a toast—and such like, I am absolutely good for nothing." And he plunged his two hands into his hair, and looked dolefully at the head of the cane I carried in my hand.

Gryce was a reassuring, middle-class presence against his wealthy suspects' excesses of ardor, perversity, and pride. Green makes it clear that her detective is "not the thin, wiry individual with the piercing eye" that dime novels of the period equated with detective skill. Instead, "Mr. Gryce was a portly, comfortable personage with an eye that never pierced, that did not even rest on *you*." He at times appears distracted, absently staring at doorknobs, buttons, inkstands, and his own fingers, and yet he does not miss anything of importance.

After the smashing success of *The Leavenworth Case*, Green changed her middle name from "Catherine" to "Katharine" (that is, she adopted her mother's name) and enjoyed an enlarged social life while continuing to write detective fiction that sold well. In 1882, possibly as a courtesy, Putnam published Green's early poetry, *The Defense of the Bride and Other Poems*, which the reviewer for *Harper's* praised as a collection of "vigorous productions" remarkable for their "masculine force and brevity."

In 1884 Green married Charles Rohlfs. Her father was suspicious of the young actor, possibly because Rohlfs was eight years younger than his established daughter, and insisted that his prospective son-in-law give up the stage, which Rohlfs agreed to do. (After the marriage Green's books appeared under the name Mrs. Charles Rohlfs.) Despite his father-in-law's injunction, Rohlf did return to acting after James Green's death. He in fact starred as the modest Gryce in his wife's dramatic adaptation of her famous novel in 1890. His wife supported this venture; indeed, quite contrary to her usual composition style, Green dictated her dramatization of *The Leavenworth Case* to her husband. In a letter that was published in the 22 April 1893 issue of *The Critic*, Green wrote, "if ever anything gushed from the brain without pause or hindrance, it was that play."

Happy in her married life, Green gave birth to two sons and a daughter: Rosamund (1885), Sterling (1887), and Roland (1892). Living in Buffalo, Anna Katharine Green Rohlfs was a churchwoman, mother, and dedicated gardener, yet most of the time she was also hard at work on another novel or keeping up her correspondence with writers such as Mary Wilkins Freeman and Arthur Conan Doyle. She was the family's principal bread-winner during her children's early years, and her energy and discipline enabled the Rohlfses to support her mother-in-law, her sister, and her husband's design studio. Her success enabled Charles Rohlfs to establish his own career, which included the creation of a spare yet elegant line of furniture that resembles the mission style. Some of his designs are part of the collection of New York's Metropolitan Museum.

Green featured Ebenezer Gryce with an array of youthful aides in *A Strange Disappearance* (1879), *Hand and Ring* (1883), *Behind Closed Doors* (1888), *A Matter of Millions* (1890), and *The Doctor, His Wife, and the Clock* (1895). Green then provided her detective with a female sidekick, Amelia Butterworth, in *That Affair Next Door* (1897), *Lost Man's Lane, A Second Episode in the Life of Amelia Butterworth* (1898), *The Circular Study* (1900), *One of My Sons* (1901), and *Initials Only* (1911). A literary descendant of Gryce's lawyer-friend in *The Leavenworth Case* in the sense that she eases the detective's entry into the social world of wealth, Butterworth is nevertheless a prototype for the elderly female amateur detective epitomized by Agatha Christie's Miss Marple. Throughout his long career Gryce, who is traced from young manhood to an age so advanced that his deductive powers are on the wane, negotiates intricate plots and deduces the truth despite Green's skillful use of red herrings and misleading clues. Like Gryce, Green had stamina, for as Collins noted, her "powers of invention" were "remarkable."

As in *The Leavenworth Case*, Green liked to reveal sordid passions behind wealthy Americans' gilded facades, but she also found crimes and criminals in rural areas, as in *Hand and Ring* and *Lost Man's Lane*. She found plentiful material for mystery in older houses, especially mansions in which she hid secret passages and fiendish death-traps of the sort found in *The Filigree Ball: Being a Full and True Account of the Solution of the Mystery concerning the Jeffrey-Moore Affair* (1903), *The Millionaire Baby* (1905), *The Mayor's Wife* (1907), and *The Step on the Stair* (1923). She also enjoyed teasing puzzles out of the latest technological innovations, including timely cablegrams in *Agatha Webb* (1899), electrical devices in *The Circular Study*, an innovative security system in *Three Thousand Dollars* (1910), and even airplanes in *Initials Only*. Yet all the while Green insisted that her fiction relied on the exploration of motives and character. Green's themes, style, and talent are shown to great advantage in *The Doctor, His Wife, and the Clock*, a chilling and plausible character study, and in *Dark Hollow*

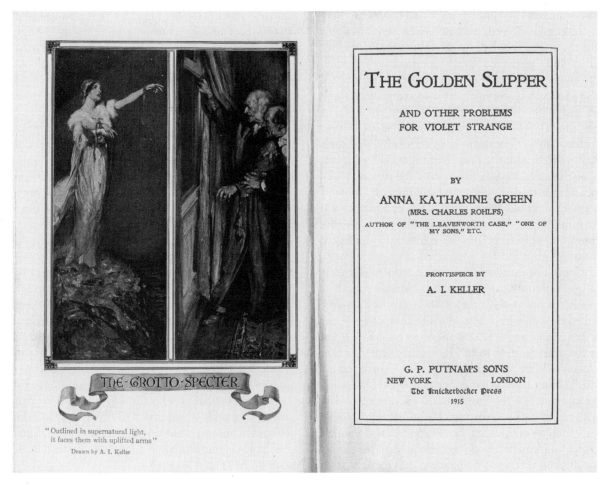

THE GROTTO·SPECTER

"Outlined in supernatural light,
it faces them with uplifted arms"
Drawn by A. I. Keller

THE GOLDEN SLIPPER

AND OTHER PROBLEMS
FOR VIOLET STRANGE

BY

ANNA KATHARINE GREEN
(MRS. CHARLES ROHLFS)
AUTHOR OF "THE LEAVENWORTH CASE," "ONE OF
MY SONS," ETC.

FRONTISPIECE BY

A. I. KELLER

G. P. PUTNAM'S SONS
NEW YORK   LONDON
The Knickerbocker Press
1915

Frontispiece and title page for Green's 1915 book, which features a young woman detective

(1914), a compelling tale of hidden guilt, honor, and remorse.

One of Green's most intriguing characters is Violet Strange, a pampered belle who appears in *The Golden Slipper and Other Problems for Violet Strange* (1915). Strange was a much more independent sleuth than Butterworth, a circumstance that Green seems to have felt some need to excuse. The sense of anomaly may explain why Green makes her most noteworthy female detective so noticeably piquant. Strange, as Green presents her to readers,

> was a small, slight woman whose naturally quaint appearance was accentuated by the extreme simplicity of her attire. . . . no other personality could vie with hers in strangeness, or in the illusive quality of her ever-changing expression. She was vivacity incarnate and, to the ordinary observer, light as thistledown in fibre and in feeling.

Depicted as "beautiful," but also as tiny, girlish, and of nervous temperament, Strange distracts onlookers with

silly prattle when engaged in detective work. "Who could dream," Green inquires rhetorically, "that back of this display of mingled childishness and audacity there lay hidden purpose, intellect, and a keen knowledge of human nature?" However, unlike Dorothy Sayers's Lord Peter Wimsey, the clubman-detective who often acts the part of a silly ass, Strange suffers enormously in her disturbing career. Publicly a witty and cultured woman, "Violet Strange in society was a very different person from Violet Strange under the tension of her secret and peculiar work."

Green heightens the tensions of her heroine's singular pursuits with frequent references to Strange's half-reluctant, half-eager attention to her lurid crimes and by indicating that, though obviously well-heeled, she seems to be impelled by financial need. Even more dramatic is the circumstance that, driven on by her desire for cash, Strange hovers near a nervous breakdown until she is rescued by a former client who asks her to be his wife. Only then does Green reveal that Strange pursued her dangerous and sometimes harrowing assignments to support an elder "sister-mother" who, though widowed, was denied a stern parent's wealth. Strange's fees have enabled her cherished elder sister to study with a European maestro in preparation for a singing career. With that career launched, of course successfully, Strange is free to accept her lover's hand and leave detecting behind. If fans knew about Sarah Green's spinsterhood and meager income from seamstress work, they might have concluded that their author worked with the same half-eager, half-reluctant air that characterizes Strange. Even if the pertinent biographical information was not widely known, Strange's near-collapse would have assured readers that Green understood ladies' proper role in life, even as she vaunted the powers of the fit, active, and intelligent American Girl.

Green also handled the topic of deductive powers in a gender-conscious way. "A woman's mind is strangely penetrating," the man who will marry Strange tells her with a sort of awe, "and yours, I am told, has an intuitive faculty more to be relied upon than the reasoning of men." Reiterating this claim in her essay "Why Human Beings Are Interested in Crime," Green asserts that in her experience, "Women have more subtle intuitions than men have–a fact which should make them valuable in actual detective work." Such an opinion can be interpreted as devaluing women's ratiocinative powers, a point that should be borne in mind when pondering the claims made regarding Green's feminism. Yet John Cornillon is quite right in his 1972 essay "A Case for Violet Strange" to note that "In eight out of nine stories" featuring the character, "the principal people she helps are women. In the one exception," he adds, "she meets and helps the man whom she will later marry." This observation should be coupled with the fact that Green's career and achievements opened up a space that women authors have occupied with élan. Strange is certainly an important precursor to Nancy Drew.

Green's books remained popular well into the twentieth century. During World War I, Roosevelt commended her for providing books that refreshed soldiers who had been harried with scenes of war. In an article titled "Anna Katharine Green Tells How She Manufactures Her Plots" in the 13 July 1918 issue of *Literary Digest,* Green agreed that her sort of

stories could "rest the mind," but she added that the creation of certain gruesome scenes was as frightening for the author as for her horripilating fans. Not all of Green's stories presented readers with scenes such as that from *The Forsaken Inn* (1890) in which a detective crawls into a sealed room to find a corpse that has moldered away there for fifteen years. Yet, Green's stories commonly relied on a quasi-Gothic sense that human passions can be strange and terrible, and only revealed, rather than resolved, by a detective's ability to probe suspects' tangled psyches and hidden acts. "Crime must touch our imagination," she observes in "Why Human Beings Are Interested in Crime," "by showing people, *like ourselves,* but incredibly transformed by some overwhelming motive."

Green's book sales dropped near the end of her unusually long career. Her final years were also marred by personal tragedy, as one son was lost in a plane crash and the Rohlfses' only daughter died. Her literary contributions were not forgotten, however, as fellow mystery writers credited Green with laying the groundwork for the fictional detective's "golden age." She helped to develop and diversify a popular and important literary genre. Along the way Green provided her successors with a wealth of guidance as to winning characterizations, spine-tingling denouements, and still-baffling labyrinths of motive, opportunity, and detective skill.

References:

John Cornillon, "A Case for Violet Strange," in *Images of Women in Fiction: Feminist Perspectives,* edited by Susan Koppelman Cornillon (Bowling Green, Ohio: Bowling Green University Popular Press, 1972), pp. 206–215;

Patricia D. Maida, *Mother of Detective Fiction: The Life and Works of Anna Katharine Green* (Bowling Green, Ohio: Bowling Green University Popular Press, 1989).

Papers:

Anna Katharine Green's papers are in private family collections and at the John Ransom Humanities Research Center at the University of Texas at Austin.

Mary Jane Holmes

(5 April 1825 – 6 October 1907)

Dorri R. Beam
University of Virginia

BOOKS: *Tempest and Sunshine; or, Life in Kentucky* (New York: Appleton, 1854; London, 1854);

The English Orphans; or, A Home in the New World (New York: Appleton, 1855);

The Homestead on the Hillside and Other Tales (New York & Auburn, N.Y.: Miller, Orton & Mulligan, 1856);

'Lena Rivers (New York & Auburn, N.Y.: Miller, Orton & Mulligan, 1856);

Meadow Brook (New York: Miller, Orton, 1857);

Dora Deane; or, The East India Uncle, and Maggie Miller; or, Old Hagar's Secret (New York: Saxton, 1859);

Cousin Maude, and Rosamond (New York: Saxton, Barker, 1860);

Marian Grey; or, The Heiress of Redstone Hall (New York: Carleton, 1863; London, 1878);

Darkness and Daylight: A Novel (New York: Carleton, 1864);

Hugh Worthington (New York: Carleton, 1865);

The Cameron Pride; or, Purified by Suffering: A Novel (New York: Carleton / London: Low, 1867);

Rose Mather: A Tale of the War (New York: Carleton / London: Low, 1868);

The Christmas Font: A Story for Young Folks (New York: Carleton / London: Low, 1868);

Ethelyn's Mistake; or, The Home in the West: A Novel (New York: Carleton / London: Low, 1869);

Millbank; or, Roger Irving's Ward: A Novel (New York: Carleton / London: Low, 1871);

Edna Browning; or, The Leighton Homestead: A Novel (New York: Carleton / London: Low, 1872);

West Lawn, and the Rector of St. Mark's (New York: Carleton / London: Low, 1874);

Edith Lyle: A Novel (New York: Carleton / London: Low, 1876);

Mildred: A Novel (New York: Carleton / London: Low, 1877);

Daisy Thornton, and Jessie Graham (New York: Carleton / London: Low, 1878);

Forrest House: A Novel (New York: Carleton, 1879);

Chateau D'Or: Norah, and Kitty Craig (New York: Carleton / London: Low, 1880);

Mary Jane Holmes

Red-Bird: A Brown Cottage Story (New York: Carleton / London: Low, 1880); republished as *Red-Bird's Christmas Story* (New York: Dillingham, 1892);

Madeline: A Novel (New York: Carleton / London: Low, 1881);

Queenie Hetherton: A Novel (New York: Carleton / London: Low, 1883);

Christmas Stories (New York: Carleton / London: Low, 1885);

Bessie's Fortune: A Novel (New York: Carleton / London: Low, 1886);

Gretchen: A Novel (New York: Dillingham / London: Low, 1887);

Marguerite: A Novel (New York: Dillingham, 1891);
Doctor Hathern's Daughters: A Story of Virginia, in Four Parts (New York: Dillingham, 1895);
Mrs. Hallam's Companion, and The Spring Farm and Other Tales (New York: Dillingham, 1896);
Paul Ralston: A Novel (New York: Dillingham, 1897);
The Tracy Diamonds (New York: Dillingham, 1899);
The Cromptons (New York: Dillingham, 1902; London: Unwin, 1902);
The Merivale Banks (New York: Dillingham, 1903);
Rena's Experiment (New York: Dillingham, 1904);
The Abandoned Farm, and Connie's Mistake (New York: Dillingham, 1905);
Lucy Harding: A Romance of Russia (New York: American News, 1905).

OTHER: "Adam Floyd," in *The Woman's Story,* edited by Laura C. Holloway (New York: John B. Alden, 1889);
"An American Abroad," in *A Cunning Culprit; or, A "Novel" Novel: A Composite Romance by Twenty Different Popular Writers* (Chicago: Hobart, 1895), pp. 269–280.

As one of the most popular writers of the nineteenth century, Mary Jane Holmes is estimated to have rivaled Harriet Beecher Stowe in earnings and stand next to E. P. Roe as probably the most widely read of American novelists writing after the Civil War. Her thirty-nine books reached sales of more than two million copies. Several of her books were still in publication long after her death and well into the twentieth century. Early in Holmes's career, Francis S. Street and Francis S. Smith contracted her to write a novel a year for serialization in their *New York Weekly* in order to compete with the formidable popularity of the *New York Ledger,* which featured E. D. E. N. Southworth. Holmes easily rose to the task, almost quadrupling the circulation of the *Weekly* in a matter of only a few years and securing her prominent position among popular writers of the last half of the century.

Street and Smith claimed that her stories were "snapped up with an avidity which proves the fair writer's popularity with the masses, and fairly entitles her to the name of 'QUEEN OF THE HUMAN HEART!'"–a fitting tribute since Holmes's novels tend to focus on matters of the heart, particularly courtship and romance. Holmes is often classed with the "domestic sentimentalists" of the mid nineteenth century, although she outlasted many of them, publishing her last book in 1905. Modern readers will find her work quite readable, and critics of the period will be interested in her version of what Nina Baym has called "woman's fiction," the story of female "trials and tri-

umphs," which Holmes leavens with humor, an unusual element in the domestic genre.

Born on 5 April 1825 and raised in a modest rural home in Brookfield, Massachusetts, Mary Jane Hawes was the fourth daughter and fifth of nine children born to Preston and Fanny Olds Hawes. Her childhood home was probably much like the one her heroine describes at the opening of the semi-autobiographical novel, *Meadow Brook* (1857):

> Far away among the New England hills stands a large old fashioned farm-house, around whose hearth-stone not many years agone, a band of merry, noisy children played, myself the merriest, noisiest of them all. It stood upon an eminence overlooking a broad strip of rolling meadow land, at the extremity of which was the old grey rock, where the golden rod and sassafras grew, where the green ivy crept over the crumbling wall, and where, under the shadow of the thorn-apple tree, we built our play-houses, drinking our tea from the acorn saucers, and painting our dolls' faces with the red juice of the poke berries, which grew there in great abundance.

The scenery of Massachusetts as well as that of Kentucky and upstate New York, where she lived as an adult, figure prominently in Holmes's fiction.

Priding herself on her attention to detail, Holmes claimed, "In writing, it is my aim to be as true to nature as possible, and I usually try to be very accurate with regard to localities,–I am even particular about the starting of trains from certain points." According to an 1870 assessment of popular writers in *Appleton's Journal,* her portrayals of small-town America helped her to achieve "an immense constituency outlying in all the small towns and rural districts" of the country. Moreover, Holmes's ability to evoke a sense of place has earned consistent praise from both nineteenth- and twentieth-century critics.

Holmes in a letter to a friend written in the 1880s described her parents as "strictly orthodox" and praised their "rigid ideas" for having "a restraining influence in my whole life." Her uncle Joel Hawes was a well-known Congregationalist minister in Hartford whose published addresses include the widely distributed "'A looking-glass for ladies;' or, The Formation and Excellence of the Female Character." The title is ironic since he rails against women receiving "fashionable" educations that enhance their ornamental status by focusing on etiquette and the parlor arts but neglect their intellect and the development of useful domestic skills. Certainly, Holmes shared her uncle's condemnation of fashionable education, a recurring theme in her novels.

The heroines in Holmes's novels generally start out poor and awkward but nonetheless are smart, resourceful, and, above all, genuine. In each novel young men are naturally attracted by the heroine's intelligence and depth of character, giving her an advantage over her vapid but beautiful rivals in a contest over the eligible beau. First, however, the Holmes heroine must attend to her education in order to blossom into a graceful, cultured, and learned specimen of womanhood. The rewards, though unanticipated by the heroine, are great and include at least one marriage offer, usually from a suitor who far exceeds her own class status. The heroine is further rewarded with a greatly improved wardrobe, elegantly understated rather than plain. It is thus that Holmes strikes a wily compromise between fashion and morality that perhaps bends the letter of her uncle's law.

Holmes's own education was decidedly rigorous. A precocious child, she began school at age three and left home to be a district school teacher in a neighboring town at the age of thirteen. When Rosa Lee of *Meadow Brook* begins to teach at the same age, she is still in pantalets rather than the full-length skirt adult women wore, a circumstance that further incites the disrespect Rosa receives from the villagers who are chagrined by the extreme youth of their new teacher.

Mary Jane Hawes evidently spent much time daydreaming. In a 20 March 1884 letter to J. C. Derby, a prominent publisher, she claimed that she could not "remember a time when a story of some kind was not bugging in my brain—and I commenced early to put my thoughts on paper." One sees further analogies to Holmes's childhood in the musing of Rosa Lee:

> Strange fancies filled my brain and oftentimes, as I sat there in the hazy light of an autumnal afternoon, there came and talked with me myriads of little people, unseen, it is true, but still real to me. . . . There, on a mossy bank, beneath a wide-spreading grapevine, with the running brook at my feet, I felt the first longings for fame, though I did not thus designate it then. I only knew that I wanted a *name* which should live when I was gone.

In *Fifty Years Among Authors, Books, and Publishers* (1884) Derby recalled Holmes's assertion that she had articulated similar "fancies" to her schoolmates, telling them that "she would write a book, and when the girls laughed and jeered at her, she grew more earnest and insisted on her assertion, saying *she would* write a book and all of them would read it too." Such an ambition is precocious indeed, for fame was not a culturally authorized desire for little girls who were supposed to prepare for a life lived almost entirely in the private sphere. Holmes, though, became a published author by the age of fifteen. The popularity that her writing eventually achieved suggests that her early prophecy was fulfilled.

Hawes matured into a woman who, as Helen Waite Papashvily records in *All the Happy Endings: A Study of the Domestic Novel in America* (1956), was "slender, tall with a little stoop to hide it." She had "curly hair and a false fringe she ordered by mail from Chicago, violet eyes, a sweet mouth, she loved everybody and everybody loved her." While teaching in her early twenties, she met Daniel Holmes, a student at Yale, and they were married in 1849, after he graduated. In a fitting demonstration of Holmes's ideal marriage of intellectual equals and competent helpmates, the couple taught together at the district school in Versailles, Kentucky, from 1850 to 1852. When Daniel decided to take up law, the Holmeses moved back east to Brockport, in upstate New York, which remained their home for the rest of their lives. The few years in Kentucky were important to Holmes, for there she gathered the material for her first novel, *Tempest and Sunshine; or, Life in Kentucky* (1854). The novel eventually proved to be one of Holmes's best sellers, rivaling in sales her *'Lena Rivers* (1856), also set partly in Kentucky. Both novels continued to sell as Holmes's popularity grew from the 1860s through the 1880s.

Tempest and Sunshine, which modern critics find to be one of Holmes's less compelling works, is unfortunately the novel most often read as representative of her writing. It is the story of two sisters, a dark, conniving, and stormy "tempest" named Julia and an upright, good-natured ray of "sunshine" named Fanny. In typical Holmes fashion, Julia's plot to break up Fanny's match with a handsome young man is foiled, and the earnest and moral heroine is rewarded with marriage while the artful, selfish Julia, whose chief ambition is a fashionable match, is punished with spinsterhood. Critic Helen Waite Papashvily has characterized this pattern as an original one: "The earlier domestic novelists had usually depicted the struggle of life as woman against man. For Mrs. Holmes it was usually woman against woman, rival against rival, youth against age, sister against sister, a meeting of opponents truly worthy and equal. The male impaired physically, mentally, morally, no longer a protagonist, came to be a trophy, a token prize for the victor."

Baym in *Woman's Fiction: A Guide to Novels by and about Women, 1820–1870* (1978) points out that Holmes portrays a shrewd insight into the psychological origins of sibling rivalry by emphasizing the constructed, rather than essential, nature of each sister's personality. Of particular interest is, as Baym puts it, Holmes's "open avowal of the exploitative possibilities of goodness, in its suggestion that one might adopt goodness as a political strategy." Holmes's savvy departure from the extreme moral earnestness of the domestic genre is characteristic of her lighter handling of its themes.

Holmes's next novel, *The English Orphans; or, A Home in the New World* (1855), is the first in a long line of what Baym calls a "picaresque fiction of upward feminine mobility." Holmes's heroine, Mary Howard, begins her ascent after she is orphaned and removed to a poor house in the first few chapters. Not only is Mary Howard destitute, but she is also plain and has two extra protruding front teeth—an alarming state of affairs for a romance heroine. Yet Mary improves herself step by step, getting the vexing teeth extracted, acquiring a teaching job, and even saving enough money to spend a year at Mount Holyoke Seminary. The bill for the rest of her education is paid for by a secret benefactor, who turns out to be, of course, a young man whom Mary had nursed back to health many years ago. He has watched Mary's blossoming at a distance until the time came for him to ask for her hand in marriage, a fitting end to Mary's struggles.

The neat resolution of *The English Orphans* is unsettled by a colorful, slightly crazy woman named Sal, whom Mary met at the poorhouse. Feminist critic Mary Kelley identifies Sal, who has a rejected novel manuscript hidden away and is working on a grammar, as one of a legion of "secret writers" in domestic fiction that reveal the ambivalence of mid-nineteenth-century women writers toward their public professions. Holmes creates an inverse relationship between Sal's sanity and her ability to use language; that is, the crazier she gets, the more eloquent she becomes. Holmes may perhaps be suggesting that in their normal, "sane" roles women are unable to express themselves truly. Moreover, the combination of a familial link discovered between Sal and Mary and Sal's residence in Mary's new home renders Sal the uneasy double of Mary. While Mary relinquishes teaching in honor of her husband's wishes, Sal chafes when he forbids Sal to publish. The two women have found a home at last, but the presence of both under one roof and one rule reveals the conflict of female ambition with domestic bliss. *The English Orphans* was not the last novel in which Holmes would feature a "secret writer," and one wonders to what extent her own success—to be measured in immense sums by the next decade—conflicted with her ideals of married domesticity. Though she may have struggled with this conflict, Holmes, unlike other women writers, never offered excuses for earning money or fame by writing.

In 1856 Holmes published her most famous work, *'Lena Rivers,* in which 'Lena, "a little specimen of Yankeeism," leaves her home in Massachusetts, "a small rural village, nestled among rocky hills, where the word fashion was seldom heard, and where many of the primitive customs of our forefathers still prevailed," to live with wealthy "stuck up" relatives on a Kentucky plantation. Many nineteenth-century readers doubtless

would share modern readers' fascination with the antiquated ways of the remote New England town revealed through Holmes's descriptions, for such places were quickly passing into history even then. The lively clash between the rustic Yankees and the haughty Anglophile Kentuckians provides further entertainment for readers: "What a pity we couldn't all have been born in England," sighs one Kentucky society matron in a rare moment of democratic expansiveness. No object escapes Holmes's ridicule, from 'Lena's rude clothes, to her Yankee grandmother's domestic parsimony, to her Kentucky aunt's feigned delicacy. By treating her heroine's charms with less than reverence or the fashionable woman's selfishness with less than horror, Holmes adopts a playfully ironic stance toward the themes of the domestic novel genre.

Holmes's humor is less consistent when it concerns racial matters. Sometimes her slaves are the witty agents of sharp critique, as is shown in Aunt Milly's remarks on her mistress in *'Lena Rivers:*

> But Lor' that's the way with more'n half the white folks. They jine the church, and then they think they done got a title deed to one of them houses up in heaven (that nobody ever built) sure enough. Goin' straight thar, as fast as a span of race horses can carry 'em Ki! Won't they be disappointed, some on 'em, and Miss Matilda 'long the rest, when she drives up, hosses all a reekin' sweat, and spects to walk straight into the best room, but is told to go to the kitchen and turn hoe-cakes for us niggers, who are eatin' at the fust table, with silver forks and napkins?

Just as often, however, blacks and abolitionists are the butt of Holmes's humor. Holmes's slaves suffer none of the psychic or physical damages of slavery other than the benign ills of selfish mistresses. The thrust of most scenes is to expose the inhumanity of the plantation mistress more than that of the system of slavery itself. Everyone—the slaves themselves, even 'Lena and Rosa who assume their married roles as mistresses of plantations with ease—is quite content with the system. Holmes keeps to her claim to "never avowedly attack the evils of the day, or write at some great principle, as some do," but her manifest complacency with the institution of slavery is itself a political stance in the highly charged years before the Civil War.

Holmes was less reticent about social issues that she deemed more appropriate to New England women's proper domestic and familial concerns than removed "political" issues such as slavery. *Meadow Brook* is more didactic than usual for Holmes, who was praised for her moral tone but was not prone to offer explicit moral instruction in her novels. The most striking instance, in which a young husband and father dies a harrowing death from alcoholism, testifies to Holmes's commitment to the temperance movement. Since she had no children, the affable and generous Holmes was able to devote a great deal of her resources to social activism. Papashvily lists a breathtaking array of Holmes's charitable activities: "she taught Sunday school, built a parish house, tithed a tenth of her rapidly mounting income, organized a temperance society, a village reading room, a literary club and, during the depression of 1893, bread and soup kitchens for the unemployed. She opened her home to students of the local schools, helped the dependents of the Union soldiers during the war and the veterans themselves on their return, gave lectures, educated two Japanese girls she met on her travels, and dispensed cookies with a lavish hand to three generations of Brockport children."

In addition to her many humanitarian projects, Holmes wrote almost constantly, publishing thirty-eight novels in a forty-nine-year career, and traveled extensively with her husband—to Europe, Russia, Asia, and all over the United States. Despite Holmes's wealth of activity, Derby records that the minister at her Episcopal church characterized her as circumscribed to Brown cottage, her home in Brockport: "while she prefers the quiet of home life, and is fond of spending her evenings in her own favorite room—the library—conversing with and listening to the reading of her accomplished husband, a gentleman of profound and varied learning, she is ever ready to open her pleasant home, for social gatherings, whenever occasion requires." By taking pains to document the achievements of Holmes's husband and her deference to him, the minister established Holmes's status as a "true woman": pious, domestic, and even submissive. Like her secular, adventurous heroines Holmes seems to have endorsed this model of womanhood while using its tenets to clear a rather liberal sphere of action for herself.

Holmes's writing shares many of the values of other domestic sentimentalists; her differences are most often those of degree (sometimes shading into ambivalence). One twentieth century critic, writing before the advent of feminist criticism that underscored the cultural work of sentimentalism, disparaged 'Lena Rivers as "a lachrymose classic"; however, most critics, contemporary and modern, acknowledge that Holmes rarely engages in sentimental effusions and laud her vigorous prose. An October 1855 review of *The English Orphans* in the venerated *North American Review* claimed that the "pathetic element stops short of mawkishness" and commended Holmes for her "exquisite" characterization, her nuanced comedy, and her natural plot. Holmes's writing also is not exces-

DAISY THORNTON

AND

JESSIE GRAHAM.

BY

MRS. MARY J. HOLMES,

AUTHOR OF

TEMPEST AND SUNSHINE.—'LENA RIVERS.—DARKNESS AND DAYLIGHT.—
MARIAN GREY.— ENGLISH ORPHANS.—HUGH WORTHINGTON.—
MILBANK.—ETHELYN'S MISTAKE.—
EDNA BROWNING, ETC., ETC.

"Those whom God has joined together let no man put asunder."

NEW YORK:
Copyright, 1878, by
G. W. Carleton & Co., Publishers.
LONDON: S. LOW & CO.
MDCCLXXVIII.

Title page for Holmes's 1878 novel, the thirteenth of twenty romances that were first serialized in the New York Weekly *and then published by Carleton*

sively sensational, for she purposed to "never deal in murders or robberies or ruined young girls; but rather in domestic life as I know it to exist."

Holmes's endorsement of a quiet realism is precisely what makes her work such an odd choice for serialization the *New York Weekly,* a cheap story paper that traded in sensationalism. Nevertheless, her sale of "Marian Grey; or, The Heiress of Redstone Hall" to Street and Smith in 1859 saved the *Weekly* from bankruptcy and began its run of heady success. Holmes's fame and fortune were sealed in 1863 when she presented the manuscript "Marian Grey" to George W. Carleton, a master of the popular market, to be published in book form.

Marian Grey involves purloined fortune and female picaresque adventure but is a resolutely moral romance. As Marian's guardian dies, he confesses that his estate was actually purchased with her inheritance and that all he owns is hers. He asks her to marry his handsome son Frederick in order to avoid exposing his theft and to prevent Frederick's immediate destitution. Marian is able to overcome the shock of the proposal because she has always been in love with Frederick. Frederick, obsessed with the beautiful Isabel, is less excited but conquers his reluctance in order to avoid poverty and disgrace. After the wedding ceremony, however, Marian learns Frederick's true feelings and flees the scene. Living hand-to-mouth under an assumed name, Marian stays away for seven years, thinking this the legal time required to annul the marriage. When she returns to free her husband, she learns that maturity has made him realize the superiority of the honest but plain Marian to the shallow, greedy Isabel. True to romantic formula, distance made her husband's heart grow fonder.

Carleton also republished Holmes's previous novels, and her sales figures soared. For each new novel that was serialized in the *Weekly* Holmes was paid between $4,000 and $6,000, depending on length, for serial rights. Then Carleton issued the novel in green cloth with gold stamping for $1.50. Holmes received royalties of fifteen percent from Carleton and, later, from his successor, George W. Dillingham. Holmes became so popular that libraries were said to have to keep twenty to thirty copies of each of her novels on the shelves. The Boston Public Library reported in 1872 that Holmes's books, along with Southworth's and Caroline Lee Hentz's, were called for more than any others. One New York bookbinder claimed it was common to have calls from the publisher to bind fifty thousand volumes of her novels at one time. Holmes's early novels, *Tempest and Sunshine, 'Lena Rivers, Meadow Brook, Marian Grey, Darkness and Daylight* (1864), and *Ethelyn's Mistake; or, The Home in the West* (1869), remained her most popular efforts and continue to be the most discussed by modern critics because they were published during the heyday of the domestic novel.

Such popularity, however, was not without its consequences. In the last quarter of the century cultural conservatives, among them many librarians, instigated a backlash against Holmes and other popular writers. She was one of sixteen "questionable" authors listed by the American Library Association. The circulation of this list resulted in the systematic eradication of many of the authors' titles from libraries across the country. Modern readers may be astonished to hear Holmes's work deemed immoral, but an 1887 reviewer of *Gretchen: A Novel* (1887)–Holmes's personal favorite–felt her popularity must be attributable to "the abundance of romantic melodrama, and the

general tendency of nearly every one of any account in the story to acquire either by shrewdness, or natural inheritance, or marriage, the control of immense wealth. . . . They are simply crude glorifications of wealth and luxury, and must have, with many, a more debasing influence than an open portrayal of vice." Such a view seems to turn a cold eye on Holmes's rags-to-riches stories in order to indict their bourgeois capitalist ethic, and it is more likely that such late-century fears stemmed from elite concerns about Holmes's primary audience. Her books were sold mostly by newsboys on railroad cars and in steamboats, an utterly democratic venue. For elites, Holmes's "sin" probably lay more in her promotion of class mobility than in her endorsement of crass materialism.

Although the reviewer may not have been forthcoming as to the true basis of his criticism, he was certainly right in pointing out Holmes's reliance on romantic melodrama. Her descriptions of an occasional moonlight rendezvous or embrace during an electric storm are worthy of milder twentieth-century romances. A vaguely sexual tension between the heroine and hero permeates Holmes's pages and keeps the reader turning them. She was skillful at prolonging such sexual tension through obstacles. The premise of *Ethelyn's Mistake,* for example, rests on a series of misunderstandings between husband and wife. Ethelyn's husband finds an old love letter to Ethelyn from an old flame who happens to be in town at the moment. Naturally, the husband assumes that Ethelyn is unfaithful. Proud Ethelyn leaves immediately when she hears the insulting charge. During the ensuing separation, Ethelyn and her husband realize how much they love each other. Their reunion is eventually effected but not until many blunders have occurred and many years have passed, giving greater pleasure to the final reunion. Thus, while lurid sensation was absent from Holmes's novels, romantic "thrills" were not.

Nineteenth-century fears about the propriety of art or, more precisely, about the propriety of calling Holmes's work art, which certainly contributed to the late-century condemnation of her books by cultural elites, have often been revisited in the twentieth century. Moved by the occasion of Holmes's death on 6 October 1907 at the age of eighty-two, several elite cultural organs put forward defenses of her work. Though the writer in the 3 October issue of *The Nation* acknowledged that her work was "barely recognized as existing by the guardians of literary tradition," he claimed that such writing required skill: "It is a common fallacy that any writer of facility could turn out books like these." The critic for the December 1907 issue of *The Bookman* agreed: "the public to which Mrs. Holmes appealed was faithful to her until the very end" because she realized that the "public which critics do not recognise holds fast to certain primitive ideals, both ethical and literary, which are unchanged amid the clash of Romantics and Realists, of Naturalists and Symbolists."

Twentieth-century scholars, particularly in the period prior to the feminist recovery of women's domestic novels, largely ignored or disparaged Holmes's work. Alexander Cowie was more respectful than most when in *The Rise of the American Novel* (1948) he offered Holmes some shelter under the umbrella of realism: "It is to be feared that our grandmothers read *'Lena Rivers* for the sake of the ingredients [of popular romance] . . . but they may have read it also for its good sense of place and its amusing delineation of Negro life and character." Doubts about the pleasures to be derived from Holmes's racial caricatures aside, such an evaluation displays the difficulties presented by traditional literary criticism of Holmes's work: it is hard to achieve a just assessment of Holmes's work when it is judged by stylistic elements used to acclaim male writers, and its content is deemed embarrassingly feminine. There are, however, important reasons to study her work on its own merits. Holmes may be valued for her witty departure from, and sometimes pointed critique of, domestic fiction, for her under-examined contributions to American humor, for nudging the domestic novel toward the women's romance novel, and, not least, for her well-documented ability to entertain.

References:

Nina Baym, *Woman's Fiction: A Guide to Novels by and about Women in America, 1820–1870* (Ithaca, N.Y.: Cornell University Press, 1978);

Herbert Ross Brown, *The Sentimental Novel in America 1789–1860* (Durham, N.C.: Duke University Press, 1940);

Esther Jane Carrier, *Fiction in Public Libraries, 1876–1900* (New York: Scarecrow, 1965);

Alexander Cowie, "The Domestic Sentimentalists and Other Popular Writers (1850–1870)," in his *The Rise of the American Novel* (New York: American Book Company, 1948), pp. 412–446;

J. C. Derby, *Fifty Years Among Authors, Books, and Publishers* (New York: Carleton, 1884);

Dee Garrison, "Immoral Fiction in the Late Victorian Library," in her *Apostles of Culture: The Public Librarian and American Society, 1876–1920* (New York: Free Press, 1979);

John S. Hart, *A Manual of American Literarture* (New York: Johnson Reprint Corporation, 1969);

Mary Kelley, *Private Woman, Public Stage: Literary Domesticity in Nineteenth-Century America* (New York: Oxford University Press, 1984);

Frank Luther Mott, *Golden Multitudes: The Story of Best Sellers in the United States* (New York: Macmillan, 1947);

Mary Noel, *Villains Galore: The Heyday of the Popular Story Weekly* (New York: Macmillan, 1954);

Helen Waite Papashvily, *All the Happy Endings: A Study of the Domestic Novel in America, the Women Who Wrote It, the Women Who Read It, in the Nineteenth Century* (New York: Harper, 1956).

Papers:

Many of Mary Jane Holmes's letters and memorabilia are held by the Seymour Library in Brockport, New York.

Thomas Janvier
(16 July 1849 – 18 June 1913)

Layne Neeper
Morehead State University

BOOKS: *Color Studies* (New York: Scribners, 1885; London: Bickers, 1886); enlarged as *Color Studies and A Mexican Campaign* (New York: Scribners, 1891);

The Mexican Guide (New York: Scribners, 1886);

The Aztec Treasure House: A Romance of Contemporaneous Antiquity (New York: Harper, 1890; London: Sampson Low, 1891);

Stories of Old New Spain (New York: Appleton, 1891; London: Osgood & McIlvaine, 1891);

The Uncle of an Angel and Other Stories (New York: Harper, 1891);

The Armies of To-day: A Description of the Armies of the Leading Nations at the Present Time (New York: Harper, 1893);

An Embassy to Provence (New York: Century, 1893; London: Unwin, 1893);

The Women's Conquest of New-York. Being an Account of the Rise and Progress of the Women's Rights Movement . . . By a Member of the Committee of Safety of 1908 (New York: Harper, 1894);

In Old New York (New York & London: Harper, 1894);

Saint Antonio of the Gardens, with Provençal translation by Mary Girard (Avignon: Roumanille, 1895);

In the Sargasso Sea (New York & London: Harper, 1898);

The Passing of Thomas; In the St. Peter's Set; At the Grand Hôtel du Paadis; The Fish of Monsieur Quissard; Le Bon Oncle d'Amérique; Five Stories (New York & London: Harper, 1900);

In Great Waters: Four Stories (New York & London: Harper, 1901);

The Christmas Kalends of Provence and Some Other Provençal Festivals (New York & London: Harper, 1902);

The Dutch Founding of New York (New York & London: Harper, 1903);

Santa Fé's Partner: Being Some Memorials of Events in a New-Mexican Track-End Town (New York & London: Harper, 1907);

Henry Hudson, a Brief Statement of his Aims and his Achievements (New York & London: Harper, 1909);

Legends of the City of Mexico (New York & London: Harper, 1910);

From the South of France: The Roses of Monsieur Alphonse, The Poodle of Monsieur Gáillard, The Recrudescence of Madame Vic, Madame Jolicoeur's Cat, A Consolate Giantess (New York & London: Harper, 1912);

At the Casa Napoleon (New York & London: Harper, 1914).

Thomas Janvier was a journalist, prolific short-story writer, and novelist who is best remembered for his fictionalized accounts of bohemian and middle-class life in nineteenth-century New York City. Much of his most interesting fiction chronicles the artistic enclave of

142

Greenwich Village and the French Quarter with its eccentric, cosmopolitan inhabitants. Janvier attempted to capture the spirit and times of New York when farmlands still rimmed the city and recently arrived immigrants sought to make their way in a new country. In his portrayals of the manners, dialects, and mores of New Yorkers he can be regarded as a local colorist, one of the dozens of regionalist writers who flourished at the end of the nineteenth century. In addition to his New York fiction the well-traveled Janvier wrote both fiction and nonfiction set in exotic Mexico and the south of France.

Like his contemporary Henry James, Janvier was interested in New York and European society and culture. However, much of Janvier's work reads as droll but rather facile prose that is almost wholly lacking in psychological depth and compelling artistry. Janvier's corpus of work suggests the entertaining but largely superficial nature of most late-nineteenth-century local-color writing. It is writing that has largely fallen out of critical favor while the work of realists such as James and Edith Wharton, more insightful observers of the New York scene, has become part of the canon of American literature.

Thomas Allibone Janvier was born in Philadelphia on 16 July 1849 to Frances de Haes and Emma Janvier. Both parents had literary inclinations; his father was a published poet, and his mother wrote stories for children. His sister, Margaret Thompson Janvier, under the pseudonym of Margaret Vandergrift, was a successful children's author. Janvier received a common-school education, began a career in business, and, abandoning that quickly, entered into journalism from 1871 to 1880 for the *Philadelphia Times,* the *Evening Bulletin,* and the *Press.* In 1878 he married Catherine Ann Drinker, a painter and author from Philadelphia. From 1881 to 1884 he explored Colorado, New Mexico, and Mexico as a journalist.

Returning from the West, Janvier settled permanently in New York, though he left the city several times for extended trips to Mexico, France, and England. His travels had a direct bearing on Janvier's literary career. His excursions in the American Southwest and Mexico led to his publication of *The Mexican Guide* (1886), a standard nineteenth-century guidebook; *The Aztec Treasure House: A Romance of Contemporaneous Antiquity* (1890), a story for adolescents; and *Stories of Old New Spain* (1891). His travels in southern France led to his publication of nonfiction accounts of the French character and customs in *An Embassy to Provence* (1893), *The Christmas Kalends of Provence and Some Other Provençal Festivals* (1902), and *From the South of France* (1912). For his interest in Provence and through his association with such writers as Mistral and Felix Gras, he was awarded honorary membership in the Society of the Felibrige for French poets and men of letters.

Color Studies (1885), Janvier's first book of collected stories, is also his most enduring work. The four stories that make up the collection were originally published in New York magazines under his nom de plume Ivory Black, and all take as their common subject the artistic community of painters in Greenwich Village. The book is notable for its finely drawn descriptions of place, its delineation of the manners and morals of New York artists, and its adroit handling of dialect. Like almost all of Janvier's work, it is light fare—a point the author emphasizes in his epigraph: "There is no moral in this book, / No purpose is there 'twixt its covers. / In truth, whichever way you look / You'll only find—a Pair of Lovers."

The title character, "Rose Madder" is an artist's beautiful daughter who will only sit for her father's execrable paintings. She is romantically pursued by the young artist Vandyke Brown and his rival, the devious McGlip. Both artists plan to enter an art competition, hoping to win money, honor, and subsequently Rose's love. Brown conceals the subject of his painting to all but Rose, and in this way some intimacy is established between the two. Before the exhibition McGlip enters Brown's studio, realizes Brown's painting is superior to his own, and defaces it. Rose discovers what McGlip has done and reveals to Brown publicly that "no matter if you have lost the medal, dear, you—you shall have *me* all the same." The hulking Cremnitz White, who subdues McGlip by choking him, complains to the elder Madder, "Ach, mein Gott, Madter! Fhy dit yoo shoost not let me shoke him and pe done mit it?" Further violence is averted, however, and Rose and Brown are married soon after. The story is as maudlin in its telling as it is predictable in its outcome but is somewhat redeemed by Janvier's local-color touches of dialect and setting.

A more interesting story in the same collection is "Roberson's Medium." Like James's celebrated "Daisy Miller" (1878), Janvier's story explores a variation on the late-nineteenth-century cultural figure that James's most popular work helped establish: the "American Girl"—the virtuous but impudent young woman who defies social conventions. Mangan Brown's younger cousin Violet Carmine unexpectedly comes to New York from a plantation in Mexico where she was raised "on the American plan; to be self-confident, and that sort of thing." Like Daisy Miller, Violet, though chastely innocent, upsets social proprieties by such acts as visiting Coney Island unescorted with the painter Rowney Mauve. Violet protests to her disapproving cousin, "Why, cousin Mangan, I thought that here in America girls could do just as they pleased." Rowney fully

THE LETTER FROM THE DEAD.

THE FIGHT IN THE CAÑON.

THE CAVE OF THE DEAD.

Illustrations by Frederic Remington from Janvier's The Aztec Treasure House *(1890)*

appreciates her violations of decorum and falls in love with her. Roberson, a painter who shares studio space with Rowney, admits to Rowney that he also loves the impetuous Violet. Bent on duping and humiliating Roberson so as to win Violet as his own, Rowney contrives a convoluted parlor trick involving a séance presided over by a fraudulent "Theosoph" during which Rowney and Violet "materialize" and kiss before the aghast Roberson.

Soon realizing that he has been fooled, Roberson reveals the scandalous kiss he witnessed to Violet's cousin and friends, thus jeopardizing Violet's reputation. To avoid further scandal, Rowney proposes marriage and Violet agrees but only if they will elope. Instead of expressing parental disapproval, Violet's father hails her "spirited way" and proclaims that love "defies conventionalities, and laughs at locksmiths, and is the true parent of Romance!" In "Daisy Miller" James shows how an American girl's innocent breaches of European social codes cause her to be sacrificed to a system that she does not fully understand; however, in Janvier's lighthearted and trivialized adaptation of the same theme, the social repercussions of Violet's transgressions are so thoroughly downplayed for the sake of romantic comedy as to be unsatisfying.

Janvier went on to become a regular contributor to *Harper's Magazine* from the late 1880s until his last years, and several of his stories were routinely collected and published by Harper, as was *The Uncle of an Angel and Other Stories* (1891). In the title story Janvier returns to the theme of the American Girl and approaches his subject with the jocund humor befitting a comedy of manners. Hutchinson Port, an elderly and patrician Philadelphian, is dismayed to find himself named the guardian of Dorothy, his eighteen-year-old niece. Dorothy proves to be a willful charge who through badgering persistence always gets her way. Referring to herself as her uncle's "angel," Dorothy insists that they vacation in Saratoga rather than Port's customary resort at Narragansett. After a month's stay, however, she concludes that Saratoga is "vulgar" and decides they should move on to Narragansett without delay. Once there, Dorothy complains about the somber company of aged Philadelphians and longs for the excitement of dances, yachting, and tennis.

In pursuit of adventure Dorothy accompanies the "scamp" Van Rensselaer Livingstone to balls and on boating expeditions. Fearing the outcome of the inevitable confrontation with her uncle that her association with the disreputable Livingstone will bring, Dorothy chooses instead to marry Pennington Brown, a tedious old Philadelphian and one of her uncle's oldest friends, who has secretly proposed marriage to her—all for the sake of not being bested by her uncle in argument.

While the plot is ridiculously improbable and the characters are merely caricatures, the story is interesting for its depiction of Saratoga and Narragansett as the playgrounds of the privileged class in the Gilded Age.

Janvier's only novel, *In the Sargasso Sea* (1898), is an unabashed adventure story, a dramatic departure in both its subject matter and style from the body of his other work. Bound for the African coast where a job awaits him, Roger Stetworth, a mechanical engineer and "a promiscuously green young fool," books passage aboard the *Golden Hind* despite being suspicious of the ship. Several days out from New York harbor, Stetworth's apprehensions prove to be well-founded. Capt. Luke Chiltin and his first mate reveal they are slavers involved in the trafficking of Africans from the west coast to Northern Africa. The captain and mate try to force Stetworth to become a part of their slaving enterprise, but he refuses and as a result is beaten unconscious and thrown overboard. Stetworth is miraculously plucked from the Atlantic by the passing *Hurst Castle* and has his wounds tended by a kindly doctor. A terrific storm nearly swamps the liner, however, and the wounded Stetworth is left behind in the ensuing chaos as the other passengers abandon the listing ship. He stays aboard the well-provisioned vessel for days as it is drawn irresistibly toward the weed-choked perimeter of the Sargasso Sea.

Stetworth finds the Sargasso Sea to be a vast ships' graveyard crowded with hundreds of wrecks that are caught in the slowly swirling eddy. He decides to venture forth from the *Hurst Castle* and, by jumping from deck to deck of the closely packed wrecks, begins to explore his strange surroundings. He quickly becomes disoriented in the maze of shipwrecks but perceives that newer ships ring the outer edge of the weed-mass and older vessels are lodged within the concentric rings further toward its center. Roving from ship to ship, Stetworth not only finds a compass and charts but also an antiquated Spanish galleon laden with hundreds of gold ingots and a cask of small jewels. Unable to haul the gold, he removes the priceless gems. He then boards a newer wreck, assembles a small seaworthy craft, and makes his way out of the Sargasso Sea where he is then rescued by a steamer.

Janvier's sole novel is exasperatingly dull because dozens of pages are given over to the repetitious, mundane business of Stetworth's search for food among the wrecks and delivery from his predicament. In one scene, for example, Janvier describes in painstaking detail how Stetworth sews beans into the shorn sleeves of his shirt and hauls them on his back. Although the book shows traces of the slight influence of Edgar Allan Poe's *The Narrative of Arthur Gordon Pym of Nantucket* (1838) and Herman Melville's early sea novels, Janvier's story is thoroughly plot-driven and lacks any vestige of metaphoric or symbolic significance.

In Great Waters: Four Stories (1901) also represents a departure from Janvier's customary comedies in that all the stories are tragic. In "A Duluth Tragedy," for instance, George Maltham comes to desolate Minnesota Point on Lake Superior to conduct some protracted business. He chances upon the home of Major Calhoun Ashley, a displaced South Carolinian with a thick southern accent, and his beautiful, wild-spirited daughter, Ulrica. In the ensuing several weeks, Maltham, who is already engaged to be married in Chicago, plays with the affections of Ulrica, and she falls deeply in love with him. Upon learning that Maltham has never been serious in his intentions toward her, Ulrica proposes that they take her small sloop out sailing. Once on the tempestuous lake, Ulrica reveals her plan to sail the ship into the maelstrom and thus destroy them both.

With its depiction of passionate but doomed love, the story is thoroughly melodramatic. However, aside from the bathos and histrionics implicit in it, Janvier's decision to present a "magnificent, commanding, defiant" woman who is "glad and eager to give herself strongly to the strong death-clasp of the waves" holds some cultural significance in turn-of-the-century fiction. While the story is far from a feminist declaration, Janvier's Ulrica does refuse to become the passive victim of aborted love and chooses instead to be an avenging actor who seeks justice for the wrong done to her.

Janvier died childless in New York City on 18 June 1913 and was buried in Moorestown, New Jersey.

His last book, *At the Casa Napoleon* (1914), was published posthumously the year after his death. The collection represents a fitting close to his literary career, for in these stories he alternately treats the residents of Greenwich Village and provincial French hamlets. The title story is itself characteristic of the majority of Janvier's oeuvre. It is set in a "Franco-Spanish-American hotel" off Washington Square. The hotel's colorful lodgers are newly relocated immigrants from Spain, Germany, and France, and Janvier shows with light, comic touches the ways in which New Yorkers are joined in common purpose toward establishing a new and richer life in America.

In his laudatory preface to Janvier's *At the Casa Napoleon,* Harper editor Ripley Hitchcock eulogizes Janvier and praises his literary contributions for their "mellowness and quaintness." Such terms, however, no longer evoke literary merit, and Hitchcock's remarks underscore that Janvier's reputation has not withstood the passing of time. There has been no substantial critical discussion of Janvier's work. While most contemporary commentators would agree that the overall quality of his writing is decidedly second-rate, Janvier's regionalist preoccupations with place, manners, and dialect impart to his work some small measure of historical significance in reflecting certain late-nineteenth-century tendencies in American fiction.

Papers:
Some of Thomas Janvier's manuscripts and correspondence are held by the Clifton Waller Barrett Library at the University of Virginia.

John Beauchamp Jones

(6 March 1810 – 4 February 1866)

Robin Grey
University of Illinois–Chicago

BOOKS: *Wild Western Scenes: A Narrative of Adventures in the Western Wilderness, Forty Years Ago* (New York: Colman / Baltimore: Hickman, 1841);

The Book of Visions: Being a Transcript of the Record of the Secret Thoughts of a Variety of Individuals While Attending Church, anonymous (Philadelphia: Moore, 1847);

Rural Sports: A Tale in Four Parts (Philadelphia: Marshall, 1849);

The Western Merchant: A Narrative . . . , as Luke Shortfield (Philadelphia: Grigg, Elliot, 1849);

The City Merchant; or, The Mysterious Failure (Philadelphia: Lippincott, Grambo, 1851);

Adventures of Col. Gracchus Vanderbomb, of Sloughcreek, in Pursuit of the Presidency; Also, The Exploits of Mr. Numerius Plutarch Kipps, His Private Secretary (Philadelphia: Hart, 1852);

The Spanglers and Tingles; or, The Rival Belles . . . (Philadelphia: Hart, 1852); republished as *The Rival Belles; or, Life in Washington* (Philadelphia: Hart, 1852);

The Monarchist: An Historical Novel Embracing Real Characters and Romantic Adventures (Philadelphia: Hart, 1853);

Life and Adventures of a Country Merchant: A Narrative of His Exploits at Home, during His Travels, and in the Cities; Designed to Amuse and Instruct (Philadelphia: Lippincott, Grambo, 1854);

Freaks of Fortune; or, The History and Adventures of Ned Lorn (Philadelphia: Peterson, 1854); republished as *Love and Money* (Philadelphia: Peterson, 1865);

The Winkles; or, The Merry Monomaniacs: An American Picture with Portraits of the Natives, anonymous (New York: Appleton, 1855);

Wild Western Scenes, Second Series; The War Path: A Narrative of Adventures in the Wilderness . . . (Philadelphia: Lippincott, 1856);

Border War: A Tale of Disunion (New York: Rudd & Carleton, 1859); republished as *Wild Southern Scenes . . .* (Philadelphia: Peterson, 1859); republished as *Secession, Coercion, and Civil War: The Story of 1861* (Philadelphia: Peterson, 1861);

Wild Western Scenes: or, The White Spirit of the Wilderness . . . New Series (Richmond: Malsby, 1863);

John Beauchamp Jones

A Rebel War Clerk's Diary at the Confederate States Capital, 2 volumes (Philadelphia: Lippincott, 1866).

OTHER: *Baltimore Saturday Visiter,* edited by Jones (9 May 1840 – 6 November 1841);

Baltimore Phoenix and Budget, edited by Jones (April 1841 – December 1841);

Madisonian, edited by Jones (8 November 1841 – 14 December 1841);

Daily Madisonian, edited by Jones (15 December 1841 – 7 April 1845);

Compact, edited by Jones (16 October 1847 – 4 December 1847);

Southern Monitor, edited by Jones (6 June 1857 – 8 April 1861).

John Beauchamp Jones was a popular novelist (particularly of the West and the South) and a well-connected literary editor and political journalist in the two decades leading up to the Civil War. Jones's fiction and activities as an editor attracted the attention of other literary notables of the period, including Edgar Allan Poe and William Gilmore Simms. His early novels, *Wild Western Scenes: A Narrative of Adventures in the Western Wilderness, Forty Years Ago* (1841), *The Western Merchant: A Narrative . . .* (1849), and *Life and Adventures of a Country Merchant: A Narrative of His Exploits at Home, during His Travels, and in the Cities; Designed to Amuse and Instruct* (1854), capture the picturesque and generally Edenic qualities of the West, where he spent his early years. His novels commend the honesty of "the People" and predict their abiding success, hearkening back to the democratic republicanism of Thomas Jefferson and to the enterprising self-reliance illustrated in Benjamin Franklin's *Autobiography* (1868). His adventure novels, including his best-seller *Wild Western Scenes,* are typically humorous, fast-paced, episodic, and filled with a cast of colorful frontier types, including Daniel Boone. In his own day this novel sold a hundred thousand copies, including translations into other languages. Many of his novels dramatize a keen awareness of the economic problems of America in the 1830s and 1840s, including the Jacksonian Bank War, the hard-currency conflict, the panic of 1837, the excesses of land speculation, and international trade imbalances. One novel, *The City Merchant; or, the Mysterious Failure* (1851), divides its focus between these economic issues and the racial tensions that culminated in race riots in Philadelphia. During the period following the Compromise of 1850 and Fugitive Slave Law, Jones increasingly focused his novels on the growing sectional antagonism between the North and the South. *Adventures of Col. Gracchus Vanderbomb, of Sloughcreek, in Pursuit of the Presidency; Also, The Exploits of Mr. Numerius Plutarch Kipps, His Private Secretary* (1852), a satire on political demagoguery in the 1850s, highlights the futility of campaigning to represent the entire nation in an environment of such intense sectional strife. His *Border War: A Tale of Disunion* (1859), another well-received novel, was one of the few attempts to imagine the Civil War before it actually began. The novel, republished as *Wild Southern Scenes,* depicts the wrongs he believed the South suffered while urging the necessity of maintaining the Union. By modern estimates Jones's importance as a literary figure rests on his regional and self-consciously American writings. His

life, like Poe's, also vividly illustrates the difficulties of American authors, particularly those whose careers straddled the Mason-Dixon line, in an emerging publishing industry that was plagued by economic instability. His importance as an historical figure derives both from his chronicles of the presidential administration of John Tyler in the *Daily Madisonian* (1841–1845), in which he wrote extensively about the president and U.S. monetary policies, and from his editorship of the *Southern Monitor* (1857–1861), in which he sought to promote the Southern cause in the North and to assuage the escalating sectional tensions. Among historians he is today best remembered for his detailed and extensive diary of the Civil War, written at the Confederacy's Richmond, Virginia, headquarters and later published as *A Rebel War Clerk's Diary at the Confederate States Capital* (1866).

Little documentary evidence exists about Jones's early years: he was born in Baltimore on 6 March 1810, and his family immigrated to Kentucky and Missouri in the Western territories, the setting of several of his early novels. Other details about his early life must be inferred from his novel *The Western Merchant,* which appears to be a thinly veiled autobiography and is the only work he published under the pseudonym "Luke Shortfield." According to the story "Luke" comes from a large family that relocated to Kentucky when he was a child of six. He acquires "the rudiments of a good English education, and an insatiable passion for books" before his father's business fails. He then briefly works on the family farm before taking a job as a deputy clerk in a lawyer's office. There he informally furthers his education by reading volumes of British and Roman history as well as English literature. He then agrees to aid his brother as a clerk and merchant in a western outpost in Missouri. Owing to their prudence and thrift, he and his brother prosper financially, and he becomes a respectable western merchant in his own right. His future as a merchant is, however, undermined by his longing to be a writer and his wistful desire to earn the love of a refined and wealthy heiress he left behind in Norfolk, Virginia. In the novel these problems are happily resolved by the heiress, who reciprocates his love, encourages his writing, and improves his financial situation.

Jones married the wealthy Frances Thomas Custis of Accomack County, Virginia, in 1840, and shortly thereafter he became the joint proprietor as well as editor of the *Baltimore Saturday Visiter.* In December 1841 Jones became the editor and the sole proprietor of a Washington newspaper called the *Daily Madisonian.* Whereas Jones's family genealogy remains sketchy, evidently by his own choosing, his marriage gave him a long and venerable set of family connections in Norfolk

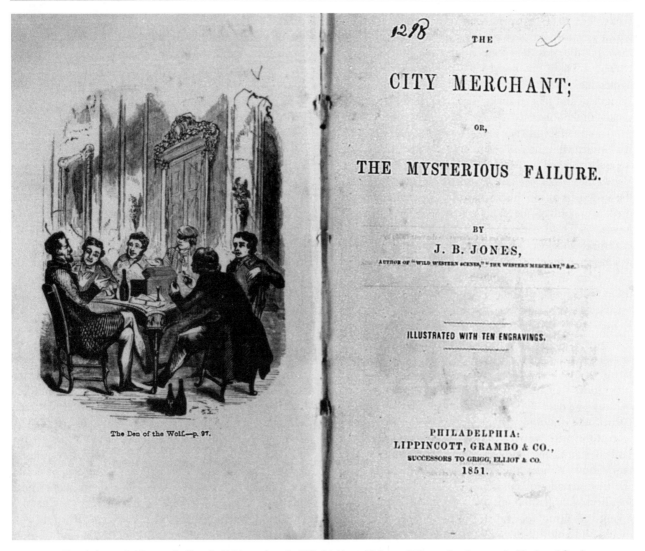

Frontispiece and title page for Jones's 1851 novel, set in Philadelphia amid the escalating tensions between the North and South

and Northampton and Accomack counties, as well as income from lands owned by the family in Virginia. His wife's family could be traced back to Martha Custis Washington and through her descendants to Mary, her great-granddaughter and the wife of Confederate general Robert E. Lee. Gov. Henry Wise of Virginia, the object of Jones's enduring political devotion, was also a kinsman of Frances Jones. Jones's talents as a writer as well as his wife's illustrious Virginia connections probably enhanced his mobility in high political circles within both the Tyler administration and the Confederacy.

In his earlier days as a writer, contributor to magazines, and subsequently editor of the *Baltimore Saturday Visiter,* Jones faced the difficult problems of a depressed publishing industry in antebellum America. He, like other writers such as Poe, resorted to magazine or newspaper editorships in order to supplement his income. Jones also

sought to gain some measure of economic and artistic autonomy by controlling his own magazine: he even bought a share in the *Baltimore Saturday Visiter* in order to publish his first novel in its pages. Like many other American authors, Jones identified at least one of the causes of his predicament and therefore supported American literary nationalism through his fervent advocacy of an international copyright law. His *Baltimore Phoenix and Budget* announced that it was "devoted to the encouragement of native talent being almost exclusively composed of American Productions." In such a precarious environment American magazinists customarily offered one another some measure of cooperation and support. Jones, in fact, sent literary contributions during Poe's editorship of *Burton's Gentleman's Magazine* and corresponded with him (6 August 1839) about the reception of *Burton's* in Baltimore. Poe likewise included Jones in volume 19 of *Graham's*

(December 1841) in his installment of "Autography," in which he analyzed the signatures as well as the literary merit of "the most noted among the living literati of the country." There Poe noted Jones's connection with "the lighter literature of Baltimore" and praised him for the "judgment and general ability" he displayed during his editorship of the *Visiter*.

Jones's first and best-selling novel, *Wild Western Scenes*, was written while he was editor of the *Baltimore Saturday Visiter* and published in Baltimore just as he was preparing to launch the *Daily Madisonian* newspaper in late 1841. Set in the wilderness on the "mad Missouri" River, some two hundred miles north of "the St. Louis settlement" in about 1800, it portrays the adventures of a small group of world-weary easterners who seek to escape the vanities and vexations of civilization and to bury themselves in some obscure retreat away from the cycle of "one striving to oppress his fellow being, that he might acquire riches and power, to be again snatched from his grasp by others." These men and women, along with their children and hired hands, seek and occasionally find "a peaceful scene, fresh from the hand of God, and unmarred by the workmanship of meaner creatures."

Jones's first novel, like many of his others, is a curious blend of light, humorous episodes of hunting parties and shooting matches; picaresque, sensational adventures with warring Indian tribes, prairie fires, and buffalo stampedes; and darker, Gothic studies of the temptations of cities, the decadence of the wealthy, and the tragic results of misguided love. The hired hands Joe Beck (an Irish immigrant) and Sneak Punk (an eccentric Vermonter) provide most of the comic elements and colorful dialogue in their hunting rivalries and practical jokes. In the adventure segments of the novel Jones tries his hand at historical fiction for the first time by introducing Boone, who guides and protects the group through the dangers of the frontier.

However, the easterners—Charles Glenn, a physician from New York and Philadelphia, and Jasper Roughgrove, trained for the ministry in England—provide the rationale for the story and add an unsettling, melodramatic element. In an exchange of intimacies late in the narrative, both these virtuous men discover that the women they loved had been ruined by bad marriages to predatory, wealthy patricians and thus both men have fled to the frontier to escape their sorrows. Although Jasper briefly recuperates his loss by marrying his ruined lover, Charles is not so fortunate. In an extraordinary and grotesque scene worthy of Poe (whose tale "Berenice" Jones may have read), Charles is called to conduct before medical students an autopsy upon a beautiful prostitute whose body miraculously escaped unscathed from a fatal fire. After opening the chest and removing the heart to examine it, he becomes

curious to see the face of the veiled cadaver and discovers—in a high state of alarm—that he is holding the heart of his lost love. Unlike Poe, however, Jones turns such dark episodes into didactic occasions for moralizing about the need for strength of character to resist temptations. The story ends on a lighter note with all virtue being duly rewarded: Charles finds love and marries, and Jasper's family is finally reunited.

William Gilmore Simms, reviewing the novel years later for the *Southern Quarterly,* suggested its plot structure was "inartistical and clumsy, but not deficient in interest." Poe, however, remarked favorably upon Jones's "series of papers of high merit now in course of publication in the 'Visitor' [*sic*], and entitled 'Wild Western Scenes,'" which Jones was at the time having published at his expense as a bound novel. It is highly probable that Poe wrote another favorable (unsigned) notice of Jones's *Wild Western Scenes* a month later in volume 20 of *Graham's* (January 1842), when Poe was still literary editor of that magazine: "Mr. Jones is a man of talent, and these descriptions of Wild Western Life evince it. We read each successive number with additional zest." Perhaps Jones's political situation seemed attractive to Poe: Jones already had the ear of President Tyler as well as his son Robert, who himself had literary aspirations. (Jones published favorable reviews of Robert Tyler's poetry in his *Madisonian.*) His newspaper was largely being supported by its official status as Tyler's organ as well as by the "executive printing" work given to it by the Senate and the president. Since Poe was known to have a keen interest in a Customs House patronage job in Philadelphia in order to support his literary ambitions, and since he had encouragement through friends that Robert Tyler meant him to have it, Poe's interest in Jones may well have been related to Jones's proximity to the Tylers.

The Daily Madisonian, which occupied Jones for the next four years, provides detailed information about the politics, literature, and economics of America during the period from late 1841 to 1845. Jones was clearly in a position to know—and occasionally to influence—the inner workings of Congress and government patronage, the economic circumstances of American writers, the currency problems of the U.S., and the mounting tensions among Americans between their national and regional identities. According to one obituary notice Jones was "during the whole of that Administration upon the most intimate and confidential relations with Mr. Webster, Mr. Upshur, Mr. Spencer and Mr. Ewing of Mr. Tyler's Cabinet; and was frequently invited to, and participated in the consultations of the leading men who gave Mr. Tyler's administration a cordial support." During his editorship of the *Daily Madisonian* he wrote articles ranging from a "Brief History of Money" to

"International Copyright," in which he announces that "Our country possesses many men of great literary genius, whose powers are lost to the world, simply because they cannot *afford to write for nothing*." In his series on the four regions of the country his announced purpose is "to show the relations existing between the different sections of the Union and the Federal Government, and to demonstrate that a resuscitation of the old Republican doctrines and measures of Jefferson and Madison . . . will conduce to the speedy and permanent prosperity of all." His article "On the Appointment of Washington Irving as Minister to Spain" congratulates the "discrimination and the justice of Mr. Tyler and Mr. Webster" in making this patronage appointment and then ponders the question of "whether a man who forms correct tastes and gives a wholesome tendency to the morals and opinions of his countrymen, is not as much a public benefactor as he who constructs a bridge or frames a bankrupt law."

Many of the economic themes and sectional concerns that dominate his novels derive from the issues he encountered in his editorship of the newspaper. Jones tended to focus on America as a nation that pitted the "hardy and honest People of the West" against the abuses of an increasingly corrupt Congress and the monopolistic impulses of the northeastern economic elite. Although he was a Whig, Jones felt persecuted by powerful coteries within Congress and exclaimed in his *Daily Madisonian* of 4 June 1842 that, even though he "had been daily with the President, the Secretaries, the office-holders and the office-seekers," he was powerless to prevent the loss of his own privilege of the executive printing. (Nor could Tyler prevent it, since the embattled president was at odds with Congress and his own Whig party.) Jones's novelistic interests and political allegiances shifted to the South during the early 1850s, but he continued to emphasize the ideal of a humble republicanism struggling against a monied aristocracy. The North represented the wealthy clique of merchants and bankers destroying the economy and fragmenting the Union for the gain of a few; the "Glorious South," according to Jones, was the last stronghold of republicanism, constitutionality, and states' rights.

Even though the loss of the government printing contract was a financial setback for him, Jones continued to edit and write for the *Daily Madisonian*. In successive issues of the paper, he spoke in ever more melodramatic terms of his rough treatment at the hands of Whig congressmen hostile to Tyler: "was it not *too* great an anti-climax to be tossed heels over head into the basement (it was base-meant) of the Capitol, and brought to the end of our career in a dark committee room? Well, there was no alternative but to divulge whatever was required of us, or to languish in prison,

and perhaps die there." Finally, in April 1845, after the departure of Tyler from office and the inauguration of President James K. Polk, Jones turned over the *Daily Madisonian* to the Democrats. Although during that administration John C. Calhoun offered Jones the position of chargé d'affaires to Naples, he declined it. Instead, he traveled in Europe in 1846, briefly edited another political newspaper, *The Compact*, in Philadelphia in 1847, and finally devoted himself to writing novels.

Although eight years had elapsed since his first novel, Jones returned to the West for the setting of his second, moderately successful novel, *The Western Merchant*. In addition to its probable autobiographical elements, the novel depicts the sensuous beauty and powerful economic appeal of the western landscape. In many ways this novel (along with the 1854 reworked and greatly expanded version titled *Life and Adventures of a Country Merchant*) resembles the immigration literature of the period–travel narratives, settlers' manuals, and railroad company pamphlets–which promoted resettlement to newly arrived Europeans and to disheartened city dwellers. The "great natural energy of character" and "wise penetration" of the region's residents are frequently praised. The significant advantages of the midwestern lands over those further west are analyzed (including the cost of an acre, the nature of the terrain, and fertility of the land). The creed of Luke Shortfield's brother Joseph clearly touts the ample economic possibilities of Missouri and of the West in general: "A young man of good character, and of a business capacity, will not long want for capital in a new country. But he must be steadfast, energetic, and never ashamed of small beginnings."

In the manner of Franklin's *Autobiography*, *The Western Merchant* and *The Country Merchant* are loosely structured by episodes, each depicting an adventure that tests a novice's character, provides him with positive and negative models of authority, and gauges his maturation and moral fiber. One positive model is Luke's father, whom he emphatically defends as man of "unimpeachable integrity" whose discretion and honor insured that despite his business failure, "every dollar was honorably offered up to his creditors." One negative model for Luke is Moses Tubal, the Jewish merchant who attempts to compete with Luke at his Missouri outpost. William Shakespeare's Shylock and his kinsman Tubal in *The Merchant of Venice* were clearly models for Jones's character, as well as for other Jewish characters in *The City Merchant* and *The Country Merchant* (where the Missouri frontier outpost is named "Venice"). Portrayed with the physical traits, broken English, deviousness, and greed associated with the most negative Jewish stereotypes, Tubal nevertheless offers an

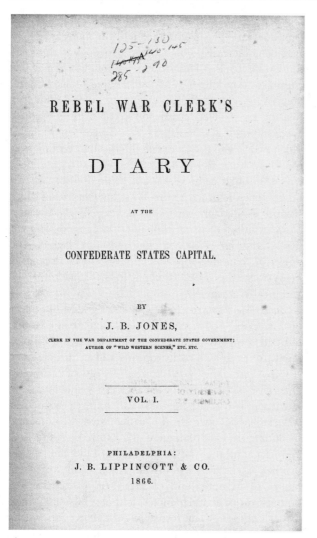

REBEL WAR CLERK'S

DIARY

AT THE

CONFEDERATE STATES CAPITAL.

BY

J. B. JONES,

CLERK IN THE WAR DEPARTMENT OF THE CONFEDERATE STATES GOVERNMENT;
AUTHOR OF "WILD WESTERN SCENES," ETC. ETC.

VOL. I.

PHILADELPHIA:
J. B. LIPPINCOTT & CO.
1866.

Title page for Jones's diary of the Civil War years, for which he became known as "the Confederate Pepys"

important lesson about the dangers and attractions of monopolies and adds an interesting complexity and variety to Jones's depiction of the frontier. In the three novels the Jewish characters' economic practices represent an alternative form of capitalism about which Jones was ambivalent. His narrators tend to display both a tacit admiration for the characters' cleverness and a sharp disdain for their financial practices. In *The Western Merchant* the astute initiate prevails over his competitor by outwitting him at his own games but then experiences sharp remorse and resolves to return to more ethical principles.

Unlike the America that Franklin depicted many years earlier, these novels also register the economic instabilities of the nation and the region, based in part upon the knowledge Jones gained while running the *Daily Madisonian*. On one occasion Luke comments upon the national monetary chaos exacerbated by the loss of the centralized (though private and corrupt) Bank of the United States. With the steady flow of foreign immigrants to his state, Missouri had been fortunate, for "the coins of Europe soon began to circulate more abundantly in Missouri than, perhaps, in any other part of the Union." "Subsequent experience," however, "has proved that the depreciated shinplasters of other states could not be kept out of circulation by all the wisdom of our rulers; and since the banishment of the U.S. Bank notes, every Missouri merchant has at times been under the necessity of submitting to the extortionate discounts of brokers, when converting the currency taken in his neighborhood into paper that would be received in the east." Luke's refusal to pay the discount rate becomes a pivotal incident in the novel, for when he decides to return to the East to ask for the hand of his beloved, he decides to keep all the money he earned as a merchant in coins. When his ship wrecks on the way, his fortune sinks along with it.

This reversal hastens his sudden change to writing as a vocation, a decision that allows Jones to comment on the plight of American authors and the instabilities of the publishing industry, where "in consequence of the precarious condition of the business of the country," most houses declined to "make any additional engagements." Luke learns what Poe already knew too well, "that not a single one in this country has ever yet realized sufficient means from the profits of his pen (the *poetic pen*) to support his family." Although he manages to earn money by writing for magazines and gets some compensation for his first novel, Luke decides that his book "failed to produce me any substantial benefit to compensate me for the labor of composition." This prompts Luke to leave Philadelphia, where his "poor works had been so prematurely buried." His vocational crisis is rendered melodramatically in passages explicitly, and perhaps satirically, recalling the intensity and despair of romantic writers. With the surprise recovery of his sunken fortune, however, his hopes are restored, and he is poised to receive the fruits of his labors and his principles.

Jones's third novel, *The City Merchant,* published in the wake of the 1850 Fugitive Slave Law and the escalating tensions between the North and South, continues the lessons useful to a merchant but changes the location to Philadelphia and introduces Jacksonian economic policies, abolitionism, and sectional tensions as major issues. *The City Merchant* contains a vivid picture of circumstances in America, particularly in Philadelphia from 1836 to 1840, and offers an uncommon Southern perspective on Northern events. Jones highlights the sharp political and social divisions among a diverse population severely tested by the economic crisis. In many respects a roman à clef portraying actual historical events and figures (including Presidents

Andrew Jackson and Martin Van Buren, bankers, and abolitionists), *The City Merchant* describes the circumstances that led to the panic of 1836–1837 and the subsequent national depression. Theories about the causes and inevitability of economic turmoil are presented in a series of conversations between a fictional Whig merchant, Edward Saxon, and Nicholas Biddle, the actual president of the Bank of the United States.

The events in the novel suggest that the panic of 1837 aggravated relations between Whig speculators on credit and Jacksonian Democrats favoring coin and a bullion-backed national currency; between Irish working-class immigrants and the free Northern blacks, their perceived rivals for jobs; and between insurgent abolitionist forces and antireform groups. Through the character of the Saxon, the first half of the novel examines the human consequences of a national economy overwhelmed by international trade imbalances, excessive speculation, and overextended credit. Saxon's foresight and his father's detailed economic diary help him to survive the economic upheaval (and profit from it) by selling his stocks and inventories for cash under the guise of a "mysterious failure." Deep cynicism about the political parties and their tactics also emerges in the early part of the novel in Jones's portrayal of the ways that the Democratic Party courted the Irish immigrants' votes with promises of patronage jobs.

In depicting the abduction of Saxon's daughters by a gang of mulatto men, the second half of the novel dramatizes the perceived threat to civil order that abolitionist efforts were said to promote. Jones represents Philadelphia as little more than a carnival of social and racial disarray excited by antislavery passion: setting the example is "Lucretia Mott walking by the side of Frederick Douglass." Indeed, the narrator laments the "great strapping negro fellows promenading the streets in sociable attitudes and familiar converse with white women; while white men walked the pavements with sooty-faced African women hanging on their arms!" Saxon, moreover, refers without hesitation to the entire population of free blacks in the city as supposed "fugitive slaves." Saxon's Irish porter, Paddy Cork, along with his comrades the Avengers, rescues the daughters on more than one occasion, but not before taking part in the burning of Pennsylvania Hall that occurred during an abolitionist meeting in May 1838. (The kidnapping of the white daughters by mulattoes may in part reflect a vengeful reversal of the Fugitive Slave Law, which was characterized by abolitionist Theodore Parker as the "hateful statute of kidnappers.") Jones's growing allegiances with the South are evident in this novel: the South is consistently depicted as the victim of Northern radicals' provocations, sustaining "such aggressions and wrongs as to

arouse their ardent spirits to frenzy." William Gilmore Simms, a strong proponent of Southern culture and institutions, favorably reviewed the novel, pronouncing it "readable," in part because of "the right-mindedness with which the author discusses the evils of abolition at the North, and the negro mania, which has done so much mischief North and South."

The novel, however, is not without nuances on the issue of race: the narrator acknowledges that the riots brought down the fury of the white population on the blacks, though "many of them were innocent of any participation"; moreover, he claims "it was a painful scene to witness the weeping women and children thronging the streets, flying from their homes" because "an indiscriminate massacre was threatened." The novel, too, traces with some sympathy and trepidation the complicated effects of interracial unions on the lives and identities of the offspring. Primarily, however, as with Jones's later and more successful novel *Border War, The City Merchant* depicts riots and other displays of social disorder to offer a cautionary tale to the Northern abolitionists who would not compromise for the sake of law and order.

A year after warning of deepening sectional tensions in *The City Merchant,* Jones returned to the issue in one of the two novels he published in 1852. *Adventures of Col. Gracchus Vanderbomb, of Sloughcreek, in Pursuit of the Presidency* is both a cynical satire on American politicians and political demagoguery as well as a humorous, spirited study of the aggressive regional identifications of northerners and southerners, affiliations that permitted no meaningful neutrality after the so-called Compromise of 1850. The North and the South, and the Mason-Dixon line separating them, literally structure the plot of the novel. Gracchus Vanderbomb's parents—a New Yorker and a Virginian—hope to create balance or neutrality by building their home exactly on the dividing line and by having their son tutored at home, thus providing their son with a nonsectional identity. Their "Halfway House," in the town of Midway, is built with identical parts on either side of the line. The Northern portion, however, is furnished only with American goods and served only by white servants, whereas the Southern portion is furnished with imported items and served only by slaves. By alternating their residences among the "Halfway House" and additional homes in Furzehill on the Hudson River and in Sloughcreek in Virginia, the family eludes regional affiliation. Later, in middle age, Gracchus is elected first to the New York legislature and then to the Virginia legislature, and he realizes that by declining both and exploiting his unique "neutrality" he might campaign for and attain the presidency. Actual politicians, the issues of the 1850s, and Roman history are all implicated in the various strategies he devises with his tutor and companion, Numerius Plutarch Kipps.

Vanderbomb's campaigns alternate between the South and the North and show that in such an environment of sectional antagonism and suspicion even his most evasive and ambiguous comments are invested with the political motives of the opposite region. In the midst of his Southern campaign he discovers that he inadvertently brought with him his white servant from Massachusetts. Therefore, even after an interrogation in the South–where he successfully obscures or evades defining his position on "the Union," "the Constitution," "the Compromise," "Freesoilism," and "the Higher Law of Mr. Drawees [William Seward]"–he is tacitly assumed to be an abolitionist intent upon stealing their slaves away into freedom. He barely escapes being tarred and feathered, only to find himself in a similar situation in the North. This time the presence of his Southern slave Juba in his party inclines them to believe he is in search of fugitive slaves to be returned to their masters. Despite his attempts to tell his audience in the vaguest possible terms what he thinks will most please them, he eventually finds himself imprisoned in a hideaway for fugitive slaves and in need of rescue. After conducting the rest of his campaign in the press (a duel with an editor results), he fails to gain the nomination of either the Southern convention in Baltimore or the Northern one in Philadelphia and ultimately fails as an independent candidate. Whereas publishers, it is noted in the novel, sought to straddle the Mason-Dixon line out of "fear to be charged with taking sides, and losing the custom of those of opposite politics," Vanderbomb sought to be perceived as a national candidate. He found, however, that in the America of the 1850s the category "national" no longer existed.

Jones temporarily retreated from the issues of antebellum America in his next novel, *The Monarchist: An Historical Novel Embracing Real Characters and Romantic Adventures* (1853). It is set during the American Revolution, an historical moment to which he returned three years later in *Wild Western Scenes, Second Series; The War Path: A Narrative of Adventures in the Wilderness* (1856). *The Monarchist* is panoramic in scope, both in terms of characters and locales (Virginia, Philadelphia, and elsewhere). Several among the large cast of characters were his wife's relatives and ancestors (the Custis family), and several scenes were set on the farm and lands owned by her family on the eastern Shore of Virginia. According to the review by Simms, himself an acknowledged master of the historical novel, the book showed substantial "reading and diligence on the part of the writer, who has scraped together a large body of interesting and curious revolutionary anecdote and illustra-

tion"; but the novel's "chief disability," according to Simms, was a "skipping from place to place, and from person to person. . . . The eye is not permitted to rest long enough on any of the parties to take much interest in any of them." Although Jones's main concern was an examination of monarchy, some characters are, in fact, more developed than Simms credits. For example, Master Wales, the central character, exhibits significant natural ability, great energy, intense loyalty, and a skill in diplomacy. Through him Jones is able to explore the alternative of monarchical government for the nascent American colonies. Wales, a Scotsman living in America, becomes convinced of the value of monarchy and makes successive attempts to have it restored. First, he attempts to have Charles Edward, the Scottish heir to the British throne, proclaimed king in America. He then tries to have the authority of King George III reestablished. Finally, he ventures to rouse monarchical ambitions in George Washington. Unsuccessful at each, he finds his most receptive audience in France's Napoleon, to whom he swears his loyalty and for whom he gives his life.

Jones's disenchantment with the operations of a democratic government, dating from his time at the *Daily Madisonian,* may have prompted his meditations on monarchy. Although he thought the potential for a meritocracy was the greatest virtue of a democracy, he was witness to such corruption and abuses of power in Congress (and later in the Confederacy) that his hopes waned that any great men would emerge to govern. He later wrote in his *A Rebel War Clerk's Diary* that a meritocracy might emerge, "provided the people have rule in the new confederacy. If we are to have a monarchy for the sake of economy and stability, I shall submit to it in preference to the domination of the Northern radicals." He evidently thought monarchy might afford the Confederacy, at least at the beginning of the war, the kind of stability that America's democracy, with its reeling economy, sectional tensions, sharp biases, and civil war, had been unable to sustain.

Although not published until 1854, Jones's next novel, *Freaks of Fortune; or, The History and Adventures of Ned Lorn,* in all probability had been written a decade earlier. (Installments of it were advertised in the 1841–1842 prospectus for his *Baltimore Phoenix and Budget.*) Reflecting Jones's familiarity with the president and his son while running the *Daily Madisonian,* the novel's dedication to Robert Tyler strongly hinted at not only the family's integrity and consequent financial disappointments but also the moral of the novel itself: "To Robert Tyler–Who, with His Father, Retired from the Presidential Mansion–As They Had Entered It–Without Fortune." The message of the novel is even more explicitly stated by the central character, Ned Lorn, an orphan dispossessed of his fortune by a weak-willed uncle and a wicked coconspirator: Ned realizes that "If I have character, . . . the fortune might contribute to my happiness—but not without it." The novel may, in fact, be a sort of loose fable of President Tyler's troubled administration and the effects of Whig political treachery on it: Jones had insinuated often in the *Madisonian* that Tyler had been dispossessed of the power and legacy he deserved by corrupt members of his own party. In the novel Ned becomes a writer and trusts that "Sooner or later merit has its reward. If long delayed, like capital well invested, the accumulated interest will come with the principle." With plot turns and characters highly reminiscent of Charles Dickens's novels, *Freaks of Fortune* centers on the concealed identity of Ned; his apparent death in a "house of refuge" during an epidemic; his rescue from there and subsequent kidnapping and concealment by those who feared his claims to the fortune; his escape and subsequent plans to prove his identity and his malefactors' guilt; his experiences as a writer of a romance (called *The Dishonored*); and his eventual reversal of fortune. The large cast of characters is equally Dickensian in that they are colorful and divided between obvious heroes (for example, Susan Meek, the child's loyal guardian, and Mr. Persever, the lawyer who seeks evidence to aid Ned's case) and manifest villains (Job Mallex, the roguish coconspirator, who later becomes a corrupt politician; Jack Cadaver, an accessory to the kidnapping and a trafficker in cadavers sold to medical students; and Mrs. Sutly, a murderer and cunning extortionist). Yet, Jones did manage to develop the plot and the characters in ways that advance some of his favorite themes and concerns, including the unregulated financial environment in America, land speculation in the West, the attraction of politics for the greedy and the corrupt, the absence of conscience among the wealthy, and the power wielded by literary editors and critics who "do not always read the books they approve or condemn."

In the same year that *Freaks of Fortune* appeared, Jones also published his reprise of *The Western Merchant* in the much expanded *Life and Adventures of a Country Merchant,* a novel distinguishable from the original in its focus upon the way new frontier cities and counties are planned and developed as well as its concern with the broader dangers of market discrepancies and fluctuations between the East and the West. Much of the earnestness of the earlier novel is replaced by comic antics and satiric playfulness. Evangelical camp meetings are, for example, satirized when two boys climb a tree and drop brandy and brimstone onto surging torch flames during the period of the minister's admonishment and exhortation to his audience. Unlike the prudent Luke of *The Western Merchant,* Napoleon Wax, the main char-

Jones shortly before his death on 4 February 1866

acter in *Life and Adventures of a Country Merchant,* demonstrates important lessons about business by making bad decisions; he nevertheless thrives in business because others intervene on his behalf to correct his mistakes.

"Nap" is depicted as an ignorant and gullible naïf, but his mistaking of a monkey escaped from a road show for a negro servant—meant as a comic interlude—reveals a more distinctly Southern bias to the character's prejudices, one that introduces to the novel a negative negro stereotype absent from the prior novel. It may be that Jones rewrote *The Western Merchant* in the hope of attracting a Southern audience. As with *The City Merchant,* which highlighted antiabolitionist efforts, this novel was also published in Philadelphia by Lippincott, Grambo, who distributed extensively in the South.

Native American characters in Jones's novels were more rarely made to conform to negative stereotypes, such as in the captivity narrative in *Wild Western Scenes: The War Path.* More often, however, they were well-drawn, individualized characters (also seen in *The War Path*) with such specific tribal affiliations as Osage, Pawnee, Comanche, and Apache. Indeed, the first and third *Wild Western Scenes* novels depict an harmonious interracial marriage between a Native American and a Caucasian and offer commentaries, especially in *Wild Western Scenes: or, The White Spirit of the Wilderness* (1863), about the nobility of Indians and the comparative savagery of whites. "I would rather trust in the honor of that chief," comments Roughgrove, "than in the honor of many of the chiefs of my own race." The savagery and hypocrisy of Christians in history is also noted by a Comanche woman, La-una, who comments, "the books I learned to read first, narrated the burning of women and children, and even English bishops, by Catholic Christians." In general, whereas Jones's Indian characters were said to suffer "degradations" from their contact with whites, this judgment was not extended to the black slaves in his novels, many of whom are depicted as obsequious, foolish, ignorant, and at best childlike. These depictions exhibit the prejudices that increasingly shaped Jones's later career as a defender of the South's right to promote its own institutions, including the institution of slavery.

By 1857 Jones and his family had taken up residence in Burlington, New Jersey, while he published a new weekly magazine out of Philadelphia titled the *Southern Monitor*. The weekly's motto was "The Union as it was, the Constitution as it is." The magazine, which he published for four years, aimed at tempering the escalating tensions in the North related to the South. The strategy Jones planned, according to a review in the *Richmond Enquirer,* was to take a populist approach: "to aid in opening the eyes of the Northern people, and enable them to see the mad course pursued by the politicians who are attempting to lead them to their ruin." Originally, however, it was conceived of in less conciliatory and more conspiratorial terms. In November 1856 Jones proposed to the Southern Convention in Savannah that a plan should be made to establish a group of "co-operating presses, in the Northern cities, devoted to the rights and interests of the slaveholding States." According to Jones "the Press . . . seems to be the lever by which the popular sentiment is moved." Noting the vast circulation statistics of the *New York Tribune,* Jones asserted: "there is reason to suppose such a gigantic engine has been a principal auxiliary in the consolidation of the vast Northern party, which menaces the constitutional rights of the South." Since a Southerner was "in the streets of a Northern city . . . now regarded as an alien, a vassal, or an enemy," the Southern press must seek to address this problem by establishing daily newspapers as well as weekly journals (for wider circulation) in four major Northern cities—Boston, New York, Philadelphia, and Baltimore. These papers were to be coordinated in their Southern perspective and published by a select corps of Southern-born editors and a vast network of pro-Southern printers and distributors. The responsibilities of these

publications were, among other things, to monitor the dispersal of import duties collected in New York but because of the Southern states; "to furnish early information on the machinations of the diabolical abolition societies, and to warn Southern readers against newspapers, . . . and books calculated to produce injury"; "to utter Southern sentiment boldly and fully in the hot-beds of abolitionism, and to send their leading articles to all the capitals of Europe."

When the Southern Convention declined to adopt his proposal, Jones took upon himself the task of publishing the vigilant but more restrained *Southern Monitor* to promote Southern interests. He knew, however, on 8 April 1861 that he had to depart immediately from Philadelphia, for he realized "that the first gun fired at Fort Sumter will be the signal for an outburst of ungovernable fury, and I should be seized and thrown into prison." He learned days later that his office "had been sacked by a mob" and numbers of people "visited my office, displaying a rope with which to hang me." Jones escaped to Richmond, joined first by his son Custis and later by his wife and their three other children.

While still in Philadelphia publishing the *Southern Monitor,* Jones wrote *Border War,* the novel that was his most significant success after the original, best-selling *Wild Western Scenes*. It was also his last complete novel; although he attempted to recapture his original success by writing *Wild Western Scenes: 1; or, The White Spirit of the Wilderness,* the severe shortage of supplies and paper during the Civil War allowed him to publish only the first of two planned volumes in Richmond in 1863, abandoning an unpublished draft of the concluding volume.

Jones's *Border War* was one of the few attempts—other than Nathaniel Beverley Tucker's *The Partisan Leader* (1836) and Edmund Ruffin's *Anticipations of the Future* (1860)—to imagine a civil war years before one actually began. Jones assumed, with good reason, that a Southerner would gain the presidency in 1860, never guessing that a split in the Democratic Party would put Abraham Lincoln in office. The novel portrays how the war would be fought with a Virginian at the helm. At first the determinedly neutral President Randolph devotes himself to assisting both sides of the conflict in ways that he thinks will preserve the Union. Gradually, however, the president withdraws his Union forces into the mountainous regions of Virginia, thereby separating the Northern rebel abolitionists from their supplies. Southward, to his rear, Randolph orders a fortified city to be built to which he retires, calls up all his Southern reinforcements, surrounds the invaders, and ends the war with much less devastation than the actual Civil War. In this novel it is the rebel factions in the North who set up a separate government, but they are unable to maintain coherent direction and stability. Northern dictators arise, and fanatical leaders slay each other. The strife of warring factions eases the way for Randolph's forces to convince the mostly leaderless rebel army to give up. Former slaves are persuaded that they, too, were better off as they were.

A romance and thwarted marriage between a Northern woman, Edith Langdon, and a Southern man, Henry Blount, is also played out against scenes of city riots depicting the "reckless sword of popular violence," roving "predatory bands" conducting guerrilla warfare for plunder, railroad sabotage, and territorial invasions initiated by the North but reciprocated by the South. The novel accurately predicts the South's uncompromising insistence upon "equality" with the North, as well as the problems of financing and supplying the war effort and the intrusion of England in seeking to make treaties or diplomatic alliances with individual states.

The imaginative evocation of the war borrows heavily from the misguided events of the English Civil War under Oliver Cromwell, from the Roman Empire, and from the Reign of Terror during the French Revolution. To these Jones adds his own prejudices and fantasies, including the roundup and deportation to Liberia of not only abolitionists (including Wendell Phillips) but also "members of Congress, and some hundreds of political parsons and newspaper scribblers"; the fortification of the federal treasury in the cities, foiling "the mobs . . . in their attempts to pillage the mint, the custom-houses, and post-offices"; and the depiction of Northern "despotism" in the person of the corrupt and self-aggrandizing Commander Ruffleton, who declares himself "Emperor for life" and destroys his support among the "Blue Caps" by issuing the "Proclamation at Richmond," in which he announces that the federal system had been "a failure" and so "Like the Romans, we should henceforth be known only as Americans. State lines were to be obliterated." He outlines the establishment of a senate by "an hereditary order of nobles–the descendants of men who had won distinction"; the representatives "were to be chosen as provided by the Constitution," and the patrician order was to be chosen by the emperor and senate from among the first families of the states, of which the South, especially Virginia, had many to contribute. Most unexpected was the announcement that slavery would "be perfectly lawful, as in Rome, everywhere within the limits of the Empire" and that "the entire Continent and adjacent islands must submit to the sway of the American Empire." Undone by a weak will, greed, and bad counsel, Ruffleton's followers desert him. The "Restoration" of the presidency and the completion of the marriage between North and South (Edith and Henry) conclude this tale, published also as *Wild Southern Scenes* in 1859 and republished in 1861 as *Secession, Coercion, and Civil War: The Story of 1861.* The novel was widely and positively reviewed for its vivid depictions of the chaos of social disorder and the consequent need to preserve the Union. During the actual war Southern sol-

diers and commanders at Richmond remarked to Jones that they too had enjoyed the novel.

A Rebel War Clerk's Diary, which Jones kept while posted at the Confederate headquarters in Richmond, offers modern historians an important, minutely detailed, though at times highly personal, account of the war and is one of his most significant contributions. After years of attempting to prevent the dissolution of the Union, he became committed to the need for secession, claiming that he preferred other terms like "rebellion" or "revolution" because they were associated with the Revolution of 1776 but that "secession by any other name would smell as sweet." The diary is rich in detail and offers important information about the Southern economy, the dissension among the members of the Southern leadership, and the texture of social life in Richmond. On the Southern economy Jones's observations range from the tremendous sacrifices made by the people to his own family's deprivations ("we are in a half starving condition . . . my wife and children are emaciated") to the foolhardy decisions made by the Confederate secretary of the treasury ("If he had recommended the purchase by the government of all the cotton, it could have been bought at 7 cents per pound; and the profits alone would have defrayed the greater portion of the expenses of the war, besides affording immense diplomatic facilities and advantages"). The diary, moreover, reveals the tensions and complexity of events: it depicts the weeks of confusion, for example, before learning of the devastating outcomes of the Vicksburg and Gettysburg battles ("the darkest day of the war") and discloses the tenuousness of alliances among the Confederate leadership: "There is an indefinable dread of conspiracy, and the President is right, perhaps, to frown upon all military organizations not subject to his orders. . . . A jealousy, I fear, is growing up between Confederate and State authority."

The diary also proffers interpretations that were shaped by Jones's own preoccupations. He repeatedly finds fault with the Southern leaders, who, he believed, were summoned from the ranks of the self-seeking and the uncouth and were lacking in the integrity he associated with the leadership of President Tyler. In noting the transfer of Confederate government gold to England for safekeeping, he remarked that "if this were known, it could hardly be accomplished, for such is the distrust of several members of the cabinet that the people would revolt. They would believe the cabinet meant soon to follow the gold. And some of our military commanders have no better opinion of them than the people." Frequently he suspects Northern-born generals in command of Southern troops of sabotaging the Southern cause ("When *will* the government put 'none but Southerners on guard?'"). Jefferson Davis's foibles, too, are exhibited with frankness, as for example with respect to Gen. P. T. G. Beauregard's hard-fought defense of Charleston: "The President is still scrutinizing Beauregard. . . . So, omitting all notice of this defense, the attention of the President seems fixed on what the general omitted to do; or what he might, could, or should have done." Despite his disappointment with Southern leaders, Jones still believed in the common man and in a meritocracy where "many a true man who this day stands forth as a private, will end as a general"; he had high hopes that the war itself would be "a mighty winnowing" in which "the wheat will be separated from the chaff."

Jones lived long enough after the Civil War both to publish his diary and to be confronted with the attempts to sort out the conflict's atrocities. (He testified on behalf of Henry Wirz and other Southern leaders charged with inhuman brutality against Union soldiers at Andersonville.) Exhausted by the privations of the war and by tuberculosis, Jones returned to Burlington, New Jersey, where he died on 4 February 1866. Because of his criticisms of Southern leadership, his memory has not been celebrated among Southerners. Nevertheless, his contributions to Southern history, to regional literature and Americana, and to our knowledge of the life of writers, literati, and the publishing industry in America remain valuable. His life and works provide important details about the conjunction among literature, politics, and economics in antebellum America.

Biography:

Clark Brockman, "John Beauchamp Jones," M.A. thesis, University of South Carolina, 1937.

References:

J. Thomas Scharf, *History of Baltimore City and County,* volume 5, part 2 (Philadelphia: Everts, 1881), p. 617;

Dwight R. Thomas, "John Beauchamp Jones," in "Poe in Philadelphia, 1838–1844: A Documentary Record," Ph.D. thesis, University of Pennsylvania, 1978, II: 828–830;

Lyon G. Tyler, *The Letters and Times of the Tylers,* 3 volumes (New York: Da Capo, 1970).

Richard Burleigh Kimball

(11 October 1816 – 28 December 1892)

Kent P. Ljungquist
Worcester Polytechnic Institute

BOOKS: *The True Life of the Scholar: An Address Delivered Before the Literary Societies of Dartmouth College, Hanover N.H., July 24, 1844* (New York: George Ambrose, 1844);

Saint Leger; or, The Threads of Life, anonymous (New York: Putnam, 1849; London: Bentley, 1850); republished as *The Saint Leger Family; or, The Threads of Life. A Novel* (London: Ward & Lock, 1855);

Cuba and the Cubans: Comprising a History of the Island of Cuba, its Present Social, Political, and Domestic Condition; Also its Relation to England and the United States, as the author of "Letters from Cuba" (New York: Hueston/Putnam, 1850);

Romance of Student Life Abroad (New York: Putnam, 1853); republished as *Students Abroad: Their Romance and Real Life* (London: N.p., 1854); republished as *Students Abroad* (New York: Putnam, 1862); republished as *A Student's Romance* (New York: Dillingham, 1893);

The Lawyer: The Dignity, Duties, and Responsibilities of His Profession (New York: Putnam, 1853);

Undercurrents of Wall-Street: A Romance of Business (New York: Putnam, 1862); republished as *Fettered Yet Free,* anonymous (New York: Carleton, 1884);

Was He Successful? A Novel (New York: Carleton, 1864); republished as *His Idol: A Novel* (New York: Carleton, 1880);

Henry Powers (Banker), How He Achieved a Fortune, and Married: A Novel (New York: Carleton / Leipzig: Tauchnitz, 1868);

To-Day: A Romance (New York: Carleton, 1870); republished as *Virginia Randall; or Today in New York,* 2 volumes (London: Bentley, 1870); republished as *An Artful Widow: A Novel* (New York: Carleton, 1881);

Collegiate Education. An Address Before the Alumni of Dartmouth College, July 19, 1871 (New York: Carleton, 1871).

OTHER: "The Sun-Dial of Isella," in *The Knickerbocker Gallery,* edited by Kimball and others (New York: Hueston, 1855), pp. 383–393;

Joseph Warren Fabens, *In the Tropics, by a Settler in Santo Domingo,* introduction by Kimball (New York: Carleton, 1863);

Fabens, *The Prince of Kashna: A West Indian Story,* edited, with an introduction, by Kimball (New York: Carleton, 1866).

159

SELECTED PERIODICAL PUBLICATIONS—
UNCOLLECTED:

POETRY

"Lines: The Earthly," *Knickerbocker Magazine,* 34 (July 1849): 45;

"The Actual," *Knickerbocker Magazine,* 36 (July 1850): 30.

FICTION

"Reminiscences of an Old Man. The Young Englishman," anonymous, *Knickerbocker Magazine,* 20 (November 1842): 458–460; 21 (January 1843): 15–23; 21 (February 1843): 161–169; 21 (April 1843): 316–318; 21 (May 1843): 450–456;

"A Sequel to *Saint Leger,*" *Knickerbocker Magazine,* 37 (January 1851): 1–12; 37 (March 1851): 251–255; 37 (May 1851): 443–449; 38 (July 1851): 60–65; 38 (October 1851): 444–448; 39 (January 1852): 76–81;

"The Man Who Never Was Young," anonymous, *Atlantic Monthly,* 7 (March 1861): 320–334.

NONFICTION

"Little Talks for Little Children," *Knickerbocker Magazine,* 56 (October 1860): 380–384;

"London," *Knickerbocker Magazine,* 56 (November 1860): 447–453;

"The Situation," *Continental Monthly,* 1 (January 1862): 1–6;

"Dickens's Two Visits Here," *New York Times,* 26 July 1891, p. 11.

Among the authors who surrounded Lewis Gaylord Clark, editor of *The Knickerbocker Magazine* during much of that magazine's distinguished life, was the businessman Richard Burleigh Kimball, who wrote stories, sketches, and essays for literary periodicals from the 1840s until the 1890s. His most celebrated work was the metaphysical novel *Saint Leger; or, The Threads of Life* (1849), which reflects the impact of German philosophic ideas. A lawyer and financier comfortable with Wall Street and its environs, Kimball explored these settings in a series of novels published after the success of *Saint Leger.*

Born in Plainfield, New Hampshire, on 11 October 1816, he was the youngest child of Richard Kimball and Mary Marsh Kimball. Descended from Richard Kimball of Suffolk County, England, who immigrated to Massachusetts in 1634, Richard Burleigh Kimball was proud of his British ancestry. His family's role in American history was also a source of pride—his uncle had served in the Continental Army under George Washington, and his maternal grandfather was among the first settlers in the White River region of Vermont. His family background gave him an appreciation of both American and world history, an appreciation that is reflected in his fictional and nonfictional writings.

Kimball attended Kimball Union Academy in Meriden, New Hampshire, from 1827 to 1830. A precocious child, Kimball passed the qualifying examinations for Dartmouth College at age eleven, but, believing him too young for university life, the college administration delayed his matriculation there for two years. After graduating Phi Beta Kappa from Dartmouth in 1834, he studied law under Judge Doe of Waterford, New York, qualifying for the bar there in 1836. Later that year he visited Paris for the first time and witnessed the social changes that were engulfing the Continent. He studied law with André Marie Jean-Jacques Dupin, a member of the French Chamber of Deputies, and attended medical lectures. His exposure to European customs and ideas is reflected in both *Saint Leger* and *Romance of Student Life Abroad* (1853) and provided him with a cosmopolitan perspective that he would apply to events in the Americas. Among his early contributions to *The Knickerbocker* in the mid 1840s was a series of letters on Cuba, which dealt with social, economic, and political conditions on the island. Because of its resources of sugar, molasses, and coffee, Cuba, the last major bastion of the Spanish colonial regime in the Americas, had strong economic appeal to potential investors in the United States. Its plantation economy also invited the critical scrutiny of outsiders, specifically for the havoc the slave trade had imposed on its native population. When rumors of revolution on the island sprang up and Cuba became the object of American expansionist designs, Kimball's interest in its affairs became even more timely. His letters on Cuba, harshly criticizing the degrading effects of the slave trade, were published as a book, *Cuba and the Cubans: Comprising a History of the Island of Cuba, its Present Social, Political, and Domestic Condition; Also its Relation to England and the United States* (1850).

Washington Irving, one of Kimball's literary models, introduced himself in his narrative persona of Geoffrey Crayon in *Tales of a Traveller* (1824) as: "I am an old traveller. I have read somewhat, heard and seen more, and dreamt more than all. My brain is filled, therefore, with all kinds of odds and ends." In an early contribution to *The Knickerbocker,* Kimball, still in his twenties, assumes the mask of an old Englishman recollecting his worldly travels. In the November 1842 issue Clark introduced a "Mysterious Correspondent," a cross between Irving's other narrative persona Diedrich Knickerbocker and the Wandering Jew, who philosophizes about vanity and human destiny. Following Clark's editorial note was Kimball's "Reminiscences of an Old Man," which offered a brief self-portrait of the worldly-wise old man, who narrates, supposedly referring to personal papers and journals, the voyage of a ship from England to Jamaica. Continuing for several issues in 1843, the old man's reminiscences focus on the last days of a dreamy, philosophical invalid in his early twenties, the victim of consumption. The series, subtitled "The Young Englishman,"contrasts youth and age and displays Kimball's talent for graphic description of ocean scenes. In addition to comprising Kimball's initial experiment with first-person narration and the tale-within-a-tale technique, "The Young Englishman" also introduces the character who became the protagonist of his most famous novel, *Saint Leger*. At the end of the series, the invalid, at the point of his demise, is identified as William St. Leger.

St. Leger was too promising a character for Kimball to discard, and Clark, overcoming some initial reluctance, began running the "Saint Leger Papers" (the serialized version of Kimball's novel) in *The Knickerbocker* in January 1845. Following the initial impact of German writers and ideas in America in the 1820s and 1830s, editors such as Clark were hostile to the extravagant supernaturalism associated with this "mystical" school of writing, the vague thinking it supposedly inspired, and the exaggerated feelings and passions it allegedly engendered. In *Saint Leger* the main character is exposed to German philosophic musings, but Kimball depicts this philosophy in a manner that would offend neither Clark nor other critics. To be sure, he presents William St. Leger within the context of Gothic conventions: there is an ancient family whose lineage extends back to the Middle Ages; a grotesque looking, moss-covered estate; and a dark prophecy that seems to hover over the family line. A Byronic villain named Vautrey threatens Saint Leger's happiness, and Kimball even invokes the portentous biblical phrase "blackness of darkness," an image also used in "The Young Englishman." Though David S. Reynolds finds aspects of Kimball's novel that place it in the tradition of the dark adventure genre, with its protagonist's restless skepticism and anguished speculations, the Saint Leger estate is no House of Usher. Unlike Edgar Allan Poe's "The Fall of the House of Usher"(1839), with its catastrophic conclusion, in *Saint Leger,* despite the protagonist's sense of doom, the prologue of the novel implies a hopeful future that can cancel out whatever hereditary curse may lurk in the background.

Book 1 of *Saint Leger* marks the narrator's initiation into the world of passion and violence, and Book 2 takes him to Germany, a "land of mystical philosophy, of wilder theories, and wilder doubts." Titillated by Goethean philosophy and charmed by an evil temptress, Saint Leger ultimately rejects these allures and eschews his pursuit of an "unintelligible mysticism." In a series of melodramatic shifts, the dark Vautrey pays for his villainy with his life, and Saint Leger aligns himself with life-nurturing forces embodied in a blond hero-

ine named Theresa. Although the setting of the novel is strictly European, Kimball's invocation of romantic nature apparently struck a chord with American readers, and the novel went through at least twenty printings by 1864.

Though the book was marred by flaws and incoherences, it won the praise of Tayler Lewis in a review in the 23 February 1849 *Literary World* for its portrayal of "the inner life" and its depiction of an agitated soul confronting an uncertain destiny. Buoyed by such praise, Clark ran "A Sequel to *Saint Leger*," its glorification of nature's healing powers further heightened, in *The Knickerbocker*. By 1853 the novel *Saint Leger* had gone into its sixth American printing, had been translated into French and Dutch, and had been republished in England and by Tauchnitz in Germany.

When installments of "A Sequel to *Saint Leger*" were appearing sporadically in *The Knickerbocker* in 1851, Kimball published "Marie Laforet," a story that drew upon his experiences abroad, in *The Knickerbocker* (September 1851). Set in France, the new story was preceded by a prologue addressed to the editor of the magazine ("My dear Clark"). Experienced with the genre of letters that described foreign settings, Kimball aimed to give readers a sense of the sweeping changes in France, which had been the setting of Irving's "Sketches in Paris in 1825," published in *The Knickerbocker* in November and December 1840. Kimball published three more stories on European life: "Students' Nonsense" in *The Knickerbocker* (December 1852); "A Story of Calais" in *The Knickerbocker* (January 1851); and "Emilie de Coigny" in the *International Magazine* (April 1852). Eventually dropping the convention of the descriptive letter, Kimball devised a new strategy of organization altogether different from the "Saint Leger Papers." He joined these tales to several other sketches to form the 1853 work *Romance of Student Life Abroad*. Although his 1836 voyage to Europe had taken him to Scotland, England, and Germany, the setting of *Romance of Student Life Abroad* is confined to France, the country in which he had studied the most extensively. An 1842 return to Europe had renewed associations of travel and student life, and events of the late 1840s had made a lasting impression on the American public and its writers. One of his companions during the 1836 stay had been O. H. Partridge, who became a respected physician in the Philadelphia area. Kimball uses his friend's name for a character in his book and incorporates details of their travel experiences into his narrative. *Romance of Student Life Abroad* is a series of interlinked tales with multiple narrators, the stories purportedly told by the members of a diverse group of medical students in Paris. The students represent different cultures (Polish, Irish, English, American, and German), and in introducing them Kimball highlights the national characteristics of each. He also takes some care in establishing the general fitness of the characters for the stories they tell.

Given the scattered publishing history of the initial group of stories, the range of comic and serious tonalities, and the crowd of nationalities represented, Kimball achieves a remarkable degree of unity in the volume. Some stories address philosophic issues in the mode of *Saint Leger* (body versus spirit), and many focus on art and artists and their attempts at representation. He also places individual tales within the context of the revolutionary era. For example, "The Story of Louis Herbois," one of the opening tales in the volume, transports the reader back to 1789 when "The revolution had begun, and soon swept everything before it." Other tales deal with the 1830s when another French revolution had subsided and Louis Philippe had been installed as king. "Pistols, blunderbusses, and 'infernal machines,'" which "none but Frenchmen know how to appreciate," evoke a time when "the excitement of politics . . . gives a zest to life." Ostensibly dealing with events of the 1830s, *Romance of Student Life* has as much to do with the events of 1848 and 1849, years of political turmoil in Europe, whose impact on American writers is discussed by Larry J. Reynolds in his *European Revolutions and the American Renaissance* (1988). People in nearly every part of Europe rebelled against conservative governments, demanding more freedom and greater democracy. Many Americans believed that these rebellions foreshadowed the final collapse of repressive European monarchy and the establishment of democracy (on the American model) across the globe. In his preface (placed playfully at the end of the volume) Kimball writes of a future when the long-awaited "day will come" and "the sacred cause of Freedom" will extend its reach everywhere.

Revolutionary events have the power to stir the imagination and unleash the passions, and the main thematic unity of *Romance of Student Life* comes from its focus on emotional fixation or romantic obsession. Several tales feature characters whose adoration of others approaches pathological extremes. Narrated by the German student Franz von Herberg, "The Terrible Picture" records the story of a dreamy, superstitious painter who falls in love with a lady of rank, a copyist at the Louvre. Finding appropriate paintings to copy, he follows her every movement and gesture, and according to the narrator of the story, his regimen is a sign of obsession. The painter's romantic and sexual longings are apparently transferred to his canvas, albeit in tortured fashion. The narrative is ambiguous about whether the painter's terrible picture is "the work of a heated and overwrought brain" or something more chilling for the painter later discovers that the object of his fascination has been killed in an accident.

The other students are shuddering spectators to this unlikely tale, but Kimball uses a narrative framing technique, having a melancholy German student tell the story of his spellbound countryman, to render its supernatural elements more credible. The story raises questions about the student-painter's sanity, but it also propounds an implicit and open-ended query about the "life-like" nature of art and its power to represent beauty in a transitory world.

Kimball also uses the tale-within-a-tale technique in "The Fair Mystery," a story of romantic or sexual obsession supposedly told by Kimball's friend Partridge. A nervous and excitable French student named Dervilly comes under the spell of a female "apparition" in the Rue Morgue and manages to gain her affection, only to have his turbulent emotions thrown into total disorder:

A mystery hung about this beautiful girl; she claimed no one for her friend, she spoke of no acquaintances, she never alluded to brother or sister, or other relation; she made no mention of her home. Besides, a strange sadness, strange in one so young, seemed to possess her, and to pervade her spirit; and while contemplating that imperturbable countenance, Dervilly at times felt an awe come over him for which he could not account, and which for moments subdued even the forces of his passion. It appeared to him then, as if he were under a spell. . . . Dervilly would forget everything in the raptures of such moments; indeed, in his ecstasy he would be driven almost to madness; for of all characters . . . hers was the one to set a youth of ardent temperament crazy. . . .

Here and in other stories Kimball comments on the fine line between immature love and unhealthy fixation. Even the confident Partridge's nerves are unsettled as he pays homage to Kimball's master by invoking Irving's "The Adventure of the German Student" (from *Tales of a Traveller*), who had attempted to flee the terror of the Revolution only to escape into a more nightmarish world:

I must admit I was, for the moment, a little tremulous. I recollected stories of devils taking possession of the dead bodies of young virgins, in order to lure young men to perdition. I thought of the tale of the German student, who, on retiring with his bride, beheld her head roll from her body, (she had been guillotined that morning,) leaving him wed to the foul fiend. In spite of me, I looked upon the pale stricken creature before me in one way or the other connected with the adversary, and holding a commission from the prince of the Power of Air.

A reviewer in *Graham's Magazine* (February 1853) found enough vitality and interest in *Romance of Student Life Abroad* to claim that it surpassed *Saint Leger*. In the July 1860 issue of *The Knickerbocker,* another reviewer called Kimball's tales of student life "decidedly more attractive" than his more abstract works.

After the success of *Romance of Student Life Abroad,* which went through several editions, Kimball turned to novels of business. *Undercurrents of Wall-Street: A Romance of Business* (1862), as its title suggests, records the fluctuations and reversals of life in America's financial center. Kimball's first-person narrator is an individual who admits "I had omitted . . . to cultivate the morale of my nature." His obsession with material success is a character trait that the novel demonstrates in unremitting detail. Despite the book's subtitle, the narrator claims he is not writing "a romance" but is actually recording a series of difficult financial circumstances starting with the Panic of 1837 and extending to the economic dislocations of the late 1850s.

Part 1 of the novel, which traces the narrator's loss of fortune, home, and spouse, contains satirical touches, evidenced by Kimball's use of comic names for personalities (Mr. Oilnut and John Bulldog, an attorney) and institutions (Screwtight and Company). This satire reinforces Kimball's use of the narrator's personal history to expose the workings of Wall Street. (The title of the narrative, as serialized in *The Knickerbocker,* in 1861 and 1862, was "Revelations of Wall-Street.") The occasionally sensationalist style, reminiscent of *Saint Leger,* becomes a vehicle of the narrator's moralizing. By the end of the novel, the satirical impulse and the moralizing tendency seem to work at cross purposes. By recording the "doleful experiences" of his narrator's downfall, Kimball apparently intended to make an ethical warning about obsession with material possessions and gain, but the novel obsessively records each petty transaction and financial reversal in such excruciating detail that the reader may never acquire sufficient moral distance of the flawed world of finance that Kimball aimed to expose. Whatever the novel's flaws, the reviewer in *The Knickerbocker* (April 1862) was enthusiastic:

> The extraordinary merit of the "Under-Currents of Wall-Street" may, in fact, be summed up in its startling, extraordinary and terrible truthfulness. . . . We are glad that a new era is dawning in novel-writing–the truthful. People are tired of romance, they want real life. . . . But it is hard to copy from life, very hard to make the common-place striking. Mr. Kimball has done it, and done it with a simple vigor that is miraculous. The secret of it all is a thorough knowledge of his subject and the art of depicting it in the fewest possible words.

Kimball had demonstrated that he could write convincingly of businessmen, their motives, strategies, tactics, and disappointments. This attention to detail is also evident in his shortest novel, *Henry Powers (Banker), How He Achieved a Fortune, and Married: A Novel* (1868). At the beginning of this work, Powers disclaims the label of "fiction" for his personal history. Once again using first-person narration, a technique that here may reflect the autobiographical sources of the events recorded, Kimball tells the story of Powers, born in a New Hampshire village, a student at a private academy, and an aspirant to a large fortune in his early twenties. Powers quickly rises in a New York firm until the Civil War sidetracks his business career. After the war he meets Horace Deams, a spokesman for the values of the new era in business. Introducing Powers to the world of financial speculation, Deams entices him and other investors into a dubious scheme to provide coal to the poor. Kimball, however, resists the moralizing tendencies of *Undercurrents of Wall-Street.* Powers does separate himself from Deams's uncertain tactics, and his marriage to Mary Worth prevents financial decline as well as his "sliding to the bottom" of the moral scale. Kimball's purpose in *Henry Powers* appears to have been simply to provide a portrait of the battle of wits among the Wall Street financiers. Near the novel's conclusion Kimball notes explicitly that "the vice of avarice–the worst of all vices–is not fostered by a Wall-Street life."

In both *Undercurrents of Wall-Street* and *Henry Powers,* Kimball relies on the intriguing surfaces of life in the business world. In *To-Day: A Romance* (1870) he attempts his longest and most ambitious novel by introducing his largest gallery of characters. He also revives most of the salient themes that occupied him throughout his career: education, Old World versus New World values, the flaws of businessmen, social life in urban settings, and metaphysical speculations. The characters in Kimball's large cast have one thing in common: most of them either attended or had contact with the Select School for Boys and Girls (Scotsenkopf), located on the banks of the Hudson River. Kimball develops his range of themes primarily through contrasting characters, especially Alfred DuBarry and Tom Castleton (similar to the contrasting characters of Vautrey and St. Leger). The character who can be identified most closely with Kimball himself is Castleton, who attends the Select School and Round Hill Academy before graduating from Dartmouth and entering the legal profession. Castleton is immature, unworldly, and unsophisticated, but he aspires to understand life completely. He shares this openness to learning with the more worldly DuBarry, who sojourns in Europe and dabbles in fashionable German philosophy. Though separated by vast distances, Castleton and DuBarry remain rivals for Clara, who embodies one of Kimball's themes as a figure of personal integrity. While trying to be a "faithful chronicler" of external events, Kimball stresses the novelist's need for sensitivity to the hidden springs of action, to motives that lie beneath the surfaces of human lives. In this context Clara emerges as a significant character not just by virtue of her attractiveness to both DuBarry and Castleton. Of refined taste, vivid imagination, and practical good sense, she lacks the surface appeal of that "fascinating young priestess," Virginia Randall, another of Kimball's female characters. Kimball points out that individuals live triple lives: an occupational life, a home life, and a personal or inner life. Since the latter constitutes personal identity, this inner life should be the domain of the novelist. In *To-Day* Kimball's narration is unwieldy and occasionally laborious in shifting setting and gathering the various threads of the story. Nevertheless, in its ambitious scope it reveals the higher responsibilities that Kimball envisioned for the novelist.

Between *Undercurrents of Wall-Street* and *Henry Powers* Kimball published another portrait of an aspirant for success, *Was He Successful? A Novel* (1864), originally serialized in *Continental Monthly* (June 1862–April 1864). He once again presents rural village values in conflict with urban commercial interests. Several of the characters experience this tension in their lives, but the central character is Hiram Meeker, a young man from Brownsville, Connecticut, who attends the Newton Institute before embarking on a business career. Meeker's business acumen impresses many of his associates, but Kimball makes it clear that Meeker is totally self-interested. He has two goals in life: to achieve success in worldly terms and to insure himself a place in the hereafter. More than in his other novels, Kimball provides a religious backdrop for the conduct of his characters, and in the person of Meeker, he presents a conformist to social and religious conventions—a dutiful churchgoer and observer of temperance principles. Though always acting from "carefully considered motives," Meeker is no melodramatic villain. Observing conventional norms of conduct, he does little to which one could take clear exception. Kimball depicts Meeker as a dutiful but morally complacent seeker of worldly success who glides from one position to another by putting little strain on his ethically underdeveloped disposition. His morality never rises above prudence; his sense of virtue never transcends policy.

Was He Successful? is Kimball's most carefully structured novel: Part 1 deals with village concerns, and part 2 describes life in New York. Set against Meeker's rise, village life declines as Kimball convincingly portrays the transition from a rural to a capitalist society. Religious practices, in particular, have been watered down in a post–Civil War society increasingly dominated by secular concerns and the demands of the economic marketplace. In part 2 his main character's moral obtuseness is delineated in his family relationships and in two romantic subplots. After breaking an engagement with one woman because her family has lost its property, Meeker becomes increasingly impressed by people with "ton," the stylish elite. He looks to polite society for a suitable partner, and there is a certain poetic justice in his marriage to a disagreeable coquette, Arabella Thorne. A significant span of time elapses between parts 2 and 3, as Meeker's children inherit his moral nature. Kimball, avoiding the melodrama of his other novels, introduces no last-minute moral reform on Meeker's part, who instead becomes even further hardened by life. Though acknowledging that a reader may dislike Meeker, Kimball remains consistent in his portrayal of an unsympathetic character whose self-interested outlook on life never broadens.

As a fiction writer Kimball drew directly from his experiences in law and finance in Wall Street offices and elsewhere. He had begun his law practice as a partner with William A. Beach in Waterford, New York, but moved to Troy, New York, in 1840. Later that year he joined his brother Elijah H. Kimball's practice on Wall Street for several months before opening his own law firm in New York City. D. T., one of the five children from his marriage with Julia Tomlinson, whom he married 17 April 1844, also became a lawyer. A successful legal practice and shrewd investments gave him financial security, which allowed him to cut back on his legal activities after 1854. His speculations in real estate led him to found the town of Kimball, Texas, and he developed a railway in southeast Texas, serving as president of the Galveston, Houston & Henderson Railroad from 1854 to 1860. Purchasing an estate in Westchester, New York, in 1859, he traveled and pursued his literary interests while working sporadically at his law firm until his early seventies.

As did Fitz-Greene Halleck and Frederic S. Cozzens, fellow writers for *The Knickerbocker,* Kimball divided his time between business and literary pursuits. He knew statesmen (William Seward, Daniel Webster, and Henry Clay), and he also cultivated contacts with literary men in the United States and abroad (Charles Dickens, William Makepeace Thackeray, Irving, Alphonse de Lamartine, and Edward Bulwer Lytton). He wrote reminiscences of some of these individuals for *The New York Times,* with his personal recollections of Dickens appearing on 26 July 1891. He had apparently finished a collection of these reminiscences, tentatively titled "Half a Century of Recollections," but he died in New York City on 28 December 1892 at the age of seventy-seven, and the volume was never published.

Well before the eponymous protagonist of William Dean Howells's novel *The Rise of Silas Lapham* (1885) invested in paint, Kimball offered his own portraits of American businessmen facing moral dilemmas in an economic marketplace that posed new challenges to individual integrity. As Wayne Westbrook has noted, "money and religion are themes closely linked" in the business novel. Though they are unmentioned by historians of business fiction, Kimball's novels offer significant attention to religious practices. Hiram Meeker is a character who embodies personal self-interest joined to a profession of religious faith that has devolved into mere practicality. Before Henry James in his novel *The American* (1877) sent Christopher Newman to France, Kimball offered his own version of Americans in Paris and their encounter with Old World values in *Romance of Student Life Abroad*. A traveler who had made the transatlantic voyage more than thirty times, Kimball merits study within the context of European-American relations in the nineteenth century.

References:

"Kimball's Student Life," *Graham's Magazine,* 42 (April 1953): 205–208;

Tayler Lewis, "The Inner Life," *Literary World,* 6 (23 February 1849): 171–174;

Perry Miller, *The Raven and the Whale: The War of Words and Wits in the Era of Poe and Melville* (New York: Harcourt, Brace, 1956);

David S. Reynolds, *Beneath the American Renaissance: The Subversive Imagination in the Age of Emerson and Melville* (New York: Knopf, 1988), pp. 193–194;

Larry J. Reynolds, *European Revolutions and the American Renaissance* (New Haven: Yale University Press, 1988);

"Richard B. Kimball," *Knickerbocker,* 59 (January 1862): 1–8;

"Richard Burleigh Kimball," *International Magazine,* 1 (January 1851): 156–157;

Emily Stipes Watts, *The Businessman in American Literature* (Athens: University of Georgia Press, 1982);

Wayne Westbrook, *Wall Street in the American Novel* (New York: New York University Press, 1980).

Papers:

There is no major collection of Richard Burleigh Kimball's papers. Some of his correspondence is held in collections at the Baker Memorial Library, Dartmouth College, and the Alderman Library, University of Virginia.

Eliza Leslie

(15 November 1787 – 1 January 1858)

Elisa E. Beshero-Bondar
Pennsylvania State University

BOOKS: *Seventy-Five Receipts for Pastry, Cakes, and Sweetmeats,* anonymous (Boston: Munroe & Francis / New York: Francis, 1828; revised, 1832; augmented, 1834); augmented as *Miss Leslie's Seventy-Five Receipts for Pastry, Cakes, and Sweetmeats* (Boston: Munroe & Francis / New York: Francis, 1846);

The Mirror; or, Eighteen Juvenile Tales and Dialogues, 2 volumes, anonymous (Boston: Munroe & Francis / New York: Francis, 1828);

Stories for Emma: Being a Series of Easy Reading Lessons, with the Syllables Divided, anonymous (Boston: Munroe & Francis / New York: Francis, 1829);

Stories for Adelaide, anonymous (Philadelphia: Ash, 1829);

The Young Americans; or, Sketches of a Sea-Voyage and a Short Visit to Europe, anonymous (Boston: Munroe & Francis / New York: Francis, 1829);

American Girl's Book; or, Occupation for Play Hours (Boston: Munroe & Francis / New York: Francis, 1831); republished as *The Girl's Book of Diversions; or, Occupation for Play Hours* (London: Tegg / Dublin: Tegg, Wise & Tegg / Glasgow: Griffen / Sydney, Australia: J. & S. A. Tegg, 1835); augmented as *The American Girl's Book* (New York & Boston: Francis, 1857);

Wonderful Travels, Being the Narratives of Munchausen, Gulliver, and Sinbad from the Original Works with Numerous Alterations . . . (Boston: Munroe & Francis / New York: Francis, 1832);

Atlantic Tales; or, Pictures of Youth (Boston: Munroe & Francis / New York: Francis, 1833);

Pencil Sketches; or, Outlines of Character and Manners (Philadelphia: Carey, Lea & Blanchard, 1833);

Laura Lovel: A Sketch . . . for Ladies Only (Lowell, Mass.: Franklin Bookstore, 1834);

Pencil Sketches; or, Outlines of Character and Manners, second series (Philadelphia: Carey, Lea & Blanchard, 1835);

Directions for Cookery: Being a System of the Art, in Its Various Branches (Philadelphia: Carey & Hart, 1837); often revised, sometimes as *Miss Leslie's Complete Cookery;*

Eliza Leslie

Pencil Sketches; or, Outlines of Character and Manners, third series (Philadelphia: Carey, Lea & Blanchard, 1837);

Althea Vernon; or, The Embroidered Handkerchief, to which is added Henrietta Harrison; or, The Blue Cotton Umbrella (Philadelphia: Lea & Blanchard, 1838);

The Tell Tale and The Week of Idleness (London: Dean & Munday, 1838);

Birth-Day Stories (Philadelphia: Anners, 1840);

The House Book; or, A Manual of Domestic Economy . . . (Philadelphia: Carey & Hart, 1840); republished as *Miss Leslie's Lady's House Book; a Manual of Domestic*

Economy . . . (Philadelphia: Baird, 1850; augmented, Philadelphia: Hart, 1850);

Mr. and Mrs. Woodbridge, with Other Tales (Providence: Cady, 1841);

Mrs. Washington Potts and Mr. Smith (Philadelphia: Lea & Blanchard, 1843);

Stories for Helen (Philadelphia: Anners, 1845);

The Young Revolutionists: Containing the Stories of Russel and Sidney; and Chase Loring: Tales of the American Revolution (New York: Francis / Boston: Francis, 1845);

The Indian Meal Book . . . (London: Smith, Elder, 1846; Philadelphia: Carey & Hart, 1847);

Kitty's Relations and Other Pencil Sketches (Philadelphia: Carey & Hart, 1847);

The Lady's Receipt-Book: Useful Companion for Large and/or Small Families (Philadelphia: Carey & Hart, 1847); augmented as *Miss Leslie's Lady's New Receipt-Book: A Useful Guide for Large or Small Families* (Philadelphia: Hart, 1850); augmented as *Miss Leslie's New Receipts for Cooking* (Philadelphia: Peterson, 1856);

Leonilla Lynmore, and Mr. and Mrs. Woodbridge; or, A Lesson for Young Wives. Also Dudley Villiers (Philadelphia: Carey & Hart, 1847);

Amelia; or, A Young Lady's Vicissitudes: A Novel (Philadelphia: Carey & Hart, 1848);

The Dennings and Their Beaux, and Alina Derlay, &c. &c. (Philadelphia: Hart, 1851);

The Maid of Canal Street, and the Bloxhams (Philadelphia: Hart, 1851);

Miss Leslie's Stories for Young People (Philadelphia: Anners, 1852);

Stories for Summer Days and Winter Nights (New York: Higgins & Kellogg, 1853);

The Behavior Book: A Manual for Ladies (Philadelphia: Hazard, 1853);

Stories for Adelaide: A Second Book for Her Little Friends (Philadelphia: Hazard, 1856);

Miss Leslie's New Cookery Book (Philadelphia: Peterson, 1857);

A First Book for My Very Young Friends (Philadelphia: W. P. Hazard, 1857);

The Meteor: A Choice Collection of Popular Melodies, designed for the use of schools, seminaries, singing classes, and family circles: together with a complete course of elementary instruction (Boston: Russell, 1867).

OTHER: *Stephanie Felicite Genlis, Eugene and Lolotte: A Tale for Children,* translated by Leslie (Boston: Munroe & Francis, 1828);

"The Little Child's Present," in *The Little Child's Book* (Boston: Munroe & Francis; New York: Francis, 1830);

Domestic French Cookery, Chiefly Translated from Sulpice Barué, translated by Leslie (Philadelphia: Carey & Hart, 1832);

The Gift, 4 volumes, edited by Leslie (Philadelphia: Carey & Hart, 1835–1839);

The Violet, 4 volumes, edited by Leslie (Philadelphia: Carey & Hart, 1837–1842);

Miss Leslie's Magazine: Home Book of Fashion, Literature, and Domestic Economy, edited by Leslie (1843);

Lydia Maria Francis Child, The Little Girl's Own Book . . . with additional sports and games by Miss Leslie (Glasgow: Fraser, 1843);

Antique American Recipes: from Eliza Leslie's Cookbooks, edited by Hope Peek (Mount Vernon, N.Y.: Constantia, 1988).

SELECTED PERIODICAL PUBLICATIONS–
UNCOLLECTED: "The Parlours, Both, Are Occupied: a new song: dedicated to the inmates of all fashionable boarding-houses throughout the United States," *Godey's Lady's Book,* 28 (February 1844): 100–101;

"Western New York, a Slight Sketch," *Godey's Lady's Book,* 31 (November 1845): 185–190;

"The Baymounts," *Saturday Evening Post,* 30 (7, 14, 21, and 28 December 1850): 1;

Autobiographical sketch, in "Personal Reminiscences of Miss Eliza Leslie," by Alice B. Haven, *Godey's Lady's Book,* 56 (April 1858): 344–350.

Literally a household word in Victorian America, Eliza Leslie taught generations of American women how to cook, behave themselves in public, and clean their houses. She also entertained them with fiction depicting ludicrously pretentious imposers upon well-bred American hospitality and tales outlining the right and wrong ways for girls to be educated and for young women to earn lasting respect from eligible bachelors. Best known for her cookbooks and incredibly detailed instructions on every conceivable topic related to conventional women's behavior and activities in the mid nineteenth century, Leslie's short stories, which appeared regularly in *Godey's Lady's Book,* ruthlessly ridiculed improprieties and introduced to American literature comic female figures whose character flaws are revealed through minute descriptions of dress, coiffure, or household dishabille.

Her only novel, *Amelia; or, A Young Lady's Vicissitudes* (1848), a Cinderella story, perfectly exemplifies a common thread running through Leslie's complete corpus of writing: American women's need for respect and how it can best be attained. Amelia stresses the importance of the genteel upbringing to which Leslie constantly exposed her readers by demonstrating how a

The Young Revolutionists:

CONTAINING THE STORIES OF

RUSSEL AND SIDNEY;

AND

CHASE LORING:

TALES OF THE AMERICAN REVOLUTION.

BY MISS LESLIE.

"This is my own, my native land."

NEW-YORK:
C. S. FRANCIS & CO. 252 BROADWAY.
BOSTON:
J. H. FRANCIS, 128 WASHINGTON STREET.
1845.

Title page for Leslie's collection of stories that present an idealized portrayal of the relationship between white and black Americans during the Revolutionary War

well-raised young woman suddenly reduced to the position of a maidservant in her crude father and cruel stepmother's inn escapes from this scene of barbaric incivility when her refined manners attract the attention and affection of a wealthy and polished gentleman whom she ultimately marries. As Nina Baym observes in *Woman's Fiction: A Guide to Novels by and about Women in America, 1820–1870* (1978), *Amelia* and Leslie's general preoccupation with etiquette and correctness underline the need for a code of gallantry to protect American middle-class women from brutal male exploitation. While Leslie's minute focus on appropriate female dress, occupation, and behavior may be difficult for many late-twentieth-century feminists to accept, her writings widely disseminated domestic customs and norms that helped shape American women social climbers and gave them a sense that they could be just as respectable and civilized as their English counterparts—

if not more so. Not only did Leslie encourage women's literacy and instruct them on how to behave at dinner parties, but her writings also served a common cause of American antebellum letters, to define a distinct and respectable American culture separate from its English and European origins.

Although she emphasized in an autobiographical sketch dated 1851 that "I have no *English* blood in me," during her childhood Leslie experienced much of the English culture that she later featured prominently and ambivalently in her writings. Born the first child of Robert and Lydia Baker Leslie in Philadelphia on 15 November 1787, Leslie moved with her family when she was five years old to England, where they remained for six years. Her father, a watchmaker by profession and a self-made Renaissance man accomplished in mathematics, drawing, and music, had served while in Philadelphia as an elected member of the American Philosophical Society, by the recommendation, according to Eliza Leslie, of Thomas Jefferson. Indeed, by her own account Jefferson and Benjamin Franklin were "warm personal friends" of her father. Despite these impressive ties, upon obtaining a partnership with Isaac Price, who promised to look after Leslie's business, the Leslie family moved to London in June 1793 to export watches and clocks to Philadelphia. During the family's sojourn in London, Eliza's two brothers were born, one of whom, Charles Robert Leslie, became a well-known painter and illustrator of Sir Walter Scott's Waverley novels.

As a child "Betsy" loved to read and draw, and of her youthful education in England she wrote:

> My father thought I could acquire sufficient knowledge for a child by simply reading 'in book,' without making any great effort to learn things by heart; and, as this is not the plan usually pursued at schools, I got nearly all my education at home. I had a French and music master, both coming to give lessons at the house, my father himself teaching me to write, and overlooking my drawing. My mother was fully competent to instruct me in every sort of useful sewing. I went three months to school merely to learn ornamental needle-work.

In keeping with her pride in her father's self-taught accomplishments and her own abilities to learn independently without rote memorization or "parroting," much of Leslie's later fiction, including "Eliza Farnham; or the Poor Scribe" and "Barclay Compton," derides the education received at finishing schools as useless. The expensively educated Miss Farnham, having managed to bribe other girls to write her lessons for her, finds after graduation that she cannot pen an intelligent letter to her fiancé, and the sailor Barclay Compton returns from sea after a year to find that his wife, who had learned Italian ballads at school but had never heard of "The Star-Spangled Banner," is utterly incapable of managing a household or servants without the help of her mother.

Unlike these characters, young Eliza soon put her education to full use. When she and her family moved back to Philadelphia in 1799 upon Price's death, they found that he had left the watch and clock business in financial shambles. Robert Leslie's health steadily declined, and when he died in 1803, Eliza and her mother opened a boardinghouse to support her younger siblings. Eliza, now sixteen years old, began teaching drawing and became locally famous for her skilled copies of artistic masterpieces. Her literary efforts had begun some years earlier when she tried her hand at pastoral poetry, which she ceased writing in disgust when her father pointed out to her an actual shepherd. Indeed, when she was about twelve or thirteen years old, she burned all her poetic attempts. Those that she later wrote appear at the end of her volumes of *Pencil Sketches; or, Outlines of Character and Manners* (1835). Her more adulatory and solemn verses praise Revolutionary War heroes and the cause of liberty, while others, such as "Lady Jane Grey," pay tribute to earlier historical figures suggested as poetic subjects by her brother's paintings.

It seems likely, given her later close attention to proper female behavior, that *The Young Ladies' Mentor,* published in Leslie's name in Philadelphia in 1803, is her own work. She did not, however, claim it in her autobiographical sketch, stating that her first writing to appear in print was *Seventy-Five Receipts for Pastry, Cakes, and Sweetmeats,* published in 1828 on the advice of her brother Thomas Jefferson Leslie, an army engineer, with whom she and her mother were living at West Point, New York. According to Eliza, so many people were requesting copies of recipes she had learned at Mrs. Goodfellow's cooking school in Philadelphia that her brother suggested "my getting rid of the inconvenience by giving them to the public in print." It did not take her long to find a publisher for these dessert recipes, which were reprinted in several editions during and after her lifetime. According to Mary Anna DuSablon in *America's Collectible Cookbooks: The History, the Politics, the Recipes* (1994), these recipes were especially welcome to beginning cooks and young wives anxious to elevate their household cuisine to suit the most highly civilized tastes—those of Europeans. Introducing her recipes in 1828 as "in every sense of the word, American," Leslie's ambivalence to fashionable European conventions appears in the same sentence: "but the writer flatters herself that (if exactly followed) the articles produced from them will not be found inferior to any of

a similar description made in the European manner." Thus, her recipes, as much of her fiction, reveal a tension between conforming to transatlantic customs and shrugging them off in favor of those uniquely "American."

Many of Leslie's fiction and conduct books, indeed, express disapproval of English customs. Far from encouraging her ever-expanding readership to adopt without question all customs from across the Atlantic, some of Leslie's most memorable advice disdains things British as utterly impractical or revolting. For example, in *The Behavior Book: A Manual for Ladies* (1853) she quite emphatically opposes the English use of finger bowls: "When the finger-glasses are sent round, dip a clean corner of your napkin into the water, and wet round your lips with it, but omit the disgusting foreign fashion of taking water into your mouth, rinsing and gurgling it round, and then spitting it back into the glass." To drive home the point about finger bowls in vivid detail, in the story "The Bloxhams" Leslie portrays the scene as the English Countess Wangledon "to the great disgust of the uninitiated part of the company . . . took two or three mouthfuls of the water, rinsed her mouth very audibly, and then spirted the liquid back again into the bowl, finishing by dipping in her fingers and wiping them with her napkin." "The Bloxhams" represents English characters as supremely impolite, insulting their more than gracious American hosts by continually remarking on their lack of manners and ignorance of English customs and by long outstaying their welcome in the American home—a sort of British invasion. Indeed, in setting the story in the late eighteenth century, Leslie re-creates a war of custom similar in spirit to the American Revolution.

It is possible that Leslie's hostile, satiric portrayal of pretentious English characters visiting America in stories such as "The Bloxhams," "Mrs. Washington Potts," and "Althea Vernon," to name a few containing the most memorable lampoons, derived from her impressions of her English sister-in-law, Harriet Stone Leslie, wife of Charles. Charles had been apprenticed as a young man in England and had found most of his work there, but on the appeals of his family and friends in Philadelphia he returned to that city to live with his wife and family. According to Ophia Smith, Charles and Eliza had long maintained a close correspondence through which they respectfully criticized each other's work. Charles often advised Eliza not to instruct her readers but rather to write more like a novelist and represent life more realistically. In turn Eliza criticized her brother's choices in color or technique, which he would revise accordingly. When her brother's family came to live in Philadelphia in 1833, Eliza was apparently anxious for them to remain for good and for her brother to

Charles Robert Leslie, Eliza Leslie's younger brother, who succeeded as an illustrator of Sir Walter Scott's novels

be established as an American artist. Charles's hopes were frustrated, however, and his wife was unhappy and wished to return home to England, a desire that left Eliza particularly miffed. The family returned to England within a year. Smith cites a bit of gossip written by Ellen Bailey, a friend visiting Philadelphia at the time, in a letter to her sisters in Ohio:

> Betsy . . . can think and talk of nothing else. She says it is too bad that Charles should be blamed when it is his most ardent wish to remain here but for the sake of domestic peace he was compelled to return his wife gave him no rest until he consented to resign and leave this horrid country. Betsy says she believes she was disappointed that she did not find the Americans in a savage state. When she discovered her error she railed out against their extravagance and ungentility. To think they eat with their knives and break their eggs in a glass. Oh shocking! Betsy says she cannot imagine what possessed Charles to marry such a woman. She is not pretty accomplished or sensible nor does she possess one qualification to render any man happy.

This spiteful representation is perhaps vividly echoed in the forms of such pretentious imposters to English fortune as the Countess Wangledon, the Montague family in "Mrs. Washington Potts," and Sir Tiddering Tattersall of "Althea Vernon," all of whom boast of their much superior and more refined English

society at American gatherings. Perhaps Leslie's motivation to write *The Behavior Book* and the vivid contrast in her fiction between refined and pretentious behavior grew out of this consciousness of foreigners snubbing Americans as culturally inferior.

While her adult fiction heavily concentrated on conflicts of etiquette as matters of principle, Leslie's first experiments with fiction writing were children's stories, published in collections such as *The Mirror; or, Eighteen Juvenile Tales and Dialogues* (1828), *Stories for Adelaide* (1829), and *Atlantic Tales; or, Pictures of Youth* (1833). One of the first writers (along with Lydia Maria Child) to produce books especially for American children with American settings and characters, Leslie again struck gold in the literary market. She was sufficiently encouraged by her success to have *American Girl's Book; or, Occupation for Play Hours* published under her name in 1831; her previous books had appeared anonymously. As was conventional for the time, her children's stories always pointed out a moral or taught a lesson, but her child characters tended to be more lifelike and believable than those of other writers. *Stories for Emma: Being a Series of Easy Reading Lessons* (1829) and *Stories for Adelaide,* originally written for her nieces, were especially instructive for beginning readers, who were aided by Leslie's practice of dividing words into syllables.

Although she initially had little confidence in her ability to write adult fiction, she entered a story contest sponsored by *Godey's Lady's Book.* According to Alice Haven's preface to Leslie's autobiographical sketch, upon finishing the manuscript "(late at night, after returning from a party), she threw it into the grate, intending to burn it in the morning. But, reading it over once more before lighting her bonfire, she thought the experiment, at least, would be no loss." Had she burned the manuscript, her most famous tale (and the *Godey's* prizewinner), "Mrs. Washington Potts," would never have appeared in print in 1832, and her long career of writing fiction for *Godey's* and *Graham's Magazine* might never have begun.

Eventually, as her writings became more widely printed, she published more cookbooks, and in 1843 she edited *Miss Leslie's Magazine: Home Book of Fashion, Literature, and Domestic Economy* for about a year before turning it over to T. S. Arthur. By this time hers had become an authoritative word on the minute details of household management and civilized behavior. *The House Book; or, A Manual of Domestic Economy* (1840), pointedly directed toward inexperienced ladies of the house rather than their servants, critiqued aristocratic conventions and elitist American boarding schools that trained wealthy young women only in frivolous, impractical arts, leaving them unfamiliar with the rudiments of domestic economy. With typical bluntness Leslie observed that

> A great change has certainly taken place since the days when, during the presidency of her husband, Mrs. Washington, followed by a servant-man with a basket, went daily to Philadelphia market; and when the all-accomplished daughters of Mr. Jefferson made pastry and confectionary in a room fitted up for that purpose in their father's mansion at Monticello.

If women complained about their servants' backwardness, these women had most likely only themselves to blame for being ignorant of how a house should be run and what orders they should give. Yet her minute instructions on how, for example, to launder particular fabrics would have been of use to households not wealthy enough to employ servants for the purpose:

> Brown French linen of very fine quality, is frequently used for ladies' travelling dresses in the summer and for gentlemen's round jackets. To prevent it from fading, it should be washed with hay, as should also brown holland aprons and petticoats. Two large handfuls of hay will suffice for one dress. Wash the dress first in cold water, without any soap, having first boiled the hay . . . Rinse it through two hay-waters, and in the last put a table-spoonful of pyroligneous acid, or vinegar of wood, (to be obtained at the druggist's) or a small tea-spoonful of oil of vitriol.

From Leslie's perspective women's education necessarily included a fairly thorough knowledge of domestic chemistry.

Concerning domestic servitude, her representation of African Americans and servant classes in her fiction reflect growing tensions concerning these issues in the antebellum United States. Contemporaneous with Harriet Beecher Stowe's *Uncle Tom's Cabin*, Leslie's "Nothing Morally Wrong" (published in *The Dennings and Their Beaux*, 1851) depicts idealistic abolitionists as foolish while at the same time representing the sound intelligence and common sense of a young mulatto servant woman named Zuby. The eccentric Miss Jonathina Judd clings to many lofty dreams to reform society—including abolishing the customs of dressing ornately for dinner and imposing on servants to arrange one's hair or clean the house. Miss Judd defies fashion in favor of her own philosophy of simplicity and self-sufficiency, wearing clothes she has made herself, and for a large portion of the story she is described as ridiculous in her ill-fitting, wrinkled gown. She is represented as so self-absorbed in her defiance of custom that she does not care how she discomfits her hostess or imposes on the servants by refusing to treat them as

such. Zuby shows much generosity and practical intelligence by explaining to Miss Judd the errors of her ways, fixing her hair, and convincing her to wear a tailor-made gown. Zuby's hard work lands Miss Judd a husband at the end of the story—thus demonstrating the importance of upholding the conventions that Miss Judd despises. Similarly, in "The Bloxhams" the obnoxious Countess Wangledon expresses her abhorrence of slavery to the black attendant, Rose, while at the same time ordering her about:

> "Poor creature!"–ejaculated the countess. She then desired Rose to unlace her boots, and while the girl was kneeling to perform the office, the countess looked at her compassionately, and said, in a melancholy tone–"Unhappy daughter of Africa!" "Please, maum, my mother's name's Phebe"–said the girl. "Miserable, ill-fated wretch! What a heart-breaking life must be yours!" "Please, maum, it don't seem to me that I'm a wretch, or miserable any way. Master's people's all well used, and we gets plenty of wictuals and clothes, and plenty of physic when we're sick, and is allowed balls. I'm a desperate dancer myself."

Rose, like other black or white servants in Leslie's stories, objects to being called miserable or wretched and takes a certain pride in doing her jobs well.

Leslie's fiction also represents free nonwhites in terms that sugarcoat their relationship with white Americans. In *The Young Revolutionists: Containing the Stories of Russel and Sidney,* set during the American Revolution, a free black family runs an army hospital in their home, while Wacuna, an old American Indian woman living alone in a secluded hut in the woods but friendly with the white families nearby, nurses a sixteen-year-old war hero, Russel, back to health and helps to save a Quaker household from being plundered by British soldiers. In representing African Americans and American Indians as supporting the cause of colonial America against the British and in portraying servants and slaves as loyal, content, and useful members of large, well-managed homes owned by whites, Leslie's fiction validates the idea of racial subservience. It mercilessly satirizes abolitionists as badly educated fools, more racist than slave owners in their self-aggrandizing pity for the downtrodden. At the same time nonwhites are depicted as vitally important to the proper American way of life that all her writing is focused on defining.

Critics found Leslie's fiction too satiric to suit entirely their tastes but applauded her for her realistic portrayal of characters, faulting her more for her choice of topics than for her treatment of them. A contemporary reviewer of her *Pencil Sketches* complained in *North American Review* in October 1833 that she always focused on the dark side of American social life and the vulgar, pretentious aspects of human nature and suggested that she could more profitably employ her considerable talents in finding qualities to praise about America. However, Irving Browne, writing in the *Critic* (11 February 1893), elevates Leslie's writing above that of Jane Austen for its "shrewdness, humor, and quiet sarcasm" as well as for its wider variety of characters and settings.

Apart from her writings, Leslie became a famous Philadelphian in her later years. Although she had grown heavy in her old age and had some difficulty walking, she was feared for her biting sarcasm and stubborn ideas. She was also valued by her closest friends for her sharp memory, wit, and large store of humorous anecdotes. She spent the last ten years of her life living at the United States Hotel, where she not only met visiting celebrities but also received visitors of her own from across the United States and from abroad. During this time she was working on a biography of John Fitch, an inventor and friend of her father, which she never completed. She died in Gloucester, New Jersey, of what Alice Haven described as "a silent but fatal disease," and is buried in St. Peter's churchyard in Philadelphia.

Letters:

Charles Robert Leslie, *Autobiographical Recollections with Selections from His Letters,* edited by Tom Taylor (London: Murray, 1860); republished, with an introduction, by Robin Hamlyn (Wakefield, U.K.: EP, 1978).

Biographies:

Marjorie Stein, *Eliza Leslie: An Early Author on American Cookery,* thesis, University of Wisconsin, 1930;

Ophia D. Smith, "Charles and Eliza Leslie," *Pennsylvania Magazine of History and Biography,* 74 (October 1950): 512–527.

References:

Nina Baym, *Woman's Fiction: A Guide to Novels by and about Women in America, 1820–1870* (Ithaca, N.Y.: Cornell University Press, 1978), pp. 84–85;

Mary Anna DuSablon, *America's Collectible Cookbooks: The History, the Politics, the Recipes* (Athens: Ohio University Press, 1994);

Susan Williams, *Savory Suppers and Fashionable Feasts: Dining in Victorian America* (New York: Pantheon, 1985).

Papers:

Many of Eliza Leslie's letters may be found in the Women Authors Collection at the Library of Congress and in the Stauffer Collection, the E. C. Gardiner Collection, and the Conarroe Papers of the Historical Society of Pennsylvania. Much of her correspondence with her lifelong friends, the Baileys, is with the Bailey family correspondence in the John H. James manuscript collection at Urbana, Ohio. Some professional correspondence may also be found with the Samuel Griswold Goodrich letters, 1822–1856, in the Clifton Waller Barrett Library at the University of Virginia Library in Charlottesville.

George Lippard

(10 April 1822 – 9 February 1854)

Michael L. Burduck
Tennessee Technological University

BOOKS: *Adrian, the Neophyte* (Philadelphia: Diller, 1843);
Original Revolutionary Chronicle: The Battle-Day of Germantown (Philadelphia: Diller, 1843);
Herbert Tracy, or The Legend of the Black Rangers: A Romance of the Battle-field of Germantown (Philadelphia: Berford, 1844); republished in *The Fourth of July, 1776, and Herbert Tracy: Two Legends of the Revolution* (Philadelphia: Severns, 1849);
The Ladye Annabel; or, The Doom of the Poisoner: A Romance by an Unknown Author, anonymous (Philadelphia: Berford, 1844); enlarged as *The Ladye of Albarone; or, The Poison Goblet: A Romance of the Dark Ages* (Philadelphia: Peterson, 1859); republished as *The Mysteries of Florence* (Philadelphia: Peterson, 1864);
The Quaker City; or, The Monks of Monk-Hall. A Romance of Philadelphia Life, Mystery, and Crime, 10 parts, anonymous (Philadelphia: Zieber, 1844–1845); revised edition, 2 volumes (Philadelphia: Peterson, 1845); republished as *Dora Livingstone, the Adulteress; or, The Quaker City* (London: Purkess/Floyd, 1848);
Blanche of Brandywine; or, September the Eleventh, 1777. A Romance, Combining the Poetry, Legend, and History of the Battle of Brandywine, 3 parts (Philadelphia: Zieber, 1846);
The Nazarene; or, The Last of the Washingtons: A Revelation of Philadelphia, New York, and Washington, in the Year 1844, 5 parts (Philadelphia: Lippard, 1846);
Legends of Mexico (Philadelphia: Peterson, 1847); republished as *Legends of Mexico; or, The Battles of Old Rough and Ready* (London: Pratt, 1849);
The Rose of Wissahikon; or, The Fourth of July, 1776. A Romance, Embracing the Secret History of the Declaration of Independence (Philadelphia: Zieber, 1847); republished in *The Fourth of July, 1776, and Herbert Tracy: Two Legends of the American Revolution;*
Washington and His Generals; or, Legends of the Revolution, by George Lippard. With a Biographical Sketch of the Author, by Rev. C. Chauncey Burr, 3 volumes (Philadelphia: Zieber, 1847); republished as *Legends of the American Revolution, "1776"; or, Washington and his Generals* (Philadelphia: Peterson, 1876);

Bel of Prairie Eden: A Romance of Mexico (Boston: Hotchkiss, 1848; Philadelphia: Peterson, 1848);
The Heart-Broken (Philadelphia: Zieber, 1848);
Paul Ardenheim: The Monk of Wissahikon (Philadelphia: Peterson, 1848);
The Entranced; or, the Wanderer of Eighteen Centuries (Philadelphia: Severns, 1849);
The Memoirs of a Preacher, a Revelation of the Church and the Home (Philadelphia: Severns, 1849); republished as *Mysteries of the Pulpit; or, a Revelation of the Church*

and the Home (Philadelphia: Barclay, 1851); enlarged as *The Memoirs of a Preacher; or, The Mysteries of the Pulpit* (Philadelphia: Peterson, 1864);

The Man with the Mask; A Sequel to The Memoirs of a Preacher, a Revelation of the Church and the Home (Philadelphia: Severns, 1849); republished in *The Memoirs of a Preacher; or, The Mysteries of the Pulpit* (Philadelphia: Peterson, 1864);

Washington and His Men: A New Series of Legends of the Revolution (Philadelphia: Severns, 1849; enlarged edition, New York: Stringer & Townsend, 1850);

The Empire City; or, New York by Night and Day, 2 volumes (New York: Stringer & Townsend, 1850);

The Killers: A Narrative of Real Life in Philadelphia, by a Member of the Philadelphia Bar, anonymous (Philadelphia: Hankinson & Bartholomew, 1850); republished as *The Bank Director's Son: A Real and Intensely Interesting Revelation of City Life* (Philadelphia: Barclay & Orton, 1851);

The Midnight Queen; or, Leaves from New-York Life (New York: Garrett, 1853);

New York: Its Upper Ten and Lower Million (Cincinnati: Rulison, 1853).

Editions and Collection: *The Monks of Monk Hall,* introduction by Leslie Fiedler (New York: Odyssey Press, 1970);

George Lippard, Prophet of Protest: Writings of an American Radical, 1822–1854, edited, with an introduction, by David S. Reynolds (New York: Peter Lang, 1986);

The Quaker City; or, The Monks of Monk-Hall: A Romance of Philadelphia Life, Mystery, and Crime, edited, with an introduction and notes, by Reynolds (Amherst: University of Massachusetts Press, 1995).

Combining an innate radicalism with a keen sense of his audience's literary tastes, George Lippard became one of the most controversial and popular writers of the mid nineteenth century. His works, dealing with a wide variety of subjects including Gothic horror, the American Revolution, moral hypocrisy, social inequality, literary cliques, and the labor movement, struck a chord with his contemporaries and allowed him to make a successful living as a professional man of letters. *The Quaker City; or, The Monks of Monk-Hall: A Romance of Philadelphia Life, Mystery, and Crime* (1844–1845), Lippard's most famous book, sold nearly one hundred thousand copies by 1854, the year of his death. Lippard proudly proclaimed that this exposé of the corruption of "finer" Philadelphia society "has been more attacked, and more read, than any work of American fiction ever published."

One of the most strikingly original literary figures of his time, Lippard unabashedly expressed his belief that true literature should never shrink from its duty of discussing the key social or moral issues facing the American people. Lippard remained a prophet of change throughout his short life. Frequently accused of indecency, he steadfastly adhered to the notion that vice must be exposed before it can be defeated. Adamant without being righteous, Lippard tempered his idealism with the realization that a moral triumph is never easily won; however, he remained committed to the notion that through literature a writer could help the United States transcend moral duplicity and create "a heart capable of generous emotions."

George Lippard was the fourth of six children. His father, Daniel L. Lippard, born in 1790, taught school in Philadelphia until he married Jemima Ford in 1815, and he then served a three-year term as treasurer of Philadelphia County. In 1820 the Lippard family purchased a farm in West Nantmeal Township, Chester County, approximately forty miles west of Philadelphia, and George Lippard was born there on 10 April 1822. Farm life proved difficult for the Lippards, and the family relocated to an old family home in Germantown, Pennsylvania. Restless and anxious to find a lucrative profession, Daniel L. Lippard and his wife, Jemima, moved to Philadelphia in 1824, leaving young George in Germantown in the care of two aunts, Catherine and Mary, and his paternal grandfather, Michael. Lippard attended the Concord School in Germantown. In 1831 came the first in a series of deaths that struck the Lippard family between 1831 and 1843. Jemima Lippard died soon after giving birth to a son, who also died. Over the next twelve years George Lippard would suffer the loss of his grandfather, his father, and two of his sisters. In 1832 Lippard's impoverished aunts sold the Germantown house and moved to the bustling city of Philadelphia. Lippard's father remarried in 1833, but he lived apart from young George and his surviving sisters. Hoping that their nephew would become a Christian gentleman, Lippard's aunts encouraged him to join the Western Methodist Episcopal Church in Philadelphia. In the summer of 1837 Lippard attended Catherine Livingston Garretson's Classical School in Rhinebeck, New York, and he planned on becoming a Methodist minister.

Lippard quickly grew disenchanted with the idea of being a cleric, and he returned to Philadelphia. In October 1837 his father, who had been running a grocery store while serving as a constable, died without leaving his son an immediate inheritance, and it became clear to Lippard that he had to seek gainful employment. A career in law seemed a wise choice, and between 1838 and 1841 Lippard worked as an assistant in the law office of William Badger, and later for Ovid F. Johnson, the attorney general of Pennsylvania from 1839 to 1845.

Having something of his father's restlessness, Lippard soon realized that a lawyer's life was less attractive than he had initially thought. In 1840 he began to write what would become *The Ladye Annabel; or, The Doom of the Poisoner: A Romance by an Unknown Author,* published in serial form in 1843 and in book form in 1844. When he finally abandoned his legal studies in 1841, he decided to devote his life to literature, and this decision was reinforced when he met John S. DuSolle, editor of the Philadelphia newspaper *The Spirit of the Times.* From January to April 1842 Lippard worked as a writer and later as a city news reporter for DuSolle's paper. Mixing fact and fiction, Lippard wrote the "City Police" column under the pen name "Billy Brier" and reported on the exploits of various criminals. In addition, Lippard wrote two columns, "The Sanguine Poetaster" and "The Bread Crust Papers," in which he satirized Henry B. Hirst and Thomas Dunn English as pretentious hack writers. He also commented on Charles Dickens's visit to America, and he was particularly amused by how many Americans were virtually worshiping this British novelist.

Encouraged by the public reception of his *The Spirit of the Times* columns, Lippard left DuSolle's paper in April 1842 in order to become a full-time fiction writer. He published his first story, "Philippe de Agramont," a Gothic tale set during the reign of King Richard II, in *The Saturday Evening Post* on 9 July 1842. A story idealizing Wat Tyler's peasant revolt against the punitive taxes levied by the king, the work reveals Lippard's sympathy for the downtrodden. In November 1842 *The Saturday Evening Post* published the serial version of Lippard's novel of the American Revolution *Herbert Tracy, or The Legend of the Black Rangers: A Romance of the Battle-field of Germantown.* In the novel Lippard mixes fact and folklore to present a story of love and intrigue set during the Revolution. *Herbert Tracy,* republished by newspapers across the nation (and subsequently published in book form in 1844), is the first of many works by Lippard devoted to the Revolutionary War.

In January 1843 Lippard began working for *Citizen Soldier: A Weekly Newspaper Devoted to the Interests of the Volunteers and Militia of the United States.* The owners, Isaac and Adam Diller, were so impressed with Lippard's editorial and writing skills that they made him chief editor in July of 1843. Lippard's trenchant criticism and his lively columns were well received by the paper's readers. *Adrian, the Neophyte* (1843) and *The Ladye Annabel* (in serial form), two medieval Gothic tales, appeared in *Citizen Soldier* in 1843. He also wrote political columns and a spirited defense of Edgar Allan Poe. Two of Lippard's most popular *Citizen Soldier* columns, "The Spermaceti Papers" and "The Walnut Coffin Papers," demonstrate his adept skill as a literary satirist. Lippard's favorite target was George R. Graham's publishing firm. Always eager to ridicule "The Grey Ham," Lippard also directed his venomous humor

Vignette title page for Lippard's 1848 novel set in Pennsylvania during the American Revolution

at "Spermaceti Sam," (Samuel P. Patterson, co-publisher of *The Saturday Evening Post*), "The Reverend Rumpus Grizzle" (Rufus Wilmot Griswold, anthologist and editor), and "Professor Peter Sun" (Charles J. Peterson, fictionist). Lippard also used these columns to praise various writers who in his opinion were carrying American literature to new artistic heights. He regularly praised Charles Brockden Brown, James Fenimore Cooper, and Washington Irving but was especially impressed with the works of Poe. The two men had met in 1842 when Lippard was working for *The Spirit of the Times.* In the November 1843 issue of *Citizen Soldier,* Lippard lauded Poe's poetry, fiction, and criticism, writing: "his mind penetrates the utmost recesses of the human soul, creating vast and magnificent dreams, eloquent fancies and terrible mysteries."

Although the public enjoyed Lippard's literary works, few critics were singing his praises. Indeed, many of the positive reviews of Lippard's works that appeared in *Citizen Soldier* were written either by Lippard himself or by

THE EMPIRE CITY

OR

NEW YORK BY NIGHT AND DAY.

BY GEORGE LIPPARD,

AUTHOR OF "WASHINGTON AND HIS GENERALS, OR LEGENDS OF THE REVOLUTION," "THE QUAKER CITY," "PAUL ARDENHEIM, OR THE MONK OF WISSAHIKON," "THE NAZARENE, OR LAST OF THE WASH-INGTONS," "BLANCHE OF BRANDYWINE," "LADYE ANNABEL," "THE MEMOIRS OF A PREACHER," "LEGENDS OF MEXICO," "THE MAN WITH THE MASK," "THE ENTRANCED, OR THE WANDERER OF EIGHTEEN CENTURIES," "JESUS AND THE POOR," "WASHINGTON AND HIS MEN," "HERBERT TRACY," &C.

NEW YORK:
STRINGER & TOWNSEND, 222 BROADWAY.
1850.

Title page for Lippard's novel about corruption among upper-class New Yorkers

one of the Diller brothers. In an attempt to strengthen his reputation, Lippard sent Poe a copy of *The Ladye Annabel* in early 1844. On 18 February 1844 Poe responded to Lippard. Poe wrote: "You seem to have been in too desperate a hurry to give due attention to details; and thus your style . . . is at times somewhat exuberant—but the work, as a whole . . . [is] richly inventive and imaginative—indicative of *genius* in its author." Poe concludes his letter by reminding Lippard that "If my opinion of 'The Ladye Annabel' can be of *any* service to you whatever, you have my full permission to publish this letter, or any portion of it you deem proper." Lippard included this letter in the book version of *Herbert Tracy* published in 1844, and the two writers were good friends thereafter.

Lippard resigned from *Citizen Soldier* in the spring of 1844, and he became increasingly involved in literary and social controversies. The reform-minded writer discussed such topics as women's rights, socialism, work laws, anti-Catholicism, and abolition. His popularity with readers

and critics grew. In the autumn of 1844, Lippard published the first installment of what would turn out to be his most famous novel. *The Quaker City; or, the Monks of Monk-Hall,* a work influenced by the "city novel" tradition popularized by the French writer Eugéne Sue, sold briskly, and when the complete novel appeared in book form in May 1845, more than sixty thousand copies were sold. Based on the famous Singleton Mercer trial of 1843, a court case in which Mercer was acquitted after killing Mahlon Heberton, who had raped Mercer's sister, the book features such elements as pornography, Gothicism, and anti-elitism. In his preface Lippard revealed his motive for writing *The Quaker City:* "That the seduction of a poor and innocent girl, is a deed altogether as criminal as deliberate murder. It is worse than the murder of the body, for it is the assassination of the soul. If the murderer deserves death by the gallows, then the assassin of chastity and maidenhood is worthy of death by the hands of any man, and in any place." Set in Monk Hall, a combination brothel/dungeon, the novel exposes the hypocrisy of Philadelphia's wealthy upper class. Lippard reserves an intense disdain for one of the most despicable figures in the novel, the Reverend F. A. T. Pyne. A Calvinist "doom and gloom" preacher known for his ardent anti-Catholic nativism, Pyne regularly visits Monk Hall to satisfy his lecherous desires. In one scene Pyne drugs and attempts to seduce his own daughter. In *The Quaker City,* Lippard also mocks Rosamond Culbertson's 1836 novel, *Rosamond,* a virulently anti-Catholic work in which the author invents a Catholic plot to capture young boys and throw them into a large meat grinder to make sausages for the unsuspecting public. Although some readers (including Lippard's former employer John S. DuSolle) were offended by what they viewed as the immorality in Lippard's book, *The Quaker City* became one of the most popular books published in the United States, and by 1849 twenty-seven editions of the work had appeared. The public was so influenced by Lippard's novel of "secret" Philadelphia life that the book prompted the New York State Assembly to enact an antiseduction law in 1849. Lippard, who always believed that literature should focus on social reform, may well have felt that the New York law vindicated him from the charge of "indecency" that was frequently leveled against *The Quaker City.*

Lippard once again turned his attention to writing and lecturing about the American Revolution. On 18 December 1845 he delivered the first historical lecture at Philadelphia's William Wirt Institute, and on 3 January 1846 the *Philadelphia Saturday Courier* published Lippard's Liberty Bell legend (which continues to be accepted as "fact" by most Americans). The *Saturday Courier* published sixty-two of his Revolutionary legends through December 1848, and because of Lippard's contributions the newspaper more than doubled its circulation.

George Lippard (portrait by an unknown artist; The Historical Society of Pennsylvania)

On 15 May 1847 Lippard married Rose New-man. With Lippard's friend the Universalist minister Charles Chauncey Burr presiding, the ceremony was conducted as a moonlight service on a cliff overlooking the Wissahikon River. In the same year Lippard published two books dealing with the American Revolution: *Washington and His Generals; or, Legends of the Revolution, by George Lippard. With a Biographical Sketch of the Author, by Rev. C. Chauncey Burr,* and *The Rose of Wissahikon; or, The Fourth of July, 1776. A Romance, Embracing the Secret History of the Declaration of Independence.* A third book published in 1847, *Legends of Mexico,* recounted stories of Zachary Taylor's 1846 campaigns in the Mexican War.

On 31 March 1848 Lippard's daughter, Mima, was born. In the summer of that year Lippard was asked to speak at the annual convention of the National Reform Congress, a group of labor activists. In his address Lippard discussed workers' rights and land reform, and the occasion marks Lippard's first foray into the American labor movement. Lippard was not yet finished being a man of letters, however, and in

December 1848 he published the first issue of his weekly newspaper, *The Quaker City* (named after his successful novel), which remained extremely popular until its last issue appeared in June 1850. In 1849 Lippard published five new serial novels in his newspaper: *The Memoirs of a Preacher, a Revelation of the Church and the Home* and *The Man with the Mask; A Sequel to The Memoirs of a Preacher, a Revelation of the Church and the Home* (both of which dealt with immoral preachers); *The Entranced; or, the Wanderer of Eighteen Centuries* (a fictionalized socialist history of the world); *The Empire City; or, New York by Night and Day* (dealing with the corruption of New York's wealthy class); and *The Killers: A Narrative of Real Life in Philadelphia, by a Member of the Philadelphia Bar* (an account of gang warfare in Philadelphia). Soon after their publication in *The Quaker City,* all of these works were republished in book form by various firms. One of the newspaper's columns, "The Quaker City Police Court," was written by Lippard under the name "Justice Poe" and doled out harsh punishments for poorly talented writers. In July 1849 Poe visited Lippard in

Philadelphia, and Lippard collected money from some of his literary friends to help the impoverished poet.

In 1849 Lippard founded a labor organization to which he was to devote the majority of his remaining years. The Brotherhood of the Union mingled ritualism, patriotism, religious tolerance, and labor reform, and the group grew rapidly. A confirmed socialist, Lippard based his political ideals not on the "scientific socialism" promulgated by Karl Marx and others but rather on a sentimental, idealistic belief in the possibility of creating a society based on mutual understanding and trust. Lippard traveled around the country lecturing on behalf of the Brotherhood of the Union speaking on such topics as the American Revolution, social reform, and spiritualism. In October 1850 the brotherhood elected Lippard to the post of Supreme Washington, a position he would hold for life. He became close to the Daughters and Sons of Liberty, a radical Philadelphia group concerned with the rights of women, blacks, and Native Americans. The reform-oriented author became one of the most important figures in the American labor movement.

Although during this period Lippard spent much of his time on social and labor reform issues, he also maintained a keen interest in literature. Shortly after Poe's death he published a moving tribute to his friend in the 20 October 1849 issue of his newspaper, *The Quaker City* (one year later he wrote a spirited defense of Poe for the newspaper). Soon after this piece appeared came the first in a series of personal tragedies. In late October 1849 his daughter, Mima, died. A son, Paul, was born in May 1850, but in less than a year he, too, died. In the spring of 1851 Lippard's wife, Rose, died of tuberculosis at the age of twenty-six. Grief-stricken, Lippard contemplated suicide, but he took strength from his role as leader of the Brotherhood of the Union, and resolved to continue his quest to improve American society.

He lectured widely between 1851 and 1854, and in 1851 published *The White Banner,* a periodical intended to help spread the reform doctrines of the brotherhood. In 1852 Lippard's friend Burr hired him to serve as literary editor of the *New York National Democrat,* a daily paper for which Lippard also wrote pieces attacking the corruption of the upper classes in New York City. After a few months Lippard decided to resume his lecturing, although in 1851 he published *The Midnight Queen; or, Leaves from New-York Life* and *New York: Its Upper Ten and Lower Million,* two critiques of social inequality.

Perhaps, in part, as a result of his hectic travel schedule, Lippard's health began to fail in 1853. Suffering from tuberculosis, Lippard continued to write almost until his final hour. He died on 9 February 1854, having established a reputation as a popular writer of Gothic and patriotic tales and as a social reformer who refused to abandon his utopian dream of shaping a more ideal American culture.

Biographies:

John Bell Bouton, *The Life and Choice Writings of George Lippard* (New York: Randall, 1855);

Joseph Jackson, "George Lippard: Misunderstood Man of Letters," *Pennsylvania Magazine of History and Biography,* 54 (October 1930): 376–391;

Roger Butterfield, "George Lippard and His Secret Brotherhood," *Pennsylvania Magazine of History and Biography,* 74 (July 1955): 291–309.

Bibliographies:

Joseph Jackson, "A Bibliography of the Works of George Lippard," *Pennsylvania Magazine of History and Biography,* 54 (April 1930): 131–154; 54 (October 1930): 381–383;

Roger Butterfield, "A Check List of the Separately Published Works of George Lippard," *Pennsylvania Magazine of History and Biography,* 74 (July 1955): 302–309;

Jacob Blanck, *Bibliography of American Literature,* volume 5 (New York: Yale University Press, 1969), pp. 405–415.

References:

Emilio DeGrazia, "Poe's Devoted Democrat, George Lippard," *Poe Studies,* 6 (June 1973): 6–8;

Hayward Ehrlich, "The 'Mysteries' of Philadelphia: Lippard's *Quaker City* and 'Urban' Gothic" *ESQ: A Journal of the American Renaissance,* 18 (1972): 50–65;

Burton R. Pollin, "More on Lippard and Poe," *Poe Studies,* 7 (June 1974): 22–23;

David S. Reynolds, *George Lippard* (New York: Twayne, 1982);

J. V. Ridley, "George Lippard's *The Quaker City:* The World of the American Porno-Gothic," *Studies in the Literary Imagination,* 7 (Spring 1970): 77–94;

Larzer Ziff, *Literary Democracy: The Declaration of Cultural Independence in America* (New York: Viking, 1981), pp. 91–107.

Papers:

Major collections of George Lippard's papers are located at The Historical Society of Pennsylvania, Philadelphia, and the American Antiquarian Society, Worcester, Massachusetts. Other collections of manuscripts and letters are held by the Free Library of Philadelphia, the Bucks County (Pennsylvania) Historical Society, the New York Public Library, the Library of Congress, and the Barrett Collection at the University of Virginia.

Charles Major

(25 July 1856 – 13 February 1913)

Mathew David Fisher
Ball State University

BOOKS: *When Knighthood Was in Flower; or, The Love Story of Charles Brandon and Mary Tudor . . . Rewritten and Rendered into Modern English from Sir Edwin Caskoden's Memoir by Edwin Caskoden* (Indianapolis & Kansas City: Bowen-Merrill, 1898; London: Sands, 1899);

The Bears of Blue River (New York & London: Doubleday & McClure, 1901);

Dorothy Vernon of Haddon Hall (New York & London: Macmillan, 1902);

A Forest Hearth: A Romance of Indiana in the Thirties (New York & London: Macmillan, 1903);

Yolanda, Maid of Burgundy (New York & London: Macmillan, 1905);

Uncle Tom Andy Bill: A Story of Bears and Indian Treasure (New York: Macmillan, 1908);

A Gentle Knight of Old Brandenburg (New York: Macmillan, 1909);

The Little King: A Story of the Childhood of King Louis XIV, King of France (New York & London: Macmillan, 1910);

Sweet Alyssum (Indianapolis: Bobbs-Merrill, 1911);

The Touchstone of Fortune, Being the Memoir of Baron Clyde (New York & London: Macmillan, 1912);

Rosalie, by Major and Test Dalton (New York: Macmillan, 1925).

Charles Major (The American Antiquarian Society)

Charles Major was one of America's most successful writers of historical romances and regional adventure novels in the late nineteenth century. His first novel, *When Knighthood Was in Flower; or, The Love Story of Charles Brandon and Mary Tudor* (1898), sold more than two hundred thousand copies in two years and remained a best-seller for more than fourteen months. Along with Maurice Thompson, George Barr McCutcheon, Booth Tarkington, David Graham Phillips, and Theodore Dreiser, Major wrote during a period when Hoosier novelists were remarkably popular. He was born in Indianapolis on 25 July 1856 to Stephen and Phoebe Major, both Irish immigrants. Having graduated from his "common school" educa-

tion in 1872, he attended Michigan University until 1875. He read law with his father, an important Indiana lawyer and judge, and was admitted to the bar in 1877. Major practiced law throughout his life; however, as Richard Banta points out in his study *Indiana Authors and Their Books* (1949), he accepted only enough cases to maintain a "respectable living," and after the success of his first two novels he only kept his office "in order to have a quiet place to work." He suspended even this nominal practice in 1885 to serve as representative to the Indiana legislature and in the same year married Alice Shaw.

Although occupied by law and politics, Major had a passion for history. His biographer, Kenneth Fallis, writes in his *When Charles Major Was in Flower* (1988): "While attending high school he passed Levi Book-walter's bookstore every day. What caught and kept his interest in the window was a complete set of Sir Walter Scott's works. It was modestly priced at $4.50, but this was beyond purchasing with his allowance. Each day as he passed the store his resolve grew stronger to own the set. He finally earned the amount and began his lifelong interest in English history." Major's interest in English history was not merely literary, however. His family, originally the D'Fys, were among the French who went to England with William the Conqueror. Major collected books on this and other historical periods, compiling an extensive library.

Major's first novel was written as a hobby, largely for his own pleasure. Originally subtitled "The Love Story of Charles Brandon and Mary Tudor, the King's Sister, and Happening in the Reign of His August Majesty, King Henry VIII Rewritten and Rendered into Modern English from Sir Edwin Caskoden's Memoir by Edwin Caskoden," the novel was characteristically inspired by Major's comprehensive study of the history of the period—in this case Francois Pierre Guillaume Guizot's *History of France,* which refers to Mary Tudor's love for her brother's friend, Charles Brandon.

Major understood well the limitations of his literary abilities. Because he felt unable to replicate accurately the dialect of the period, Major tells the story of Mary Tudor's romantic relationship with Charles Brandon through Edwin Caskoden, who himself is translating into modern language a memoir written by his ancestor Sir Edwin Caskoden, a member of Henry VIII's court. Brandon was appointed to the court after impressing the king by avenging the deaths of his brother and father. Returning from the "continental wars," Charles, his older brother, and his father gamble away most of their battle pay playing dice with Sir Adam Judson. It is soon revealed that Judson has cheated the Brandons, and in the insuing duel both Charles's father and brother are killed. Charles, however, wins the duel when he slashes his sword "lengthwise through Judson's eyes and the bridge of his nose, leaving him sightless and hideous for life."

Princess Mary falls in love with Brandon at first sight, vexing her brother the king, who had unsuccessfully attempted to arrange marriages for Mary in the past with more appropriately elevated suitors. Employing a device that he used throughout his historical romances, Major offers another pair of lovers as foils for this budding relationship; in this case, Sir Edwin is in love with Lady Jane Bolingbroke, Princess Mary's lady in waiting.

Brandon and Mary's relationship is soon dramatically altered, however, upon the death of the wife of the French king, Louis XII. Seeking to strengthen political ties with marriage bonds, Louis asks Henry for Mary's hand. Of this arrangement Edwin reports: "Louis was an old man, and an old Frenchman at that; full of French notions of morality and immorality; and besides, there were objections that can not be written, but of which Henry and Mary had been fully informed. She might as well marry a leper. Do you wonder she was full of dread and fear, and resisted with desperation of death?" Mary and Brandon attempt to escape to New Spain by boat, with Mary unsuccessfully disguising herself as a man. When sailors insult and attack her, Brandon retaliates; consequently, they are kicked off the ship, and Brandon is sent to the Tower of London.

Mary is eventually forced to wed Louis but resolves "to make life a burden to the Father of his People." In addition to generally avoiding his romantic advances, she changes the meal schedule so that the king eats a heavy meal late at night and provokes him to drinking "as much as brother Henry." Further, "she took the king on long rides with her on cold days, and would jolt him almost to death, and freeze him until the cold tears streamed down his poor pinched nose, making him feel like a half-animated icicle, and wish that he were one in fact." Mary's plan works: the king dies and she is allowed to return to England to marry Brandon.

When Knighthood Was in Flower was a best-seller for fourteen consecutive months, going through two more printings within a year of its publication. The reviewer in the *Chicago Times-Herald* compared Major favorably to Anthony Hope, a popular romance writer of the time. In 1899 the novel was dramatized by Paul Kester for the popular actress Julia Marlowe, who later became a lifelong friend of the Majors. Despite an initially tepid response, a revised version of the play opened in New York in 1901 to more positive reviews. Film versions were produced in 1908 and 1922, and in 1953 *When Knighthood Was in Flower* was the basis for Walt Disney's *The Sword and the Rose.*

Though Major continued to reside in Shelbyville, Indiana, the fame brought about by his first novel resulted in many opportunities for the Major family. In 1901 the couple was invited to the White House to meet President William McKinley and dined with Samuel Clemens "at the famous Delmonico's in New York City."

Also in 1901 Major published his second novel, *The Bears of Blue River.* Set in the 1820s, "when Indiana was a baby state," the novel is the first of Major's attempts to explore a local theme. The novel's main character, "Little Balser" Brent, is a young boy of thirteen or fourteen who with the help of his friend Tom

Fox embarks on a series of adventures, all focused on the killing of the many bears that ranged over the Indiana wilderness. In the first chapter Little Balser kills a six-hundred-pound bear that attacks the boy during a fishing trip. Later he helps an eloping couple who are being pursued by the woman's father. When the couple is wed, the husband gives him a "smooth-bore carbine" in exchange for his help. After this episode the narrative becomes a string of loosely connected stories of Little Balser's encounters with bears, usually in the company of his brother Jim, Tom Fox, and his young love, Liney Fox. With the help of his dogs, Tige and Prince, Little Balser kills several bears, including the legendary "One-Eared Bear" and the "fire bear." This novel and Major's other two regional adventure stories are most notable for their use of Indiana dialect, settings, and manners.

Major's literary reputation continued to grow with the publication of *The Bears of Blue River*. In 1902 he was invited to sit on a literary panel including James Whitcomb Riley, McCutcheon, and Mary Catherwood. For his third novel, *Dorothy Vernon of Haddon Hall* (1902), he returned to the historical romance, setting the action in England in 1567. As in *When Knighthood Was in Flower,* Major employs a distant narrator to relate the story, in this case Malcolm Vernon, Dorothy Vernon's cousin; he also reuses the dramatic device of an ill-suited arranged marriage.

The novel opens with Malcolm journeying to Haddon Hall to wed Dorothy Vernon. Though Malcolm has not seen her for seven years and is sixteen years older than she is, Dorothy's father wishes to join Malcolm's father's estate with his own through this union. Malcolm is disappointed in Dorothy, finding her headstrong and childish, but develops a serious interest in her companion, Madge. However, Sir John Manners, whom Malcolm meets on his journey to Haddon Hall and subsequently befriends, falls in love with Dorothy. Unfortunately, Sir John's father and Dorothy's father are sworn enemies. A series of dramatic encounters follows, resulting in Dorothy's imprisonment. John writes to Dorothy, explaining that he has rescued Mary, Queen of Scots, who was once John's lover, from her imprisonment.

Jealous of Mary's previous relationship with John, Dorothy betrays her to Queen Elizabeth, and she is subsequently sent back to prison. Though John's role in Mary's liberation is discovered, Elizabeth grants him a royal pardon at Dorothy's request, and the two starcrossed lovers are wed. Malcolm and Madge, whose relationship has continued to build throughout the novel, are likewise married. Like Major's first historical romance, *Dorothy Vernon of Haddon Hall* was adapted for the stage and later the screen.

Marion Davies as Mary Tudor in the 1922 movie adaptation of When Knighthood Was In Flower, *one of three screen versions of Major's best-known work*

Dorothy Vernon of Haddon Hall was followed in 1903 by *A Forest Hearth: A Romance of Indiana in the Thirties,* in which Major returned to the Indiana frontier. Blending the romantic dimension of his historical romances with the backwoods setting of *The Bears of Blue River,* this novel tells the story of Dic Bright and Rita Bays, who like the characters in Major's romances are beset with seemingly impossible obstacles. Rita's mother insists that she marry an older man, Mr. Williams, whom Dic faces in a duel in the novel's crucial scene. Williams shoots first, wounding Dic in the thigh, but Dic refuses to kill Williams. Dic is assisted by Billy Little, the community's unofficial banker, who sends him to New York to earn enough money to return and marry Rita. When Rita's brother Tom embezzles money from the family's business, Billy Little prevents Tom's arrest and provides the necessary money to save the Bays' business. Rita's father, showing uncharacteristic resolve, has Billy take Rita to Dic, and the two are married.

Though not as financially successful as his two previous historical romances, Major's *Yolanda, Maid of Burgundy,* published in 1905, was reviewed favorably.

The reviewer for *The New York Times* (2 December 1905) wrote, "It is a story bristling with intrigue and adventure, with meetings after dark, and love and scorn and villainy and fine ladies traveling unattended, and mystery galore, and always through it all runs the theme of love—the love of a brave man for a beautiful girl." Major again employs a distant first-person narrator, Sir Karl de Pitti, tutor to Count Maximilian, the young son of the impoverished duke of Hapsburg. Max's father tries to better his kingdom by arranging a marriage for his son with the young princess of Burgundy, but his query to the duke of Burgundy is not answered. To distance Max from these courtly intrigues, Sir Karl volunteers to take the young count out to see the world beyond the castle walls. The two set out incognito on a journey replete with harrowing adventures.

During one of these exciting episodes both Sir Karl and Max are wounded, and while recovering from their injuries in a monastery they are employed by George Castleman, the duke of Burgundy's advisor, to escort him safely back to Burgundy. Upon their arrival, Max is introduced to Castleman's wife, his daughter Antoinette, and Antoinette's "cousin," Yolanda—actually one and the same person, and not Castleman's daughter at all. Max falls in love with Yolanda, and throughout much of the book he entertains suspicions that the princess and Yolanda are actually the same person; but she continues to fool him, hoping that he will love her for her character and not for her kingdom. When an evil nobleman, Count Calli, attempts to force his attentions on Yolanda, Max intercedes, breaking the count's wrist. Both Max and Sir Karl are imprisoned until Max challenges Calli to a duel.

During the duel Max's horse is mysteriously injured, and he is thrown to the ground. Just as Calli is about to administer the deathblow, the princess, who everyone agrees greatly resembles Yolanda, throws herself on Max to save him. The duke discovers that Calli is responsible for the treachery, and the count is promptly hanged. Because he demonstrated remarkable bravery, the duke invites Max, along with Sir Karl, to join his troops in battle against Switzerland. The campaign is disastrous, and in the end Duke Charles is killed. Though he knows that marriage to the princess would save his father's duchy from insolvency, when he returns with what remains of Burgundy's army Max proposes marriage to Yolanda. Yolanda finally reveals her identity; the two are married; and their kingdoms are united.

Major was invited to the White House for the second time in 1908, this time to meet President Theodore Roosevelt. That year he also published his sixth novel, *Uncle Tom Andy Bill: A Story of Bears and Indian Treasure,* a sequel to *The Bears of Blue River,* again set in his native Indiana. The reviewer for the December 1908 *Bookman* hailed it as "a new juvenile which will receive a ready welcome," and a critic for the 12 December *Outlook* called it "a true and lively picture of life half a century ago in what is now the middle west, but was then the frontier." The main character of the novel is an old man who regales his family's small children with stories of his adventures with Balser Brent from the earlier novel. On a cold winter night, Tom Andy Bill recalls, an Indian, Wyandotte, wanders half-frozen and close to death into the boys' campsite. While they nurse him back to health, he rants about a cave filled with gold. In the spring the boys head for Cincinnati to sell their furs.

During the trip to Cincinnati and back Tom Andy Bill and Little Balser endure several dramatic adventures, including being rescued from a gang of thieves by a young girl named Mab, with whom Tom Andy Bill falls in love. When he and Balser journey to Cincinnati to sell another season's furs, they are taken prisoner by a tribe of Indians but are released when they discover that Wyandotte is chief of the village. Their Indian friend is dying, however, and on his deathbed he reveals the exact location of the cave of gold. The boys locate the gold, but meanwhile one of Mab's relatives has kidnapped her and forced her to marry against her will. Seven years later Mab and her daughter manage to escape and return to Tom for protection. Mab lives only three more years, but Tom and her daughter live happily as a family after her death.

In his next novel, *A Gentle Knight of Old Brandenburg* (1909), Major widened his literary scope, setting his narrative in eighteenth-century Germany. The story's protagonist, Fritz, is actually Frederick Henry, heir to Bayreuth, sent away by his father to avoid a purely financially arranged marriage. During his travels he is captured by the Prussian army, but he so impresses the king that he is eventually promoted to captain of the king's grenadier regiment. Characteristically, Fritz assumes a false identity and falls in love with the Princess Wilhelmina. Wilhelmina loves Fritz but has been ordered to marry either Adolph of Schwedt or the Duke of Weissenfels.

Adolph, demonstrating his nobility, offers to help the lovers by initiating the wedding and then withdrawing his offer in favor of Fritz's. Weissenfels discovers this deception and tries to attack the king; however, as the captain of the grenadiers, Fritz defends the king and slays Weissenfels. After several complicated plot twists, Fritz reveals his identity, and he and Wilhelmina are wed. As Adolph watches the couple ride away from the castle, however, he dies of a broken heart. Critical opinion of Major's seventh novel was again split between that expressed by the writer from *The Saturday Review* (26 March 1910), who wondered if "there was any crying need for a piece of book-making like this," and that of

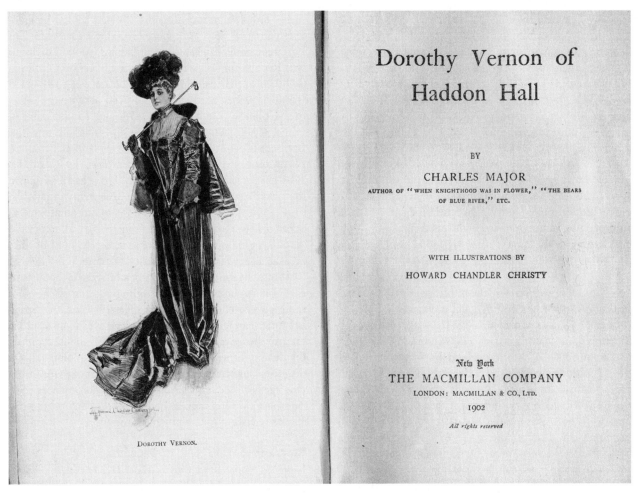

DOROTHY VERNON.

Dorothy Vernon of Haddon Hall

BY

CHARLES MAJOR

AUTHOR OF "WHEN KNIGHTHOOD WAS IN FLOWER," "THE BEARS
OF BLUE RIVER," ETC.

WITH ILLUSTRATIONS BY

HOWARD CHANDLER CHRISTY

New York
THE MACMILLAN COMPANY
LONDON: MACMILLAN & CO., LTD.
1902
All rights reserved

Frontispiece and title page for Major's third novel, set in England in 1567

the critic for the *Spectator* (15 January 1910), who wrote, "Readers who remember Mr. Major's 'Dorothy Vernon' will expect a good story, and will not be disappointed."

In his next historical romance, *The Little King* (1910), Major opted against the use of a first-person narrator. The story concerns the young King Louis XIV and his nurse, "Sweet Mam'selle." In her attempts to relieve Louis's boredom, Mam'selle often surreptitiously takes the boy out into the streets of the city. The narrative focuses on one such escapade, during which Louis meets Louise, a young slum girl whose father had been imprisoned for attacking a nobleman who had insulted his daughter. When the young Louis and Mam'selle return to the castle, he orders the release of Louise's father. Louis demands that Louise move into the castle, but in her unhappiness she convinces him to leave with her through a secret tunnel. The two seek refuge with a woman who can only offer them her floor because she has had to sell her furniture to pay the "house tax." In the morning she is arrested for stealing bread to feed her children, and Louis returns to the castle to effect her release. The novel

ends unhappily when friends of Mam'selle and her fiancé, Jean Breton, are murdered by the villainous Cardinal Mazarin. Mam'selle and Jean are then forced to flee Paris, and the story concludes with Louis vowing revenge upon the cardinal. Fallis suggests that this uncharacteristically pessimistic ending represents Major's attempt to account for Louis's tyrannical reign.

In 1912 Major saw the publication of his last novel, *The Touchstone of Fortune, Being the Memoir of Baron Clyde*. Once again employing the setting characteristic of all of his historical romances except *The Little King*, this story involves the exiled court of the merry monarch, Charles II. True to form, the narrator, Edwin, Baron of Clyde, tells the story, which focuses on the protagonist, Frances Jennings, a maid of honor in the queen's court, and her romance with the exiled George Hamilton. Early in the novel, Hamilton, having been accused of murder, returns to the court disguised as an old man. When Frances is mysteriously kidnapped and imprisoned in a tower, Hamilton, Edwin, and Frances's friend Betty rescue her. Dressed as a man, Betty attempts to scale the walls to Frances's chambers, falls, and is rescued by Edwin. Edwin loses Charles's favor when the king discovers his role in Frances's escape; it is revealed that the king himself had Frances imprisoned for spurning his advances. George Hamilton must flee France but returns in disguise to purchase Dunkirk for King Louis XIV. He succeeds in his negotiations and takes Frances with him when he leaves. Edwin gives up his title and marries Betty, and the two happy couples reunite in France. Critics generally concurred with the reviewer for the *Literary Digest* (4 May 1912), who judged *The Touchstone of Fortune* "a romantic and exciting story," but several reviewers noted a general lack of narrative and plot control. The critic for the *Nation* (2 August 1912) allowed that Major had managed a "general fidelity to the flavor of the period" but considered the novel "a mere confection, to be tasted and forgotten."

In the year following the publication of *The Touchstone of Fortune* Major and his wife embarked on a business trip to England. Major's health, which had begun to trouble him during a trip to Canada in 1911, continued to decline. While in England he met critic James Milne, who wrote of Major: "Behind his talk there was a deep human knowledge of English history such as few, even deliberate English students of history, can hope to possess. There was hardly a yard of historic London which he could not clothe in the romantic color of the past." Suffering more acutely from his illness, Major returned home in November 1912 and was diagnosed with liver cancer. The disease spread rapidly, and on 13 February 1913 Major died.

Twelve years after Major's death his wife allowed the publication of *Rosalie* (1925), an unfinished text that was completed by Test Dalton. The story is narrated by the protagonist, Dr. John Alden Collingwood, who is falsely accused of murder. He escapes with the help of a young woman, Rosalie, who had encouraged him during his trial. Though Collingwood loves Rosalie, he is thirty years older than she and is unable to profess his love because he is a condemned man. Rosalie, however, helps Collingwood flee to Canada; the two are shipwrecked and finally, passing themselves off as uncle and niece, find refuge in a mission directed by the benevolent Father Ignace and the evil Gabriel Du Barr. Du Barr repeatedly attempts to kill Collingwood in order to win Rosalie for himself, and he finally reports Collingwood to the British authorities. The novel ends when Rosalie's father and a British official arrive with news that Collingwood has been pardoned for his alleged crime. Collingwood and Rosalie are married, and Du Barr commits suicide. Few reviewers appreciated this posthumous novel: the reviewer for *The New York Times Book Review* (14 June 1925) referred to it as "a structure that stands but between whose boards many cracks are to be found. It is like a house built by an amateur carpenter as compared to one put together by an expert."

The lukewarm response to *Rosalie* was likely due in part to the waning popularity of period romance at that time. During the two decades or so that the historical romance enjoyed its astounding popularity, Major's novels were consistently best-sellers. When the Spanish-American War ushered in a period of realism in literature, however, romantic novels, with their emphasis on distant times and settings, unwieldy coincidences, disguises, and false identities, seemed out of place in the new age. Consequently, Major's historical romances have been largely forgotten, although his Indiana adventure stories remain popular juvenile literature.

Biography:

Kenneth Fallis, *When Charles Major Was in Flower: A Biography of the Shelbyville Author* (Shelbyville, Ind.: Shelby County Historical Society, 1988).

References:

Howard G. Baetzhold, "Charles Major: Hoosier Romancer," *Indiana Magazine of History,* 51 (March 1955): 31–42;

Anton Scherier, "Charles Major," *Indiana Magazine of History,* 45 (September 1949): 265–267.

Papers:

Charles Major's correspondence and other materials are housed in the Purdue University Library, West Lafayette, Indiana.

James McHenry
(20 December 1785 – 21 July 1845)

Maureen Ann Sullivan
University of Alaska, Fairbanks

BOOKS: *The Bard of Erin and Other Poems Mostly National* (Belfast: Smyth & Lyons, 1808);

Patrick: A Poetical Tale Founded on Incidents Which Took Place in Ireland During the Unhappy Period of 1793 (Glasgow: M'Kenzie, 1810);

The Pleasures of Friendship: A Poem in Two Parts, to Which Are Added a Few Original Irish Melodies (Pittsburgh: Eichbaum & Johnston, 1822); revised and enlarged as *The Pleasures of Friendship . . . to Which Are Added a Few Other Poems and Original Melodies* (Philadelphia: Poole, 1825); revised and enlarged *as The Blessings of Friendship and Other Poems* (London: Wightman & Cramp, 1825); revised and enlarged as *The Pleasures of Friendship and Other Poems* (Philadelphia: Grigg, 1828; enlarged again, 1830); republished as *The Pleasures of Friendship* (Philadelphia: Grigg & Elliot, 1836);

Waltham: An American Revolutionary Tale in Three Cantos (New York: Bliss & White, 1823);

The Wilderness; or, Braddock's Times: A Tale of the West, 2 volumes, anonymous (New York: Bliss & White, 1823); republished as *The Wilderness, or The Youthful Days of Washington*, 3 volumes, as Solomon Secondsight (London: Newman, 1823);

The Spectre of the Forest; or, Annals of the Housatonic, a New-England Romance, 2 volumes, anonymous (New York: Bliss & White, 1823; London: Newman, 1823);

O'Halloran; or, The Insurgent Chief: An Irish Historical Tale of 1798, 2 volumes, anonymous (Philadelphia: Carey & Lea, 1824); republished as *The Insurgent Chief; or O'Halloran*, as Solomon Secondsight (London: Newman, 1824);

The Hearts of Steel: An Irish Historical Tale of the Last Century, 2 volumes, anonymous (Philadelphia: Poole, 1825; London, 1825);

The Usurper: An Historical Tragedy in Five Acts (Philadelphia: Harding, 1829);

The Betrothed of Wyoming: An Historical Tale, anonymous (Philadelphia: Principal Booksellers, 1830);

The Feelings of Age, to Which Is Added The Star of Love: Poems (Philadelphia: Banks, 1830);

Meredith; or, The Mystery of the Meschianza: A Tale of the American Revolution, anonymous (Philadelphia: Principal Booksellers, 1831);

To Britannia (London: Stephenson, 1839);

The Antediluvians; or, The World Destroyed: A Narrative Poem in Ten Books (London: Cradock, 1839; Philadelphia: Lippincott, 1840).

PLAY PRODUCTIONS: *The Usurper,* Philadelphia, Chestnut Street Theatre, 26 December 1827;

Love and Poetry; or, A Modern Genius, Philadelphia, Walnut Street Theatre, 5 December 1929;

The Maid of Wyoming, Philadelphia, Arch Street Theatre, 28 January 1831.

OTHER: *American Monthly Magazine,* volumes 1–2 (1824), edited by McHenry.

SELECTED PERIODICAL PUBLICATIONS—
UNCOLLECTED: "Ellen Stanley, or The Victim of Vanity," *Philadelphia Album,* 3 (30 July 1828): 65–67;

"The Outlaw of Slimish," *Philadelphia Monthly Magazine,* 2 (November 1828): 36–57;

"American Lake Poetry," anonymous, *American Quarterly Review,* 11 (March 1832): 154–174;

"Decline of Poetry," anonymous, *American Quarterly Review,* 15 (June 1834): 448–473.

James McHenry's name is unfamiliar to most readers today, though he enjoyed considerable popularity as a poet, playwright, novelist, and critic during his life. McHenry's contributions to literature should not be forgotten, however, as he was the first American fiction writer to explore both Irish legendary themes and the state of affairs in Northern Ireland.

Little is known of the early life of McHenry. He was born on 20 December 1785 in Larne, Ireland. His parents, George and Mary Smiley McHenry, raised their son in Larne's seceding Presbyterian church. He had a hunched back, to which he refers in his writing, most likely the result of a childhood injury. When McHenry was twelve years old, his father died. He received some schooling in Latin and Greek by the Reverend John Nicholson, but his later education remains a mystery. He might have attended a Scottish university, studying medicine and theology. McHenry's memoir, attached to the 1841 edition of *The Poems of the Pleasures,* states that his mother wished him to become a clergyman, but he wanted to become a doctor. An unpublished poem located in McHenry's manuscript notebook, "A Keepsake: To a Young Lady on Leaving Ireland for the University of Glasgow, Oct. 21, 1810," mentions science, but the university has no records of him as a medical student. He loved a woman named Ellen, but he did not tell her of his love because he was afraid of rejection because of his deformity. She became the subject of at least three works: a short narrative, "Ellen Stanley, or The Victim of Vanity" (1828); "Ellinor's Grave" (1828), a poem written in response to her suicide in 1828, about which she disclosed her plans to McHenry in a letter; and *O'Halloran; or, The Insurgent Chief: An Irish Historical Tale of 1798* (1824), a novel in which the heroine bears her name. McHenry married Jane Robinson in 1812 or 1813, and they moved to Belfast, where he worked for an apothecary before opening his own medical office. On 28 June 1814 McHenry's first son, Alexander Robinson, was born. That same year a literary journal in Belfast made McHenry its editor; while the name of the journal is unknown, it is known that James Sheridan Knowles contributed to it.

In 1816 McHenry set out for America. It seems that the McHenrys moved among various cities for the first few years, arriving in Harmony, Pennsylvania, in 1819. McHenry presented two medical papers in 1821 and 1822, the sum of his contribution to medical literature. He moved to Pittsburgh, where he wrote *Waltham: An American Revolutionary Tale in Three Cantos* (1823), a narrative poem about the American Revolution. He finally settled in Philadelphia in 1823, where he opened a medical office. He also began writing fiction, publishing two novels that year, *The Wilderness; or, Braddock's Times: A Tale of the West* and *The Spectre of the Forest; or, Annals of the Housatonic, a New-England Romance.* In 1824 McHenry and his wife opened a dry-goods store that sold Irish linens and other types of cloth. He also became the editor for *The American Monthly Magazine,* but financial difficulties made this endeavor short-lived.

McHenry's year with *The American Monthly* made him many enemies among the Eastern literati. He held definite opinions about what literature should be and voiced these opinions in the magazine, as well as in the *American Quarterly Review,* for which he served as poetry critic starting in 1828. McHenry scathingly criticized nearly every contemporary author whose novel did not satisfy his own requirements for good fiction. Sketching characters and drawing scenes, he said, is not the same as writing a well-constructed story, and he took to task several popular writers, including Washington Irving, James Fenimore Cooper, and Sir Walter Scott, suggesting that Scott would be better off if he never touched a pen again. In his article "American Lake Poetry" in the March 1832 issue of the *American Quarterly Review,* he also deprecated several poets, notably N. P. Willis and William Cullen Bryant, attacking them for their lack of originality and asserting that most of their works were not worth reading. Needless to say, his opinions were unpopular, and it might be inferred that the harsh critiques of his own writing directly resulted from his blunt censures of so many of his contemporaries.

In 1827 McHenry became the literary editor of *The Philadelphia Album* and also published several of his own poems for the paper. His first daughter, Mary, was born in 1827; Jane was born in 1830; and Ellen was born in 1834. Neither Jane nor Ellen lived past the age of three.

McHenry became a U.S. citizen in October 1828, but he was still active in the Irish community in Pennsylvania. In the summer of 1829 the Association of the Friends of Ireland made McHenry chairman of the arrangements committee for the planned celebration of Ireland's Catholic Emancipation Act, which eliminated restrictions on the political and civil rights of Roman Catholics in Britain and Ireland. Three hundred and fifty people attended the celebration, and both McHenry's poem "An Address," which he read, and a song he composed, "The Champion of Erin Has Broken Her Chains," were later printed in the local papers. McHenry's activities in the Irish community of Philadelphia also led him to work against the reelection bid of President Andrew Jackson in 1832, although from 1819 to 1829 he had been a staunch supporter of Jackson's, contributing biographical sketches of him to *The National Gazette.*

The Pleasures of Friendship: A Poem in Two Parts, to Which Are Added a Few Original Irish Melodies (1822), McHenry's second collection of poems, was probably his most popular. The title poem carries a didactic message about the healing power of friendship over 1,200 lines of heroic couplets. The poem is a sort of pastiche, made up of short narrative passages epitomizing friendship. Most of the other poems in the volume were shorter lyrics. The collection encompassed the idea that friendship is one of man's greatest joys and should be recognized as a healing power. McHenry saw nine American and English editions of this collection published in his lifetime, and it was reviewed extensively and favorably. Each subsequent publication included most of McHenry's minor verse written up to that time.

McHenry's first novel, *The Wilderness,* is an historical romance mainly notable because George Washington is a central character. The story centers around the Fraziers, the first Ulster immigrant family in American fiction, and their trials during the French and Indian War. Gilbert Frazier settles in Pennsylvania with his family in the early 1750s and adopts Maria, the daughter of a Frenchman who has disappeared. Maria falls in love with Charles Adderly, the protagonist of the novel, who was sent by the Ohio Company to build a fort on the Ohio River. Tonnaleuka, an educated Indian, is a close friend of the Fraziers and is considered to be a prophet by his own people. When Adderly is captured by Indians, Tonnaleuka engineers his escape. Young Col. George Washington, commander of an expedition to Ohio, also falls in love with Maria and professes his love to her, but she does not tell him that she has already pledged herself to Adderly. The villain, De Villiers, also loves Maria and will stop at nothing to get her.

McHenry intertwines historical background with his own inventions, making many historical characters such as Washington perform imagined feats. He intimates at the end of the novel that Washington devoted himself to his country because of his unrequited love

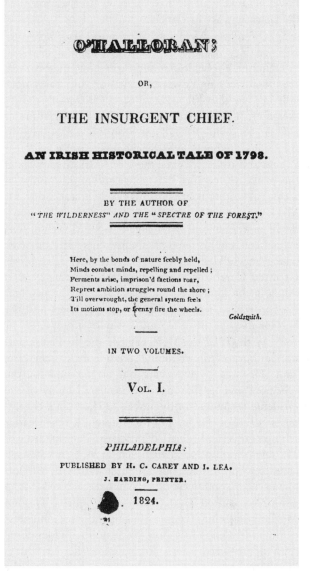

Title page for McHeenry's 1824 novel, the first by an American to dramatize the political conflicts in Northern Ireland

for Maria. *The Wilderness* introduces some of the stock romantic situations that McHenry uses repeatedly in his later novels, for example, the capture of the heroine by the villain.

The Wilderness sold 1,500 copies and was published in England with the subtitle "The Youthful Days of Washington." Of course, McHenry encountered more than his share of detractors who harshly criticized *The Wilderness.* Particularly caustic was the reviewer for the *New England Magazine* (June 1832), who refers to Gilbert Frazier as "an Irish bog-trotter" and condemns McHenry's use of Northern Irish dialect in the novel, arguing that criticism of *The Wilderness* was impossible "seeing that it is not written in English." Other critics noted that it should not be classified as an American novel because while it takes place in America, most of the characters are foreigners.

O'Halloran, McHenry's first novel with a wholly Irish setting, deals with the Irish rebellion of 1798. O'Halloran, a rebel leader and Protestant landlord, rescues the drowning Edward Barrymore, and Barrymore falls in love with Ellen Hamilton, O'Halloran's granddaughter. A recluse named Saunders asks Barrymore to aid him in saving O'Halloran from his affiliation with the United Irishmen, who believe in the union of Great Britain and Ireland. When the United Irishmen hear of this plan, they capture Barrymore and imprison him in a cave. A young poet named McNelvin, a stand-in for McHenry, overhears a plot to have Barrymore murdered in France and helps him escape. McNelvin also loves Ellen, but his timid nature prevents him from ever telling her. O'Halloran, however, promises Ellen to Sir Geoffrey Carebrow in exchange for donating needed funds to the United Irishmen. At the end the penitent Carebrow dies, leaving all his money to Ellen, and the heroine marries the noble and just Barrymore.

With *O'Halloran* McHenry became the first American author to write about the situation in Northern Ireland. He was twelve years old at the time of the rebellion, and he may have remembered many of the incidents recounted in the novel. O'Halloran's character is based on Henry Joy McCracken, a rebel leader who was tried and executed in Belfast. The character of McNelvin was undoubtedly based on McHenry himself character: both share an unrequited love for a girl named Ellen; both were poets; and both suffered from a deformity caused by a childhood injury. Though McHenry falls into the trap of using the stock situations of romantic fiction—the story turns on the hidden identities of key characters, for example—he introduces Northern Irish local color and political themes into the American novel. The novel sold well, and there were four European editions of *O'Halloran,* including a French translation. Again, many of McHenry's enemies found fault with this novel, criticizing the style and language and accusing the author of too closely imitating Scott's *Waverly* (1814).

The Hearts of Steel: An Irish Historical Tale of the Last Century (1825) was published as the second in what McHenry intended to be a series of Irish novels. Set in County Antrim in the middle of the eighteenth century, the novel presents Edmund M'Manus, or Munn, a bulking Catholic who learned eternal animosity for the Rosendale family from his father because the Rosendales captured the M'Manus family castle generations back, during the Protestant invasion of William of Orange. Munn's life goal is to exact revenge on the Rosendale family. Isabella, the Protestant offspring of Bernard, Munn's brother, becomes the love object of

the good and noble Frederick Rosendale, who heads north on duty to subdue the agrarian insurrectionist group the Hearts of Steel. Munn has joined this secret society, whose main intent is to combat the evils of absentee landlordism through terrorist methods. Frederick and Isabella are captured and kept in adjoining cells in a cave by Forsythe, a Hearts of Steel leader who wants Isabella for himself. As in other McHenry novels, the hero and heroine manage a miraculous escape. Finally, the leaders of the Hearts of Steel are captured and brought to trial. Of course, Frederick and Isabella marry, uniting the families of Rosendale and M'Manus forevermore.

Despite its repetition of conventional romantic elements, *Hearts of Steel* is unusual for its historical depiction of the ills of absentee landlordism. While McHenry clearly does not condone the methods of the agrarian insurrectionist groups, he demonstrates his empathy for the plight of those northerners who suffered at the hands of the English. More socially conscious than its predecessors, this novel differs from McHenry's earlier works in that it is not merely historical; it offers social commentary, focusing on the problems caused by England's imposed authority on Ireland rather than the alienation of Catholics and Protestants.

McHenry's first effort as a playwright brought great distress to his life. Although not published until two years after its first production, *The Usurper* was first performed at Philadelphia's Chestnut Street Theatre on 26 December 1827. Maybe more than any other work, this play caused considerable suffering in McHenry's personal life. The play is based on the Irish legend of Cova, son of Ugaena Mor, who kills his brother, Leary Lorc, and all his children except one, Maen. Not unlike *Macbeth, The Usurper* shows how exorbitant ambition causes the deterioration of a character. Important because it is the first tragedy in the United States based on a legendary Irish theme, *The Usurper* still contains several of the romantic elements commonplace in McHenry's work, such as a case of hidden identity and the capture of the heroine by the villain.

McHenry had an agreement with the play's stage manager, Francis C. Wemyss, that *The Usurper* would continue its run only as long as it made money, but the profits from the second performance did not even cover the staging of the play. McHenry asked that the play be allowed to have a third performance, and instead of refusing, Wemyss wrote up a vindictive announcement for the third performance calculated to sully McHenry's name. The third performance did not take place, and this set of circumstances undermined McHenry's literary reputation.

The Usurper also cost McHenry his church. Presbyterianism at the time was quite strict in its opposition to drama, considering the stage to be dangerous to the soul. The Eighth Presbyterian Church of Philadelphia, of which McHenry was a member, offered the dramatist an ultimatum: he must give up the play or the church. He chose the play. In fact, his daughters, Mary and Jane, were not baptized until 5 February 1833, one day before three-year-old Jane died; it can be surmised that McHenry knew the infant was quite ill and begged the church for mercy to have both daughters baptized. McHenry was never pardoned by his church and did not become the member of any church again. Public perception of him was mixed; he was attacked in New York for his unwelcome intrusions into the fields of literature and criticism, but in Philadelphia he was still greatly respected and admired.

The Betrothed of Wyoming: An Historical Tale (1830) and Meredith; or, The Mystery of the Meschianza: A Tale of the American Revolution (1831) were a departure from McHenry's earlier works. In The Betrothed of Wyoming the villain, Butler, tries to incite the Native Americans against the colonists in Pennsylvania and, like several other McHenry villains, endeavors to obtain the virtuous heroine, Agnes, by any means possible. Once he captures Agnes, she is forced to make a choice: submit or watch others die because of her refusal. The characters are static, and although the book went through two editions, it received little critical attention.

Set in Philadelphia in 1778, Meredith depicts the tensions caused by the Revolution in the Meredith family. Elias Meredith is a Quaker, and his nephew is a patriot. Mary Ballantyne, the daughter of Adam Ballantyne, a Scottish immigrant, is corrupted by Meredith's enemy, the Tory villain named Harris, and she feigns her death. When Harris repeatedly sees her apparition, he becomes quite afraid. McHenry employs conventional romantic devices again but also borrows Gothic conventions, such as when he uses the "ghost" of Mary Ballantyne. The novel presents a series of exhilarating incidents and several violent scenes, but it also competently renders the Quaker way of life and their attitudes toward war. It was not heavily reviewed, and Blanc regards it as inferior to The Wilderness.

In 1839 McHenry visited Ireland and then London, where he published his epic poem The Antediluvians; or, The World Destroyed: A Narrative Poem in Ten Books, which he meant to be his masterpiece. The poem consists of ten books of blank verse. Set in the time of Noah, before the flood, Jethuran, a good man in wicked times, is condemned to death for his refusal to worship a false statue, and the diabolical giant Shalmazar places Hadallah, Jethuran's daughter, in his harem. God sends Japhet, Noah's heir, to her rescue. The poem ends with the flood and the destruction of the wicked. The preoccupation of many Americans with the end of the world

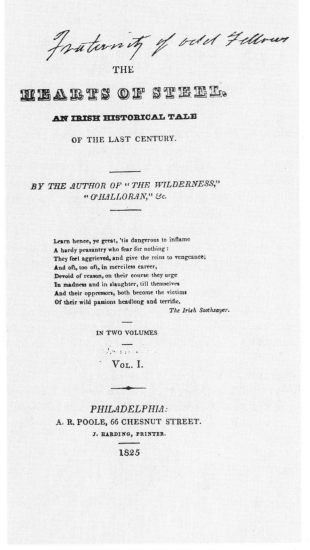

Title page for McHenry's 1825 novel, in which a Northern Irish terrorist group revolts against England oppression

had roots in the Bible, and the apocalyptic theme of McHenry's poem mirrors the mind-set of many nineteenth-century readers.

McHenry intended to show humans in their fallen state, and he wanted a subject that would be universal, one in which he could show his poetic powers to the world. Blanc argues that McHenry fails, succeeding only in diminishing the Scriptures to the level of melodrama. Viciously attacked by Blackwood's Edinburgh Magazine, Graham's Magazine, and The Knickerbocker Magazine, the poem marks end of McHenry's literary career.

Although his writing career came to an end, McHenry remained active in politics. He was involved in several endeavors: he entreated to make Philadelphia the state capitol of Pennsylvania; he attempted to establish a transatlantic steamship line; he lobbied for Philadelphia businessmen who were seeking tax exemptions for soda ash and bleaching; and he served on a committee that organized a public dinner for the friends of President John Tyler. In 1842 he was appointed the U.S. consul at Londonderry, Ireland. Although taking the position also meant that he would be paid less than what he currently made, he accepted it because of his respect for President Tyler. He went to Ireland the following spring, and once in office he attempted to stretch his powers further than was allowed. He issued certificates to linen merchants a few miles outside his district, even though he was forbidden to do so. He wrote to the secretary of state complaining about the restriction, arguing that he relied on the fees collected from the merchants to meet the expenses of his office rent. He also requested transfers to places where he might make more money, but he was denied. He could not afford even to pay for the passage of his wife and children from Philadelphia.

In July of 1845 McHenry became ill while in Larne and died a few days later in a hotel just miles from his birthplace. He died in his homeland serving the country of his adoption.

Biography:
Robert E. Blanc, *James McHenry (1785–1845): Playwright and Novelist* (Philadelphia: University of Pennsylvania Press, 1939).

References:
Charles Fanning, ed., *The Exiles of Erin: Nineteenth-Century Irish-American Fiction* (Notre Dame, Ind.: Notre Dame University Press, 1987), pp. 78–89;

"Memoir of James McHenry, M.D.," in *The Poems of the Pleasures* (Philadelphia: Lippincott, 1841), pp. 273–282;

Fanning, "The Profession of Novelist: James McHenry and Charles Cannon," in his *The Irish Voice in America: Irish-American Fiction from the 1760s to the 1980s* (Lexington: University Press of Kentucky, 1990), pp. 39–71;

Ellis Paxson Oberholtzer, *The Literary History of Philadelphia* (Philadelphia: Jacobs, 1906), pp. 213, 215–219;

Francis Courtney Wemyss, *Twenty-Six Years of the Life of an Actor and Manager* (New York: Burgess, Stringer, 1847), pp. 141–147, 157;

John Wilson, review of *The Antediluvians, Blackwood's Edinburgh Magazine,* 46 (July 1839): 119–144;

Guy R. Woodall, "Robert Walsh's War with the New York Literati: 1827–1836," *Tennessee Studies in Literature,* 15 (1970): 25–47.

S. Weir Mitchell

(15 February 1829 – 4 January 1914)

Laura Dassow Walls
Lafayette College

BOOKS: *Researches upon the Venom of the Rattlesnake; with an Investigation of the Anatomy and Physiology of the Organs Concerned* (Washington, D.C.: Smithsonian Institution, 1860);

Researches upon the Anatomy and Physiology of Respiration in the Chelonia, by Mitchell and George R. Morehouse (Washington, D.C.: Smithsonian Institution, 1863);

The Children's Hour, by Mitchell and Elizabeth W. Sherman (Philadelphia: Published for the Benefit of the Sanitary Commission, 1864);

Gunshot Wounds, and Other Injuries of Nerves, by Mitchell, Morehouse, and William W. Keen (Philadelphia: Lippincott, 1864); revised and enlarged as *Injuries of Nerves and Their Consequences* (Philadelphia: Lippincott, 1872);

The Wonderful Stories of Fuz-Buz the Fly and Mother Grabem the Spider, anonyomous (Philadelphia: Lippincott, 1867);

Wear and Tear, or Hints for the Overworked (Philadelphia: Lippincott, 1871; revised, 1887);

Fat and Blood: And How to Make Them (Philadelphia: Lippincott, 1877); revised as *Fat and Blood: An Essay on the Treatment of Certain Forms of Neurasthenia and Hysteria* (Philadelphia & London: Lippincott, 1884);

Nurse and Patient, and Camp Cure (Philadelphia: Lippincott, 1877);

Hephzibah Guinness; Thee and You; and A Draft on the Bank of Spain (Philadelphia: Lippincott, 1880);

Lectures on Diseases of the Nervous System, especially in Women (Philadelphia: H. C. Lea's Son, 1881; enlarged edition, Lea Brothers, 1885; London: Churchill, 1885);

The Hill of Stones and Other Poems (Boston & New York: Houghton, Mifflin, 1883);

In War Time (London: Macmillan, 1884; Boston & New York: Houghton, Mifflin, 1885);

Researches Upon the Venoms of Poisonous Serpents, by Mitchell and Edward T. Reichert (Washington, D.C.: Smithsonian Institution, 1885);

S. Weir Mitchell

Roland Blake (Boston & New York: Houghton, Mifflin, 1886);

A Masque and Other Poems (Boston & New York: Houghton, Mifflin, 1887);

Doctor and Patient (Philadelphia & London: Lippincott, 1888);

Prince Little Boy and Other Tales Out of Fairy-Land (Philadelphia: Lippincott, 1888);

Far in the Forest: A Story (Philadelphia: Lippincott, 1889; London: Macmillan, 1901);

The Cup of Youth and Other Poems (Boston & New York: Houghton, Mifflin, 1889);

A Psalm of Deaths and Other Poems (Boston & New York: Houghton, Mifflin, 1890);

Address Before the Congress of American Physicians and Surgeons September 23d, 1891. The History of Instrumental Precision in Medicine (Philadelphia: University of Pennsylvania Press, 1891); enlarged as *The Early History of Instrumental Precision in Medicine. An Address Before the Second Congress of American Physicians and Surgeons, September 23rd, 1891* (New Haven: Tuttle Morehouse & Taylor, 1892);

Characteristics (New York: Century, 1892; London: Macmillan, 1901);

The Mother and Other Poems (Boston & New York: Houghton, Mifflin, 1893);

Francis Drake: A Tragedy of the Sea (Boston & New York: Houghton, Mifflin, 1893);

Mr. Kris Kringle: A Christmas Tale (Philadelphia: Jacobs, 1893);

Two Lectures on the Conduct of the Medical Life. Addressed to the Students of the University of Pennsylvania and the Jefferson Medical College (Philadelphia: University of Pennsylvania Press, 1893);

When All the Woods Are Green: A Novel (New York: Century, 1894; London: Macmillan, 1901);

Philip Vernon: A Tale in Prose and Verse (New York: Century, 1895);

A Madeira Party (New York: Century, 1895);

Clinical Lessons on Nervous Diseases (Philadelphia & New York: Lea Brothers, 1897);

Hugh Wynne: Free Quaker, Sometime Brevet Lieutenant-Colonel on the Staff of His Excellency General Washington, 2 volumes (New York: Century, 1897; revised, 1897; London: Unwin, 1897; revised, New York: Century, 1908);

The Adventures of François: Foundling, Thief, Juggler, and Fencing-Master During the French Revolution (New York: Century, 1898; London: Macmillan, 1898);

Ode on a Lycian Tomb (New York: Privately printed, 1899);

The Wager and Other Poems (New York: Century, 1900);

The Autobiography of a Quack and the Case of George Dedlow (New York: Century, 1900; London: Unwin, 1900); republished in *The Autobiography of a Quack and Other Stories* (New York: Century, 1901; London: Macmillan, 1901);

Dr. North and His Friends (New York: Century, 1900; London: Macmillan, 1900);

Circumstance (New York: Century, 1901);

A Comedy of Conscience (New York: Century, 1903; Edinburgh: Douglas, 1904);

Little Stories (New York: Century, 1903; London: Warne, 1919);

New Samaria and The Summer of St. Martin (Philadelphia & London: Lippincott, 1904);

The Youth of Washington, Told in the Form of an Autobiography (New York: Century, 1904; London: Unwin, 1904; revised, New York: Century, 1910);

Constance Trescot: A Novel (New York: Century, 1905);

A Diplomatic Adventure (New York: Century, 1906);

Pearl Rendered into Modern English Verse (New York: Century, 1906; enlarged, Portland, Me.: Mosher, 1908);

A Venture in 1777 (Philadelphia: Jacobs, 1908);

The Red City: A Novel of the Second Administration of President Washington (New York: Century, 1908; London: Macmillan, 1908);

The Comfort of the Hills and Other Poems (New York: Century, 1910);

The Guillotine Club and Other Stories (New York: Century, 1910);

John Sherwood, Ironmaster (New York: Century, 1911);

A Brief History of Two Families: The Mitchells of Ayrshire and the Symons of Cornwall (Philadelphia: Privately printed, 1912);

Westways, A Village Chronicle (New York: Century, 1913; London: Unwin, 1914).

Collections: *The Collected Poems of S. Weir Mitchell* (New York: Century, 1896);

The Works of S. Weir Mitchell, Author's definitive edition, 16 volumes (New York: Century, 1905–1910);

The Complete Poems of S. Weir Mitchell (New York: Century, 1914).

Although now largely forgotten, S. Weir Mitchell was once a celebrity: a prominent Philadelphia physician, America's foremost neurologist, and a best-selling author. Mitchell's controversial "rest cure" for neurasthenia was administered to such literary figures as Edith Wharton, Charlotte Perkins Gilman, and Virginia Woolf, and he is remembered for his pioneering work on the biochemistry of snake toxins, the phenomenon of "phantom limbs" in amputees, and the causes and treatment of neuralgia and neurasthenia. Mitchell published several medical textbooks and hundreds of scientific papers and also pursued a successful literary career.

Mitchell's most famous novel was *Hugh Wynne: Free Quaker, Sometime Brevet Lieutenant-Colonel on the Staff of His Excellency General Washington* (1897), an historical romance of the American Revolution that sold more than half a million copies. His literary production was prodigious as he wrote twelve more novels, eight volumes of poetry, and dozens of short stories and novellas. His best novels, though not of the first rank, are readable and entertaining, offering serious and wide-ranging commentary on social issues and presenting some memorable characters animated by his clinical understanding of mental illness. Indeed, Mitchell was the first novelist in America to fully use the insights of psychiatry.

Silas Weir Mitchell was born and lived out his life in Philadelphia, a city with which he strongly identified and in which he set much of his fiction. He was the son and grandson of doctors: his father, John Kearsley Mitchell of Virginia, was famous as both physician and poet, reviewed kindly by none other than Edgar Allan Poe. His mother, Sarah Matilda Henry, raised her nine children in a strict Presbyterian household. Young Weir (he disliked his rustic first name) grew up frail and bookish, but when he began spitting up blood (a symptom of tuberculosis) at age sixteen, he cured himself by taking up a vigorous outdoor life and thus building up his resistance to the disease.

Mitchell attended the University of Pennsylvania, but when his father's health failed he felt compelled to withdraw and choose a career so he could support the family. He selected medicine over the objections of his father, who predicted failure, and grew into his studies, completing the standard two-year curriculum at Jefferson Medical College in 1850. After a further year of medical study in Paris and travel in Europe with his sister Elizabeth (with whom he was close until her death in 1874), he returned in 1851 to join his father's practice, which he took over in 1855. His marriage to Mary Middleton Elwyn in September of 1858 was followed by the birth in 1859 of their son John, who became a doctor, and the birth in 1862 of a second son, Langdon, who became a writer.

The smooth progression of Mitchell's life was interrupted by the Civil War, which devastated him personally but propelled him to international fame and provided some of his best writing material. Despite his expertise, Mitchell could not prevent his wife's death from diphtheria in 1862. During the war, while his sister Elizabeth cared for his sons, he worked as a contract surgeon at a Philadelphia army hospital. Weir became interested in the most difficult cases of nerve damage, especially in the mental causes of physical paralysis. He went to work as a scientist, applying research methods learned in Paris and eventually writing up his voluminous notes as *Gunshot Wounds, and Other Injuries of Nerves* (1864). He later expanded his work as *Injuries of Nerves and Their Consequences* (1872), a classic medical text still in use during World War I. Mitchell gave early recognition to the condition that in the early twentieth century came to be known as "shell shock" (later called "post-traumatic stress syndrome"), arguing that its sufferers were medically ill rather than malingering.

Frontispiece for Mitchell's Hugh Wynne *(1897), in which a Quaker participates in the Revolutionary War as a spy*

Although a nervous breakdown in 1864 forced him to scale back his work, Mitchell continued both to see patients and to pursue research into neurological disorders. He rose to popular and professional fame in the 1870s through his writings and the establishment of his famous teaching clinic at the Orthopedic Hospital and Infirmary for Nervous Diseases. In 1874 his marriage to Mary Cadwalader secured his place as a "Philadelphia Brahmin." He was deeply fond of their only child together, Maria, and when diphtheria took her suddenly in 1898 at the age of twenty-two, his grief resulted in his best poem, *Ode on a Lycian Tomb* (1899). Literature began to be his dominant interest in the 1880s, but he continued to be showered with honorary degrees and accolades from the medical profession and to publish on paralysis, hysteria, and epilepsy until his death in 1914.

Mitchell's career presents an unusual blend of literature and science, habits of mind that he believed were complementary and mutually enhancing. He used his fiction to dramatize the characters, psychoses, and moral dilemmas he encountered as a doctor while his poetic imagination generated his most creative scientific insights. Mitchell felt that the enlargement of his pursuits beyond science made him a better doctor. The two halves of his achievement may be seen to good advantage in his first published fiction, "The Case of George Dedlow," which appeared in *The Atlantic Monthly* in July 1866. The story is a Poe-like tale narrated with clinical detachment by a doctor whose Civil War wounds necessitate the amputation of both his arms and his legs. The anonymous story (submitted by Dr. William Henry Furness, to whose daughter, Mrs. Caspar Wister, Mitchell had shown it, and published without Mitchell's knowledge) was taken as fact by so many readers that the publisher received letters of condolence and contributions of money.

Fictionalizing his scientific observations allowed Mitchell to go beyond the standard clinical case study and explore in imagination the "metaphysics" of a man without limbs. The story allowed him to discuss the phenomenon of the "phantom limb," the strong sense reported by nearly all of his amputee patients that their missing limb was still present. Unlike other doctors, Mitchell believed that these reports offered an insight into the workings of the nervous system. Moreover, he inferred that a person's sense of identity or "selfhood" was inextricably bound up with bodily existence. Thus Dedlow's loss of body results in his being "less conscious of myself, of my own existence," uncertain "if I were really George Dedlow or not." Dedlow concludes that "a man is not his brain, or any one part of it, but all of his economy, and that to lose any part must lessen this sense of his own existence." To dramatize this insight Mitchell rather whimsically ends the story with a seance at which Dedlow summons up his lost legs. Momentarily he restores his "self-consciousness. I was reindividualized, so to speak." To everyone's wonder Dedlow then strides across the room on invisible legs before collapsing again helplessly on his two stumps.

The notion that body and mind are an integrated whole informs all of Mitchell's writing. His friend and fellow novelist Oliver Wendell Holmes advised him to secure his medical career before venturing further into fiction, and it was nearly twenty years before Mitchell went beyond writing the occasional poem or short story. In the 1870s he published two best-selling books of medical advice that expanded his view of the indivisibility of bodily and mental health. In his "little sermon" *Wear and Tear, or Hints for the Overworked* (1871)–a book so popular the first edition sold out in ten days–he warned the rising American middle class against its bad habits of overwork, poor diet, and lack of exercise, all of which he argued would lead to nervous collapse. Doubtless drawing on his own boyhood experience, Mitchell advocated rest, good food, and vigorous outdoor exercise as both prevention and cure. He detailed

his advice in his later writings as the "camp cure," whereby ailing ladies and gentlemen, even whole families, were to spend a summer living in tents, hiking, swimming, and boating. The argument, which was developed in *Doctor and Patient* (1888), formed the basis for his novel *John Sherwood, Ironmaster* (1911).

Mitchell believed that the dangers of stress for women were particularly acute. Both climate and custom threatened the health of American womanhood, and overwork of the brain before the age of seventeen put at serious risk the health and "womanly usefulness" of American girls. Mitchell, however, was deeply ambivalent about a woman's proper destiny. On the one hand he asserted that girls should be raised exactly like boys, in an outdoor life with plenty of sports and exercise, and that no woman should be prevented from following a "male" career in science and medicine. Yet, on the other hand, he cautioned that women were unsuited to "brainwork" until after adolescence and warned that it was socially undesirable for women to follow careers more appropriate for men. As he put it in *Doctor and Patient,* "For most men, when she seizes the apple, she drops the rose."

Mitchell's ambivalence toward women is fully seen in his notorious "rest cure," which he advanced in the medical literature in the early 1870s and then later in the best-selling *Fat and Blood: And How to Make Them* (1877). Mitchell's cure found international acceptance: by 1892 *Fat and Blood* had been translated into German, Russian, French, and Italian, and elements of the rest cure were praised and adopted by Sigmund Freud. In the introduction to his book Mitchell specified the treatment's target: "chiefly women of a class well known to every physician,–nervous women, who, as a rule, are thin and lack blood." Believing that the best therapy for their nervous condition lay in restoring their bodily health, Mitchell prescribed prolonged seclusion, which meant removal of the patient from her codependent caregivers; bed rest, from a few hours a day to as much as eight solid weeks; massage and electrical treatment to exercise the muscles; and a rich diet based on large quantities of milk. Evidence suggests that many women responded gratefully and positively to the treatment and that Mitchell, rather than dismissing their complaints, took them seriously. Written testimony, however, also documents the destructive potential of his cure.

For all his talents and accomplishments, Mitchell is perhaps best known as the doctor who nearly drove Charlotte Perkins Gilman to insanity. In her autobiography *The Living of Charlotte Perkins Gilman* (1935), she writes that after a month of being "fed, bathed, rubbed" she was sent home with instructions to "'Live as domestic a life as possible. . . . Have but two hours' intellectual

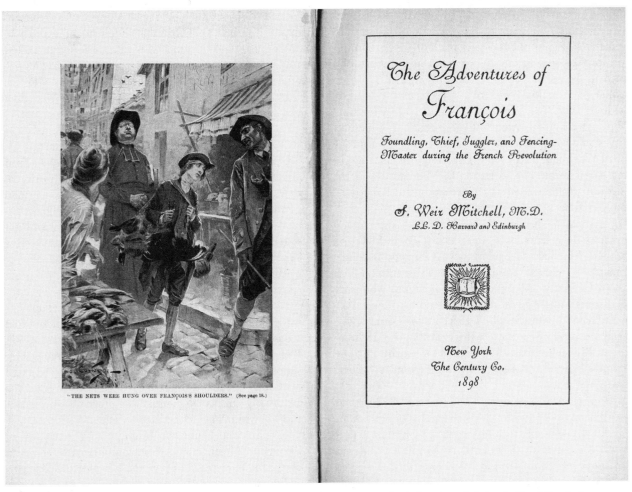

"THE NETS WERE HUNG OVER FRANÇOIS'S SHOULDERS." (See page 18.)

The Adventures of
François
Foundling, Thief, Juggler, and Fencing-
Master during the French Revolution

By
S. Weir Mitchell, M.D.
LL. D. Harvard and Edinburgh

New York
The Century Co.
1898

Frontispiece and title page for Mitchell's 1898 book, in which a thief saves a noble family from the mob during the French Revolution

life a day. And never touch pen, brush or pencil as long as you live.'" Gilman obeyed "and came perilously near to losing my mind." She fictionalized her experience in "The Yellow Wallpaper" (1891), written to reach Mitchell "and convince him of the error of his ways." In the story Gilman's unnamed narrator is isolated in the manner of the rest cure by her husband-doctor, John, until she goes quite mad. Implicit in the story is Gilman's rebuttal to Mitchell, that "pen, brush, or pencil" are not the disease but the cure–a cure overlooked by Mitchell in his certainty that a woman's intellectual life posed a danger to her reproductive health. Gilman sent Mitchell a copy of her story and claimed that he got her message, a claim for which no corroboration has been found in Mitchell's papers.

Mitchell began to turn seriously to literature when he was at the apex of his medical career and certain that literary success would not jeopardize his professional reputation. He wrote his novels during the long summer vacations his family spent at Newport, Rhode Island, from 1877 to 1890, and, from 1891 until

his death, at Bar Harbor, Maine. For his first novel, *In War Time* (1884), which was first serialized in *The Atlantic Monthly,* Mitchell drew on his years as a surgeon in the Civil War. The novel's protagonist, Dr. Ezra Wendell, is a contract surgeon stationed at a Philadelphia army hospital patterned after the Filbert Street Hospital where Mitchell began his studies of war wounds, and the action begins with the traumatic moment in summer 1863 when the Gettysburg casualties are pouring in. Ezra's successful treatment of one of them, Major John Morton, sweeps him into the Philadelphia aristocracy.

Ezra's merits, however, do not match his aspirations: he is a flawed man, lacking both professional and personal courage. His weakness sets in motion the two major themes of the novel, character and class. Through Ezra, Mitchell traces the decline of a decent but morally weak man who lacks drive and develops the shameful capacity to take advantage of others. His decline is motivated by his deep desire to climb socially, for in living beyond his means Ezra must break into money given him in trust for an orphan girl, Hester Gray, whom he is raising with the help of his staunch spinster sister, Ann. Eventually his moral compromises and professional incompetence result in the death of a patient, the major's elder son, destroying Ezra's professional life and his hopes of marriage to the wealthy widow Alice Westerley, who loses all respect for him. Through his story Mitchell suggests that Ezra's mediocrity would have been adequate in an earlier day, but the Civil War changed the temper of American life, energizing social ambition and raising the "standards" of the medical profession, creating demands ruinous to the morally weak.

Mitchell's first novel won praise from his contemporaries. In a letter of 2 April 1885 George Meredith praised Mitchell's elevation of psychology into art: "You have evolved the story from the characters. I look about me in my country vainly for an author who is up to that high-water mark of fiction." Another friend, William Dean Howells, used his first "Editor's Study" column in *Harper's New Monthly Magazine* (January 1886) to praise Mitchell's characterizations of decaying Puritanism, his handling of local color, and the book's "artistic quiet."

Mitchell's next novel, *Roland Blake* (1886), was published two years after his first, and for the rest of his life he would keep to the pace of bringing out a new novel every two or three years. His subject in his second novel was again the Civil War, but Mitchell shifted from social realism to genteel romance. Named for the legendary Roland and the mystical poet William Blake, Mitchell's hero combines the virtues of both. As Mitchell comments, "Men of practical capacity who are also imaginative are advantaged thereby: large ranges of the possible lie open to their reason, and the improbable is not set aside as foolish." Roland faces the dilemma of whether or not to expose the double-dealing of the Confederate spy Richard Darnell to the grandmother of the lovely Olivia Wynne, who is caring for Darnell's invalid sister Octopia. Roland, a gentleman, does not want to reveal to Octopia that her brother Richard, a Northerner, has sold out to the South, unless he has no other choice.

The real interest of the novel, which ends predictably with the self-destruction of the villainous Darnell and the union of hero and heroine, lies in the character of Octopia, a fictional version of the kind of grasping, neurotic hypochondriac Mitchell was famous for treating in real life. Octopia's knowledge of a dark family secret—the suicide of Olivia's father—enables her to manipulate the Wynnes into catering to her demands. The burden falls unfairly on bright young Olivia, who rebels and flees with her grandmother into hiding on Cape May. By the time Octopia and her scheming

brother discover their refuge, Blake is at last ready to expose Darnell and Olivia is independent enough to enter into a relationship with him. The break in her routine of dependence helps even Octopia to reform, and she marries the fussy Addenda Pennell, who will care for her whims as before he cared for his ailing clocks.

Mitchell's third novel, *Far in the Forest: A Story* (1889), set in the physical and moral wilderness of northern Pennsylvania, is a quick-paced and even lurid adventure tale that portrays the innate superiority of inherited nobility. Baron John Riverius, a German immigrant, overcomes the suspicions and violent resistance of the superstitious, poverty-ridden, and whisky-soaked frontier folk to organize them into a productive local timber economy. At the same time he manages to rescue a well-bred widow, Elizabeth Preston, from the American woods.

Showing Mitchell's interest in technical experimentation, *Characteristics* (1892) is the first of his two "conversation novels" (the second is *Dr. North and His Friends,* 1900). In these novels Mitchell forgoes plot almost entirely to follow the wide-ranging intellectual discourse of his alter ego, Dr. Owen North, and his exquisitely cultivated friends: the lawyer Fred Vincent and his wife, Anne, the historian Clayborne, the artist Victor St. Clair, and the bright young Alice Leigh, whom Dr. North cures of her ambition to become a doctor by marrying. In *Dr. North,* Mitchell develops two additional characters: Xerxes Crofter, a cagey railroad magnate, and Sibyl Maywood, a young woman who is beautiful but considered "deformed" because one shoulder is slightly higher than the other. Sibyl's love for and rejection by St. Clair leads to her psychological imbalance, allowing Mitchell to delineate a case of split self or "double consciousness"—one side of her personality writes love letters to St. Clair, of which the other side lacks all knowledge. Both conversation novels—but particularly the second—earned respect and praise. They are a valuable index to the mind and culture of genteel America.

Mitchell took his reader back to the forest in the novel *When All the Woods Are Green: A Novel* (1894). Basing this minor work on his love of outdoor vacations and summer fishing trips, he portrays the woods not as a wilderness but as a nostalgic playground. It was his first book published by the Century company and initiated an important financial relationship. After 1894 sales of Mitchell's fiction remained high enough to bring him an average annual royalty of $10,000 from that publisher alone.

Mitchell achieved his greatest success in 1897 with *Hugh Wynne,* the historical romance set in Philadelphia during the American Revolution that established

Mitchell examining a patient at the Clinic of the Orthopædic Hospital in Philadelphia

his name and literary reputation. Mitchell's mild technical experimentation continued: to broaden the point of view beyond the first-person narration of the aged Hugh Wynne, Mitchell has him incorporate the diary of his close friend Jack Warder, whose voice both supplements and contests the old man's memories. Though he wrote it in only six weeks, Mitchell spent seven years researching the novel, which is steeped in historical detail that further slows the action already prolonged by the reticence of the aging narrator.

As a youth Hugh Wynne faced the moral quandary posed by his Quaker identity. Although unwilling to take up arms, he participates in the revolutionary cause as a spy and a courier even though it costs him his Quaker faith, the love and trust of his cold and imperious father, and nearly his family fortune. The plot centers on the machinations of Hugh's cowardly and scheming cousin, Arthur Wynne, a British officer who insinuates himself into the affections of Hugh's loyalist father in an attempt to secure title to the ancient family estate in Wales and the love of the beautiful Tory loyalist Darthea Peniston. Despite her politics, Darthea is loved as well by both Hugh and his best friend Jack, ambiguously described as both sturdy and a "sweet girl-boy." In the end she gives her heart to Hugh, "a great, strong, masculine fellow."

The appeal of the book lay in its affirmation of the moral values modeled by the honorable and courageous Hugh and the tender-hearted, jovial, and equally courageous Jack. Many of the subsidiary characters are well-drawn, particularly the somber general George Washington and Hugh's aunt, Gainor Wynne, a tough-minded, independent spinster who wields her considerable wealth and social power in a spirited defense of the revolutionary cause and her beloved Hugh.

Mitchell seems particularly concerned with presenting the proper ideals of manhood. Hugh Wynne has strength, integrity, vitality, physical prowess, Emersonian self-reliance, and a love for nature. He is slow to anger but will not be whipped, whether by schoolyard bullies, the adolescent vices of drinking and gambling, an authoritarian church, or the British Empire. Wynne's struggle for independence from the Quaker law of his father is directly paralleled with America's struggle for independence from Britain: the final letter disowning Hugh from the Quaker church is dated 4 July 1776. Aunt Gainor, who brings him the letter, declares triumphantly, "You are free at last"—and in the next breath adds the news of Congress's vote for the Declaration of Independence.

Although the Pennsylvania Quakers objected to Mitchell's portrait of them and published a pamphlet offering corrections of his treatment of their customs and manners during the Revolution, praise was generally widespread. "It has rained congratulations," exulted Mitchell in his correspondence. He was particularly pleased by Thomas Bailey Aldrich's remark to him that "there are two great American novels 'The Scarlet Letter' and 'H. W.'" One reviewer for the November 1898 issue of *The Century Illustrated Monthly Magazine* noted that Mitchell had in his historical novel caught the temper of the contemporary moment–the advent of the Spanish-American War–when America had resolved, Hugh Wynne-like, "to take its place on the world's stage and play its fit part in the responsibilities, the rewards, and the sacrifice of empire." Buoyed by such praise, Mitchell's life from then on was governed more by his literary success than by his fame as a doctor.

Mitchell turned next from the American to the French Revolution, and just a year later he produced the fast-moving, picaresque romance *The Adventures of François: Foundling, Thief, Juggler, and Fencing-Master During the French Revolution* (1898). Mitchell drew on his student days in Paris to create the atmosphere for the book, which he called the true narrative of a family servant. The novel follows the descent of France into the insanity of the revolution through the eyes of its curiously amoral hero, François. An orphan with a beautiful voice and an ever-laughing disposition, François is raised as a choirboy, but when his adolescent voice breaks, he escapes from the organized brutality of Notre Dame cathedral to the chaotic savagery of the streets. François rises in "that pit of crime and bestiality" by learning to juggle and read palms; then he and his little dog Toto fall in with a fencing master to whom François becomes an assistant.

As the revolution gathers and breaks, François and Toto bob atop the stream of events, bits of flotsam with many casual friends, a few mortal enemies, and no loves. François, who is willing to steal anything but refuses to do anyone harm, eventually becomes involved with a noble family whom he saves from the Terror by leading them through the catacombs of Paris. In gratitude they give him a home for life, a gift that reforms the thief as no moral teaching ever could. Yet environment is not all: in Mitchell's words, "character was the more despotic parent in this resolute man, who could wrestle strenuously with circumstance." Or as the noblewoman he saves concludes: "He had many delicacies of character, but that of which nature meant to make a gentleman and a man of refinement, desertion and evil fortune made a thief and a reprobate." That François "naturally" gravitates to nobility reinforces Mitchell's frequent theme that a natural aristocracy should be allowed to rise and govern. (He delicately reminds readers that it was the French nobility, not the

commoners, who fought for America's freedom.) Mitchell called it "the book of my affections," and reviewers were generally enthusiastic.

Dr. North and His Friends was followed by *Circumstance* (1901), a sharply observed Jamesian social satire with a crowded cast of characters in which Mitchell again explores how various characters bear up or fail under the test of life's "circumstances." He treated the same theme more successfully four years later when after several revisions he published *Constance Trescot* (1905), a fast-paced, intense, and tightly focused study of monomania, "the devil of one idea." Mitchell thought his book "the best American tragic novel" and believed it was "the best of my own novels"–the latter remark, at least, confirmed by modern critics. Contemporary reviewers, though, focused on Mitchell's insistence that his book was based on a true story and doubted the veracity of his claim.

The heroine of the novel, Constance, is a Boston blue blood raised by her wealthy atheist uncle, Rufus Hood, to lack all religious and spiritual beliefs. Brought up to be "natural," she is beautiful, vital, and exudes a sexual power that charms everyone she meets. "This girl, this woman, is a creature of instincts," says her uncle Rufus. "She loves and hates with animal fidelity; and once she is set on doing anything, neither saint nor devil can change her." Her tender instincts and passion are aroused by the frail, intellectual lawyer George Trescot, crippled in the shoulder while fighting for the Union. "He is my religion," she declares. In 1870 Uncle Rufus agrees to their marriage on the condition that the impecunious George become Rufus's agent in St. Ann, Missouri, where George is to defend Rufus's property claims and settle some festering land disputes. The Boston newlyweds must tread carefully in the explosive landscape of the Reconstruction South. Although the Trescots prove skillful peacemakers, they cannot conquer the Southerners' champion, the moody, distrustful, and passionate lawyer John Greyhurst. Moments after winning his case in court, George approaches the defeated Greyhurst to hand him a generous offer of settlement. Mistaking George's gesture of reaching into his coat pocket, Greyhurst whips out a pistol and shoots him dead on the spot.

This shocking turn comes halfway through the novel, which then shifts from social to psychological concerns: What will Contance do? Mitchell tracks the steady decay of Constance's personality as she becomes consumed by a monomaniacal desire for revenge. To a protesting friend, she replies that "nothing on earth will move me." The town acquits Greyhurst of murder, but Constance has pronounced her own verdict. True to her name, she returns to St. Ann to stalk Greyhurst, thwart his every wish, and deny him "a life that would

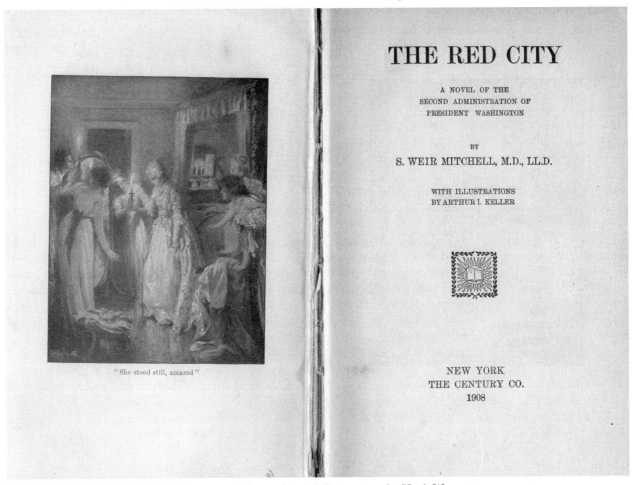

THE RED CITY

A NOVEL OF THE
SECOND ADMINISTRATION OF
PRESIDENT WASHINGTON

BY

S. WEIR MITCHELL, M.D., LL.D.

WITH ILLUSTRATIONS
BY ARTHUR I. KELLER

NEW YORK
THE CENTURY CO.
1908

"She stood still, amazed"

Frontispiece and title page for Mitchell's 1908 sequel to Hugh Wynne

atone for the past," ultimately driving him to put a bullet through his temple and fall "at her feet—dead." Her purpose completed, Constance drifts into listless neurosis, driving away her friends and family, even her loyal sister Susan. At the end she is morbid, selfish, and chillingly alone. Without Christian principles, Constance lacks the moral basis to transcend either "the deadly instinct" of an animal or "the conventional morals and opinions" of her "social world." As a woman, she lacks the basic resource of open violence, a man's power to "call him out and kill him." She is left with nothing but the insidious power to destroy from within. Mitchell's moral drama also has political overtones, as the reader is led to consider whether the North and the South have the ethical principles needed for peace and reconciliation.

The weight of political schism on the fortunes of self and family again dominates Mitchell's *The Red City: A Novel of the Second Administration of President Washington* (1908), which he dedicated to Howells, "a friend of many years." In this sequel to *Hugh Wynne,* Mitchell returns to the French Revolution, this time from the perspective of a fledgling America during President Washington's second term. Expectations must have been high for the book, which was serialized for $12,000, Mitchell's highest price yet; it and *Constance Trescot* each sold approximately fifty thousand copies.

Philadelphia, the "Red City" of the title, is the refuge to which the hero of the novel, the Vicomte René De Courval, flees with his ailing mother after the brutal murder of his father by a Jacobin mob upon his exposure as an aristocrat by the villain Carteaux. But Philadelphia in 1792 is hardly a placid retreat for the French émigrés, for here too they find a country tearing itself in two. On one side are the Federalists, led by Alexander Hamilton, the party of balance and reason and "strong central rule"; on the other, Thomas Jefferson's Republicans, "gone mad in their Jacobin clubs," certain that "we were in danger of a monarchy" and gone "all for France and for Citizen Equality, who, as Hamilton foresaw, might come to be the most cruel of tyrants." Looming above all is the grave, noble, and exhausted

President Washington, holding the young country together against the twin tyrannies of English monarchy and French anarchy.

The aristocratic young René receives in the New World "nature's baptismal regeneration of mind and body," plus the assistance of both Hugh Wynne and Aunt Gainor and the guidance of the incognito German nobleman "Johann Schmidt." In the Quaker home of Mary Swanwick, he grows to manhood through meeting the challenges variously posed by hard work, the slave revolt in Haiti, Philadelphia's yellow-fever epidemic, American politics, and the manipulations of the treacherous Carteaux, whom René finally defeats. Like Mitchell's other high-born émigrés, however, at the end of the novel René turns his back on the New World to assume his proper place in the Old, though he takes as his wife the lovely Quaker commoner Margaret Swanwick. The European's Ben Franklinesque rise from poverty and exile to wealth and power assume a distinctive character in its American setting, for in honorably meeting each test, René proves himself to be one of nature's true aristocrats, a one-man argument for American federalism. At the last the reader learns that he becomes a general in Napoleon's army.

In his 1911 "camp cure" novel *John Sherwood, Ironmaster* Mitchell further explores the regenerative power of New World nature. John Sherwood, a bookish, shy young orphan, grows up alienated from people but enamored of machines and "the poetry of invention" until on the verge of his career as an industrial magnate he is cut down by tuberculosis. Leaving his old life and "ruined hopes" behind, John moves to inherited property on the north coast of Maine with his loyal and "doglike" black servant Dodo. The forced idleness in the Maine woods not only restores his health but also teaches him the spiritual value of nature and "the pleasure of simple observation unaided by science or explanatory wisdom." Moreover, recovered health and contact with nature renew his relation to humanity: John is drawn into the sparse society of the woods. In his wise resolution of a lurid and complicated plot twist involving paranoia and murder, he shows himself fully redeemed, worthy of the love of the newly widowed Helen Norman. The novel ends with the promise of their marriage within the warmth of a new circle of friends.

In 1909 Mitchell's colleagues honored his achievements by electing him president of the American Neurological Society, the culminating tribute to his long career in medicine; his literary career concluded four years later with the publication of *Westways: A Village Chronicle* (1913). He had begun and abandoned the book around 1866, but at age eighty-two Mitchell returned to his early effort, reworking it into one of his strongest novels. It is his final examination of the trauma of the Civil War, showing its effects on the people of Westways, an ironmill town in the Pennsylvania Alleghenies, and particularly on the Penhallows, owners of the mill and the town's first family.

With a regional realism reminiscent of Harriet Beecher Stowe's *Oldtown Folks* (1869), Mitchell follows the overprotected John Penhallow and the energetic tomboy Leila Gray as they grow up together into adulthood and face division and loss as a result of the war, experiences that leave them older, wiser, and free at last to marry each other. The canvas is broad and full of incident as Mitchell again treats many of his favorite themes: the poignant contrast in the destinies of boy and girl, so alike as children and yet so differently fated; the dull, grim horrors of war and the pain of the war-torn family, in which Ann Grey Penhallow, from Maryland, and her husband, James, must somehow compromise their opposed beliefs about slavery if they are to survive the war without hurting each other; the benevolent leadership of America's natural nobility, as the Penhallows guide the town morally and nourish it economically; the honest, constant loyalty of the escaped slave, Josiah, to his saviors, the Penhallows; and the clinical sickness of Peter Lamb, the drunken parasite whose hereditary weakness was exacerbated by the indulgences of others, who sells out Josiah, commits arson, theft, and rape, attempts to murder James, and is finally shot as an army deserter. Critics have praised *Westways* as a more mature and finer work than the better-known *Roland Blake,* with well-drawn characters and a sense of reality.

S. Weir Mitchell died abruptly after a week's illness at the age of eighty-four on 4 January 1914. He was thus spared knowledge of World War I, which would show many of his contemporaries the hollowness of the genteel values he treasured and promoted in his life, writing, and medical practice. Yet, for all their gentility, Mitchell's novels are inhabited by a surprising array of failures and criminals; paranoids, schizophrenics, and neurotics; suicides and even murderers—all of them based on his clinical experience and original research. His clinical detachment enabled him to deal with external symptoms more readily than the internal workings of the mind and heart, generally preventing his characters from taking on a life of their own. Nevertheless, his unflinching scientific realism allowed him to portray such characters sympathetically, not as villains but as human beings caught in the grip of forces beyond their control. He proved himself a skillful storyteller.

Although he was a progressive in science, Mitchell in his social and literary views was almost reactionary. Though called a literary realist, Mitchell despised "the recent realistic atrocities of Zola." Though he influenced Sigmund Freud, he once threw a library book on

Freud into the fire in disgust. Though honored by Walt Whitman for his generous financial assistance and free medical advice, Mitchell renounced their friendship after discovering that Whitman had deprecated his poetry. In a memorial address his friend Owen Wister noted that it was "preposterous to suppose" that Balzac or Flaubert knew more of evil, sorrow, or pain than Mitchell, but that unlike them, he had emerged "from his own hard early struggle and his long experience of human excrescences, writing the literature of Encouragement not Discouragement." While Mitchell's conformity to upper-class values and ideals account for the datedness of his writing, it is also the reason that the student of psychological and social realism, of medicine, of gender studies, and of American culture will find much of value in his works.

Biographies:

Anna Robeson Burr, *Weir Mitchell: His Life and Letters* (New York: Duffield, 1929);

Nolie Mumey, *Silas Weir Mitchell, the Versatile Physician (1829–1914): A Sketch of his Life and His Literary Contributions* (Denver: Range Press, 1934);

Ernest Earnest, *S. Weir Mitchell, Novelist and Physician* (Philadelphia: University of Pennsylvania Press, 1950);

Richard D. Walter, *S. Weir Mitchell, M.D.–Neurologist: A Medical Biography* (Springfield, Ill.: Charles C. Thomas, 1970).

References:

Catherine Golden, "'Overwriting' the Rest Cure: Charlotte Perkins Gilman's Literary Escape from S. Weir Mitchell's Fictionalization of Women," in *Critical Essays on Charlotte Perkins Gilman*, edited by Joanne B. Karpinski (New York: G. K. Hall, 1992): 144–158;

Kelley Griffith Jr., "Weir Mitchell and the Genteel Romance," *American Literature,* 44 (May 1972): 247–261;

Barrie Hayne, "S. Weir Mitchell," *American Literary Realism 1870–1910,* 2 (Summer 1969): 149–155;

Debra Journet, "Phantom Limbs and 'Body-Ego': S. Weir Mitchell's 'George Dedlow,'" *Mosaic,* 23 (Winter 1990): 87–99;

Joseph P. Lovering, *S. Weir Mitchell* (New York: Twayne, 1971);

Suzanne Poirier, "The Physician and Authority: Portraits by Four Physician-Writers," *Literature and Medicine,* 2 (1983): 21–40;

Poirier, "The Weir Mitchell Rest Cure: Doctor and Patients," *Women's Studies,* 10 (1983): 15–40;

Arthur Hobson Quinn, "Weir Mitchell, Pioneer and Patrician," in his *American Fiction, an Historical and Critical Survey* (New York: Appleton-Century, 1936), pp. 305–322;

David M. Rein, *S. Weir Mitchell as a Psychiatric Novelist* (New York: International Universities Press, 1952);

Talcott Williams, "Dr. S. Weir Mitchell; Physician, Scientist, and Author," *Century Magazine,* new series 35 (November 1898): 136–140.

Papers:

The unpublished papers of S. Weir Mitchell are housed in the College of Physicians Library, Philadelphia, and the Library of the University of Pennsylvania. Letters from Mitchell to William Osler are held in the Osler Library, McGill University. Much of Mitchell's correspondence is held at Duke University and the Duke University Medical Center, the New York Public Library, Harvard University, the Historical Society of Pennsylvania, Johns Hopkins University, the University of Virginia, and Yale University Library.

Elizabeth Stuart Phelps
(H. Trusta)
(13 August 1815 – 30 November 1852)

Patricia D. Maida
University of the District of Columbia

BOOKS: *Little Kitty Brown and Her Bible Verses,* anonymous (Philadelphia: American Sunday-School Union, 1851; London & Edinburgh: Thomas Nelson, 1855);

The Sunny Side; or, the Country Minister's Wife, as H. Trusta (Philadelphia & New York: American Sunday-School Union, 1851);

The Angel over the Right Shoulder, anonymous (Boston: Jewett, 1852; London: Low, 1858);

Kitty Brown and Her City Cousins, anonymous (Philadelphia & New York: American Sunday-School Union, 1852; London & Edinburgh: Thomas Nelson, 1855);

Kitty Brown and Her Little School, anonymous (Philadelphia: American Sunday-School Union, 1852; London & Edinburgh: Thomas Nelson, 1855);

A Peep at "Number Five"; or, A Chapter in the Life of a City Pastor, as Trusta (Boston: Phillips, Sampson, 1852);

The Sunny Side and A Peep at "Number Five," as Trusta (London, 1853);

Kitty Brown Beginning to Think, anonymous (Philadelphia: American Sunday-School Union, 1853; London & Edinburgh: Thomas Nelson, 1855);

The Last Leaf from Sunny Side, as Trusta (Boston: Phillips, Samson, 1853);

The Tell-Tale; or, Home Secrets Told by Old Travellers, as Trusta (Boston: Phillips, Samson, 1853);

Little Mary; or, Talks and Tales for Children, as Trusta (Boston: Phillips, Samson, 1854).

During her thirty-seven years Elizabeth Stuart Phelps combined a literary career with the roles of mother, homemaker, and minister's wife. Her place in American literary history traverses religious and gender lines to the frontiers of realistic fiction. Phelps, who also wrote for the magazine market and produced a series of religious children's books, is best known for her realistic novels. Her legacy was carried on by her daughter, who took her mother's name and established her own career as an author.

The second of nine children of Abigail Wooster Stuart and the Reverend Moses Stuart, Elizabeth Wooster Stuart was born on 13 August 1815 into a strict Calvinist New England family with roots going back to the seventeenth century. Her father was a well-known clergyman, scholar, and professor of Greek and Hebrew literature at Andover Theological Seminary in Massachusetts. By his example and direction the entire family was stimulated to pursue religious and intellectual endeavors. In a memoir Elizabeth's sister Sarah Stuart Robbins described Andover as a closely knit community where "strict Puritan rules governed every household," and at home the Reverend Stuart demanded absolute order and discipline, his children believing him to be "chosen and set apart." Reading and writing were emphasized, and it is not surprising that Elizabeth and two of her sisters, Sarah and Abbie, became professional writers.

Because Abigail Stuart was chronically ill, Elizabeth was often called on to care for her siblings and assume a mother's social role. As a consequence she learned early how to manage a home. Elizabeth was more like her father than her mother, however. As Carole Farley Kessler has pointed out, she was said to resemble him both physically and intellectually. An excellent student, Elizabeth received her early education in Andover; at age sixteen she was enrolled in the Mount Vernon School in Boston, where she studied for two years.

Even as a child she had written stories for her family and friends. Her first published fiction was written while she was a student at the Mount Vernon School. During that time she became a protégée of the Reverend Jacob Abbott, a founder of the school and later the author of the successful Rollo books, an educational children's series. Under his influence she produced articles for the religious magazine that he edited,

Elizabeth Stuart Phelps with two of her children, Mary Gray and Moses Stuart Phelps, circa 1850

using the pseudonym H. Trusta (an anagram of Stuart), which she used for all her subsequent writings that were not published anonymously.

In September 1842 Elizabeth Stuart married Austin Phelps, a Calvinist clergyman who was much like her father. The Phelpses settled in Boston, where he was pastor of the Pine Street Church. As a pastor's wife she became immersed in the religious and social concerns of the church. Her years in Boston are said to have been among her happiest. She gave birth to two children in Boston: Mary Gray (born in 1844) and Moses Stuart (born in 1849). Her daughter became the subject of Phelps's *Little Mary; or, Talks and Tales for Children,* published posthumously in 1854. The book is a record of the child-rearing practices she used successfully with Mary and is an effort to demonstrate how parents can inculcate religious, social, and ethical values in their children.

In 1850, when Austin Phelps was appointed professor of rhetoric at Andover Theological Seminary, the family moved back to Andover, an environment Elizabeth knew well. Her father, then a widower, was still on the faculty, although close to retirement.

Despite the demands placed on her, Phelps made time to study and write. Although for most of her life she suffered from severe headaches, caused by an undiagnosed chronic illness, she was a tireless worker. Known for her superior intellect, she was determined to maintain a reflective life, believing in the traditional Puritan values of self-study and social responsibility. In her autobiography, *Chapters from a Life* (1896), Mary Phelps (Elizabeth Stuart Phelps Ward) provided a glimpse of her mother's routine

Now she sits correcting proof-sheets, and now she is painting apostles for the baby's first Bible lesson. Now

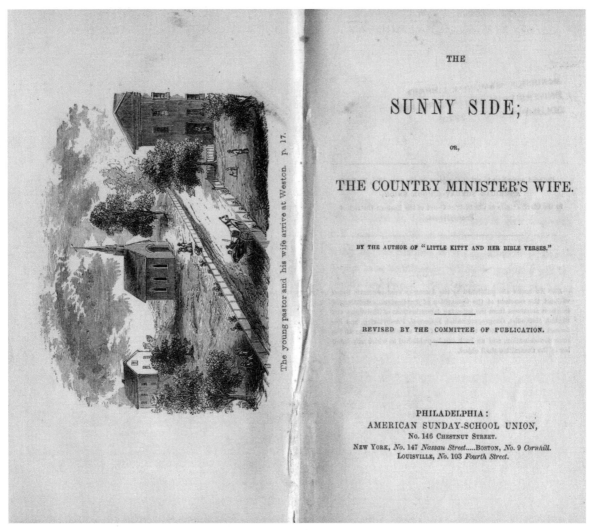

The young pastor and his wife arrive at Weston. P. 17.

THE

SUNNY SIDE;

OR,

THE COUNTRY MINISTER'S WIFE.

BY THE AUTHOR OF "LITTLE KITTY AND HER BIBLE VERSES."

REVISED BY THE COMMITTEE OF PUBLICATION.

PHILADELPHIA:
AMERICAN SUNDAY-SCHOOL UNION,
No. 146 CHESTNUT STREET.
NEW YORK, No. 147 Nassau Street.....BOSTON, No. 9 Cornhill.
LOUISVILLE, No. 103 Fourth Street.

Frontispiece and title page for Phelps's first novel, based on her experiences as a minister's wife

she is writing her new book, and now she is dyeing things canary-yellow in the white-oak dye—for the professor's salary is small, and a crushing economy was in those days one of the conditions of faculty life on Andover Hill. Now—for her practical ingenuity is unlimited—she is whittling little wooden feet to stretch the children's stockings on, to save them from shrinking; and now she is reading to us from the old, red copy of Hazlitt's "British Poets," by the register, upon a winter night.

Phelps no doubt felt the pressure of time and the fragility of life as she hastened to accomplish her goals. In addition to writing, she also lectured at Boston University, where she presented a course on the modern novel. An 1880 history of Abbot Academy reveals that although Phelps was in "delicate health," she volunteered "to give the same course of lectures to the young ladies of the academy."

Inspired by Abbott, Phelps published her own religious stories for young people—the Kitty Brown series, from 1851 to 1853. In simple prose these four books recount the spiritual development of a preteen girl. In *Kitty Brown Beginning to Think* (1853), for example, Kitty experiences religious conversion after a series of encounters with people in her community. The plot traces the awakening of her conscience and spiritual identity as she observes other young people such as Rosa Day, who "was always so industrious," and concludes that the behavior of good people is a consequence of being a Christian. Questioning the sudden death of a friend, Kitty does not passively accept Rosa's assurance "that God had taken him, that he was perfectly happy." Instead she wrestles with the concept of death until she herself is "born again." As a young adult, Elizabeth herself had experienced a personal reli-

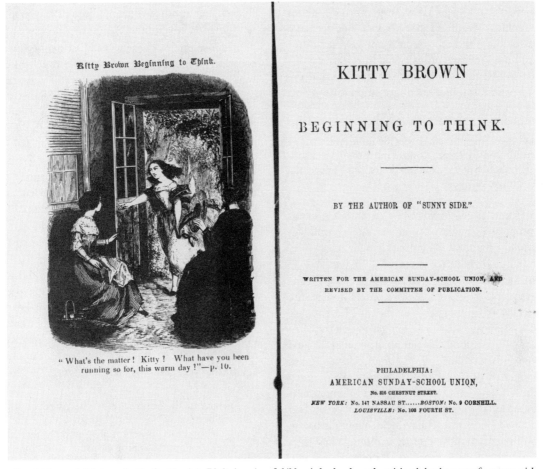

Frontispiece and title page for the final book in Phelps's series of children's books about the spiritual development of a young girl

gious conversion—although in her case the process was so wrenching that she became physically ill.

Phelps used her personal experiences in much of her nonfiction and fiction. She used the family journal she had kept for several years when she wrote her first novel, *The Sunny Side; or, the Country Minister's Wife* (1851). The book includes characteristics of the typical domestic novel, emphasizing household routine and social milieu, while providing portraits of husband and wife sharing the burden of his ministry. Phelps developed a realistic style, using a third-person narrator along with first-person journal accounts. In *Notable American Women* (1971) Ola Elizabeth Winslow praised "the easy flow of the story and natural idiom of the conversation" and said of the characters, "These are real people, and the circumstantial details of their daily lives is authentic."

Phelps further developed her skills in *A Peep at "Number Five"; or, A Chapter in the Life of a City Pastor* (1852), an autobiographical novel about her Boston years. The focus of this coming-of-age story is on Lucy, who is sixteen when she leaves school to marry Mr. Charles Holbrook, a newly ordained minister. ("Num-

ber Five" is the address of the little house that the Holbrooks rent in Boston.) The narrator observes, "Are not ministers' wives, then, heavily burdened? Let their prematurely care-worn and anxious faces, and their physician's bills answer." Lucy Holbrook, however, is resilient and cheerful, making friends with people in the community who help her. She also becomes an advocate for slaves and abused women and children.

Phelps experimented with voice by integrating letters from Lucy to her best friend, Mary, into the third-person omniscient narration of the novel. Lucy's early letters candidly reveal her youth and inexperience as they recount how she felt on attending her first church service in Boston:

Now this first Sabbath had been a great bugbear to me. I had thought of it with a beating heart. I knew it would prove a trying ordeal. To begin with, I was puzzled how to dress. I supposed I ought to wear something a little bridish, and yet I did not wish to dress on the Sabbath in any such way as would attract attention.

A subsequent letter relates how she is unable to control a fit of nervous laughter during a church service: "I needn't tell you, Mary, my infirmity about laughing. What wouldn't I have given not to have laughed then; but I did and I could not help it." After her husband takes charge of his own church, Lucy discovers that as the minister's wife she has become the center of attention among the congregation. She writes to Mary of her initial discomfort:

> I was no longer one of them, I was the minister's wife. Every head seemed turned toward me, and I found myself in the midst of a sea of eyes. Right–left–before–behind,–eyes, eyes, eyes.

These early letters are in the voice of a girlish Lucy, but as the novel progresses, she develops into a mature, confident woman–and there is a corresponding change in her voice.

The plot and characterization of *A Peep at "Number Five"* are deliberately understated. Ever the realist, Phelps avoided emotional responses and recorded instead the practical details of running a household. The couple's major task is balancing their small budget so that they can buy books as well as food. At one point, having decided that Lucy spends too much on groceries, Charles takes over the family shopping. With light humor the narrator describes how Lucy deals with a clergyman dinner guest after Charles forgets to buy food. He and Lucy also find humor in the situation when Lucy accidentally burns the few pieces of bacon they have in the pantry. When they cannot afford a carriage to meet social obligations, Lucy walks. (In fact, she walks most of the time.) A Victorian silence prevails over the arrival of Lucy and Charles's first child. A new chapter begins with the unnamed baby, later called Miss Tot, already ensconced in the household. Although life becomes more complicated with a child, the Holbrooks continue to grow in their roles. As the narrator points out, experience teaches both the minister and his wife "the cost of the profession." Thus Phelps presented her readers with an insider's view of the lives of a minister and his wife.

The physical and emotional stress in Phelps's personal life took its toll. In 1852 she became pregnant with her third child. During this pregnancy her son Stuart had to be nursed through a serious illness, and her father died unexpectedly. In poor health herself, she gave birth to a son, Amos Lawrence, in August. Despite doctors' efforts, she continued to decline. Her daughter, who was eight years old at the time, later described being sent home from school after being told that her mother had died:

> I took my little brother's hand without a word, and we trudged off. . . . I remember perfectly that we were very gaily dressed. Our mother liked bright colors on children. The little boy's coat was of red broadcloth, and my cape of a canary yellow, dyed at home in white-oak dye.

In fact, her mother did not die that day but a month later, on 30 November 1852.

Since Phelps chose to veil her identity by using the pseudonym H. Trusta and because much of her work was published posthumously, she did not receive personal recognition during her lifetime. Her use of a pseudonym for even her adult fiction, her best work, underscores her desire to work without the demands or the criticism that name recognition would have brought. The sales of her books reveal her success: *The Sunny Side; or, the Country Minister's Wife* sold one hundred thousand copies, and *A Peep at "Number Five"* sold twenty thousand copies in the first months after its publication. Her novels were also published abroad and sold well.

After Phelps's death her family made a concerted effort to establish her literary reputation. Her husband prepared her unpublished works for publication and wrote a personal memoir. Mary Gray Phelps took her mother's name. Determined to follow in her footsteps as a writer, she later achieved renown as Elizabeth Stuart Phelps Ward. Perhaps the most insightful evaluation of Elizabeth Stuart Phelps's position in American literary tradition is given by her daughter:

> The author of "Sunnyside," "The Angel on the Right Shoulder," and "Peep at Number Five," lived before women had careers and public sympathy in them. Her nature was drawn against the grain of her times and of her circumstances; and where our feet may find easy walking, hers were hedged.

References:

Carole Farley Kessler, "A Literary Legacy: Elizabeth Stuart Phelps, Mother and Daughter," *Frontiers: A Journal of Women's Study,* 5 (Fall 1980): 28–33;

Kessler, "'The Woman's Hour': Life and Novels of Elizabeth Stuart Phelps, 1844–1911," dissertation, University of Pennsylvania, 1977;

Philena McKeen and Phoebe McKeen, *Annals of Fifty Years: A History of Abbot Academy* (Andover, Mass.: Draper, 1880);

Austin Phelps, "Memorial of the Author," in *The Last Leaf from Sunny Side* (New York: Sheldon, 1853);

S. S. Robbins, *Old Andover Days: Memories of a Puritan Childhood* (Boston: Pilgrim Press, 1908);

Elizabeth Stuart Phelps Ward, *Austin Phelps: A Memoir* (New York: Scribners, 1891);

Ward, *Chapters from a Life* (Boston & New York: Houghton, Mifflin, 1896).

Papers:

Some of Elizabeth Stuart Phelps's papers are held at Boston University.

E. P. Roe

(7 March 1838 – 19 July 1888)

E. Kate Stewart
University of Arkansas at Monticello

BOOKS: *Barriers Burned Away* (New York: Dodd & Mead, 1872; London: Routledge, 1874; revised edition, New York: Dodd, Mead, 1885);

Play and Profit in My Garden (New York: Dodd & Mead, 1873);

What Can She Do? (New York: Dodd & Mead, 1873; London: Edmunston & Douglas, 1875);

Opening a Chestnut Burr (New York: Dodd & Mead, 1874; London: Routledge, 1874; revised edition, New York: Dodd, Mead, 1884);

Gentle Woman Roused (New York: National Temperance Society, 1874);

From Jest to Earnest (New York: Dodd & Mead, 1875; London: Warne, 1875);

A Manual on the Culture of Small Fruits (Newburgh, N.Y.: Journal of Printing Establishment, 1876);

Near to Nature's Heart (New York: Dodd & Mead, 1876; 2 volumes, London: Ward, Lock & Tyler, 1875);

A Knight of the Nineteenth Century (New York: Dodd, Mead, 1877; London: Ward, Lock, 1877);

A Face Illumined (New York: Dodd, Mead, 1878; London: Ward, Lock, 1878);

Success with Small Fruits (New York: Dodd, Mead, 1880; London: Seeley, 1880);

A Day of Fate (New York: Dodd, Mead, 1880; London: Ward, Lock, 1880);

Without a Home (New York: Dodd, Mead, 1881; 2 volumes, London: Ward, Lock, 1881);

Edward Payson Roe's Catalogue of Small Fruits and Grape Vines (Newburgh, N. Y.: Journal Printing House, 1882);

An Unexpected Result and Other Stories (New York: Dodd, Mead, 1883; London: Routledge, 1883);

His Sombre Rivals: A Story of the Civil War (New York: Dodd, Mead, 1883; London: Warne, 1883);

A Young Girl's Wooing: A Love Story (New York: Dodd, Mead, 1884; London: Warne, 1884);

Nature's Serial Story (New York: Harper, 1885; London: Sampson Low, 1884);

An Original Belle (New York: Dodd, Mead, 1885; London: Ward, Lock, 1885);

Driven Back to Eden (New York: Dodd, Mead, 1885; London: Ward, Lock, 1886);

He Fell in Love with His Wife (New York: Dodd, Mead, 1886; London: Ward, Lock, 1886);

The Hornet's Nest: A Story of Love and War (New York: Dodd, Mead, 1887);

The Earth Trembled (New York: Dodd, Mead, 1887; London: Ward, Lock, 1887);

Found Yet Lost (New York: Dodd, Mead, 1888; London: Ward, Lock, 1888);

"Miss Lou" (New York: Dodd, Mead, 1888; London: Ward, Lock, 1888);

The Home Acre (New York: Dodd, Mead, 1889);

Taken Alive and Other Stories With an Autobiography (New York: Dodd, Mead, 1889).

Collections: *Birthday Mottoes Selected from the Writings of E. P. Roe,* edited by Lyman Abbott (New York: Dodd, Mead, 1882); *A Bunch of Violets,* selected by Irene E. Jerome (Boston: Lee & Shepherd, 1888);

A Brave Little Quakeress and Other Stories (New York: Dodd, Mead, 1892);

The Works of E. P. Roe, 19 volumes (New York: Collier, 1900).

SELECTED PERIODICAL PUBLICATIONS–
UNCOLLECTED: "The Strawberry in History and Poetry," *Publishers' Weekly,* 9 (19 June 1880): 627–629;

"Letter to the Editor," *Literary World,* 19 (4 August 1884): 248;

"International Petty Larceny," *Publishers' Weekly,* 15 (9 January 1886): 47–48;

"How to Succeed in Literature," *Home and School Supplement: An Illustrated Educational Monthly* (December 1886): 165–169;

"My First Novel: *Barriers Burned Away,*" *Cosmopolitan,* 3 (July 1887): 327–329;

"The Elements of Life in Fiction," *Forum,* 5 (April 1888): 226–236;

"*Queen of Spades* and 'A Native Author Called Roe,'" *Lippincott's Monthly Magazine,* 42 (1888): 459–500.

Upon the death of E. P. Roe, *Publishers' Weekly* noted that he was one of the most widely read authors of the 1870s and 1880s. The fact that more than five million copies of his novels were sold during the closing decades of the nineteenth century testifies to his acceptance by the public. Roe has not, however, been praised by literary critics. If he is mentioned at all in critical assessments of nineteenth-century fiction, he is relegated to the position of a third-rate hack who produced predictable, didactic narratives that feature the conversion of at least one individual to Christianity. Yet the popularity of E. P. Roe's fiction makes him a worthy subject for literary examination. His themes and situations spoke to American culture in the later nineteenth century. Particularly notable are Roe's use of native landscapes, his promotion of American ideals, and his treatment of natural disasters. In the age of burgeoning realism he called for literature that was actual but rejected the principles of a photographic realism.

Born on 7 March 1838 in Modena, New York, Roe was the seventh child of Peter and Susan Williams Roe. Roe's father, who had failed to succeed in the wholesale grocery business in New York City, had become a farmer in the upstate New York community where he provided his family with a modest, comfortable home. The parents provided their children with a nurturing environment. Roe learned to revere his staunch Whig ancestors who played a vital role in securing America's independence. His invalid mother instructed him and his siblings in the Bible and such religious classics as John Milton's *Paradise Lost* (1867). Both father and mother were avid gardeners and passed on their love of nature. Peter Roe imparted social consciousness to his children by word and deed. He was the first abolitionist in Orange County, New York.

Roe began his schooling at a private, coeducational institution that was run by his older brother Alfred. Between 1857 and 1859 Roe chose the ministry as his profession, having undergone a conversion experience at the Presbyterian church near the school. After attending a boarding school for two years, Roe entered Williams College, where despite being plagued by serious eye problems that prevented his finishing the formal course of study, he distinguished himself as a speaker and writer. Rest and outdoor recreation relieved his eye condition so that he could enter Auburn Seminary in 1861. Finishing that phase of his formal training, Roe was ordained to the ministry by the North River Presbytery in Somers, New York, in 1862.

Roe's first pastoral duties were as a chaplain during the Civil War. He served ably in this position and contributed weekly reports to the *Evangelist,* a Presbyterian magazine. Driven by a desire to complete his seminary training, Roe attended Union Theological Seminary in New York in early 1863. His strong patriotic sense influenced him to return to the chaplaincy after a semester. Later that year he took another leave to marry his childhood friend, Anna Sands.

After the war Roe returned to New York and in 1866 became the pastor of the First Presbyterian Church in Highland Falls, a mile from West Point. During the first year of his pastorate, the energetic Roe established a church library, began cultivating a garden for both fun and profit, and organized the financing for a church building program. In his ministry Roe preached a practical gospel that reflected his early childhood training and would become the hallmark of his fiction.

Roe might have spent his life as a Presbyterian minister had he not felt compelled to visit Chicago in the wake of the historic fire of October 1871. Walking the streets and observing the destruction, Roe conceived the idea for *Barriers Burned Away* (1872), a monumentally successful first novel that was the result of a year of intense effort. The novel chronicles the life of Dennis Fleet, an educated, gifted man of faith who is handicapped by poverty. Following the death of his father, Fleet goes to Chicago to eke out an existence and is initially frustrated in his attempts to find employment. Eventually August Ludolph, an aristocratic German who disdains anything American and shows utter contempt for religion, hires him as a general flunky at his art museum. When Ludolph learns that Fleet has genuine taste and talent, he gives the young man increasing responsibilities in designing art displays.

The love interest in the novel is Christine, Ludolph's daughter, who is drawn to Dennis Fleet though she shares her father's views and hopes to soon travel to Germany with him to claim their places in the aristocracy. For his part Fleet believes his poverty, lack of social standing, and deep Christian faith are insurmountable obstacles in the relationship. When the fire breaks out, however, he proves himself a hero by risking his own life to save others, even those who had treated him shabbily when he first came to Chicago. Because of the fire Ludolph dies in his magnificent art building and Fleet converts Christine to Christianity as the couple stands on the shore of Lake Michigan surrounded by destruction. Although they are left with nothing, they can now forge a life together.

In *Barriers Burned Away* Roe introduces some of the basic themes and motifs of his fiction. He saw the favorable presentation of a viable faith in his stories as his especial ministry, and the conversion experience is central to his work. In most of his novels a Christian manages to bring the unbeliever to faith, thereby paving the way for the happy ending. Roe pays particular attention to the religious climate of the day, here presenting the religious skepticism of the rabidly German Ludolphs. Coming on the heels of the enthusiasm for the German Higher Criticism of the Bible, the novel portrays well the waning of orthodoxy in America during the nineteenth century. Roe's patriotism is evident in his negative portrayal of the Ludolphs because of their aversion to anything American. As he would in subsequent writings, Roe discloses the evils of alcoholism. Dennis Fleet befriends the Bruder family who are near destruction because of Berthold Bruder's advanced alcoholism. Fleet secures employment for one of the young sons in the family. He keeps Berthold, a once gifted painter, sober when he hires the elder Bruder to give him art lessons.

Perhaps one of the most interesting features of *Barriers Burned Away* is Roe's focus on the disaster itself. While the Chicago fire lends authenticity to the setting, it also becomes a vehicle for his religious themes. The catastrophe causes the errant characters to recognize the true value of human life; in a more narrow sense it brings together the lovers, ensuring that they will leave

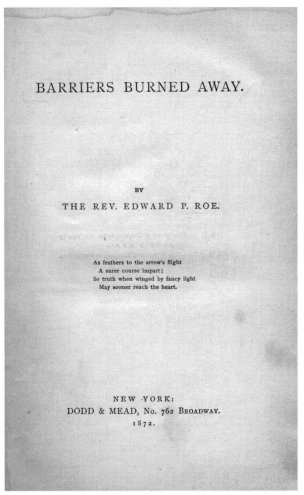

Title page for Roe's first book, a novel that depicts the devastation caused by the 1871 Chicago fire

behind the destruction and rebuild for the future. Roe emphasizes that despite the destruction wrought by the disaster the human spirit prevails and endures.

In his second novel, *What Can She Do?* (1873), Roe presents as his primary character Edith Allen, a strong, independent female character in the mold of Christine Ludolph. When the death of her father forces Edith and her mother and sisters to give up their posh New York existence and find a means of survival, Edith decides that a home-garden business could provide much needed support for her family. Malcolm McTrump, a successful local gardener, shares his expertise with her, giving Edith confidence that she can prosper by growing fruits and vegetables and instilling in the hardened young woman a practical theology based on the love of God. Edith also has a secret helper in her gardening enterprise, Arden Lacey, a poor neighbor of strong character who has fallen in love with her. At first angered when she discovers that Arden has been tending her garden at night, Edith, who is developing a more gentle, Chris-

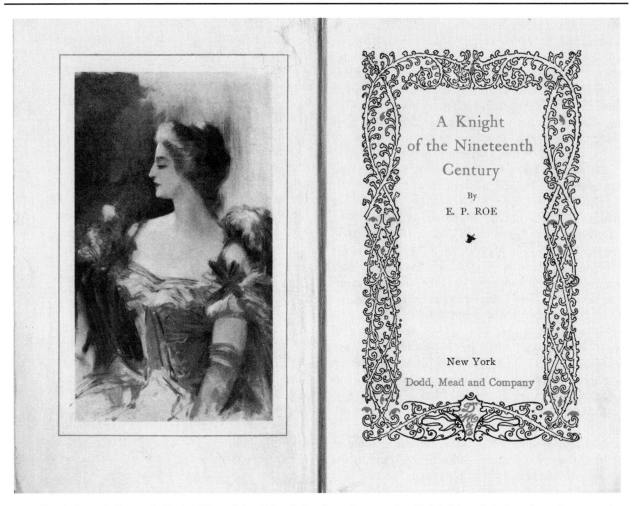

Frontispiece and title page for Roe's 1877 novel, in which a dissipated man becomes a "good knight" through the love of a good woman

tian spirit, comes to realize that he was motivated by friendship and concern. Although a drought that threatens her garden causes Edith to suspect that God has abandoned her, the rains come in time to save her strawberries, the sale of which allows her to pay off some of the family mortgage and give the Allens a financial cushion. In the end Edith and Arden marry.

What Can She Do? appeared the same year Roe published his first nonfiction work, *Play and Profit in My Garden* (1873), in which he details how he managed to earn more than $2,000 by growing fruits and vegetables on a two-acre patch. The parallels between the books are unmistakable as Roe, like his character, found that strawberries proved to be a profitable crop. Throughout his literary career Roe published several treatises on gardening and landscapes. *A Manual on the Culture of Small Fruits* (1876) and *Success with Small Fruits* (1880) are other how-to books on tending a garden for profit. In *The Home Acre* (1889) Roe gives instructions on planting the ideal kitchen garden on one acre. The latter book

differs from the others in that Roe outlines the specific arrangements for small gardens that utilize every inch of space in a pleasing design.

Roe's third novel, *Opening a Chestnut Burr* (1874), features Walter Gregory, a young man who was reared in the Christian faith but who departs from his early training. When Gregory works himself to the point of collapse in the city, his benevolent employer sends him home for rest and recuperation. He stays with the Waltons, a worthy family who reside in the old Gregory homestead. There is a mutual attraction between him and Annie Walton, the upright daughter of the family, but he is chagrined by her piety while she is disturbed by his skepticism. The reader, even one who has little or no knowledge of Roe's work, quickly discerns that Walter and Annie will eventually overcome all obstacles and marry once Walter comes to see the light. Its predictability notwithstanding, *Opening a Chestnut Burr* is notable for its vivid descriptions of the landscape of the Highland on the Hudson area. The novel also contains some interesting commentary on shady Wall Street practices, for Charles Hunting, Annie's would-be husband, uses sharp practices to cheat Walter and his business associates. Roe offers little analysis of the unscrupulous business, but his use of it is an indication that such matters were becoming a social concern.

As he was writing *Opening a Chestnut Burr* Roe began to be troubled by his health. When his doctor advised that maintaining both a pastorate and a writing career would debilitate him physically, Roe chose to resign his pastorate at Highland Falls. He did not lessen his writing pace, however. In *Gentle Woman Roused* (1874) he depicted a woman activist in the temperance cause. Shortly after leaving the ministry, he published the comic novel *From Jest to Earnest* (1875), in which Lottie Marsden, a self-absorbed socialite, decides to play a joke on a sincere ministerial student by pretending to be in love with him. Although the jest enjoys some success initially, Lottie soon realizes the worth of Frank Hemstead, and the two marry. Roe fully developed his theme of patriotism in *Near to Nature's Heart* (1876), an historical novel set during the American Revolution. Combining the themes of religious skepticism and pride in country in this work, Roe depicts George Washington as both the national and religious hero.

In *A Knight of the Nineteenth Century* (1877) Roe interweaves his main themes. He confronts contemporaneous religious issues by exposing the sham Christianity of the members of an affluent congregation who spurn Egbert Haldane, an unkempt, dissipated man, when he attends their church. He emphasizes the temperance theme by showing the great difficulties that Haldane encounters before he is converted to Christianity, becoming a "good knight" through the love of a good woman. After his conversion, Haldane becomes a doctor and serves ably in the Civil War both as a doctor and a chaplain. Although he served in the Union army, Haldane marries Laura Romeyn, who has Southern relatives to whom Haldane extends kindnesses during a yellow-fever epidemic. The novel thus shows Roe's love of the whole country, both the North and the South.

Roe's next two novels, *A Face Illuminated* (1878) and *A Day of Fate* (1880), explore the disparity between appearance and reality. Both works feature young women who from a distance appear attractive and sincere; closer scrutiny, though, reveals the two to be shallow and superficial. The hero of *A Face Illuminated* is an artist, Harold Van Berg, who seeks to capture a spirit of goodness in his paintings. One of his subjects, Ida Mayhew, appears to possess this quality; but when he carefully examines her face, Van Berg realizes her lack of depth. Roe, of course, develops the story line so that appearance and reality join. Ida converts to Christianity and becomes the manifestation of ideal beauty.

In *A Day of Fate* Richard Morton is a newspaper editor in New York City who–like Walter Gregory in *Opening a Chestnut Burr*–dedicates himself so fiercely to his work that he must escape to the country to recuperate. At a Quaker meeting he spots his "ideal" woman, Adah Yocomb. Adah, though, lacks depth and interests herself only in clothes and men. During a visit to the Yocomb's home, Morton meets Emily Warren, a rather dowdy music teacher who possesses genuine goodness. Eventually Morton realizes that he loves Emily and God and they marry.

In a variation on his temperance theme Roe examines drug addiction in *Without a Home* (1881). The principal character, Mildred Jocelyn, must make her way in the world after her father loses his business and social standing because of his opium habit. While Roe certainly does not condone intemperance, he stresses compassion in dealing with the substance abuser. As in the case of Egbert Haldane in *A Knight of the Nineteenth Century,* Roe shows that once the addiction is abandoned the addict can become a productive member of society.

In several of his novels Roe uses the Civil War as a background from which he develops the plot. In each of the novels that touches the war, Roe preaches a doctrine of not only salvation but also of reconciliation. Sensitive to the attitudes of Southerners, Roe gently calls for an end to regional conflicts that would only divide the "re-united" United States. *His Sombre Rivals: A Story of the Civil War* (1883) includes vivid details of war scenes with which Roe would have been familiar. Alford Graham and Warren Hillard, close friends, vie for the affections of Grace St. John. When Hillard is killed in the war, Grace is so devastated that she falls ill and suffers amnesia. Graham marries her to save her life and to honor his departed friend. The couple then moves to Virginia. *An Original Belle* (1885) features graphic scenes from the Battle of Gettysburg. The plot focuses on Marian Vosburgh, a righteous and independent woman who influences her suitors to become upstanding men.

One of Roe's last novels, *The Earth Trembled* (1887) recalls his first book, for again his focus is a disaster. Shortly after the earthquake of August 1886 in Charleston, South Carolina, Roe visited the site of destruction. The resulting novel concerns not only the natural disaster of the earthquake but also the long-term consequences of the man-made disaster of the Civil War. Roe depicts the tensions between the sons and daughters of the Old Confederacy, the "new" Southerners, and Yankees who have moved to Charleston for business purposes. In the end the groups are brought together through the hardships caused by the earthquake. Just as he had done for

Chicago in the wake of the fire in *Barriers Burned Away,* Roe at the conclusion of *The Earth Trembled* prophesies the complete renewal of Charleston.

Following Roe's death on 19 July 1888, which was attributed to a heart attack brought on by overwork, his primary publisher brought out *The Home Acre* (1889), *Taken Alive and Other Stories With an Autobiography* (1889), and *A Brave Little Quakeress and Other Stories* (1892). In these as in his earlier works Roe demonstrated his love of country, nature, and God, the themes that made him one of the most popular writers in nineteenth-century America.

Bibliography:

Katherine M. Babbitt, "E. P. Roe: A Preliminary Check List," thesis, State University of New York, Albany, 1971.

Biographies:

Mary A. Roe, *E. P. Roe: A Reminiscences of His Life* (New York: Dodd, Mead, 1899);

Sidney Forman, *A Hudson Highlands Social History: The Writings of Edward Payson Roe* (Fort Montgomery, New York: Sidney Forman, 1983).

References:

Glenn O. Carey, *Edward Payson Roe* (Boston: Twayne, 1985);

Ann Harrold-Doering, "Enough of Both Worlds: The Novels of E. P. Roe," dissertation, Bowling Green State University, 1974;

Philip Mathew Johnson, "America's Native Author: E. P. Roe and the Strategies of Religious Fiction," dissertation, University of Texas at Dallas, 1996;

Spencer Park Lane, "E. P. Roe: A Study of Popular Taste in Nineteenth Century American Fiction," thesis, University of Missouri–Columbia, 1948;

David S. Reynolds, *Faith in Fiction: The Emergence of Religious Literature in America* (Cambridge, Mass.: Harvard University Press, 1981), pp. 204–206.

Papers:

A collection of E. P. Roe's manuscripts is housed at the Clifton Waller Barrett Library at the University of Virginia. These materials include primarily horticultural and religious writings, mostly dated before Roe began his literary career.

Edgar Saltus

(8 October 1855 – 31 July 1921)

Carol Sue Hubbell and Lawrence I. Berkove
University of Michigan–Dearborn

BOOKS: *Balzac* (Boston & New York: Houghton, Mifflin, 1884);

The Philosophy of Disenchantment (Boston & New York: Houghton, Mifflin, 1885);

The Anatomy of Negation (New York: Scribner & Welford, 1886; London: Williams & Norgate, 1886; revised, Chicago: Belford, Clarke / London: Drane, 1889);

Mr. Incoul's Misadventure (New York: Benjamin & Bell, 1887; London: Greening, 1903);

The Truth about Tristrem Varick (Chicago & New York: Belford, Clarke, 1888; London: Routledge, 1889);

Eden: An Episode (Chicago: Belford, Clarke, 1888; London: Routledge, 1889);

A Transaction in Hearts: An Episode (New York: Belford, Clarke, 1889; London: Routledge, 1889);

The Pace That Kills: A Chronicle (Chicago: Belford, Clarke / London: Drane, 1889);

A Transient Guest and Other Episodes (Chicago: Belford, Clarke / London: Drane, 1889);

Love and Lore (New York: Belford, 1890);

Mary Magdalen: A Chronicle (New York: Belford, 1891); republished as *Mary of Magdala: A Chronicle* (London: Osgood & McIlvaine, 1891);

Imperial Purple (Chicago: Morrill, Higgins, 1892; London: Greening, 1906);

The Facts in the Curious Case of H. Hyrtl, Esq. (New York: Collier, 1892);

Madam Sapphira: A Fifth Avenue Story (New York & Chicago: Neely, 1893);

Enthralled: A Story of International Life Setting Forth the Curious Circumstances Concerning Lord Cloden and Oswald Quain (London: Tudor, 1894; New York: AMS, 1969);

When Dreams Come True: A Story of Emotional Life (New York: Collier, 1894; London: Transatlantic, 1895);

The Lovers of the World, 3 volumes (New York: Collier, 1896–1897?);

Purple and Fine Women (New York: Ainslee, 1903; London: Shurmer Sibthorp, 1903);

Edgar Saltus, 1890

Wit and Wisdom from Edgar Saltus, edited by G. F. Monkshood and George Gamble (London: Greening, 1903);

The Pomps of Satan (London: Greening, 1904; New York: Kennerley, 1906);

The Perfume of Eros: A Fifth Avenue Incident (New York: Wessels, 1905; London: Grant Richards, 1905);

Vanity Square: A Story of Fifth Avenue Life (Philadelphia & London: Lippincott, 1906);

Historia Amoris: A History of Love, Ancient and Modern (New York: Kennerley, 1906; London: Sisley, 1906);

213

republished as *Love throughout the Ages* (London: Sisley, 1908);

The Lords of the Ghostland: A History of the Ideal (New York: Kennerley, 1907; London: Laurie, 1908);

Daughters of the Rich (New York: Kennerley, 1909; London: Grant Richards, 1909);

The Monster (New York: Pulitzer, 1912);

Oscar Wilde: An Idler's Impression (Chicago: Brothers of the Book, 1917);

The Paliser Case (New York: Boni & Liveright, 1919);

The Imperial Orgy: An Account of the Tsars from the First to the Last (New York: Boni & Liveright, 1920);

The Gardens of Aphrodite (Philadelphia: Privately printed for the Pennell Club, 1920);

The Ghost Girl (New York: Boni & Liveright, 1922);

Parnassians Personally Encountered (Cedar Rapids, Iowa: Torch Press, 1923);

The Uplands of Dream, edited, with an introduction, by Charles Honce (Chicago: Covici, 1925);

Victor Hugo and Golgotha (Chicago: Covici, 1925);

Poppies and Mandragora, by Saltus and Marie Saltus (New York: Vinal, 1926).

OTHER: Honoré de Balzac, *After-Dinner Stories from Balzac,* translated by Saltus as Myndart Verelst, with an introduction by Saltus (New York: Coombes, 1886);

Théophile Gautier and Mérimée Prosper, *Tales before Supper from Théophile Gautier and Mérimée Prosper,* translated by Saltus as Verelst, with an introduction by Saltus (New York: Brentano's, 1887);

Jules Amédée Barbey d'Aurevilly, *The Story without a Name,* introduction by Saltus (Chicago: Belford, 1891);

Wolfgang Menzel, *Germany from the Earliest Period,* translated by Mrs. George Horrocks, includes a chapter by Saltus (New York: Collier, 1898);

Alfred Rambaud, *Russia,* translated by Leonora B. Lang, includes a chapter by Saltus (New York: Collier, 1898);

J. Talboys Wheeler, *India and the Frontier States of Afghanistan, Nipal and Burma,* includes a chapter by Saltus (New York: Collier, 1899);

W. L. George, *A Bed of Roses,* introduction by Saltus (New York: Boni & Liveright, 1919);

Oscar Wilde, *Salomé, The Importance of Being Earnest, Lady Windermere's Fan,* introduction by Saltus (New York: Boni & Liveright, 1919).

SELECTED PERIODICAL PUBLICATIONS–
UNCOLLECTED: "The Impostor," *Ainslee's,* 39 (May 1917): 1–37;

"After the Ball," *The Smart Set,* 67 (January 1922): 93–99.

For many years Edgar Saltus has been loosely associated with the bohemian and decadent movements in literature. He has also been inaccurately categorized as a disciple of Oscar Wilde and as a mere popularizer of Arthur Schopenhauer. His talent for clever phraseology has often been noted, as well as his ability to produce shudders in some of his readers, but he has been given little credit for versatility of style or originality of thought. Although Saltus was undeniably attracted to Schopenhauerian philosophy, his own viewpoint was not totally defined by it. Saltus saw limitations in Schopenhauer, and his writings reveal an attitude that transcends pessimism. His was by no means a one-track talent; in addition to popularizing what he called "the philosophy of disenchantment," Saltus also wrote intriguing fictionalized history, somewhat in the manner of Walter Pater, and he displays a wide-ranging and sophisticated sense of humor.

Saltus's interest in pessimism and his affinity for French literature were cultivated during the European education of his youth. He was born on 8 October 1855 into a wealthy, socially prominent New York family for whom travel and study in Europe was a matter of course. Because of this background Saltus was occasionally–and unfairly–accused of snobbery for his focus in his fiction on the rich and traveled. He grew up in New York, was included in the social register, and was comfortable in London and Europe. Saltus wrote of the world he knew, but he was often critical of the social elite.

Edgar's father, Francis Henry Saltus, inherited wealth and was an innovative businessman who received international recognition for inventing the rifled-steel cannon. When Edgar was seven years old, his parents separated, and he remained with his mother, the former Eliza Howe Evertson, while his half brother, Francis, left for Europe with his father. Saltus's third wife, Marie, in her biography of her husband, reports that Saltus was denied nothing within the power of his adoring mother and that later in life he admitted he had been indulged. His first two marriages ended in divorce, with scandalous accusations by Helen Sturgis Read, his first wife, prompting such headlines as "An Erotic Writer's Erotic Adventures." A source of lingering pain in his life was his unsuccessful custody fight for his only daughter, Elsie, when his second marriage ended. Edgar and Elsie Smith Saltus were separated before the birth of their daughter, but she denied him a divorce, and he remarried only after her death. His marriage to Marie Giles in 1911 lasted until his death in 1921, and she describes it as a satisfying, albeit sometimes turbulent, one.

Saltus's literary taste was broad but discriminating, ranging from the classics to contemporary European literature and including a few American writers. His most generous praise was for his French favorites, such as Honoré de Balzac, Jules d'Aurevilly, Gustave Flaubert, and Victor Hugo. In *Victor Hugo and Golgotha* (1925) he called Hugo's best works "perhaps as enduring as anything fashioned by man can be." Carl Van Vechten, in his *Excavations* (1926), claimed that Saltus "annexed the horrors of Hugo," and others have seen the possible influence of Hugo's *L'Homme qui rit* in Saltus's *Enthralled: A Story of International Life Setting Forth the Curious Circumstances Concerning Lord Cloden and Oswald Quain* (1894). Saltus called Henry James "the great master of English prose" in *Collier's* (16 December 1897) and in *The Philosophy of Disenchantment* (1885) refers approvingly to James's *The Portrait of a Lady* (1881) as a believable picture of life that ends in the complete disenchantment of the heroine.

Saltus's career as a writer coincided with that of Oscar Wilde. The two men had a friendly relationship, sharing a sophisticated wit and an aesthetic bent. Although Saltus defended Wilde's character and genius in *Oscar Wilde: An Idler's Impression* (1917), it is doubtful that he saw him as a master to be emulated. He called Wilde a "third rate poet who occasionally rose to the second class but not once to the first."

Saltus credits the idealistic and unconventional Ralph Waldo Emerson with having opened his eyes. In an 1896 *Collier's* column he wrote, "I began to see, and what to me was even more marvelous, I began to think." Respectful but vague references to Emerson appear throughout Saltus's works, and in *The Philosophy of Disenchantment* he refers to Schopenhauer as "this Emerson in black."

Saltus's first published book, the biography *Balzac* (1884), was praised as a graceful, vivacious, and informative work, a welcome addition to American knowledge of Balzac. With the publication of *The Philosophy of Disenchantment,* his second book and the cornerstone of his reputation, and then *The Anatomy of Negation* (1886), however—although the strength of Saltus's style was again acknowledged—the books' controversial philosophical attitudes of pessimism and skepticism were less appreciated.

Among twentieth-century critics Saltus has had admirers, such as Van Vechten, James Huneker, and Charles Honce, but others, including H. L. Mencken, harshly accused Saltus of style without substance. Mencken's assessment of Saltus continued a theme begun by others but was in part a reaction to the 1925 publication of Marie Saltus's biography. In contrast to the popular view of her husband as cynical and sophisticated, she presents a sympathetic Saltus capable of tenderness and playfulness but with his idiosyncrasies and occasional impetuousness exposed. The degree to

Edgar Saltus at sixteen

which Marie Saltus's book and Mencken's denunciation influenced Saltus's reputation cannot be measured. His popularity had faded many years earlier. A revival of interest in Saltus did not materialize, even with the republication of many of his works in the 1920s and the production of two motion pictures based on his novels: *The Paliser Case* (1920) and *Daughters of the Rich* (1923).

After spending two semesters at Yale and before earning a law degree from Columbia in 1880, Saltus spent several years in Europe and is reported to have studied at the Sorbonne and in Heidelberg and Munich. During these years of heightened European interest in Schopenhauer and pessimism, Saltus was drawn to the literary style and mood of French novelists and poets and, in philosophy, found Schopenhauer especially persuasive.

The Philosophy of Disenchantment is a lucid, witty explanation of Schopenhauer's pessimistic philosophy that life consists of suffering with no hope of happiness. Relief from pain is complete only in annihilation. In life suffering always outweighs any fleeting moments of joy. Saltus carefully reports Schopenhauer as identifying the Will, or Genius of the Species, as the relentless force behind man's irrational but irresistible urge to live and reproduce. Without completely endorsing every element of Schopenhauer's philosophy, Saltus affirms the view that life is "an affliction," with any hope of happiness only an illusion. Hence, disenchantment for Saltus is the removal of the illusion, the "enchantment" that interferes with seeing life accurately. The prospects for contentment are greater for the pessimist who expects suffering, he suggests, than for one with high expectations since "it is the accidental nature of the sorrow that gives its sting."

Schopenhauer student Eduard von Hartmann's *Philosophy of the Unconscious,* published in 1869, was also a topic of discussion during Saltus's student years in Germany. Although Hartmann is not a significant figure in the history of psychology, his pre-Freudian theories played a role in the European debate over the existence of an unconscious mind. Saltus devotes a chapter in *The Philosophy of Disenchantment* to Hartmann and recounts admiringly his experience calling upon Hartmann at his home in Berlin and receiving patient and gracious explanations to his questions about philosophy. Saltus found a conception of pessimism that was "not a gospel of desolation" in Hartmann's contented attitude and his normal life, which included a wife and children—a significant contrast to Schopenhauer.

In *The Anatomy of Negation,* which he called "a history of anti-theism from Kapila to Leconte de Lisle," Saltus identifies the roots of pessimistic thought in the early Buddhist negation of the value of life and traces it through time. This second philosophical work dwells less on hopelessness, however, and more on the value of reasoned skepticism. He is particularly critical of reward-and-punishment theology and affirms the value of those throughout history who have had the courage to deny prevailing dogma.

In 1887 Saltus published the first of sixteen novels, most of which feature disenchantments related to unrequited love and the effects of careless assumptions. In *Mr. Incoul's Misadventure* (1887) Saltus delves into the darker side of human nature in a story in which irony prevails; the novel ends with a murder and a suicide after the vicious Mr. Incoul jumps to the circumstantial conclusion that his wife has been unfaithful. This work has been called one of Saltus's best, mainly on the basis of its suspenseful entertainment. It has been praised for its vividly described bullfight scene and the suicide's final moments.

The Truth about Tristrem Varick (1888), however, Saltus's second novel, better demonstrates his sense of humor and his capacity for complexity. It also manifests Saltus's significant divergence from Schopenhauer, a trend the philosophical justification of which he explicitly developed eighteen years later in *Historia Amoris: A History of Love, Ancient and Modern* (1906). The pessimistic theme of *The Truth about Tristrem Varick* is qualified by

a satirical and sometimes playful treatment of idealism in a story of faithful though unrequited love. The hero's name connotes both knightliness and sadness. His schoolboy acts of chivalry and, later, the inclusion of the name "Iseult" among those he fancies appropriate for the beautiful Viola Raritan, recall the medieval love story "Tristan and Iseult" and hint at Tristrem's romantic notions of his life and fate. Falling in love with Viola, a young woman he has just met, Tristrem assumes that because she is lovely she is worthy. Through a series of such rash assumptions he idealizes Viola and his own obsession with her. He rationalizes her signals of disinterest to suit his dream and continues to pursue her, eventually assuming the role of her protector to the point of murdering her dishonorable lover. The story ends with the prospect of Tristrem's execution, which a romantic might view as the tragic death of a broken-hearted lover.

Tristrem, however, is more a comic than tragic figure. His name and rather melancholy sentimentality could well have been inspired by Laurence Sterne's satirical novel *Tristram Shandy* (1759–1767). Both title characters are sympathetic but unsuccessful in love and comically sad. The "truth" about Tristrem, like the "life and opinions" of Tristram Shandy, is comprised of a string of absurdities. The narrators of both books use subtle humor and a posture of total seriousness to achieve ironies that steadily deepen their themes. Confusion develops between illusion and reality, emotion and reason, and, in the case of Tristrem, virtue and vice. Tristrem mistakes his emotional vision for truth and pursues a dream as if it were reality.

The end of the novel reveals an irony within Tristrem's character: his difference from, but similarity to, his father. The emotionally responsive and kind-hearted Tristrem appears to be totally unlike his cold, rejecting father, who arbitrarily disinherits him after hastily and wrongly concluding that Tristrem is not his son. Tristrem just as arbitrarily, however, although with a sense of nobility, gives away his fortune after his grandfather finds a way to have the will legally reversed. In a final irony, Tristrem, like his father, acts upon faulty assumptions and pursues a distorted idea of justice.

Saltus's novels reinforce the values he identifies, in his philosophical books and essays, as most important: skepticism and compassion. In *Mr. Incoul's Misadventure,* despite the humorous title, Mr. Incoul is a clear villain. He is cold, calculating, and vicious in seeking retribution when he suspects his wife has been unfaithful. The book's title-page quotation from the biblical book of Deuteronomy, "And thine eye shall not pity," is ironically fulfilled in Mr. Incoul's complete lack of compassion. In the case of Tristrem Varick, Saltus leads the reader to sympathize with Tristrem in spite of his blundering behavior because he means well. The ambiguities in *The Truth about Tristrem Varick,* with its ironic picture of life as both tragic and comic, provoke compassion.

In the short story "A Transient Guest" (published in *A Transient Guest and Other Episodes,* 1889) another wealthy young New Yorker, Tancred Ennever, falls instantly and overpoweringly in love with a woman he has just met on a visit to the island of Sumatra. His naive assumptions and rationalizations lead him to entertain unrealistic expectations and indiscreetly declare his love. The irresistible woman is a widow, Mrs. Lyeth, the fiancée of Tancred's host, General Van Lier. The general's beautiful young daughter, Liance, is attracted to Tancred, but she cannot compete in his eyes with Mrs. Lyeth. When the general finds a love letter Tancred wrote to Mrs. Lyeth, she tells him it was intended for Liance; however, Tancred admits to the general within Liance's hearing that he has no interest in her. Having offended his host, Tancred leaves on the next boat, barely escaping the wrath of the general's demure daughter. As a farewell gift Liance sends a basket of poisoned treats to Tancred; when he tosses one to his pet dog, the animal immediately dies. Saltus's depiction of a vindictive woman challenges the tendency among most writers of his era to place women upon a pedestal as the nobler sex.

Love, in Saltus's novels, does not always lead to disenchantment. In *Eden: An Episode* (1888) a blameless but somewhat mysterious husband is suspected when his wife, Eden, allows circumstantial evidence to destroy her trust in him. In the end her reasonableness and his patience allow him to explain himself and restore her confidence. This novel is less complex than the earlier two but is of interest for its focus on misunderstanding and premature judgment—dominant themes in Saltus's fiction.

The novel *A Transaction in Hearts: An Episode* (1889) is said by Marie Saltus to be based in part on Saltus's own experience. It involves a theme that is common in his fiction: men in love who assume too much and behave foolishly. The novel features a young minister, Christopher Gonfallon, whose wife of a few years, suffering from chronic neuralgia, has lost attractiveness to him. He becomes infatuated with his sophisticated sister-in-law, Claire, and declares his love to her, assuming her interest in him. Claire appears to be flippant and shallow but reveals herself at the end to be more selfless and honest than her minister brother-in-law. She tells Gonfallon plainly that it is her sister, Ruth, who loves him, provoking some soul searching that leads him back to his wife.

Imperial Purple (1892) represents one of Saltus's few attempts at historical fiction; it is a flamboyant and

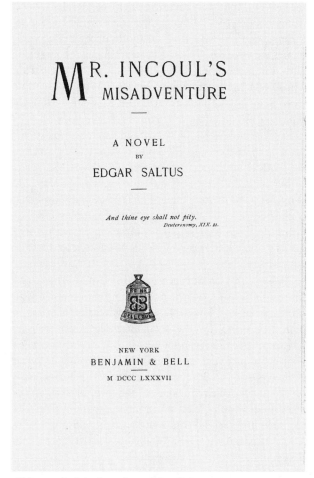

Title page for Saltus's 1887 novel, in which a cruel man exacts revenge after wrongly suspecting his wife of an affair

impressionistic account of Roman excesses and perversities. The novel was widely praised and valued as an illustration of Saltus's unique style rather than as accurate history. A picture of the caesars of Imperial Rome in a luxuriously draped parade of corruption, it may be read as a study in the corruptibility of human nature and the insatiability of power. It is usually seen simply as an opportunity for Saltus to venture into the sensuous and wicked splendors of a decadent past. This reinforced the aura of wickedness imputed to him by his popular "erotic" novels, tame by today's standards, and his troubled marriages.

At least one of Saltus's novels was clearly inspired by events of his own life. *Madam Sapphira: A Fifth Avenue Story* (1893), published two years after Saltus's divorce from Helen Read, is a protest against her well-publicized accusations of infidelity. In the novel a manipulative wife accuses her innocent husband of infidelity in order to free herself to remarry. Among the similarities to real life, both Saltus and the fictional hero, Carol Nevius, are away in Europe when the accusations against them are printed in the newspapers. The wife of the novel, Hilda (née Snaith), then marries her lover, Ablaut; the year following her divorce from Saltus, Helen Read married William Oothout. Saltus cleverly names the lover in *Madam Sapphira* "Ablaut," a linguistic term for a variation in vowels within the same root word, which rhymes with Oothout. With this subtle word play Saltus implies that only a slight difference separates the man and his fictional counterpart.

The biblical Sapphira, wife of Ananias, was struck dead as the penalty for deception (Acts 5:1–10). When the truth about his wife fully impacts Nevius, he refers to her as "Madam Sapphira" and imagines her tombstone with the words "Here lies Hilda Snaith, and that is all she ever did." He is angry enough to contemplate murdering her and fills a perfume bottle with anhydrous prussic acid. He is not callous enough to dispatch it, however.

Fittingly, Carol Nevius is cast as an attorney. The impact of Saltus's own legal training, while not put to professional use, is detectable in his works. It arises in plot details such as the legal loophole discovered by Tristrem Varick's grandfather, in distinctions between justice and pity such as appear in *Vanity Square: A Story of Fifth Avenue Life* (1906), and in Saltus's significant focus on the misuse of circumstantial evidence. In *Madam Sapphira* he counters Helen's accusations with an alternate scenario in which an innocent husband is framed. Van Vechten called the book "malicious" for its inferences damaging to the Read family.

After Saltus's divorce he found both his public standing and his finances diminished, and he focused less on novels and began writing for various journals. In 1893 he began a weekly column for *Collier's* and wrote frequent articles for the *New York Journal* as well as *Cosmopolitan, The Smart Set,* and *Ainslee's*. His essays communicate a cautious view of the Industrial Revolution and ambivalence about nineteenth-century America. Saltus would not accept the prevailing optimism about the advance of technology and capitalism. As early as *The Philosophy of Disenchantment* he had called progress "the chimera of the present century," and in his later, often humorous, journalism he often chided the greedy capitalist or lamented the loss of beauty which accompanies "utility."

Saltus said on more than one occasion that in history, romance, or literature "it is the shudder that tells," and the shudder produced by the perversity and romantic intrigue in his works has been cited as evidence that sensation, not truth, was his objective, that he was simply offering his readers the sensuality and the horrors they were looking for. Saltus expanded on this idea of the reader's ambivalent response to portrayals of evil in the essay "Human Hyenas" in *The Pomps of Satan* (1904), in which he wrote, "though hyenas alarm,

they also attract." If the shudder was a key literary effect for Saltus, however, it was also a part of the reality he saw. He was attracted to realism in the sense of facing the truth about life even when it contradicts tradition or desire. He admired this quality in both Emerson and Schopenhauer, two men who saw very different truths.

It has been insufficiently recognized that Saltus was not a total believer in Schopenhauer. As early as his encounter with Hartmann, he put his own stamp on pessimism, and in *The Philosophy of Disenchantment* he calls Schopenhauer's extreme and celibate asceticism an "eccentric theory." Indeed, Saltus's three marriages, as well as other reported love affairs, demonstrate his rejection of asceticism. Although he saw men's dreams of happiness as illusions, he did not completely reject the possibility of real love.

In *When Dreams Come True: A Story of Emotional Life* (1895) an idealistic, wealthy young writer, Tancred Ennever, matures through suffering and self-analysis and, ultimately, finds real love. The beautiful and gentle Sylvia realizes she does not love Tancred after agreeing to marry him, and in despair he sails for Europe. On board the ship he again meets Sylvia's friend Mme. Bravoura, a widow. As they converse and spend time together, Tancred finds himself falling in love with this woman of grace and maturity. He realizes he hardly knew Sylvia.

Much of the novel's action consists of a series of misinterpretations based on circumstantial evidence. Just after Tancred and Mme. Bravoura become engaged, Tancred's mother, having misread Sylvia, notifies him that she still loves him. Tancred wants to do the honorable thing and decides, happily, that his loyalty belongs to Mme. Bravoura. A further misunderstanding leads Tancred to believe that Mme. Bravoura, known as Jack, manipulated circumstances and lied in an effort to attract him and his money. When he in effect accuses her of this, she parts from him with dignity. Tancred returns home to find that Sylvia does not love him and that he was wrong about Jack. He dreams of the opportunity to beg her forgiveness but believes that to ask would be an insult.

Following the advice of novelist Alphabet Jones, a witty, cynical, and sometimes wise recurring character in Saltus's novels, Tancred loses himself in his writing. In Europe, researching the "heroines of love," he fails to find historical examples of love that ends happily. Unexpectedly, Tancred discovers Mme. Bravoura at an Italian villa, where he pours out his heart and finds himself loved and forgiven.

Mme. Bravoura lives up to the suggestion of her name. In contrast to the reticent and vacillating Sylvia, Jack is boldly forthright and sure of her purpose and

*Portrait of Marie, Saltus's third wife, who stimulated his interest in
mysticism and the occult*

her heart. The noble Tancred outgrows his earlier
visions of chivalrous romance and finds a woman
whose maturity enables confidence and stability. In
spite of history's warning, the novel ends with Jack and
Tancred enjoying real love, whose survival after suspicions and misunderstanding is enabled by his humility
and her forgiveness. Saltus thus allows for the possibility of love that rises above mere instinct. At the time of
publication he had recently married his second wife,
Elsie Smith Saltus.

In *Historia Amoris,* an essayistic account of love's
influence and evolution in human history, Saltus again
diverges significantly from Schopenhauer in his view of
the possibilities of love, particularly that between a man
and a woman. For Saltus, Schopenhauer defined love as
merely an instinct, a manifestation of a universal Will
that he named the Genius of the Species. Through this
force one is duped into believing a union with a particular partner will produce happiness, but love merely provides a means of producing the next generation and
then vanishes, its purpose completed, leaving the lovers
disillusioned. Hartmann endorsed Schopenhauer's theory but explained instinct in terms of a universal
"Unconscious" will. This force, according to Hartmann, is the "essence" of life itself and directs the survival and progressive evolution of the species with

unerring though unconscious clairvoyance. This purpose is accomplished through a natural process of sexual selection. Saltus, however, finds both Schopenhauer's
theory and Hartmann's explanation of it flawed
because they do not account for unrequited love.
Because Schopenhauer conceived of Will as selecting
and manipulating human generation by love, unrequited love appears to be a failure of the system. Hartmann offered the theoretical explanation that while a
man may be attracted to a woman who is the best available complement for him, it does not necessarily follow
that he is the most qualified for her. She may be of a
superior makeup or may have met another, better
match who attracts her. Saltus does not see love as necessarily directed toward the goal of improving the species, however. Humans fall in love with the unworthy
or the disinterested. For Saltus unrequited love, as portrayed in the character of Tristrem Varick, is incompatible with the concept of direction by unerring instinct.

Saltus, in contrast to Schopenhauer, sees love's
potential for lifting man above mere instinct or passion.
He finds in love something intrinsically noble as well as
beautiful. Rather than refining the species, love brings
out the best in the individual. According to Saltus, both
Schopenhauer and Hartmann confuse instinct with sentiment. Love, which has lifted humanity out of its prim-

itive state and accounts for the "heightened stature of the soul," he says in *Historia Amoris,* is based on sentiment, not instinct.

In *Vanity Square* Saltus offers an entertaining mystery featuring a bored member of the leisure class. His peaceful life is disrupted when he becomes attracted to a woman of deceptive beauty. Stella Sixmuth, a nurse who cultivates an illusion of personal saintliness, is attracted to Gerald Uxhill's money. While devotedly nursing his sick child and then his wife, Maud, she subtly undermines his marriage and slowly poisons Maud. Circumstantial evidence points to Uxhill as the poisoner. The plot serves as the backdrop for excursions into philosophical and psychological concepts, some of which are digressive demonstrations of Saltus's interest in the emerging field of psychology.

Illusions of intellectual and moral superiority are unveiled in this novel. Uxhill and Miss Sixmuth discuss how "tedious" the majority are and how they lack purpose. "All they require is to be comfortable," Stella asserts. Uxhill claims that "Vanity Square," in particular, contains a "lot of damned nobodies, talking about nothing."

The novel ends with Uxhill contentedly satisfied and believing he has matured through suffering. When he and Maud learn that Miss Sixmuth, now in London, has married a wealthy husband whose previous wife died in Stella's care, Maud expresses guilt. To protect their daughter, Mowgy, from the publicity, they kept silent about Stella's attempt at murder. After reminding Maud that Mowgy means more to them than a stranger, Uxhill rationalizes that "True justice is pity. It was in that spirit we let her go." Saltus's law training ensures that he understood the definition of justice and its distinction from pity. The novel has been criticized for a "fairy-tale" ending, but the happy ending is an illusion framed in irony. Uxhill, in spite of his self-congratulation, is as vain as the rest of Vanity Square and as eager for his own comfort.

The Lords of the Ghostland: A History of the Ideal (1907) offers Saltus's conception of the history of religious belief. He repeats some material from *The Anatomy of Negation* and challenges orthodoxy by commenting on the similarities and shared roots of various beliefs. While he is skeptical of all religions, however, his tone is more sympathetic toward man's need to believe. It is not simple belief that disturbs Saltus but claims to sole proprietorship of truth and conformity to creeds that become superstitions. He writes of a past when the lower-class Egyptian, denied access to the divine, prayed to jackals and scorpions and says, "It was ridiculous but human. He too would have a part, however insensate, in the dreams of all mankind." Interestingly, the book ends with an acknowledgment of Saltus's own

emerging attraction to reincarnation, calling it perhaps a dream, but a beautiful ideal. While *The Lords of the Ghostland* received some positive reviews, it is less systematic than *The Philosophy of Disenchantment* and *The Anatomy of Negation,* prompting Percival Pollard's judgment that Saltus's words had lost their connection to ideas and become "simply an exhibition of virtuosity."

Marie Saltus is credited with converting her husband to theosophy, and Saltus's later works are said to reflect this change of perspective. Whatever value Saltus ultimately accorded to theosophy, his interest in Eastern mysticism, reincarnation, and occult possibilities far predated his relationship with Marie. In *The Philosophy of Disenchantment* he calls the modern pessimist "a Buddhist who has strayed from the Orient," and his comments throughout his writings reveal his knowledge of ancient beliefs.

In assessments of Saltus there is the suspicion that he saw dangers, discrepancies, and perversities all around him but lacked the courage, discipline, or genius to grapple with solutions. His critics claim, variously asserting a failure of nerve, a need to please his readers, or simple confusion, that Saltus was hindered by a lack of conviction. Saltus, however, would perhaps assert that his commitment was less to pessimism than to skepticism. He made it clear that he feared too-rigid convictions more than he feared ambiguity. In *The Lords of the Ghostland* and *The Anatomy of Negation,* for example, he made the point that religious dogmatism leads to intolerance, while skepticism leads to greater compassion.

Accused of placing style before substance, Saltus did not deny a strong orientation toward verbal artistry. He acknowledged on more than one occasion, "In literature, only three things count—style, style polished, style repolished." He strove to write with wit and eloquence and manifested both cynical and playful humor. In tongue-in-cheek essays, quips, and satirical fiction he used sly humor to both entertain and challenge. In the essay "Truffles and Tokay" he commented on literature's capacity for revelation: "The sculptor has his chisel, the musician his piano, the painter his brush. The novelist has but his brain. . . . The novelist is the instrument and the instrumentalist. He chisels the impalpable, attunes the inaudible and paints the unseen." Although Saltus appeared to have had no overt intent beyond amusement, he had a deeper sense that a novelist has some larger duty. "Paramount of all," he says in "The Morality of Fiction," reprinted in *Love and Lore* (1890), the novelist "should let no work go from him that does not instil [*sic*] some lesson and make men, and women too, the better and the wiser for his prose."

A central theme for Saltus is the promotion of skepticism as an antidote to naive assumptions and blind tradition. This skepticism challenges thought, and because the skeptic suspends judgment, it promotes tolerance. Suggesting in "Truffles and Tokay" that the apprehension of truth does not eliminate a sense of mystery, he says that the best "books" will not be found in the library. He recommends "the book of Nature, a treatise that all philosophers begin and none of them finish" and "the book of Destiny, which all thinkers consult and none can construe."

The truth, to Saltus the skeptic, was always complex and never final or complete. In *The Anatomy of Negation* he writes: "The veil of Maya is unraised. The most we can do to lift it is to finger feebly at the edges." Ultimately, Saltus was disenchanted even with pessimism.

Biographies:

Marie Saltus, *Edgar Saltus, the Man* (Chicago: Covici, 1925);

Claire Sprague, *Edgar Saltus* (New York: Twayne, 1968).

References:

Van Wyck Brooks, *The Confident Years* (New York: Dutton, 1952), pp. 113–117;

Benjamin de Casseres, *Forty Immortals* (New York: Seven Arts, 1926), pp. 88–93;

Ramsey Colles, "A Publicist: Edgar Saltus," *Westminster Review,* 162 (October 1904): 463–474;

Elbert Hubbard, "Heart to Heart Talks with Philistines by the Pastor of His Flock," *Philistine,* 25 (October 1907): 129–143;

Harry Levin, "The Discovery of Bohemia," in *Literary History of the United States,* edited by Robert E. Spiller and others (New York: Macmillan, 1953), pp. 1072–1074;

Eric McKitrick, "Edgar Saltus of the Obsolete," *American Quarterly,* 3 (Spring 1951): 22–35;

H. L. Mencken, "Edgar Saltus," in his *Prejudices: Fifth Series* (New York: Knopf, 1926), pp. 277–282;

Gorham B. Munson, "The Limbo of American Literature," *Broom,* 2 (June 1922): 250–260;

Morse Peckham, "Edgar Saltus and the Heroic Decadence," *Tulane Studies in English,* 23 (1978): 61–69;

Percival Pollard, *Their Day in Court* (New York: Neale, 1909), pp. 81–87;

Ruth E. Stephenson, "Literary Techniques, Background and Ideas of Edgar Saltus," dissertation, University of Wisconsin, 1953;

Arthur Symons, "Edgar Saltus," in his *Dramatis Personae* (Indianapolis: Bobbs-Merrill, 1923), pp. 263–269;

Carl Van Vechten, "Edgar Saltus," in his *Excavations* (New York: Knopf, 1926), pp. 89–128;

Beverly E. Warner, "Practical Pessimism," *New Englander and Yale Review,* 229 (June 1888): 432–442.

Papers:

The Beinicke Library at Yale University holds a significant archive of Edgar Saltus's papers. Claire Sprague also mentions other collections, such as the Clifton Waller Barrett Collection at the University of Virginia, the Brander Matthews Collection at Columbia University, and the Henry E. Huntington Library.

William Joseph Snelling
(Solomon Bell)
(26 December 1804 – 24 December 1848)

Mary R. Reichardt
University of St. Thomas

BOOKS: *Tales of the Northwest; or, Sketches of Indian Life and Character, by a Resident Beyond the Frontier,* anonymous (Boston: Hilliard, Gray, Little, & Wilkins, 1830);

Tales of Travels West of the Mississippi, as Solomon Bell (Boston: Gray & Bowen, 1830);

Truth: A New Year's Gift for Scribblers, anonymous (Boston: Foster, 1831); revised and augmented as *Truth, a Gift for Scribblers, with Additions and Emendations* (Boston: Printed for the Author, 1831; revised again, Boston: Mussey, 1832);

The Polar Regions of the Western Continent Explored: Embracing a Geographical Account of Iceland, Greenland, the Islands of the Frozen Sea, and the Northern Parts of the American Continent . . . Together with the Adventures, Discoveries, Dangers, and Trials of Parry, Franklin, Lyon, and other Navigators, in Those Regions (Boston: Reed, 1831);

Tales of Travels in Central Africa: Including Denham and Clapperton's Expedition, Park's First and Second Journey, Tuckey's Voyage up the Congo, Bowditch's Account of the Mission to Ashantee, Clapperton's Second Expedition, and Caillie's Travels to Timbuctoo, as Bell (Boston: Gray & Bowen, 1831);

Tales of Travels in the North of Europe: Including Brooks' Travels in Lapland, Conway's Travels in Norway, Sweden, and Denmark and Granville's Travels in Russia and Poland, as Bell (Boston: Gray & Bowen, 1831; Boston: Gray & Bowen / Philadelphia: Key & Mielke, 1831; Boston: Gray & Bowen / New York: Collins & Hannay, 1831);

A Brief and Impartial History of the Life and Actions of Andrew Jackson. By A Freeman, anonymous (Boston: Stimpson & Clapp, 1831);

Exposé of the Vice of Gaming, as It Lately Existed in Massachusetts: Being a Series of Essays and Reports with Notes and Emendations Originally Published in the New-England Galaxy (Boston: Snelling, 1833);

The Rat-Trap; or, Cogitations of a Convict in the House of Correction, anonymous (Boston: Thomson, Weeks, Jordan, 1837; revised, 1837).

Editions: *William Joseph Snelling's Tales of the Northwest,* edited, with an introduction, by John T. Flanagan (Minneapolis: University of Minnesota Press, 1936);

Tales of the Northwest, Masterworks of Literature Series (New Haven: College & University Press, 1975).

OTHER: "Te Zahpahtah: A Sketch From Indian History," anonymous, in *The Token: A Christmas and New Year's Present,* edited by S. G. Goodrich (Boston: Gray & Bowen, 1831): 143–151;

"Nonona: A Tale of Indian Fortitude," anonymous, in *Youth's Keepsake: A Christmas and New-Year's Gift for Young People* (Boston: Broaders, 1835), pp. 91–111;

"A Night in the Woods," in *The Boston Book. Being Specimens of Metropolitan Literature, Occasional and Periodical,* edited by Henry T. Tuckerman (Boston: Light & Horton, 1836), pp. 40–48;

Eugène Sue, *The Lover's Chase,* translated by Snelling (Boston: Published for the author, 1845).

SELECTED PERIODICAL PUBLICATIONS–UNCOLLECTED: "The Fortunes of Mendokaycheenah," anonymous, *New-England Magazine,* 3 (October 1832): 290–296;

"Shoankah Shahpah," anonymous, *New-England Magazine,* 4 (March 1833): 187–195;

"The Last of the Iron Hearts," anonymous, *American Monthly Magazine,* 1 (March 1836): 239–244.

William Joseph Snelling was not a man to be ignored. In his relatively brief life, every role he assumed—explorer, interpreter, journalist, editor, author, critic, reformer—was played with an energy so intense it inevitably earned him the respect of many admirers and the scorn of an equal number of enemies. Though his published work runs the gamut from children's literature to inflammatory rhetorical essays, Snelling is best known today for his short stories detailing the lives and lore of Native American tribes in what is now the upper Midwest.

Born in Boston on 26 December 1804, William Joseph Snelling was the only child of Elizabeth Bell and Josiah Snelling, a military officer who won distinction at the battle of Tippecanoe in 1811. After his mother's death in 1810, William lived with relatives while attending Luther Stearn's school in Medford, Massachusetts, while his father, who married his second wife, Abigail Hunt, in 1812, continued with his military career. In 1818 William entered the United States Military Academy at West Point, New York. His father was appointed commander of the U.S. Fifth Infantry in 1819, and the following year the regiment went west to Fort St. Anthony (later renamed Fort Snelling), near present-day St. Paul, Minnesota.

With the characteristic restlessness that was to mark his entire career, William Snelling left West Point at age sixteen and headed west to join his father. After wintering with a band of Dakota Indians, probably near Prairie Du Chien, Wisconsin, Snelling arrived at the fort in 1821. For the next seven years he led a life full of adventure, working as a fur trader and army scout. His knowledge of the Dakota language and culture made him useful on many occasions as an interpreter. He also played an important role as mediator between the white settlers and Native American tribes dwelling in the vicinity of the fort and in the suppression of an uprising by Winnebago Indians in 1827.

He married Dionice Fournier, a French-Canadian woman, at Fort St. Anthony in 1826, but she died the following year. After his father's death early in 1828, Snelling returned to Boston, where he embarked on a career as an author and journalist. Writing primarily under the name Solomon Bell, he published several realistic travel and adventure books for children over the next few years, including *Tales of Travels West of the Mississippi* (1830), the popular *Tales of Travels in Central Africa: Including Denham and Clapperton's Expedition, Park's First and Second Journey, Tuckey's Voyage up the Congo, Bowditch's Account of the Mission to Ashantee, Clapperton's Second Expedition, and Caillie's Travels to Timbuctoo* (1831), and the equally popular *The Polar Regions of the Western Continent Explored: Embracing a Geographical Account of Iceland, Greenland, the Islands of the Frozen Sea, and the Northern Parts of the American Continent; Together with the Adventures, Discoveries, Dangers, and Trials of Parry, Franklin, Lyon, and Other Navigators, in Those Regions* (1831). He also wrote an anonymously published biography, *A Brief and Impartial History of the Life and Actions of Andrew Jackson. By A Free Man* (1831). During this period his long verse satire, *Truth: A New Year's Gift for Scribblers* (1831), established him as a

William J. Snelling's father, Col. Josiah Snelling

caustic yet perceptive critic of the state of early-nineteenth-century American letters. Mock epic in tone, the poem outraged authors whom Snelling pronounced mere poetasters and hacks; the work threw literary Boston into an uproar. Although he scorned many writers of large ego and small talent ("Moths, millers, gnats, and butterflies, I sing"), Snelling's venom was particularly directed at those who depicted Native Americans as stereotypes, especially those who romanticized them as "Noble Savages." Of John Augustus Stone's popular play *Metamora; or, The Last of the Wampanoags: An Indian Tragedy in Five Acts* (1829), for example, Snelling writes,

Here's St-ne, for instance, with his Indian piece,
His broken English, clap-traps, paint, and grease,
Throws mother Nature into ague fits,
And for his pains five hundred dollars gets.

On the other hand, *Truth* also enhanced the reputations of those writers such as William Cullen Bryant whose work Snelling praised as genuine art. Published in

Fort Snelling in Minnesota, named after Colonel Snelling. William Snelling was a fur trader and army scout here from 1821 to 182 8 (sketch by Major John Bliss, 1833; from Marcus L. Hansen, Old Fort Snelling, 1819–1858, *1958)*

revised and augmented editions in 1831 and 1832, *Truth* was an influential if not infamous document in its time and remains a notable contribution to American satiric verse. It especially warrants comparison with James Russell Lowell's *A Fable for Critics* (1848), which it anticipated by seventeen years.

Between 1828 and 1848 Snelling was a regular contributor of fiction, nonfiction, and poetry to a variety of magazines and newspapers, including *The New-England Magazine, The North American Review,* and *The American Monthly.* He also published pieces in gift books or literary annuals, such as *Youth's Keepsake: A Christmas and New-Year's Gift for Young People.* He served stints as editor of both the *New-England Galaxy* and *The Boston Herald.* As a journalist Snelling threw himself vigorously into reform campaigns. While editor of the *New-England Galaxy,* for example, he used his position to attempt to abolish gambling in Boston. Snelling published a collection of his editorials on the topic, *Exposé of the Vice of Gaming, as It Lately Existed in Massachusetts: Being a Series of Essays and Reports with Notes and Emendations Originally Published in the New-England Galaxy* (1833), in order to help defray his legal expenses. In 1837, having served a four-month jail sentence for public drunkenness, he published a rambling pamphlet advocating prison reform, *The Rat-Trap; or, Cogitations of a Convict in the House of Correction.* Snelling's second wife, Mary Leaverett, whom he had married sometime after he returned to Boston,

died in 1837. He married for a third time on 2 March 1838. His wife, Lucy Jordan, with whom he had three daughters, bore the youngest eight months after his death.

While best known in his time for the publication of *Truth,* Snelling is recognized today primarily for his contributions to the development of the American short story. Soon after returning to Boston from the frontier, he began composing short fiction based on his experiences living among Native American tribes in what would become the upper Midwestern part of the United States. Ten such stories were collected in *Tales of the Northwest; or, Sketches of Indian Life and Character, by a Resident Beyond the Frontier,* published in 1830; others, such as "Te Zahpahtah" (1831) and "The Last of the Iron Hearts" (1836), as well as several narrative poems such as "The Snow Shoe," were never collected. Since Spelling typically published his work either anonymously or using a pseudonym, it is likely that other uncollected pieces have remained unidentified. For example, the stories "The Fortunes of Mendokaycheenah" (1832) and "Shoankah Shaphah" (1833), both published in *The New-England Magazine,* were probably written by Snelling, but his authorship has not been verified.

Snelling's stories are lively and compelling narratives designed, as he states in his preface to *Tales of the Northwest,* to portray Native Americans in a realistic manner. Aware that some aspects of Native American life were already vanishing as the West began to open, Snelling sought to record his experiences for future ages. He particularly wished to correct stereotypes of Native Americans promulgated by contemporary writers. In "The Last of the Iron Hearts," for instance, he writes,

> It is an ungrateful task to write an Indian tale as it should be written; and, what is more, the man is not in America who can do it; or if he be, he has not yet made his appearance in print. So the brave and unfortunate race, so deeply wronged by our fathers and ourselves, pass away, and no data are left to posterity by which to understand their character, save the dull records of incompetent or one-sided chroniclers, and the vague speculations of hasty travellers. . . . we are not going into a dissertation, but beg leave to assure our readers that the Indian is not the ferocious brute of Hubbard and Mather, or the brilliant, romantic, half-French, half-Celtic Mohegan and Yemassee created by Symmes and Cooper. How can men, however talented, describe what they never saw?

Evoking his own experience, Snelling insisted that one "must live, emphatically, *live,* with Indians; share with them their lodges, their food, and their blankets, for years, before he can comprehend their ideas, or enter into their feelings."

Although sometimes lapsing into more of a romantic sensibility than he would have cared to admit, Snelling certainly comes closer than any writer of the period to realistically depicting Native Americans. His Native American characters are complex human beings whose difference from whites is primarily due to circumstantial, not racial factors. In fact, Snelling sought to emphasize the two races' essential similarity. "There are wise and good men among Indians, but they are few and far apart, as in civilized nations, and about in the same proportion to their numbers," he wrote in *Tales of the Northwest;* "they have as many of the vices and follies of human nature as other people, and it is believed no more. . . . the heart of man beats neither slower nor faster under a blanket than beneath a coat or waistcoat." Throughout his writing Snelling strove for realistic description. In his 1980 article "Antipode to Cooper: Rhetoric and Reality in William Joseph Snelling's 'The Bois Brulé'" Todd Gray Willy points out how Snelling's unadorned description of an Indian territory fort vividly contrasts with James Fenimore Cooper's romanticized and picturesque portrait of Fort William Henry in *The Last of the Mohicans* (1826). Snelling, who had seen his father direct much of the construction of Fort St. Anthony, which was not completed until 1823, paints a less romantic and more squalid picture:

> The reader must not suppose that the Forts of the Indian country are constructed to the rules of Vauban. On the contrary, there are mere stockades of pickets around the stores and dwellings of the traders and their people. These edifices are built of logs, rudely squared by the axe and plastered with clay. They contain a heterogenous population, Indians, whites, and their squaw wives and half breed children, dogs, and in consequence, fleas unnumerable. . . . Besides this, a trading fort is the sanctuary of all evil odors.

Although they sometimes lack unity and read more like sketches than polished short stories, Snelling's tales are engaging. Several of the stories in *Tales of the Northwest* retell Native American legends and take place before the arrival of white settlers. Other stories depict the cultural conflict resulting from the increasing white encroachment on Native American lands or from intertribal tensions. Throughout all of the stories, however, Snelling is less interested in depicting ethnographic details than in exploring the psychology of his Native American and white protagonists. "The Captive" concerns an Indian youth who, overcome by a sudden impulse, shoots the two white men for whom he is serving as a scout. When caught, tried, and sentenced to execution for the crime, he goes to his death with stoic courage, accepting full responsibility for his act. "The Hohay" is based on an Indian tale of warfare between two tribes over a woman stolen by her lover, and "Weenokhenchah Wandeeteekah" is a tragic Indian romance in which one wife kills herself and her baby because her husband has preferred his other wife to her. "La Butte des Mortes" details the 1725 battle between the French and the Sac Indians. "Charles Hess" is a fictionalization of an actual incident in the life of a white frontiersman who married an Indian woman. While Hess is hunting one day, his family is slaughtered in a Dakota raid, and the old man is forced to beg the chief for the life of his one surviving daughter. "The Bois Brulé," by far the longest story in the volume, takes as its plot the reception of a "half-breed, William Gordon" by both Native American and white societies. Exploring the socially taboo subject of miscegenation (a topic Cooper flirts with but finally avoids in *The Last of the Mohicans*), Snelling envisions in his protagonist some type of reconciliation between the white and red races as he speculates on a new breed of men rising in the west: "The halfbreeds of the North-west are physically a fine race of men. The mixture of blood seems an improvement on the Indian and the white. By it, the muscular strength of the one, and the easy grace, and the power of endurance of the other, are blended."

Tales of the Northwest was well received. A critic in the July 1830 issue of *The North American Review* wrote that the work's "descriptions of nature, both living and inanimate, have a striking air of truth and fidelity, and the style of execution is marked throughout with great freedom and power." Nearly a century later, Fred Lewis Pattee claimed in his *Development of the American Short Story* (1923) that Snelling's "Indian stories are undoubtedly the best written during the early period."

Snelling died of apoplexy, or "congestion of the brain," in 1848 at the age of forty-four in Chelsea, Massachusetts, and was buried in Boston. A combative journalist and early champion of the power of the press to effect social reform, Snelling was also one of the first to call for realism in fiction, prefiguring the intense debate on the issue following the Civil War. Along with Washington Irving and Nathaniel Hawthorne, he was among the first American writers to produce a unified collection of short fiction. His stories remain significant as perhaps the most accurate fictional portrayals of the upper Midwest's Native American groups written during the early national period; as such, they are important early local-color narratives relating many facts about Native American and frontier life.

References:

Lucille B. Emch, ed., "An Indian Tale by William Joseph Snelling," *Minnesota History,* 26 (September 1945): 211–221;

Elizabeth Evans, "William Joseph Snelling: Still a Forgotten Critic," *Markham Review,* 5 (Fall 1975): 15–20;

John T. Flanagan, "William Joseph Snelling, Forgotten Critic," *Philological Quarterly,* 16 (October 1937): 376–393;

Flanagan, "William Joseph Snelling's Western Narratives," *Minnesota History,* 17 (December 1936): 437–443;

Todd Gray Willy, "Antipode to Cooper: Rhetoric and Reality in William Joseph Snelling's 'The Bois Brulé,'" *Studies in American Fiction,* 8 (Spring 1980): 69–79;

Willy, "Literary Realism as Anti-Racism: The Case of William Joseph Snelling," *Old Northwest,* 15 (Fall 1991): 143–161;

Allen E. Woodall, "William Joseph Snelling, 1804–1848: A Review of His Life and Writings," dissertation, University of Pittsburgh, 1932;

Woodall, "William Joseph Snelling and the Early Northwest," *Minnesota History,* 10 (December 1929): 367–385.

Papers:

The largest collection of William Joseph Snelling's papers and other memorabilia is at the Minnesota Historical Society, St. Paul.

Elizabeth Stoddard

(6 May 1823 – 1 August 1902)

Jennifer Hynes

BOOKS: *The Morgesons* (New York: Carleton, 1862; revised edition, New York: Cassell, 1889);

Two Men: A Novel (New York: Bunce & Huntington, 1865; revised edition, New York: Cassell, 1888);

Temple House: A Novel (New York: Carleton, 1867; revised edition, New York: Cassell, 1888);

Lolly Dinks's Doings, as His Mother, Old Mrs. Dinks (Boston: Gill, 1874);

Poems (Boston & New York: Houghton, Mifflin, 1895);

The Morgesons and Other Writings, Published and Unpublished, by Elizabeth Stoddard, edited by Lawrence Buell and Sandra A. Zagarell (Philadelphia: University of Pennsylvania Press, 1984).

OTHER: *Remember! A Keepsake,* edited by Richard Henry and Elizabeth Stoddard (New York: Leavitt, 1869); republished as *Readings and Recitations From Modern Authors* (Chicago & New York: Belford, Clark, 1884).

SELECTED PERIODICAL PUBLICATIONS– UNCOLLECTED:

POETRY

"Sunset," anonymous, *Russell's Magazine,* 1 (June 1857): 223;

"A Woman's Dream," anonymous, *Harper's Monthly,* 15 (June 1857): 77;

"Still Unknown," anonymous, *Harper's Monthly,* 24 (December 1861): 83;

"Mary Booth," *New York Evening Post,* 2 March 1863, p. 1;

"Childless," *Harper's Monthly,* 30 (May 1865): 696;

"The Perverse," *Harper's Monthly,* 46 (May 1873): 830;

"The Difference," anonymous, *Harper's Monthly,* 40 (February 1875): 322;

"The Story of the Leaf," *Independent,* 48 (12 November 1896): 1509.

FICTION

"Our Christmas Party," anonymous, *Harper's Monthly,* 17 (January 1859): 202–205;

"My Own Story," anonymous, *Atlantic Monthly,* 5 (May 1860): 526–547;

Elizabeth Stoddard

"What Fort Sumter Did For Me," anonymous, *Vanity Fair,* 3 (25 May 1861): 241–243;

"Gone to the War," anonymous, *Vanity Fair,* 4 (21 December 1861): 275–276;

"Eros and Anteros," *New York Leader,* 22 February 1862, pp. 2–3;

"A Partie Caree," *Harper's Monthly,* 25 (September 1862): 466–479;

"Tuberoses," *Harper's Monthly,* 26 (January 1863): 191–197;

"Sally's Choice," *Harper's Weekly,* 7 (30 May 1863): 342;

"Osgood's Predicament," *Harper's Monthly,* 27 (June 1863): 52–61;

"The Prescription," *Harper's Monthly,* 28 (May 1864): 794–800;

"Gull's Bluff," *Harper's Monthly,* 31 (July 1865): 208–213;

"The Chimneys," *Harper's Monthly,* 31 (November 1865): 721–732;

"Lucy Tavish's Journey," *Harper's Monthly,* 35 (October 1867): 656–663;

"Unexpected Blows," *Harper's Monthly,* 36 (December 1867): 64–74;

"The Inevitable Crisis," *Harper's Monthly,* 36 (January 1868): 248–256;

"Accidents Will Happen," *Putnam's,* new series 1 (April 1868): 487–498;

"My Uncle," *Public Spirit,* 3 (April–June 1868): 50–55, 81–87, 173–178;

"The Visit," *Harper's Monthly,* 37 (November 1868): 802–809;

"Captain Bond," *Hearth and Home,* 1 (2 January 1869): 28–29;

"Becky Bradley," *Hearth and Home,* 1 (23 January 1869): 75–76;

"Bester My Grandfather," *Hearth and Home,* 1 (20 February 1869): 141;

"A Violin Stop," *Putnam's,* new series 3 (February–March 1869): 176–184, 277–286;

"Boots," *Appleton's Journal,* 2 (30 October 1869): 324–327;

"Me and My Son," *Harper's Monthly,* 41 (July 1870): 213–221;

"The Tea-Party," *Appleton's Journal,* 6 (7 October 1871): 400–405;

"A Dead-Lock and Its Key," *Harper's Weekly,* 15 (4 November 1871): 1042–1043;

"About Misers," as Betsy Drew, *Aldine,* 5 (May 1872): 99;

"Out of the Deeps," *Aldine,* 5 (May 1872): 94–95;

"Concerning Two Voyages," *Harper's Weekly,* 16 (22 June 1872): 490–491;

"In the Garden," as Drew, *Aldine,* 5 (July 1872): 138;

"A Woman's Eternity," as Elizabeth B. Leonard, *Aldine,* 5 (October 1872): 204–205;

"Interludes," *Aldine,* 6 (March 1873): 52–54;

"The Ball on the Ice," as Leonard, *Aldine,* 6 (April 1873): 77–78;

"Young Martin and Old Martin," *Aldine,* 6 (June 1873): 116–117;

"Waiting at the Station," *Harper's Bazar,* 6 (26 July 1873): 470–471;

"Nature's Forest Volume," *Aldine,* 6 (August 1873): 161–162;

"On the Trap," as Leonard, *Aldine,* 6 (September 1873): 181;

"The Swanstream Match," *Appleton's Journal,* new series 5 (October 1878): 336–347;

"Love Will Find Out the Way," *Harper's Monthly,* 45 (September 1882): 567–576;

"Merely a Young Woman," *Harper's Weekly,* 29 (6 June 1885): 362–363;

"A Study for a Heroine," *Independent,* 37 (24 September 1885): 1246–1248;

"Among the Haunts of the Pioneer Novelist," *Independent,* 41 (12 September 1889): 1171;

"Niagara Falls," *Independent,* 41 (3 October 1889): 1268;

"In Town Again," *Independent,* 41 (7 November 1889): 1457;

"The Threads Leading to Thanksgiving," *Independent,* 41 (28 November 1889): 1592–1595;

"Polly Dossett's Rule," *Harper's Monthly,* 80 (January 1890): 267–278;

"Book-Makers," *Independent,* 42 (27 February 1890): 273;

"The Quest of Memory," *Independent,* 42 (3 April 1890): 448;

"The Calico Magpie," *Independent,* 42 (3 July 1890): 940;

"Betty's Downfall," *Independent,* 43 (23 April 1891): 620–621;

"A Wheatfield Idyl," *Harper's Monthly,* 83 (September 1891): 571–581;

"Mrs. Jed and the Evolution of Our Shanghais," *Independent,* 43 (3 September 1891): 1330–1331;

"My June Jaunt," *Independent,* 44 (21 July, 8 August, 25 August 1892): 1008, 1146–1147, 1182–1183;

"My 'Twa Dogs," *Independent,* 45 (20 July 1893): 970–971;

"A Day in an Old Country House," *Independent,* 46 (16 August 1894): 1045–1046;

"Aux Italiens," *Independent,* 47 (17 January 1895): 70–71;

"An Exposition of Ignorance," *Independent,* 47 (11 July 1895): 922.

NONFICTION

"From Our Lady Correspondent," seventy-five biweekly columns for the *San Francisco Daily Alta California,* 8 October 1854 – 28 February 1858;

"Hearth and Home Travels," *Hearth and Home,* 1 (8, 15, 22, 29 May 1869): 315, 331, 348–349, 364;

"A Literary Whim," *Appleton's Journal,* 6 (14 October 1871): 440–441;

"Women in Art–Rosa Bonheur," as Leonard, *Aldine,* 5 (July 1872): 145;

"Literary Folk As They Came and Went With Ourselves," *Saturday Evening Post,* 5 (20, 30 June 1900): 1126–1127, 1222–1223.

Elizabeth Stoddard earned little popular notice and moderate critical attention in her day, but she has since been recognized as an early experimenter with realism. Her three novels demonstrate an attention to the psychological intricacies of characters and an attempt to avoid whitewashing life with stock sentiment. Much of Stoddard's short fiction, written for magazines with the hope of quick financial gain, tends toward the standard plots and sentimental rhetoric of the women's fiction of her day, but some of her stories stand out as honest portrayals of character or distinctive situations. Because of her focus on hidden passions and the darker side of domestic life, modern critics have compared her fiction with that of Romantic writers such as Nathaniel Hawthorne and the Brontë sisters.

The oldest of two daughters and six sons born to Wilson and Betsy Drew Barstow, Elizabeth Drew Barstow was born on 6 May 1823 in the coastal town of Mattapoisett, Massachusetts. While her father's successful shipbuilding business allowed the family to enjoy prosperity and a respected social position during most of Elizabeth's childhood, occasional business failures checked the Barstows' security. In 1837 and again in 1840–1841 Elizabeth attended Wheaton Female Seminary, where she disliked the overt evangelical Protestant atmosphere and pressure to conform. Much of her true education came from reading works she selected from the library of a local Congregationalist minister, Thomas Robbins, including the classics of eighteenth-century English literature.

Many of the details of life in the isolated coastal town of Mattapoisett, as well as Elizabeth's experiences as the privileged daughter of a shipbuilding father and her turbulent relationship with her only sister, appear in her fiction, most notably in her first novel. By the time she visited New York in the fall of 1851, she had enough interest in literature to attend literary evenings at the home of Anne Lynch. Her first publication came in October 1852, when "Phases," a reverie, appeared in George and Evert Duyckinck's *Literary World*.

In December 1852 Elizabeth Barstow married Richard Henry Stoddard. The poor son of a sea captain, Richard Stoddard struggled to earn a living by writing poetry in an outdated Romantic mode and taking on whatever literary hackwork he could find. In 1853 he landed a job in the New York Custom House with the help of Nathaniel Hawthorne (who was a distant cousin of Elizabeth). Richard held this job for sixteen years, and in 1866 he assisted Herman Melville in also finding a position there. Because of their impoverished circumstances, the Stoddards moved frequently, living in boardinghouses and apartments in Brooklyn and Manhattan.

By 1854 Elizabeth Stoddard was polishing her poetry with the help of her husband and publishing poems in *The Knickerbocker Magazine*. Richard praised his wife's verse to outsiders, but within their literary circle more pointed, sophisticated criticism of each member's writing was the norm. The candid nature of the "Genteel Circle"—as the group of poets that included Richard

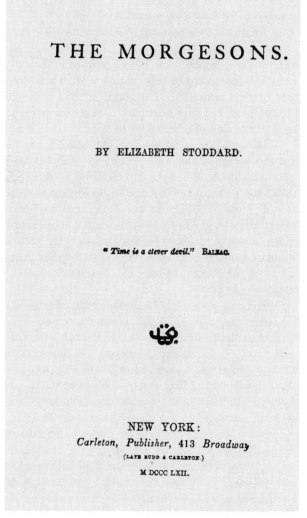

THE MORGESONS.

BY ELIZABETH STODDARD.

" *Time is a clever devil.*" BALZAC.

NEW YORK:
Carleton, Publisher, 413 Broadway
(LATE RUDD & CARLETON.)
M DCCC LXII.

Title page for Stoddard's first novel, set in a coastal village that closely resembles her hometown of Mattapoisett, Massachusetts

Stoddard, Bayard Taylor, and George Henry Boker was called—might have contributed to Elizabeth Stoddard's decision to continue her apprenticeship by writing for a newspaper three thousand miles from home, the *San Francisco Daily Alta California*. From October 1854 through February 1858 Stoddard contributed a biweekly column to the newspaper, discussing literary, artistic, dramatic, social, and political occurrences in New York and commenting on politics in Europe. Other incentives might have been a desire to maintain ties with her favorite brother, Wilson, who had gone to the West Coast during the gold rush, and the Stoddards' need for the twelve dollars per column that her letters earned. Headed "From Our Lady Correspondent" and signed "E.D.B.," Stoddard's columns became the most popular regular feature of the newspaper. During the late 1850s and early 1860s Stoddard also published poetry and short stories in *Harper's Monthly*, *The Atlantic Monthly*, *Van-*

ity Fair, and other magazines and newspapers, earning as much as $100 for a piece of short fiction.

All three of the Stoddards' sons predeceased their parents. Wilson Stoddard, born in 1855, died of scarlet fever in 1861. Another son, born deformed in the early spring of 1859, died in July of that year. Their third son, Edwin Lorimer Stoddard, born in 1863, survived to adulthood, but after beginning a successful career as an actor, he died of tuberculosis in 1901.

When Thomas Wentworth Higginson made his first visit to Emily Dickinson's home in Amherst, Massachusetts, he described the experience in a 16 August 1870 letter to his wife: "I shan't sit up tonight to write you all about E.D. dearest but if you had read Mrs. Stoddard's novels you could understand a house where each member runs his or her own selves." All three of Stoddard's novels deal with characters who pride themselves on their individualism and their somewhat isolated styles of living.

Her first novel, *The Morgesons* (1862), is generally considered her most important. It is a first-person, semi-autobiographical account of the childhood and early adulthood of Cassandra Morgeson, daughter of a wealthy shipbuilding father and an inhabitant of a coastal town much like Mattapoisett. Although the novel recounts the heroine's entrance into adulthood and eventual marriage, these traits are its only similarities to the popular women's fiction of the day, which Stoddard repeatedly derided. Rather than being the nineteenth-century ideal of the true woman (pure, pious, domestic, and submissive), Cassandra abhors the evangelical Protestantism of her townsmen, falls in love with a married man and feels no shame, and shows revulsion toward the drudgery of domestic life. Indeed, the novel does not idealize romantic love. Cassandra's sister, Veronica, is married to an incurable alcoholic and gives birth to a mentally retarded child. While Stoddard's contemporaries found *The Morgesons* something of a puzzle with its spare dialogue and idiosyncratic characters, modern critics have been impressed with Stoddard's realism and the differences between her novel and the usual women's fiction of her day. Sandra Zagarell has argued that the main focus of *The Morgesons* is on Cassandra's search for a role outside those conventionally prescribed for women. Sybil Weir and Stacy Alaimo have both pointed out Stoddard's use of the bildungsroman tradition, which she altered slightly to focus on a female character.

Stoddard's other two novels do not include the same sort of memorable characters as *The Morgesons.* Also set in a coastal town, *Two Men* (1865), which has third-person narration rather than the distinctive first-person narration of *The Morgesons,* focuses on another family of individuals and the outsiders who attempt to

join it. When a carpenter with socialist leanings, Jason Auster (the first of the "two men"), marries into the wealthy and prominent Parke family, he finds it impossible to be more than the dependent husband of his wealthy wife, Sarah. A cold woman who harbors a love for her adventurous, absent cousin, Osmond Luce, Sarah bears one son, whom she names Parke to indicate his allegiance to her maternal lineage. The second of the "two men," Osmond returns briefly to the Parke manor to leave his illegitimate daughter, Philippa—yet another interloper into the Parke clan. Eventually the two outsiders, Jason and Philippa, bond with an honest love that is stronger than any of which the Parkes are capable. *Two Men* also includes a sexual episode between the young Parke Auster and a beautiful mulatto woman, a scene considered scandalous by many of Stoddard's contemporaries. Stoddard's narrator draws no moral lesson from this incident. As Ann Jerome Croce has pointed out, Stoddard aimed not to teach morality but to examine human nature honestly. Modern critics have written little about *Two Men.* Maurice Kramer calls *Two Men* the bleakest of Stoddard's novels, with its cast of cold, shallow characters and its theme of passion as either hypocritical or lawless.

Like her first two books, Stoddard's third novel, *Temple House* (1867), is set in a coastal village and details the lives of a household of individuals. The inhabitants of Temple House, a run-down mansion belonging to the Gates family, live in decayed gentility and a harmony of isolation. Retired sea captain Argus Gates spends his days loafing and contemplating nature (a means of finding peace common in Stoddard's novels) while his brother's wife and daughter, Roxalana and Temple Gates, share the sparsely furnished shell of a home and ponder their neighbors' lives. Temple's closest friend, the wealthy Virginia Brande, seeks a respite in Temple House from her insane mother, her overbearing father, and the pushy suitor her father is trying to force her to marry. While most of the townspeople misunderstand the strange, apparently heathen habits of the Temple House dwellers, Virginia appreciates the honesty and lack of ceremony she finds there. So isolated are the members of the Gates family that even after Temple Gates marries and bears a child she is unable to feel any connection to her helpless infant. While Argus Gates finds a spiritual union with Sebastian Ford, a mysterious sailor whom he saves from a shipwreck, this friendship is one of the few instances in which a Temple House dweller is able to relate to another human being. As in *Two Men, Temple House* ends with a love match between two seemingly incompatible characters. Maurice Kramer finds a kind of grudging transcendentalism and an appreciation of spiritual affections in the novel while Richard Foster has defined the major theme of *Temple House* as the spiritual decay of the New England ruling classes, depicted through the contrast between the poor but spiritually rich Gates family and the wealthy but soulless Brandes.

After the publication of her last novel, Stoddard concentrated on writing short fiction and poetry for magazines. Between 1867 and 1873 Stoddard sold some three dozen stories and sketches and one dozen poems. Many were produced with quick income in mind, but several rank among her best work. Published in *Hearth and Home* in 1869, three accounts of people from her native town–"Captain Bond" (2 January), "Becky Bradley" (23 January), and "Bester My Grandfather" (20 February)–show Stoddard's skill at depicting regional characters. "Collected by a Valetudinarian" (*Harper's Monthly,* December 1870), one of a handful of Stoddard's stories that have been republished in modern editions or anthologies, is written in the form of a woman's reactions to inspecting the journal of a female writer. It is of interest for its similarities to Stoddard's own diary of 1866 and for its innovative form. After Richard Henry Stoddard became editor of *The Aldine* in 1871, Elizabeth began contributing to this magazine regularly. A series of six sketches that she wrote for *The Aldine* was expanded into her only children's book, *Lolly Dinks's Doings* (1874). Focusing on the childish antics of her son Edwin Lorimer Stoddard (Lolly), this book is a curious blend of fairy stories, satire, and incidents that took place in the Stoddards' home. Among the favorable contemporary criticism of *Lolly Dinks's Doings* was the comment that it ranked with Lewis Carroll's *Alice in Wonderland* (1865).

Mired in poverty and illness and despairing of ever achieving literary fame, Stoddard wrote little after 1874. When revised editions of all three of her novels were published in 1888 and 1889, they caused a small flurry of attention among critics and readers who had become more receptive to Stoddard's realism. Some of this attention must have been owing to Edmund Clarence Stedman's favorable preface to *Two Men.* Requests for stories and poems encouraged Stoddard to take up her pen once again, but the small revival of interest in her work soon faded. Among those who noticed Stoddard's writing was the influential editor and realistic fiction writer William Dean Howells, who helped Stoddard find a publisher for a collection of her verse, *Poems* (1895), most of it previously published in magazines.

A final tribute to the aging Stoddard occurred in 1901, when her three novels were reprinted from the plates of the 1888–1889 edition. No revival of interest ensued this time. The few reviews that were written referred to Stoddard's fiction as out of date. She died of double pneumonia on 1 August 1902 and was buried in Sag Harbor, New York.

References:

Stacy Alaimo, "Elizabeth Stoddard's *The Morgesons:* A Feminist Dialogue of Bildung and Descent," *Legacy,* 8 (Spring 1991): 29–37;

Lawrence Buell, "Provincial Gothic: Hawthorne, Stoddard, and Others," in his *New England Literary Culture: From Revolution Through Renaissance* (Cambridge: Cambridge University Press, 1986), pp. 351–370;

Ann Jerome Croce, "Phantoms From an Ancient Loom: Elizabeth Barstow Stoddard and the American Novel, 1860–1900," dissertation, Brown University, 1988;

Croce, "A Woman Outside Her Time: Elizabeth Barstow Stoddard (1823–1910) and Nineteenth-Century American Popular Fiction," *Women's Studies,* 19 (1991): 357–369;

Richard Foster, "The Fiction of Elizabeth Stoddard: An American Discovery," in *Geschichte und Fiktion: Amerikanische Prosa im 19. Jahrhundert / History and Fiction: American Prose in the 19th Century,* edited by Alfred Weber and Hartmut Grandel (Gottingen, Germany: Vandenhoeck & Ruprecht, 1972), pp. 161–193;

Foster, introduction to *The Morgesons* (New York: Johnson Reprint, 1971);

Alfred Habegger, "The Chains of Literature: Elizabeth Stoddard and Henry James," in his *Henry James and the "Woman Business"* (New York: Cambridge University Press, 1989), pp. 85–101;

Leila Assumpcao Harris, "The Marriage Tradition in the Novels of Elizabeth Stoddard," dissertation, Texas Tech University, 1990;

Susan K. Harris, "Projecting the 'I'/Conoclast: First-Person Narration in *The Morgesons,*" in her *19th-Century American Women's Novels: Interpretative Strategies* (Cambridge: Cambridge University Press, 1992), pp. 152–170;

Harris, "Stoddard's *The Morgesons:* A Contextual Evaluation," *ESQ: A Journal of the American Renaissance,* 31 (1985): 11–22;

John B. Humma, "Realism and Beyond: The Imagery of Sex and Sexual Oppression in Elizabeth Stoddard's 'Lemorne Versus Huell,'" *South Atlantic Review,* 58 (January 1993): 33–47;

Dean H. Keller, "Mrs. Stoddard's 'Stories,'" *American Notes & Queries,* 7 (1969): 131–132;

James Kraft, "An Unpublished Review by Henry James," *Studies in Bibliography,* 20 (1967): 267–273;

Maurice Kramer, "Alone at Home with Elizabeth Stoddard," *American Transcendental Quarterly,* 47–48 (1980): 159–170;

James H. Matlack, "*The Alta California*'s Lady Correspondent," *New York Historical Society Quarterly,* 58 (1974): 280–303;

Matlack, "Early Reviews of *Walden* by the *Alta California* and its 'Lady Correspondent,'" *Thoreau Society Bulletin,* 131 (1975): 1–2;

Matlack, "Hawthorne and Elizabeth Barstow Stoddard," *New England Quarterly,* 50 (1977): 278–302;

Matlack, "The Literary Career of Elizabeth Barstow Stoddard," dissertation, Yale University, 1967;

Nancy Kay McQuistion, "Psychological Realism in Elizabeth Stoddard's *The Morgesons*," thesis, Texas A&M University, 1988;

Edmund Clarence Stedman, "Mrs. Stoddard's Novels" and "Mrs. Stoddard's Poems," in his *Genius and Other Essays* (New York: Moffat, 1911), pp. 154–165;

Richard Henry Stoddard, *Recollections, Personal and Literary,* edited by Ripley Hitchcock (New York: Barnes, 1903);

Sybil Weir, "*The Morgesons:* A Neglected Feminist Bildungsroman," *New England Quarterly,* 49 (1976): 427–439;

Weir, "Our Lady Correspondent: The Achievement of Elizabeth Drew Stoddard," *San Jose Studies,* 10, no. 2 (1984): 73–91;

Sandra A. Zagarell, "Legacy Profile: Elizabeth Drew Barstow Stoddard (1823–1902)," *Legacy,* 8 (Spring 1991): 39–49;

Zagarell, "The Repossession of a Heritage: Elizabeth Stoddard's *The Morgesons*," *Studies in American Fiction,* 13 (1985): 45–56.

Papers:
Elizabeth Stoddard's materials are scattered in some two dozen research libraries, often catalogued along with those of her husband, Richard Henry Stoddard. Major collections of her correspondence and manuscripts are at the New York Public Library, the Columbia University Library, the Boston Public Library, the American Antiquarian Society, the Colby College Library, the Middlebury College Library, the Houghton Library at Harvard University, the Library of Congress, the Historical Society of Pennsylvania, and the Henry E. Huntington Library at San Marino, California.

William Leete Stone

(20 April 1792 – 15 August 1844)

Boyd Childress
Auburn University

BOOKS: *Letters on Masonry and Anti-Masonry, addressed to the Hon. John Quincy Adams* (New York: Halsted, 1832);

Tales and Sketches–Such as They Are, 2 volumes (New York: Harper, 1834; Glasgow: Griffin, 1848);

Stories for Children, Founded in Fact (Concord, N.H., 1834);

Stories for the Nursery in Words of One or Two Syllables (Philadelphia: Morgan, 1834);

Matthias and His Impostures; or, The Progress of Fanaticism, Illustrated in the Extraordinary Case of Robert Matthews and Some of his Forerunners and Disciples (New York: Harper, 1835);

The Mysterious Bridal and Other Tales, 3 volumes (New York: Harper, 1835);

Maria Monk and the Nunnery of the Hotel Dieu; Being an Account of a Visit to the Convents of Montreal and Refutation of the "Awful Disclosures" (New York: Howe & Bates, 1836); republished as *Maria Monk's "Awful Disclosures" Completely Exposed; or, A Visit to Montreal and An Examination of the Hotel Dieu Nunnery* (London: Andrews, 1836);

Ups and Downs in the Life of a Distressed Gentleman, as "the author of 'Tales and Sketches, such as they are'" (New York: Leavitt, Lord / Boston: Crocker & Brewster, 1836);

Letter to Doctor A. Brigham on Animal Magnetism: Being an Account of a Remarkable Interview between the Author and Miss Loraina Brackett while in a State of Somnambulism (New York: Dearborn, 1837; revised edition, 1837);

The Witches: A Tale of New-England, anonymous (Bath, N.Y.: Underhill, 1837); republished as *Mercy Disborough: A Tale of New England Witchcraft* (Bath, N.Y.: Underhill, 1844);

Life of Joseph Brant-Thayendanegea: Including the Border Wars of the American Revolution, and Sketches of the Indian Campaigns of Generals Harmar, St. Clair, and Wayne, 2 volumes (New York: Blake, 1838);

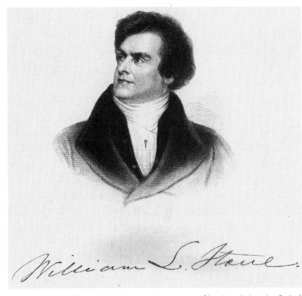

(American Antiquarian Society)

The Life and Times of Red-Jacket, or Sa-go-ye-wat-ha, Being the Sequel to the History of the Six Nations (New York & London: Wiley & Putnam, 1841);

The Poetry and History of Wyoming: Containing Campbell's Gertrude; with a Biographical Sketch of the Author by Washington Irving, and the History of the Wyoming from its Discovery to the Beginning of the Present Century by William L. Stone, by Stone, Thomas Campbell, and Washington Irving (New York & London: Wiley & Putnam, 1841);

Uncas and Miantonomoh: A Historical Discourse Delivered at Norwich, (Conn.,) on the Fourth Day of July, 1842, on the Occasion of the Erection of a Monument to the Memory of Uncas, the White Man's Friend, and First Chief of the Mohegans (New York: Dayton & Newman, 1842);

Border Wars of the American Revolution, 2 volumes (New York: Harper, 1843);

The Life and Times of Sir William Johnson, bart., 2 volumes, by Stone and William Leete Stone Jr. (Albany: Munsell, 1865).

OTHER: *Reports of the Proceedings and Debates of the Convention of 1821, Assembled for the Purpose of Amending the Constitution of the State of New York: Containing All the Official Documents, Relating to the Subject, and Other Valuable Matter,* edited by Stone and Nathaniel H. Carter (Albany: Hosford, 1821);

"Narrative of the Festivities Observed in Honor of the Completion of the Grand Erie Canal," in *Memoir, Prepared at the Request of a Committee of the Common Council of the City of New York and Presented to the Mayor of the City, at the Celebration of the Completion of the New York Canals,* by Cadwallader D. Golden (New York: Printed by order of the Corporation of New York, 1825), pp. 289–408;

"The Dead of the Wreck," in *The Atlantic Souvenir for 1831* (Philadelphia: Carey & Lea, 1831), pp. 164–193;

"The Grave of the Indian King," in *The Forget-Me-Not* (Philadelphia: Carey, Lea & Carey, 1831), pp. 101–118;

"Murdered Tinman," in *The Forget-Me-Not* (Philadelphia: Carey, Lea & Carey, 1833), pp. 273–290;

"The Skeleton Hand," in *The Forget-Me-Not* (Philadelphia: Carey, Lea & Carey, 1834), pp. 129–151;

"Uncle Zim," in *The Forget-Me-Not* (Philadelphia: Carey, Lea & Carey, 1835), pp. 311–313;

"Life in the Woods," in *The Forget-Me-Not* (Philadelphia: Carey, Lea & Carey, 1836), pp. 55–79;

"Burial of the Immigrant's Babe," in *The Remembrancer; or, Fragments for Leisure Hours . . . Compiled by the Association for the Improvement of Juvenile Books* (Philadelphia: T. Ellwood Chapman/Marshall, Williams & Butler, 1841), pp. 78–81.

SELECTED PERIODICAL PUBLICATION–UNCOLLECTED: "The Spectre Fire-Ship," *Knickerbocker Magazine,* 3 (May 1834): 361–370.

Journeyman newspaperman, editor, essayist, historian, and biographer as well as author of short fiction, William Leete Stone was a Federalist supporter whose role as a political advocate overshadowed the significance of his career as an author and historian of Indians during the American Revolution. In addition to his *Maria Monk and the Nunnery of the Hotel Dieu; Being an Account of a Visit to the Convents of Montreal and Refutation of the "Awful Disclosures"* (1836), *Life of Joseph Brant-Thayendanegea: Including the Border Wars of the American Revolution, and Sketches of the Indian Campaigns of Generals Harmar, St. Clair, and Wayne* (1838), and *The Life and Times of Red-Jacket, or Sa-go-ye-wat-ha, Being the Sequel to the History of the Six Nations* (1841), Stone is best remembered as one of several targets of libel suits filed by America's first great romantic historical novelist, James Fenimore Coo-

per. From 1821 until just before his death in 1844, Stone edited the influential *New York Commercial Advertiser,* advocating support for the Erie Canal, emancipation of slaves, and education. At the same time he was adamant in his opposition to women's rights and woman suffrage. His many books established Stone as a minor author of histories of New York State and New England. His two volumes of short fiction and regional legends contributed to the new nation's struggle for a literary identity. Yet the appearance of a review of Cooper's *History of the Navy of the United States of America* in Stone's newspaper in 1839 led to years of litigation for libel, resolved only after Stone's death in 1844, an episode that is curiously overlooked in entries on Stone in standard reference works.

Stone was born on 20 April 1792, in New Paltz, New York, in the Shawangunk Mountains. His father was William Stone, a Congregationalist minister, Yale graduate, and Revolutionary War soldier. William Stone lived through the major engagements of White Plains, Brandywine, and Monmouth (all American defeats); was present when Benedict Arnold's British contact, Maj. John Andre was executed; and was remembered for carrying a Hebrew Bible and the works of Josephus in his knapsack. After his graduation from Yale, William Stone accepted a church position in New Paltz, where his son was born. The Reverend Stone soon left the church and took up farming along the Susquehanna River, where his son worked the fields by day and learned Latin at night. The area was heavily populated by Native Americans among the other settlers; such an environment, when coupled with Stone's vivid imagination, provided the setting for many of his works. Although living on the frontier, Stone acquired a rudimentary education in classical Latin and Greek and theology, courtesy of his father. Stone's own aspirations overcame those of his strong-willed father, however, and he left home at age seventeen to apprentice at a newspaper office in nearby Cooperstown.

Cooperstown was a rural hamlet in 1809, but it was home to the *Cooperstown Federalist,* a newspaper of modest circulation and influence that provided Stone with his first journalism experience. Col. John H. Prentiss, the owner of the *Federalist,* had begun another paper, the *Herkimer American,* which he left under the charge of an incompetent brother. Stone was sent to neighboring Herkimer and soon took charge of the entire enterprise with Thurlow Weed, who had worked under Stone in Cooperstown as an assistant. Like Stone, Weed was later a target of Cooper's libel suits. Stone bought the paper, but less than a year later he moved to Hudson, where he purchased the *Northern Whig.* Here he also briefly edited two short-lived literary magazines, the *Lounger* and the *Spirit of the Forum.* He relocated again, to the state capital at Albany in 1816, where he bought still another newspaper, *The Albany Daily Advertiser*. The *Daily* merged with *The Albany Gazette,* but the business failed in 1818. During his tenure in Albany, Stone was married on 31 January 1817, to Susannah Pritchard Wayland, whose father was the Reverend Francis Wayland of Saratoga Springs. Stone's new brother-in-law was Francis Wayland, who was president of Brown University from 1827 to 1855. After *The Albany Gazette & Daily Advertiser* failed, the newlyweds moved to Hartford, Connecticut, in 1819, where Stone became editor of the influential Federalist newspaper the *Hartford Mirror*. With support for the Federalists all but dead by then, the once lively political organ gradually became a literary paper and gazette, more in line with Stone's true interests. He was vital in the formation of a Hartford literary club, which briefly published a magazine titled *The Knights of the Round Table.* After two years in Hartford, Stone returned to his native New York and took control of the *New York Commercial Advertiser* in 1821. In twelve years Stone had worked on or owned five newspapers in five communities, but he remained in New York after 1821.

Personally, Stone was good-natured and cheerful, with a persistent resolution to improve and educate himself. He read voraciously and sought out associations with educated people, especially authors such as Cooper, Washington Irving, Robert Charles Sands, and James Gates Percival. His industriousness was legendary among those who knew him and with whom he worked. Stone's father urged him to write plainly and with precision, stressing grammar and accuracy. Writing years after Stone began his career in newspapers and literary magazines, his father warned him that he wrote "with a pen dipped in vinegar."

The father's characterization certainly applies to much of Stone's newspaper writings, as is clearly evidenced in the *New York Commercial Advertiser,* the best known and most prosperous newspaper of its day. Stone's predecessor at the *Commercial Advertiser* was Noah Webster. Stone was both fortunate and skillful as an editor and was able to attract some excellent writers. Frank Luther Mott praised Stone's talent and admired his reputation as a writer of history. In his editorials Stone was an opponent of slavery, a staunch advocate of internal improvements in the form of the Erie Canal, and a supporter of the Clintonians. From his association with Gov. De Witt Clinton, Stone acquired the title "Colonel," which followed him for the rest of his life. Most of his surviving correspondence is addressed to Colonel Stone, and the press of his day widely referred to him as such. In 1828 Stone supported John Quincy Adams in the presidential campaign against Andrew Jackson, and the *Commercial Advertiser* became a Whig

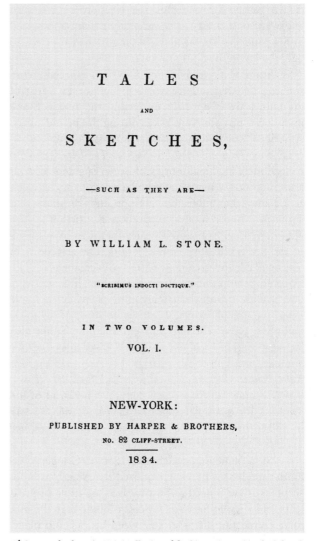

TALES

AND

SKETCHES,

—SUCH AS THEY ARE—

BY WILLIAM L. STONE.

"SCRIBIMUS INDOCTI DOCTIQUE."

IN TWO VOLUMES.

VOL. I.

NEW-YORK:

PUBLISHED BY HARPER & BROTHERS,

NO. 82 CLIFF-STREET.

1834.

Title page for Stone's 1834 collection of Gothic stories set in colonial and revolutionary America

paper—and still later a Republican organ. Stone's opposition to slavery included an outlined plan for emancipation. Another of Stone's causes was the Greek struggle for independence. His campaign to raise money for relief of the Greeks resulted in sending food, clothing, and financial aid to the struggling nation.

Stone's acrimonious pen earned him more than one vituperative response to his editorial stances on political issues. He feuded with several editors but none more than William Cullen Bryant, influential editor of the *New York Evening Post.* Bryant supported the Jacksonian Democrats, while Stone, the old Federalist, opposed the party of the common man. After Stone wrote that no gentleman could possibly support Jackson, Bryant took exception in the form of a physical attack on his larger, stronger opponent. On 20 April 1831 Bryant accosted Stone on the way to his office and set to beating him over the head with a whip. As a small crowd gathered Stone took the weapon from Bryant and went on his way. The next day Bryant apologized in his paper for the incident, saying he had no right to take the law of libel into his own hands.

Stone was a rather prolific writer, especially considering the demands of a newspaper career. Most of his books are historical, concerning the region Stone knew best, upstate New York, during the period of the American Revolution. His first important work, however, was *Tales and Sketches–Such as They Are* (1834), a collection of fictional stories of New England legends and traditions, which established a relationship between Stone and the publishers Harper and Brothers and earned for him a modest reputation as a fiction writer, although his short fiction is nearly forgotten by students of the literary history of the period. The selections in *Tales and Sketches* include a variety of accounts of colonial and revolutionary America. Although Stone took liberty with historical accuracy in his sketches, he made extensive use of historical settings in most of his tales, and they were readable and entertaining. Stone also found a market for them in several magazines, literary annuals, and gift books such as *The Forget-Me-Not, The Knickerbocker Magazine, The Atlantic Club Book, The Token, The Gift*, and *The Biographical Annual*. "The Dead of the Wreck," for example, appeared in *The Atlantic Souvenir* in 1831, three years before the two-volume *Tales and Sketches* was published.

Stone's fiction, much like that of Cooper, was influenced by his times. He utilized the American landscape and had a need to portray it as an arena of great feats. His debt to Sir Walter Scott is obvious in the intimate connection he asserts between history and place. As did many of his fellow Americans, Stone wrote out of a desire to create an American literary establishment, despite the inability of most to make a living from their writing. Stone's contributions were minor compared to many of the icons of early American literature, but he wrote several works of short fiction, most of them collected in *Tales and Sketches*.

Among Stone's better stories is the long story (later published separately, in book form) "Mercy Disborough," considered the best literary use of witchcraft before Hawthorne's "Young Goodman Brown" (1835). Like many of his works of fiction, Stone based "Mercy Disborough" on an historical event–a seventeenth-century Connecticut trial for witchcraft. Mercy Disborough and another young woman are accused and tried, and Mercy is found guilty of witchcraft and sentenced to be burned to death. Claiming her innocence throughout, Mercy is rescued by Indians, illustrating another theme common to much of Stone's writing–the heroic role of Native Americans on the New England frontier. The story is well told and lively, with decent character

development. Another tale, "Grave of the Indian King," occurs during King William's War, and once again Indians are featured. As the Onondaga hear of the advance of an overwhelming French force, they flee their homes, leaving only the old chief to face the enemy. Before his death at the hands of France's Indian allies, the chieftain delivers his last prophecy, predicting the fall of the French and the eventual rise of the English. Stone's use of Indian materials is clear in the words of the aging prophet, still another example of his utilizing what he knew best.

The longest sketch in the two volumes is "The Mysterious Bridal," an eerie tale set in Connecticut in the last quarter of the eighteenth century. Young Samuel Talcott is born into a well-to-do farm family on Thanksgiving Day. From an early age Samuel demonstrates clairvoyant ability; he can divine the whereabouts of a lost cow or a schooner late for arrival. Considered extremely intelligent by all whom he encounters, he excels in his studies at Yale; but at a gala to celebrate his graduation and return home, Esther Peabody, an old woman many consider to be a witch, predicts evil will befall Samuel and his father five years in the future. Samuel meets and falls hopelessly in love with the siren-like Cora, whom he encounters several times over the next few years but with whom he never develops a true relationship. Nearly five years later Samuel is forced to marry Cora in New York. The marriage changes him for the worse in appearance, mood, and his physical health. Five years to the day after old Esther's prediction, Samuel dies. At his funeral she suddenly reappears and speaks of the misfortunes of the Talcotts, then dies herself. As the story ends it is revealed that Esther is the half-sister of the elder Talcott. "The Mysterious Bridal" is not Stone's best work, but his use of local color, and especially the history and various legends of the region, is representative of his style.

Also found in *Tales and Sketches* are Gothic tales typical of national literature of the period. Set during the American Revolution, "The Skeleton Hand" tells the story of a young woman who disappears on the eve of her wedding and whose skeleton is discovered ten years later. Covering a twenty-five year span, the tale focuses on the murderer, Roswell Thornton, who kills the bride-to-be only after she is driven insane from the terror of her abduction. The guilt-ridden Thornton subsequently puts himself in the path of every imaginable danger–the revolutions in the American colonies and France, pirates and warring Indians, and a yellow-fever epidemic in Philadelphia. In the end the skeletal hand of the woman's remains points to Thornton as the murderer, and he is executed for his crime. "The Skeleton Hand" is again reminiscent

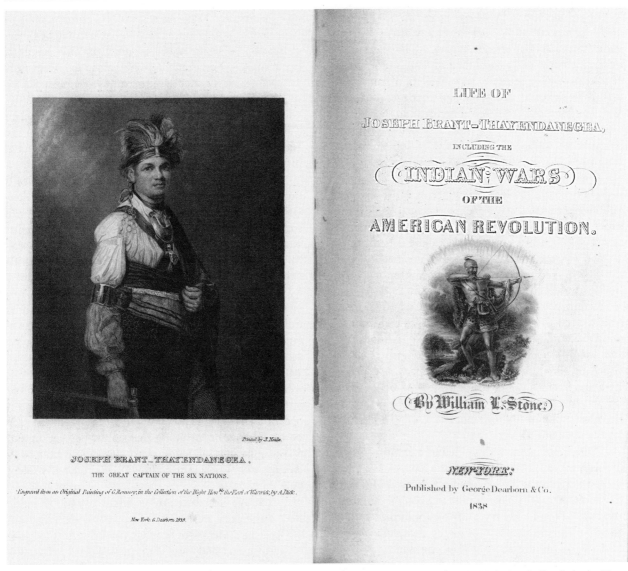

Frontispiece and title page for Stone's biography of the Mohawk military leader who fought in support of the British during the Revolutionary War

of Scott. Another macabre tale is entitled "The Dead of the Wreck," a first-person narrative of a shipwreck in 1828, unusual among Stone's tales in that it takes place well after the Revolution; it also features some of his best writing. In the story a ship sets sail from Quebec to Labrador, runs into a gale, and is rescued by another vessel. When the second ship encounters a winter storm and is wrecked on Anticosta Island in the Gulf of St. Lawrence, the survivors slowly freeze and starve to death. Those hardy enough to survive the cold begin to suffer from starvation and turn to cannibalism, until finally the narrator is the only survivor. He completes the narrative as he awaits his inevitable fate.

"The Spectre Fire-Ship," generally considered Stone's best piece of short fiction, was apparently completed too late for inclusion in *Tales and Sketches*.

Another shipwreck tale, the story was published in *The Knickerbocker* for May 1834; it is in the spirit of other supernatural tales written for *The Knickerbocker* by William Leggett, John Waters, James Hall, and various anonymous writers. "The Spectre Fire-Ship" is set in 1785, and the narrator of the tale, a seaman named Samuel Hoyt, is rescued after the brig *Dove* is shipwrecked off the coast of Connecticut. After six days adrift Hoyt and three shipmates are rescued aboard the *El Dorado,* under Captain Warner. Warner is a respected ship's captain, but the rescued sailors soon discover him to be highly disturbed, perhaps consumed by the devil. Rumored to have once been a pirate, Warner reveals to the ship's mate he has made a pact with the devil and must surrender himself the following Friday night. The night before the final encounter Warner sees a fire ship. Although unseen by others, the fire ship closes on the *El Dorado* and sends out a boat for Warner on Friday afternoon. No one else sees a boarder but Warner. That night, the fire ship is completely consumed in flames and is visible to the crew of the *El Dorado* as well as Warner. The captain is locked in his cabin but manages to break away and jumps into the sea. The fire ship then disappears. The remaining crew solemnly brings the ship into port at Antigua, where they abandon the vessel completely. As Hoyt relates the story, no sailor will ever again sign on the *El Dorado*.

The characters of "The Spectre Fire-Ship" are skillfully developed, as is the plot, which builds suspensefully to the point when the crew thinks they see the fire ship. Literary critics have judged the story better than most Gothic tales of the time, finding it in many ways reminiscent of Christopher Marlowe's *Dr. Faustus* (1604). The story has its basis in the legend of an incident off the Rhode Island coast in 1738, but Stone altered the tale somewhat. Interestingly, Stone's son, William Leete Stone Jr., published virtually the same story under the same title in *Potter's American Monthly* in 1881, almost fifty years after "The Spectre Fire-Ship" first appeared in print. Stone's son added a note that the fantastic tale was related to his father by Dr. Noah Stone of Oxford, Connecticut, who heard it from an eyewitness.

In general Stone's short fiction compares favorably with other leading writers of the day such as Cooper and Hawthorne. Nearly half of the pieces in *Tales and Sketches* were originally published in literary annuals of the day, such as *The Forget-Me-Not,* published by the respected Philadelphia firm of Carey, Lea, and Carey. Collectively, Stone's short fiction represents an overlooked contribution to his country's emerging national literature, one that deserves the attention of literary historians seeking to understand early American prose fiction.

Other than "Mercy Disborough," which was published in book form as *The Witches: A Tale of New-England* in 1837 and again under its original title in 1844, Stone's only long fictional work was *Ups and Downs in the Life of a Distressed Gentleman* (1836). The novel is not autobiographical; although Stone reportedly based it on his own knowledge of the "gentleman" of the title. Intended as satire, it is the story of Daniel Wheelwright of New Jersey, who grows up in the Mohawk River valley. The son of a coach maker, young Daniel is sent off to college to train as a minister, a profession for which he shows no inclination. He follows with the study of medicine but again demonstrates little aptitude, settling instead for the life of a merchant. Wheelwright is duped out of his investment but lands on his feet when a claim against the government falls into his lap. He loses his

new fortune in a lottery scheme and, upon returning to New York, winds up in prison. Wheelwright's new enterprise, a steamboat company on Lake George, north of New York City, is ruined when the boat burns just before her maiden trip. Fortune once more shines on Wheelwright in the form of marriage to a wealthy widow, but the relationship ends on a sour note when she is proved a fraud. Stone's story concludes with the "distressed gentleman" finally turning to coach making, his father's initial vocation.

Ups and Downs in the Life of a Distressed Gentleman is not particularly well written but is not without entertaining comic scenes. Harmless as it may seem, the small book created quite a stir in Stone's life when it was brutally reviewed by Edgar Allan Poe in the *Southern Literary Messenger*. Stone and Poe had crossed swords before in the literary press, but their previous exchanges paled in comparison to Poe's sarcastic review of *Ups and Downs in the Life of a Distressed Gentleman*. Poe called the book "ineffective daubing" and a "public imposition." Poe concludes that the book belonged among the "quack advertisements" in Stone's *Commercial Advertiser*. A reviewer in *The Knickerbocker* (June 1836) was much kinder to Stone. Years later Poe again shared his low esteem for Stone in *Graham's Magazine* (December 1841), when he questioned Stone's abilities as a newspaperman, concluding that public perception and private opinions of Stone were at opposite poles and that no honest observer had ever recognized any talent in Stone.

During Stone's tenure as editor of the *Commercial Advertiser* he also ran afoul of Cooper. As early as 1826 the two considered themselves friends. At Cooper's request Stone had sent him newspapers while the former was in Europe, although there is little extant correspondence between the two other than a February 1827 letter from Cooper to Stone. By the 1830s the two were political enemies. After the publication of Cooper's *History of the Navy of the United States of America* (1839) and subsequent negative reviews, Stone was one of several editors Cooper sued—others were Thurlow Weed, Park Benjamin, and even Horace Greeley. Between 1837 and 1843 Cooper filed fourteen libel suits and even two charges for criminal libel as he carried on his own private war against the press. At issue in each case was a review of Cooper's account of the Battle of Lake Erie during the War of 1812. Stone published a review by William Alexander Duer in the newspaper in four installments during June 1839. Duer, president of Columbia College from 1829 until 1842, had called into question Cooper's assessment of the role of Lt. Jesse Elliott, whom Cooper raised to sharing heroic status with Commo. Oliver Hazard Perry, generally considered the true hero of Lake Erie. Instead of targeting Duer, Cooper sued Stone, claiming the review was "written with a base motive," and the reviewer charged Cooper with purposefully distorting history. After several delaying tactics by Stone, a trial was held beginning 16 May 1842. The proceedings took four days, with Cooper arguing his case for hours at a time. A panel of three attorneys decided the case in Cooper's favor, declaring Stone had libeled the novelist. The monetary award, however, was only $250 plus $50 for court costs. In addition Stone had to reprint the seventeen-page award in his newspaper. Stone published an apologetic yet sarcastic editorial in the *Commercial Advertiser* along with the award. The editorial claimed that Duer was offended by the award and had offered to pay Stone's fee. Cooper considered the award a great victory, apt retribution for the attack on his work.

This was not the end of the feud between Cooper and Stone, however. In July 1843 Stone printed a letter supposedly from Cooper in which Cooper expresses impatience over not yet receiving his award, which he needs to invest on Wall Street. Cooper sued again and won another $250 judgment in September 1843, which a state court of errors reversed in July 1845, nearly a year after Stone's death.

This episode is the most intriguing of Stone's lengthy career as an editor and author, yet standard biographical references make no mention of either case, and Stone's own son devotes just one page to it in his one-hundred-page memoir of his father. In contrast Cooper's correspondence is rife with references to Stone and libel, and Cooper's biographers generally mention their subject's obsession with Stone and other newspaper editors.

Of all Stone's writings, none had more immediate impact than his fifty-six-page pamphlet *Maria Monk and the Nunnery of the Hotel Dieu,* published in 1836. Stone stepped into the middle of the Maria Monk controversy and the fervent anti-Catholicism stirred by Monk's *Awful Disclosures of the Hotel Dieu Nunnery of Montreal,* published earlier that year. Monk was a troubled young Protestant woman who had entered Montreal's Hotel Dieu convent with the intention of becoming a nun. She told of a life of sex at the pleasure of the convent's priest, of children born, baptized, and then strangled, and of the murder of those who refused to follow the demands of the priests. The book sold twenty-six thousand copies in its first six months and was, as Ray Allen Billington has termed it, "by far the most influential single work of American nativistic propaganda in the period preceding the Civil War." *Awful Disclosures* did as much to ignite opposition to Catholicism as Harriet Beecher Stowe's *Uncle Tom's Cabin* (1852) did to marshal forces against slavery.

The publication of *Awful Disclosures* ignited latent anti-Catholic sentiment in the New York press. Stone was a Protestant, but he deplored the exploitative attacks on the Catholic Church. In the fall of 1836 he was in Montreal and was granted access to the nunnery. He checked details of Monk's *Awful Disclosures* and, finding no evidence to verify her claims, proclaimed the priests and nuns innocent. Stone also met with Monk and concluded she had never even been in the Hotel Dieu. *Awful Disclosures* bore the imprint of Howe and Bates, but Howe and Bates were really employees of the publishing firm of Harper and Brothers, who feared customer repercussions if they actually published the volume; the dummy firm was set up to protect Harper. Ironically, Harper published three of Stone's books as well, and his refutation of Monk also carried the imprint of Howe and Bates.

Stone was immediately attacked in newspapers, by the Protestant Reformation Society, and in a pamphlet titled *Evidence Demonstrating the Falsehoods of William L. Stone* (1836). A book-length poem, *The Vision of Rubeta; an Epic Story of the Island of Manhattan* (1838), satirized Stone, his investigation of the Hotel Dieu, and Stone's fellow newspaper editor, Charles King of the *New York American.* In defense of his father, William Leete Stone Jr. responded in his 1866 memoir to the lengthy verse, correctly ascribing authorship of the work to Laughton Osborn, and labeling it clever but gross, obscene, and vitriolic toward Stone. A satirical drama, most likely the work of Osborn as well, followed the same year but was probably never performed. Stone was labeled a dupe of the Catholics and called "Stone-blind"; yet his work had done much to discredit Monk's claims of abuses. She published a sequel, *Further Disclosures by Maria Monk,* in 1837, which met with little success. The Maria Monk episode and the Cooper trials constitute Stone's most widely recalled legacy.

Stone's first published volume of history was *Life of Joseph Brant-Thayendanegea: Including the Border Wars of the American Revolution,* published in New York by Alexander Blake. For years Stone had attempted to collect manuscripts and other records of the Indians of the New York and New England areas. While most of Stone's collected material concerned Indian agent Sir William Johnson, he concentrated on other figures as well—Brant being one. The biography of Brant was as much a history of Indian campaigns of the Revolution, especially the armies under Generals Nicholas Herkimer, Barry St. Leger, and "Mad" Anthony Wayne. Brant was a Mohawk who led much of the Iroquois nation against the colonials during the Revolution. Formally educated in New Hampshire, he was baptized a Christian. He sided with the British during the war, primarily to protect the future of Indian lands. Controversial throughout his life, Brant was demonized among frontier settlers but was an effective Indian leader. The book was recognized for its use of primary resources, and Stone's writings incorporated the verbatim text of many historical documents. His preservation efforts proved to be a significant step in raising awareness in New York of the importance of collecting and providing accessibility to the state's historical records. The New York State Historical Agency was created in 1838 for that purpose, and Stone was a proponent of these efforts.

In his biography of Brant, Stone researched the Seneca massacre of American settlers at Wyoming in the Mohawk River valley. Stone concluded Brant was not at Wyoming–a conclusion that was counter to popular history at the time but has subsequently proven to be accurate. Stone claimed he later traveled to the region and discovered several survivors of the massacre who affirmed his assertions. Stone's biography of Brant, as well as others of his histories, are still cited in more contemporary historical scholarship.

Stone's next history was *The Life and Times of Red-Jacket, or Sa-go-ye-wat-ha,* published in1841. In this book Stone closely followed the methods he had used in *Life of Joseph Brant,* utilizing extensive notes and documents he had been collecting for years and reproducing various primary records within his text. Red Jacket, whose Indian name means "he causes them to be awake," was an Iroquois chief with a fondness for red jackets whose war record during the Revolution was far less distinguished than his oratorical skills. He was a major figure in treaty negotiations between the United States and the Iroquois Nation but enjoyed a greater reputation for his leadership powers during the War of 1812, again as a spokesman for Native American rights. Critics charged Red Jacket with benefiting from the sale of Indian lands, but Stone's Red Jacket is an admirable figure, more a hero than the vain figure he was. In general Stone's second effort at biography was well received.

Stone's final major history, the two-volume *Border Wars of the American Revolution,* published in 1843 as part of Harper's Family Library, concerned the wars along the frontier of colonial expansion, most of them involving Native Americans on either side of the conflict. Stone once again drew on select documents and included them within the text of the book, much of which was a rehashing of his earlier biographies of Brant and Red Jacket; indeed, the publication of *Border Wars* followed his earlier books by only five years. The work remains Stone's most readable.

Stone's histories are organized in the typical nineteenth-century style, divided into chapters of nearly equal length that are in turn outlined in the table of con-

tents. Stone had a habit of introducing his histories with a reference to one of Aesop's fables, in which a lion tells a forester that a statue of a man standing over a vanquished beast proves not that man is superior to the beasts but that beasts cannot make statues. Stone used the analogy to compare the fates of Indians and whites on the frontier, a circumstance for which the Indians had not been allowed to offer their own narrative. Stone was not a pure apologist for the Indian enemies of the frontier colonials, but he did take their side. He wrote of Indian exploits and heroism but did not report Indian exploitation, which was a common literary theme when whites and Indians later fought on the western frontier. Neither exciting nor bland, Stone's writing was workmanlike. Some critics have argued that it is difficult to determine where fact ends and fiction begins in his history, but generations of historians have found Stone a reliable source, and his preservation of source material is still useful for researching the Native American experience during the Revolution. Stone was typical of contemporary historical novelists such as Cooper and Robert Montgomery Bird in that all utilized a romantic or heroic style to incorporate Indians and Indian lore into their works.

Stone's other writings were significant, but his histories are his most important contribution to the national literature. His best-selling work was the exposure of Maria Monk, but other books by Stone enjoyed local success. *Matthias and His Impostures; or, The Progress of Fanaticism, Illustrated in the Extraordinary Case of Robert Matthews, and Some of His Forerunners and Disciples* (1835) was an exposé similar to Stone's refutation of Monk. *The Poetry and History of Wyoming* (1841) was a republication of Bristish poet Thomas Campbell's *Gertrude of Wyoming, A Pennsylvanian Tale* (1809), that included Washington Irvings's 1810 biographical sketch of Campbell and Stone's own history of the region. *Uncas and Miantonomoh* (1842) was a lengthy discourse which grew from a commemorative speech Stone delivered on 4 July 1842 to mark the erection of a monument to the Mohican chief Uncas. His earliest writing outside of newspapers was an account of the completion of the Erie Canal published in November 1825. Among his many writings, this may be Stone's most cited.

William Leete Stone left behind one work that was published after his death. Before his death Stone had written nine chapters of a book on Indian agent Sir William Johnson, the most controversial of British agents on the colonial frontier. Johnson was revered by Indian leaders and feared by settlers. Twenty years after Stone's death his son completed the work, publishing *The Life and Times of Sir William Johnson, bart.* (1865). Following in his father's footsteps, William Leete Stone Jr. was an historian who published several books of Revolutionary War history. Much of the biographical information on Stone is from a sketch of his life written by his son and published in an 1866 edition of Stone's biography of Red Jacket. Obviously sympathetic, the son's life of his father fills in gaps on the senior Stone's career and his causes and includes entries from a diary Stone kept in 1829 while on a tour of central New York State.

Stone was an important figure in initiating interest in preserving archival materials in New York State. He led the movement to establish the New York State Historical Agency, an organization for preserving historical records. Stone was unsuccessful in promoting a mission to Europe to recover manuscripts and records related to New York and its history. He was also active in benevolent associations such as New York's Institution for the Deaf and Blind and the Society for the Reformation of Juvenile Delinquents. He was a New York City school commissioner for several years and superintendent in 1833–1834. Stone became ill in the fall of 1843 and died on 15 August 1844 after a long and painful illness. His short fiction remains part of an interesting chapter in the nation's literary history.

Biographies:

William Leete Stone Jr., "Memoir of the Author," in *The Life and Times of Sa-go-ye-wat-ha, or Red Jacket, by the late William Leete Stone, with a Memoir of the Author, by his Son* (Albany: Munsell, 1866), pp. 9–101;

Stone Jr., *The Family of John Stone, One of the First Settlers of Guilford, Connecticut* (Albany: Munsell, 1888), pp. 45–97.

References:

James Franklin Beard, ed., *Letters and Journals of James Fenimore Cooper,* 6 volumes (Cambridge, Mass.: Belknap Press of Harvard University Press, 1960–1968);

Ray Allen Billington, "Maria Monk and Her Influence," *Catholic Historical Review,* 22 (October 1936): 283–296;

Neal Frank Doubleday, "William Leete Stone as Storyteller," in his *Variety of Attempt: British and American Fiction in the Early Nineteenth Century* (Lincoln: University of Nebraska Press, 1976), pp. 160–175;

Sidney P. Moss, *Poe's Literary Battles: The Critic in the Context of His Literary Milieu* (Carbondale: Southern Illinois Press, 1963), pp. 50–70;

Edgar Allan Poe, "Ups and Downs in the Life of a Distressed Gentleman," *Southern Literary Messenger,* 2 (June 1836): 455–457.

Ruth McEnery Stuart

(21 May 1849? – 6 May 1917)

Kathryn B. McKee
University of Mississippi

BOOKS: *A Golden Wedding and Other Tales* (New York & London: Harper, 1893);

Carlotta's Intended and Other Tales (New York & London: Harper, 1894);

The Story of Babette, A Little Creole Girl (New York: Harper, 1894; London: Osgood & McIlvaine, 1895);

Gobolinks, or Shadow-Pictures for Young and Old, by Stuart and Albert Bigelow Paine (New York: Century, 1896);

Sonny: A Story (New York: Century, 1896); republished as *Sonny: Tales* (London: Century, 1896); republished as *Sonny: A Christmas Guest* (New York: Century, 1897; London: Hodder & Stoughton, 1905);

Solomon Crow's Christmas Pockets and Other Tales (New York: Harper, 1896);

In Simpkinsville: Character Tales (New York & London: Harper, 1897);

The Snow-Cap Sisters: A Farce (New York & London: Harper, 1897);

Moriah's Mourning and Other Half-Hour Sketches (London & New York: Harper, 1898);

Holly and Pizen and Other Stories (New York: Century, 1899);

Napoleon Jackson: The Gentleman of the Plush Rocker (New York & London: Century, 1902);

George Washington Jones. A Christmas Gift that Went A-Begging (Philadelphia: H. Altemus, 1903; London: Charles H. Kelly, 1904);

The River's Children: An Idyl of the Mississippi (New York: Century, 1904);

The Second Wooing of Salina Sue and Other Stories (New York: Harper, 1905);

Aunt Amity's Silver Wedding and Other Stories (New York: Century, 1909);

Sonny's Father in which the Father, now become Grandfather, a Kindly Observer of Life and a Genial Philosopher, in his Desultory Talks with the Family Doctor, Carries along the Story of Sonny (New York: Century, 1910);

Ruth McEnery Stuart

The Haunted Photograph, Whence and Whither, A Case in Diplomacy, The Afterglow (New York: Century, 1911);

Daddy Do-Funny's Wisdom Jingles (New York: Century, 1913);

The Cocoon: A Rest-Cure Comedy (New York: Hearst's International Library, 1915);

Plantation Songs and Other Verse (New York & London: Appleton, 1916).

SELECTED PERIODICAL PUBLICATIONS—
UNCOLLECTED: "A People Who Live Amid
    Romance," *Ladies Home Journal,* 14 (December
    1896): 7–8;
"The Author's Reading in Simpkinsville. A Mono-
    logue," *Century,* 60 (August 1900): 612–619;
"Value of Folklore in Literature," *New York Times Review
    of Books,* 12 October 1913, pp. 544–545;
"American Backgrounds for Fiction: VI–Arkansas,
    Louisiana, and the Gulf Country," *Bookman,* 39
    (August 1914): 620–630.

A full-length photograph of Ruth McEnery Stuart
graces the cover of the 16 December 1899 issue of *Harper's
Bazar;* she is identified in the caption as one of the "American Authoresses of the Hour." The article inside features
photographs of Stuart's New York home and information
about her hobbies. Such details undoubtedly appealed to
her vast and devoted readership, largely composed of
women who, like Stuart, stood balanced on the edge of a
new century that promised greater opportunities and freedom than women had ever experienced before. The
women of the 1890s looked to figures such as Stuart for
leadership.

Moving to New York from New Orleans after the
success of her first published stories, Stuart established herself as a leading writer in the 1890s and won renown both
as an accomplished hostess and as a devoted advocate of
women's rights. Given the decline of Stuart's reputation
following her death in 1917, the author of the *Harper's
Bazar* feature about her, Candace Wheeler, was prescient
in choosing her as an authoress "of the hour." Stuart, however, is also an authoress of the hour in the sense that her
work offers the modern reader valuable insight into the
cultural concerns of the time in which she wrote, the
uncertain transition between centuries that both intimi-
dated and excited Americans.

Dubbed "the laureate of the lowly" by Mildred L.
Rutherford in *The South in History and Literature* (1906),
Stuart consistently received praise during her lifetime
for realistically portraying three downtrodden segments
of Southern society: Italian Americans in New Orleans,
Arkansas farmers and small town residents, and African Americans. Readers considered her representations
of African American life among her best work, and Joel
Chandler Harris reportedly wrote to Stuart shortly
before his death: "You have got nearer the heart of the
negro than any of us." Calling herself a "friendly chronicler," Stuart explains in her December 1896 *Ladies
Home Journal* article, "A People Who Live Amid
Romance," that she set out to rectify the northern focus
on "ill-selected and misleading localities, with the inevitable result of false impressions, and, sometimes, of
ill-founded prejudices."

Stuart's contemporaries approved of the South she
gave to the world. Edwin Lewis Stevens in *The Library of
Southern Literature* (1907) praised "her own natural and
unconscious optimism through which she sees her South
suffused with the roseate glow of sentiment and romance."
Unlike her fellow Louisiana writers Kate Chopin, Grace
King, and George Washington Cable, Stuart never ventures into complicated interracial issues such as miscegenation, preferring to rely on easily identifiable stereotypes of
both black and white characters. Her portrayals of African
American characters and their relationships with whites
began to be attacked shortly after her death, and most
recent critics of Stuart's work have objected to her reliance
on what at the time were already viewed as romantic
images of the antebellum South.

Stuart was born Mary Routh McEnery on 21 May,
probably in 1849, though some biographical sources give
dates as late as 1856. (When she moved to the North she
changed *Routh,* an old spelling from her mother's family, to
Ruth to avoid confusions and misspellings.) Her father,
James McEnery, immigrated to America from Ireland and
eventually became a well-respected cotton merchant,
planter, and slaveholder in Marksville, Louisiana. He married Mary Routh Stirling, the daughter of a prominent
local family. Their daughter grew up in New Orleans,
where the family moved so that James McEnery might be
nearer the customhouse. Details about Mary Routh
McEnery's early education are sketchy. By her own
account, much of her schooling took place on the streets of
New Orleans, where she absorbed the richly diverse dialects and habits of the immigrant, Creole, and African
American neighborhoods of the port community. Despite
her self-professed affinity with the downtrodden, Stuart's
upper-class standing meant that in her youth she made her
observations from the vantage point of class privilege.
Such a perspective is often apparent in the stories she
wrote later.

In response to her family's straitened financial circumstances after the Civil War, Mary Routh McEnery
and her sister Sarah taught at a local school for girls. In
1879 she met her thrice-widowed cousin, Alfred Oden Stuart, on a trip to Arkansas. She remained in Arkansas for
four months, ostensibly to teach, but at the end of that
period married Alfred Stuart, thirty-one years her senior
and the father of eleven children, many of them grown. A
wealthy cotton planter, Alfred Stuart was a leading citizen
of Washington, Arkansas, where the couple made their
home. Ruth McEnery Stuart credited her experience in
Washington with providing much of the background she
later built on in her fiction, particularly in her black dialect
sketches. As she is quoted in E. F. Harkins and C. H. L.
Johnston's *Little Pilgrimages Among Women Who Have Written
Famous Books* (1901), "most of my negro character-studies
have come from my association with the negroes while [in

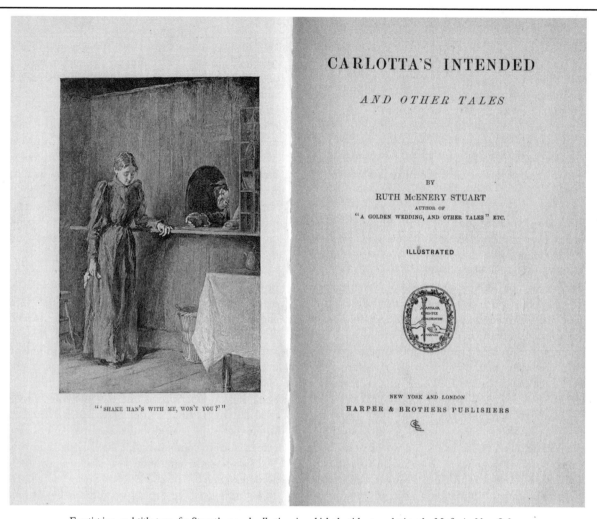

"'SHAKE HAN'S WITH ME, WON'T YOU?'"

CARLOTTA'S INTENDED

AND OTHER TALES

BY

RUTH McENERY STUART
AUTHOR OF
"A GOLDEN WEDDING, AND OTHER TALES" ETC.

ILLUSTRATED

NEW YORK AND LONDON
HARPER & BROTHERS PUBLISHERS

Frontispiece and title page for Stuart's second collection, in which the title story depicts the Mafia in New Orleans

Arkansas]. We lived right among them—there were hundreds of negroes to one white person."

While in Arkansas Stuart began to turn to a literary career. She organized Washington's D.O.T. (Dear Old Town) Club, a reading group for local women, and within that circle she shared a parody of Edgar Allan Poe's "The Raven," her first extant literary work. It was events, more than her interest in writing per se, however, that propelled her to authorship. Her husband died of a stroke three years after she gave birth to a son, Stirling, in 1880. Although she maintained a residence in Arkansas until 1888, Stuart spent much time after her husband's death with her own family in New Orleans. As she recalled for a reporter, "It is the old story—the bread-and-butter question. . . . Except for this necessity, I do not know that I should have begun to do any serious work."

Charles Dudley Warner's interest in Stuart's fiction was largely responsible for her initial successes. In the summer of 1887 Stuart and her sister Sarah met Warner, then editor at *Harper's Monthly Magazine,* at a resort in

North Carolina. They must have discussed Stuart's literary ambitions because shortly thereafter she forwarded two stories to him: "Uncle Mingo's 'Speculatioms'" and "Lamentations of Jeremiah Johnson." He retained the latter for *Harper's New Monthly Magazine* and sent the former to *The Princeton Review,* where in January 1888 it became Stuart's first published work. Both stories reflect the tone and content of much of Stuart's subsequent writing and of local color fiction generally, then at the height of its popularity.

Each tale is told by a white, presumably male, narrator who recalls for the reader the childlike antics of African American characters. The narrator in "Uncle Mingo's 'Speculatioms,'" for example, pities the elderly and ailing title character, who has gone out into the world to earn money for his impoverished former mistresses. When questioned about his decision to leave his own family behind, Mingo seems unconcerned. He is far more worried as to "'who gwine to look arter we's white folks?'" Just before he dies, Mingo instructs the narrator to deliver his earnings to the white family who once owned him, and the narrator welcomes the opportunity to execute his duties as a Southern gentleman. "Lamentations of Jeremiah Johnson" shows the playful humor that distinguishes much of Stuart's fiction. Set in Washington, Arkansas, this story relies on wordplay and comic physical incongruities, two of Stuart's common tactics for creating humor. "Lamentations of Jeremiah" is the name of the title character. He is his parents' tenth child, having been preceded by nine sisters, all of whom died before their brother's birth. Consequently, Lamentations is regularly outfitted in their dresses, a circumstance that, at twelve years of age, he perceives as a direct threat to his budding masculinity: "'Ef I could jes grown past dem gal frocks, I'd be willin' ter die de nex' minute, 'caze den I could die like what I is, an' 'spect myself as I on'y kin 'spect myself in breeches!'"

In the late 1880s or the early 1890s Stuart moved to New York to be nearer her publishers. New York City and the literary community at Onteora in the Catskill Mountains served as her homes from that time until her death. Warner, whose patronage smoothed her transition to a literary life, encouraged editors to accept her submissions, which began appearing regularly in *Harper's Bazar* and *Century Illustrated Monthly Magazine*. She joined several women's clubs. In *Gender, Race, and Region in the Writings of Grace King, Ruth McEnery Stuart, and Kate Chopin* (1989) Helen Taylor characterizes her as more devoted to suffrage than any other transplanted Southern female writer and discusses at length the conflict Stuart undoubtedly felt between her upbringing as a Southern woman and her open support for revamped definitions of femininity.

In addition to black dialect poems and tales such as "Uncle Mingo's 'Speculatioms'" and "Lamentations of Jeremiah Johnson," Stuart's first book, *A Golden Wedding and Other Tales* (1893), includes one of Stuart's early Simpkinsville sketches, "The Woman's Exchange of Simpkinsville." It was the first in a series of stories that featured white characters from a small, imaginary Arkansas town who speak in dialect about the comic and tragic events in their close-knit community. In this extended tale twin spinster sisters, Sarey Mirandy Simpkins and Sophia Falena Simpkins, confront personal financial difficulties by turning their parlor into a market where the women of the town can sell their baked goods and handiwork, minus a commission deducted by the sisters for the use of their home and the benefits of their managerial skills. Their good natures and generosity actually prevent their making a great deal of money, but the independence they secure finally has little to do with actual wealth. In breaking free of the roles typically assigned them by the community, the Simpkins sisters assert a vision of female selfhood similar to the one that Stuart herself advanced.

Stuart's next books—*Carlotta's Intended and Other Tales* and *The Story of Babette, A Little Creole Girl,* both published in 1894—cemented her national reputation. Both works include an edge of realism not evident in the rosy sentimentalism of Stuart's earlier collection. In the lengthy title story of *Carlotta's Intended,* set in a cosmopolitan New Orleans plagued by the first significant appearance of the Mafia in America, she incorporates Irish, Italian, and German dialects to recount the thwarted love of an Irish shoemaker, Pat Rooney, for an Italian girl, Carlotta, whom he has watched grow up and intends to marry. The story chronicles the innocence of their love for one another—hers because she is but a teenager, his because despite his advanced age Carlotta is Pat's first love. After defending Carlotta from rumors that she wanted to marry a member of the New Orleans Mafia, Pat is marked for death by this group. The heartbroken Pat, who learns that Carlotta actually loves a boy her own age, dies not from a Mafia knife but by drowning when he frees a kitten caught near the river's edge. Carlotta later visits Pat's grave in the company of her husband and their children. Although a reviewer for the 1 July 1894 issue of *The New York Times* responded with an impatience then coming to dominate critical treatments of regional writing—"The field of dialect fiction has been greatly overworked lately"—Stuart's depiction of the Mafia and the tensions it introduced into New Orleans society is noteworthy for its realism.

The Story of Babette is also set in New Orleans and suggests both the diversity of the city and the hard edge beneath its glamour. In this novel a Creole girl, abducted as a child by a poor Italian woman who lured her away in hopes of securing a monetary reward that might save her own family from penury, is returned to her family as an adult. Although Babette is restored to her rightful place among New Orleans's prominent families, the Italian family remains disenfranchised, living in squalor beyond the city. Stuart presents the unbridged gap between these residents of the same locale, the kidnapping suggesting the tensions that often gave rise to violent clashes between factions of New Orleans society.

Despite the similarities in plot and theme characterizing Stuart's eleven short story collections, the tone of her work varies widely from sketch to sketch, making generalizations about her fiction difficult. The title story of *Solomon Crow's Christmas Pockets and Other Tales* (1896), for example, fits squarely within the paternalistic tradition of plantation fiction, featuring patronizing and moralistic white characters whose superior racial sensibilities are necessary to regulate the behavior of the lazy, thieving black characters. Chief among these minor-league criminals is the comical child Solomon

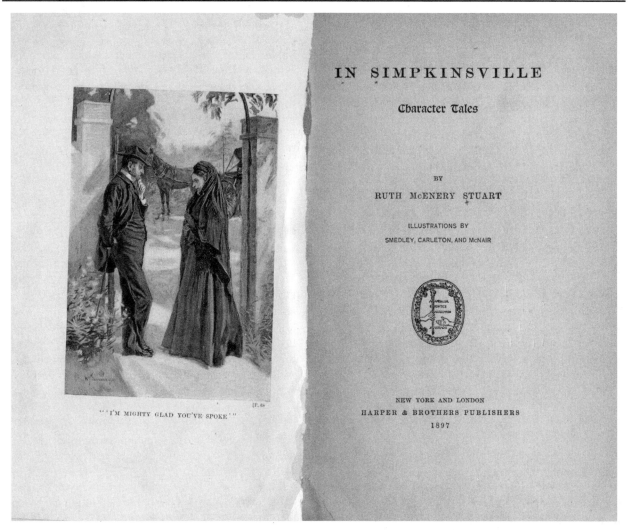

IN SIMPKINSVILLE

Character Tales

BY

RUTH McENERY STUART

ILLUSTRATIONS BY
SMEDLEY, CARLETON, AND McNAIR

NEW YORK AND LONDON
HARPER & BROTHERS PUBLISHERS
1897

"'I'M MIGHTY GLAD YOU'VE SPOKE'"

Frontispiece and title page for Stuart's 1897 book that includes "The Unlived Life of Little Mary Ellen," in which the community participates in a distraught woman's delusion

Crow, called "Solomon" by his mother because his visage appeared so wise at birth and "Crow" by the neighborhood children because he is so black. The white people for whom he works only allow him to wear clothes out of which they have cut the pockets. They reward the reformed Solomon at Christmastime with a new suit, outfitted with many pockets. The racist overtones of this and many other Stuart stories may trouble modern readers.

In other stories, though, Stuart features strong black characters, making sweeping conclusions about Stuart's racial attitudes problematic. "Blink," a story also included in *Solomon Crow's Christmas Pockets,* tells a different tale of the relationship between a black character and her former mistress. Here an aspiring female writer, serving as Stuart's surrogate, turns to the pen as a way of supporting her family in its postbellum decline. She receives guidance from her mammy, who listens to the stories read aloud and identifies their weaknesses, including an overabundance of unrealistic circumstance and elevated diction. "'Write down some *truly truth* what is *ac-chilly happened,*'" Mammy counsels her pupil, whose work meets with immediate success when she follows this advice. While the story also includes a number of gratuitously sentimental details, it finally offers a portrait of two strong women successfully making their own way in a reconstructed society they scarcely recognize, redefining their roles both in the world at large and in relationship to one another.

Stuart's best-selling book was *Sonny: A Story* (1896), reprinted eleven times before 1914. The title character of this series of sketches is the precocious, undisciplined son of Deuteronomy and Martha Jones, white residents of a small town in Arkansas. He is his parents' only child, born to them late in life after nearly twenty years of marriage. The reader first meets the family only a few hours after Sonny's birth and follows his progression through adolescence, courtship, and marriage. Sonny never speaks directly, however, and what begins as an account of a mischievous young boy's antics becomes the story of his father's life. Deuteronomy's ostensible auditor is an unnamed doctor, who appears periodically to interject questions in what is otherwise a stream of pithy observations, comic moments, and exaggerated descriptions, as well as a running commentary on the social and political events of his day.

In one of the funniest sketches, "Sonny's Christening,'" Sonny refuses to be baptized because he equates the procedure with vaccination, which he also refuses. When Sonny develops an infection in his foot due to a splinter that he will not let his mother remove, she sends for the rector to have him baptized, in case he should die. In response, Sonny crawls first under the bed and then up a tree in the butter-bean arbor, forcing all of the adults out into the pouring rain to coax him down. From his treetop perch Sonny orders everyone christened. Sonny's father explains to the rector "'thet the rites o' the church didn't count for nothin' on our farm, next to the rights o' the boy!'" and so both the narrator and his wife are rebaptized. The narrator finally proposes that the rain descending from heaven be considered blessed, and the rector, desperate to save himself if no one else, agrees. Dedicated to her son, Stirling, *Sonny* includes many of Stuart's own thinly veiled reflections on being a parent. Because she served Stirling as both mother and father, Stuart undoubtedly felt comfortable extending herself into the mind of her protagonist's father.

Stuart often mixes the trappings of sentimental literature with a startling realism and a dark comedy that can unsettle the reader. One of her most popular and striking tales is "The Unlived Life of Little Mary Ellen," collected in *In Simpkinsville: Character Tales* (1897). The story exposes through the eyes of the community one woman's dementia; having been abandoned by her fiancé at the altar, the title character imagines that a large wax doll is the child she bore for the man who jilted her. All of the characters surrounding Mary Ellen cooperate in perpetuating her fantasy. The doctor makes house calls to treat the doll, and the servants tend to it as though it were human. At the story's climax, a dog steals Mary Ellen's "child" from its cradle and drags it through the yard until it is scarcely recognizable. Mary Ellen arranges for the doll's funeral, and then quietly dies herself during the service. Readers and critics have been haunted by this story that is recognized as being atypical for Stuart. In a September 1897 review in *Harper's* Laurence Hutton called it "the most complete piece of work which has yet come from Mrs.

Stuart's pen." Taylor in *Gender, Race and Region* finds the story powerful because it questions "gender definitions within the community by featuring a female emotional breakdown." Stuart returned in other stories to the mental health of women and the strategies females develop for managing the circumstances of their lives.

In "A Note of Scarlet," included in *Holly and Pizen and Other Stories* (1899), Stuart uses an unlikely female character to explore the constraints of gender. One of her most complex and unconventional stories, "A Note of Scarlet" details one day in the life of Miss Melissa Ann Moore, a spinster who lives with her brother's family and is chiefly renowned for the mats she makes as gifts—always the same style and always the same moss green color. Her routine is interrupted when one day she inexplicably makes a red mat; Miss Melissa then finds she is able to break with convention on a larger scale. She stays home from church, begging off with a fictitious headache. Knowing that she is behaving sinfully but unable to stop herself, Miss Melissa then goes on a fishing expedition that yields thirty fish and an encounter with Silent Si, a mysterious deaf and mute creature of indeterminate gender. Complicating Si's sexual identity is her racial identity. She is thought to be a voodoo woman escaped from a plantation or a black man afflicted with strange white spots, signaling either that he has leprosy or that he is being transformed through some magical spell into a white man. As she cleans the fish that she and Si have caught, Miss Melissa raises a song that mingles with the songs of the birds, and "it was as if the long-pent joy that ought to have expressed itself through years of living had suddenly burst forth, demanding right of way."

Although "A Note of Scarlet" ends rather conventionally and typically for a Stuart short story of middle-aged romance, its light-hearted conclusion does not undermine its significance. A projection of Miss Melissa's own sensuality and her desire for release from the self-imposed regimen of her daily routine, Si literally escorts Melissa beyond the boundaries of the life she has known. Their communication without words finally speaks volumes about the power of human connection between like-minded individuals and the freedom that comes from stepping beyond the labels and expectations constructed in language.

In the second tale of *Holly and Pizen and Other Stories*, "Queen O'Sheba's Triumph," Stuart features one of her complex African American female characters. The title character leaves Broom Corn Bottom for New York City, where she intends to make her fortune and her future. Her initial optimism fades, however, and she is reduced to working as a scullery maid at a Harlem boarding house. For the benefit of her friends and family back home, Queen O'Sheba spins a shimmering

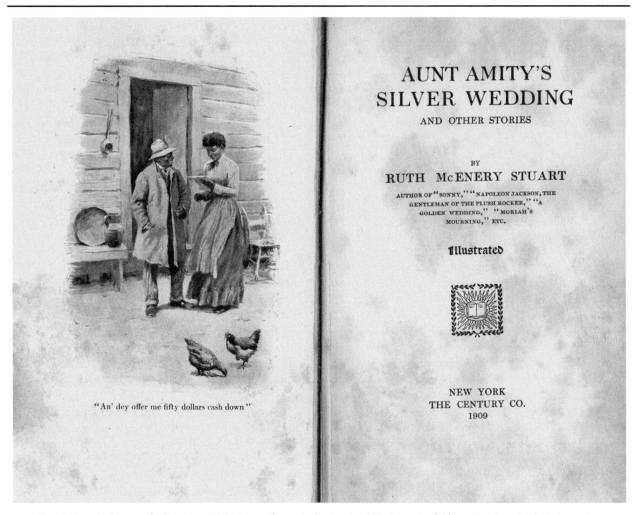

AUNT AMITY'S
SILVER WEDDING
AND OTHER STORIES

BY
RUTH McENERY STUART

AUTHOR OF "SONNY," "NAPOLEON JACKSON, THE
GENTLEMAN OF THE PLUSH ROCKER," "A
GOLDEN WEDDING," "MORIAH'S
MOURNING," ETC.

Illustrated

NEW YORK
THE CENTURY CO.
1909

"An' dey offer me fifty dollars cash down"

Frontispiece and title page for Stuart's 1909 book, one of several collections in which she wrote of African Americans in plantation settings

account of her life, which their visit threatens to expose. She quickly devises a scheme whereby she cashes in her funeral policy in advance. Her guests arrive just in time to attend her lavish funeral while she watches the proceedings, Tom Sawyer–like, from the back of the funeral parlor, taking particular pleasure in the minister's suggestion that she died from fast living. Strangely Sheba actually does die during the funeral service, fainting when she leaps up to confess all. Nonetheless she proves one of Stuart's most memorable and intriguing female characters, noteworthy for her remarkable independence and ingenuity that transcend the stereotypical characteristics of black female characters. This story has attracted the attention of modern readers and critics, who have pointed to it when redeeming Stuart from charges of excessive sentimentality.

From 1892 until her death Stuart earned money by reading aloud from her own work. She spoke throughout the country, fulfilling a three-week engagement in Chicago, for instance, in 1895. Audiences particularly

praised the authenticity of her characters' dialect. Taylor asserts that "by the early twentieth century Stuart was established as one of the best known and most admired of all the Southern women who had come north to make their literary reputations and fortunes." At the peak of her literary productivity, the period between 1895 and 1900, Stuart enjoyed monetary security, and in the decade between 1895 and 1905 she was considered one of the best-paid writers in the country. Contemporary critics and fellow writers praised her work, and she counted among her friends the leading authors of the day, including George Washington Cable and Mark Twain. In 1897 Kate Chopin observed, "Sympathy and insight are the qualities, I believe, which make her stories lovable, which makes them linger in the memory like pleasant human experiences. . . ."

Stuart wrote steadily from 1888 until 1905, when Stirling died after falling from an upper-story window of the home he shared with his mother. He had been trying to enter the house after having been inadvertently locked out in the snow. Rumors that he was intoxicated at the time wounded Stuart deeply. She frequently alluded in her correspondence to the intensity of her sorrow, and on at least one occasion compares her mental state to insanity. Her writing career ground to a halt for the four years following Stirling's death. With *Aunt Amity's Silver Wedding and Other Stories* (1909) she returned to the short-story settings and characters types that had earlier secured her fame, although by that time the popularity of local color had cooled substantially.

In the sequel to the popular *Sonny* collection, *Sonny's Father in which the Father, now become Grandfather, a Kindly Observer of Life and a Genial Philosopher, in his Desultory Talks with the Family Doctor, Carries along the Story of Sonny* (1910), Stuart allows Sonny to do what her own son was unable to do—become a well-respected professional man, husband, and father. Sonny, though, figures even less prominently here than he did in the previous series of sketches. Although Stuart includes many comic, entertaining moments in *Sonny's Father,* she also enters into the far more serious business of cultural criticism. Under the guise of the narrator's amiable and digressive musings, she introduces contemporary topics that an aging farmer might well have broached but that a woman would traditionally have been expected to shun. Through her masculine persona she comments on the Spanish-American War, the reform movement, and the conflict between tradition and progress that gripped the South and the nation on the eve of a new century. Behind the demeanor of a drawling small-town narrator is a cosmopolitan woman who was politically aware and recognized in Sonny's father an acceptable instrument for expressing her views.

Stuart's most pointed exploration of feminist themes occurs in her final novel, *The Cocoon: A Rest-Cure Comedy* (1915), a comic exposé of one woman's trip to a rest-cure facility, likely based on the treatment Stuart received following her son's death. Having suffered from broken sleep and anxiety for some time, Blessy Heminway, a New York socialite, travels to Seafair Sanitarium in Virginia to rest. Through the letters she writes to her husband, Jack, back home and the entries in her diary, she creates a record of her stay for her as yet unborn "daughter, not sons." Blessy finds the treatments at Seafair singularly dull. She must spend extended periods of time ensconced in comforters and reclined on cots on the roof (cocooning).

Blessy's chief complaint is the humorlessness of the institution, until she finds herself embroiled in the romances of the exotic characters she meets. She initiates a series of practical jokes but believes she may have gone too far in her masquerade as a single woman when one of the other patients seems to be planning to marry her. Her husband shows up just in time to restore Blessy to her more conventionally ordered life in New York. It seems likely that *The Cocoon* is the fulfillment of Stuart's intention, once mentioned to a reporter, to write the "story of a girl in modern times meeting problems in the light of 'feminism' as it flourished today." Critics, though, expressed disappointment in its sentimentality and slapstick humor. Yet even if the comic resolution is finally unsatisfying, the narrator's physical confinement illustrates the barriers erected against exploring issues related to women's mental health, probably linked in the protagonist's case to her failure to have a baby. Critics have regularly linked *The Cocoon* to Charlotte Perkins Gilman's "The Yellow Wallpaper." In both works the women are forbidden to write, but violate that rule as a means of preserving themselves from genuine madness.

In her final collections Stuart continued to write of the scenes and characters of plantation life that had initially attracted her audience. *Daddy Do-Funny's Wisdom Jingles* (1913) and *Plantation Songs and Other Verse* (1916) are heavily illustrated volumes of black dialect poetry. Dedicated to "the Memory of those faithful brown slave-men of the plantations throughout the South," *Daddy Do-Funny's Wisdom Jingles* contains ninety short poems attributed to the venerable narrator. Although many are intended strictly to entertain, some are playful comments on societal issues, as does "The New Rich" in its portrait of the recently elevated "'Sis' Mush A. Roon.'"

Stuart uses examples from *Daddy Do-Funny's Wisdom Jingles* in her impassioned defense of dialect literature, "Value of Folklore in Literature," which appeared in the 12 October 1913 issue of *The New York Times Review of Books.* Her obvious impatience with critics of the genre goes beyond self-defensiveness. She speaks of the general relationship between literature and culture when she explains that "they are too vividly alive to become fixed, these dialects; too open to approach; and so it behooves us to entrap them in transit, for they bring to us half-shades and iridescence with moving power in depicting elemental emotions."

Plantation Songs, Stuart's final book, is divided into three sections: "Plantation Songs," "Songs of Life and Love," and "Just for Fun." Verse in the first section offers largely conventional portraits of plantation life in black dialect, while the poems of part two are elevated in tone and theme and are structurally conventional. Particularly notable is the poem "Brotherhood," a clear reflection on World War I and a lamentation for the peace obscured by "the battle-smoke of wars . . . / While doomed men in red-darkness fight / (With a groping sense of wrong or right)."

At the time of her death in New York City on 6 May 1917, Stuart had published more than twenty books in a twenty-three-year period. The writer of her obituary in *The New York Times* observed that "at no time did her writings indicate that she had given up anything of her early youth spent in the South." It is from that girlhood that Stuart drew the images that recur in her fiction, many of them originating in the stereotypes of the Old South that are fundamental to late-nineteenth-century writing from that region. Yet, Stuart was not simply an emissary of the plantation school, and it is just as much a disservice to the complexity of her work to view her exclusively as a social commentator or as a feminist. Raised on the ideal of an Old South, she wrote at times with an eye for the uncharted relationships possible in a New South.

References:

Dorothy H. Brown, "Ruth McEnery Stuart: A Reassessment," *Xavier Review,* 7, no. 2 (1987): 23–36;

Mary Frances Fletcher, "A Biographical and Critical Study of Ruth McEnery Stuart," dissertation, Louisiana State University, 1955;

Joan Wylie Hall, "Ruth McEnery Stuart," *Legacy,* 10, no. 1 (1993): 47–56;

E. F. Harkins and C. H. L. Johnston, "Ruth McEnery Stuart," in *Little Pilgrimages Among Women Who Have Written Famous Books* (Boston: L. C. Page, 1901), pp. 255–265;

Ethel C. Simpson, "Ruth McEnery Stuart: The Innocent Grotesque," *Louisiana Literature,* 4 (Spring 1987): 57–64;

Simpson, ed., *Simpkinsville and Vicinity: Arkansas Stories of Ruth McEnery Stuart* (Fayetteville: University of Arkansas Press, 1983);

Judy E. Sneller, "Bad Boys / Black Misfits: Ruth McEnery Stuart's Humor and 'The Negro Question,'" in *Images of the Child,* edited by Harry Eiss (Bowling Green, Ohio: Bowling Green University Popular Press, 1994), pp. 215–228;

Sneller, "'Sambo' and 'The Southern Lady's Humor and the (Re) Construction of Identity' in the Local Color Fiction of Ruth McEnery Stuart," in *Gender, Race, and Identity,* edited by Craig Barrows and others (Chattanooga, Tenn.: Southern Humanities Press, 1993), pp. 237–245;

Helen Taylor, *Gender, Race, and Region in the Writings of Grace King, Ruth McEnery Stuart, and Kate Chopin* (Baton Rouge: Louisiana State University Press, 1989).

Papers:

The Ruth McEnery Stuart Papers, containing correspondence, manuscripts, and collected reviews, are housed in the manuscripts department of Howard-Tilton Memorial Library, Tulane University, New Orleans, Louisiana.

H. E. Taliaferro
(Skitt)
(4 March 1811 – 2 November 1875)

Ed Piacentino
High Point University

BOOKS: *The Grace of God Magnified: An Experimental Tract* (Charleston, S.C.: Southern Baptist Publication Society, 1857);

Fisher's River (North Carolina) Scenes and Characters, by "Skitt," "Who Was Raised Thar" (New York: Harper, 1859).

Collections: *Carolina Humor: Sketches by Harden E. Taliaferro,* edited by David K. Jackson (Richmond, Va.: Dietz Press, 1938);

The Humor of H. E. Taliaferro, edited, with an introduction, by Raymond C. Craig (Knoxville: University of Tennessee Press, 1987).

H. E. Taliaferro is best known for a single book, *Fisher's River (North Carolina) Scenes and Characters, by "Skitt," "Who Was Raised Thar"* (1859), a collection of humorous sketches and tales in the tradition of antebellum Southern frontier humor, a subliterary mode which enjoyed popular currency between the 1830s and the end of the Civil War. Taliaferro, a Baptist preacher on the Alabama frontier for most of his adult life, never achieved the popular acclaim accorded authors such as Augustus Baldwin Longstreet, Johnson Jones Hooper, Thomas Bangs Thorpe, and George Washington Harris, whose works helped to shape the contours and to establish the conventions commonly associated with the school of Old Southwestern humor.

Hardin Edwards Taliaferro, christened Mark Hardin Taliaferro (pronounced Tolliver), was born 4 March 1811 on a farm on the Little Fisher River in Surry County, North Carolina, an area located in the northwestern section of the state bordering Virginia's Blue Ridge Mountains. He was the eighth child of Charles and Sallie Burroughs Taliaferro. Taliaferro's grandfather, John Taliaferro, a Baptist preacher and teacher, had been a Revolutionary War surgeon, migrating from Pittsylvania County, Virginia, to Surry County in 1779. Taliaferro's father was a prosperous landowner and farmer and a devout Primitive Baptist

H. E. Taliaferro

who represented Surry County in the North Carolina legislature in 1811, 1812, and 1813. Known as Hardy or "Skitt" during his boyhood years Taliaferro remarks in the preface to *Fisher's River* that he spent many happy days during his youth working as a tub-boy for grist mills located on Fisher River. As a tub-boy, Taliaferro loaded the mill hoppers with grain and filled sacks with the processed meal. This experience had its long-range fringe benefits, the most important of which for Taliaferro's future as an author of backwoods humorous sketches was listening to local raconteurs recount tall tales and anecdotes, some of which he would subsequently remember and incorporate into *Fisher's River*.

Because in the 1820s Surry County afforded young people little opportunity for advancement, in 1829 the eighteen-year-old Taliaferro left home, migrating to Roane County in east Tennessee, where three older brothers Charles, John, and Richard engaged in farming and tanning. Taliaferro worked in his brothers' tanyard, learning a trade he would practice off and on for most of the rest of his life. While in Roane County in 1831 Taliaferro was baptized in the Prospect Missionary Baptist Church, where his oldest brother Charles served as pastor; and in the spring of 1832 he was licensed to preach. He began preaching on Sundays and farming and tanning during the rest of the week. Recognizing the need for additional education if he hoped to continue in the ministry, Taliaferro entered Madisonville Academy in nearby Madisonville, Tennessee, where he studied for about a year. While in Madisonville, Taliaferro also came to know the family of John Henderson, a local printer, and in 1834 he married Henderson's daughter Elizabeth. During the next year, Taliaferro did some preaching in area churches, and his first child, Nancy, was born.

In 1835 Taliaferro and his family moved farther south near the frontier post of Talladega, Alabama, where his cousin Green Taliaferro McAfee, a judge, resided. In the 1830s Alabama was still sparsely settled frontier country and lacked the population and resources to support young family men, like H. E. Taliaferro, who pursued a ministerial vocation. Consequently, in addition to his weekend preaching in small Baptist churches in the area, Taliaferro farmed and ran a tanyard. About a year after Taliaferro's arrival in Talladega, his father-in-law, John Henderson, and his family also migrated there. One of Henderson's sons, Samuel, also a Baptist preacher like Taliaferro, became the pastor of a church in Talladega, and subsequently rose to prominence as a leader among Alabama Baptists.

Taliaferro himself became a respected figure in Alabama Baptist circles during the next twenty years. He pastored several rural churches, engaged in church affairs at both the local and state levels, served on important church committees, and was chosen to deliver sermons at state Baptist conventions. His family was also growing—in the early 1840s his second daughter, Adelaide, was born.

In the 1840s Taliaferro first began to display his writing talents, chiefly in the form of sermons, four of which he published in the Virginia Baptist Preacher. One of these sermons, "The Covenant of Redemption," he delivered initially at the Baptist State Convention in Marion, Alabama, on 19 November 1846. In 1845, when a controversy erupted between the American Baptist Home Mission Society of Boston, which refused to appoint a slaveholder as a missionary among the Indians, and the proslavery Alabama Baptist Convention, the Southern Baptist Convention was founded. Taliaferro's attitude toward the slavery controversy was that of a moderate. According to Raymond Craig, "he counseled patience and reason, and believed in compromise and pragmatic good faith"; however, as did many Southerners of his time, Taliaferro staunchly proclaimed that Northern interference in the South's affairs should not be tolerated, and he apparently saw nothing wrong with slavery.

In 1851, at the age of forty, Taliaferro suffered a spiritual crisis of intense magnitude which precipitated in him serious doubts about his faith. His personal anxiety concerning his religious faith, by his own admission, stemmed from the period of his baptism and of his being licensed to preach in Roane County, Tennessee, nearly twenty years earlier. During this period of spiritual uncertainty, Taliaferro discovered Jonathan Edwards's well-known account of his own spiritual despondency and subsequent conversion in his "Personal Narrative" (1765). In 1857, in what may have been an act of therapeutic confession, Taliaferro published his first book—a graphic rendering of his own "personal narrative," *The Grace of God Magnified: An Experimental Tract*. The first edition consisted of two thousand copies. In it Taliaferro lamented being "an unholy man ministering in holy things." His professed intent in this book—a combination of narrative, personal letters, biblical quotations, brief excerpts from books, and the whole of Edwards's conversion tract—was, in his words, "to give . . . a plain and truthful account of the grace of God bestowed on me after many years." After a long period of doubt and despair regarding the uncertainty of his spiritual salvation, Taliaferro came to a self-realization. Proclaiming near the end of *The Grace of God Magnified* that he was a "redeemed, saved sinner, trusting alone in Jesus for salvation," he expressed his eagerness to preach again, accepting his humble role as God's servant. A poignant account of what it is like to be in the throes of spiritual despondency, *The Grace of God Magnified* was republished in 1858.

Taliaferro's activities in the 1850s also included journalism. In 1853 when the *Alabama Baptist*, a periodical serving as an organ of communication for Baptist preachers and laymen, was moved to Tuskegee, Alabama, its name was changed to the *South Western Baptist*. Two years later, the editor Samuel Henderson, Taliaferro's brother-in-law, invited Taliaferro to join him in Tuskegee as junior editor and co-publisher. According to Richard Walser, soon after Taliaferro joined the *South Western Baptist*, "an improvement in the writing of the articles was . . . noticeable. Famous authors were quoted more frequently, books were reviewed, and a light touch crept in occasionally." During most of his tenure with the *South Western Baptist,* which mainly published news items about Baptist churches and associations and various Baptist activities taking place in Alabama, the paper was financially successful; and by 1860 it had nearly five thousand subscribers. In his efforts to keep the *South Western Baptist* fiscally solvent, Taliaferro solicited additional advertising and traveled the state to try to collect overdue fees from delinquent subscribers.

From time to time Taliaferro wrote humorous anecdotes for the *South Western Baptist* under the signature "H. E. T." One such anecdote, part of an article in the 1 March 1860 issue about Taliaferro's observations during his travels in backwoods Alabama, describes a rustic man from St. Clair County, who has never seen a train before, but is eager to ride on the "critter" to Selma. In Taliaferro's recollection of the scene and the exchange of words between the conductor and the St. Clair man, the reader perceives a conflict of cultures, a scenario frequently found in antebellum Southern frontier humor:

> He went to the Conductor before it [the train] started, and said, "See here, Mister, I wants to ride on yer waggin to Selmy, what is the price? Here is the rinktum." "Never mind," said the Conductor, "wait till we get on board." "No, sir-ree," said the persistent man, "take the short stuff right now, it's burnin' my pocket. You'll know me when I come on." . . . The whistle blow'd, and the Conductor saw the young man standing some distance off, and hallowed him to "come on board." Our hero commenced making a rapid search for a "board," but was not successful, and finding a shingle, gathered it with both hands, came dashing into the cars, holding it up in triumph, exclaiming, "Mister, Mister, I can't find a board, won't this shingle do?" It was received, and on he went in wonderment to "Selmy."

In July 1858, when Sam Henderson resigned the editorship of the *South Western Baptist,* Taliaferro became senior editor and invited John E. Dawson, a Georgia minister, to join him as co-editor and co-owner of the paper. Taliaferro met with some controversy during the war. In the 6 March 1862 issue he announced that the paper would suspend publication. Taliaferro based his decision on several practical factors: the scarcity of paper, ink, and other supplies needed to keep the newspaper operational, the inflated costs of a wartime economy, the loss of staff who left the paper to join the war effort, and the widespread neglect of patrons to pay their subscriptions. Many Alabama Baptists condemned Taliaferro's action as rash, and Henderson, the former editor, resurrected the *South Western Baptist* briefly; how-

FISHER'S RIVER

(NORTH CAROLINA)

SCENES AND CHARACTERS.

BY "SKITT,"

"WHO WAS RAISED THAR."

ILLUSTRATED BY JOHN M'LENAN.

NEW YORK:
HARPER & BROTHERS, PUBLISHERS.
FRANKLIN SQUARE.
1859.

Title page for Taliaferro's second book, the only collection of his fiction published during his life

ever, the paper was published only infrequently for the remainder of the war.

From a literary standpoint, one of the most significant events in Taliaferro's life in the 1850s was a two-week trip in the summer of 1857 to Surry County, the place of his roots, which he had not visited for nineteen years. While there he went to see the graves of his parents and reacquainted himself with many of his old friends and neighbors. More important, his return to this mountain community he called home became the impetus for the composition of his second and last book, *Fisher's River (North Carolina) Scenes and Characters.* Published pseudonymously under Taliaferro's boyhood nickname, "Skitt," by Harper and Brothers in the fall of 1859, *Fisher's River* is the work on which the author's reputation rests. Like Augustus Baldwin Longstreet, the author of *Georgia Scenes* and at one time a minister himself, Taliaferro, as a Baptist preacher, likely wished to remain anonymous as the author of a collection of backwoods humorous sketches so as not to damage his reputation. In fact, in the preface to his book, Taliaferro claims that he had not actually intended to publish these humorous sketches, but friends who had read them had persuaded him to do so.

Fisher's River comprises twenty-three chapters, seventeen focusing on North Carolina scenes, principally those set in the northwestern section of Surry County during the 1820s. Thirteen engravings, the work of John McLenan who also illustrated many of the humorous books of Mortimer Neal Thomson ("Doesticks"), a popular northeastern urban humorist and contemporary of Taliaferro, pictorially complement the text. In the preface Taliaferro calls Surry County a "romantic section [that] produces a people equally as romantic" and indicates that the book's intent was to save "from Oblivion's fell grasp the scenes and stories of an earlier time." Furthermore, he hopes the sketches of *Fisher's River* will "contribute a mite toward our country's stock of humorous literature." To help carry out this purpose Taliaferro seems to have resorted to self-promotion, using the pages of the *South Western Baptist*. In the 10 November 1859 issue, which includes a brief notice predicting brisk sales (which Taliaferro may have written himself), *Fisher's River* was applauded as "a fair specimen of Southern backwoods vernacular, [with] a naturalness about the delineation which will make the reader feel easy in the perusal." Contemporary reviews of *Fisher's River* were laudatory. Writing in January of 1860, a reviewer in the *Southern Literary Messenger*, a periodical to which Taliaferro would subsequently contribute additional humorous sketches in the early 1860s, observed that the material of *Fisher's River* had value as social history and resembled Longstreet's *Georgia Scenes* (1835). A. H. Guernsey, in the July 1862 issue of *Harper's New Monthly Magazine*, generously appraised *Fisher's River* as "one of the half dozen clever books of American character and humor" and also favorably compared Taliaferro's collection to *Georgia Scenes*." More recent critical appraisals of Taliaferro's book have also been complimentary. In his 1965 *South Atlantic Quarterly* article Tristram P. Coffin perceived the significance of the *Fisher's River* sketches in the manner in which "they utilize the actual folklore of the Surry County area, in their fidelity to folk sources, and in the way they relate folk material to the culture from which it springs." Cratis D. Williams in 1968 called *Fisher's River* "perhaps the most important book portraying the social life and customs of the Southern mountain people to appear before the Civil War."

Whether Taliaferro actually knew Longstreet's *Georgia Scenes*, or Joseph Beckham Cobb's *Mississippi Scenes: Or, Sketches of Southern and Western Life* (1851)—works whose titles Taliaferro seems to echo in the extended title of his own book, *Fisher's River (North Carolina) Scenes and Characters*—remains conjectural. What can be definitely ascertained about *Fisher's River,* however, is Taliaferro's indebtedness to the tradition of Old Southwestern humor, as indicated by the oral quality, subject matter, and style. Like many of the practitioners of antebellum Southern frontier humor, Taliaferro employs the frame device. Typically, he introduces his vernacular yarn spinners and sets the scenes for the stories they tell. Sometimes several of the tales and anecdotes are grouped together and told by the same narrator, with the framework providing the natural connections between individual pieces. Unlike earlier writers, such as Sarah Kemble Knight and William Byrd II who had depicted backwoods scenes and characters critically and condescendingly, Taliaferro employed a gentle brand of humor and treated characters sympathetically. After all, "Skitt" Taliaferro, who was born and raised in Surry County, considered himself to be one of these people.

In addition many of the tales and sketches of *Fisher's River* fit neatly into the categories of subject matter that Hennig Cohen and William B. Dillingham in their anthology, *Humor of the Old Southwest* (1994), have used to classify the diverse range of topics and plots employed by Southern frontier humorists. Among the subjects Taliaferro treats are: hunting and animal stories (Uncle Davy Lane's sketches and tales); camp meetings, sermons, and religious exercises (Johnson Snow's "The Night Meeting," "He Joins the Church," and "He Apostasizes"; Charles Gentry's "Origin of the Whites" and "Jonah and the Whale"; "Outdone"; and "Straw! Straw, More Straw Here"); travelers and visitors ("Glassel and the Owl" and "Ham Rachel of Alabama"); militia drills ("Famus or No Famus"); courtship and marriage ("Dick Snow's Courtship," "The Wedding," and "A Declaration of Love"); fights ("A Quarter-of-a Dollar Fight," "Fight at the Quaker House," and "Fight about a Kipskin"); practical jokes ("Uncle Billy Preaches"); drinking and drunkenness ("The Convert" and "A Call to the Ministry"); and the naive countrymen in the city ("Tare and Tret. An Alabama Tale"). Because so much of the material in *Fisher's River* treats subjects of a religious nature, either directly or indirectly, more so than in sketches by other humorists of the Old Southwestern school, Raymond Craig notes that Taliaferro may be aptly designated the "humorist of frontier religion."

Like other Southwestern humorists, Taliaferro has several of his characters recount tall tales whose details have been enlarged to preposterous proportions. Unlike his counterparts of the Old Southwest, however, in *Fisher's River* Taliaferro drew extensively on personal memories of humorous anecdotes and tales told to him in his youth by actual Surry County natives such as Uncle Davy Lane, Johnson Snow, Larkin Snow, and Oliver Stanley, each showcasing a natural penchant for storytelling. Uncle Davy Lane, a local gunsmith, nar-

BENDING BUCKSMASHER.

Illustration by John McLenan for Taliaferro's Fisher's River (North Carolina) Scenes and Characters, *depicting Taliaferro's narrator Uncle Davy bending his rifle's barrel so he can shoot around a mountain*

rates outlandish animal and hunting tales, one after another, in the best deadpan manner. Typical tall tales, Davy's anecdotes detail humorous personal adventures involving incredible incidents. For example, in "The Horn-Snake," Davy relates an encounter with a large snake that grips its tail in its mouth forming a hoop and that rolls down the mountain after the frightened hunter, eventually attaching itself to a tree with his stinger. Davy then describes that he shoots the snake with his gun "Bucksmasher," only to discover that the tree "were dead as a herrin'; all the leaves was wilted like a fire had gone through its branches." Even more outlandish is "The Pigeon Roost," a variation of a well-known Baron Munchausen tale about the horse hanging from a church steeple. Davy recounts how his horse, which he had hitched to the limb of a tree where a large flock of pigeons was roosting, was lifted forty feet into the air—"swingin' to a limb, danglin' 'bout 'tween the heavens

and the yeth like a rabbit on snare-pole"–after he begins shooting.

In yet another anecdote of tall-tale proportions, "The Escape from a Whale," Oliver Stanley, who migrated to Surry County from the seacoast, tells an entertainingly personalized version of the Jonah story in graphic detail. He effects his escape from the whale's belly by cleverly lighting his pipe, causing the whale, in Stanley's words, to "gin me a rucktion, and sent me 'bout a hundred feet right up to'ads the good world."

Another of Taliaferro's Surry County raconteurs featured in *Fisher's River* is the Reverend Charles Gentry, an African American Baptist slave preacher, whose "theology was not always sound, yet a good deal of it was original" and who "had a penchant for controversy" because he continually challenged "established views . . . upsetting them by the force of his cataract voice and rail-mauling gestures, if not by argument." Of the two folk sermons the Reverend Gentry delivers, the better is "Jonah and the Whale," which Gentry emphatically insists to be "de true varsion of Jonah and the whale." The whale, according to Gentry's account, "cum up and lick him [Jonah] down like salt–hardly a bug moufful fur sich a big whoppin feller"; and the bewildered Jonah, trapped in the whale's belly, inquires repeatedly, "'O lord, what hab I done?'," to which the whale responds, "'Hush yer mouf.'" Jonah uses his fingernails to "claw and scratch the fish's paunch" in his effort to free himself. As a consequence, in the bizarre conclusion, Gentry notes that the whale becomes so sick that he swims rapidly toward shore, "'and, sure 'nuff, he gin one great big hee-ho, and out cum Jonah right on de flat of he back on the bank.'" Like other works of Southern frontier humor, *Fisher's River* is aimed at a white audience; and Taliaferro, though he portrays his slave preacher sympathetically, nevertheless keeps Gentry's character well within the bounds of the accepted popular racial stereotype of the inferior black man, relegated to the role of an entertainer of white people and object of ridicule.

A key recurring feature of the colorful vernacular style of *Fisher's River,* yet another indication of the direct influence of Southern frontier humor on Taliaferro's book, is the use of oral speech patterns, best demonstrated through exaggerated, incongruous comparisons. Every sketch or anecdote, narrated by Taliaferro's rustic and uneducated yarn spinners, contains graphic and amusing examples of this device. In describing a large panther, in the hunting tale, "The Panther," for instance, Uncle Davy Lane points out, "Thar he sot on a limb, his eyes shinin' away like new money, slappin' his tail jist like a cat gwine to jump on a rat." In "The Escape from the Whale" Oliver Stanley, one of Taliaferro's most talented and entertaining wordsmiths, figuratively recounts his kidnapping by sailors in a series of vivid animal similes: "they nabbed me quick as a snappin' turkle, put a gag in my mouf quicker nur yer could bridle a hoss, a bandage on my peepers, tied me hand and foot like a hog." In "Ham Rachel of Alabama," the concluding sketch of *Fisher's River,* Ham, a loquacious rustic, "a lean, gaunt-looking specimen of freakish humanity, about five feet eight inches high, stoop-shouldered, long-armed, and knock-kneed, with a peaked dish face, little black restless eyes, long keen nose, and big ears," creates an immediate humorous impression by sprinkling his description of the presidential candidate Gen. Zachary Taylor with incongruous domestic images: "he has fout the Mexicans, and licked 'um all up, like a cow licks up salt, and has kivered the nation with glory, like a bed-quilt kivers a bed."

Following the publication of *Fisher's River,* Taliaferro remained busy, spending much of his time attend-

ing to his increased responsibilities as senior editor of the *South Western Baptist,* as a Baptist minister serving several rural churches, and as a man who had to attend to the needs and interests of his family. Still, he managed to direct some of his energy to literary endeavors. In the summer of 1860 he wrote George William Bagby, editor of the *Southern Literary Messenger,* offering to contribute, under the pseudonym of "Skitt," as time would permit, occasional humorous sketches for the *Messenger,* if Bagby was interested. At Bagby's request, between November 1860 and October 1863, Taliaferro submitted for publication nine humorous sketches, exploiting, for the most part, similar subjects and rustic characters as those found in *Fisher's River.* Unlike the sketches of *Fisher's River,* however, Taliaferro's authorial voice dominates these narratives. "Some Chapters in the Eventful Life of Captain Robert Exquisite"(1862) which Taliaferro described in a letter to Bagby, 29 October 1860, as a "humorous satire upon exquisite, bombastic talkers, those bores of the literary world," is an extended narrative consisting of nine chapters. In it, Robert, who, because of his verbosity, pomposity, and foolish behavior, becomes an object of self-mockery. Several of the other *Messenger* pieces–"Parson Squint, by Skitt, Who Has Seen Him"(1861), "Tasting Religion" (1862), "Sketch by Skitt: Johnson Snow and Uncle Davy Lane" (1862), and "Deacon Crow" (1863)– humorously treat religious topics. "Tasting Religion," the best of the four, depicts a backwoods protracted meeting in which Dick Snobbs, who falls asleep during the services, becomes the victim of a prank (a young man puts salt in his mouth while Dick is asleep). Dick awakens suddenly, and the congregation erroneously believes he has experienced conversion until he abruptly exclaims: "I don't know–how religion–if this is religion–tastes to the rest on ye–but it tastes to me monsteraciously like salt. If it's no better tasted nur this–a man's jist as well of thout it as with it–and a leetle better." "Sketches by Skitt: Johnson Snow at the 'Hottle'" (1863), accentuates to ridiculousness the naïveté and ignorance of countrymen coming to the city. Two humorous Civil War sketches: "The Desperade"(1862)– the title being a mispronunciation of "dress parade"– featuring a sexually eager and persistent young wife who desperately desires to spend one night with her husband before his regiment departs for the front; and "Militeer Power" (1862), featuring a naive rustic, Silas Simpkins, who unsuccessfully tries to board a train reserved for military use–further demonstrate the range and diversity of Taliaferro's comedic subject matter. "Duck Town, by 'Skitt,' Who has been 'thar'" (1860), his first submission to Bagby–a sketch of a mining area in Tennessee and its unusual inhabitants–rounds out Taliaferro's contributions to the *Southern Literary Messen-*

The Pigeon-Roost

Illustration by McLenan for Taliaferro's short story "The Pigeon-Roost," about a horse lifted aloft after Uncle Davy shoots the pigeons weighing down the branch to which he had tethered it

ger. In 1938 David K. Jackson collected Taliaferro's *Messenger* pieces in *Carolina Humor: Sketches by Harden E. Taliaferro.*

Although Taliaferro had hoped, as he told George Bagby, to publish a second edition of *Fisher's River* and to include in it sketches he had submitted to the *Southern Literary Messenger,* his plans never materialized. He continued to reside in Tuskegee, preaching in several rural churches and writing occasionally for the *South Western Baptist* until federal troops forced the paper to suspend operations in April 1865. Perhaps because of financial difficulties attributable to a depressed economy in Alabama, and because he needed supplementary income to support his family, he returned to the tanning business, opening his own tanyard in Tuskegee near the end of the Civil War. About the same time the war ended, Taliaferro became editor of a new weekly newspaper, the *Tuskegee News.* Though religious news was the primary focus of the *Tuskegee News,* Taliaferro still included items for the moral edification of readers and some humorous pieces reprinted from other newspapers. Taliaferro remained editor of the *News* until the late 1860s.

With the demise of the Confederacy and the emancipation of slaves, the American Baptist Home Mission Society of Boston, responding to the requests of African American freedmen, spearheaded an effort in the South to establish separate churches for blacks and to provide training for African Americans desiring to enter the Baptist ministry. To provide training for black ministers, the Home Mission Society, though much despised by Southern Baptists, actively recruited white Southern Baptist ministers to direct these efforts. In Alabama few white ministers volunteered to assist, and only three were actually appointed for this task, Taliaferro being one of them. Although he had supported the institution of slavery, Taliaferro had always included blacks in his ministry, and he believed white Southerners—not "Yankees"—should educate the freed slaves. Between 1869 and 1872, Taliaferro helped to train black ministers in small communities near Tuskegee and to organize the first Baptist State Convention for black Alabama Baptists.

In the spring of 1873 Taliaferro left Alabama and returned to Loudon, Tennessee, the area where he had been ordained and had gotten his start in the ministry forty-one years earlier. During the last two years of his life Taliaferro continued to be active in the Baptist Church, joining the Loudon Baptist Church and holding various positions, including Moderator of the Providence Baptist Association in 1875. Taliaferro died in Loudon on 2 November 1875, at the age of sixty-four.

While known in his lifetime as an ardent and pious Baptist preacher and as a conscientious and dedicated publisher and denominational editor, Hardin E. Taliaferro has since become critically recognized as a creditable backwoods humorist, his reputation resting on *Fisher's River (North Carolina) Scenes and Characters*. In his markedly sympathetic and gently humorous depiction of frontier life in Fisher's River, Taliaferro not only combined folklore motifs and features of Old Southwestern humor to create a lively and entertaining amalgam, but he also did something that no other Southern backwoods humorist had ever done before: presented memorable and engaging anecdotes and stories told by yarn spinners he had actually known in Surry County, North Carolina. In his transcription of authentic folk materials, Taliaferro anticipated a strategy similar to the one Joel Chandler Harris would subsequently employ when he appropriated and then transformed the animal tales he heard Georgia slaves recount in his boyhood into his Uncle Remus stories in the 1880s. As a final testament to H. E. Taliaferro's achievement, E. B. Teague, a fellow Baptist minister in Tuskegee who had known him, generously acknowledged in an obituary published in the *Alabama Baptist* on 6 January 1876, Taliaferro's talent and appeal as a backwoods humorist: "His colloquial powers were fine, and his humor most spontaneous and rich."

Bibliography:

Richard Walser, "Biblio-biography of Skitt Taliaferro," *North Carolina Historical Review*, 15 (1978): 375–392.

References:

Ralph Steele Boggs, "North Carolina Folktales Current in the 1820's," *Journal of American Folklore*, 47 (1934): 269–288;

Tristram P. Coffin, "Harden E. Taliaferro and the Use of Folklore by American Literary Figures," *South Atlantic Quarterly*, 64 (1965): 241–246;

Hennig Cohen and William B. Dillingham, eds., *Humor of the Old Southwest* (Athens: University of Georgia Press, 1994);

James H. Penrod, "Harden E. Taliaferro, Folk Humorist of North Carolina," *Midwest Folklore*, 6 (1956): 147–153;

Cratis D. Williams, "Mountain Customs, Social Life, and Folk Yarns in Taliaferro's *Fisher's River Scenes and Characters*," *North Carolina Folklore Journal*, 16 (1968): 143–152.

Frederick William Thomas

(26 October 1806 – 27 August 1866)

Benjamin F. Fisher
University of Mississippi

BOOKS: *An Address Delivered Before the Hamilton County Agricultural Society at the Annual Exhibition, September 27, 1832* (Cincinnati: Hamilton County Agricultural Society, 1832);

The Emigrant, or Reflections While Descending the Ohio, anonymous (Cincinnati: Alexander Flash, 1833);

Address Delivered on the Fourteenth Anniversary of the Institution of the Order of Independent Odd Fellows in the United States (Cincinnati: Published by Direction of the Lodges, 1834);

Clinton Bradshaw; or, The Adventures of a Lawyer, 2 volumes, anonymous (Philadelphia: Carey, Lea & Blanchard, 1835);

East and West: A Novel by the Author of "Clinton Bradshaw," 2 volumes, anonymous (Philadelphia: Carey, Lea & Blanchard, 1836);

An Address Delivered before the Erodelphian Society of Miami University, at Its Thirteenth Annual Celebration, August 7th, 1838 (Oxford, Ohio: Printed by W. W. Bishop, 1838);

Howard Pinckney: A Novel by the Author of "Clinton Bradshaw," 2 volumes, anonymous (Philadelphia: Lea & Blanchard, 1840; London: J. Clements, 1841);

The Beechen Tree: A Tale Told in Rhyme (New York: Harper, 1844);

Sketches of Character, and Tales Founded on Fact (Louisville: Office of the *Chronicle of Western Literature and Art,* 1849);

An Autobiography of William Russell, by the Author of "Clinton Bradshaw," & C, anonymous (Baltimore: Gobright, Thorne, 1852);

John Randolph, of Roanoke, and Other Sketches of Character, Including William Wirt. Together With Tales of Real Life (Philadelphia: A. Hart, 1853).

OTHER: "A Chapter from the Adventures of a Lame Gentleman," in *The Gift: A Christmas and New Year's Present for 1839,* edited by Eliza Leslie (Philadelphia: Carey & Hart, 1838), pp. 168–178;

"War Song of Seventy-Six," in *Selections from the Poetical Literature of the West,* edited by William D. Gal-

Frederick William Thomas (painting by Thomas D. Jones, American Antiquarian Society)

lagher (Cincinnati: U. P. James, 1841), pp. 193–195;

"'Tis Said that Absence Conquers Love," in *The Poets and Poetry of America,* sixteenth edition, edited by Rufus W. Griswold (Philadelphia: Parry & Macmillan, 1856), p. 408.

SELECTED PERIODICAL PUBLICATIONS— UNCOLLECTED:
POETRY
"Stanzas to Helen," *Southern Literary Messenger,* 4 (July 1838): 473–474;

"Retrospections," *American Museum of Literature and the Arts,* 1 (September 1838): 86–88;

"A Poet to His Sister," *Knickerbocker Magazine,* 14 (March 1840): 233;

"Woman," *Ladies' Companion,* 14 (January 1841): 141;

"Anacreontic Farewell," *Ladies' Companion,* 15 (May 1841): 14;

"To Ianthe of Louisiana," *Ladies' Companion,* 15 (June 1841): 94;

"Extracts from an Unpublished Poem: The Meeting of the Lovers," *Graham's Magazine,* 19 (July 1841): 38–39;

"A Belle at a Ball," *Graham's Magazine,* 19 (September 1841): 119;

"Song of the Western Steamboat-Men," *Knickerbocker Magazine,* 22 (October 1843): 333–334;

"Stanzas: To My Sister," *Knickerbocker Magazine,* 28 (October 1846): 344–345;

"A Health," *Knickerbocker Magazine,* 29 (May 1847): 29.

FICTION

"Early Home Records," *Knickerbocker Magazine,* 14 (September 1839): 213–221;

"Early Home Records. Number Two," *Knickerbocker Magazine,* 14 (December 1839): 483–490;

"Old Nat," *Ladies' Companion,* 14 (February 1841): 154–161.

In *Edgar Huntly* (1799) Charles Brockden Brown exhorted aspirant American authors to focus on the West as useful material for creating a genuinely indigenous literature. Frederick William Thomas takes a place with others such as James Kirke Paulding, Washington Irving, Timothy Flint, and James Hall who responded, at least in part, to Brown's call. *Clinton Bradshaw; or, The Adventures of a Lawyer* (1835), Thomas's first novel, and *The Beechen Tree: A Tale Told in Rhyme* (1844) became popular among American readers, and reviewers gave careful consideration to his writings; however, Thomas's publications have sustained little popularity since their own day. He is accorded scantiest notice in the long standard histories of American fiction by Arthur Hobson Quinn and Alexander Cowie, and he is ignored elsewhere in accounts of the American novel.

Most biographical accounts of Thomas–including one of his own sent to Edgar Allan Poe in late 1841–offer many inaccuracies. Indeed, as was the case with his friend Poe, for many years Thomas has had wrong dates given for his birth. In *The Literature of the Middle Western Frontier* (1925) Ralph L. Rusk rectifies inaccuracies concerning Thomas's life and writings, chiefly by reference to periodical sources that were overlooked by others and to Thomas's autobiographical notes, used by J. H. Whitty in his edition of Poe's poems (1911).

Born on 26 October 1806 to Ebenezer Smith and Ann Fonerden Thomas, in Providence, Rhode Island, Frederick William Thomas spent his early years in Charleston, South Carolina, and then, when his family moved to Ohio, he stayed with relatives in Baltimore, presumably because of a leg injury that his parents feared would be exacerbated if he made the rugged trip West. In Baltimore he was admitted to the bar in 1828. Three years later he moved to Cincinnati, where his father edited the *Commercial Daily Advertiser.* Thomas assisted his father while once again conducting a law practice, and during the next decade he pursued other journalistic and literary activities, such as editing the *Democratic Intelligencer* for six months. His contributions to newspapers have never been completely collected nor systematically recorded. Thomas also traveled extensively throughout the Midwest, garnering materials that were put to good use in his creative works.

Thomas's first book, *The Emigrant, or Reflections While Descending the Ohio* (1833), an attempt to create word pictures of nature in verse, betrays the influence of Thomas Gray, William Wordsworth, and George Gordon, Lord Byron as well as other literary antecedents to whom the speaker alludes. The speaker's reflections encompass separation from his beloved, the demise of the Indians who formerly inhabited the Ohio River region in which he travels, and the intense appeal of the West to his patriotic sentiments. *The Beechen Tree* descends from the verse narratives of Byron and Sir Walter Scott; Byron's comic sense, notably as it is couched in feminine rhymes, is apparent in this tale of thwarted love that ultimately impels the protagonist into the West to forget his old life and begin anew in that region of opportunity.

Several of Thomas's short poems were included in prestigious contemporaneous anthologies–for example, revised editions of Rufus W. Griswold's *The Poets and Poetry of America* (he had been relegated to an appendix in the first edition in 1842) or *The Poets and Poetry of the West,* edited by William T. Coggeshall (1860), which includes an error-riddled memoir of Thomas–but more recent anthologists of nineteenth-century American verse have included no selections from his works. He also wrote songs that were published as sheet music and in anthologies, such as "War Song of Seventy-Six" in 1841. Thomas's name once commanded sufficient respect to be favorably mentioned as a contributor to renowned literary annuals such as *The Gift,* edited by Eliza Leslie, or to be sought as a contributor to the *Baltimore American Museum,* a short-lived periodical at the close of the 1830s.

Thomas's associations with Poe, however, have done more than his short works to keep his name alive. In his edition of Poe's writings, Thomas Ollive Mabbott has attempted to sift fact from myth concerning the Thomas-Poe relationship. The two authors' correspondence sheds light on Poe's hopes for political office during the administration of John Tyler in the 1840s and other topics of a more literary nature. Moreover, Thomas's "Chapter from the Adventures of a Lame Gentleman," a story in *The Gift: A Christmas and New Year's Present for 1839* (1838), reads almost as if it were a follow-up to Poe's own 1838 tales "How to Write a *Blackwood's* Article" and "A Predicament" in delineating the narrator's overwrought emotionalism within a comic framework. This autobiographical tale about adventures on a river boat was favorably noticed in such prestigious periodicals as *The Knickerbocker Magazine* and *Burton's Gentleman's Magazine* and is also noteworthy as an anticipation of such better-known representatives of American humor as T. B. Thorpe's "The Big Bear of Arkansas" (1841) or Mark Twain's *Adventures of Huckleberry Finn* (1884).

Thomas's novels represent his greatest literary achievement. The first, *Clinton Bradshaw,* was rightly discerned by Poe and others as an attempt to Americanize Edward Bulwer-Lytton's renowned novel, *Pelham; or, The Adventures of a Gentleman* (1828), a book remembered as the most worthwhile specimen of the British "fashionable" or "silver-fork" novel much admired during the 1820s and 1830s. Such fiction portrayed wealthy characters modeled on actual persons. *Clinton Bradshaw,* like *Pelham,* centers on its hero's activities in upper-class society in an unspecified eastern locale, possibly near Baltimore. An aspiring young lawyer, Bradshaw manages ultimately to wend his way through a difficult, if wholly sentimental, love affair culminating in marriage to the customary insipid heroine. Along the way, he sustains several brushes with criminals, successfully defends an innocent girl against murder charges, indulges in "only-the-boys" dinners and revels, and too frequently intones passages from Byron, Scott, and other literary favorites of the day. Unlike *Pelham,* however, *Clinton Bradshaw* features neither flippancy toward upper-class society and its outlook during the author's own day nor any of the slang with which Bulwer-Lytton liberally sprinkled his pages. Thomas's novel also does not present sensuality as blatant as that in *Pelham. Clinton Bradshaw* further anticipates the novel of urban underworld life as popularized by Charles Dickens, notably in *Oliver Twist* (1837–1838) or *Our Mutual Friend* (1864–1865). Bradshaw's performances in court may be seen as forerunners to the courtroom scenes that enliven many television crime shows.

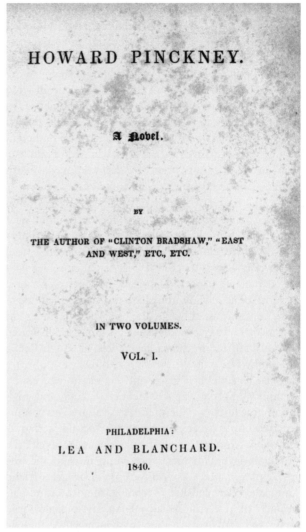

HOWARD PINCKNEY.

A Novel.

BY

THE AUTHOR OF "CLINTON BRADSHAW," "EAST AND WEST," ETC., ETC.

IN TWO VOLUMES.

VOL. I.

PHILADELPHIA:
LEA AND BLANCHARD.
1840.

Title page for Thomas's third novel, set near New York City (courtesy of Special Collections, Thomas Cooper Library, University of South Carolina)

Far more interesting, Thomas's second novel, *East and West: A Novel by the Author of "Clinton Bradshaw"* (1836), reveals more of his modifications of the crime novel (another genre popularized by Bulwer-Lytton, Dickens, and William Harrison Ainsworth in Great Britain) to reflect American situations. Thus it ranks with novels such as Paulding's *Koningsmarke* (1823) or William Gilmore Simms's *Martin Faber* (1833) or *The Scout* (1854), wherein their authors attempted to graft American literary materials onto stocks of established Gothicism. *East and West* is more emphatically western in substance than *Clinton Bradshaw.* Thomas adapted materials then being used by writers of frontier humor—for example, the sympathetic presentation of the ebullient rustic, Blazeaway, along with disparagement of the foppish Gothic-sentimental antagonist (who goes West only to create trouble for the hero and heroine and who, drunkenly planning to murder the latter, falls over the rail of the steamer on which they are journeying and drowns). These elements combine with the aspirations toward great democratic freedom and its accompanying successes in the unproved West, making *East and West* another American work typical of its day. Symbolically, an American spirit that developed from westward expansion puts behind it the puerilities of over-refined Eastern urbanism, as well as the defects that many American readers and critics found inherent in literary Gothicism. *East and West,* while less bombastically patriotic in tone than *The Emigrant,* nevertheless hymns the potential in the American West.

The backdrop in *Howard Pinckney: A Novel by the Author of "Clinton Bradshaw"* (1840) is a rural setting near New York City. The characters divide interestingly between lower-class types who speak convincingly and upper-class sorts who converse among themselves with stilted pretentiousness. Thomas's handling of Europeanized Gothic villainy in treating the fate of the antagonist, as contrasted with the superior qualities of nationalistic American characters, is more sophisticated than it had been in the earlier novels, although Pinckney embodies traits of the Byron–Bulwer-Lytton protagonist in American guise, and his inamorata, Fanny Fitzhurst, has the vaguely defined beauty and high moral qualities of heroines typical in early-nineteenth-century American romance. Pinckney's characterization displays an artistic advance over the protagonists in Thomas's preceding novels, and the hero's observations, as well as those of his great friend Langdale, offer plausible psychological portraiture, particularly of love relationships. Sexuality, violence, jealousy, and brutality are more convincing here than in Thomas's other fiction. Reviewers found the characters compelling but the dialogue faulty; Thomas's intent to create more consistent comedy than he had previously attempted may account for the disparity between his well-conceived characters and their utterances. Nevertheless, *Howard Pinckney* may be designated as Thomas's outstanding achievement in fiction. Similarities to detective fiction are discernable in the later chapters. Consequently, Poe's low estimate of *Howard Pinckney* in comparison with *Clinton Bradshaw,* expressed in a 23 November 1840 letter to Thomas, may have stemmed from anxiety over Thomas's drawing too near the methods in Poe's own detective tale, "The Murders in the Rue Morgue," which did not appear until April 1841.

During these years Thomas had relocated to Cambridge, Maryland, and Washington, D. C., where he once more practiced law, dabbled in politics, and wrote little. He died in Washington on 27 August 1866. His last novel, *An Autobiography of William Russell, by the Author of "Clinton Bradshaw," & C* (1852), drew heavily

and tediously on his own early experience, including his move from the South to Baltimore and then westward. That Thomas's creativity was flagging is evident in his reworking of material used years earlier in shorter sketches, along with a customary drunken antagonist, without imparting any new vitality to such substance. Plot and characterization lack whatever excitement went into the making of his earlier works. *Sketches of Character, and Tales Founded on Fact* (1849) includes three pieces of short fiction: "Boarding-School Scenes; or, A Frolic among the Lawyers," "Mary M'Intyre Has Arrived," and "The Unsummoned Witness" (first published in *Ladies' Companion,* November 1840), all redolent of the timeworn situations and characters in comic or Gothic-sentimental fiction. A sensational courtroom scene followed by pursuit and the bringing down of a vicious murderer enliven the second tale, though little life is breathed into the first. "Mary M'Intyre" reads rather like a watered-down Paulding satire on pretentious affection. The first tale was recycled into *An Autobiography of William Russell.* The remaining pieces in *Sketches of Character* are portraits of William Wirt, Simon Kenton (expanded from material published first in the *Cincinnati Mirror,* December 1833), and John Randolph of Roanoke; these pieces reappear in *John Randolph, of Roanoke, and Other Sketches of Character, Including William Wirt. Together With Tales of Real Life* (1853). Some of these articles appeared originally in the *Chronicle of Western Literature and Art,* published in Louisville, Kentucky.

Frederick William Thomas's novels remain worthy of notice as experiments toward creating a truly American literature during years when literary nationalism gained increasing credence in the United States. The novels stand as transition pieces between the episodic creations of Tobias Smollett and the greater sophistication in creating the same kind of fiction in *Adventures of Huckleberry Finn;* with the latter they also share propensities for employing Mississippi and related river settings. Thomas transplanted the Byronic Hero, along with his literary kinsman, the Bulwerian Dandy, into American situations. In such respects he has generally been overlooked in favor of other Americans of his time who were inspired by Byronism, such as Poe, Simms, or even the youthful John Greenleaf Whittier. The fashionable-novel elements in Thomas's fiction foreshadow those in the novel of manners in the hands of Henry James and Edith Wharton. Given the paucity of details and documentation concerning Thomas's personal life, scholars can only imperfectly assess the autobiographical elements in his productions. *Howard Pinckney,* Thomas's most significant accomplishment in fiction writing, despite his own preference for *Clinton Bradshaw,* is worth reconsideration for the plausible sophistication of its recognizable prototypes in American contexts.

References:

William T. Coggeshall, ed., *The Poets and Poetry of the West* (Columbus, Ohio: Follett, Foster, 1860), pp. 184–186;

Alexander Cowie, *The Rise of the American Novel* (New York: American Book Co., 1948), pp. 226–227, 789;

"Increase of Novel Writing," *American Monthly Magazine,* 6 (November 1835): 228–237;

Joseph Holt Ingraham, "Biographical Sketches of Living American Poets and Novelists. No. I. Francis [*sic*] William Thomas, Esq.," *Southern Literary Messenger,* 4 (May 1838): 297–301;

William Ellery Leonard, *Byron and Byronism in America* (New York: Columbia University Press, 1905);

Mary E. Phillips, *Edgar Allan Poe, the Man,* 2 volumes (Chicago: Winston, 1926);

Edgar Allan Poe, *Collected Works of Edgar Allan Poe,* 3 volumes, edited by Thomas Ollive Mabbott (Cambridge, Mass.: Harvard University Press, 1969–1978);

Poe, *The Complete Works of Edgar Allan Poe,* 17 volumes, edited by J. A. Harrison (New York: Crowell, 1902);

Poe, *The Letters of Edgar Allan Poe,* revised edition, 2 volumes, edited by John Ward Ostrom (Port Washington: Gordian Press, 1966);

Arthur Hobson Quinn, *American Fiction: An Historical and Critical Survey* (New York: Appleton-Century, 1936), p. 131;

Quinn, *Edgar Allan Poe: A Critical Biography* (New York: Appleton-Century-Crofts, 1941);

Ralph L. Rusk, *The Literature of the Middle Western Frontier* (New York: Columbia University Press, 1925);

Dwight Thomas and David K. Jackson, *The Poe Log: A Documentary Life of Edgar Allan Poe, 1809–1849* (Boston: G. K. Hall, 1987);

Emerson Venable, ed., *Poets of Ohio* (Cincinnati: R. Clarke, 1909), pp. 51–55, 354;

William Henry Venable, *Beginnings of Literary Culture in the Ohio Valley, Historical and Biographical Sketches* (Cincinnati: R. Clarke, 1891), p. 290;

J. H. Whitty, ed., "Memoir," in *The Poems of Edgar Allan Poe* (Boston: Houghton Mifflin, 1911), pp. xix–lxxxvi.

Papers:

An archive of Frederick William Thomas's papers is part of the Griswold Collection at the Boston Public Library, Massachusetts.

Daniel Pierce Thompson

(1 October 1795 – 6 June 1868)

Lucia Z. Knoles
Assumption College

BOOKS: *The Adventures of Timothy Peacock, Esquire; or, Freemasonry Practically Illustrated,* anonymous (Middlebury, Vt.: Printed by Knapp & Jewett, 1835);

May Martin; or, The Money Diggers: A Green Mountain Tale (Montpelier, Vt.: Walton, 1835; revised edition, Burlington, Vt.: Goodrich, 1848); augmented as *May Martin and Other Tales of the Green Mountains* (Boston: Mussey, 1852)–includes stories from *Lucy Hosmer* and *The Shaker Lovers;*

The Green Mountain Boys: A Historical Tale of the Early Settlement of Vermont, 2 volumes, anonymous (Montpelier, Vt.: Walton, 1839; London: Cunningham, 1840; revised edition, Boston: Mussey, 1848);

Locke Amsden; or, The Schoolmaster: A Tale, anonymous (Boston: Mussey, 1847);

Lucy Hosmer; or, The Guardian and Ghost: A Tale of Avarice and Crime Defeated (Burlington, Vt.: Goodrich & Nichols, 1848);

The Shaker Lovers; or, Virtue and Innocence Triumphant (Burlington, Vt.: Goodrich & Nichols, 1848);

An Address Pronounced in the Representatives' Hall, Montpelier, 24th October, 1850, before the Vermont Historical Society, in the Presence of Both Houses of the General Assembly (Burlington, Vt.: Free Press Office, 1850);

The Rangers; or, The Tory's Daughter, a Tale, 2 volumes, anonymous (Boston: Mussey, 1851);

Gaut Gurley; or, The Trappers of Umbagog: A Tale of Border Life (Boston: J. P. Jewett / Cleveland: Henry P. B. Jewett, 1857); republished as *The Demon Trapper of Umbagog: A Thrilling Tale of the Maine Forests* (Philadelphia: Columbian, 1890);

The Doomed Chief; or, Two Hundred Years Ago, anonymous (Philadelphia: Bradley, 1860; Philadelphia & Boston: Evans, 1860);

History of the Town of Montpelier . . . Together with Biographical Sketches of Its Most Noted Deceased Citizens (Montpelier, Vt.: Printed by Walton, 1860);

Centeola: and Other Tales, anonymous (New York: Carleton, 1864);

Daniel Pierce Thompson (after a portrait by T. W. Wood)

Green Mountain Boy at Monticello: A Talk with Jefferson in 1822, introduction by Howard C. Rice Jr. (Brattleboro, Vt.: Book Cellar, 1962).

OTHER: "Montpelier," in *Gazetteer of the State of Vermont,* by Zadock Thompson (Montpelier, Vt.: Walton, 1824), pp. 188–189;

The Laws of Vermont, of a Public and Permanent Nature, Coming Down to and Including the Year 1834, compiled by Thompson (Montpelier, Vt.: Printed by Knapp & Jewett, 1835);

"Great Wolf Hunt on Irish Hill," in *Vermont Historical Gazetteer* (Montpelier: Vermont Watchman and State Journal Press, 1882), IV: 69–72;

"Life, Character and Times of Ira Allen," in *Proceedings of the Vermont Historical Society for the Years 1908–1909* (Montpelier, Vt.: 1909?), pp. 87–172.

SELECTED PERIODICAL PUBLICATION– UNCOLLECTED:"A New Anecdote of Washington," *Harper's New Monthly Magazine,* 30 (December 1864): 74–76.

During the mid nineteenth century Daniel Pierce Thompson of Vermont enjoyed a period of considerable popularity as an author of historical romances. Generally regarded as an imitator of James Fenimore Cooper, Thompson never achieved critical success even during his heyday, and few reviews of his work exist. The only exception to this critical silence came with the publication of *Locke Amsden* (1847), a novel of education about a young Vermont teacher that preceded Edward Eggleston's *The Hoosier Schoolmaster* (1871) by more than two decades. Thompson's overblown style and contrived plots have not worn well and are unlikely to attract a wide audience in the future. Students of antebellum American attitudes toward education and literacy, however, will continue to find much of interest in *Locke Amsden,* and Thompson's is also a valuable example of the fervor for discovering an American past that swept the United States during the first half of the nineteenth century.

Thompson's origins may help account for his patriotic enthusiasms. The grandson and namesake of the Daniel Thompson who fell at the Battle of Lexington, Daniel Pierce Thompson was born on 1 October 1795 under the shadow of the Bunker Hill memorial in Charlestown, Massachusetts. Five years later he moved with his parents, Rebecca Parker and Daniel Thompson Jr., and his sisters, Fanny, Charlotte, and Rebecca, to a small farm near Berlin, Vermont. This relocation, necessitated by his father's business failures, shaped the course of Thompson's sensibility and eventual career. Not settled until 1787, Berlin township had almost seven hundred residents when the Thompsons arrived in 1800. Thus, young Thompson found himself surrounded by the kind of visible reminders of pioneer life most likely to stir a boy's imagination.

One incident in particular probably set in motion Thompson's historical curiosity. The family farm was located on the Stevens branch of the Winooski River, so named to commemorate an early tragedy of the region. Rejected in love, Stevens had attempted to escape his romantic woes by seeking refuge on the river. Too demoralized to make the necessary efforts to ensure his survival, he had died while making a too-long postponed attempt to catch a fish. Buried by passing hunters, the corpse of the tragic lover was unexpectedly exposed in 1806 by the plow of the eleven-year-old Thompson and his father. As Thompson later remembered, "the sight of these remains, as they were thrown out by the deep furrow that was made lengthwise through them, with the rust-eaten jackknife lying in the midst, palpable to view, caused it to become one of the most vivid of my early recollections, and subsequently led me to make minute inquiries of the oldest settlers in all that related to the unfortunate hunter."

An equally fateful discovery occurred in 1811, when Thompson spotted a water-soaked volume at the bottom of a stream and thus acquired his first book. Many of his later allusions are to verses he memorized from this collection of English poetry. A just estimate of the value this treasure held for Thompson can be derived from his description of the almost visceral pain the hero of his semi-autobiographical novel *Locke Amsden* experienced when bereft of books.

Thompson's determination to get an education was at odds with his father's belief that it would have no practical benefit. Thompson won over his father, however, after raising the funds necessary for schooling. Thompson used a silver dollar from his grandmother to buy and raise a sheep that, through a series of trades, he eventually parlayed into a valuable team of oxen. He then began to teach himself from an arithmetic book, a copy of Virgil, and Latin texts he had purchased with money earned by trapping and selling muskrat and mink. In 1815, after three Latin lessons for which he paid a local Dartmouth graduate a total of thirty-seven and one-half cents, Thompson moved thirty miles away to prepare for college by living and studying in the home of a clergyman. In his enthusiasm for learning, he devoured all of Virgil in just twelve weeks and was ready to move on to the Randolph-Danville Academy by the fall of 1816. Throughout this period Thompson "boarded round" as a schoolmaster in rustic northern Vermont communities during the winter and assisted his father and brother on the farm during the summer months.

Thompson entered Middlebury College in 1817. In an 1850 address at his alma mater, Thompson recalled his arrival at Middlebury as a

poor untutored, unfriended boy, who had never seen books but in visions, whose almost every merit, indeed, consisted in

The dream, the thirst, the wild desire,
Delirious, yet divine—to know—.

Despite the miscellaneous nature of his academic training, Thompson was able to graduate in a little more than two years, receiving his degree in 1820. He

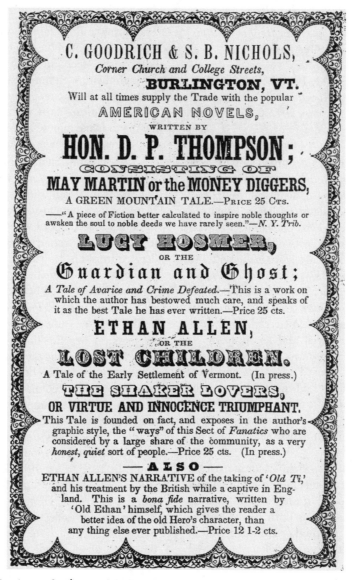

Advertisement for Thompson's books on the back cover of his novel Lucy Hosmer *(1848)*

reported that he published some essays and stories during his college career, but none has survived.

After leaving Middlebury, Thompson spent three or four years studying law while working as a tutor for a wealthy family in Virginia. The high point of this period in his life remained vivid in Thompson's recollection more than forty years later, when he published "A Talk with Thomas Jefferson" in *Harper's New Monthly Magazine* (May 1863). In response to the young law student's request for an interview, the former president had invited Thompson to Monticello for dinner and conversation.

After Thompson returned to Montpelier in 1823 or 1824, he opened a law office, entered politics, took up historical investigations, began writing, and enjoyed the simple leisure pursuits afforded by small-town life.

For Thompson these various activities seemed to be all of one piece. He based some of his fictional works on information he garnered as part of his legal practice, while he acquired other background for his writing in conversations with farmers he encountered during fishing expeditions.

The first literary product of these conversations appeared in 1824, when Thompson's history of the early settlement of Berlin and Montpelier was published as part of Zadock Thompson's *Gazetteer of the State of Vermont*. Years later Thompson described how he had "visited, for the purpose of collecting materials for that task, the most intelligent settlers of Montpelier and the neighboring towns, and made minutes of the facts and incidents." In virtually all the prefatory notes he wrote for his publications, fiction and nonfiction,

Thompson insisted that his works were based on the notes he had taken during interviews with firsthand witnesses. When introducing novels or short stories, he generally added a remark that he had altered facts in the interest of producing better fiction.

Thompson married Eunice Knight Robinson of Troy, Vermont, in 1831. They had six children: George Robinson (1834), Alma (1837), William Penn (1839), Frances (1842), Daniel Greenleaf (1850), and Charles Sumner (1851).

During the same years in which he was beginning his family, Thompson's political and literary activities started to escalate. Within two years of his return to Vermont, Thompson had been made register of probate for Washington County, and from that point on he held a series of political offices over the course of about thirty years. After serving as clerk of the Vermont House of Representatives for three years, he was chosen by the governor to compile *The Laws of Vermont, of a Public and Permanent Nature, Coming Down to and Including the Year 1834,* which was compiled in 1834 and published in 1835. Thompson became judge of probate in 1837 and continued to be known as Judge Thompson even after leaving that position in 1840.

Thompson produced two other works in 1835: *The Adventures of Timothy Peacock, Esquire; or, Freemasonry Practically Illustrated* and *May Martin; or, The Money Diggers: A Green Mountain Tale. The Adventures of Timothy Peacock* is a satirical tract with an almost eighteenth-century flavor. Published anonymously, it was part of the anti-Masonic frenzy that broke out following the mysterious disappearance of William Morgan, author of a book alleged to expose the secrets of the Masonic order. The stylistic and substantive excesses of Thompson's piece later prompted him to feel some embarrassment. Given the scant attention the work received, however, it had no real effect on Thompson's reputation or the course of the controversy.

Thompson tasted his first literary success that same year, however, when his novel *May Martin; or, The Money Diggers* was chosen to receive the prize of fifty dollars offered by *The New-England Galaxy* for best original tale. Thompson learned of the competition after most of his story was completed, having begun writing "rather as an agreeable relaxation from the professional labors and studies of the day than with any view of publication." Basing his narrative on a local tale about treasure hunters in the mountains of Vermont, Thompson added further interest by connecting it to the famous Canadian counterfeiter Stephen Burroughs, whose *Memoirs* (1798) had been popular among New England readers. (Thompson later included counterfeiters in at least two other stories, "The Rustic Financiers" and "The Counterfeiters.") As a final touch, Thompson

added a romance plot loosely based on historical circumstances. This same blend of history and romance also characterizes much of Thompson's subsequent work.

Although Thompson secured a copyright for *May Martin; or, The Money Diggers* and had the pleasure of seeing a "large edition" of it completely sold out, he received little benefit from the more than fifty editions that subsequently appeared. For all his career Thompson was the victim of weak American copyright laws and the absence of international copyright agreements. In America the fact that *May Martin; or, The Money Diggers* had been printed in a newspaper made it possible to pirate the tale with impunity. In his introduction to the 1852 edition of *May Martin and Other Tales of the Green Mountains* Thompson commented that many editions had appeared "without thanks, return, or benefit, to the author, save the compliment involved in the act, which is, indeed, something, since it is not every work that is worth stealing." As Thompson's son Daniel later reported, the novelist discovered that "literature has few pecuniary rewards." Moreover, a reviewer in *The Literary World* in 1851 hypothesized that the cheap chapbook editions through which many readers were exposed to Thompson's fiction may have accounted for the lack of critical attention he received.

Thompson's most popular novel, *The Green Mountain Boys: A Historical Tale of the Early Settlement of Vermont,* appeared in 1839. Sometimes reminiscent in spirit to Sir Walter Scott's *Ivanhoe* (1819), Thompson's novel describes in glowing terms the role the Green Mountain Boys played in the property dispute that began in 1769 between Vermont settlers and New York landowners and in the American Revolution. Although historically these two episodes were separated in time, Thompson conflated them in the interests of "unity of design." Thus, volume one, which describes the early exploits of the Green Mountain Boys in their skirmishes against unscrupulous land agents, concludes with a dramatic scene in which a captured Green Mountain leader is rescued by a wily bear of a man who turns out to be Ethan Allen. When Allen arrives on the scene, he dramatically announces the Battle of Lexington (1775): "Blood—American blood—has been shed!" With this device the book achieves a neat shift from the regional to the national stage without causing any disruption to the plot.

Interwoven with these events is the kind of plot familiar to readers of sentimental romances. The dashing Colonel Warrington of the Green Mountain Boys—a fictionalized portrait of the Revolutionary war hero Seth Warner—competes with an unscrupulous Tory land speculator for the hand of the lovely Alma Hendee. The novel includes an inheritance swindle, a long-lost son with an identifying tattoo, a rape prevented by a timely swoon, and two deathbed confessions. In the final chapters of the novel Warrington's best friend is revealed as the long-lost son and heir, Warrington himself reappears "lazarus-like" after being reported dead on the battlefield, and a larger-than-life Ethan Allen is released from a British prison just in time to take part in the festivities surrounding the four weddings that bring the narrative to a close.

The Green Mountain Boys enjoyed great popularity during the middle of the nineteenth century and was widely recognized as "the classic of Vermont." The novel found an appreciative audience even outside of America and was republished in London and Leipzig. Thompson's unsuccessful attempt to solicit a review from Henry Wadswoth Longfellow seems to suggest that Thompson was also interested in cultivating critical attention, a feat he did not accomplish.

When *The Green Mountain Boys* has been noticed by critics, it has generally been characterized as an inferior version of a Cooper novel. Certainly settlers, backwoodsmen, and Indians populate a world of forests, cabins, and caves in the fiction of both men. The tendency to place Thompson in Cooper's shadow, however, has had the unfortunate effect of obscuring those qualities that set Thompson apart from his better-known contemporary. One distinctive element of Thompson's writing is his use of humor; a comic tone prevails throughout volume one of *The Green Mountain Boys* as the band responds to enemy attacks with the kinds of spirited pranks commonly found in folktales.

While Thompson's wilderness has been criticized as less vibrantly imagined than Cooper's, Thompson himself criticized Cooper's depiction of the woods and backwoodsmen as unrealistic. Moreover, although Thompson expressed a love of nature and a respect for the skills of those who can face its challenges, his fiction has no Natty Bumppo figure to provoke nostalgia for an unspoiled wilderness. Instead, the settlers are Thompson's heroes. Although the actual Seth Warner was a backwoodsman of little education, his fictional counterpart in *The Green Mountain Boys* is described as "rather an amateur woodsman than one from habit or necessity." The nature of Warrington's relationship with the wilderness is an expression of his cultivation; a Green Mountain Boy comments that the lieutenant "is fond of looking at prospects—scenery I think he calls it."

In his preface Thompson seems to disavow any literary claims, saying that he wrote "without consulting, as perhaps he should, the models to be found in the works of approved writers in this department of literature." Instead he identifies himself primarily as a historian who has worked "from the imperfect published histories of the times, from the private papers to which

he has had access, and more particularly from the lips of the few aged relics of that period who actively participated in the wild and stirring scenes which peculiarly marked the settlement of this part of the country." Thompson's vision of himself as a historian helps to explain the underlying unity of his various interests. A founder of the Vermont Historical Society in 1838 and its first secretary, he was later elected its librarian and cabinet keeper. Thompson's passion for collecting historical documents, artifacts, and particularly testimonials reflected the national obsession of his day, as Americans' search for a past led to the rise of state and local historical societies across the country, particularly in New England.

In 1846 Thompson served as secretary of the State Education Society, and it may have been at this time that he wrote his lecture for teachers titled "Results to be aimed at in Instruction and Discipline." The following year he expressed his educational theories in fictional form, publishing *Locke Amsden* and dedicating it to the "friends of popular education and self-intellectual culture in the United States." Semi-autobiographical in content, the book describes the struggles of a young Vermont farm boy to acquire an education and then to teach others.

Notably crisper in style than Thompson's other works, the book functions essentially as a narrative argument on behalf of the principle that "Knowledge is Power." It proposes education as the basis of better farming, better government, and a better quality of life. In the course of the novel Locke wins over his students by appealing to their imaginations, moving from specific examples to general principles. His success is also based on treating his scholars as human beings rather than as brutes. Locke joins forces with a few other intelligent individuals to accomplish feats such as stamping out an epidemic and rescuing a woman from a burning building. While one of Locke's associates is a well-educated doctor, the other is an illiterate farmer who is a splendid example of the benefits and the limitations of self-culture.

By describing the challenges Locke faces as a schoolmaster in each of three communities, Thompson outlined some major threats to American education in his day. The dangers of illiteracy are evident in Horn of the Moon, an isolated mountain community where Locke is faced with students for whom "mere brute force, had unfortunately been made the subject of predominating applause" and with parents who regarded knowledge of mathematics as a sign of conspiring with the devil. In the aptly named Mill-Town Emporium, civic leaders are interested only in providing students with utilitarian skills, while the leading townspeople in Cartersville aggravate class divisions by removing their children from the "common school" to an academy providing "genteel education" in "crow-quill penmanship," French, fashionable pronunciation, and piano.

In addition to positive reviews from such publications as *The North American Review* and *The New York Tribune*, *Locke Amsden* also provoked approving comments from educators, including Horace Mann, Longfellow, Cornelius Conway Felton, and Harvard president Jared Sparks. While there are strong parallels between the elements of *Locke Amsden* and Eggleston's better-known novel, there is no evidence to suggest that Eggleston was familiar with Thompson's work before he wrote *The Hoosier Schoolmaster*. Excerpts from both works are included in Hubert M. Skinner's *The Schoolmaster in Literature* (1892), and Eggleston's introduction to that anthology includes a favorable reference to *Locke Amsden*.

Thompson returned to the romance form that had first brought him renown to write *Lucy Hosmer; or, The Guardian and Ghost* and *The Shaker Lovers; or, Virtue and Innocence Triumphant*, both published in 1848. These collections of fictionalized accounts of regional events were republished in 1852 in *May Martin and Other Tales of the Green Mountains*.

The same civic spirit that prompted Thompson's interest in history and education caused him to take over as editor of *The Green Mountain Freeman* in 1850. Once a Jeffersonian Democrat, Thompson was by this time a member of the Anti-Slavery Party and a supporter of the Republicans. Like the Republicans and most of his fellow Vermonters, Thompson was opposed to the extension of slavery and used the paper as an abolitionist organ, rallying support for causes such as the admission of Kansas as a nonslave state. He sold *The Green Mountain Freeman* in 1856.

During his years as a newspaperman, Thompson did not dedicate himself solely to journalism. Throughout this period he wrote poetry, delivered lyceum lectures, and continued his historical writing. In 1850 Thompson delivered the annual Vermont Historical Society address to a joint session of the General Assembly. His speech on the Vermont Council of Safety during the Revolution was criticized by his fellow townsman E. P. Walton, who asserted that Thompson built "superstructures of fiction upon a very narrow basis of fact." Nevertheless, when he incorporated the same material into *The Rangers; or The Tory's Daughter, a Tale* (1851), his sequel to *The Green Mountain Boys*, Thompson regarded the novel as his most historically accurate to date because of "the author's greater anxiety to give a true historic version of the interesting and important events he has undertaken to illustrate." The dedication to Jared Sparks and the presence of many footnotes in the novel seem to underscore this point.

The appearance of *May Martin and Other Tales of the Green Mountains*, a collection of previously published fiction by Thompson, attests to the continuing popularity of his works. From that point on, however, attention to his works dwindled, as Thompson continued to move between his two hardly distinguishable roles as historical romancer and historian. In 1857 he produced *Gaut Gurley; or, The Trappers of Umbagog: A Tale of Border Life*, yet another romance based on a local legend. The most notable aspect of this tale of the murder of fur trappers is its loving descriptions of nature and life in the wild. Thompson strayed from his usual material in 1860 to write *The Doomed Chief: or, Two hundred Years Ago*, a novel set during King Philip's War (1675–1676) in colonial New England. Thompson based his romance on information gathered from such sources as Cotton Mather's *Magnalia Christi Americana* (1702), the life of John Eliot by S. Francis in Jared Spark's *Library of American Biography* (1834–1848), Benjamin Thatcher's *Indian Biography* (1832), Jonathan Carver's *Travels through the Interior Parts of America in the Years 1766, 1767, and 1768* (1778), Peter Folger's *A Looking Glass for the Times* (1676), and Thomas Church's *Entertaining Passages Relating to Philip's War* (1716). Elected town historian in 1859, Thompson returned once again to nonfiction to write *The History of the Town of Montpelier* (1860), which combines an informal chronological narrative with a series of biographies of early citizens of the area.

Although all his writing to that point had celebrated local history, Thompson's historical interests were broadened when he visited his daughter Alma Thompson Burrows in Wisconsin during the winter of 1863–1864 and saw ancient Indian burial mounds. This experience led to the publication of his final historical romance, "Centeola; or the Maid of the Mounds," collected in *Centeola: and Other Tales* (1864).

Another story in this book, "The Unfathomable Mystery," is a fictionalized account of a crime in Vermont that involved the disappearance of a traveling peddler and the immediate display of inexplicable prosperity on the part of two townspeople. Never brought to trial because of a lack of evidence, the two suspects bought and burned all available copies of *Centeola: and Other Tales*.

During the last years of his life Thompson suffered a series of strokes that left him partially paralyzed, and he lived under straitened circumstances. Yet he continued to write on the subjects closest to his heart. In 1863, the year President Abraham Lincoln issued the Emancipation Proclamation, Thompson returned to the notes he took during his 1822 visit to Monticello and published "A Talk with Thomas Jefferson" in *Harper's New Monthly Magazine*. Their topics of conversation closely paralleled Thompson's interests. The two men discussed slavery, Jefferson's philosophy of education, and his opinion of the accuracy of a biography of Patrick Henry. That article was followed by "New Anecdote of Washington" in *Harper's New Monthly Magazine* (December 1864). A myth-making story based on information provided by Seth Warner's son, it describes a "noble-looking" George Washington descending unexpectedly on the widow of the Vermont patriot and giving her "a bag of silver money" adequate to discharge her crushing debts and mortgage. It is easy to recognize the characteristic Thompson method in the introduction of the story: "We will let Mr. Warner . . . relate the memorable incident in question in his own language; which, by the aid of the minutes before us, we know we can repeat substantially, and we think very nearly literally. . . ." Thompson wrote yet another biographical note in the same year: "Life, Character and Times of Ira Allen" (*Proceedings of the Vermont Historical Society for the Years 1908–1909,* 1909?) celebrates the role Ethan Allen's brother played in the Revolution and later the founding of the State University of Vermont.

When he died on 6 June 1868 at the age of seventy-two, Thompson left behind the unfinished manuscript for a novel, "The Honest Lawyer." It would have made an excellent title for his biography. Thompson was fondly remembered by his neighbors as a cheerful friend and good citizen, particularly beloved by the many boys who routinely badgered him for stories.

What little critical attention has been accorded Thompson since his death has evaluated his merits as a romancer of the Cooper school and found him wanting. It is important to recognize, however, that Thompson criticized Cooper repeatedly on the grounds that his fiction was unrealistic and insufficiently American in spirit. In an unpublished lecture, "American Romances," Thompson complained that Cooper intended "to inspire undue respect for aristocratic distinction, while our national feeling as entertained and exhibited by the great mass of the people, has found, in our estimation, but a feeble portrayal in the efforts of his pen. . . ." For Thompson this defect was not so much literary as a lapse of patriotism. Although Thompson was a Republican during his later years, his best novels and histories continued to express his Jeffersonian vision of well-ordered communities of cultured farmers and workers, cooperative neighbors, and enlightened citizens.

His writings may be understood best as an example of the early- and mid-nineteenth-century patriotic enthusiasm for discovering an American past. When Thompson gave his readers a jolly, larger-than-life Ethan Allen minus the complications that troubled more scrupulously factual historians, he manufactured a legend calculated to satisfy Americans hungry for heroes. Thompson seemed to see himself as engaged in an enterprise not unlike that of his friend Jared Sparks, who edited the popular volume of Washington's papers and a series of biographies of American figures. Each author, in his own way, used historical materials to generate portraits of heroes for an audience eager for positive depictions of the "American character." The citizens of Vermont who erected a memorial to Thompson in 1915 seem to have understood this achievement when they inscribed on the tablet: "He who faithfully records the deeds of heroes and pioneers plays his full part in the consummation of their benefit to posterity."

Biographies:
Biographical Encyclopaedia of Vermont of the Nineteenth Century (Boston: Metropolitan, 1885), pp. 256–260;
John E. Flitcroft, *The Novelist of Vermont: A Biographical and Critical Study of Daniel Pierce Thompson* (Cambridge, Mass.: Harvard University Press, 1929).

Papers:
Most of Daniel Pierce Thompson's papers were destroyed when his house burned shortly after his death. Many of his surviving literary manuscripts, research notes, correspondence, and other documents can be found at the Vermont Historical Society in Montpelier. There are smaller collections at the Wisconsin Historical Society and the Beinecke Library, Yale University.

John Townsend Trowbridge
(18 September 1827 – 12 February 1916)

David E. E. Sloane
University of New Haven

BOOKS: *Kate, the Accomplice; or, The Preacher and Burglar: Story of Real Life in the Metropolis,* as Paul Creyton (Boston: Star Spangled Banner Office, 1849);

Lucy Dawson; or, The Bandits of the Prairie: A Romance of the Far West, Being a Tale of Crime and Daring Founded on Facts, as Creyton (Boston: Williams, 1850);

Father Brighthopes; or, An Old Clergyman's Vacation, as Creyton (Boston: Phillips, Sampson, 1853; revised edition, Boston: Lee & Shepard, 1892);

Hearts and Faces; or, Home-Life Unveiled, as Creyton (Boston: Phillips, Sampson, 1853);

The Deserted Family; or, Wanderings of an Outcast, as Creyton (Boston: Crown / Philadelphia: Bradley, 1853);

Burrcliff: Its Sunshine and Its Clouds, as Creyton (Boston: Phillips, Sampson, 1854);

Martin Merrivale: His X Mark, as Creyton (Boston: Phillips, Sampson / New York: Derby, 1854);

Ironthorpe: The Pioneer Preacher, as Creyton (Boston: Phillips, Sampson / New York: Derby, 1855);

Neighbor Jackwood, as Creyton (Boston: Phillips, Sampson, 1857; revised edition, Boston: Lee & Shepard, 1895);

Neighbor Jackwood: A Domestic Drama in Five Acts (New York & London: S. French, 1857);

The Old Battle-Ground (New York: Sheldon, 1860);

The Drummer Boy: A Story of Burnside's Expedition, anonymous (Boston: Lothrop, Lee & Shepard, 1863); republished as *Frank Manly, the Drummer Boy: A Story of the War* (Boston: Gill, 1876);

The Vagabonds (New York: Gregory, 1863);

Cudjo's Cave (Boston: Tilton, 1864);

The Ferry-Boy and the Financier, anonymous (Boston: Walker, Wise, 1864);

The Little Rebel, anonymous (Boston: Tilton, 1864);

The Three Scouts (Boston: Tilton, 1865);

Coupon Bonds (Boston: Ticknor & Fields, 1866);

Lucy Arlyn (Boston: Ticknor & Fields, 1866);

The South: A Tour of its Battle-fields and Ruined Cities, A Journey through the Desolated States, and Talks with the People: Being a Description of the Present State of the Country (Hartford, Conn.: Stebbins, 1866); repub-

John Townsend Trowbridge

lished as *A Picture of the Desolated States; And the Work of Restoration: 1865–1868* (Hartford, Conn.: Stebbins, 1868); abridged as *The Desolate South,* edited by Gordon Carroll (New York: Duell, Sloan & Pearce / Boston & Toronto: Little, Brown, 1956);

Neighbors' Wives (Boston: Lee & Shepard, 1867);

The Vagabonds, and Other Poems (Boston: Fields, Osgood, 1869);

The Story of Columbus (Boston: Fields, Osgood, 1870);

Lawrence's Adventures Among the Ice-Cutters, Glass-Makers, Coal-Miners, Iron-Men, and Ship-Builders (Boston: Fields, Osgood, 1871);

Jack Hazard and His Fortunes (Boston: Osgood, 1871); republished in *How to Rise in the World; or, Every-*

271

Day Progress (London: Warne, 1875); republished in *Who Won at Last; or, Every-Day Progress* (London & New York: Warne, 1884?);

A Chance for Himself, Or Jack Hazard and His Treasure (Boston: Osgood, 1872);

Coupon Bonds and Other Stories (Boston: Osgood, 1873);

Doing His Best (Boston: Osgood, 1873); republished in *How to Rise in the World; or, Every-Day Progress* (London: Warne, 1875); republished in *Who Won at Last; or, Every-Day Progress* (London & New York: Warne, 1884?);

Fast Friends (Boston: Osgood, 1875);

The Emigrant's Story and Other Poems (Boston: Osgood, 1875);

The Young Surveyor (London: Sampson Low, Marston, Low & Searle, 1875); republished as *The Young Surveyor; or, Jack on the Prairies* (Boston: Osgood, 1875);

Coupon Bonds: A Play in Four Acts (Boston: Baker, 1876);

The Great Match, and Other Matches, anonymous (Boston: Roberts, 1877);

The Book of Gold and Other Poems (New York: Harper, 1878);

His Own Master (Boston: Lee & Shepard / New York: Dillingham, 1878);

Bound in Honor; or, A Harvest of Wild Oats (Boston: Lee & Shepard / New York: Dillingham, 1878);

Young Joe and Other Boys (Boston: Lee & Shepard / New York: Dillingham, 1880);

The Silver Medal (Boston: Lee & Shepard / New York: Dillingham, 1881);

A Home Idyl and Other Poems (Boston: Houghton, Mifflin, 1881);

The Pocket-Rifle (Boston: Lee & Shepard / New York: Dillingham, 1882);

The Jolly Rover (Boston: Lee & Shepard / New York: Dillingham, 1883);

Phil and His Friends (Boston: Lee & Shepard / New York: Dillingham, 1884);

The Tinkham Brothers' Tide-Mill (Boston: Lee & Shepard / New York: Dillingham, 1884);

Farnell's Folly (Boston: Lee & Shepard / New York: Dillingham, 1885);

The Satin-Wood Box (Boston: Lee & Shepard / New York: Dillingham, 1886);

The Little Master (Boston: Lee & Shepard / New York: Dillingham, 1887);

His One Fault (Boston: Lothrop, Lee & Shepard / New York: Dillingham, 1887);

Peter Budstone: The Boy Who Was Hazed (Boston: Lee & Shepard / New York: Dillingham, 1888);

The Lost Earl With Other Poems and Tales in Verse (Boston: Lothrop, 1888);

A Start in Life: A Story of the Genesee Country (Boston: Lee & Shepard / New York: Dillingham, 1889);

Biding His Time; or, Andrew Hapnell's Fortune (Boston: Lee & Shepard / New York: Dillingham, 1889);

The Adventures of David Vane and David Crane (Boston: Lothrop, 1889);

The Kelp-Gatherers: A Story of the Maine Coast (Boston: Lee & Shepard / New York: Dillingham, 1891);

The Scarlet Tanager and Other Bipeds (Boston: Lee & Shepard / New York: Dillingham, 1892);

The Fortunes of Toby Trafford (Boston: Lee & Shepard, 1893);

Woodie Thorpe's Pilgrimage and Other Stories (Boston: Lee & Shepard, 1893);

The Prize Cup (New York: Century, 1896);

The Lottery Ticket (Boston: Lee & Shepard, 1896);

A Question of Damages (Boston: Lee & Shepard, 1897);

Two Biddicut Boys and Their Adventures With a Wonderful Trick-Dog (New York: Century, 1898);

My Own Story With Recollections of Noted Persons (Boston: Houghton, Mifflin, 1903);

A Pair of Madcaps (Boston: Lothrop, Lee & Shepard, 1909).

Collection: *The Poetical Works of John Townsend Trowbridge* (Boston: Houghton, Mifflin, 1893).

OTHER: *Our Young Folks,* edited by Trowbridge (1870–1873).

"Trowbridge, are you still alive?," burst out Mark Twain when he encountered John Townsend Trowbridge at Thomas Bailey Aldrich's funeral in 1908. "You must be a thousand years old. Why I listened to your stories while I was rocked in the cradle." As recorded in Albert Bigelow Paine's *Mark Twain, A Biography* (1912), Trowbridge countered that his earliest infant smile was at one of Twain's jokes. Twain was probably closer to the truth, for though both men had written in the same genres for more than half a century, Trowbridge was eight years Twain's senior and had published his first work in periodicals several years before his more famous peer. Their careers and writing, however, were a marked contrast. Whereas Twain's portrayal of Europe, the Southwest, and the West rose to the level of visionary literature, Trowbridge's more modest descriptions of the New England character and political and personal agenda remained minor.

In 1916, six years after Twain's death left the world in mourning, Trowbridge's passing was marked by only a handful of brief, respectful obituaries. He was praised for his extended series of boys' books and a few volumes of poetry. Although Trowbridge had prized his poetry highly, his best-remembered verses are two popular poems, a burlesque of Yankee ingenuity titled

"Darius Green and His Flying Machine" and a sentimental elocution piece, "The Vagabonds." During his
lifetime Trowbridge creditably edited several magazines, fraternized with the greatest writers of his era,
and wrote a variety of serious works of poetry and fiction. He was regarded by contemporaries as a spokesman for the northeastern Yankee viewpoint, respected
for his insights into his own region and its characters
and characteristics, for his views of the South and racial
issues, and for his understanding of the issues of childhood and growing up. His overall production, including
short stories and moralistic adventure books for boys,
exceeded forty volumes.

The eighth of nine children of Windsor Stone
Trowbridge and Rebecca Willey Trowbridge, John
Townsend Trowbridge was born shortly after midnight
on 18 September 1827 in a log cabin in Ogden, Monroe
County, New York, six miles west of the Genesee River.
Originating from England, members of the Trowbridge
family migrated to America in 1634, establishing themselves first in Boston and then in New Haven. Trowbridge's parents were pioneer farmers, and the boy was
raised in a two-story frame farmhouse within sight of
the Erie Canal, which had opened two years before his
birth. Brought up a Calvinist, which he believed did
more to destroy than strengthen his faith in a divine
Providence, he peopled his imaginary world with supernatural beings, including fairies and gremlins.

Trowbridge's formal education as a boy occurred
in a one-room schoolhouse. At fifteen he discovered
and taught himself French. At the public library he
encountered the works of such writers as Sir Walter
Scott; George Gordon, Lord Byron; James Fenimore
Cooper; William Shakespeare; and Plutarch as well as a
variety of European and American melodramas. Looking back on his formative years in *My Own Story With
Recollections of Noted Persons* (1903), he declares that his
study of Latin "threw a flood of light on the grammar
of my own language, like a lantern shining backward
on a path one has been treading in the dark."

The reader can perhaps best gain a sense of
Trowbridge's boyhood, with its opportunities for a boy
of pluck and honesty and its difficulties with competing
boys and with nature, through his novel *A Start in Life:
A Story of the Genesee Country* (1889). In *My Own Story*
Trowbridge records that he spent the Fourth of July of
his fifteenth year at home, alternately reading and plow-
ing corn, rather than at the festivals. He presents the
episode both as typical of his independent, bookish
development on his parents' farm and as the happiest
Fourth of July in his life.

Trowbridge began writing verse at thirteen, and
his first poem appeared in in the *Rochester Republican*
(New York) when he was sixteen. In the fall of 1844,

Illustration by F. O. C. Darley for Trowbridge's The Vagabonds *(1863)*

following the death of his father, Trowbridge left the
farm and enrolled at the Lockport classical school for
one year. His second work, "New Year's Address," was
published by the *Niagara Courier* on 1 January 1845. He
taught school in Illinois and in Lockport, New York,
before making his way with a trunk of manuscripts to
New York City in May 1847 to begin his literary career
in earnest.

In New York, Trowbridge worked as an engraver
as he pursued his literary interests, discovering Broadway theater, reading French writers such as Eugéne
Sue, Honoré de Balzac, Victor Hugo, and George Sand,
and trying to establish himself as a professional author.
He had the good fortune to be befriended by Mordecai
M. Noah, proprietor of the *Sunday Times*. Noah introduced him to publishers, including Charles W. Holden
of *Holden's Dollar Magazine,* where Trowbridge published
a couple of stories on backwoods life. He soon published his first piece in the New York *Knickerbocker Magazine,* then the major literary journal in America, but
without attribution or pay.

In August 1848 Trowbridge moved to Boston, the
city where he spent the rest of his literary life. Trowbridge was quickly caught up in the cultural and intellectual life of what was then considered the "Athens of
America." He attended Jenny Lind's concerts and the
lectures of Theodore Parker, wielding his "mighty
moral sledge" against slavery and "Religion cased in

creeds," as Trowbridge wrote in one admiring sonnet. He was also moved by William Lloyd Garrison, William Douglas, and Harriet Beecher Stowe. B. P. Shillaber of the Boston *Carpet-Bag* was among his friends.

The weeklies provided a ready market for his short stories, and he wrote for *The Yankee Blade* and other journals. At twenty-one he became editor of *The Yankee Nation* for a year. He then was employed as an editor on *The American Sentinel,* but his satiric article on slave-catching and southern secession in early 1851 alienated conservative readers and contributed to the demise of the journal. He did not work again as an editor until he joined *Our Young Folks* in 1865—and turned again to writing fiction.

Father Brighthopes; or, An Old Clergyman's Vacation (1853) was among Trowbridge's early works. He wrote it under the pseudonym Paul Creyton, which he used for his first nine books, in response to a request for a "domestic" story by Moses D. Phillips, one of Boston's leading publishers. The book features Mr. Rensford, an elderly clergyman-schoolmaster who tells stories to encourage good behavior in his youthful friends. Later, from 1865 through 1867, Trowbridge published several "Half Hours with Father Brighthopes" in *Our Young Folks.* His ability to combine simple morality with an emphasis on scene and event makes them better reading than the didactic stories from the American Tract Society and other purveyors of moral tales for children.

Martin Merrivale: His X Mark (1854), Trowbridge's first extended work of fiction, was published serially and written, like most of his works, in bursts of episodic plot action and with numbers in print before the conclusion was written. A satiric tale of Boston life, the novel presents two Boston families, one newly rich, the other in aristocratic decay. Some of the characters were drawn from Trowbridge's experience. The writing is clear and direct, and Trowbridge shows skill in setting scenes and developing episodes, displaying a talent for scene-painting and episodic development. Trowbridge believed that the adventures of the green, young writer in Boston, who encounters the two families, were the best parts and that the sentimental and melodramatic parts were the poorest.

In the preface to *Ironthorpe: The Pioneer Preacher* (1855), a novel based around the westward journey of pioneers in the early part of the century, Trowbridge claims that "Its scenes have their foundation in truth." While Trowbridge's characters often show a realistic crudeness of speech and the scenes he draws are carefully observed, the larger-than-life Ironthorpe is plainly derivative of the Byronic hero. Despite his melodramatic rescues of unfortunates in snowstorms, Ironthorpe is not a figure of unalloyed virtue: he deserted a socially pretentious eastern wife who might have transformed herself

religiously as he had done. His problematic personal history makes him something of a mysterious outcast.

Neighbor Jackwood (1857), Trowbridge's first widely successful work of fiction, achieved a degree of notoriety because in its conclusion the New England hero is romantically united with the octoroon heroine he has rescued from slavery and sexual exploitation at the hands of a villainous slave hunter. The novel reflected the gathering antislavery sentiment in New England following the Fugitive Slave Law of 1850, which required that non-slave owners participate in the capture of runaways. Trowbridge found, however, that many readers disliked the antislavery theme and were appalled at the idea that the white hero would marry the mixed-blood heroine.

In the melodramatic but arresting novel, Charlotte, an improbably saintly escaped slave, finds her way to Jackwood's farm, where she is granted hospitality and protection. Trowbridge weaves local-color vignettes of "down easters" through the developing romance between Charlotte and Hector Dunbury, a hero who, like Ironthorpe before him, clearly reflects Trowbridge's early love of Byron and Scott. Largely tangential to the complicated plot that features escapes, chases, the restoration of true love and filial affection, and the punishment of vice, both grave and petty, neighbor Jackwood appears only at climactic points to articulate the ideas implicit in the melodrama. In his homely manner he advocates the cause of humanity and opposition to slavery.

In a preface to the 1895 edition of his frequently republished work, Trowbridge describes how he wrote *Neighbor Jackwood* after the publication of Harriet Beecher Stowe's *Uncle Tom's Cabin* (1852) and reveals that the publisher withheld his novel for a time so that it would not be smothered in the "dust" of the more famous work. He adopted a play from the novel, *Neighbor Jackwood: A Domestic Drama in Five Acts* (1857), which appeared on the Boston stage with some success. Trowbridge claimed that proslavery and antislavery viewers engaged in a hissing match that threatened to become a riot on its opening night.

Trowbridge married Cornelia Warren of Lowell, Massachusetts, in May 1860. His wife died in March 1864, six weeks after giving birth to a son, Windsor Warren Trowbridge, who was cared for by Sarah Adelaide Newton. Trowbridge would marry Newton on 4 June 1873, and together they would have two daughters and one son.

Cudjo's Cave (1864) was another of Trowbridge's deeply felt—and widely read—polemical novels against slavery. The two chief figures of the novel are Cudjo, an animalistic escaped slave driven mad by the horrible abuses of slavery, and Pomp, another escaped slave, but

"THE LISTENER UNDER THE WINDOW SCOWLED."
Page 13.

THE SCARLET TANAGER

AND

OTHER BIPEDS

BY

J. T. TROWBRIDGE

BOSTON
LEE AND SHEPARD PUBLISHERS

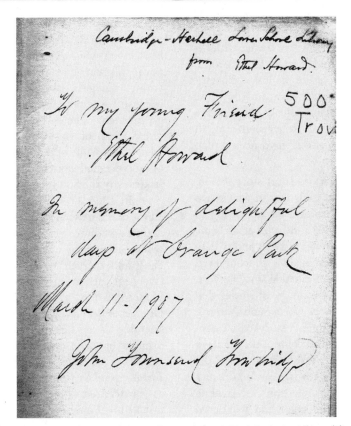

Frontispiece and title page, with an endpaper inscription, for one of Trowbridge's books for children (Thomas Cooper Library, University of South Carolina)

a Byronic figure who seems like an African king in the American wilderness. Pomp glories at one point in showing some white hunters trapped by fire "that even the despised black may, under God's providence, be of some use to the white men, besides being their slave." In the plot involving guerrilla fighting during the Civil War, wilderness fires, and Cudjo's mysterious caves, Cudjo dies, but Pomp escapes to reappear in *The Three Scouts* (1865). Although melodramatic, the novel has powerful action scenes and a seemingly accurate rendering of ugly racism and black and poor-white dialects. Because he had never visited the South, Trowbridge in *My Own Story* laments that the action and characters were "portrayed more from without" and called the novel an "inferior work." The reviewer for *The North American Review* (April 1864) complained that as a "sensation story of to-day" it not only was overly melodramatic but also presented several characters who were unnatural and unconvincing.

Throughout his career Trowbridge's shorter works were a significant component of his literary production. With Stowe, Oliver Wendell Holmes, Henry Wadsworth Longfellow, James Russell Lowell, and Ralph Waldo Emerson, Trowbridge contributed to the first number of *The Atlantic Monthly* in 1857. His first important poem, "The Vagabonds," appeared in *The Atlantic Monthly* in March 1863. The poem presents a drunken beggar telling his life story. He travels with his dancing dog, Roger, and begs for coins to buy food. The vagabond's despair is rooted in the loss of his girl, who became a virtuous parson's wife, and now the tramp looks forward to the land where lodgings are free, "the sooner, the better for Roger and me." It remained for decades an international favorite as a platform piece.

Trowbridge's most important short story, "Coupon Bonds," has a comic local-color plot in which two boys trade lost bonds for marbles. First appearing in *The Atlantic Monthly* in September and October of 1865, it was republished in paper covers in 1866 and widely distributed by bankers as propaganda to counter a financial panic. In 1873 it became the title story for *Coupon Bonds and Other Stories,* an anthology of stories that had been published in *The Atlantic Monthly* and *Harper's;* the volume includes another notable story of accidentally developed virtue, rich in local color of the Pennsylvania oil country, titled "The Man Who Stole the Meeting House." The reviewer for *Appleton's Journal* (1 February 1873) praised the collection as rivaling Stowe's stories of New England color and wondered why *Neighbor Jackwood* was not more widely read. Trowbridge periodically gathered his stories in subsequent collections as his career progressed.

In June 1865 Trowbridge moved into a house in Arlington, Massachusetts, just west of Cambridge, that would be his home for the rest of his life. Having undertaken a mortgage and hating the idea of debt under even the best of terms, Trowbridge accepted the proprosal of Lucius Stebbens, one of the major Hartford publishers of subscription books, that he tour and describe the states of the Confederacy following the war. This tour provided the material for *The South: A Tour of its Battle-fields and Ruined Cities, A Journey through the Desolated States, and Talks with the People: Being a Description of the Present State of the Country* (1866) and *Neighbors' Wives* (1867).

In anecdote after anecdote of his travel volume—which was republished in 1868 as *A Picture of the Desolated States; And the Work of Restoration: 1865–1868* and as *The Desolate South* in 1956—Trowbridge shows that the ugly racism of Southern whites was deep, profound, and unshaken. As one respondent commented, "The great trouble in this country is, the people are mad at the niggers because they are free." Another says, "When you hear that the country is ruined, and the niggers won't work, the trouble is in them that make the complaint, and not in the niggers. My niggers say to me, 'Massa Joe, we ought to work mo'e'n we ever did befo'e; for once, we just worked for our victuals and clothes, and now we're getting wages besides.'"

Trowbridge describes a devastated and dispirited land. Even white planters have their stories to tell: "I never was married, and never had a home. When I was young, the girls said I smelt like a wet dog; that's because I was poor. Since I've got rich, I'm too old to get married." The choice and portrayal of subjects indicate a strain of melancholy that Trowbridge acknowledged even while optimistically insisting on the promise of a redeemed society. The volume clearly demonstrates why the South failed to embrace Reconstruction.

In 1865 Trowbridge also became a contributing editor of the newly founded *Our Young Folks*. He became managing editor from 1870 to 1874, losing the position when the journal was bought by Scribner and Company and merged with *St. Nicholas*. He wrote extensively for the periodical, both short stories and poems. Under various pseudonyms, including Augustus Holmes and Harvey Wilder, he published a variety of scientific essays and studies of industries, which he brought out as a loosely constructed novel, *Lawrence's Adventures Among the Ice-Cutters, Glass-Makers, Coal-Miners, Iron-Men, and Ship-Builders,* in 1871. Illustrated, the book, as Trowbridge admitted, had more the look of an instructional manual for boys than a work of fiction.

Although Trowbridge had established his reputation as a writer with his local-color fiction, his attacks on slavery, and his reportorial tour of the South, poetry

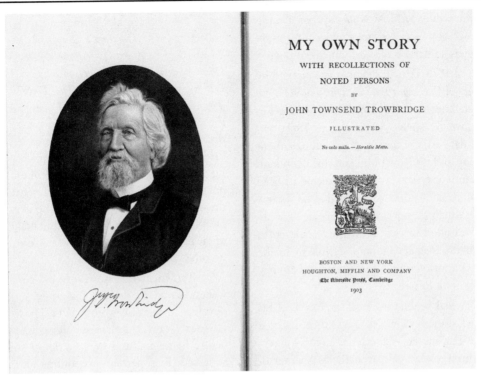

Frontispiece and title page for Trowbridge's 1903 autobiography

was still his first love. In *My Own Story* he flatly states, "My best, fullest, and most thoughtful work has been woven into my poems; yet I find myself far more widely known as a story-writer than as a poet." *The Vagabonds, and Other Poems* (1869), his first collection, is a mixed work that features both romantic clichés such as dryad-haunted woods and ruddy auroras as well as realistic local-color touches. In the title poem Trowbridge presents a portrait and is true to the tenets of realism in not intruding his judgment of the vagabond into the poem. Although thoroughly sentimental, the poem provides more of an implicit commentary on the reentry into society by war-shocked veterans than a cursory reading might at first suggest.

Trowbridge can best be understood as a transitional poet. While he used some of the most stilted of genteel poetic clichés, he was an early and steadfast supporter of Walt Whitman's vigorously realistic poetry. Like other poets of the post–Civil War period, Trowbridge was part of the gradual movement in which the bucolic local-color setting of field and forest was beginning to be replaced by an increasingly imposing urban landscape arrayed against the virtues of the simple and the naive. An obvious transitional poem is "The Wolves," which develops a social theme by turning the country image into the cliché of "the wolf at the door":

Know ye the fiend that is crueller far
Than the gaunt grey herds of the forest are?

Swiftly vanish the wild fleet tracks
Before the rifle and woodman's axe:
But hark to the coming of unseen feet,
pattering by night through the city street!
. . . .
Shudder not at the murderer's name,
Marvel not at the maiden's shame.
. . . .
He giveth little who gives but tears,
He giveth his best who aids and cheers.
He does well in the forest wild
Who slays the monster and saves the child;
But he does better, and merits more,
Who drives the wolf from the poor man's door.

Trowbridge uses the image of the wolf to suggest a host of problems—crime, economic upheaval, and societal transformation—that America was only beginning to face. Other poems in the volume are similarly didactic.

The Vagabonds, and Other Poems also includes the often anthologized portrait of the comic Yankee inventor, "Darius Green and his Flying-Machine." First published in *Our Young Folks* in March 1867, the poem tells the story of a not-very-shrewd Yankee who creates a winged flying machine to astonish the nation and all creation. Landing in a heap, he moralizes, "Wal, I like flyin' well enough, / . . . but the' ain't such a thunderin' sight / O' fun in't when ye come to light." Other poems present local-color vignettes. "The Charcoalman" and "The Wonderful Sack" are notable for Trowbridge's attempt to capture the world of working-class Americans. In his choice of material, if not always in his manner, Trowbridge is an early realistically inclined poet.

In the fall of 1870 Trowbridge was encouraged by one of the owners of *Our Young Folks* to write a novel to be published in installments. Titled *Jack Hazard and His Fortunes,* it ran through twelve numbers in 1871 and launched a popular series of boy-book adventures about an Erie Canal boy and his Newfoundland dog. Although the novel has dramatic episodes, the story seems artificial as Jack's self-reformation too easily explains his escape from a degraded situation and parentage to a life of forthright integrity and good works. Trowbridge claimed to have dashed off the installments and sent them to the printer almost without revision. *Jack Hazard and His Fortunes* appeared in book form in 1871.

Trowbridge was in the middle of the fourth of his five Jack Hazard stories when *Our Young Folks* merged with *St. Nicholas.* The success of the series and its longevity were based on Trowbridge's strengths as a writer of fiction. He had the ability to engagingly realize local scenes and characters such as a profane canal boatman, alcoholic coal burners, and village families and farmers. Although these are third-person narratives, Trowbridge allows his characters to grapple with moral problems instead of lecturing on them as author. Jack directly voices his hope to break away from the dirt and squalor of canal life: "I'd be different if I could; but how can I be?" Stealing a hat, swearing oaths, and running for his life from his brutal father, Jack must develop his own moral toughness and stand up to a variety of ugly bullies. He has much in common with Twain's Huckleberry Finn, though Huck is by far the more powerful creation.

Trowbridge continued writing serials and short works for *St. Nicholas* and for Daniel Ford's *Youth's Companion* through the late 1880s. "Young Joe," the title piece for the collection *Young Joe and Other Boys* (1880), was one of the best of these stories, again featuring a character with some affinity to Huck Finn. His stories were fitted to the needs of the popular juvenile periodicals, and they were subsequently republished in various individual volumes and in four series of stories. This writing provided Trowbridge a comfortable income for the time, allowing for various trips and the development of a summer property in Kennebunkport, Maine. The stories were often touted as more true-to-life than the didactic stories of other writers, showing boys who performed bad deeds as well as good and spoke a natural language.

Trowbridge also continued to write poetry. His collections *The Emigrant's Story and Other Poems* (1875), *The Book of Gold and Other Poems* (1878), *A Home Idyl and Other Poems* (1881), and *The Lost Earl With Other Poems* (1888) were gathered in *The Poetical Works of John Townsend Trowbridge* (1893). Local color abounds in these poems, which feature farmers, seamen, widows, drunks, misers, poets, and scheming females. Trowbridge differs from more pretentious contemporaries by his reliance on a strong narrative line in his verse. His poems convey homely details of setting, speech, and dress rather than describing emotions in abstract lyrics. Despite his penchant for sentimentality, Trowbridge often provides a more realistic sense of his world than do other poets of the period.

Trowbridge is not the most adventurous of the writers using local-color materials and attempting to develop a realistic voice. Bret Harte in prose and Charles Godfrey Leland in verse had surpassed him before he began, and Will Carleton and others would supersede him, perhaps accounting for the eclipse of his reputation even before his death. His adventure stories, though, continued to sell into the twentieth century. A 1909 republication of *The Pocket-Rifle* (1882) advertises eight of his novels and twenty-three of his stories for boys. His many such works perhaps justify his commenting as part of his reflection on the obscurity of his poetry, "I don't know but that, after all, the most satisfactory monument I could choose would be to live in the hearts and memories of mothers and boys."

References:

John Burroughs, "J. T. Trowbridge," *Scribner's Monthly,* 9 (November 1874): 32–36;

Rufus A. Coleman, "Trowbridge and Clemens," *Modern Language Quarterly,* 9 (June 1948): 216–223;

Coleman, "Trowbridge and Shillaber," *New England Quarterly,* 20 (June 1947): 232–246;

Coleman, "Trowbridge and Whitman," *PMLA,* 63 (March 1948): 262–273;

William Dean Howells, "Editor's Easy Chair-III," *Harper's Monthly Magazine,* 108 (February 1904): 481–482.

Papers:

The most important collections of John Townsend Trowbridge's papers are at the Huntington Library in California, Johns Hopkins University, the Boston Public Library, Harvard University, and the University of Virginia.

Lew Wallace

(10 April 1827 – 15 February 1905)

Dennis W. Eddings

Western Oregon University

BOOKS: *The Fair God; or, The Last of the 'Tzins: A Tale of the Conquest of Mexico* (Boston: Osgood, 1873; London: Ward, Lock, & Bowden, 1873);

Commodus: An Historical Play (Crawfordsville, Ind.: Privately printed, 1876; revised edition, 1877); revised and republished in *Harper's Monthly,* 78 (January 1889): 171–193;

Ben-Hur: A Tale of the Christ (New York & London: Harper, 1880);

Life of Gen. Ben Harrison, bound with *Life of Hon. Levi P. Morton,* by George Alfred Townsend (Philadelphia, Chicago & Kansas City: Hubbard / Boston: Guernsey / Cincinnati: Morris / Denver: Perry / San Francisco: Bancroft, 1888); separately published as *Life of Gen. Ben Harrison* (Philadelphia, Chicago & Kansas City: Hubbard / San Francisco: Bancroft, 1888);

The Boyhood of Christ (New York: Harper, 1889);

The Prince of India; or, Why Constantinople Fell, 2 volumes (New York & London: Harper, 1893);

Address of Gen. Lew Wallace at the Dedication of Indiana's Monuments on the Battlefield of Shiloh, Tennessee. . . . (Crawfordsville, Ind.: News-Review, 1903);

Lew Wallace: An Autobiography, 2 volumes (New York & London: Harper, 1906).

SELECTED PERIODICAL PUBLICATIONS–
UNCOLLECTED: "The Capture of Fort Donelson," *Century,* 19 (December 1894): 284–308;

"The Boyhood of Christ," *Harper's Monthly,* 74 (December 1886): 3–18;

"An Address to the Cadets at the United States Naval Academy," *Harper's Weekly,* 38 (23 June 1894): 586;

"My Own Account of the First Day at Shiloh," *Book-lovers' Magazine,* 7 (January 1906): 72–77.

Lew Wallace

Lew Wallace's literary reputation rests solidly on the brawny shoulders of *Ben-Hur: A Tale of the Christ* (1880). While exact sales figures are unknown, in 1944 Harper, the publisher, estimated the book had sold more than two million copies. If to that is added an extremely popular stage production that opened in New York on 29 November 1899, touring annually until 1920, and two epic motion-picture versions, the latter frequently shown on television, then the total number of people who have encountered Judah Ben-Hur and his rivalry with the noble Roman Massala, culminating in the famous chariot race, is quite staggering, perhaps more than any other work by an American author. Yet Wallace's influence on American literature, with one exception, is minimal at best. That one exception, however, is highly significant. Carl Van Doren credits the popularity of *Ben-Hur* with breaking through the moral opposition of rural America to the novel as a literary form, thus creating a far larger audience for future writers. Wallace's other two historical romances, though, are virtually unknown, and his campaign biography of Benjamin Harrison, while quite accurate, is more an historical oddity, like Nathaniel Hawthorne's 1852 biography of Franklin Pierce or William Dean Howells's 1850 biography of Abraham Lincoln, than a significant work in its own right. Somewhat anachronistically writing historical romances at a time when the new realism of Howells, Mark Twain, and Henry James was flourishing, Wallace belonged temperamentally (and stylistically) to the older tradition of Sir Walter Scott and James Fenimore Cooper. Wallace's great theme was the loss of family and heritage, perhaps more fitting a general who fought for the Confederacy rather than the Union. As melodramatic personally as the characters who inhabit his romances, Wallace nonetheless was a man of his age.

Lewis Wallace, the second of four sons born to David Wallace, governor of Indiana from 1838 to 1840, and Esther Test Wallace, daughter of John Test, the first U.S. congressman from Indiana, was born on 10 April 1827. Raised in Crawfordsville, Indiana (his mother died in 1834), Wallace was an indifferent student, frequently escaping school to spend time wandering the fields and streams of the surrounding countryside. He claims in *Lew Wallace: An Autobiography* (1906) that his formal schooling, such as it was, ended at age sixteen. While his formal education may have been haphazard, Wallace was a voracious reader who took advantage of his father's fairly extensive library. One encounter, in 1843, was with William Hickling Prescott's three-volume *History of the Conquest of Mexico* (1843). The work fired Wallace's imagination and led to the commencement of what would eventually become *The Fair God; or, The Last of the 'Tzins: A Tale of the Conquest of Mexico* (1873), a project taken on, according to his autobiography, as much for self-discipline as for literary glory.

In 1846 Wallace raised a company of troops, the First Regiment, Indiana Volunteers, and joined the Mexican War. His dreams of military glory, though, were frustrated by inactivity in the backwaters of the campaign. That frustration increased when his unit was finally ordered to the front, only to be sent back to their dismal bivouac in Texas before reaching their destination. Still, the expedition had one clear advantage for Wallace: his interest in and love for Mexico was intensified through firsthand observation. Consequently, when he returned to Indianapolis in 1847, he relieved the tedium of studying law (a profession he loathed) by reworking the draft of *The Fair God,* which he completed in 1853. He was dissuaded from seeking a publisher, however, by Charles White, president of Wabash College.

With the firing on Fort Sumter, Wallace was summoned by the governor of Indiana to assist in meeting Lincoln's call for volunteers. Wallace plunged into the challenge with abandon, again forming his own regiment. As colonel of the 11th Regiment, Indiana Volunteers, Wallace distinguished himself by leading a surprise raid on Romney, Virginia, netting arms and supplies as well as much desired notice from his superiors and a Northern public avid for any positive news from the war. Promoted to brigadier general in October, Wallace joined General Grant's forces in the capture of Forts Henry, Heiman, and Donelson. His actions there led to his promotion to major general; he was the youngest at the time to hold that rank. To this point, it appeared that the Civil War would provide Wallace the glory and fame for which he desperately wished. A far less distinguished moment occurred, however, at the battle of Shiloh, 6–7 April 1862. Surprised early on the morning of 6 April by a Confederate assault, Union forces were driven back on the Tennessee River. Grant summoned Wallace and his troops, camped about six miles from the battlefield, to join the battle. Wallace led his army toward the position the Union forces had occupied the previous evening, before the assault.

As a result of this error, a six-mile march turned into fifteen, and the long-expected Wallace arrived at nightfall after fighting for the day had ceased. He never lived down his tardy arrival at the scene of battle and never stopped trying to exonerate himself. Various assignments in the backwaters of the war left Wallace vexed, although he performed admirably. His moment of at least partial redemption came in July 1864 at the Battle of Monocacy, when a badly outnumbered force under Wallace's command detained a rebel force advancing on Washington, effectively saving the city from occupation.

Wallace's service with the army did not end with Appomattox. He was the second-ranking officer on the military commission that tried and sentenced to death those charged with the assassination of President Lincoln. He then served as president of the commission that tried and condemned Henry Wirz, warden of the infamous Andersonville prison. Even after that duty Wallace did not rejoin his family in Crawfordsville, returning instead to Mexico for seven months (1866–1867), where he actively assisted Benito Juarez in the campaign to oust Maximilian and reestablish constitutional government in Mexico. When he finally returned to Indiana, Wallace was at loose ends. He found work at his in-laws' bank and the law dissatisfying and unrewarding. Consequently, he turned to the work he had begun twenty years earlier, *The Fair God.*

The Fair God, published in 1873, purports to be a translation from the Spanish of Fernado DeAlva, a sixteenth-century Aztec historian. The impetus for the romance, Cortez's conquest of Mexico, is related through the adventures of Aztecs, royal and common. The commoner Hualpa, a great hunter, seeks a warrior to serve. He fastens on Guatamo, the 'Tzin, who, in love with Montezuma's daughter, is exiled through the plotting of his rival for her hand, Iztlil. Through it all lurks Cortez, the fair (white) god Montezuma fears. After many intrigues, battles, and escapes, the inevitable happens: Cortez vanquishes the Aztecs, and the death of all is imminent. The melodramatic is a staple of Wallace's writing, and *The Fair God* is not exempt from it, although Wallace manages to treat the "heathen" Aztecs with sympathy and understanding. Montezuma's failure to attack Cortez, despite superior numbers, is traceable to religious beliefs grounded in prophecy. Hualpa is courageous; Guatamo is noble. The sense that something fine and valuable has been lost to an inevitable progress, a theme reminiscent of Cooper, comes through despite the conventional characters, stilted dialogue, and frequently bombastic prose. Despite the faults of *The Fair God,* one strength shines through: scenes of battle or action, such as Hualpa's fight with the panther, are forcefully told. Himself a man of action who had witnessed war and who honored courage, Wallace was at his best when writing of battles. The book was well received, selling more than seven thousand copies in the first year.

With the success of *The Fair God* Wallace turned his attention to a lifelong ambition, to be a playwright. He wrote "Our English Cousin" (unpublished), then turned to the past, where he felt more comfortable, writing *Commodus: An Historical Play,* privately published at his own expense in 1876. The play involves the efforts of Maternus, unjustly exiled by the evil Commodus, to regain his position and free Rome from tyranny by raising an army to invade the capital and assassinate the emperor. When he is betrayed by a trusted lieutenant, Maternus meets his death with noble Roman virtue. Efforts to produce the play came to naught, but as with *The Fair God,* Wallace continued to work on it over the next twenty years. The play was commercially published in *Harper's Monthly* in January 1889 (but has never been acted).

In 1878 Wallace was appointed territorial governor of New Mexico, where he was subjected to several letters (and a few threats) from William Bonney, the notorious Billy the Kid, who to a great extent symbolized the outlawry and anarchy Wallace was sent to suppress. While in New Mexico, perhaps as a relief from the futility of trying to stop the range wars and feuding that dominated the scene, Wallace completed *Ben-Hur.*

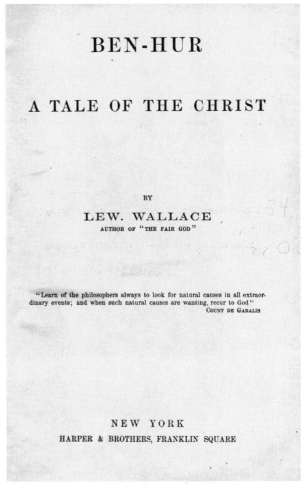

Title page for Wallace's 1880 novel based on the fall of the Jewish prince Judah Ben-Hur to the position of Roman galley slave and his subsequent rise in the Roman world

The book that made him famous was apparently begun in 1873 and included extensive research into the history and geography of Roman Judea. The book that evolved is well known. Judah Ben-Hur is betrayed out of his fortune and birthright by the Roman Massala. Ben-Hur survives slavery on the galleys; fights off assassins; bests Massala in a chariot race; finds his long lost mother and sister, who are cured of leprosy by a divine miracle; meets and weds a fair maiden; and in the end is restored to his noble position. Wallace once more gives his penchant for melodrama free rein, but *Ben-Hur* is superior to *The Fair God.* The plot is tighter, and the characters are more human and believable. Dialogue remains stilted, but the action scenes are tighter and more thrilling (most notably in the justly famous chariot race) than in his earlier effort. As an example of the historical romance, *Ben-Hur* deserves its reputation. While sales were slow at first, to Wallace's disappointment, by 1881 they began to increase, reaching an astonishing 45,000 copies in 1886–1887.

The chariot race in the two popular motion-picture versions of Ben-Hur: *(top) Francis X. Bushman as Messala and Ramon Navarro as Ben-Hur in the 1925 movie; (bottom) Charlton Heston (at left) as the title character in the 1959 movie*

While Wallace succeeded in New Mexico in terms of finishing *Ben-Hur,* he did not succeed in bringing peace to that troubled territory. Instead, in 1881 President James A. Garfield, entranced with the novel, called Wallace back to Washington and named him minister to Turkey, where he served until his return to Indiana in 1885. Wallace proved an able minister, becoming close friends with the Sultan Abdul-Hammid, testified to by the sultan's breaking tradition by shaking hands with an infidel. In 1888 Wallace was deeply involved in the presidential campaign of his friend William Henry Harrison, for whom he wrote a campaign biography in one month. But even while writing that biography, Wallace was involved in another project of much greater scope, yet another historical romance, this one even more ambitious than *Ben-Hur.*

The Prince of India; or, Why Constantinople Fell (1893) had its genesis in President Garfield's offhand suggestion that Wallace write a book with Constantinople as its setting. Again his research was painstaking, enforced this time by his actually visiting the scene during his ministry to Turkey. His subject was the fall of Constantinople in 1453. The element of romance involves the Princess Irenè, beloved by both Mahommed and Constantine, and the ubiquitous figure of the Wandering Jew, the Prince of India who assumes Christian or Moslem guise to further his goal of uniting religions into a single, peaceful whole. *The Prince of India,* larger and more ambitious than Wallace's earlier romances, is also more adventurous and better written. As in his first romance, Wallace again treats the sense of loss and disaster brought about by the human inability to understand or accept a different culture. This time, however, he has a central figure actively engaged in breaking down such barriers. Such improvements in conception and execution, alas, were no guarantee of success. The book sold one hundred thousand copies in six months; then sales dropped off precipitously. What Wallace considered his finest effort was also his least successful.

From 1895 on Wallace remained more and more in Crawfordsville, with occasional speaking tours, attendance at Civil War reunions, and (as an offshoot of *The Prince of India*) the writing of "The Wooing of Malkatoon," a poem based on a thirteenth-century legend of Prince Othman, who foretold the conquest of Constantinople and was consequently awarded the maiden Malkatoon. The poem was published, with *Commodus,* by Harper in 1897. That same year Wallace, at the urging of Harper, began work on his last literary project, *Lew Wallace: An Autobiography,* perhaps the most interesting and instructive of his books. Although he only lived long enough to trace his life as far as the defense of Washington in 1864—his wife finished in almost shorthand fashion the remainder of volume two—Wallace creates in himself his most forceful character, in the process revealing his melodramatic nature; his desire for fame, glory, and wealth; and his propensity for self-justification. In short, the autobiography makes evident the personality behind many of Wallace's fictional characters.

Lew Wallace will never have the literary reputation of such contemporaries as Twain, James, or Stephen Crane. His flair for the melodramatic and his overwrought prose strike an artificial note in a time more used to the realistic treatment of material. While the historical romance remains a popular form in American literature, matters of style and taste have passed Wallace by. Moreover, his works lack that intrinsic value that could make them rewarding despite the obstacles his style and tendency to moralize create. Nonetheless, the success of *Ben-Hur* and its incorporation into the popular imagination suggests that Wallace's name will continue as part of the American literary tradition. How appropriate, then, that he came to be known, and remains known, as Ben-Hur Wallace, linking together creator and creation.

Bibliography:

Dorothy Ritter Russo and Thelma Lois Sullivan, "LW," in their *Bibliographical Studies of Seven Authors of Crawfordsville, Indiana* (Indianapolis: Indiana Historical Society, 1952), 305–416.

Biographies:

Irving McKee, *"Ben-Hur" Wallace: The Life of General Lew Wallace* (Berkeley: University of California Press, 1947);

Robert E. Morsberger and Katherine M. Morsberger, *LW: Militant Romantic* (New York: McGraw-Hill, 1980).

References:

Paul Gutjahr, "'To the Heart of the Solid Puritans': Historicizing the Popularity of *Ben-Hur,*" *Mosaic: A Journal for the Comparative Study of Literature,* 26 (1993): 53–67;

James D. Hart, *The Popular Book; A History of America's Literary Taste* (New York: Oxford University Press, 1950);

Allene Stuart Phy, "Lew Wallace and 'Ben-Hur,'" *Romantist,* 6–8 (1982–1984): 2–10;

Lee Scott Theisen, "'My God, Did I Set All of This in Motion?' General Lew Wallace and *Ben-Hur,*" *Journal of Popular Culture,* 18 (1984): 33–41;

Carl Van Doren, *The American Novel* (New York: Macmillan, 1921).

Papers:

Material on Lew Wallace is extensive and may be found in the following depositories: the General Lew Wallace Study, Crawfordsville, Indiana; the Lew Wallace Jr. Collection, Southport, Connecticut; the J. K. Lilly Jr. Collection of the Lilly Library, Indiana University, Bloomington; and the W. H. Smith Library, Indianapolis.

Anne Warner

(14 October 1869 – 1 February 1913)

Karen L. Morgan

Mardigian Library, University of Michigan–Dearborn

BOOKS: *An American Ancestry* (Minneapolis: Hall, Black, 1894);

His Story: Their Letters, anonymous (Chicago: Drake, 1902);

A Woman's Will (Boston: Little, Brown, 1904);

Susan Clegg and Her Friend Mrs. Lathrop (Boston: Little, Brown, 1904; London & Cambridge: Dean & Son, 1904); republished in *Susan Clegg: Her Friend and Her Neighbors* (Boston: Little, Brown, 1910);

The Rejuvenation of Aunt Mary (Boston: Little, Brown, 1905; London: Gay & Bird, 1907);

Seeing France with Uncle John (New York: Century, 1906; London: Gay & Bird, 1906);

Susan Clegg and Her Neighbors' Affairs (Boston: Little, Brown, 1906; London: Gay & Bird, 1906); republished in *Susan Clegg: Her Friend and Her Neighbors* (Boston: Little, Brown, 1910);

Susan Clegg and a Man in the House (Boston: Little, Brown, 1907);

An Original Gentleman (Boston: Little, Brown, 1908);

The Panther: A Tale of Temptation (Boston: Small, Maynard, 1908);

Seeing England with Uncle John (New York: Century, 1908; London: Gay & Hancock, 1908);

In a Mysterious Way (Boston: Little, Brown, 1909);

Your Child and Mine (Boston: Little, Brown, 1909);

Just Between Themselves: A Book About Dichtenberg (Boston: Little, Brown, 1910; London: Unwin, 1910);

How Leslie Loved (Boston: Little, Brown, 1911); republished as *Leslie's Lovers* (London: Unwin, 1911);

When Woman Proposes (Boston: Little, Brown, 1911);

Sunshine Jane (Boston: Little, Brown, 1914; London: Religious Tract Society, 1914);

The Gay and Festive Claverhouse: An Extravaganza (Boston: Little, Brown, 1914);

The Taming of Amorette: A Comedy of Manners (Boston: Little, Brown, 1915);

The Tigress (New York: Watt, 1916);

The Rejuvenation of Aunt Mary, a Three-Act Comedy (New York: S. French, 1916);

Anne Warner (photograph by Hana, London)

Susan Clegg and Her Love Affairs (Boston: Little, Brown, 1916).

PLAY PRODUCTION: *The Rejuvenation of Aunt Mary: a Three-Act Comedy,* New York, Garden Theatre, 15 October 1907.

SELECTED PERIODICAL PUBLICATIONS–UNCOLLECTED: "An Author's Year," *Bookman* (New York), 27 (March 1908): 23–24;

"Amazing Widow," *Collier's,* 55 (12 June 1915): 5–6; (19 June 1915): 11–12; (26 June 1915): 18–19; (3 July

1915): 12–13; (10 July 1915): 11–12; (17 July 1915): 10–11;

"Later Troubles of Susan Clegg," *Ladies' Home Journal,* 32 (December 1915): 25; 33 (January 1916): 22; 33 (February 1916): 24; 33 (March 1916): 18; 33 (April 1916): 28;

"Anita and the Seven Boys," *Canadian Magazine,* 54 (April 1920): 486–492.

In her day Anne Warner was considered one of the best American humorists. Although her humor is less subtle, she was compared to New England writer Mary E. Wilkins Freeman. Warner's character Susan Clegg was compared to Alice Hegan Rice's Mrs. Wiggs, and she also has much in common with Marietta Holley's Samantha. Warner's reputation is based on her Susan Clegg stories, which are almost entirely written in the form of anecdotes told by Susan Clegg to her neighbor and friend Mrs. Lathrop, who rarely says anything but is a wonderful listener. Warner's greatest wit is displayed when Susan shares her opinions on men, many of which remain as fresh as when they were first written. It is difficult to place the Susan Clegg stories geographically. One review describes Susan Clegg as "a New England gossip," but there are no particular references to New England in the stories. Minnesota and upstate New York are also possible locations. In addition to five volumes of the Susan Clegg stories, most of which first appeared in magazines, Warner wrote several light novels, some of which are set in Europe. These books were most frequently recommended, if at all, for "summer reading" and "idle hours." They include two humorous travel books, *Seeing France with Uncle John* (1906) and *Seeing England with Uncle John* (1908), light romances in which she caricatured the American tourist in Europe while also providing information for the prospective traveler.

The daughter of attorney William P. Warner and his wife, Anna Elizabeth Richmond Warner, Anne Richmond Warner was born on 14 October 1869 in St. Paul, Minnesota. Her family was part of elite St. Paul society. She was educated at home by her mother, and married Charles Ellis French on 12 September 1888. Born in 1847 in Columbia, South Carolina, French had moved to Minneapolis in 1880 and was in the flour-and-grain industry. The Frenches had two children, Charles Jr. and Anne. By 1905 the couple had divorced amicably, with Charles French retaining custody of their son and Anne Warner taking custody of their daughter. While making frequent trips back to the United States, Warner and her daughter lived in Germany from 1905 until April 1911. After spending several months in St.

Paul, they settled permanently in England the following fall.

Anne Warner's first book, *An American Ancestry* (1894), was a genealogy of her husband's family. She is said to have published an unnamed travel volume in 1894, and in 1901 she published her first short story. The anonymously published novel *His Story: Their Letters* (1902) is attributed to Warner. A light story of love and marriage, it is characterized by the sort of humorous dialogue that she used in most of her later works.

Warner used her life in Germany as background for several works, including the first novel published under her name, *A Woman's Will* (1904). Rosina, a young American widow traveling in Europe, both pursues and evades Count Von Ibn, a German musical genius. She has no plans to end a year of blissful widowhood, but she is overwhelmed by her attraction to Ibn, who says of a woman's relationship to a genius, "The women were not meant to be the genius, only to help him and rest him after his labor." *The New York Times Saturday Review of Books* (18 June 1904) recommended this book for summer reading, noting that its "chief charm" is the count's conversation.

In 1904 Warner also published four short stories in *The Century Illustrated Magazine,* which with the addition of "The Minister's Vacation" were published as *Susan Clegg and Her Friend Mrs. Lathrop* at the end of that year. In this first collection Susan, a spinster in her early forties, hopes to marry as soon as her bedridden father dies. After Mrs. Lathrop suggests that a feather bed sometimes speeds the dying process, Susan provides one, and her father dies within a day. Susan is amazed at the effectiveness of the remedy and immediately sets about looking for a husband, approaching several single men in their small town without success. Only later, when Susan receives an inheritance from her father, do some of these bachelors change their minds. By then, however, she has decided that a husband might be a lot of trouble. While her paralyzed father would stay put, she could not depend on a husband to stay at home. Written in rural dialect, the Clegg stories are "phonographically accurate," according to the reviewer for *Reader Magazine* (December 1904), who went on to say: "There is a great deal of satisfaction to be had out of the Susan Clegg stories. They are all humor, and humor of an obvious, tangible sort." The reviewer also called the stories "fresh" and "interesting." The reviewer for *The Arena* (November 1904) agreed, with reservations, saying: "There is no denying the fact they are clever sketches, abounding in bright sayings and very true to a certain phase of life among simple-minded people who live almost wholly on the surface of being. . . . we doubt

Frontispiece by W. J. Enright for Susan Clegg and Her Friend Mrs. Lathrop *(1904), the first of Warner's books featuring these popular rural characters*

if our readers will take special pleasure in them." Yet, Warner's reputation was built on these stories.

Both rural and urban in setting, *The Rejuvenation of Aunt Mary* (1905) tells of Jack Denham's wealthy, elderly Aunt Mary, who holds the purse strings as he throws himself into one scrape after another. While she is patient with him at first, she finally cuts him out of her will and goes to New York City to find out what he is doing. Instead of disapproving, as she expected, she enjoys herself. Jack arrives at a happy ending, aided by Mrs. Beulah Rosscott, a young widow he hopes to marry. Like many of Warner's widows, Beulah is reluctant to give up her freedom for a second marriage. Warner adapted this novel for the stage, and the dramatic version was produced in New York City in 1907. In an article in the March 1908 issue of *The Bookman* (New York) Warner commented, "Clyde Fitch . . . said that one's sensations were indescribable when one saw one's characters on the stage. My sensations certainly

were indescribable." She may have agreed with *Harper's Weekly* (30 November 1907), which suggested the play should have remained "a readable story."

Warner's next book, *Seeing France With Uncle John*, published in 1906, was first serialized in *The Century Illustrated Magazine* from June to October of that year. The story of an uncle traveling with his two nieces, Yvonne and Edna, the book alternates Yvonne's charming letters to her mother with Uncle John's comments on the landscape and culture of France, as well as on traveling with two young women: "Your mother has trusted you girls to me and I haven't drawn a quiet breath since." The nieces outwit their uncle with the help of their suitors. The reviewer for *The New York Times Saturday Review of Books* (8 December 1906) commented that "the present book falls so far below what she has taught her readers to expect that even her enemies, if she has any, must be sorry that she has published it."

Also in 1906 Warner published another short-story collection, *Susan Clegg and Her Neighbors' Affairs* (1906). These stories, some published earlier in *Redbook, Reader Magazine,* and *The Century,* continue Susan Clegg's narrative to her friend Mrs. Lathrop. In the first section, "Mrs. Lathrop's Love Affair," the recently widowed Deacon White has decided to propose to Mrs. Lathrop, probably because she is the only single woman in town who has not expressed any interest in him. As Susan says, "He said he jus' felt he'd enjoy the revenge o' stayin' single. But he said it didn't take him long to see's stayin' single is a privilege no woman's goin' to allow a man whose wife's dead." In part two of this tale Susan reports to Mrs. Lathrop that an automobile is in town running over everything. It is driven by two men, "One steers in goggles, 'n' the other jumps in 'n' out 'n' settles for the damages." The deacon is one of the casualties, and when he is taken to Polly Allen's to recover, Susan rightly predicts Polly will be the next Mrs. White. The second section, "Wolf at Susan's Door," includes the stories of the weddings of Lucy Dill to Hiram Mullins, and Polly Allen to Deacon White. The reviewer for *The New York Times Saturday Review of Books* (8 December 1906) wrote that the Susan Clegg stories "deserve a place among the choice specimens of American humorous literature—which means the best humorous literature in the world."

As Warner wrote in her 1908 article in *The Bookman*, 1907 was a busy year for her. After spending a few days with a friend in Indianapolis in April 1907, she wrote,

> I came to Chicago and arranged *Susan Clegg and a Man in the House* in eleven days. Then I went to New York and worked on the play [*The Rejuvenation of Aunt Mary*]

for six weeks. . . . Then I was ill for six or seven weeks, after which I wrote *Seeing England with Uncle John,* having done the necessary reading during my illness. I finished the book September 7th and wrote eight short stories, and then, October 5th, I came East to see the play staged. . . . On my way home in November I stopped at Rochester and made a 40,000-word draft for a new book. . . . now I am writing some short stories preparatory to beginning to really write that book.

Susan Clegg and a Man in the House (1907) is a collection of anecdotes held together by Susan's narration about taking a lodger, Elijah Doxey, the young editor of the local paper, to "learn a little of what it would mean to have a man in the house." When she examines his things and discovers a locked box, she is obsessed with finding out what it contains: "A trustin' nature is one thing to have around an' a distrustin' nature is another thing, an' I can tell you that there's somethin' about feelin' as you ain't trusted as makes me take my hands right out of my bread dough an' go straight upstairs to begin lookin' for that key again." She is horrified to discover that the box contains Elijah's flute. She is sure she will not be able to prevent him playing it or stand the sound of it. "It is very easy to take a man into your house but once a woman has done it an' the man is settled, nobody but a undertaker can get him out in any way as is respectable accordin' to my order of thinkin'." While she attends church, she worries about what Elijah might be doing at home, he being "of a inquirin' disposition." When Elijah is taken ill, 'Liza Emily, one of the many young ladies infatuated with him, comes over to help. As Susan comments, "I think any girl as is willin' to do her nine-tenths can have a time tryin' to be happy with him. If she ain't happy long it won't be Elijah's fault for he's just as sure his wife'll be happy as any other man is." After three months, Elijah moves elsewhere, and Susan reports what she has learned to Mrs. Lathrop: "I don't like the way of a man in the house, Mrs. Lathrop,—they seem to get like they thought you enjoyed havin' them around. I can't see where they ever got the idea in the first place, but it certainly does seem to stick by 'em most wonderful." While Elijah is lodging with her, Susan goes to the Convention of Women's Clubs and is mistaken for another person named Susan Clegg, who writes stories and wants Susan to stay with her. She reports to Mrs. Lathrop, "I felt that no matter how kind she was I wouldn't never be able to be happy anywhere where I had to be around with a woman who talked all the time," a sly commentary on Susan herself. The reviewer for *The New York Times Saturday Review of Books* (26 October 1907) was enthusiastic: "Susan is a positive joy, and the reading world owes Anne Warner a vote of thanks for her contribution to the best of American humor; she

has created a character genuinely quaint, original, and sympathetic, and we hope that she will continue to delight us with the adventures of Susan Clegg and her friends."

Warner's next book, *An Original Gentleman* (1908), is a collection of twenty-two short stories, a mélange of American local-color tales and stories set in Europe, most previously published in magazines such as *Lippincott's* and *Redbook*. In addition to the long title story, the collection includes "The Twelve Little Broilers," a tale set in the South with African American characters, and "Jane and Her Genius," the story of a girl who becomes a writer. In the same year, Warner published *The Panther: a Tale of Temptation,* an allegorical story in which a large man and a woman with silver-blue eyes must renounce "temptation" for reasons never stated. There is no happy ending to this story, nor does it include any humor. It is not one of Warner's best efforts.

Warner rounded out one of her most productive years with *Seeing England With Uncle John* (1908), again alternating letters from Yvonne to her mother with Uncle John's commentary. In this book Yvonne and her husband, Lee, travel from their home in Oxford to Liverpool to meet Uncle John, who has already set off on his own adventure. The young couple spends the rest of the book a step behind Uncle John and his trunk, until they finally catch up with him back in Oxford. This light romance and guidebook is indexed and furnishes details on points of interest for the traveler.

Warner's *In a Mysterious Way* (1909) is a mixture of local-color writing and a mystery involving visitors to a small town in upstate New York. Mrs. Ray, one of Warner's boundlessly energetic countrywomen, runs the post office, keeps boarders, bids for the job of whitewashing the school, and makes new clothes out of old for her neighbors, while paying close attention to the out-of-town visitors Alva and her friends Lassie and Ronald. The reviewer for *The New York Times Saturday Review of Books* (22 May 1909) approved of Mrs. Ray but wrote, "It seems rather a pity that Anne Warner, one of our cleverest humorists, does not follow the natural bent of her talent, instead of writing mediocre novels with a 'problem' flavor."

Your Child and Mine (1909) is a collection of children's stories, many of which had appeared in magazines. In her preface Warner assured children of their importance: "there is no telling what you have locked up in your future." Among the stories is "The Surrender of Cornwallis," in which a child gives up his desire to be called by his name instead of "baby" to please his ailing mother. In "The Practical Care of a Fairy" Nora learns from a fairy how to care for pets.

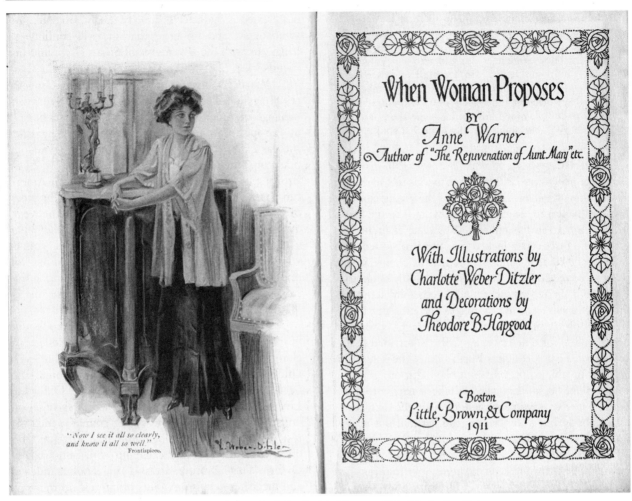

Frontispiece and title page for the last book by Warner published during her lifetime

Just Between Themselves: A Book About Dichtenberg (1910), about three couples on a holiday in an out-of-the-way German village, gives the impression that vacationing in Germany requires stamina and careful planning. Also published in 1910 was *Susan Clegg: Her Friend and Her Neighbors,* which comprises the previously published *Susan Clegg and Her Friend Mrs. Lathrop* and *Susan Clegg and Her Neighbors' Affairs.*

Warner again used a German setting in *How Leslie Loved* (1911), in which the title character, a young American widow, travels around Germany, flirting with eligible gentlemen and trying to avoid the man whom she is destined to marry. Eventually she finds that telling others how wonderful Hugo is renders him desirable in her eyes, too, and marriage results.

By the time Warner decided to settle permanently in England in 1911, her celebrity was such that her move was the subject of a story in *The New York Times* (3 September 1911). Warner told the reporter,

This country is really very young, very crude . . . and it is difficult for the people, especially the women, to feel what my work means to me and to respect it. Women of America, though they are petted and pampered as nowhere else, are not expected to enter the real world of affairs. The men do no take them into it with them, and so they cannot grasp what my serious work may mean to me.

Warner's comments did little to endear her to the American reading public. Clinging to her theosophic beliefs, however, she remained serene in the face of criticism.

The last book by Warner published during her lifetime was *When Woman Proposes* (1911). Nathalie Arundel, a wealthy, young American widow living in England, sees Capt. Francis Mowbray, a soldier, at a party and immediately decides to marry him. The convoluted plot seems to suggest that an expenditure of capital can bring about almost anything. As the newlyweds take a hansom cab to her house after their wedding, Nathalie makes her position clear:

I've never had any love-making in all my life, and I don't want to be cheated out of it. I haven't been able to help doing the way I've done . . . because you were so dead-set in your ideas, and I saw in the very first of it that expecting you to do anything towards getting us married would be a piece of folly that never would come out anywhere . . . and so I've done all the work. But I think you ought to make it up to me now–don't you?

In 1912, within a few months of Warner's move to England, her former husband died, and within the year her son, Charles, a student at the University of Virginia, also passed away. She survived him by only a few months, dying on 1 February 1913. New books by Warner continued to be published through 1916, and stories appeared in magazines as late as 1920, attesting to her industry and that of her executor, who was probably her brother Richard Warner.

One of these posthumous publications is *Sunshine Jane* (1914), an optimistic story set in rural America. In the spirit of Eleanor Porter's title character in *Pollyanna* (1913), Jane, a trained "Sunshine Nurse," visits her aunts, Matilda Drew and Susan Ralston, allowing Matilda, who has been a miserly caretaker to Susan, to take a holiday. Susan has pretended to be an invalid because, as she puts it, "It was the pleasantest way to get along . . . Matilda wasn't here very long before I see that if her patience wasn't to give out, I'd got to begin to fail. I went to bed, and I've failed ever since." Others in the community benefit from Jane's sunny disposition and her practice of looking for the best in every situation.

Flirtation is the theme of several of Warner's last works. In *The Gay and Festive Claverhouse: An Extravaganza* (1914), set in England, Claverhouse, a charming man-about-town, has been mistakenly diagnosed with a fatal illness, an error which results in his marriage to his devoted cousin Madeleine. In *The Taming of Amorette: A Comedy of Manners* (1915), Amorette, a young widow in Europe, marries Geoffrey Girard, who encourages her to continue the relentless flirtations that were her entertainment before marriage. She finds that this behavior is not after all what she wants, and through her husband's indulgence she becomes a happy wife. *The Tigress* (1916) begins with Nina Darling, a heartless flirt, refusing yet another invitation to flee from her unsatis-

factory marriage: "Oh, why can't you men appreciate being petted and amused, without imagining that it must be inspired by adoration and coupled with a desire for life-long attachment?" she says to Gerald Andrews. Like a jungle cat, Nina flirts her way through a tangled plot to a happy ending.

Warner's final posthumously published book, *Susan Clegg and Her Love Affairs* (1916), is written in a less conversational style than her earlier Susan Clegg stories, with more narration and much less dialect. The book recounts the return of Mrs. Lathrop's unprepossessing son, Jathrop, who has made a fortune prospecting for gold in the Klondike. He decides to rebuild his mother's old home and the home of her old friend Susan Clegg. Returning to visit his mother for Christmas, Jathrop brings the bald, red-bearded Mr. Kettlewell, a friend even richer than himself. Subject to nightmares in which he acts out his dreams, Kettlewell invades Susan's home and leaves her tied up and gagged for five hours. Nonetheless, Susan and Kettlewell are entranced with each other, and by the end of the book they are married, Kettlewell's peculiarities outweighed by his charm and fortune.

Meriting further study and a wider audience, Warner's Susan Clegg stories are an important contribution to American literature. *The Bookman* (New York) obituary for Warner (April 1913) assessed her place in American letters: "With these stories–*Susan Clegg and her Friend Mrs. Lathrop, Susan Clegg and a Man in the House* and *Susan Clegg, Her Friend, and Her Neighbours*–she attained a place in the little circle of American women humorous writers who have achieved distinction."

References:

"Anne Warner Explains Why She Forsook America," *New York Times,* 22 October 1911, V, p. 12;

Emily Toth, "A Laughter of Their Own: Women's Humor in the United States," in *Critical Essays on American Humor,* edited by William Bedford Clark and W. Craig Turner (Boston: G. K. Hall, 1994), pp. 199–215;

Nancy Walker, "Susan and Tish: Women's Humor at the Turn of the Century," *Turn-of-the-Century Women,* 2 (Winter 1985): 50–54.

Charles Wilkins Webber

(29 May 1819 – 11 April 1856?)

Richard P. Benton
Trinity College, Hartford, Connecticut

BOOKS: *Jack Long; or, Shot in the Eye: A True Story of Texas Border Life,* anonymous (New York: Graham, 1846);

Old Hicks, the Guide; or, Adventures in the Camanche Country in Search of a Gold Mine (New York: Harper, 1848); republished as *Adventures in the Camanche Country, in Search of a Gold Mine* (Glasgow: Griffin, 1848);

The Gold Mines of the Gila: A Sequel to Old Hicks, the Guide, 2 volumes (New York: DeWitt & Davenport, 1849); revised as *The Prairie Scout; or, Agatone the Renegade: A Romance of Border Life* (New York: DeWitt & Davenport, 1852);

The Hunter-Naturalist: Romance of Sporting; or, Wild Scenes and Wild Hunters (Philadelphia: Bradley, 1851); republished as *Romance of Natural History; or, Wild Scenes and Wild Hunters* (Philadelphia: Lippincott, Grambo, 1852); republished as *Wild Scenes and Wild Hunters of the World* (Philadelphia: Bradley, 1852); abridged as *The Romance of Forest and Prairie Life: Narratives of Perilous Adventures and Wild Hunting Scenes,* anonymous (London: Vizetelly, 1853); republished as *Romance of Sporting; or, Wild Scenes and Wild Hunters* (Philadelphia: Lippincott, 1865); republished as *Wild Scenes and Wild Hunters; or, The Romance of Sporting* (Philadelphia: Claxton, Remsen & Haffelfinger, 1875);

The Texan Virago; or, The Tailor of Gotham and Other Tales (Philadelphia: Lippincott, Grambo, 1852);

The Wild Girl of Nebraska (Philadelphia: Lippincott, Grambo, 1852);

Tales of the Southern Border (Philadelphia: Lippincott, Grambo, 1853);

Yieger's Cabinet. Spiritual Vampirism: The History of Etherial Softdown, and Her Friends of the "New Light" (Philadelphia: Lippincott, Grambo, 1853);

Wild Scenes and Song-Birds (New York: Putnam, 1854);

"Sam"; or, The History of Mystery (Cincinnati: Rulison / Philadelphia: Quaker City, 1855); abridged as *Historical and Revolutionary Incidents of the Early Settlers of the United States, with Biographical Sketches of*

(American Antiquarian Society)

the Lives of Allen, Boone, Kenton, and Other Celebrated Pioneers* (Philadelphia: Rulison, 1859).

SELECTED PERIODICAL PUBLICATIONS– UNCOLLECTED: "Adventures; or, Wild Life on the Texas Frontier," as A Kentuckian, *New World,* 8 (23 March 1844): 354–357; (6 April 1844): 425–439; (13 April 1844): 451–454; (20 April 1844): 482–485; (4 May 1844): 542–545; (18 May 1844): 608–611; (1 June 1844): 669–672; as C. Wilkins Eimi, a Kentuckian, *New World,* 9 (6 July 1844): 2–4; (20 July 1844): 71–76;

"Instinct, Reason, and Imagination," as Eimi, *U.S. Magazine & Democratic Review,* 15 (October 1844): 408–418;

"Adam Baker, the Renegade: A Tale of the Texas Frontier," as Eimi, *Columbian Magazine,* 2 (November 1844): 193–201;

"The Remonstrance," as Eimi, *U.S. Magazine & Democratic Review,* 15 (December 1844): 595–596;

"American Ornithology," as Charles Winterfield, *American Review,* 1 (March 1845): 262–274;

"About Birds and Audubon," as Winterfield, *American Review,* 1 (11 April 1845): 371–383;

"The Mocking Bird—An Indian Legend," as Winterfield, *American Review,* 1 (1 May 1845): 497–501;

"Metaphysics of Bear Hunting," as Winterfield, *American Review,* 2 (August 1845): 171–188;

"Adventures on the Frontier of Texas and Mexico, no. 2," as Winterfield, *American Review,* 2 (October 1845): 365–384; (November 1845): 504–518; (December 1845): 599–613; 3 (January 1846): 1–17;

"Birds and Poets Illustrating Each Other," as Winterfield, *American Review,* 3 (February 1846): 129–143;

"Hawthorne: Review of His Writings," *American Review,* 4 (September 1846): 296–316;

"The Viviparous Quadrupeds of North America . . . of John James Audubon and the Rev. John Bachman," *Literary World,* 1 (13 March 1847): 127–149; (20 March 1847): 152–154; (10 April 1847): 224–226;

"North American Foxes: The Viviparous Quadrupeds of North America of Audubon and Bachman," *Southern Quarterly Review,* 1 (April 1848): 403–457;

"Hunting the Wild Cat," *Graham's Magazine,* 38 (March 1851): 139–143;

"The Boy Hunter," *Graham's Magazine,* 29 (July 1851): 10–16;

"Trout Fishing in Jessup's River," *Godey's Lady's Book,* 43 (October 1851): 204–207.

According to John William Rogers, Charles Wilkins Webber was "the first fiction writer of importance to use Texas as his theme." His fiction was based largely on his own experiences, as was the early work of his contemporary Herman Melville; in fact, an anonymous reviewer in the *U.S. Magazine and Democratic Review* (May 1848) compared Webber's novel *Old Hicks, the Guide; or, Adventures in the Camanche Country in Search of a Gold Mine* (1848) favorably to Melville's *Omoo: A Narrative of Adventures in the South Seas* (1847). Acknowledging that *Old Hicks* "is not finished with the care and polish of *Omoo*," the reviewer said that "there is in it far more earnestness and poetry . . . while it has the same

remarkable *vraisemblance* of that popular work." Webber's novel is, according to the reviewer, even superior to Melville's "in the confidence it inspires of its truth."

Webber was born on 29 May 1819 in Russellville, a small town in southern Kentucky, to Augustine Webber, a physician, and Agnes Maria Tannehill Webber. He had an irregular education at home, reading works by Homer, Ovid, William Shakespeare, and John Milton as well as by contemporary authors such as Sir Walter Scott, James Fenimore Cooper, and William Cullen Bryant. An amateur naturalist who later became a close friend of John James Audubon, Webber particularly admired Bryant's nature poems. Seeking adventure, in 1838 Webber left Russellville for the two-year-old Republic of Texas, where he joined the Texas Rangers. In 1843 he returned to Kentucky and briefly studied medicine before enrolling in the fall of 1843 at Princeton Theological Seminary with the intention of becoming a Presbyterian clergyman. That ambition, too, was soon given up, and in 1844 he moved to New York City to pursue a career in journalism. A series of nine "sketches" based on his experiences in Texas were published in *The New World: A Weekly Family Journal of Popular Literature, Science, Art and News* from March through July 1844 under the title "Adventures; or, Wild Life on the Texan Frontier" under the pseudonym "C. Wilkins Eimi, a Kentuckian."

In February 1845 Webber published his best-known story, "Jack Long, or Lynch Law and Vengeance, a Tale of Texas Life," in *The American Review: A Whig Journal of Politics, Literature, Art and Science,* using his own name; the story appeared simultaneously in *The United States Magazine and Democratic Review* as "The Shot in the Eye: A True Story of Texas Border Life" under the C. Wilkins Eimi pseudonym. It was published in book form, anonymously, in 1846 as *Jack Long; or, Shot in the Eye: A True Story of Texas Border Life.* The story is set in lawless Shelby County, east Texas, where the affluent cotton planters have hired a group of vigilantes, the Regulators, to maintain order. The Regulators, however, have proved to be little better than the horse thieves, cattle rustlers, gunmen, and bandits they were set up to control. One day Jack Long, a hunter who is an artist with his Kentucky rifle, beats the leader of the Regulators, Hinch, a bully and braggart, in a shooting match. Thereafter Hinch and his Regulators harass Jack at every opportunity. Finally they lasso him when he goes to his spring, unarmed, to fetch water for his wife. They strip him and beat him unconscious in front of his horrified wife and children. After Jack recovers from the assault, residents of Shelby County begin to discover the dead bodies of Regulators, each of them shot through the eye. The tale was particularly admired by Edgar Allan Poe, who thought its construction approached perfection.

Another series of four tales appeared in *The American Review* from October 1845 through January 1846 under the title "Adventures on the Frontier of Texas and Mexico" and the pseudonym "Charles Winterfield." In 1848 Webber became assistant to the editor of *The American Review*. Published that same year, his novel *Old Hicks, the Guide* is the story of an expedition through Texas and New Mexico in 1839–1840 in search of legendary gold. The narrator of the autobiographical stories is Webber, a Texas Ranger captain. The other members of the party are the seven Rangers he has handpicked for the expedition; the guide, old Hicks, a mountain man who speaks Indian languages; Dr. Martin, a physician-actor-naturalist-inventor who supplies comic relief; Emily L'Enville, a French beauty with whom the narrator falls in love; and Albert, Count Beauford, a confidence man and roué who tricked Emily into a false marriage and who is also the war chief of a band of Comanches. One of the Rangers, Jack Lanville, is Emily's long-lost brother; another, Dolphin Larry, is a liar and a lecher. The narrator kills Dolphin Larry when he finds "the libidinous monster" sexually assaulting Emily. The novel is filled with scenes of violence, including battles with the Indians and the lynching of two horse thieves, but it also includes lyrical descriptions of the beauty of the natural surroundings.

In 1849, in Boston, Webber was married to an artist-naturalist who later contributed twenty-five colored lithographs to his *Wild Scenes and Song-Birds* (1854). Also in 1849 he suffered a severe financial loss when the horses he had purchased for a gold-seeking expedition to the Colorado and Gila Rivers were stolen by Comanches in Corpus Christi, Texas. Webber also conceived of the idea of importing camels from the Near East into Texas to be used for transporting people and goods across the Great Plains. He obtained a charter from the New York legislature to form a company for this purpose, but apparently he took the matter no further.

The American Review went out of business in 1852. Some of Webber's autobiographical stories of life on the Texas frontier were collected the following year as *Tales of the Southern Border*. A representative tale is "The Border Chase: A First Day with the Rangers." The narrator, identified as Webber or "Old Kentuck," is the guest of the owner of a cotton plantation on the Brazos River. His host is informed that a slave who escaped from the plantation has been captured and is being held for the reward by a merchant in San Antonio. The narrator and the plantation owner ride to San Antonio and find the slave in chains; deciding that he is unlikely to

escape, they visit a nearby tavern. There they encounter a group of young men, dressed in Mexican sombreros and serapes worn over buckskin suits; each is armed with a pair of pistols and a bowie knife. The men, who greet the two strangers with "manly and straight-forward courtesy," belong to a regiment of Texas Rangers commanded by the stalwart Col. John Coffee Hays. (Hays was a real person, although in 1840, when the story takes place, he was a captain, not a colonel.) The narrator is struck with admiration for the Rangers and asks Hays if he might become one of them. The colonel promptly welcomes him into the regiment, and the other men toast him and dub him "Old Kentuck." The next day the narrator and his planter friend return to the merchant's house, where they learn that the slave escaped with the aid of a Mexican vaquero and has crossed the border at Laredo.

Also published in 1853, *Yieger's Cabinet. Spiritual Vampirism: The History of Etherial Softdown and Her Friends of the "New Light"* is a departure from Webber's usual themes. The novel is a satire of contemporary movements such as transcendentalism, utopianism, abolitionism, mesmerism, mental healing, vegetarianism, feminism, temperance, and spiritualism. The main character, Etherial Softdown, a spiritualist medium and popular lecturer on mental healing, seems to have been modeled on the spiritualist poet Achsa W. Sprague. Etherial Softdown is a "vampire" because she seduces men and drains them of their manhood.

In 1855 Webber joined the mercenary army of the filibuster William Walker, who had been asked by the Liberal Party of Nicaragua to help it overthrow the ruling Conservative Party. Webber was apparently killed in the battle of Rivas on 11 April 1856.

Webber is practically unknown to students of American literature today. Although Edgar Allan Poe was an admirer of *Jack Long; or, Shot in the Eye*, Webber's writing is often sentimental, his characterizations shallow, and his plots weak; but he knew how to develop suspenseful action, and his writing abounds in marvelous descriptions of scenery.

Bibliography:
Generosa Callahan, *Bibliography of Charles Wilkins Webber* (Austin: University of Texas at Austin Library, 1944).

References:
"Frontier Life," *United States Magazine and Democratic Review*, 22 (May 1848): 424–432;
Edwin Gaston Jr., "Charles W. Webber, *Old Hicks, the Guide* (1848)," in his *The Early Novel of the Southwest* (Albuquerque: University of New Mexico Press, 1961), pp. 221–222;

Mabel Major and others, *Southwest Heritage: A Literary History, with Bibliography,* revised edition (Albuquerque: University of New Mexico Press, 1948), p. 81;

Sanford E. Marovitz, "Poe's Reception of Charles Wilkins Webber's Gothic Western 'Jack Long; or Shot in the Eye,'" *Poe Studies,* 4 (June 1971): 11–13;

Edgar Allan Poe, "Tale Writing–Nathaniel Hawthorne," *Godey's Lady's Book,* 35 (November 1847): 252–253; republished in *The Complete Works of Edgar Allan Poe,* 17 volumes, edited by James A. Harrison (New York: Crowell, 1902), XIII: 141–154;

David S. Reynolds, *Beneath the American Renaissance: The Subversive Imagination in the Age of Emerson and Melville* (New York: Knopf, 1988);

John William Rogers, *Finding Literature on the Texas Plains, with a Representative Bibliography of Books on the Southwest by J. Frank Dobie* (Dallas: Southwest Press, 1931), p. 39;

William J. Scheick, *The Half-Blood: A Cultural Symbol in 19th Century American Fiction* (Lexington: University of Kentucky Press, 1979);

Henry Nash Smith, "The Innocence and Wildness of Nature: Charles Wilkins Webber and Others," in his *Virgin Land: The American West as Symbol and Myth* (Cambridge, Mass.: Harvard University Press, 1950), pp. 77–83.

Edward Noyes Westcott

(27 September 1846 – 31 March 1898)

Jeffrey B. Kurtz
Pennsylvania State University

BOOKS: *David Harum: A Story of American Life* (New York: Appleton, 1898; augmented edition, New York: Dover, 1960); excerpted in *The Christmas Story From David Harum,* edited by William H. Crane (New York: Appleton, 1900);
The Teller: A Story (New York: Appleton, 1901).

A banker for most of his life, Edward Noyes Westcott blended characteristics of the realism and local-color movements that emerged after the 1850s in his novel *David Harum: A Story of American Life* (1898). A significant contribution to popular fiction at the turn of the century, Westcott's book may be associated with the regional writing that emerged after the Civil War, works that exploited local customs and dialects in fiction or verse.

Born in Syracuse, New York, the third child of Amos and Clara Babcock Westcott, Westcott spent most of his life in his native city. Drawn early to banking, he left school at sixteen to assume a position as a junior clerk in the Mechanics' Bank of Syracuse. He worked there until 1866, when he went to New York City to take a position in the office of the Mutual Life Insurance Company. Two years later he returned to Syracuse and began work as a teller in the First National Bank. He later became a cashier in the banking firm of Wilkinson and Company. His ambition was complemented by his gifts for singing and composing music. He also found time to write several pamphlets for the Reform Club of New York, of which he was a member. He married Janet Dows in 1874, and they had three children, two sons and a daughter.

In 1880 Westcott organized the banking and brokerage firm of Westcott and Abbott, which proved a successful financial venture until the failure of an allied firm brought hardship on the business. He later served as the secretary of the Syracuse Water Commission, but he resigned from that position in 1895 because of steadily failing health. He died from tuberculosis at age fifty-one, before the publication of his only novel.

David Harum is marked by its rustic setting and use of humor, mainly in the proverbial wisdom and social commentary of the title character. Westcott's fictional ren-

Edward Noyes Westcott, 1889

dering of a rural New York town exhibits the tone and characteristics of much "b'gosh" fiction. David Harum, while certainly a trickster, is also a proverbial "crackerbox philosopher." His aphorisms, including statements such as "A reasonable amount of fleas is good for a dog–they keep him f'm broodin' on bein' a dog," express a commonsense wisdom that resonated with readers.

As a banker Westcott surely encountered many different classes of people, and their sundry character traits are colorfully presented in *David Harum.* The novel is a story of success and ingenuity, of the triumph of and necessity for common wisdom and country lore amid industrialization and urban alienation. Set in Homeville, New York, it is the story of an uneducated country banker, David Harum, and his relationship with his business associate, John Lenox, who came to Homeville from New York City after the death of his father to work as a teller in Harum's bank. The novel highlights Harum's relationships with particular clients, including crooked real-estate dealers whom he physically removes from his office and an elderly widow whom Harum absolves of responsibility for her mortgage because her late husband had taken the young Harum to the circus. This man, says Harum, was the first person who "ever treated me human up to that time. He give me the only enjoy'ble time 't I'd ever had . . . . an' he gin me the fust notion 't I'd ever had that mebbe I wa'n't only the scum o' the earth, as I'd ben teached to believe."

The day-to-day business of the bank is sparsely treated as David Harum and his stories entertain and educate Westcott's readers. Harum is a cantankerous and endearing character with a gift for colloquial speech, which infuses his stories about his past with humor and common appeal. While Harum's vernacular sometimes offends Lenox's upper-class pretensions and sensibilities, the country banker and clever horse trader never alienates his new business partner and friend. Lacking the formal education of a contemporary industrial baron, Harum has made his own sort of empire in Homeville, one grounded in the principles of integrity, fairness, generosity, and simplicity.

Lenox is a sophisticated but sincere cosmopolitan, a world traveler gifted with a beautiful, refined singing voice. In his mid twenties when his father died, he had dropped out of college after two years, showed no inclination for medicine or scholarship, and had grown impatient with his clerkship in a law firm. After his father's death he determined that working in a country bank removed from hectic city life might provide him a new beginning.

Harum and Lenox grow close to one another, and by the end of the novel the older man evinces a fatherly affection for his younger partner. At one point late in the story Lenox confesses to Harum, "Your house has grown to be more a real home than any I have ever known, and you and your sister are like my own people."

Also significant to the story is Lenox's relationship with Mary Blake, a young woman he met and for whom he developed an intense affection during a return voyage from Europe. Separated after their arrival in the United States, they are reunited six years later when Lenox takes an ocean voyage to help relieve his influenza. They eventually marry and settle in Homeville, name their first child after Harum, and are made heirs to his fortune.

Contrasting the manners and customs of urban and rural life, the novel shows Westcott's keen eye for the details of both cultures. The result is an interesting portrayal of how people from different regions and social classes interacted with each other in the late nineteenth century and managed from time to time to discover common ground. Harum is an Everyman: he is most comfortable when discussing horse trading and Homeville's shifting weather patterns; yet he exhibits an uncanny financial intelligence, and his sincerity and integrity resonate deeply. His willingness to help people who are down on their luck, insecure with their finances, or just uncertain of their station in life makes him extremely popular with most of Homeville's residents. His intelligence keeps him beyond the reach of those who might take advantage of such a genuinely good-natured person. Westcott's novel may be seen as a subtle argument for the place of the country philanthropist in late-nineteenth-century American culture.

David Harum achieved considerable popular success. While Westcott had found it difficult to secure a contract with a publisher for the book (Jacob Blanck reports, for example, that one publisher rejected the book on the grounds that it was "vulgar and smelled of the stables"), the novel eventually went through six printings in twelve weeks and sold more than four hundred thousand copies in the two years following its publication. The story also was adapted and popularized for stage and film.

References:

Richard G. Case, "The Westcott and David Harum," *Courier,* 10 (Winter 1973): 3–14;

William H. Crane, preface to *The Christmas Story From David Harum,* edited by Crane (New York: Appleton, 1900), pp. v–ix;

Henry Glassie, "The Use of Folklore in *David Harum,*" *New York Folklore Quarterly,* 23 (September 1967): 163–185;

Forbes Heermans, introduction to *David Harum: A Story of American Life* (New York: Appleton, 1898), pp. v–viii;

Helen Sargent Hitchcock, "David Harum Philosophizes Again," *New York Times Magazine,* 17 July 1938, pp. 10, 16;

Carrie Belle Parks, introduction to *David Harum: A Story of American Life* (New York: Appleton, 1931), pp. vii–xix;

Syracuse Libraries, special David Harum issue, 11 (February 1918);

Arthur T. Vance, *The Real David Harum* (New York: Baker & Taylor, 1900).

Papers:

The major collections of Edward Noyes Westcott's papers are at Syracuse University Library, Columbia University Library, and the Syracuse Public Library.

Frances Miriam Whitcher

(1 November 1812 – 4 January 1852)

Robyn M. Preston
University of Southern Mississippi

See also the Whitcher entry in *DLB 11: American Humorists, 1800–1950.*

BOOKS: *The Widow Bedott Papers* (New York: Houghton, Osgood, 1855; London: Warne, 1883);
Widow Spriggins, Mary Elmer, and Other Sketches, edited by Mrs. M. L. Ward Whitcher (New York: Carleton, 1867).

Her work "called forth a general burst of praise from one end of the Union to the other," said Louis A. Godey of Frances Miriam Whitcher, a pioneer in the creation of a female humorist tradition in American literature. In her brilliant social satires, collected in book form after her death as *The Widow Bedott Papers* (1855) and *Widow Spriggins, Mary Elmer, and Other Sketches* (1867), Whitcher tried to show that women's search for status was leading them deeper into degradation by forcing them to compete with one another on the grounds of wealth and other superficialities. Through her sketches Whitcher sought to open women's eyes to the folly of their behavior. For modern readers the sketches give insight into the domestic lives of women in the first half of the nineteenth century and shed new light on the history of the feminist movement in America.

Frances Miriam Berry was born in Whitesboro, New York, on 1 November 1812, the thirteenth of fifteen children of Lewis Berry, the owner of an inn, and Elizabeth Wells Berry. A precocious child, she could recite poetry at age two, before she could read, and she composed poetry by dictation before she learned to write. She was also a talented caricaturist. Even these childhood works often had a satirical bite; in the introduction to *Widow Spriggins, Mary Elmer, and Other Sketches* her friend Alice B. Neal quotes her as saying that she despaired over her "undesirable gift of a remarkably strong sense of the ridiculous." Berry attended the village school and the local academy and took French lessons in Utica.

Frances Miriam Whitcher (courtesy of the Dunham Public Library, Whitesboro, New York)

During the 1820s and 1830s Whitesboro, along with many other American communities, was the scene of various social and moral reform movements that grew out of the religious revival known as the Second Great Awakening. While Berry did not participate in these movements, she observed them with a keen eye. In 1838 Berry—who was, according to her sister Kate, "shy and sensitive to a painful degree"—made one of her few ventures into the public arena when she joined the Moenian Circle, a literary group dedicated to the Greek god of satire, Momus, and formed in response to the reform activity going on in Whitesboro. Her participation in the Moenian Society marks the beginning of her literary career: it was for this group that she composed the eleven-chapter spoof, "The Widow Spriggins," which she read at society meetings a chapter at a time. Berry made her first appearance in print in 1839, when the weekly *Rome Gazette* published the work under the pen name "Frank."

"The Widow Spriggins" is a burlesque of Regina Maria Roche's *The Children of the Abbey* (1796). Permilly Ruggles (who later becomes the Widow Spriggings) is an uneducated country woman who models her every move on Roche's aristocratic heroine, Amanda. The plot centers on Permilly's imagined betrothal to Philander, the alias of a man named Johnson, who amuses himself by pretending to court her. The humor of the sketches involves Permilly's unsuccessful attempts at gentility and her determination to appear educated. The collision of aristocratic values with country bumpkin manners results in a narrative filled with malapropisms, misspellings, and incongruities. The other women admire Permilly for what they think is her sophisticated speech; one exclaims, "I never heerd nobody use eleganter language in my life!" The ridicule of women who aspire to be genteel is a central theme of Whitcher's later work.

The first appearance of Whitcher's best-known character came on 1 August 1846, when Joseph C. Neal published "The Widow Bedott's Table Talk" in his *Saturday Gazette*. This first story began a series that was immensely popular: "The 'Table Talk' makes a sensation," said Neal. Continuing to use the pseudonym "Frank," Berry contributed eight more Widow Bedott sketches to the *Saturday Gazette* from the fall of 1846 through the spring of 1847; Neal called them the best works of their kind that his magazine had ever printed. Set in fictional Wiggletown, the sketches focus on the "no holds barred" determination of the widow Priscilla Bedott, a loud, self-indulgent, pretentious gossip, to find a new husband, but the plots are less important than Berry's biting satire of female hypocrisy, gossip, and other vulgarities. "The Widow Bedott's Table Talk" is a rambling, pointless monologue in dialect in which Bedott talks about her dead husband, Deacon Hezekiah Bedott. In the sketches that follow, the chief targets of the author's wit are sentimentality and the plight of women who have no meaningful role beyond the domestic sphere. Berry debunks the sentimental image of widowhood as pathetic, lonely, and deserving of pity and charity by creating the hardy, boisterous Widow Bedott.

In 1846 Berry left the Presbyterian faith in which she had been raised and became a member of St. John's Episcopal Church; she was soon engaged to the pastor, Benjamin William Whitcher, and they were married on 6 January 1847. In March she published what she thought would be the last sketch in the Widow Bedott series. In this piece a third-person narrator takes over to relate the activities of the Widow Bedott, who is thoroughly displeased with everyone in Wiggletown and a complete failure in her attempts to snare a husband.

In April William Whitcher was called to the ministry of Trinity Episcopal Church in Elmira, New York. Meanwhile, the Widow Bedott sketches had attracted the attention of Louis Godey, and in early 1847 *Godey's Lady's Book* began publishing a new series of Whitcher's sketches. Aunt Maguire of fictional Scrabble Hill, the central figure of these sketches, is the younger sister of the Widow Bedott. Melissa Poole Maguire, however, is a dramatically different character from her sister. Though she, too, speaks in dialect, Aunt Maguire is not the butt of Whitcher's jokes, as her sister is; rather, she is a voice of reason and common sense and a critic of arrogance and hypocrisy. In the Aunt Maguire sketches Whitcher makes the transition from burlesque to social satire.

By July 1847 Whitcher had moved to Elmira, and two of her Aunt Maguire sketches had appeared in *Godey's Lady's Book*. Her new surroundings had a significant impact on Whitcher's satire. The people of Elmira were, she claimed in a 27 June 1847 letter to her sister Kate, "very clever, well meaning people, but . . . rather low in the intellectual scale." She complained about the women's preoccupation with "cooking, fixing, scandal & quilting," the last of which they carried to an extent "beyond belief." Her observations of her neighbors, along with her experiences as a minister's wife, provided the material for her best work.

The third Aunt Maguire sketch, "Aunt Maguire's Account of Parson Scrantum's Donation Party," appeared in the March 1848 issue of *Godey's Lady's Book*. Donation parties were given for ministers and their families by members of the congregation to supplement the ministers' small salaries; while the motives were benevolent, the parties placed the families in the demeaning position of being recipients of charity. Whitcher dreaded her own first donation party; in a letter to Kate dated 8 November 1847 she wrote: "I expect it will be a trying time to me. . . . But the congregation would be offended if we should decline." While her party was a success, the fictional donation party of the Reverend Mr. Scrantum and Mrs. Scrantum is humiliating: the guests bring mere trinkets as gifts, engage in a food fight, and criticize the Scrantums as poor hosts. Aunt Maguire indicts both the guests and an institution that requires clergymen and their wives to endure such treatment. Written and sent to *Godey's Lady's Book* before the Whitchers' donation party took place, the sketch appeared five months after the party, and the residents of Elmira were highly displeased. Though Whitcher published the sketch anonymously, her neighbors were

Whitcher's husband, the Reverend William Benjamin Whitcher

her authorship and led to the Whitchers' removal from Elmira. Based on her observations of the sewing group begun by her husband's female parishioners, "Aunt Maguire's Account of the Contemplated Sewing Society at Scrabble Hill" appeared in the November 1848 issue of *Godey's Lady's Book.* That piece and a subsequent sketch about the first meeting of the group enraged many of the women in the town. "Miss" (actually Mrs.) Samson Savage, the chief target of Whitcher's satire, displays all the characteristics so detested by the author: arrogance, hypocrisy, and lack of sensitivity to the feelings of others. When Mrs. Savage does not get her way with the Reverend Tuttle, a thinly disguised William Whitcher, she tells her fellow sewing society members: "I despise Tuttle, and I'll tell him tew his face when I git a chance. Ye don't ketch me a slanderin' folks behind ther backs and then soft-soapin' 'em to their faces, as some folks dew." The sewing society was organized to raise funds for charity, but the women become too wrapped up in gossip and other trivialities to accomplish anything.

Though the Sewing Society sketches were published anonymously, Whitcher's characters were too thinly veiled for her fellow Elmirans not to recognize themselves in the stories. On 25 May 1848 the *Elmira Gazette* reprinted "Aunt Maguire's Account of Parson Scrantum's Donation Party," and on 28 December 1848 it reprinted one of the sewing society sketches. In January and February 1849 the paper reprinted three of Whitcher's new Widow Bedott sketches and claimed that "the author of these articles resides among us." The controversy that soon raged was good business for *Godey's Lady's Book:* sales of the magazine rose to forty thousand copies monthly as readers tried to identify the originals of the characters in the sketches. The Whitchers, however, paid a price for Miriam's humor as William's parishioners accused him of ridiculing them in his sermons. Faced with the threat of a lawsuit from an angry church member who thought that his wife was the model for Mrs. Samson Savage, William Whitcher began looking for employment elsewhere. In March 1849 Miriam Whitcher's father became ill, and she moved back into her parents' home to attend to him. She never returned to Elmira, remaining in Whitesboro after her father died. Meanwhile, her husband, who was having difficulty finding a permanent parish, took temporary positions in Saratoga Springs and Oswego. As a result the couple was separated for long periods.

beginning to see reflections of themselves in the denizens of Scrabble Hill, and rumors that Whitcher was the author were spreading.

While writing the Aunt Maguire sketches for *Godey's Lady's Book,* Whitcher also revived the Widow Bedott for the *Saturday Gazette.* Neal had died in July 1847, and his wife, Alice, had taken over the magazine. Whitcher's move from Whitesboro to Elmira was reflected in the new series in the Widow Bedott's move from Wiggletown to Scrabble Hill, the home of her sister. The first sketch, "The Widow Bedott Resolves to Leave Wiggletown," appeared in the *Saturday Gazette* on 4 December 1847. The Scrabble Hill Widow Bedott sketches center on the widow's pursuit of and marriage to the Reverend Mr. Sniffles; they end with the widow boasting of her conquest and vowing to return to Wiggletown to show him off. The Widow Bedott remains as Whitcher first created her: she is loud, crude, and utterly a fool.

The two Aunt Maguire sketches that followed "Aunt Maguire's Account of Parson Scrantum's Donation Party" substantiated the community's suspicions of

A third and final series of four Widow Bedott sketches began in the *Saturday Gazette* on 16 June 1849 with "The Rev. Mrs. Sniffles at Home"; it ended with "The Rev. Mrs. Sniffles Abroad." The former Widow Bedott, in all her boisterous glory, exits the series

Jan 12. 1849

Elmira ~~Dec 12th~~ 1849

Happy new Year to you all dear father & mother & sisters & brothers. We thought you would feel rather anxious to hear from us after my alarming letter. So after I got my chores done up & fixed myself for calls (if I should have any.) I sat down to drop you a line to let you know that we got thro' the Sunday with whole skins. There was no demonstration on the part of the belliggerents. The church was crowded all day. The Arnots were not there the old woman never comes, but the girls do occasionally they are a curse to the church. it will never prosper here till they leave it. The commotion caused by the article is as great as ever & every body insists upon applying Mrs Samson Savage to Mrs Arnot. She goes by the name every-where & her admirers or echoes are called the "Stillman family". The young men of whom I spoke in a letter some time ago as being the beau [Capt. Hustady] of Mrs T (the woman who thought herself preached at) is called universally "Cappen Smalley" & they say it cuts him to death. A gentleman, one of our friends. the Mr Chamberlain who went east with me once. says that he attended a very large party last week. where Mrs Arnot & the echoes were present. & for the first time, they behaved with propriety and did not "nopolise" all the conversation. But they are perfectly outrageous against me & William too. As yet we cannot tell what will be the result. I confess

First page of a 1 January 1849 letter from Whitcher to her family describing the reaction of the citizens of Elmira to her sketch "Aunt Maguire's Account of the Contemplated Sewing Society at Scrabble Hill" (courtesy of New-York Historical Society, New York City)

Illustration by Whitcher for her sketch "The Rev. Mrs. Sniffles at Home" in the Saturday Gazette, *16 June 1849*

throwing all of her energy into climbing the social ladder.

Back home in Whitesboro, Whitcher, feeling that she had some unfinished business, wrote one more sketch. In "Aunt Maguire's Visit to Slabtown," which was published in the December 1849 issue of *Godey's Lady's Book,* she puts the sewing society scandal into perspective and satirizes the hypocrisy and vindictiveness of her former Elmira neighbors. The fictional Slabtown is just as obsessed with gentility as Scrabble Hill. During Aunt Maguire's visit there, the latest issue of *Godey's Lady's Book* arrives with a story about a town's upheaval over a sewing society. The residents of Slabtown are convinced that their town is the focus of the sketch and that their minister's wife is the author until Aunt Maguire confesses that she is the cause of the commotion: her conversations with Louis Godey about the Scrabble Hill sewing society had inspired him to write and publish the piece.

Whitcher had had a stillborn child in the spring of 1848; on 6 November 1849 she gave birth to a daughter whom she named Alice, after her friend Alice Neal. Her three sketches titled "Letters from Timberville" were published in *Godey's Lady's Book* in 1849 and 1850. Unlike her previous sketches, "Letters from Timberville" uses a "proper" narrator to set up the action of the story before turning it over to a colloquial narrative voice.

Begun in the spring of 1851, "Mary Elmer" was Whitcher's last piece of fiction, written so that her daughter would have something "useful" to read. Oddly, this work resembles the sentimental fiction that Whitcher had spent her career satirizing. The title character displays many of the characteristics of such popular sentimental heroines as Ellen Montgomery in Susan Warner's *The Wide-Wide World* (1850) and Little Eva in Harriet Beecher Stowe's *Uncle Tom's Cabin* (1852). Like Ellen Montgomery, the angelic Mary Elmer is sent to work as a servant and is mistreated by her employer, a harsh, cruel woman. Though she sent a few chapters of "Mary Elmer" to Godey, Whitcher died before finishing the work. William Whitcher's second wife completed the story and published it in 1867 in the collection *Widow Spriggins, Mary Elmer, and Other Sketches.*

Whitcher's health began to deteriorate in late 1850, and she died of tuberculosis on 4 January 1852. In 1855 Neal published Whitcher's collected Widow Bedott sketches as *The Widow Bedott Papers;* the book was highly successful, selling more than one hundred thousand copies in nine years and going through several editions. In 1879 the humorist David R. Locke ("Petroleum V. Nasby") adapted the Widow Bedott sketches as a play, *Widow Bedott; or, A Hunt for a Husband,* with the popular comedian Neil Burgess in the role of the widow. *Widow Spriggins, Mary Elmer, and Other Sketches* was also successful, though not to the extent of *The Widow Bedott Papers.*

By the turn of the century the demand for dialect humor had disappeared, and Whitcher sank into obscurity. Frequently anthologized female humorists such as Marietta Holley are, however, indebted to Whitcher's innovative style. In a letter to Joseph Neal, Whitcher had written: "I fear criticism; I fear 'the world's dread laugh.' I fear a repulse, a failure." Though she received criticism from her neighbors, Whitcher stood up to her fear and exposed the foolishness of women's behavior. Critics often categorize her as antifeminist, but her satire was really aimed not at women but at a society that kept them from attaining meaningful roles and condemned them to trivialities.

Biographies:

Kate Berry, "Passages in the Life of the Author of Aunt Maguire's Letters, Bedott Papers, Etc.," *Godey's Lady's Book,* 47 (July 1853): 49–55; (August 1853): 109–115;

Linda A. Morris, *Women's Humor in the Age of Gentility: The Life and Works of Frances Miriam Whitcher* (Syracuse, N.Y.: Syracuse University Press, 1992).

References:

Linda A. Morris, "Frances Miriam Whitcher: Social Satire in the Age of Gentility," in her *Last Laughs: Perspectives on Women and Comedy* (New York: Gordon & Breach, 1988), pp. 99–116;

Morris, ed., *Women Vernacular Humorists in Nineteenth-Century America: Ann Stephens, Frances Whitcher, and Marietta Holley* (New York: Garland, 1988);

Thomas F. O'Donnell, "The Return of the Widow Bedott: Mrs. F. M. Whitcher of Whitesboro and Elmira," *New York History,* 55 (1974): 5–34;

Nancy Walker, *A Very Serious Thing: Women's Humor and American Culture* (Minneapolis: Minnesota University Press, 1988).

Papers:

Frances Miriam Whitcher's papers are held at the New-York Historical Society, New York City.

Theodore Winthrop
(22 September 1828 – 10 June 1861)

Jonathan Wells
University of Michigan

BOOKS: *A Companion to the Heart of the Andes* (New York: Appleton, 1859);

Cecil Dreeme (Boston: Ticknor & Fields, 1861; Edinburgh: Paterson, 1883);

John Brent (Boston: Ticknor & Fields, 1862; Edinburgh: Paterson, 1883);

Edwin Brothertoft (Boston: Ticknor & Fields, 1862; Edinburgh: Paterson, 1883);

The Canoe and the Saddle: Adventures Among the Northwestern Rivers and Forests; and Isthmania (Boston: Ticknor & Fields, 1862; London: Low, 1863);

Life in the Open Air and Other Papers (Boston: Ticknor & Fields, 1863); republished in part as *Love and Skates* (New York & London: Putnam, 1902);

The Life and Poems of Theodore Winthrop, edited by Laura Winthrop Johnson (New York: Holt, 1884);

Mr. Waddy's Return, edited by Burton E. Stevenson (New York: Holt, 1904).

Theodore Winthrop wrote five books, traveled throughout the world, and served in the Civil War before his death in 1861 at the age of thirty-two. The first Union officer killed in the war, Winthrop died just as his literary career was being launched. All five of his full-length books were published posthumously between 1861 and 1863, and all went through multiple editions. Beginning with the publication of *Cecil Dreeme* in 1861, Ticknor and Fields sold thousands of Winthrop's novels to a wartime northern reading public that eagerly consumed Winthrop's tales, appreciating their romantic excitement and rousing adventure. In part the popularity of his books was a consequence of the mythology that sprouted almost immediately around the felled Union officer, a mythology willingly accepted by Northerners who held him up as an admirable combination of wealth, family, education, and literary talent. Yet, just as rapidly as Winthrop's star rose at the beginning of the war, his literary reputation had faded by its end.

"Theodore Winthrop's life," wrote his friend George William Curtis, "like a fire long smouldering,

(American Antiquarian Society)

suddenly blazed up into a clear, bright flame, and vanished." Winthrop's popularity as a writer was the product of a moment in American history when he symbolized the vitality and promise of the American ideal.

Winthrop's family background amplified his importance as a symbol of New England pride and heritage. His father, Francis Bayard Winthrop, was a direct descendant of Massachusetts governor John Winthrop; his mother, Elizabeth Dwight Woolsey Winthrop, was related to Jonathan Edwards and Timothy Dwight. Thus, from the time of his birth on 22 September 1828, Winthrop was surrounded by examples of erudition and accomplishment that were difficult to follow. He was provided with the finest training and education that New England could offer. For most of his life Winthrop remained itinerant, unambitious, and ambivalent on a career. Sent to study at Yale University in 1843 at the age of fifteen, Winthrop was soon expelled for misconduct and, given his family's association with the school, placed his relatives in an embarrassing position. After apologizing, he was allowed to return to Yale the following year, and a renewed devotion to his studies earned him the praise of instructors who recognized Winthrop as one of the brightest young men at the school. Named poet and philosopher for the class of 1848, Winthrop believed that on graduation his days of mischief and aimlessness had ended and that the successful prosecution of his studies augured well for the future.

After graduation, however, Winthrop rapidly descended into despondency, sloth, and self-pity. He seemed uninterested in a clerical or legal career, the two most obvious choices for a young man of his family background and education, and he thought it wise to avoid further schooling until he had made up his mind. Still, his lack of direction nagged at him. "I am disposed," he wrote in his journal in July 1848, "to think that the quality I need most is *decision* immediate and sure; procrastination is fatal to strength of character." Unable to settle on a course of action for further study and suffering from ill health, Winthrop decided in 1849 to undertake the grand tour of Europe that so many antebellum intellectuals found rewarding. As he set sail for London in July 1849 on a trip that was supposed to last only a few months, Winthrop did not know that he would spend most of the next five years away from home.

Between 1849 and 1851 the Yale graduate traveled throughout Europe, visiting England, France, Germany, Holland, Switzerland, Greece, and Italy. Accounts of his experiences in Europe reveal that he spent most of his time searching for fun and adventure. When Winthrop finally returned to America in 1851, he remained long enough only to secure an appointment in Panama with the Pacific Mail Steamship Company. In his letters from Panama to his mother in New England, modern observers may obtain a glimpse of Winthrop's interest in nature and evidence of his ability to describe the environment in rich detail that characterized his novels and adventure tales. Winthrop returned to his native soil in 1853, stopping first in San Francisco and then traveling north to Portland and Vancouver for a tour of the Northwest. These adventures provided the experience necessary for Winthrop's first attempt at a book-length manuscript, *The Canoe and the Saddle* (1862). Compared in the post–Civil War period with Henry David Thoreau's *Walden* (1854), *The Canoe*

and the Saddle exhibits Winthrop's main strength as a writer: his ability to describe nature and scenery vividly. The tale was probably written on his trek back to New York from the West across the plains in 1853, when his recollections of the Northwest were still fresh. *The Canoe and the Saddle* offers elaborate descriptions of the Columbia River, Puget Sound, and the Cascades as well as Native Americans he happened across in his travels. Recounting a trip through the lush fir trees of the Cascade Mountains, Winthrop remarked: "Unlike the pillars of human architecture, chipped and chiselled in bustling, dusty quarries, and hoisted to their site by sweat of brow and creak of pulley, these rose to fairest proportion by the life that was in them, and blossomed into foliated capitals three hundred feet overhead." This record of stirring adventures set against a backdrop of magnificent natural beauty made *The Canoe and the Saddle* a popular success, one that was republished as late as 1957.

Winthrop finally returned home to stay in March 1854, ending a period of travel and adventure that provided ample material for his novels. Settling in New York, Winthrop discovered a new resolve to devote significant time and energy to writing and a legal career. Admitted to the bar in 1855, he began in earnest to establish a healthy law practice and to devote the rest of his attention to his writing. He wrote many poems on a wide range of subjects. Reflecting his interest in ancient history and mythology, most of these poems went unpublished until his sister collected them in *The Life and Poems of Theodore Winthrop* (1884). Although committed to writing and practicing law, Winthrop could not resist an adventure and accompanied his artist friend Frederick Church on a trip through the Adirondacks and the Maine woods in 1856, an adventure that Winthrop wrote about in *Life in the Open Air and Other Papers* (1863). Just as *The Canoe and the Saddle* describes the natural beauty of the Northwest, *Life in the Open Air* offers readers a narrative of the striking natural wonders that Winthrop witnessed as he canoed on Maine waterways, particularly the flora around Mount Katahdin. Trees were one of Winthrop's favorite subjects, and he described the "white birch, paper-birch, canoe-birch [that] grow large in moist spots near the stream where it is needed. Seen by the flicker of a camp-fire at night, they surround the intrusive traveller like ghosts of giant sentinels." The stories of camping, fishing, and hiking reveal Winthrop's love and reverence for nature, as well as his delight and sense of triumph in thwarting the unexpected dangers presented by life in the outdoors.

Life in the Open Air marked the beginning of a period of considerable literary activity for Winthrop. He developed a close personal and professional friendship with Curtis, whom he met in New York in 1852 and who recognized Winthrop's talents. Little is known about their first meeting, but the two young writers frequently met for long discussions about life and literature. Curtis's private encouragement to take his writing more seriously led Winthrop to his most productive years. From 1856 to 1861, Winthrop produced *Cecil Dreeme*, *John Brent* (1862) and *Edwin Brothertoft* (1862).

The only work Winthrop published before his death, however, was *A Companion to the Heart of the Andes* (1859), an extended essay that accompanied the exhibition of a painting by Frederick Church. Winthrop published little until he mustered the courage to send "Love and Skates," a story about skating on the Hudson River, to *The Atlantic Monthly* early in 1861, winning praise and acceptance from editor James Russell Lowell.

In the 1850s Winthrop became increasingly interested in the mounting hostility between the North and South. A critic of slavery, he campaigned briefly for Free Soil presidential candidate John C. Frémont in 1856, and by 1861 he staunchly opposed secession and determined not only to help preserve the Union but also to contribute what he could to end slavery. In April 1861 Winthrop joined the New York Seventh Regiment and marched with the troops to Washington, D.C. While in the capital city he saw little action, but his intelligence and intense desire to serve the Union cause made him an important aid to Gen. Benjamin Butler. When the Seventh Regiment returned to New York, Winthrop stayed behind to serve under Butler as military secretary with the rank of major at Fort Monroe in Virginia. In early June, Winthrop found himself in the middle of the action at the Battle of Big Bethel. There he was shot through the heart and killed on 10 June 1861. Newspaper reports throughout the North bemoaned the premature death of the Union major, while Southern papers honored Winthrop for his valor in battle.

The importance of Winthrop's death was magnified not only by the fact that he was the first Union officer to fall but also because, at almost that same time, his essay on the Seventh Regiment was published in the June issue of *The Atlantic Monthly*. "Our March to Washington" lent poignancy to the Union cause as Winthrop recounted in dramatic fashion the hardships faced by men marching to war, hardships that were at least partly ameliorated by the camaraderie and sense of purpose felt by the troops. The next issue of *The Atlantic Monthly* included another essay by Winthrop, "Washington as a Camp." Northerners saw a promising young man, a man worthy of his rich New England heritage, struck down by the Confederacy. In death Winthrop instantly became famous.

To seize on Winthrop's celebrity the Boston publishing house of Ticknor and Fields agreed to publish Winthrop's manuscripts, beginning with *Cecil Dreeme* in

October 1861. The novel opens with a short biography by Curtis that added to Winthrop's heroic reputation. The hero of *Cecil Dreeme*, Robert Byng, has much in common with Winthrop himself. Both return from lengthy trips abroad to languish in indecision about a future course of action. The novel is set among the haunting Gothic rooms of Chrysalis College in New York, where Byng travels after many years in Europe. Byng, a scientist by trade and by inclination, soon learns that in his lengthy absence from New York mysterious events, particularly the "suicide" of a childhood friend named Clara Denman, have disrupted life in the city. At the center of the troubles is a heartless, greedy, but bewitching character named Densdeth who seduces and controls men and women through his financial power and charm. It was Densdeth, Byng believes, who caused Clara's suicide by trying to force her hand in marriage. Yet, Byng is mysteriously drawn to Densdeth, and he seeks out the advice of Mr. Churm, a father figure and mentor, and Cecil Dreeme, a fellow boarder at Chrysalis College with whom Byng becomes close friends. As the mystery unfolds it becomes clear that to escape marriage to Densdeth, Clara disguised herself as a man named Cecil Dreeme. Near the end of the novel Densdeth is murdered by one of the men whom he had seduced into his plot to wed Clara. Byng is shocked to learn that his best friend and confidant is a woman, but he forgives Clara and understands her deceit. The gloomy setting and the description of Densdeth's cruelty, Winthrop's biographer Elbridge Colby points out, reminded not a few readers of Edgar Allan Poe. "In wild beasts," Winthrop wrote in *Cecil Dreeme*, "the cry reveals the character—so it does in man,—a cross between a beast and a soul. If beast is keeping soul under, he lets the world know it in every word his man speaks." *Cecil Dreeme* represented a significant advance in literary sophistication over *The Canoe and the Saddle* and *Life in the Open Air*, rich as they were as narrative tales. *Cecil Dreeme*, Colby suggests, "is the writing of a master of prose," and the novel solidified Winthrop's posthumous reputation as an author of merit.

Quick to follow after *Cecil Dreeme* were *John Brent*, published in January 1862, and *Edwin Brothertoft*, published just seven months later in July. The leading character of *John Brent*, like the hero of *Cecil Dreeme*, has much in common with Winthrop. The story relates John Brent's venture across the plains on a return trip to the East, no doubt similar to the one Winthrop experienced in 1853. Along the way Brent encounters Mormons, Indians, and settlers, but the story centers around Brent's attempts to rescue Ellen Clitheroe, the kidnapped daughter of a once-wealthy English aristocrat. Brent, who has fallen in love with Ellen, frees her from her captives but loses track of her after the chase is over. He searches for his lost love, and the story ends with Brent finally catching up with her in London. In contrast to the plot of *Cecil Dreeme,* which reveals its mysteries slowly through foreshadowing and clues, the story of *John Brent* is exciting, fast-paced, and driven by action.

Edwin Brothertoft combines the staged battle between good and evil that characterizes *Cecil Dreeme* with the high adventure that marks *John Brent,* but *Edwin Brothertoft* was a departure for Winthrop in that it was set in the romantic turmoil surrounding the American Revolution. It received mixed reviews from critics, who concluded that the novel did not demonstrate any advancement over Winthrop's previous works.

The title character, who hails from an aristocratic family, returns from a lengthy trip in Europe only to languish in indecision about his future. A devoted patriot, Brothertoft is dismayed when his wife favors the Tories and flees his familial responsibilities to join the American army. He returns to his home and family only when he hears of his daughter's impending marriage to a British officer. Foiling the marriage plans, he then rescues his estranged wife from a fire. Near death from burns she has suffered, she laments her transgressions, and husband and wife are joined again briefly before she dies in his arms.

Although a few scholars in the twentieth century have tried to reestablish Winthrop's reputation in American literary history, their efforts have gone largely unheeded. Already by the end of the war Winthrop was beginning to drift out of the collective American memory. His early reputation, formed at the zenith of northern optimism and sense of righteousness at the start of the sectional conflict, was buried under the extended tragedy of the war. His life and literary career illuminate not only the struggles of an individual author to overcome self-doubt and aimlessness but also the trials of a nation searching for meaning in the midst of civil war.

References:

Elbridge Colby, "George William Curtis and Theodore Winthrop," *Nation,* 102 (29 June 1916): 706–707;

Colby, *Theodore Winthrop* (New York: Twayne, 1965);

George William Curtis, "Theodore Winthrop," *Atlantic,* 8 (August 1861), 242–251; republished as "Biographical Sketch of the Author," in *Cecil Dreeme* (Boston: Ticknor & Fields, 1861), pp. 5–19;

Ellsworth Eliot Jr., *Theodore Winthrop* (New Haven: Yale University Press, 1938);

Willard E. Martin Jr., "The Life and Works of Theodore Winthrop," dissertation, Duke University, 1944;

H. Dean Probst, "Theodore Winthrop: His Place in American Literary and Intellectual History," dissertation, George C. Peabody College for Teachers, 1964;

Eugene T. Woolf, *Theodore Winthrop: Portrait of an American Author* (Washington, D.C.: University Press of America, 1981).

Papers:

The Theodore Winthrop papers at the New York Public Library comprise a wide range of materials, including Winthrop's college essays of the 1840s, journals and letters he wrote on his many trips abroad, and the manuscripts for nearly all of his book-length works.

Lillie Buffum Chace Wyman

(10 December 1847 – 10 January 1929)

Loretta Woodard
Marygrove College

BOOKS: *Poverty Grass* (Boston & New York: Houghton, Mifflin, 1886);

American Chivalry (Boston: Clarke, 1913);

Interludes and Other Verses (Boston: Clarke, 1913);

Elizabeth Buffum Chace, 1806–1899: Her Life and Environment, 2 volumes, by Wyman and Arthur Crawford Wyman (Boston: Clarke, 1914);

The Strange Case of Edgar Allan Poe (Boston: N. p., 1923);

Gertrude of Denmark: An Interpretive Romance (Boston: Marshall Jones, 1924);

A Grand Army Man of Rhode Island (Newton, Mass.: Graphic Press, 1925);

Syringa at the Gate (Boston: Marshall Jones, 1926).

OTHER: "Work of Anti-Slavery Women," in *Woman's Work in America,* edited by Annie Nathan Meyer (New York: Holt, 1891), pp. 392–398.

SELECTED PERIODICAL PUBLICATIONS–
UNCOLLECTED: "Studies of Factory Life: The Village System," *Atlantic Monthly,* 62 (July 1888): 16–17;

"From Generation to Generation," *Atlantic Monthly,* 64 (August 1889): 164–177;

"Colored Churches and Schools in the South," *New England Magazine,* 3 (February 1891): 785–796;

"A Southern Study," *New England Magazine,* 4 (June 1891): 521–531;

"Black and White," *New England Magazine,* 5 (December 1891): 476–481;

"Peasant Life in Russia," *Chautauquan,* 15 (April 1892): 57–61;

"Harriet Tubman," *New England Magazine,* 14 (March 1896): 110–118;

"Girls in a Factory Valley," *Atlantic Monthly,* 78 (September 1896): 391–403; (October 1896): 512–517;

"The Light That Never Failed," *New England Magazine,* 20 (March 1899): 87–95;

"The Bravest of the Brave," *Brownies Book,* 1 (November 1920): 336–339;

"Girls Together: Sketches From Life, Part I," *Brownies Book,* 2 (April 1921): 109–111;

Lillie Buffum Chace Wyman in 1873 (engraving after a drawing by Edward Clifford)

"Brave Brown Joe and Good White Men," *Brownies Book,* 2 (November 1921): 318–320;

"Mark Hanna," *Opportunity,* 3 (March 1925): 83–84.

Activist, essayist, poet, and biographer, Lillie Buffum Chace Wyman was a late-nineteenth-century writer who was virtually unknown outside New England reformist circles. Shaped and nurtured by the antislavery and women's rights movements, she wrote stories and essays, appearing in popular periodicals between 1877 and 1925, that advocated prohibition, equal rights for women, and equality for all races and classes. Wyman's most significant contributions to American letters are her depictions of conditions in New England factory villages and her advocacy of social reform and personal growth, all of which link her to nineteenth-century Realist writers such as Rebecca Harding Davis, Elizabeth Stuart Phelps, and Sarah Orne Jewett.

Elizabeth (Lillie) Buffum Chace was born on 10 December 1847 in Valley Falls, Rhode Island, to Samuel Buffington Chace and Elizabeth Buffum Chace. The eighth child and oldest living daughter of ten children, Lillie was raised in an antislavery household by parents who were followers of the abolitionist William Lloyd Garrison and who conducted an underground railroad station for slaves escaping to the North. Samuel Chace was a successful Quaker textile manufacturer and a strong supporter of his wife's public work for the abolitionist cause. Serving as president of the Rhode Island Woman Suffrage Association (RIWSA), Elizabeth Chace was a well-known activist in the abolitionist and women's rights movements for sixty years. Her father, Arnold Buffum, had been the first president of the New England Anti-Slavery Society, which he had helped found in 1832. He and Elizabeth Chace's four sisters, all staunch Quakers, supported and encouraged her activism. Elizabeth Chase was a major influence in Lillie's life, encouraging her to read abolitionist material, especially Garrison's newspaper, *The Liberator;* to attend annual antislavery meetings in Providence and Boston; and to visit and to see other antislavery activists and their children. While still in her teens, she acted as her mother's secretary, writing letters to speakers and scheduling abolitionist meetings. Lillie Chace would become her mother's assistant in social reform movements and the keeper of the abolitionist legacy.

Before attending the public high school in Central Falls in 1863, Chace was taught at home by tutors, governesses, and her mother, a former schoolteacher. For a short time in 1864 she attended Codman Hill, a boarding school in Milton, Massachusetts. In the fall of the same year Chace entered Dio Lewis's Family School for Young Ladies in Lexington, Massachusetts, which provided a pivotal experience in her education. There she enjoyed some measure of independence, cultivated invaluable friendships, and immersed herself in studying the writings of William Shakespeare under the tutelage of the abolitionist Theodore Weld. In 1866, at the age of eighteen, Chace left school and returned home to live with her family. The Civil War had ended, and the emancipation of the slaves meant that the abolitionist movement had won. Lillie Chace, who had been raised an abolitionist and had always expected to join in the struggle when she finally came of age, experienced a great personal and vocational crisis. She was diagnosed as suffering from neurasthenia, a mental illness characterized by feelings of fatigue, inadequacy, and lack of motivation. In the fall of 1866 her condition worsened,

and by December of the same year she was a patient in Lewis's sanatorium. From there she wrote her good friend Anna Dickinson, urging her to "Live, my dear Anna, for there is work to be done, and there are hearts to be gladdened." In the same letter Chace wrote of herself that her life "glides by, and brings me no definite aim, no purpose, no prospect thereof."

In spite of her difficulties, by the end of the 1860s Chace had assumed the role of her mother's assistant, although she still felt a sense of purposelessness at the demise of the abolitionist movement. During this time she also occupied herself with horseback riding, playing the piano, attending parties, shopping, traveling, and writing. Wyman's eighteen-month tour of Europe with her mother in 1872 helped her to come to terms with her political and personal losses. Writing, which she gained experience in by covering reform events, now became an outlet for her to cope with loneliness and despondency.

Chace established a modest reputation as an author writing letters and articles for such major reform periodicals as *National Antislavery Standard* and *Woman's Journal,* the organ of the American Women's Suffrage Association. Her breakthrough came with her most critically acclaimed short story, "The Child of the State," which appeared in the *Atlantic Monthly* in September 1877, to promote her mother's reform interests. Published under the pseudonym S.A.L.E.M., an acronym for Lillie and her siblings Samuel, Arnold, Edward, and Mary, it established her as an effective writer of critical realism.

Based on graphic data her mother had collected on the reform school for girls, and based also on her own observations of life among the working class, Chace's story chronicles the plight of orphan Josie Welch, a "child of the state" who enters a reform school at the age of ten and by the story's conclusion has descended into a life of criminality and sordidness, ending up in prison. Wyman implies that Josie's fate and the fate of others like her is to remain "a child of the state," unless institutions are radically changed.

Thematically, the story expresses class and gender inequity, two of the most dominant themes in Chace's writing. One of the best examples of gender inequity in the story is the description of the boys in the reform school who are taught a useful trade to gain a sense of respect, while the girls are taught only domestic service. No incentives are provided for girls such as Josie, whose low self-esteem and unrecognized intelligence have led to her misfortunes. According to Wyman, such treatment of girls naturally sets up failure and is an unconscionable crime of ignorance.

The climactic dialogue between the woman visitor and superintendent of the institution regarding the

POVERTY GRASS

BY

LILLIE CHACE WYMAN

BOSTON AND NEW YORK
HOUGHTON, MIFFLIN AND COMPANY
The Riverside Press, Cambridge
1886

Title page for Wyman's first book, a collection of stories about the working class

unjust treatment of the girls effectively reinforces Chace's thesis. The superintendent tells her: "Oh, the girls! Well—the girls are a great deal worse. Women always are worse than men, you know, when they are bad. There's a peculiar devil in women, somehow, begging your pardon." When the woman asks outright if the girls are reformed, she is given a quick reply: "No; there is no possibility of reforming the girls. It is merely a house of correction for them, and serves a very good purpose in keeping them out of mischief for a few years, at least." Layered with negative images and thinking, Chace's sparse yet sympathetic documentary style paints a dismal picture of sadistic and uncaring attendants and middle-class women visitors powerless to effect change.

In October 1878 Lillie Buffum Chace married John Crawford Wyman, a former Garrisonian abolitionist and widower twenty-five years her senior. Their only child, Arthur Crawford Wyman, was born in September 1879. After her marriage Lillie Buffum Chace Wyman continued publishing fiction in the *Atlantic*

Monthly, focusing specifically on the conditions of working-class life.

In 1886 most of Wyman's *Atlantic Monthly* stories published between 1877 and 1882 were collected in *Poverty Grass.* Writing in his February 1887 "Editor's Study" column in *Harper's Magazine,* William Dean Howells praises her as a writer of "absolute and unswerving realism" who has written some "powerful sketches." In the preface to the collection Wyman describes her stories as "studies of people of different races . . . who struggle against odds, and reach whatever growth they attain through difficulty." She further explains that she has "tried to be both realistic and ideal, because I believe that the ideal is the most real element in life." Together, these eight "simple, grim, true to misery" sketches, grounded in facts and aimed at consciousness-raising, make a compelling commentary on social ills.

Several of the stories in *Poverty Grass* focus on similar inequities and make similar pleas for cross-cultural, or cross-class, cooperation. "Saint or Sinner," set entirely in a factory village, reflects the dreariness and poverty of the lives of the mill workers. "Hester's Dower" represents a departure into the preindustrial golden age of New England agrarian life, where Hester Arnold, a seamstress, struggles to maintain her own independence and dignity. "And Joe" is a multilayered story juxtaposing the life of factory laborers and owners seen through the eyes of Theodora Justice, the daughter of a manufacturer, and Joe, a half-witted epileptic boy who is living in the streets. In "Valentine's Chance" John Valentine, a young doctor who has taken up residence in a New England factory village, is mysteriously drawn to the beautiful and vital Rose, a young French Canadian factory operative. Although the narrative takes place against the background of labor agitation in the mills, "A Stranger, Yet at Home" is a touching love story that deals with the internal conflicts of Prudence Warner, a lovelorn spinster, and Darius Kingman, a young upper-class widower who had lived in China for many years before returning to the village where he had been raised as a Quaker. "Bridget's Story" highlights the hardships experienced by Bridget's friend, Ellen McKiernan, a factory operative who had raised seven children. The final story in the collection, "Luke Gardiner's Love," which was not previously published in the *Atlantic Monthly,* is a romantic love story in which Wyman demonstrates how a female operative's innocence is imperiled by the factory system.

Wyman briefly interrupted her own writing on factory operatives to become her mother's caretaker and reform assistant in the 1880s. In March 1887 she edited, with the assistance of her husband and Kate Austin, a colleague, two issues of *The Amendment,* a special campaign newspaper published by her mother's RIWSA. Wyman's four-part series of essays titled "Studies of Factory Life," an exposé of the factory system, appeared in the *Atlantic Monthly* between July 1888 and January 1889. "Girls in a Factory Valley" followed in October 1896. Concerned with equal rights and the social conditions in the South and in Russia, Wyman published her essays "A Southern Study," "Colored Churches and Schools in the South," and "Black and White" in *New England Magazine* in 1891. "Peasant Life in Russia" appeared in *Chautauquan* in April 1892, in conjunction with her work for the Friends of Russian Freedom.

After Wyman lost her mother in 1899 and her husband in September 1900, she tried to find a way to express her internal struggles and sorrow through writing. After she moved from Valley Falls to Newtonville, Massachusetts, in 1913, her writing lacked a unifying focus—she wrote memoirs of abolitionists, nostalgic remembrances, poetry, literary criticism, and racial protests.

Almost three decades after *Poverty Grass,* Wyman published her second book, *American Chivalry* (1913), a collection of biographical sketches, some of which had earlier appeared in the *New England Magazine.* The strength of the work lies in her detailed portraits of her beloved abolitionists. With authority, precision, and great intensity she highlights the lives and activities of individuals such as the former president of the Anti-Slavery Society, Wendell Phillips; her tireless reformist mother; her mother's sister Rebecca Buffum Spring; abolitionists Stephen Symonds Foster and his wife, Abbey Foster (also a pioneer in the woman suffrage movement); the evangelist and reformer Sojourner Truth; and her husband. With the exception of her husband, all of these activists were idols of Wyman's abolitionist childhood. One of the most moving, detailed sketches is that of Sojourner Truth—according to Wyman, "what people cared most to hear from her lips was the many stories of her own varied experiences."

Although Wyman's strong reverence for the past, which precipitated and shaped much of her thinking, remains in the forefront, her writing is rescued from monotonous hagiography by the interweaving of personal reminiscences and anecdotes. A somber tone is noticeable in her attempt to bring closure to the deaths of these "knights," including her husband, and to the paradoxical grief she had experienced as one of the abolitionist children who were, as she wrote in "From Generation to Generation," published in the *Atlantic Monthly* (August 1889), "trained for a conflict in which they were not permitted to fight."

Wyman published two volumes of poetry, *Interludes and Other Verses* (1913) and *Syringa at the Gate*

(1926). Both collections include poems referring to the people, places, and events of the antislavery movement and to Wyman's earlier life. There is little in these poems of permanent interest, and some of the poems make personal references so ambiguous that only the author could interpret their meaning. Although the writing style is generally simplistic and repetitive, Wyman occasionally experiments with form and uses imagery effectively.

All of the poems are similar in structure and content, with some of her best poems being two- to six-line epigrams describing abolitionists such as Garrison, Lucy Stone, Julia Ward Howe, and John Brown. A twenty-page, fifteen-part ode is dedicated to "Wendell Phillips the Hermes." Wyman had called Phillips "the great moral revolutionist" in *American Chivalry;* in the ode she writes:

> Thus, while he lived, there was a man who cared
> If well or ill the throbbing millions fared,
> He broke his heart to use for service bread;
> He filled the Altar cup with his own wine—
> The Vintage flow from forth his love benign;—
> But mourn ye, Nations, now, for Phillips dead!

In the poem "Songs From the Cloister of Age" Wyman dedicates verses to her dead husband, to her mother, and to Samuel, her dead brother, who "vanished from eyesight forever."

Many of the elegiac verses dedicated to her husband in *Interludes* and *Syringa at the Gate* attest to Wyman's devastation at his death. "For me," she mourns, "the chant of earthly joy is done, / No more the singing birds of life arise. . . ." A melancholy tone throughout Wyman's poetry seems to reflect her loneliness and personal difficulties. In "Orchard Blossoms" Wyman's preoccupation with the symbolic imagery of trees, flowers, grass, and birds suggests that she temporarily transcends her grief in her symbolic world of the "orchard," where "a blossom uprising, / Like a star below, / . . . is lovely as ever" and "its fragrance comes to you."

One of Wyman's most ambitious literary projects was undertaken at the suggestion of her older brother Arnold Buffam Chace. *Elizabeth Buffum Chace, 1806–1899: Her Life and Its Environment,* her two-volume, seven hundred-page biography of her mother, was published in 1914. In it Elizabeth Chace's personal life is juxtaposed with her public activism to, as Wyman writes in her preface, "present a vivid portrayal of an earnest woman's life in its environment." The biography is overloaded with facts, letters, and information on diverse subjects, seemingly intended to impress on the reader the life of an amazing mother and activist whose tireless efforts effected change before she died at the age of

Wyman's mother, Elizabeth Buffum Chace, and Wyman's husband, John Crawford Wyman

ninety-three. Unfortunately, the flow of the work is broken by recurrent reproductions of full or excerpted letters, making for occasionally tedious reading.

Although Wyman's failure to distance herself from the narrative may be seen as a flaw in the biography, in actuality her personal observations of Elizabeth Buffum Chace's personality and temperament, especially her "autocratic" nature, are what make the biography effective. Wyman's use of the biographical form seems to be a way for her to analyze her mixed feelings regarding her mother's death and to perpetuate the abolitionist legacy.

By the early 1920s Wyman found a new direction in her writing. Seeking to promote more positive relations between whites and blacks, she published a series of stories in *The Brownies Book,* an African American children's magazine then edited by W. E. B. DuBois. Her subject of developing racial tolerance, rather than dwelling in past abolitionist glories, is significant in the development of Wyman as a writer. The chief value of such stories as "The Bravest of the Brave," a reworking of part of the story "Black and White" (November 1920) and "Girls Together: Sketches from Life, Post I" (April 1921) lies partly in Wyman's strong awareness of the "terrible trail of pain, passion, and prejudice" slavery left behind and partly in her convincing tone.

In 1924, at the age of seventy-seven and in poor health, Wyman drew on her lifelong interest in William

Shakespeare to write a book titled *Gertrude of Denmark: An Interpretive Romance,* based on Shakespeare's play *Hamlet.* In *Gertrude of Denmark* Wyman downplays the adultery of Gertrude, Hamlet's mother, reduces Hamlet's role to a minor one and expands Gertrude's role, displaying remarkable perception in probing her inner life. In Wyman's book Gertrude evolves as a "virtuous, high-minded and much-wronged woman" who married Claudius, Hamlet's uncle, swiftly after her husband's sudden death, partly because she disliked the idea of going into a convent, but mainly to ensure Hamlet's eventual succession to the throne of Denmark.

Although Wyman questions Gertrude's maternal instincts, she rescues her from her status as a "defenseless" female character, indirectly critiquing Shakespeare's limiting characterization of women. The book reveals Wyman's own views and attitudes on the problems women face in defining themselves as wives and mothers.

Responses to Wyman's *Gertrude of Denmark* were mixed. A reviewer in *Theatre Arts Monthly* (August 1924) claimed that Wyman's "frankly intuitional and sentimental" presentation "weakens the value of what critically and historically handled might be an interesting contribution to the study of *Hamlet.*" However, a June 1924 review in *The Bookman* called it a "friendly, 'civilized,' humorous, beautiful, and assertive entry into the lists of Shakespeariana," and a reviewer for the *Spring-*

field Republican observed that "whether we are convinced or not, this romance of Hamlet and his mother . . . is likely to stay in our memory."

Wyman's next work, *A Grand Army Man of Rhode Island* (1925), is a memoir that pays homage to eighty-seven-year-old Augustine Mann, from her hometown of Valley Falls. During the Civil War, Mann had been an army surgeon with the rank of lieutenant. With remarkable detail and precision, Wyman dramatically recounts his enlistment, capture, and confinement as a prisoner of war in Richmond and his bravery. At the heart of the book is the section depicting the inhumane treatment of the prisoners who "picked lice off their bodies and their malodorous clothing." Wyman has interspersed her own memories of Mann's wife and her childhood friend Sarah Bucklin with her narrative of Mann's Civil War experiences. Although the thirty-three-page memoir has little artistic merit, Wyman, through her nostalgic remembrances, has once again accurately recaptured a past that she was unable to relinquish.

Though Wyman suffered from vision problems that left her partially blind by 1915, she pursued several research projects related to her antislavery past near the end of her life. As her health declined, she spent the last years of her life in solitude as an invalid. The eighty-one-year-old Lillie Buffum Chace Wyman died at her home in Newtonville, Massachusetts, on 10 January 1929. Little known in her own time and largely forgotten after her death, since the early 1990s her writings have gained some attention from scholars studying her within the context of nineteenth-century Realism.

References:

William Dean Howells, "Editor's Study," *Harper's Magazine,* 74 (February 1887): 482–483;

Howells, "Notes: Recent Novels," *Nation,* 43 (30 December 1886): 547–549;

Jane Atteridge Rose, "Recovering Lillie Buffum Chace Wyman and 'The Child of the State,'" *Legacy,* 7 (Spring 1990): 39–43;

Martha Tuck Rozett, "Gertrude's Ghost Tells Her Story: Lillie Wyman's *Gertrude of Denmark,*" in *Cross-Cultural Performances: Differences in Women's Re-Visions of Shakespeare,* edited by Marianne Novy (Urbana: University of Illinois Press, 1993), pp. 70–85;

Elizabeth Cooke Stevens, "'From Generation to Generation': The Mother and Daughter Activism of Elizabeth Buffum Chace and Lillie Chace Wyman," dissertation, Brown University, 1993.

Papers:

Major collections of Lillie Buffum Chace Wyman's papers, including manuscripts for unpublished works, are located at the John Hay Library, Brown University; the Moorland–Springarn Research Center, Howard University; and the Boston Public Library Antislavery Collections.

Books for Further Reading

Baym, Nina. *Novels, Readers, and Reviewers: Responses to Fiction in Antebellum America*. Ithaca, N.Y.: Cornell University Press, 1984.

Baym. *Woman's Fiction: A Guide to Novels By and About Women in America, 1820–1870*. Ithaca, N.Y.: Cornell University Press, 1978.

Bell, Michael Davitt. *The Development of American Romance: The Sacrifice of Relation*. Chicago: University of Chicago Press, 1980.

Berthoff, Warner. *The Ferment of Realism: American Literature, 1884–1919*. New York: Free Press, 1965.

Brooks, Van Wyck. *The World of Washington Irving*. New York: Dutton, 1944.

Brown, Herbert Ross. *The Sentimental Novel in America, 1789–1860*. Durham, N.C.: Duke University Press, 1940.

Buell, Lawrence. *New England Literary Culture: From Revolution Through the Renaissance*. Cambridge & New York: Cambridge University Press, 1986.

Cady, Edwin. *The Light of Common Day: Realism in American Fiction*. Bloomington: Indiana University Press, 1971.

Carter, Everett. *Howells and the Age of Realism*. Philadelphia: Lippincott, 1954.

Cawelti, John G. *Adventure, Mystery and Romance: Formula Stories as Art and Popular Culture*. Chicago: University of Chicago Press, 1976.

Charvat, William. *The Profession of Authorship in America, 1800–1870*, edited by Matthew J. Bruccoli. Columbus: Ohio State University Press, 1968.

Chase, Richard. *The American Novel and Its Tradition*. Garden City, N.Y.: Doubleday, 1957.

Chielens, Edward E., ed. *American Literary Magazines: The Eighteenth and Nineteenth Centuries*. New York: Greenwood Press, 1986.

Clark, Robert. *History, Ideology and Myth in American Fiction, 1823–52*. London: Macmillan, 1984.

Coultrap-McQuin, Susan. *Doing Literary Business: American Women Writers in the Nineteenth Century*. Chapel Hill: University of North Carolina Press, 1990.

Cowie, Alexander. *The Rise of the American Novel*. New York: American Book Company, 1948.

Davidson, Cathy. *Revolution and the Word: The Rise of the Novel in America*. New York: Oxford University Press, 1986.

Dekker, George. *The American Historical Romance*. Cambridge & New York: Cambridge University Press, 1987.

Denning, Michael. *Mechanic Accents: Dime Novels and Working-Class Culture in America*. London & New York: Verso, 1987.

Douglas, Ann. *The Feminization of American Culture*. New York: Knopf, 1977.

Elliott, Emory, gen. ed. *The Columbia History of the American Novel*. New York: Columbia University Press, 1991.

Etulain, Richard W. *A Bibliographical Guide to the Study of Western American Literature*. Lincoln: University of Nebraska Press, 1982.

Folsom, James K. *The American Western Novel*. New Haven: College and University Press, 1966.

Freibert, Lucy, and Barbara A. White, eds. *Hidden Hands: An Anthology of American Women Writers, 1790–1870*. New Brunswick, N.J.: Rutgers University Press, 1988.

Fryer, Judith. *The Faces of Eve: Women in the Nineteenth-Century Novel*. New York: Oxford University Press, 1976.

Habegger, Alfred. *Gender, Fantasy, and Realism in American Literature: The Rise of American Literary Realism in W. D. Howells and Henry James*. New York: Columbia University Press, 1982.

Harris, Susan K. *19th-Century American Women's Novels: Interpretive Strategies*. Cambridge & New York: Cambridge University Press, 1990.

Hart, James D. *The Popular Book: A History of America's Literary Taste*. New York: Oxford University Press, 1950.

Henderson, Harry B. *Versions of the Past: The Historical Imagination in American Fiction*. New York: Oxford University Press, 1974.

Hoffman, Daniel. *Form and Fable in American Fiction*. New York: Oxford University Press, 1961.

Kelley, Mary. *Private Woman, Public Stage: Literary Domesticity in Nineteenth-Century America*. New York: Oxford University Press, 1984.

Kolb, Harold. *The Illusion of Life: American Realism as a Literary Form*. Charlottesville: University Press of Virginia, 1969.

Leisy, Ernest. *The American Historical Novel*. Norman: University of Oklahoma Press, 1958.

Long, Elizabeth. *The American Dream and the Popular Novel*. Boston: Routledge & Kegan Paul, 1985.

Mainiero, Lina, ed. *American Women Writers: A Critical Reference Guide From Colonial Times to the Present*, 5 volumes. New York: Unger, 1979–1994.

Martin, Jay. *Harvests of Change: American Literature 1865–1914*. Englewood Cliffs, N.J.: Prentice-Hall, 1967.

Matthiessen, F. O. *American Renaissance: Art and Expression in the Age of Emerson and Whitman*. London & New York: Oxford University Press, 1941.

McNall, Sally Allen. *Who Is in the House? A Psychological Study of Two Centuries of Women's Fiction in America, 1795 to the Present*. New York: Elsevier/Nelson, 1981.

Moss, Sidney P. *Poe's Literary Battles: The Critic in the Context of His Literary Milieu*. Durham, N.C.: Duke University Press, 1963.

Mott, Frank Luther. *Golden Multitudes: The Story of Best Sellers in the United States*. New York: Macmillan, 1947.

Mott, *A History of American Magazines*, 5 volumes. Cambridge, Mass.: Harvard University Press, 1938–1968.

Papashvily, Helen Waite. *All the Happy Endings: A Study of the Domestic Novel in America, The Women Who Wrote It, The Women Who Read It, in the Nineteenth Century*. New York: Harper, 1956.

Petter, Henri. *The Early American Novel*. Columbus: Ohio State University Press, 1971.

Porte, Joel. *The Romance in America: Studies in Cooper, Poe, Hawthorne, Melville, and James*. Middletown, Conn.: Wesleyan University Press, 1969.

Quinn, Arthur Hobson. *American Fiction: An Historical and Critical Survey*. New York & London: Appleton-Century, 1936.

Radway, Janice. *Reading the Romance: Women, Patriarchy, and Popular Literature*. Chapel Hill: University of North Carolina Press, 1984.

Reynolds, David S. *Beneath the American Renaissance: The Subversive Imagination in the Age of Emerson and Melville*. New York: Knopf, 1988.

Rubin, Jr., Louis D., gen. ed. *The History of Southern Literature*. Baton Rouge: Louisiana State University Press, 1985.

Samuels, Shirley, ed. *The Culture of Sentiment: Race, Gender, and Sentimentality in Nineteenth-Century America*. New York: Oxford University Press, 1992.

Shapiro, Ann R. *Unlikely Heroines: Nineteenth-Century Women Writers and the Woman Question*. New York: Greenwood Press, 1987.

Slotkin, Richard. *The Fatal Environment: The Myth of the Frontier in the Age of Industrialization, 1800–1890*. New York: Atheneum, 1985.

Smith, Henry Nash. *Democracy and the Novel: Popular Resistance to Classic American Writers*. New York: Oxford University Press, 1978.

Smith, Herbert F. *The Popular American Novel, 1865–1920*. Boston: Twayne, 1980.

Spengemann, William. *The Adventurous Muse: The Poetics of American Fiction, 1789–1900*. New Haven: Yale University Press, 1977.

Spiller, Robert E., ed. *The American Literary Revolution, 1783–1847*. New York: New York University Press, 1967.

Stern, Madeleine B., ed. *Publishers for Mass Entertainment in Nineteenth Century America*. Boston: G. K. Hall, 1980.

Taft, Kendall B., ed. *Minor Knickerbockers: Representative Selections*. New York: American Book Company, 1947.

Tompkins, Jane. *Sensational Designs: The Cultural Work of American Fiction, 1790–1860*. New York: Oxford University Press, 1985.

Van Doren, Carl. *The American Novel, 1789–1939*, revised and enlarged edition. New York: Macmillan, 1940.

Zboray, Ronald J. *A Fictive People: Antebellum Economic Development and the American Reading Public*. New York: Oxford University Press, 1993.

Ziff, Larzer. *The American 1890s: Life and Times of a Lost Generation*. New York: Viking, 1966.

Contributors

Dorri R. Beam . . . . *University of Virginia*

Richard P. Benton . . . . *Trinity College, Hartford, Connecticut*

Lawrence I. Berkove . . . . *University of Michigan–Dearborn*

Elisa E. Beshero-Bondar . . . . *Pennsylvania State University*

Michael L. Burduck . . . . *Tennessee Technological University*

Bruce Guy Chabot . . . . *Texas A&M University*

Boyd Childress . . . . *Auburn University*

John D. Cloy . . . . *University of Mississippi*

Joseph L. Coulombe . . . . *University of Tennessee at Martin*

William Crisman . . . . *Pennsylvania State University, Altoona*

Joseph Csicsila . . . . *Eastern Michigan University*

Dennis W. Eddings . . . . *Western Oregon University*

Grace Farrell . . . . *Butler University*

Benjamin F. Fisher . . . . *University of Mississippi*

Mathew David Fisher . . . . *Ball State University*

Anne Razey Gowdy . . . . *Tennessee Wesleyan College*

Robin Grey . . . . *University of Illinois–Chicago*

Wade Hall . . . . *Bellarmine College*

Carol Sue Hubbell . . . . *University of Michigan–Dearborn*

Jennifer Hynes . . . . *Beaumont, Texas*

Charles Johanningsmeier . . . . *University of Nebraska–Omaha*

Lucia Z. Knoles . . . . *Assumption College*

Jeffrey B. Kurtz . . . . *Pennsylvania State University*

Kent P. Ljungquist . . . . *Worcester Polytechnic Institute*

Bennett Lovett-Graff . . . . *Woodbridge, Connecticut*

Patricia D. Maida . . . . *University of the District of Columbia*

Kathryn B. McKee . . . . *University of Mississippi*

Karen L. Morgan . . . . *Mardigian Library, University of Michigan–Dearborn*

Layne Neeper . . . . *Morehead State University*

Ed Piacentino . . . . *High Point University*

Robyn M. Preston . . . . *University of Southern Mississippi*

Mary R. Reichardt . . . . *University of St. Thomas*

Jane Atteridge Rose . . . . *Georgia College and State University*

Barbara Ryan . . . . *Michigan Society of Fellows*

Heidi M. Schultz . . . . *University of North Carolina at Chapel Hill*

David E. E. Sloane . . . . *University of New Haven*

E. Kate Stewart . . . . *University of Arkansas at Monticello*

317

Maureen Ann Sullivan .... *University of Alaska, Fairbanks*
Laura Dassow Walls .... *Lafayette College*
Daniel A. Wells .... *University of South Florida*
Jonathan Wells .... *University of Michigan*
Justin R. Wert .... *University of Mississippi*
S. J. Wolfe .... *American Antiquarian Society*
Loretta Woodard .... *Marygrove College*

Cumulative Index

Dictionary of Literary Biography, Volumes 1-202
Dictionary of Literary Biography Yearbook, 1980-1997
Dictionary of Literary Biography Documentary Series, Volumes 1-19

Cumulative Index

DLB before number: *Dictionary of Literary Biography,* Volumes 1-202
Y before number: *Dictionary of Literary Biography Yearbook,* 1980-1997
DS before number: *Dictionary of Literary Biography Documentary Series,* Volumes 1-19

C

E

H

Cumulative Index

I

N